In Face of Mystery

In Face of Mystery

A Constructive Theology

Gordon D. Kaufman

Harvard University Press
Cambridge, Massachusetts
London, England 1993

Printed in the United States of America
10 9 8 7 6 5 4 3 2 1

This book is printed on acid-free paper, and its binding materials have been chosen for strength and durability.

Library of Congress Cataloging-in-Publication Data

Kaufman, Gordon D.
In Face of Mystery : a constructive theology / Gordon D. Kaufman.
p. cm.
Includes bibliographical references and index.
ISBN 0-674-44575-9
1. Theology, Doctrinal—Introductions. I. Title.
BT65.K24 1993
230—dc20
92-9059
CIP

For all those friends and colleagues
in distant places and here at home
who have shared with me their profoundly different
religious, cultural, and philosophical orientations

Contents

Part IV Constructing a Concept of an Ultimate Point of Reference: God

Preface

In 1975 I published a small volume entitled *An Essay on Theological Method* in which I argued that theology is, and always has been, an activity of "imaginative construction" by persons attempting to put together as comprehensive and coherent a picture as they could of humanity in the world under God. This view contrasts rather sharply with more conventional conceptions according to which the work of theologians is understood to consist largely in exposition of religious doctrine or dogma (derived from the Bible and other authoritative sources). I argued, however, that this traditional way of thinking tended to obscure the important respects in which human creativity was always involved in theological activity: the materials with which theologians worked were clearly products of the imaginative creativity of previous generations, and the imagination and creativity of each new theologian was itself called upon at every point in his or her work. I tried to show that the powers of the human imagination are the principal instrumentalities which make theological work possible; and that the central theological ideas of God, humanity, and the world are—in a radical way not true of many other concepts—human imaginative constructs. Once this is understood, I contended, theology should become an activity of *deliberate* imaginative construction, carried out as self-consciously and responsibly as possible. A major part of the *Essay* was devoted to sketching what this means and how it is to be accomplished.

Since the publication of those programmatic reflections, I have been experimenting in my teaching and writing with imaginative construction as a theological method. Not until now, however, have I felt sufficiently confident about my proposals and sufficiently practiced in their use to attempt to work out a full-scale reconception of Christian theology along the lines they suggest.

Many are doubtful about the feasibility or the appropriateness of projects like this which seek to analyze and transform an overall faith-perspective or religious world-picture. Some hold that it is foolish to suppose that humans are capable of reconstructing the symbolic frameworks within which they have their experience and do their thinking. Others maintain that life (at least in our time) is so fragmentary and pluralistic that it is pointless to attempt to work out conceptions or pictures which draw it all together into a meaningful whole. Still others think that the attempt to work through and set out a "Christian" conception of God, humanity, and the world for today must represent an inappropriate continuance, in our modern pluralistic world, of the religious imperialism of the Christian past. What may appear (from a Christian point of view) to be the most deep-cutting criticism of all has been made by liberation theologians. Gustavo Gutierrez, for instance, has said that "The question is not how we are to talk about God in a world come of age, but how we are to tell people who are scarcely human that God is love and that God's love makes us one family."* A statement like this is sometimes lifted out of context and used to support the contention that theologians today should not concern themselves centrally with the question of who or what God is but instead should join together with other Christians in direct attack on the massive inhumanity, oppression, and injustice in the world, thus bringing to those who are poor and oppressed the message and spirit of the loving God's redemptive power.

I would like to say a word here about this last contention. (The others will be given full consideration as this book unfolds.) It would be a mistake, I think, to regard this as expressing a proper criticism of the program of theological reconception and construction that I undertake here. For it is not simply skepticism about the God-symbol, so widespread in western academic circles, that I am principally concerned to address. Of at least equal importance is a set of issues raised by the liberation theologians themselves: What are we to make of the fact that Christian institutions, communities, and traditions have been responsible for so much oppression and suffering in human history? Why have they been so easily corrupted into serving the interests of the powerful in oppressing the poor, the weak, women, people of color? Why have they so often supported the exploitation of third-world peoples and, indeed, of planet Earth? Why have they so frequently allied themselves with groups wielding unprincipled power in the world? With questions like these in mind, liberation theologians have themselves become highly critical of many aspects of traditional patterns of theological thinking, pointing out that sweeping claims made about God, justice, mercy, love,

*"Two Theological Perspectives: Liberation Theology and Progressivist Theology," in *The Emergent Gospel: Theology from the Developing World*, ed. S. Torres and V. Fabella (London: Geoffrey Chapman, 1978), p. 241. This quotation was called to my attention by Sharon Welch.

peace, reconciliation, and the like have in fact helped to sustain the inhuman and oppressive conditions under which many of "God's children" have had to live. On their own argument, thus, we simply dare not continue to employ traditional Christian symbols uncritically, however meaningful and attractive some of these symbols may seem. Theological ideas often prove to be dangerous and destructive when used without critical examination and careful reconstruction.

The liberation theologians are certainly correct in holding that there is no justification for focusing Christian theology on essentially speculative games of interest only to elite intellectuals; Christian theology which does not contribute significantly to the struggles against inhumanity, injustice, and the other serious evils in our world has lost sight of its deepest *raison d'être*. But for precisely this reason theologians must always take a thoroughly critical stance toward received traditions, and they must never hesitate to undertake drastic reconstruction when it becomes clear that traditional practices or beliefs can contribute to dehumanization. Simply to take the innocence and correctness of widely accepted theological symbols for granted, as the remark of Gutierrez I have quoted (when taken out of context as it is here) might seem to suggest, and moving forward with banners flying in the effort to transform the world, may well only add to our deepest human problems. It is becoming increasingly evident, for example, that for the sake of what we have regarded as our human well-being we have been exploiting—and often destroying!—the capacities of planet Earth to sustain life, including human life. If we wish to be fully responsible men and women, thus, we must pay much more attention to what is happening to the web of life as a whole when we take up our concerns about justice, humaneness, and our overall well-being.

With these considerations in mind I can state a basic conviction that underlies this book: that it is of fundamental importance—if we are truly to help bring about a more humane and just order in human affairs, and are to give proper attention to the ecosystem within which human life falls—for us men and women to think through carefully, in the light of modern knowledges, the questions of who or what we humans are, what sort of world this is in which we find ourselves, which God must be served. Our concepts of God and of Christ must be reconceived with attention to our modern understandings of ourselves and of the universe, and to our new consciousness of the destructiveness we humans have worked in the world as well as on our fellow humans. Only as we grasp more fully the ecologically interdependent character of everything in our world will we move into a position to understand why and how traditional claims about the human transcendence of nature, including our "right" and "duty" to "subdue" nature (Gen. 1:28–29), have been so destructive. And only as we appreciate more fully the actual interconnectedness of all humans with one another will we discern clearly the extent of the injustice and oppression which our religious (and other) institutions, symbols, and hierarchical structures have been creating and sustaining for so long. We dare not continue to use our received religious symbols without carefully analyzing and assessing not only what they supposedly "mean" but also their actual effects on ongoing human life and the world at large. Radical theological reconception and fresh theological construction are thus not simply elite academic exercises: they are demanded today because of the dangerously increasing destructiveness of powerful evils in our human world—evils which in our time, as we well know, can lead all too easily to the complete obliteration of human existence (and much other life) on this pianet.

I cannot in these prefatory remarks sketch the specific methods of critical analysis and imaginative construction that will be employed in this book, nor can I take up their problematic aspects. I am well aware that some who are familiar with the approach to theology which I have been developing in recent years regard it as, in a double sense, somewhat abstract and speculative: it has seemed to them to be concerned with issues that have little to do with actual problems faced by many women and men today; and they have supposed it not to be grounded in a living faith and piety. I hope that what has just been said—very briefly, to be sure—about the reasons for undertaking radical theological criticism and reconstruction will testify to the questionableness of the first charge. With regard to the second, a few remarks may here be added.

The position on which I have been working, and which I attempt to articulate in detail in this book, expresses, I think, four fundamental dimensions of my own faith and piety. These are (a) my deep sense of the ultimate mystery of life; (b) my feeling of profound gratitude for the gift of humanness and the great diversity which it manifests; (c) my belief (with this diversity especially in mind) in the continuing importance of the central Christian moral demand that we love and care for not only our neighbors but even our enemies; and (d) my conviction (closely connected with this last point) that the principal Christian symbols continue to provide a significant resource for the orientation of human life. In the theology set out in this book I attempt to express both my piety toward and my gratitude to the ultimate mystery which we daily confront. The sense of gratitude for the gift of our distinctive human qualities leads me to impute to this mystery a certain tension or movement toward humanization, even humaneness; but my piety toward the mystery *qua* mystery compels me to acknowledge that when we say such things as this we come up against the very limits of our language and our minds, we really do not know what we are saying. Partly in consequence of this awareness that it is ultimately mystery within which we live,

I try in my theological work to develop a framework that acknowledges and fully affirms the radically pluralistic character of human life, a framework which can accommodate many different religious (and secular) perspectives (so long as they are genuinely humanizing), and which permits the use of quite diverse mythical and metaphysical symbols (so long as they are recognized to be symbols and are not reified). My convictions about mystery and about human diversity demand, of course, that I also allow a significant place for, and grant the integrity of, those who believe they can say much more—in more detail and with more certitude—about the religious meaning of our common human existence than can I.

I must grant that the carefully qualified, and in certain respects agnostic, stance elaborated in this book does not provide the intense emotional satisfaction, or the sort of personal empowerment, characteristic of positions which believe themselves justified in proclaiming more concrete and specific certitudes about God, humanity, and the world. Its weakness in this respect (if that is what it is) is the obverse of its fear of every fanaticism or idolatry, so often the consequence of personal commitment given too quickly and fully to reified symbols. But it is a stance that provides a distinctive empowerment of its own: namely to open ourselves to everything human, to every position and claim; to listen sympathetically to every kind of experience—Christian, communist, Buddhist, deconstructionist, radical feminist, Muslim, liberal humanist, Nazi; to search for the human in everyone. And it encourages deep concern for the full range of modes and dimensions of being in our world, respect for every expression of the ultimate mystery of things. This is an empowerment for radical inclusiveness rather than exclusiveness, an empowerment that encourages gratitude and respect for the humanity of every person and community, not only for those who happen to agree with us. And thus the profound awe which we feel before the mystery from which all this magnificent diversity streams forth may begin to expand into a deep love and loyalty to that mystery—to expand, that is to say, into faith in the God who truly humanizes yet thoroughly relativizes us all.

The basic outlines and much of the content of this book have been worked out in lectures at Harvard University during the past fifteen years or so, and the direction they have taken has been much influenced by the questions and criticisms and intense discussions of issues in those classes; I am deeply grateful for all that my students and my teaching assistants have contributed to my thinking. Some of the central ideas in this book were first presented to wider publics in series of lectures at various other universities. In this connection I wish to thank especially the Electors to the Sarum Lectureship of Oxford University for the invitation to give the Sarum Lectures in 1986, and also Professor Maurice Wiles, who was my host during those weeks; this invitation gave me the opportunity to try out an earlier version of material now found in Chapters 1, 3, 6–10, and 17–20, and I benefited much from questions posed by listeners and from discussions with them. I also lectured and taught, as these ideas were germinating, in various other settings around the globe: the United Theological College in Bangalore, India; Doshisha and Ryukoku Universities in Kyoto, Japan; the University of South Africa in Pretoria; Manchester University in England; and various colleges and universities in North America. I am much indebted to the National Endowment for the Humanities, which supported the final full year of work on this book, 1990–91, by awarding me a Fellowship for University Teachers. During the spring term of that year I was able to lecture on materials drawn from this final stage of writing at the Chinese University in Hong Kong, Peking University, Fudan University (in Shanghai), the Nanjing Union Theological College, and Ewha Women's University in Seoul, Korea. Discussions with colleagues in all of these places proved helpful to me in many ways.

In these quite diverse settings—especially those outside the West—I was always especially concerned to explore issues connected with human religious and cultural pluralism and with the question of the directions human history now seems to be moving. My understanding of these matters and my reflection on their implications for Christian theology today have been greatly broadened and deepened by these consultations and conversations with teachers and students in many different places. It gives me great pleasure, therefore, to be able to dedicate this work to these theological and philosophical colleagues and friends around the globe, who have so greatly enriched my life and that of my wife, Dorothy, and who have taught me how indispensable to human existence and the ongoing human project is our cultural and religious diversity.

Among the many individuals who have helped me in various ways in the preparation of this text, five in particular must be singled out here for special mention. Professors Sheila Davaney of Iliff School of Theology and James Gustafson of Emory University and Mr. Sathianathan Clarke read with great care a penultimate version of the manuscript; their detailed comments and questions on various points in that text helped me to nuance better certain contentions and also saved me from several outright errors. Professor Deborah Haynes of Washington State University designed and prepared the fine set of figures without which it would have been almost impossible to explain clearly certain complex matters; and Ms. Joanne Swenson took major responsibility for preparation of the indexes. I am very much indebted to these five friends for the time and effort they have given on my behalf. I wish to thank them, and my excellent editors at Harvard University Press, Ms. Peg Fulton and Ms. Camille Smith, for helping to make this a better book.

Despite the emphasis in this work on the necessity today to develop fresh understandings of the theological significance of religious and cultural pluralism, I cannot claim to present here a theology that takes adequate account of the rich insights to be found in other traditions. I am not a scholar of comparative religions, and I can make no claims to more than a superficial experience and knowledge of cultures outside the West. I write, thus, as a western Christian theologian who has begun to glimpse something of the richness and importance of the world beyond the West, and beyond Christian frameworks, for understanding the deepest problems of life and death; and who is intent, therefore, on finding ways to remove the barriers which block off our modern western Christian ways of experiencing and thinking from this wider world beyond. It is clear today that all humans are becoming increasingly interconnected and interdependent in many ways; and that we dare not, therefore, continue to live and think simply in the limited terms which our much too parochial traditions have bequeathed to us. None of us exists, of course, as a universal or generic human mind, however much we may aspire to take the wider world into account in our thinking and writing. And it will be clear to my readers, I am sure—especially those formed by other cultural and religious traditions, as well as those of different race or gender—that I write here, inevitably, from a modern western Christian point of view and as a white male living and working largely in academia, with whatever limitations these characteristics entail and whatever insights they make possible.

I make no claims, thus, to universality for the theological position presented. It is a proposal that attempts to take into account certain of the most pressing problems of religious, cultural, social, and historical understanding and interpretation faced by educated modern western people; but for many in other circumstances it may seem abstract, obscure, impious, just plain pointless. The conversation in our pluralistic world about ultimate questions of life and death requires a wide range of voices if it is to address the diverse needs of women and men today. And it is important, I believe, that the perspective I have sought to articulate here be a part of that ongoing discussion. I gladly send it forth, therefore, to find whatever place it can within the larger conversation about the meaning of human historical existence.

Credits

The following publishers have given permission for the use of materials by Gordon D. Kaufman and published by them in earlier versions:

For extracts from *The Theological Imagination: Constructing the Concept of God,* © 1981: Westminster/John Knox Press.

For extracts from *Theology for a Nuclear Age,* © 1985: Westminster/John Knox Press and Manchester University Press.

For extracts from "Mystery, Critical Consciousness, and Faith," in *The Rationality of Religious Belief: Essays in Honour of Basil Mitchell,* ed. W. J. Abraham and S. W. Holtzer, © 1987: Oxford University Press.

For extracts from "Religious Diversity, Historical Consciousness, and Christian Theology," in *The Myth of Christian Uniqueness,* ed. J. Hick and P. F. Knitter, © 1987: Orbis Books and SCM Press.

The University of California Press has given permission for quoting two lines from Ai Qing published in Perry Link, *Roses and Thorns: The Second Blooming of the Hundred Flowers in Chinese Fiction (1979–1980),* © 1984 The Regents of the University of California.

The Division of Christian Education of the National Council of the Churches in the USA has given permission to quote from the Revised Standard Version of the Bible, © 1946, 1952, 1971; unless otherwise indicated, all biblical quotations are drawn from this translation.

I am the Alpha and the Omega,
the first and the last,
the beginning and the end.

Revelation 22

No one has ever seen God;
if we love one another, God abides in us
and his love is perfected in us.

1 John 4

. . . theology . . . is a constructive task.

Paul Tillich

Yes, you have got to assemble bits of old material.
But into a *building*.

Ludwig Wittgenstein

God and the Devil
Are both human images.

Ai Qing

Part I

Introduction: Theology as Construction

. . . what is called knowledge in everyday parlance, is only a small island in a vast sea that has not been traveled . . . Hence the existential question for the knower is this: Which does he love more, the small island of his so-called knowledge or the sea of infinite mystery?

Karl Rahner

Theology means taking rational trouble over the mystery.

Karl Barth

I extend the horizon of my senses by the imagination . . . The imagination is the original organ of religion.

Ludwig Feuerbach

1. The Question of God

"If there is no God, everything is permitted."
"The suffering of just one innocent child makes belief in God intolerable."

These two remarks attributed to Ivan in *The Brothers Karamazov,*[1] taken together, epitomize the way in which the question of God impinges on us today. On the one hand, having inherited a tradition in which all reality, all goodness, value and meaning, all rightness and normativity were believed to derive from and to be grounded upon the one eternal Source of all that is, we find ourselves continually searching for a foundation adequate to orient and ground our lives. And if such a foundation no longer seems discernible, we may feel that we are beginning to slip into a nihilism in which anything and everything goes. So the loss of God—or of certainty about God—may seem to be the beginning of the breakdown of our humanity. From this point of view, the threat of ecological destruction and the terror of nuclear holocaust appear to be apocalyptic symbols of the situation into which we humans have moved in modern history.

On the other hand, many in our time have become especially sensitive to how implausible, indeed unacceptable or even intolerable, is the understanding of God which we have inherited. Not only has the reality of God become widely questioned because of our increasing conviction that the modern scientifically described world has no place for such a being; but in addition the massive outbreaks of evil in our time have made the notion that human life is under the loving care of a Father-Creator, who governs all that is, simply incredible. Oppressed peoples—blacks, women, "third world" persons—have protested loudly that the destructive domination of much of the world by a white male elite class during recent centuries has been fostered and legitimated partly by corrupted forms of belief in this very God; and ecological writers have been able to show a connection of western theistic religious beliefs with the unrestrained exploitation of the resources of our planet and the life-threatening pollution of our environment. Massive human suffering, therefore, both of humans and of other forms of life, seems to be significantly attributable to faith in and (supposed) service to the God of western religious traditions. Even if we could still believe in such a God, and could orient our lives in terms of "his" commands, would we want to do so?

Historically, this ambivalence about God is closely connected with the movement of western culture, during the last two or three centuries, from a significantly "religious" orientation to one much more "secular." But its significance is more than merely historical. It is part of a deep uncertainty in modern consciousness about our own human existence, our freedom in the world and our responsibilities. Are we humans responsible simply to ourselves for the shape we give our lives and our society, and for what we do to the environment that surrounds and sustains us and which has brought us forth? Or must we understand our existence in terms of norms and values and realities that do not derive from us and to which we will be held accountable willy-nilly? The question about God is the question whether there is some extra-human reality in relationship to which human existence gains its being and its fulfillment, some ultimate point of reference in terms of which our human life and its problems and possibilities must be understood.

We do not know how to answer this question. Our symbol "God," heavy with the mythic overtones of our religious traditions, suggests a kind of being—an all-powerful sovereign, creator, and king of the universe—which no longer seems intelligible in our world, and which, moreover, may today deeply offend our moral sensibilities. To worship such a God, or to attempt to understand human existence in relationship to such a God, may thus seem to require a fundamental compromise of our moral and intellectual integrity (if we do not close our eyes to the self-deception in which we are engaged). Yet we have no other symbol in our western traditions which directs us so definitely toward an ultimate point of reference in terms of which all being and life, meaning and value, can be understood. Notions like "Nature" or "Universe" suggest an all-comprehensive inclusiveness; but it is not clear how human freedom and moral responsibility, human consciousness of meaning, human culture, the human quest for an understanding of our world and of our place within the world—in short, all those features of our lives that we value most—are to be interpreted in terms of such concepts, since their impersonal and abstract character has no intrinsic or necessary connection with these specifically human concerns. To our modern sensibility the natural order seems essentially impersonal and without purpose: what it would mean, therefore, to orient human existence and the quest for meaning in life simply in relationship to the Universe or to Nature is very obscure. It is not that interpretations of these symbols which make room for our specifically human concerns could not be devised; such moves are always possible. But the usefulness of abstract notions of this sort for interpreting human and humane concerns stands in sharp contrast with the richness of the symbol *God,* which has built into it from the ground up, so to speak, indissoluble connections with the themes of human freedom, responsibility, and meaning. If it is human orientation in life and in the world with which we are concerned, the symbol "God" presents itself—despite the serious problems connected with it—as the most powerful and significant in our (western) languages and traditions.

The long history of this symbol (from which stems much of its questionableness) gives it certain distinct advantages for orienting human life which no other western symbol can approach. Our major religious institutions, which still shape in decisive ways the lives of multitudes of people, take God as the central focus of worship, orientation, and service; our literary, artistic, and philosophical traditions are full of allusions to or reflection on God; our principal political and social institutions and practices were formed in connection with, and still formally reflect, respect for and devotion to God as the source and continuing foundation of human life. So despite its highly problematic character, this symbol is still very much alive in our culture, and there is every reason to explore carefully its potential for continuing to serve as the principal focus for orientation and devotion in modern life. Martin Buber has made the point well:

> ['God'] is the most heavy-laden of all human words. None has become so soiled, so mutilated. Just for this reason I may not abandon it. Generations of men have laid the burden of their anxious lives upon this word and weighed it to the ground; it lies in the dust and bears their whole burden. The races of man with their religious factions have torn the word to pieces; they have killed for it and died for it, and it bears their fingermarks and their blood. Where might I find a word like it to describe the highest! If I took the purest, most sparkling concept from the inner treasure-chamber of the philosophers, I could only capture thereby an unbinding product of thought. I could not capture the presence of Him whom the generations of men have honoured and degraded with their awesome living and dying. I do indeed mean Him whom the hell-tormented and heaven-storming generations of men mean. Certainly, they draw caricatures and write 'God' underneath; they murder one another and say 'in God's name' . . . And just for this reason is not the word 'God,' the word of appeal, the word which has become a *name,* consecrated in all human tongues for all times? We must esteem those who interdict it because they rebel against the injustice and wrong which are so readily referred to 'God' for authorization. But we may not give it up . . . We

> cannot cleanse the word 'God' and we cannot make it whole; but, defiled and mutilated as it is, we can raise it from the ground and set it over an hour of great care.[2]

What distinctive features characterize an orientation of human life that makes God its center? There is much to be said about this, but I wish here to call attention to two fundamental points complementary to each other. In the first place, to make God the central symbol in terms of which human existence is understood is to acknowledge that at its deepest level human life confronts us as profound mystery, as beyond our ken. We really do not know, and we can see no way in which we will ever be able to plumb, the ultimate meaning of human life—or whether there is such a thing as "ultimate" meaning. We have many questions about ourselves and our world: What is a truly "good" life, and how could one possibly know? Are some forms or modes of life more "authentically" human than others? Are there any identifiable basic problems, or malformations, or diseases of human existence or of the mind (what our religious traditions have called "sin") for which solutions or cures (salvation) can be found? What, if anything, are we humans here for? Are some religious or philosophical or moral or scientific traditions of more value than others in addressing these matters, or are all in diverse ways both helpful and misleading, leaving us in a relativistic confusion from which there is no escape? Should the world, and human existence within it, be understood most fundamentally with reference to "God"? to "material energies"? to "life"? to "Brahman"? to "Nirvana"? Or should we try to banish all such questions from our minds and live out our existence, so far as possible, simply in terms of the day-to-day issues and problems we immediately confront? And so on and on. It is this ultimate mystery (or these many mysteries) with which our lives and our world confront us that is emphasized by notions of God's "transcendence" of all that we are or can be, all we can know or even imagine—notions like God's "infinity," God's "absoluteness," God's "eternity," God's "all-powerfulness," God's "aseity." Such terms stress that the reality of God is beyond our comprehending or imagining; that is, that the ultimate reality with which we have to do, and thus the ultimate context of our lives and our world, is, in the last analysis, mystery. It is in terms of that which is beyond our understanding that we must, finally, understand our human situation.

Secondly, the more powerfully this dimension of mystery in God is emphasized, the more clearly the reality and significance of our own finitude comes into view. To be oriented on God—on the ultimate mystery in things—is to be aware of ourselves as limited in power and knowledge and in many other ways, to be aware that at virtually every point of our being and action we are dependent on and relative to what is beyond us, not under our control;

it is, in short, to be aware that we are "creatures." This does not mean, of course, that we can know nothing at all about ourselves or our world, that we live simply in a kind of inscrutable darkness. Nor need it imply that we have no significant powers or capabilities which we can exercise effectively to get along in life, that we have no real "freedom." But it does mean that all our knowing and acting are necessarily limited and restricted in important ways. It behooves us, therefore, to make no pretensions to understanding or knowledge beyond our proper reach; to be continually alert to the respects in which we are shaped by the concrete historical and cultural and psychological contexts in which we live; to take care that we do not seek to extend our powers or control beyond what is justifiable. In short, the symbol "God" calls us to a continuous awareness of our limitedness, our relativity. It is an important question, of course, just what is the "proper reach" of our knowledge and just what exercise of our powers is "justifiable." My contention here is that attempting to orient human life in terms of the symbol "God"—that is, attempting to live "under" God—has the complementary consequence of demanding that we live in a posture of continuing examination and reexamination of such issues. Such orientation should help us to become better aware, therefore, of our actual situatedness in the world and of our very particular responsibilities and freedoms in the concrete historical situation in which we find ourselves.

I certainly do not claim that everyone's use of the symbol "God" has been characterized by the particular dialectic of mystery and finitude which I have just sketched in a preliminary way. I do claim that these are prominent dimensions of the meaning which the word "God" has borne in western history and culture, and that it is important to call them to mind as we begin our theological reflection and construction—our exploration of the meaning of the symbol "God" in light of our present understanding of human existence in its cosmic context, and our reconception of humanity and the world in light of what we (eventually) take the word "God" to indicate.

If we choose to think of our existence in terms of the dialectic of God and the human to which I have just alluded, we will have to acknowledge from the outset that our own insight into and understanding of things, our moral intuitions and ethical standards, cannot be regarded as the highest court of appeal in the discrimination of truth and error, right and wrong, good and evil: all such human standards—however indispensable in our thinking and acting—must be regarded as subject to a higher tribunal symbolized by the name "God." When we invoke the symbol "God" in this connection, thus, we seek to focus our attention on a point of reference beyond the reach of our own insight and understanding, the ultimate resource on which our conceptions of right and good and true depend: God is the corrective of—that is, "God" is the name for that, whatever it might be, which serves to transform and correct—all our relativities, biases, and corruptions. Everything we know and do and believe is colored by our own private interests (as Freud, with his theory of "rationalization," saw clearly), and by our social position (as Marx's theory of "ideology" points out), and by the values and meanings acknowledged as important in our particular culture and social group (as the historical relativists have insisted). None of our values, norms, or insights (including those of our religion) can, therefore, claim absoluteness; however important they may be to us, they are always relative to our own needs, our language, our social problems and structures, our race and gender and class, our cultural setting. The word "God" is intended to refer us to a point beyond all these relativities, a point by reference to which we gain some sense of the inadequacy and relativity of our own positions. Being conceived as transcendent of every human perspective and situation, it can be accepted as corrective of them all. (In these remarks, of course, I am not addressing the question whether some being named "God" actually exists, but rather am setting out certain aspects of the meaning or content which, in our religious and cultural traditions, the symbol "God" has come to bear. Much more will need to be said about these matters as we proceed.)

The notions of God's "transcendence" or "absoluteness," central to the meaning of the symbol, suggest that God is to be conceived as not bound by any of the psychological or cultural relativities or interests which obscure our insight and understanding, making these always something less than true or right. Such a reference point "beyond the world" relativizes—that is, enables us to become sensitive to the relativity of—the values and meanings of our culture *in* the world: every claim, every norm (whether religious or secular), in every historical period becomes subject to criticism. Above all, such an ultimate point of reference can alert us to the likelihood that in our devotion to our own beliefs and practices and institutions we are involved in idolatries that need to be questioned and (perhaps drastically) corrected, even though we ourselves fail to see at just what points they are deficient or corrupted. Thus, human existence oriented on God may exemplify a combination of genuine humility with deep moral conviction—instead of the fanaticism that often accompanies human convictions, both religious and nonreligious, about truth and right. Faith in God, if God is taken seriously as the ultimate point of reference in terms of which all else is to be understood and relativized, means living with a certain tension in all our moral and intellectual convictions and judgments, a tension demanding that we always take into account their questionableness and thus the necessity to revise, correct, and refine them. It is a tension that must leave us always unsatisfied with our own insights and understanding, a tension always urging us to reach beyond our present position.

The symbol "God" is perhaps the most complex and dialectical of any bequeathed to us by western traditions. We should not be surprised, therefore, that it is difficult to formulate clearly its meaning or that our attempts to do so prove both inconclusive and controversial. The word "God" has many dimensions of meaning, many nuances, many uses, and we can never do justice to them all. The search for fundamental orientation in human life, however, appears to underlie most of the serious uses of this symbol. This is what is involved in acts of worship and prayer, in the asking for God's "will" in confusing moments of decision and for God's "help" in difficult situations; and it is gratitude for the guidance and strength believed given by God, and wonder that such profound meaning and support are available to help orient humans in this world, that is expressed in the worshipper's adoration and praise. "For from him and through him and to him are all things [as Paul put it]. To him [therefore] be glory forever" (Rom. 11:36). "God" is our western name for the ultimate reality with which humans have to do, that in terms of which all life gains its meaning, that from which to be separated is death. God, thus, is that ultimate point of reference in relation to which all else—including especially our human existence—should be understood.

Attempting to grasp this notion of an ultimate center of orientation and worship raises some difficult problems. How is devotion to God, as expressed, for example, in the activity of worship, to be related to the rest of life? to the need to earn a living or to the desire for play, the desire to forget the serious and the somber in life? How is it to be connected with our intense personal experiences of friendship, love, and hatred? Or to the ordinary pleasures of food, sex, physical exertion? How is devotion to God related to other loyalties important to us, such as family and friends or our nation? how related to other causes to which we are committed? to justice? truth? democracy? to working toward a more humane world? Humans enjoy, and necessarily must pursue, many diverse values and goods in this life: how are all these to be related to *God,* the ultimate Value and ultimate Good? How are we to divide our attention, energy, loyalties, and work between all these others and God? Jesus said, "You shall love the Lord your God with all your heart, and with all your soul, and with all your mind, and with all your strength" (Mk. 12:30). What could this conceivably mean in face of all these other goods and values to which we are (quite properly, it would seem) devoted? These questions confront us with the problem of God and the idols—those rivals of God for our interest and commitment—an issue which arises as soon as we try to understand what it means to say that God properly claims our full loyalty and devotion.

The notion of God, thus, as the ultimate point of reference and the only appropriate object of worship and devotion, generates immediately and unavoidably a second notion, the concept of the *idol*—the concept of that which we often, perhaps almost always, confuse with God. According to the logic of the concept of God, these rivals of God for our devotion and loyalty, though they promise fulfillment and meaning and life, ultimately bring destruction and death; it was this central religious problem of distinguishing God from the idols that was at the heart of the struggles in ancient Israel reported in the Old Testament. "Faith in God" and the "worship of God" are clearly never simple straightforward matters, for it is important that it be *God,* not an idol, in whom our faith is placed. But how can we ever be certain of anything as elusive as that? What are needed are criteria for distinguishing God from all idols, criteria that will enable us to recognize which claims to deity are false and deceitful and misleading, and which are true. Thus, the central issue of theology emerges right out of the heart of religious devotion and worship: Who or what is truly God? How can we recognize God, how distinguish God from idols? How can we ascertain that the "God" we are worshipping and serving is not an idol? However abstract and complex theological reflection may sometimes become, it has its origins in the profoundest quest of the religious life, the quest for God. If God were an object or reality directly and immediately apparent for all to see and recognize, no such quest would be required. The issue arises because God, taken by religious faith to be the most important reality to human existence, is also in many respects the most hidden from us. Central to our investigations here will be the attempt to address this issue of God and the idols, and to formulate criteria for distinguishing idols from God.

Once the importance of this problem is acknowledged, a door is opened to innumerable other issues. What sort of criterion is appropriate for distinguishing the "ultimate point of reference" from all proximate or penultimate matters? Is it essentially a metaphysical criterion which we need here, a criterion which will enable us to distinguish ultimate Reality from all partial realities or unrealities? Or is it the epistemological distinction of truth from error which would be most helpful? Is it perhaps some moral distinction of good from evil which is wanted? Or is it rather the religious contrast of the holy from the profane? Any or all of these suggestions might seem plausible.

Perhaps the question about criteria should not be framed in such an abstract way; perhaps it should be seen as fundamentally a question about the metaphors or images—or types of metaphors and images—in terms of which God is conceived and understood. Is it *philosophical concepts*—for example, "ultimate reality," "being," the distinction between "personal" and "impersonal" principles or realities—that should be given priority in attempts to think of God? Or are *mythic images*—"Lord of history," "Judge of all the earth," "King of the universe," "our Father in heaven"—more appropriate? Or should God be conceived by means of some combination of both these modalities, or perhaps in some other terms distinct from each of them? Are certain modalities of language more prone to idolatrous uses than others? If so, which ones? And why is this the case? It is evident that once the importance of the question of God and the idols is posed, a Pandora's box opens before us. No longer is it possible to avoid questions like: What can we properly mean by "God"? How can we decide this? What is it that makes some views on these matters preferable to others? A wide range of theological and metatheological issues comes before us.

In the long history of theological reflection many of these issues have been explored, and contemporary theologians cannot afford to neglect the insights of earlier generations. But the vast growth of knowledge in the natural and human sciences during the past few centuries also bears significantly on these matters and must, therefore, be taken into account in theological reflection today. It is clear that the word "God," like all other words, grew up in and through a history, its use and meaning changing and developing in accord with the needs, interests, and practices of many different peoples. The question of the meaning of this word, then, cannot be answered simply through abstract philosophical or theological argument; it must be explored with the aid of modern sociological and psychological and linguistic tools. Such explorations, we today understand, should not be directed primarily toward the discovery of some unchanging "eternal form" or some "authoritatively revealed" dogma. They must be directed, rather, to what the word "God" has actually *meant* in human discourse. Why has it been important, to communities and to individuals, to devote themselves to what they called "God"? What sort of meaning or value did—and does—such a stance have for people? How has "sin" or "estrangement from God" been experienced and understood? To what have "bondage to idols" and "salvation" referred? These are all largely historical, sociological, and psychological questions.

There are other more strictly sociological dimensions to the meaning of the word "God." What is the significance, for example, of the fact that devotion to "God" has been connected with important and powerful institutions in society—with churches, synagogues, and temples, with priesthoods and special rituals and worship practices, with distinctive patterns of life? How and why do religious ideas and claims lead persons, and indeed whole societies, to organize or reorder their lives in certain distinctive ways, legitimizing and encouraging some patterns and condemning others? What range of social functions does "God-talk" perform? What are its political and economic uses—and misuses or abuses? What significance is to be given the fact that wars are often fought "in the name of God"? It is clear that studies drawn from cultural anthropology and sociology, from history and linguistics, from psychology and comparative religions all must be taken into account in theological work today. None of this, however, should occasion surprise since (as we have noted) the question of God and the question of the meaning of human existence are so intimately interconnected. Whatever has been learned in the human sciences, then, about society, culture, and personality in general, and about the role and significance of religious symbols, institutions, and practices in particular, must be integrated into our modern theological conceptions. Account must be taken of the contemporary understanding of the interconnection of the spiritual dimensions of life with its biological and economic dimensions; Freudian questions about the role of sublimation and repression in life, Marxist questions about oppressive social institutions and about ideology, and sociobiological questions about the interconnection of all forms of life and about the genetic foundations of human institutions and practices, must all be explored. An interpretation of God for the contemporary world can easily make moves that are naively idolatrous if it does not avail itself of the most subtle and sophisticated insights of the human sciences.

The symbol "God," however, has bearing not only on human existence and its problems. From a very early period it has been closely connected with cosmological questions and interpretations: God has been regarded as the Creator of the heavens and the earth, the Source and Governor of the entire natural order as well as human life. When one translates these notions into modern terms, a further series of large and difficult questions arise for theology. How is God to be related to the vast universe of which we learn in contemporary astrophysics? How is this overarching context within which all life on planet Earth falls to be understood theologically? What can it mean to speak of God in a world believed to have issued from a "big bang" fifteen billion years ago, a world in which entropy may well have the last word? If theological claims are to be intelligible and relevant to today's world, they must be formulated in close interconnection with modern cosmological, evolutionary, and ecological ideas. Most contemporary theological reflection has almost completely ignored this task, and this has contributed substantially to the increasing implausibility of the symbol "God" in the modern intellectual world. It has also made it possible for dangerously idolatrous uses of "God" to persist into modern times, uses which have helped create the ecological crisis we face today and which continue to thwart efforts to address that crisis effectively.

It might well seem, then, that our attempt to work out an understanding of God should begin with a consideration of the nature of the world in which we live, and the nature and problems of human existence. The human is, after all, we ourselves; humanity is directly available to us. And the world is all around us, much of it known to us through modern science. We surely can say much about humanity, what our central human problems are, and what brings human fulfillment (salvation); and we can say a good bit about the world. If we can get these matters clear, it might seem, we will be in a better position to see what we might call "God"—presumably that in relationship to which salvation or fulfillment comes to us humans in this world.

To proceed straightforwardly along this path, however, would be seriously misleading; and it is important that we see why this is the case. We must not take for granted that "the human" and "the world" are relatively stable and well-known points of reference, immediately accessible to us and dependable, while God is a kind of speculative answer to our deepest human needs or an extrapolation from certain cosmological ideas. To make assumptions of this sort would be to understand the idea of God as essentially a kind of function of our notions of the human and the world; and that would be a mistake. God is supposed to be the Creator of all that is: that is, according to the logic of the concept of God, we and the world are functions of God, not God a function of us and our needs; God is the ultimate point of reference in terms of which the human and the world are to be understood, not the human and the world the principal points of reference for understanding God. We would be profoundly misconceiving things if we tried to develop an understanding of God simply out of, or on the basis of, our understandings of the human and the world. And we would be conceiving our present task much too simplistically if we supposed we could develop an adequate anthropology and cosmology without simultaneously taking up specifically theological concerns and requirements.

With this point in mind, some might argue that the proper theological order requires us to work out our conception of God first, then develop our notions of the human and the cosmos in terms appropriate to our understanding of God. Traditionally the doctrine of God has been regarded as the first and primary doctrine of Christian theology: for example, in the *Summa Theologica* of Thomas Aquinas the first forty-three questions are devoted to God, and Book One of John Calvin's *Institutes of the Christian Religion* is on the knowledge of God. The understandings of the world and of humanity, then, have been worked out (or so it has seemed) in terms largely laid down by the conception of God.

To conceive theology as proceeding in this sort of direct serial order, however, is also much too simplistic. In fact it has never been possible for theologians to begin simply and directly with God. God is not an object immediately available to human beings, to be perceived, examined, described, interpreted. Where is God? Who is God? What is God? How could we possibly begin simply and directly with God? Whatever was thought or said about God was always based on a tradition (including the Bible) which had already developed through a long history and was shaped by the experience and reflection of many generations. The theologian's work, thus, was really directed toward apprehending, interpreting, and elaborating the complex of meaning tagged by the word "God" in the traditions within which, and on the basis of which, he or she was working. This was a pattern of meaning, moreover, which was always interconnected with other central meaning-complexes, such as those indicated by such words as "humanity," "the world," and "evil," and it was not understood independently of these connections. So theological reflection actually proceeded—though this was not always clearly perceived—only through complex dialectical moves in which the interdependence of a number of key concepts was taken into account; it was never a straightforward linear deductive process.

Contemporary theologians, similarly, must develop their conceptions of God, the world, and the human in dialectical interrelationship with one another, instead of trying to derive any of these from the other(s) in linear fashion. We must work out a conception of human life and the world which makes intelligible our talk about God, if we are to understand who or what God is; and similarly we must develop our conception of God in intelligible connection with our understanding of the human and the world. From a modern point of view it is not possible to understand human existence apart from its wider situatedness in the ecology of life on this planet; and, of course, planet Earth can be understood only within the context of the solar system and the wider universe. So our anthropological work leads ineluctably into cosmology, and these two together must be developed in interconnection with our specifically theological interests and ideas. Theologians today, as Francis Fiorenza has argued, must develop their thinking within a "wide reflective equilibrium" in which a number of very complex factors are continually qualified and nuanced by balancing them over and against each other.[3]

We cannot, of course, begin with everything at once. How, then, should we get under way? Where should we begin? It is important for us to remember that all of the words and concepts we have been using so freely here—"God," "world," "humanity," and so on—are, after all, *human* words and concepts. They were created by human beings as they sought to come to terms with the problems of life, and they function exclusively within human languages. Hence, if we examine (some of) the functions and uses of these terms with which we are working, we may find a way to begin our theological work. For example, if we wish to understand who or what it is that we are speaking of—or trying to speak of—when we say "God," we should examine what those humans who use this word mean by it. What function does the notion of God play in their speech, their thought, and their lives? What are humans trying to do when they speak of or to God, when they devote themselves to God in service and worship? We must look carefully at our human practices, seeking to see what function(s) talk about and devotion to God have in human existence. Thus we are brought back to anthropology again as a starting point for developing an understanding of God.

This does not mean, however, that we have simply returned to our position of a moment ago, for we now are aware of the complex interconnectedness of the notions of God and the human and the world. On the one hand, we can say, any attempt to understand God must begin with our human practices and speech; for "God" is a human word and a human idea, and only by seeing what we humans are trying to do when we speak of God or worship God will we be able to understand this word and this idea. This implies that if we are to have a plausible notion of who or what God is, we shall have to develop simultaneously a conception of human life, within which talk about God is, in fact, intelligible; this is one thing we will be attempting to do in this book. But, on the other hand, it seems apparent that for any position that takes God seriously (certainly for any Christian position) God will need to be conceived as the ultimate point of reference in terms of which all else—the entire world with which we humans have to do—is understood. So our human existence itself, and our world, can properly be understood only in terms of what God is and what God is doing with us humans and with the world, as well as what God requires of us humans. In this respect, the understanding of the human and the world to which we come must be derivative from our understanding of God—and, for Christian faith, from what Jesus Christ reveals of God. These complex interconnected contentions we shall also attempt to take into account in this book. (I should observe here that these preliminary formulations of the problematic with which we will be concerned are, of necessity, grossly oversimplified, and thus in many respects misleading. In the course of our work we will discover that the interrelations of God, humanity, and the world—here articulated in more or less traditional, commonsense terms—will need to be rather drastically reconceived. Such reconception is a major objective of this volume.)

Thus we must deal with the anthropological and cosmological presuppositions of our talk of God as well as the anthropological and cosmological consequences of such talk; and we must deal with the theological presuppositions of our understanding of humanity and the world as well as the theological consequences of this understanding. We must concern ourselves both with how it is possible for us to speak of God at all, what it is that we are trying to do when we speak of God, and also with the question of what it means to understand who or what we humans are, what our problems might be and what our proper flourishing.

However difficult and complex the issues thus far discussed may seem, it is important to complicate them further. The central question for theology is not merely, or even preeminently, who or what God is, or how God is to be distinguished from the idols; nor is it what humanity is, and what the central problems of human existence are. It is not primarily a speculative question, a problem of knowledge, at all. Most fundamentally it is a *practical* question: How are we to live? To what should we devote ourselves? to what causes give ourselves? Put in religious terms: How can we truly serve God? What is proper worship? As we noted above, it is out of this practical concern that theology arises in the first place. Now that we have seen how complex and difficult is the question of the meaning of the symbol "God," we must come back once again to this issue. Problems of the religious life and of religious ethics, problems of human abilities and aptitudes, of motivation and discipline, of human aspirations and goals for life, must now all be added to the questions of meaning and knowledge which we have been discussing. All the practical problems of living and acting thus become central issues for theology; nothing in all of life is irrelevant or to be ignored. Of course, we should have realized this from the beginning: in western traditions God has been regarded preeminently as the "Maker of heaven and earth," the "Creator of all things visible and invisible." It should not surprise us, then, to learn that coming to understand who or what God is cannot be separated from plumbing the depths and scaling the heights of the entire world of human experience and imagination.

By now it should be clear how ambitious—indeed, impossible—is the task we have begun to set for ourselves. It is important that we recognize this clearly at the outset and that we not forget it. In the course of our investigations we will be considering in detail some of the issues briefly mentioned in this chapter, along with many others; we will be scrutinizing them, analyzing them, making inferences and deductions, drawing conclusions. This intensive work may lead us to think that we are really beginning to get the problems of human life and the question of God under significant control. That would be a serious mistake, an illusion often fostered by theological work. What we will have gained control of will be at most something of our own manufacture; to simply identify this directly with the mystery of God would be idolatry. As we proceed, we will find it necessary constantly to remind ourselves that what we are seeking to explore and understand in our theological work is ultimately beyond our ken, so we must conduct our theological inquiry in a spirit of humility and continuing self-criticism, a spirit of openness and of humor. Anselm grasped the issue well when he defined God in a conceptually elegant expression as that "than which nothing greater can be conceived."[4] But he did not deceive himself about the adequacy of this achievement, for later he went on to say: "O Lord, thou art not only that than which a greater cannot be conceived, but thou art a being greater than can be conceived."[5] To grasp what we mean by "God" we will need to stretch our powers of conception and understanding to their limits, all the while recognizing that our every formulation falls short of its goal.

The fact that the question of God will inevitably draw us into depths we cannot manage should not lead us either into despair over our efforts to understand or into cynicism about theology. On the contrary. It is precisely through exercising our intellectual and other powers to the utmost that we come to discover our true limits—and thus gain some glimmer of what is meant by the symbol "God," with its reference beyond those limits. If and as we thus gain some dim sense, some bare understanding, of who or what God is, we will also come to a profounder awareness of the range and power of the idols before whom we all too easily and too often bow. Our theological work, we may dare to hope, will give us a greater sensitivity to the many faces which idolatry wears in our world, and in this way help to open us to God.

It is necessary to make one more preliminary remark here. This book will not address the issues raised by all the diverse religious traditions which have attempted to come to grips with the question of God (though I will need to take some account of these various traditions, since a central issue with which we will be concerned in these pages is the religious pluralism of our world). Our inquiry will be much more specific and limited than that.[6] We will be attempting to develop a viable contemporary *Christian* interpretation of God, humanity, and the world. The special constraints this will place upon us, and the possibilities it will open for us, will come clearer as we proceed. Before such matters can be intelligently discussed, however, it is necessary to consider how, in view of the ultimacy of the mystery to which the symbol "God" points, it is possible to do theological work at all. To questions of theological method, therefore, we now turn.

2. Theology: One-Dimensional, Two-Dimensional, or Holistic?

How should we proceed in our attempt to develop a Christian interpretation of God, humanity, and the world appropriate to contemporary life? Where should we begin? What path should we follow? In the past religious reflection has usually understood itself to be based, for the most part, on an authoritative tradition which, it was assumed, contained or presented in some way the Truth about life, that which brings salvation (healing, wholeness, fulfillment) to human beings. This has been true not only of Christian, Jewish, and Moslem theologies; it was true of Hindu, Buddhist, and much other religious reflection as well. Usually this Truth was believed to be located in a scripture, a sacred text or collection of texts, from which it could be extracted if the correct methods of exegesis and interpretation were followed. Of course, there was always much dispute about which methods were correct and also about what the scripture meant. But all parties were agreed on one fundamental principle: scripture contains ultimate Truth, and it is the task of religious study to ascertain what this Truth is and to interpret it. Hence, religious writing around the world has often manifested an essentially authoritarian structure; it was intended to be simply commentary on and explication of authoritative sacred texts, rather than critical analysis of those texts or fresh creative thinking.

This has also been true of Christian theology, the sacred text being the Bible.[1] However, although the authority of the Bible was usually taken for granted in theological reflection, engaging in such reflection inevitably tended to undercut that authority in certain ways. The Bible presents to its readers a very peculiar subject, *God;* and this creates difficult problems for human reflection (as we have already begun to note). Though the idea of God has itself been used to undergird biblical authority throughout much of Christian history—in the claim that the Bible was "divine revelation" or the "word of God" and was thus absolutely authoritative—the recognition that absoluteness belongs ultimately to God alone tends (as we shall see) to undermine every other alleged authority. Thus, belief in God has, in the long run, worked to weaken the Bible's authority rather than support it.

It is largely with political metaphors that the Bible constructs its picture of the world. God ("YHWH" in the Hebrew Bible/Old Testament) is presented as the world's lord and king as well as its creator, and the universe is seen as basically a "kingdom" which God rules from on high. To this end he—for this is clearly a male deity—gives humanity a fundamental law to order human life; he sends prophets and other messengers with special communiqués; he governs human affairs through earthly kings and emperors, whose activities he is directing (however unbeknownst to them). Ultimately God will bring history to its intended end or goal, which he had predetermined for it from the beginning. According to the New Testament, the great climactic movement of history toward this final consummation is already under way: God initiated it when he sent his only son, Jesus Christ, to earth, and it will be completed when Jesus returns on the clouds of heaven, finally to bring in the divine kingdom.

This picture of the world, developed with the aid of political symbolism, was worked out in considerable detail and with many nuances. At its center, of course, was *God* (not the Bible) and the story of what God has done and is doing: God was the reality to be worshipped and served; the Bible was of interest and importance only because it tells this story of God. As the medium through which God becomes known, however, the Bible was indispensable. It was often viewed, thus, as the very "word of God," as the "divine revelation" through which God makes Godself[2] known to humans. But the Bible's authority is in every respect derivative. It is because the Bible is believed to contain *revelation,* revealed Truth from the Lord of the universe, that it is regarded as authoritative. This means, on the one hand, that the Bible has had immense authority for believers; but it also means, on the other, that there is a principle which can undercut that authority completely: God. If there seems any reason to suppose God might be in some respects other than as portrayed in the Bible, or if the Bible turns out to be significantly unclear or ambiguous in its picture of God, biblical authority will be seriously damaged.

Because of this (potential) tension between the biblical text and the central subject-matter of that text, Christian theology has never been simply a one-dimensional hermeneutical enterprise, limited entirely to the explication of texts; it has also always been critical and constructive in character, concerned with working out more adequate ways to conceptualize God. All such constructive efforts, of course, involved moving in some way beyond what was given in the Bible, either by drawing on extra-biblical materials or through new creative insights. Hence, however much theologians have understood their work to be essentially hermeneutical in character, it has, in fact, always involved much more than this.

Since God was portrayed in the Bible essentially as a person or agent—an active being conceived on a political and personal model—who was working creatively and redemptively in the world, it seemed reasonable to assume that knowledge of God could be acquired in a variety of ways. Some believed the love and care of God could be directly experienced, or that a "mystical union" with God was possible; others, understanding that all nature was God's handiwork, made inferences about God's existence and nature on the basis of their observations of the world roundabout them. What could be learned about God in these ways was often harmonious with what the Bible taught: then scripture seemed confirmed as true. But it was also always possible for a conflict with scriptural images and claims to emerge. Thus, for example, mystical experience (in the traditions stemming from Plotinus and Pseudo-Dionysius) of an ultimate Unity or Ground underlying all else seemed to suggest a reality very different from the personal agent-God of the Bible; and philosophical claims that ultimate reality must be completely changeless Being (Parmenides) or an Unmoved Mover (Aristotle) proved difficult to reconcile with the biblical picture of God as continuously active in the world and responsive to humans, eventually becoming incarnate in history in the man Jesus. Above all, the growing knowledge of the natural world—especially as that developed in the increasingly convincing picture worked out by Copernicus, Galileo, and Newton and culminating in modern geology, biology, and astrophysics—made the biblical "three-story" universe seem curiously antique, requiring correction in fundamental ways. Not surprisingly, Christians have frequently refused to face the difficult problems posed by issues like these, and have instead attempted simply to reassert the truth of what they took to be "the biblical story," making the smallest possible adjustments in it. Mere "human speculation," it was claimed, must always give way before "divine revelation." This sort of authoritarian move was made especially by Protestants (both during the Reformation and subsequently) attempting to overcome what they regarded as serious corruptions in Christian thinking, practice, and doctrine. And it is still often found in modern neo-orthodoxies as well as fundamentalisms. It is based on the (mis)conception that theology can and should be an essentially one-dimensional hermeneutical enterprise.

As theologians have become aware of the full significance of these tensions between biblical and nonbiblical ideas and images, however, they have been forced to face openly the question of the relationship of biblical authority to other sources of theological insight and knowledge. Thus, theology came to be understood in largely two-dimensional terms, and questions about the relationship of "revealed theology" to "natural theology" or of "special" to "general" revelation, of "reason and revelation" or of "revelation and experience," became important. It has always been difficult, however, to relate these two dimensions to each other in a way that would successfully preserve the full authority of the biblical revelation; and some openly admitted that human reason was here confronted with paradoxes which it could not overcome. But since it was God, the ultimate mystery beyond all human comprehension, about which humans were trying to think here (it was argued), they should not be surprised if their lowly human concepts got into tangles. Theologians were thus able to persuade themselves that, for example, God can quite properly be thought of both as the Unmoved Mover or Being itself (as required, supposedly, by rational philosophical reflection) and as the incarnate Son deeply involved in the vicissitudes of a very particular history—though we mere humans are unable to see how these notions can be reconciled with each other. With the revelationally grounded authority of scripture taken for granted, Christians felt themselves required to *believe* certain things to be true—particularly if implied by major Christian doctrines—even though they could not understand how this could be the case or just what it meant. There are, of course, many ways to diminish or moderate the paradoxes of such an approach—as the work of a Thomas Aquinas, for example, shows—but the underlying tensions have always remained.

What is feared most, of course, by those who take authoritarian positions of this sort, is that the tensions between biblical and other claims (endemic to every two-dimensional theology) will call into question the scriptural claims themselves, and suggest that God is in significant ways *other* than as portrayed in the Bible, thus implying that the scriptural portrait is, at least in certain important respects, misleading or erroneous. Thus the authority of revelation—and consequently of traditional theology as a whole—would be seriously undercut, and the doors would be opened wide to quite diverse ways to think of God. God might be conceived, for example, as the creator of the world but not its governor (Deism); as Nature (Spinoza); as Being (a principal medieval, as well as modern, view), or as Nonbeing or the Void (certain mystics); as in principle unknowable (Hume, Kant, and many others). In all these moves, with extra-biblical ideas and knowledge becoming important factors in making theological judgments, the Bible rapidly loses its much vaunted authority. And in due course it is realized that the very claim about the Bible's "authoritative revelation" is itself grounded on human judgments and decisions, namely the decisions and judgments of those church authorities and others who first made that claim in the early periods of Christian history. Once this is recognized, it becomes apparent that these judgments, no more than any others, can properly be shielded from critical scrutiny and reconsideration.

A 2-Dim'l
view = taking
the Bible as authori-
tative; we to
in interpret it with
Reason, experience,
etc.

A two-dimensional view is, thus, inherently unstable; and the theologian seems always to be fighting a losing battle, being forced to retreat to some new position where it is hoped a firm stand can be made. Whenever new experience, or recently developed scientific theories, or new modes of philosophical reflection call into question what had been regarded as revealed truth, it becomes necessary to reformulate the theological claims; each time this happens, of course, they become less credible. The history of modern theology has been the story of repeated defeats in this unceasing struggle with secular orientations and knowledges. As this embarrassing history has unfolded, it has become increasingly clear that theological assertions and claims can no longer be given the privileged position they once had. They must be—and in fact are—reviewed and reformulated constantly like all other claims to knowledge; and the criteria for this critical and constructive theological work—as with all other human cognitive activity—are rooted in nothing other than our human powers to reflect, to reason, and to judge. Our major theological ideas, as well as the criteria governing theological reflection and construction, have in fact emerged within the ongoing activity of human religious and theological reflection over hundreds of years; and they continue to live, and are increasingly refined, in the reflective and constructive work of theologians—and many others—today. Recognizing this, it is no longer appropriate to ground any theological claims uncritically on the traditional mythology of a special divine revelation by the Lord of the world. All such claims must today be subjected to critical scrutiny and reconstruction.

Criticism
of
revelation ✓

This sort of understanding, toward which theological reflection over the centuries has been increasingly moving in spite of itself, may seem to express what is in many respects a complete reversal of the one-dimensional authoritarianism that, for many centuries, characterized most Christian theology. Here human reason and experience appear to have become the ultimate judge and arbiter of all theological contentions, including those deriving directly from the Bible; and thus a second sort of one-dimensional approach has, especially since the period of Enlightenment, become increasingly prominent. Consider, for example, the not uncommon argument that the only theological contentions that may properly be regarded as valid or true are those grounded simply and directly in "experience." On the face of it, this may seem plausible enough, but there are, in fact, many different kinds and orders, levels and dimensions of experience, and quite diverse ways of approaching and interpreting these. Without additional guiding principles, methods of procedure, and criteria of judgment (themselves not directly supplied by experience), it would be impossible to know how to proceed in moving from "experience" to theology; for sharply different ways of theologizing can all quite properly claim an experiential basis. There can be, for example, *psychological* approaches, which may argue from certain specific sorts of experience (of the "holy" or the "sacred," or of "awe" or "forgiveness" or "prayer," or of "conversion" or "mystical union" or other "heightened" states of consciousness) to theological claims; *sociological* approaches, as with liberation theologies and their concern for structures of "oppression" in human existence; *phenomenological* approaches, which describe and analyze the nature of religion or religious experience (or human experience in general), and then attempt to ground theology on that description and analysis; *history of religions* approaches, which attempt to study the vast panorama of human religious history and experience, drawing theological conclusions from what is learned there; *gender* approaches, in which claims may be made about unique female or male capacities or experiences to which theology must be accountable; *metaphysical* approaches, which present as a basis for theological reflection some particular theoretical conception of the world that is claimed to give the fullest or most adequate interpretation of the wide reaches of human experience; and so on and on. It is evident that "human experience" is a vague and amorphous concept, and simple appeal to it actually tells us little about how theological positions are or should be constructed; a one-dimensional experientialism is, thus, no more feasible in theology than a one-dimensional biblicism.

Most theologians in the modern period have recognized this (including many focusing on one or another of the types of experience mentioned above), and in their methodological reflection have attempted, therefore, to retain some version of a two-dimensional conception, with theology understood to be built up by balancing what is drawn from divine revelation with what is given by human experience/reason.[3] Paul Tillich's "method of correlation"—according to which divine revelation provides definitive "answers" to the fundamental "questions" posed for humans by reason and experience[4]—represents a recent influential attempt to state carefully one view of the methodological implications of such an understanding. With the breakdown of neo-orthodoxy in the second half of the twentieth century, however, Tillich's formulation of the method of correlation—especially his assumption that theologians work directly with a divine or revelatory given—has seemed increasingly dubious to many.[5] Hence, instead of attempting to correlate "revelation" with the contemporary situation (as Tillich proposed), it has been suggested that the theological task is to bring what is of central meaning or significance in Christian scripture or tradition—for example, the fundamental themes of the "Christian classics" (Tracy) or the earliest Christian "kerygma" (Ogden)[6]—into significant connection with contemporary life and its problems. Theology thus continues to understand itself as having an indispensable hermeneutical dimension, but the principal "given" to be interpreted has been scaled down from the absoluteness of divine revelation to the relativity of a particular historical tradition.

A good argument can be made for this reconception of the theological task. Humans always live out of traditions of value and meaning which give form to their lives and their experience and in terms of which they understand themselves and their world; and the Christian tradition has served the West in this way for centuries. It would be foolish to scuttle all Christian values, Christian understandings of the meaning of human life, Christian ethics—as expressed, for example, in emphasis on the unique significance of each individual person, and on the importance of responsible and loving human relations—simply because these can no longer be legitimated by belief they were divinely revealed; or, for that matter, simply because we cannot "scientifically confirm" them. Christian theology today, thus, can quite properly be understood to have the important cultural task of studying this tradition, retrieving and critically assessing its variant forms and ascertaining what has given it its cultural and human significance and power—thus defining carefully what in the nineteenth century was called the "essence of Christianity"—and then setting this out in ways which make it available for addressing urgent contemporary problems.

F. D. E. Schleiermacher's attempt early in the nineteenth century to define Christianity's "essence" through developing a theology grounded on a reading of the Christian "self-consciousness"[7] presents the first great modern example of this way of interpreting Christian faith and theology. Schleiermacher was followed by many others in the nineteenth century who took a similar "confessional" approach (that is, an approach in which theology becomes essentially an exposition of what a particular group believes and values), a development that reached a high point, perhaps, with Adolf Harnack's famous book *The Essence of Christianity.*[8] This was quickly followed, however, by Ernst Troeltsch's critical analysis of the concept of "essence of Christianity" itself,[9] and his massive historical work showing that Christian faith, as presented by most modern theologians, was in fact largely a configuration of modern liberal western values. Troeltsch showed that the belief that there is some historically demonstrable "essence of Christianity" (as Schleiermacher, Harnack, and others had supposed) is simply false: every attempt to grasp and assess what Christianity has been in the past, and what it can mean for modern life, will necessarily be relative to the standpoint of each particular writer, and thus subjectivistic and ambiguous. Moreover, his study of nonwestern cultures and religions led Troeltsch to conclude that the embeddedness of Christianity in western culture meant that its traditional universalistic claim to possess a truth valid for all humanity must itself be put into question:[10] at best theologians might speak of Christian truth as appropriate to and necessary for western civilization and those formed within it. The "essence of Christianity" confessional approach, thus, has shown itself to be vague, subjectivistic, undisciplined, and at best pertinent only to the West.[11]

Many theologians continue, however, to work within the two-dimensional framework of correlational theology, apparently believing that more methodological precision in clarifying its procedures will overcome the difficulties inherent in it.[12] Schubert Ogden and David Tracy,[13] for example, have argued in recent years for such a theology: the Christian theologian is, on the one hand, to analyze and interpret the foundational documents of Christianity, and then, on the other, to correlate the central themes found in those documents with the themes and problems of contemporary life. This proposal, though a direct descendant of Tillich's "method of correlation," has (at least in Tracy's version) put aside Tillich's revelationally grounded claim that the final "answer" to all the most fundamental human problems is to be found in "the Christian message." That claim has, in effect, been reduced to the contention that the basic Christian themes are still important for modern culture—a much more modest affirmation than that made in Tillich's revelationally grounded theology.

This is obviously a significant change: if one no longer takes seriously Christianity's claim to universal validity, the justification for a single-minded focus on the Christian tradition as the principal basis for theological work seems to have disappeared. Human history, as Troeltsch saw clearly, has produced many great traditions of value and meaning; why, then, investigate only (or chiefly) the Christian heritage in attempting to find orientation for modern life? Troeltsch regarded such theological work as having some justification, despite its essentially parochial character, because in his time the several great civilizations appeared to exist in relative independence from one another, each with its own proper integrity; Christian theology, thus, precisely because of its relativity to the West, could still perform important services within that culture. But today we are steadily moving toward "one world." All of humankind is already economically interdependent in many ways; modern means of communication and transportation put all parts of the globe in continuous touch with one another, so that the relative isolation which allowed diverse cultures to develop independently is rapidly disappearing; we all live under a common ultimate threat of ecological disaster and nuclear annihilation today, and this makes rapid movement toward much fuller human cooperation around the globe imperative. In today's world, then, it hardly seems justifiable for theology—understanding itself now to be working not with the "absolute Truth" of divine revelation but principally with the resources of meaning and value carried in human traditions—to confine itself to only one major line of human history, however rich and fruitful that line has been and may continue to be. "Essence of Christianity" theologies, or programs which advocate addressing the problems of contemporary life simply through "correlating" them with the major themes found in the classical Christian documents, are really no longer adequate to or appropriate within our contemporary human situation.

There is another reason for calling such tradition-focused programs into question, an internal theological reason. As we have seen, a central Christian theme—indeed, the most fundamental of all Christian themes—is *God.* In the authoritative documents of the tradition, however, God is never presented as simply of parochial Christian or Jewish interest, merely the principal symbol of a particular religious community: God is taken to be the creator of the world and the savior of all peoples, the ultimate reality behind all that exists and all that happens. God is a reality, therefore, important to all humans everywhere (whether this is known to them or not). However, even though on the face of it this is a correct and appropriate interpretation of the meaning of the symbol "God," it seems less and less adequate today—in view of what we know about the significance of some of the weighty symbols in other religious traditions, symbols with respect to which similar sorts of claims can be (and have been) made—to attempt to justify thinking of God in this way solely on the basis of the import which the symbol has had in a single line of human tradition going back a few thousand years. With respect to this point, the absolutism of the older one-dimensional theologies—both the hermeneutical theology which emphasized that God had revealed Godself decisively in the Bible, and those experiential or rational theologies that attempted to develop carefully argued metaphysical positions—expressed more clearly what is really at stake in theological work than have confessional approaches. The seeming modesty of the latter actually conceals a kind of hidden arrogance and idolatry. Arrogance, because they assume the right to speak of the ultimate reality with which all humans have to do on the basis of what is openly acknowledged to be a single preferred tradition;[14] idolatry, because, in grounding their claims exclusively on mere human tradition (instead of, for example, God's supposed revelation), they give absoluteness to what is admittedly a historically relative set of human values and concepts instead of to God alone.

Again, this is stated arrogantly, but it need not be so.

What can be done with respect to these problems? If theology may not understand itself any longer as largely a matter of straightforward explication and interpretation of Christian traditions and/or experience, what should it do and be? Should it be understood (as some recommend) as the "science of religion," the attempt to understand and interpret the full range of human religious experience, ideas, practices, institutions? That is certainly one way to go, and it emphasizes a point that must be taken very seriously today, namely the importance of the (scientific and historical) study of religion for theological work.* "Religion" is, however, an enormously diverse and diffuse sphere of human existence, including wide ranges of perspectives and prac-

*Contemporary theory about human religiousness and the religions will be taken up explicitly in this book in a number of places, and is an underlying theme implicit throughout; in addition to what follows in the present chapter, see especially Chapters 3, 4, 6, 16, and 28.

tices, institutions and symbolisms. Moreover, it is not at all clear that there is any way, at this time, in which the descriptive and historical study of this vast and complex field can (or should attempt to) develop norms or standards coherent enough and specific enough to provide effective orientation and guidance for contemporary human life—a central theological objective. If the normative dimension of theology is to be maintained, it will be necessary at many points to introduce and employ insights into and conceptions of value and meaning, goodness and rightness. These cannot, however, be drawn from all traditions at once without falling into insoluble problems of mutual cancellation and/or contradiction. Theologians, therefore, will need to conduct their explorations and reflections in terms of some particular meaning-and-value complexes, some frameworks of interpretation which command their respect and commitment; but whatever frameworks are employed today must be open enough and comprehensive enough to allow considerable freedom and experimentation in the investigation of the many issues pertinent to the orientation and guidance of contemporary life. Although the symbol "God" has often been understood in narrow and oppressive ways in the past, for those formed by western cultural, religious, and linguistic traditions, this symbol—which is intended to designate the ultimate point of reference for all experience and activity, indeed all reality—probably meets this desideratum more adequately than any other available. (We will see, as we proceed, why and how this is the case.) In my opinion, thus, theology today should (in accordance with its etymology) continue to make the exploration and interpretation of the meaning and significance of God a central feature of its work.

The entire argument of this book may be regarded as a justification for this claim.[15] At this point I would like to sketch briefly some of its implications for our understanding of the theological task today. The word "God" is ordinarily used to indicate or invoke that which will supposedly provide us with proper orientation in life and adequate motivation in face of the most severe crises of life. That is, the idea of God is the idea of that—whatever it might be—which is absolutely trustworthy and unfailing, that to which we can turn in an hour of great confusion or dire need, that to which we can give ourselves without reservation. Putting this in more familiar religious language: only God (as distinguished from all idols, who will ultimately fail us) is the proper object for our unqualified loyalty, devotion, and worship. We may well question whether any reality corresponds to this idea, but before that question can be taken up, we must get clear what we mean by "God," with what sort of idea we are here working. It is evidently not the notion of some ordinary object of experience: all such objects are finite, limited, and relative in many ways. Indeed, idolatry (as we have noted) is precisely the confusion of such this-worldly objects with God.

The symbol "God," thus, claims to present us with a norm or criterion or reality—what I call an "ultimate point of reference"—in terms of which all else may be assessed and understood. For just this reason it is impermissible for theologians to take any religious tradition's authoritarian claims about God as an unquestioned foundation for theological work: all such claims must themselves be critically examined to see whether and in what respects they may be idolatrous. Nor may the claims of any tradition to be grounded on divine revelation be uncritically accepted: the idea of God itself (I am suggesting) forbids this. Theologians today must take full responsibility for all the concepts they use and all the claims they advance. They may no longer evade accountability by advocating positions simply because they seem well grounded in tradition or in what earlier generations regarded as divine revelation.

What does this mean for our actual theological practice? All religious ideas, after all—including the idea of "God"—have been created in and are carried by one or more traditions, and they become available to us only in and through communities that are committed to these traditions, that seek to orient their lives in terms of them, that attempt continually to criticize, reform, and develop them further. God is never available to us as an object we can directly inspect and examine; God becomes known to us, if at all, through the commitments, devotion, loyalty of God's devotees, as the object or focus toward which they direct themselves. This means that only in and through appropriation (and/or study) of Christian history and Christian traditions (including the Bible) can the God of Christian faith come into view for us. If we live primarily out of other traditions, or focus our interest and study primarily on other value-orientations and ways of life—Hindu, Buddhist, Marxist, secular humanist, Americanist—other values will become known to us, other foci will (increasingly) demand our commitments and loyalty, other gods will be worshipped. The human spirit everywhere has demonstrated its capacity to create traditions of value and meaning which then provide frameworks within which life can be oriented and ordered. The traditions of God-talk are such human creations which had their beginnings at least four thousand years ago. We can understand what this talk is and means—in all its variations and nuances—only by studying these traditions and attempting (at least imaginatively) to appropriate them, making their commitments ours.

Does this mean, then, that theology must, in fact, inevitably and necessarily accept the authority of tradition as its foundation? Have we, in spite of what I argued earlier in this chapter, worked ourselves back into an authoritarian position?

It would be a mistake to draw that conclusion. Let us recall what has already been said about the mystery within which human existence falls. We really know very little of what we are or who we are, with what realities we have to do in life, what meaning human existence has or can have. In the course of history many different views on these matters have appeared, and some of these have become formative of the great religious traditions. Within each tradition of commonly accepted symbols, rituals, and meanings, there is also, of course, much disagreement and argument. Within our own western and Christian traditions the questions of who or what God is, what can be known of God, how God is related to us and our lives, are all subject to dispute: God is by no means a clear-cut well-known reality. Indeed, the symbol "God" (as I suggested) itself points to the great mystery of life, the deepest and most profound issues about which we do not know what to say. This has been recognized from a very early period of Hebraic religious understanding and reflection: when Moses first heard a voice speaking to him from the "burning bush," he inquired as to who or what this was; the only answer he got was "I am what I am . . . I will be what I will be" (Ex. 3:14n RSV). It is important that we remember these limitations on our knowledge of the ultimate mystery of things as we proceed.

Although the human spirit has no way of overcoming the mystery of life, it is also true that we are not able simply to live with a blank, empty Void. So humans create *pictures,* pictures of what they think the world is like, pictures of what they imagine are the ultimate powers or realities with which they must deal; and they create rituals through which they enact their own roles among these realities and powers. We tell ourselves stories which depict the human situation in this world, and in our lives we attempt to act out our own parts in these stories. Great imaginative pictures and stories and rituals of this sort have become collected in the historical traditions of value and meaning and practice which we know as the religions.

These brief reminders of life's ultimate mysteriousness bring us to a position from which can be formulated an understanding of theological method somewhat different from those thus far discussed. Christian theology should have as a central focus, as I have been suggesting, the attempt to understand the meaning and use of the symbol "God" in the traditions that have developed it. This symbol cannot, however, be approached adequately in either a one-dimensional or two-dimensional way, for it is *holistic* in its emphasis: it has to do with the source and ground and meaning of *all that is.* Since much about the world (as we presently understand it) was completely unknown to our religious traditions, and this significantly affects the way in which God has been conceived, theologians dare not simply take over traditional ideas; we must be prepared to criticize every use and interpretation of the symbol "God" that has appeared to date. In connection with what criteria can such critical analysis be carried on? Our reflections in the past several paragraphs suggest three.

1. If God is to be the ultimate point of reference for understanding and orienting *us* in the world in which *we* live, then our contemporary experience and knowledge and problems must themselves function as a criterion to be taken into account in criticizing conceptions of God received from tradition and in formulating notions adequate for today. (The contemporary feminist critique of the patriarchal character of all traditional God-talk provides an interesting and important example of the direct application of this criterion in much current theological reflection and analysis.) That is, God must be understood as in meaningful relationship to, and thus significantly relevant to, our *contemporary* human life with its particular problems. This criterion will, of course, be employed rather differently in different local situations, since each such situation confronts men and women with its own unique problems. In this respect theology is always heavily influenced by contextual factors, and should acknowledge this openly.

2. We could not formulate even this first criterion if we did not take the central meaning of the symbol "God" (as it has been conveyed to us through the traditions we take seriously) to be (as I have just suggested) significantly holistic in its major bearings. What we take to be the "central meaning" of the symbol thus serves as a second criterion in theological work. But just what this central meaning is, and how it should be understood, is itself a highly controversial issue. So a major task which every theologian must confront is the development and presentation of an interpretation of what he or she takes to be the meaning of the symbol "God." I am not here proposing that (as these remarks might suggest), instead of an "essence of Christianity" approach, it is the "essence of God-talk" that we should make controlling in theology. "Essence of Christianity" approaches begin with the assumption that there is an unchanging kernel or core of truth underlying and expressing itself in the various forms in which Christianity has appeared in history, and every theologian's primary task is to ascertain what that "essence" is and to articulate it as adequately as possible for a new time. This is clearly an ahistorical way of thinking about Christian faith and theology, as the concept of essence itself suggests. I do not believe, however, that there is any such essence of God-talk to be discovered through a close inspection of theistic traditions; the approach I am proposing is based on a different understanding. I take the underlying issue which drives theological reflection to be this: In view of the ultimate mystery within which our existence falls, how are we humans to orient ourselves in the world? When we look at the traditions and practices we have inherited for resources to answer this question, we can see quickly that the symbol "God" has functioned as a major vehicle of human orientation in the past (at least for western men and women); and we may decide to explore what it can offer with respect to the major problems women and men face in life today. We

cannot begin to do this, of course, without making some (at least tentative) decisions about what this symbol means (or can be interpreted to mean) and what resources it can offer. This can be done responsibly only through imaginative extrapolation from earlier understandings and formulations (with relevant historical studies in mind) to the contemporary context of life and reflection. It should be noted now that all the activity projected here is heuristic; no essentialistic claims need be made at any point.

3. As I have been suggesting throughout, theological work must be carried on with full awareness that ultimately human life is ensconced in mystery, and this must properly qualify and relativize all our theological claims. But precisely because of the mystery, we must do the best we can in defining the situation of human beings in the world and under God: what is required, thus, is a multidimensional approach, one that takes into account (so far as possible) the major features of human experience, pertinent aspects of our knowledge of ourselves and of the world in which we live (as these are apprehended in our local situation and in the natural and human sciences today), insights drawn from artists, poets, philosophers, and others. All of this must be brought together imaginatively and creatively into a holistic picture or conception of human existence in the world and under God—but never forgetting the ultimate mystery which pervades everything we are saying.

With these several criteria before us, the overall task of Christian theology today becomes clear: theologians should attempt to construct conceptions of God, humanity, and the world appropriate for the orientation of contemporary human life. As we have been observing, these notions are (and always have been) human creations, human imaginative constructions; they are our ideas, not God's. What is needed in each new generation is an understanding of God adequate for and appropriate to human life in the world within which it finds itself, so that human devotion and loyalty, service and worship, may be directed toward God rather than to the many idols that so easily attract attention and interest. In and through such theological construction—carried through with whatever moves of imaginative creativity we can bring to the task, and with as much methodological self-consciousness as we can muster—it is hoped that the most serious problems confronting us humans today can be identified, and that we may gain some insight into appropriate ways to address them. To these issues we will be directing ourselves throughout the remainder of this book.

Theology: 1 Dimensional = Fundamentalism, of one or other sort
2 Dimensional = Methods of correlation
Holistic = p. 339. Define a concept of God, using tradition (see above, top of page) and multiple sciences today. ? [I think he is simply saying that theol. must be open to science, other spheres of culture, and other religions. Fine.]

3. Theology as a Human Imaginative Task

It is a truism that theology is a human enterprise, but unfortunately not all approaches to theology have been developed with that truth clearly in mind. This truism implies that our particular human capacities and interests, our training and our social location, our practices and habits and customs will all influence our theological work. It also implies that the presuppositions we as theologians make about the human—about human capacities as well as human limitations, about the interconnections, or the independence, of our thinking and our other activities, about the significance of the fact that we are at once sociocultural and biological creatures—will affect in many ways our theological work. It is important that we attempt to make all of these matters as clear to ourselves as possible, so we can examine them critically and can take them into account as we proceed. I would like, therefore, to introduce my contention that theology is, and always has been, fundamentally a work of the human imagination by sketching briefly some of the anthropological presuppositions which lie behind it.[1]

It is widely held today that human beings can best be understood as what we might call "sociocultural animals." We are biological organisms growing out of, but remaining a part of, the great chain of life that has evolved on planet Earth, and it is only as certain very specific needs are met—for nourishment, metabolism, exercise, elimination, social interaction, and the like—that we as individuals are able to live at all. We now know, moreover, that the biological foundations of human life cannot be adequately described in individualistic terms: we are each part of the great interconnected network that is life, and our survival depends on continuing complex interactions with that network. The foundation of our human existence, then, on which all else is built and of which it is a modification, is a very complex organic structure. In short, we are "animals."

But we are *sociocultural* animals. That is, what is specifically and most distinctively *human* about our existence is far from being merely biological. All our vital functions are heavily qualified and transformed by the cultural patterns which we have learned through interaction with other human beings from infancy onward. The significance of this point, which will be discussed in much more detail in later chapters, can be brought out by a few brief observations.

First, it is in and through social interaction that we acquire language. This is no superficial matter, since it is in the terms provided by the language we learn that all our conscious experience is formed. It is our language that gives us the names with which we identify and classify the many items of experience; language specifies the principal relations and qualities which the events and objects of experience can be expected to have; and it provides the principal medium of communication through which we relate to other human beings. It is important to note here that the language we learn is always culturally and historically specific; and it is shaped by our education as well as by our class, race, and gender. In other times, at other places, people speak languages very different from ours. In consequence, different features of experience are attended to, different interests expressed, different attitudes formed; in many respects, therefore, these become quite different sorts of people from us.

But, second, it is not only language that determines these deep differences. As we mature from infancy onward, gradually—through learning many distinctive social roles and practices—we come to fit ourselves and our behavior into the social patterns and the social structures which provide the contexts of our lives. Every society is a complex of patterns of interaction among the groups and persons which constitute it, each with different parts to play. From early on in human history it was impossible for each individual to develop expertise in every area of life, so some became weavers and others warriors, some gardeners and others hunters, and some became chiefs—that is, those who coordinated and maintained and protected the orderly practice and interrelation of all these specializations, so they would serve the well-being of the group as a whole. Without the development of such systems of diverse, highly specialized statuses and roles, human life could never have reached the enormous complexity which it now everywhere manifests.

Specialization made possible a high development of particular skills, and this in turn transformed human life in decisive ways, producing new kinds of experience and activity. The fine arts, politics, religious meditation and reflection on the meaning of life all began to appear, later to be followed by philosophy, mathematics, and the sciences. So, in the patterns played out in the activities of women and men, in the quantity and the quality of what they perceived as needs that must be met, in the interests to which they gave more and more of their attention and time, the animal basis of human life was increasingly qualified and transcended. Moreover, all these developments (like the growth of language) were also historically and culturally specific. Very different patterns of roles and tasks appeared in different historical periods and different societies. So the persons emerging within those societies were formed in quite diverse ways: they came to have different skills, different interests, different needs, and they entered into diverse sorts of relationship to other persons. In short, they became distinctively different types of human beings.

Third, as a further specification of these points about language, roles, and specializations, it is important to note the extent to which we acquire our values and ideals through our social location and through the social interactions in which we engage. What seems important in life—indeed, what *is* important to each of us—is very much a function of the culture and subculture in which we live and of the roles we are called upon to play. The conceptions of what a *good* human life is develop historically in each group in connection with felt social and cultural needs, and each person emerging in this cultural matrix thinks of and molds herself or himself in terms of these cultural ideals. The virtues that are stressed and the vices that are avoided are thus culturally defined and relative; and the sorts of acts and activities valued as beautiful, to be cherished and cultivated, are shaped by the culture. The claims to truth that are credible, the patterns of social organization regarded as just or proper, conceptions of the *right* way to treat fellow human beings—all such ideals and values, which orient human life and serve as standards for evaluating different alternatives confronting persons and communities, take quite different forms in diverse historical and cultural settings. Accordingly, human aspirations and hopes, human ways of thinking about life and the world, take very different shapes.

When we say, then, that humans are "sociocultural animals," it is quite as important to emphasize the "sociocultural" as the "animal." All humans eat; they must eat to survive. But no humans simply consume food as do other animals. They eat with chopsticks or with forks and knives, or with no utensils at all but using the right hand only, never the left; they cook some or all of their food, preparing it with special spices and condiments; they regularly eat three meals a day, or two, or one; they fast in certain culturally prescribed periods and ways; they accept as edible only certain vegetables or meats which in other cultures are regarded as revolting or poisonous; and so on. Though our eating is certainly in response to biological need, in almost every detail it is culturally formed.

Now these sociocultural animals—or rather, some of them—also speak of God, and to God; they think of themselves as living "under" God, and they profess faith "in" God. How are we to understand this? We must note immediately that it is only *some* men and women in some cultures (or subcultures) that are engaged in this activity. That is, whatever its biological roots may be, this is essentially part of the culturally formed side of human existence, that which has to do with values and ideals, with the conceptions of what human life is all about, with the meaning of human existence. Let us consider for a moment how this sort of religious activity and belief might have emerged.

The developing sociocultural animals which were to become humans increasingly ordered their lives and oriented themselves (in the packs or tribes in which they lived) with the aid of their emerging language and consciousness: they searched for food, they organized hunting parties, they planned communal defense—all in terms which were supplied by the growing language which they gradually created and refined over many generations, and passed on to the young in the form of traditions. Their life thus gradually became *cultural* in form, that is, activity ordered by words, thoughts, articulated feelings and desires, deliberate purposes, deliberately trained skills and arts, ideas. With this emergence into language and culture, increasingly complex forms of consciousness and self-consciousness appeared; and human behavior accordingly developed in important new ways. No longer was it a matter simply of following biological drives or instincts. Now humans were organizing their lives increasingly in terms of (a) their greater awareness of their own needs, including what we might call their "inwardly felt" needs for joy, peace, understanding, affection, and the like, and (b) their conceptions of the objects and powers in the world roundabout them, especially those which most directly affected them, either by significantly meeting their increasingly complex needs or by posing threats.

In time, the more imaginative or poetic women and men began to articulate stories and songs, pictures and ideas, of human life in its context.[2] These drew together and organized in new ways various aspects of experience, and they helped sharpen perception of certain features of the environment. These early ("mythic") versions of what would later become religious and philosophical conceptions of "human existence" and "the world"—retold and expanded generation after generation—depicted human life in imaginative fashion, showing the major problems to be faced and the tasks to be performed; and they presented a view of the setting within which human life fell (the world) and of the powers and beings that must be dealt with if life were to go on. Telling and retelling these cycles of stories provided a symbolic context within which it was possible to reflect more deeply on human existence, elaborating details and articulating further the understanding of the human and the world. Eventually, in those cultures which invented or otherwise acquired writing, forms of expression became more fixed, thus enabling new modes of detailed analytical reflection and consciousness to appear. Attention could be focused on particular characters or patterns or other features of stories, questions could be asked about these, and thus they could be developed further in new imaginative ways. Ultimately, articulated self-conscious *worldviews* appeared, each with its own interpretation of the possibilities and the problems of human life.

Thus, for example, human life could be seen as basically a kind of journey through hazardous territory, with wild beasts and other monsters to be overcome as one sought to make one's way home; or it might be grasped in the metaphor of a great warfare between forces of "light" and forces of "darkness." The human soul (the "I," the self, consciousness) might be portrayed as having fallen out of its proper home in heaven above and become trapped in a physical body from which it must find some way to break free; or the very sense of self, or of possessing a soul, might be seen as a terrible illusion, the product of ignorance and misunderstanding, that veil of maya from which arise all human problems but which right insight can dispel. Humans could be seen essentially as citizens or subjects in a kind of cosmic political order ruled by a God/king; or human existence might be held to be simply a product of accidental collocations of material atoms, or of blind evolutionary processes, that could just as well have formed quite different patterns or have gone other directions.

In the course of history men and women have developed many different worldviews, many different interpretations of the place and significance of human life in the world, quite diverse conceptions of the central human tasks and problems and of the solutions to those problems. Every great civilization—indeed, every isolated tribe—worked out one or more such symbolic frames in its effort to understand, to orient, and to interpret human existence; and human lives, institutions, practices, and values were shaped and reshaped in accord with these symbolic visions of Reality and the human. Thus arose the great religious traditions of humankind. It was in their religious rituals, beliefs, and institutions that women and men found an interpretation of what their existence was all about and how life was to be lived, and thus gained orientation in the world. Or rather: in and through their unavoidable search for orientation in life, for an understanding of their existence and for an interpretation of how life was to be lived, men and women created and developed the great religious traditions—elaborate patterns of symbols and rituals—which at once gave meaning to life and enabled them to find meaning in it.

It is important to recognize, of course, that these early women and men did not understand themselves to be in this way straightforwardly creating symbolic traditions of value and meaning to be bulwarks against the Void, the ultimate Mystery of existence. They understood themselves, rather, as coming to see how things actually are, what human life is really all about. No people, certainly no individual, created from scratch a conception of the world and of the human place within that world. Every individual and community which has come to consciousness and self-consciousness has done so within the context of a symbolic tradition already in place, a tradition handed on by the elders, the mothers and the fathers, as that wisdom about the human condition which was requisite for living. Each new generation, then, living and working within that framework of understanding, handed it on to the next, having made (perhaps quite unconsciously) such alterations as its own experience demanded. In their stories and their epigrams they set out what they understood of the world, how things really are; and in their injunctions and laws they prescribed the form life must take for humans to survive and flourish. No one understood herself or himself to be creating or constructing a symbolic picture of the world and of the human: it is only from our modern vantage point, looking back (with the aid of several centuries of historical work increasingly informed by a cross-cultural understanding) at the many great and diverse cultural and religious traditions which have appeared in the course of human history, that we can see how much all of this must have been a product of human imaginative creativity in face of the great mysteries of life. This creativity has developed quite diverse, indeed contradictory, pictures and understandings of human existence and the setting within which it falls, and of the realities with which human beings must come to terms.

It is within the context of this sort of general understanding of the origin and development of human religious institutions and patterns of symbolization, it seems to me, that we must seek to grasp the meaning and significance of "God-talk." Some of the frames of orientation which humans have created present what is called "God" as the ultimate reality in terms of which all else must be understood. In ancient Israel, the ancestor-culture of a number of these, God was depicted as the creator of the world and its continuing sovereign. Among God's creatures are human beings, to whom God has granted an unusual measure of freedom, creativity, and consciousness like God's own; indeed, humans were said to be created "in God's image" (Gen. 1:26–27). In this conceptual frame, men and women are presented as living within an ongoing historical movement toward the realization of God's ultimate purposes; and they are able to participate actively in that movement, either responding positively to the Creator-God's sovereign rule or, in various ways, rebelling against it. This story/worldview, developed in ancient Israel out of earlier near eastern conceptions, was decisively modified (for some) by the impact of the life, death, and supposed resurrection of a first-century Jew whom we know as "Jesus." The followers of Jesus—believing that in and through him God had taken, or was taking, the decisive step to bring history to its consummation—moved throughout the Roman world, bringing their message to Gentiles as well as Jews. In this migration from its Jewish birthplace to the larger Hellenistic world, Christianity took on many new religious practices, was increasingly interpreted in terms of Greek philosophical ideas and perspectives, and was influenced by Roman social and political attitudes and institutional patterns. But throughout it continued to proclaim *God* (and God's representative, Jesus the Christ), as the origin, center, and goal of human life, the only One capable of bringing it to fulfillment (salvation).

It is this particular strand of the complex, immensely various understandings of human existence and the world—this strand focused in and upon "God"—that we are seeking to investigate, understand, and critically reassess and reconstruct in our theological work here. How, now, should this be done? Actually, in the preceding paragraphs of this chapter, which briefly summarize widely accepted contemporary views about the growth of culture and the history of religions (including the beginnings of Judaism and Christianity), our reconstructive work has already begun. Our point of departure here was the contemporary understanding of human beings as sociocultural animals who gain orientation in life through imaginatively creating worldviews in terms of which they understand themselves and the overall context within which they live. We then took note of the emergence in ancient Israel of a frame of orientation focused on *God* as the ultimate point of reference in terms of which all else must be understood, a frame that was decisively modified and further developed during the beginnings of the Christian movement. In this exposition human talk about God, ideas of God, devotion to God, service of God have all been seen as features of, and thus functions of, a particular symbolical pattern for orienting human life, a particular world-picture. This is a significantly different way of understanding both humanity and God from that found in traditional Christian reflection, and it is important that we note clearly the differences.

Traditional Christian theology was developed from *within* a Christian world-picture (that is, within "Christian faith"), but it did not grasp the significance of that fact in the same way in which I have been presenting it here. Christians have, of course, often maintained that the reality and nature of God and the fact and significance of human creatureliness and sin are not really directly perceptible or understandable from any and every human standpoint or experience; indeed, they have maintained that these are clearly visible and rightly understood only by what they called the "eyes of faith," that is, only by those nurtured by the biblical traditions cherished in the churches. Thus faith was seen as prerequisite to proper understanding of the human condition and God: "I believe in order that I may understand," said Augustine.[3] In this sort of affirmation it is clearly acknowledged that Christian beliefs, life, and understanding are in some special way a function of the Christian standpoint or worldview (that is, of what was called Christian "faith"). But this observation, not being informed by a general theory of symbolic worldviews (as I am proposing) easily became the basis for exclusivistic Christian claims; for example, Cyprian's well-known declarations that "there is no salvation outside the Church," and "you cannot have God for your father unless you have the Church for your mother."[4] Along with these claims went derogation of other positions and points of view as false and even diabolical. Unfortunately this out-and-out Christian chauvinism has not been confined simply to the early periods of Christian history; it has been operative throughout most of the Christian era, and it is still widespread today, particularly in more conservative or traditional theological circles.

The fact that Christian ideas, attitudes, and life are all in a significant way a function of what I call the "Christian worldview" has, thus, frequently been sensed and expressed in Christian history; and it has been understood that both God and humankind are seen in quite different ways from within this symbolical frame than from without it. When (modern) concepts such as "worldview" or "interpretive scheme" or "frame of orientation" are introduced to explicate the meaning of these facts, they are placed in a new light. For such notions are intended to indicate that the complex symbolical structures of meaning, value, and concept, which define and give particular shape to a given cultural or religious orientation or tradition, are produced in the course of the creation of culture. These concepts, thus, give a role and significance to human cultural creativity—that is, to the constructive powers of the human imagination—in forming religious beliefs and attitudes, institutions and practices, which was never seriously contemplated in traditional theological reflection. It is a role and significance, moreover, with no specific implications whatsoever about the absoluteness or the finality of Christianity in comparison with other religious perspectives.

We are clearly moving here toward a rather different understanding of the symbol "God," and thus also to a different conception of theology, from what has been traditional. Instead of simply assuming that God, as grasped in Christian faith, is the Ultimate Reality with which all humans have to do, and then proceeding to set out what this must mean for human life, its problems and possibilities, we begin with an awareness that all talk of God belongs to and has its meaning within a particular symbolical frame of orientation for human life which emerged in a particular strand of human history. The symbol "God," like the rest of language and like other important religious symbols around the world, was created as the women and men in that historical movement gradually put together a world-picture which enabled them, with some measure of success, to come to terms with the exigencies of life. This symbol, then (like all others), must be understood as a product of the human imagination. This does not mean that God has no reality, is "merely imaginary"; symbols such as "tree" and "I" and "world"

The point: Xtian standpoint was seen as absolute, and not a socio-cultural creation.

A genetic account of the emergence of a concept of God by human creativity vs one that is given *

* There is something missing here. What FS called the given or gracious element in the experience to which the concept corresponds seen too in HRN

The symbol card is not empty.

and "light-year" have also been created by the human imagination, and that certainly does not imply either their falsity or emptiness. What it does mean is that this symbol (like all others) will need to be regularly subjected to criticism and testing, as we seek to see whether it continues to do the work for which it was created, whether it can continue to function significantly in human life. When such examination reveals serious problems, it becomes necessary (as with all our symbols) to engage in reconception and reconstruction—or, if this is not possible, to drop the symbol altogether.

What does this mean for Christian theology? If we understand the sociocultural dimension of human existence in the sense I have been urging here, Christian faith (like every other faith) will be seen as one symbolical perspective, one worldview, which has developed in and through a long history alongside other traditions, many of which are vying for the attention and loyalty of us all today. When one applies the concept "worldview" to one's own tradition in this way, one is simultaneously distinguishing that tradition from, and yet relating it to, other worldviews. This involves a certain distancing of oneself from one's tradition, taking a step back from simple and direct commitment to it. We now see the great theologians of Christian history, for example, not simply as straightforwardly setting out the truth that is ultimately saving for all humanity (as they have often been understood in the past), but rather as essentially engaged in discerning and articulating and reconstructing one particular perspective on life among many. Reflective interpretation of Christian faith today will involve similar activities of discernment and reconstruction; however, these must now be taken up much more self-consciously. This change in degree of self-consciousness transforms the critical questions for Christian theology. Instead of asking, What are the principal doctrines or ideas prescribed by tradition for Christians to believe, and how should we interpret these today? it now becomes necessary to direct attention to questions like, How does one articulate a worldview—in this case, the Christian picture of the world—and how does one assess its significance for human life today? Refocusing religious reflection in this way leads one to attend to a rather different agenda from that followed by most theologians in the past. Rather than concentrating on traditional doctrines and dogmas and their systematic presentation in a new historical situation, one must search for, and attempt to bring into view, the configuration or pattern of symbols and categories—the basic conceptual and symbolic framework—which gives Christian perspectives their structure and order and experiential flavor. If it proves possible to formulate and articulate this symbolic pattern, one may begin to explore whether it is well fitted to order, interpret, and provide orientation for contemporary life.

This antithesis may be too sharply drawn.

A human frame of orientation, of course, is given its full character and meaning by a complex pattern of institutions and customs, words and symbols, liturgical practices and moral claims, stories and myths which are handed down from generation to generation, shaping and interpreting the experience of those living within it. It is my contention, however, that not all these expressions and patterns and practices are of equal weight. The basic structure and character of a world-picture are determined largely by a few fundamental categories which give it shape and order; and these are connected and interrelated in various ways by the wider vocabulary of terms and symbols used in ritual and meditation, ideology and story, which provide concreteness and fill in details of an overall picture—or rather, a historically developing complex of pictures—that is able to accommodate and interpret the infinite variations and details of the experience of many generations. This configuration of basic defining terms or symbols—worked out in many different ways, with different nuances of meaning and diverse behavioral and institutional implications—I call the "categorial structure" of the world-picture. The initial task of Christian theologians today (in my view) is to formulate—on the basis of thoughtful reflection on the multiplicity of Christian institutions, practices, and liturgies, Christian philosophies, theologies, and myths—a conception of the categorial pattern of symbols that informs them. With this categorial pattern in mind, the theologian is in a position, on the one hand, to engage in the most fundamental sort of analysis and criticism of Christian worldviews, taking into account insights and understandings provided by other religious and secular positions, both ancient and modern; and, on the other hand, to proceed to construction of a contemporary Christian understanding of human life, the world, and God. In Chapters 6 and 7 I shall set out, and begin the critical examination of, the understanding of "the Christian categorial scheme" which I propose to employ through most of this work.

Any examination of the history of theology, indeed of the history of religious reflection in the West going back at least to the great Old Testament prophets, will show that changes in old ideas, and the introduction of new ones to address new historical contingencies, were occurring almost constantly—that is, that what I am calling imaginative theological construction and reconstruction has been going on throughout the Christian past (though this was seldom recognized until modern times). Since we are now aware of the importance this imaginative activity has in the development and transformation of religious symbols and theological conceptions, we are in a position to engage in it deliberately and self-consciously in ways not possible in the past, thus bringing a fuller, more critical methodological discipline to theological work.

In the theological reconstruction of the Christian categorial scheme to be undertaken in this book, every effort will be made to maintain significant continuity with the Christian tradition. In particular, we will seek to see how and why (in this framework for orienting human existence) that which was called "God" was regarded as the proper focus for human devotion, service, and worship—indeed, for all of human life; that is, why God was taken to be the ultimate point of reference in terms of which all else was to be understood. We will see, I think, that this was because God was believed to be that which makes possible human flourishing and fulfillment (salvation). That this is true is not, of course, something that can simply be taken for granted; it is a question that will need to be investigated—with the dangers of falling into an idolatry of tradition always in mind. Before this question can be addressed, however, two others must be carefully considered: (1) How is "human flourishing and fulfillment" to be understood? In what does it consist, and how do we ascertain this? (2) If we assume that by "God" we mean that reality (whatever it might be) orientation on which brings flourishing and fulfillment to human life, how is this God, the bringer of salvation, to be conceived? Who or what should be taken as God—the "God" of traditional Christian faith or perhaps some other? In view of the profound mystery within which (as I have been suggesting) human life falls, it should be evident that the answers to neither of these questions will be obvious or simple. Indeed, finding a way to come to terms with them will turn out to be a major part of the theological task.

We are now in a position to summarize the program of constructive theology which we will be following here. First, in face of the ultimate mystery of life, we must find some way of developing criteria for deciding what human flourishing and fulfillment might consist in. It will not be possible to address this issue without exploring what sorts of beings we humans are, what are the deepest and most significant problems we face, and what alternative ways of addressing these problems have thus far proved fruitful. These obviously are massive questions which it is presumptuous for anyone to pretend to be able to answer. Yet, addressing them always has been a central feature, not only of Christian theology but of every claim (religious or secular) to speak of human wholeness, well-being, or salvation. Regardless of their difficulty, then, we must attempt to bring these issues, as they present themselves to us in contemporary life, into some manageable focus. The resources of the social sciences and the humanities, of the biological and physical sciences, of philosophical reflection and poetic insight, as well as of Christian and other religious traditions, will all need to be drawn upon as we try to gain a more adequate understanding of our common human nature and our situatedness in the world.

Second, in connection with this attempt to understand better what we humans are, we will need to develop criteria to guide us as we construct our conception of a focus for orientation, devotion, and service which will most effectively facilitate human flourishing and fulfillment—that is, which can guide our construction of the image/concept of God. Which models, metaphors, images, concepts are most appropriate for imagining or thinking that to which we should give ourselves with unqualified devotion today?—if, indeed, we should so give ourselves at all. Should God be thought of in largely personal terms, as a king or lord, as a father or mother or friend? or impersonally, as the ground of being, first cause, being-itself, the absolute? Should God be thought of in highly metaphorical terms, as light, love, the most high? or in largely negative terms, as wholly other, in-finite, incomprehensible, mystery? What sorts of characteristics can properly be attributed to God: omnipotence? omniscience? love? forgiveness? speech? miracle-working? impassibility? Should we, indeed, think of the focus of human orientation and devotion as "God" at all? or would some other symbol be more appropriate? In a methodologically self-conscious constructive theology none of these questions can be settled simply by noting that "the Bible says . . ." or "tradition holds . . ." or "Jesus said . . ."; that is, they cannot be settled simply by appeal to authority.

Two reasons for rejecting any such appeal, even to the authority of a supposedly divine revelation, may be mentioned here. The first is a strictly theological reason. As we have seen, for the Christian symbol-system God alone is the only proper ultimate authority; to take anything other than God as authoritative is idolatrous. At the outset of our inquiry, then, the extent to which ideas or emphases found in tradition are to be regarded as from God must remain an open question to be investigated. There is no *theological* warrant—whatever traditional warrant there may be—for taking over images or conceptions or points of view from the Bible or tradition simply because these are supposed (in the tradition) to come from God. The second reason for rejecting authoritarian modes of theological argument is of a more anthropological sort. As we have noted, all understandings of the world and of human existence are human imaginative constructions, grown up in a particular historical stream to provide orientation in life for those living in that history. But at any given time it is always an open question whether the conceptions and values and perspectives inherited from the past remain suitable for orienting human existence in the new present: this is a question to be investigated, never a position which can simply be taken for granted.

Questions about the significance or validity of traditional conceptions, then, must be left entirely open at the outset of our theological investigations. They can be settled only in the process of our constructive work. Precisely this openness in all our theological reflection is demanded by the symbol "God" itself, which, as we have seen, is the ultimate point of reference in the Christian categorial scheme, that in terms of which all else—including our theological procedures—must be understood. If we push this self-critical dimension of the symbol "God" to its limit—as we must in fully critical theological work—the viability and usefulness of this symbol itself must be made a question to be carefully investigated. Only if and as we are able to show that this symbol, properly constructed, can and does have important significance and use in modern life, are we justified in continuing to advocate its employment: the intention of the symbol itself—to designate that focus for human worship, affection, and orientation, devotion to which brings salvation—demands this. When the dialectic of God and the idols is pressed in this way, we can see that the symbol "God" carries within itself a potentially inexhaustible principle of criticism. It is, in fact, a principal root of the critical spirit in modern culture,[5] a spirit that must continuously inform our constructive theological work, if it is to provide us with criteria and principles that will enable us to distinguish God from those idols which most seriously threaten human life today.

4. Theological Construction and Faith

Traditional Christian and Jewish faiths present a picture of humanity living in a world created by a loving God to be the context for human life. God continues to work in this world toward the realization of the well-being and salvation of humanity (as well as the other creatures) and will ultimately bring all creation to a perfect consummation as the divine purposes are realized. Human beings are to live out their lives in steady responsiveness to God's will, made known through Torah, through prophecy, and above all (for Christians) through Jesus Christ.

This notion that the world has been created and shaped by a loving God as the appropriate context for the realization of free and loving persons within a community of love and freedom is far from congruent, or even compatible, with the picture of the universe, and of human life within the universe, presented by modern history and science. Here the universe appears to be essentially a material order of whirling energies, within which, on planet Earth, life has gradually emerged through a long, slow, impersonal evolutionary process, governed by survival of the fittest. Humans gradually clawed their way to a position of unusual power in the ongoing struggle to survive, as they developed increasingly complex sociocultural patterns of life, but they are far from having brought their lives into anything approximating a truly humane order; on the contrary, they regularly produce enormities like Auschwitz, Hiroshima, and Vietnam. It is hard to see any thread of loving divine guidance running through human history as we have come to understand it. In any case, the universe as described by modern science and history—a relatively unified and well-defined picture, taken for granted by most contemporary educated persons—seems to have no place for the sort of divine being spoken of in the traditional religious mythology.

The modern idea of "universe" or "world" is an all-inclusive one, the idea of *all there is,* the structured totality of all that exists. To speak, then, of some reality or being—God—who exists somehow beyond the world, transcending it as its creator and lord, not only strains credulity; it borders on being unintelligible. How could there be something beyond or outside "all there is"? The concept of universe that we take for granted in most of our thinking and experience drives us toward thinking of God either (a) as *in* the world, one of the realities that exists, or (b) as not a reality in any clearly thinkable sense at all. In either case the traditional image/concept of God is in trouble: if we prefer (a), with what intra-mundane reality is God to be identified? If (b), how is "God" to be understood, if not as some sort of reality? Neither of these alternatives seems to fit the meaning or many of the uses of the traditional symbol. Modern cosmology no longer presents us with a picture of the world as a tight mechanistic order, but even the open-textured, looser-structured universe of contemporary thought is still a *uni*verse, the structured whole of all that is, and it is not clear how God is to be related to this.

A principal reason, I think, why A. N. Whitehead's thought has attracted considerable interest among theologians (despite the relative lack of interest in it shown by contemporary philosophers) is that it presents a conception of the world, of reality, which has an important place for what Whitehead calls "God." Whether this God can do the work of the "God" of Christian and Jewish traditions is an open and much discussed question, but in the absence of other well-thought-out alternatives to Whitehead's cosmology many theologians have felt pressed simply to take it over and do the best they can. I do not propose to move in that direction with the theological construction in this book. Doubtless there is much to be learned from Whitehead about contemporary conceptualization of the world, but in my opinion we theologians must do our own work with respect to the question of God, not simply take over someone else's. We must explore carefully the basic conceptual scheme within which the inherited notion of God had its place and meaning, and then see whether it is possible to reconstruct that scheme in such a way as to take account of contemporary experience and knowledge.

If this is done effectively, we will be in a position to judge whether the symbol "God" can continue to be viable and significant for orienting human life as it is experienced in the modern world. It is important to take seriously the possibility that theistic faith may be dying in the face of modern experience no longer tractable to it. Of course, this may be for the good. Perhaps the time when Christian faith or Jewish faith could significantly orient human life is moving into the past. Perhaps the symbol-systems of these religious traditions have done most of their historical work, and we should give them up in favor of some other frame(s) of orientation. If that is the case, it is important that we recognize it and that we try to discern the sort of worldview now required. We will be able to make responsible judgments on issues of this sort with respect to the Christian faith only if we carefully examine its pattern of symbols and concepts, attempting to see whether thoughtful reconstruction of some of its features will facilitate its receiving and interpreting the fullness of contemporary experience; apart from this its power significantly to orient human life today will continue to diminish. If our inquiry leads us to the conclusion that no amount of reconstruction will enable the Christian framework to perform these functions for modern life, we should be prepared to discard it. Theology conceived as imaginative construction must be open to all such possibilities.

In order to be in a position to assess the Christian symbolic framework, we need to consider briefly how "worldviews" or "conceptual frames" bring order to human life and what happens when they begin to fail.[1] A worldview or world-picture is working well when (1) it performs the indispensable task of providing communities and individuals with order and orientation in life, that is, when it is able successfully to organize and interpret the experience of women and men in such a way that they can come to terms with it and life can go on; and when (2) this orientation provides sufficient meaningfulness and motivating power to enable them to continue to struggle even against serious adversities and troubles, indeed catastrophes. Of course no conceptual frame fits all dimensions of experience perfectly and answers to every problem that might arise; in consequence there have always been persons like Job and Ecclesiastes, or Camus and Sartre, who have cried out against the unintelligibility, indeed the utter meaninglessness, of what they were living through. Conceptual and imagistic frames of the sort we are considering are created as humans, in their attempts to address the problems and evils of life with which they must come to terms, put together imaginative pictures of the world and of human life which make some sense of its main features; no such human construction, however, is inclusive enough or detailed enough or profound enough to comprehend and interpret every feature or dimension of life, to anticipate every novelty that might appear. It is, after all, the ultimate mystery of things we are up against here, the ultimate limits of our understanding. A certain amount of strain, then, will pervade every frame of orientation, every interpretive scheme, and sometimes, in moments or periods of serious crisis or great historical change, the strain may increase to the breaking point: then a new and profoundly different way of understanding the world and the human place within the world may be required in order to make sense of things.

Claims are often made, by both Catholic and Protestant theologians, that theological work must begin with Christian faith, that it is essential to accept the Bible as God's revelation in order to do Christian theology, that the church's fundamental affirmations must be regarded as authoritative for faith and life. I want to argue, however, that all such authoritarian moves actually express not the vitality of faith but its threatening breakdown. It is necessary to make an authoritarian demand of this sort only when a conceptual frame no longer makes sense of experience, and has thus begun to seem useless or meaningless. Appeals to divine revelation as the ultimate authority in theology, therefore, should be regarded as a warning flag: they are made when the theological conceptual frame is not working as well as it should, and needs careful scrutiny and possibly drastic reconstruction. Here the book of Job can be instructive, for it is about the breakdown of a traditional frame of orientation, a frame represented by Job's friends but one which Job himself (suffering on his ash heap) can no longer accept: it simply does not make sense of his experience. Job is the hero of this story, not because of his faithfulness to traditional views, but precisely because he dares to question the way in which these views interpret suffering and evil in human affairs. He even hurls his doubts and objections into the face of God.

My point is this: in a time when fundamental religious or theological claims are heavily questioned, when they seem dubious or unintelligible or even absurd, it is a serious mistake to invoke the *authority* of the major symbols of the tradition as the principal basis for theological work. This may appear to work for a while, but in the end it will only produce greater strains in the system. We see once more, then (from another point of view), why theological work grounded principally on what is claimed to be authoritative "revelation" is simply not appropriate today. The concept of revelation is itself a part of the conceptual scheme which has become questionable, and it is the overall scheme, therefore, which now must be carefully examined and possibly reconstructed. Doubtless there are some to whom this questionableness is not apparent, or who choose to ignore it. There is certainly nothing wrong with that; people may do theology in whatever way they choose. But for those who find serious problems or difficulties with the Christian worldview, there is no alternative to careful critical examining of its most fundamental symbols and claims, and then rebuilding in whatever ways seem necessary. This is what we shall be doing in the course of this book. I will sketch out what I take to be the fundamental categorial scheme that has given Christian faith-perspectives their structure, and then I will present a reconstruction of that scheme that I believe is appropriate for today.

Questions about the fundamental meaning and usefulness of the principal categories of a frame of orientation do not arise when those categories are working properly, that is, when they succeed in organizing experience and life into a relatively intelligible whole. At such times there is no need to question the basic metaphors, images, and concepts which constitute the understanding of the world; rather, they are straightforwardly employed in the normal ordering and understanding of life. For many persons today notions like "experience," "meaning," "interpretation," "life," "self," "universe," "time," "nature," and the like all have this kind of more or less unquestioned status, and therefore we use these notions daily in organizing our "lives" and our "experience" [*sic*] and in "interpreting" these to "ourselves" [*sic*]. Certainly interesting and significant philosophical questions can be raised about all these terms: they are ambiguous in important respects, not clearly defined, possibly not entirely coherent, and their precise referents are hard to specify. Nonetheless, we constantly use (and presuppose) these and many others like them as fundamental reference points or anchors which organize and order the complex conceptual web within and by means of which we do all our thinking, understanding, and experiencing; and the conceptual scheme which they help to structure provides us with a world sufficiently intelligible to enable us to live and act and think with some effectiveness.*

If and when certain fundamental features of our world begin to crack apart, as may be happening today, and our trust in some of our language begins to break down, we can go in either of two directions. We can insist that our most fundamental terms or categories do in fact stand for and refer to *realities,* to things that are *really there:* "Time *is* real; how else could one understand flow and change?" "Each of us *is* an individual self; it is unthinkable that our 'selfhood' might be just a cultural or linguistic construction." "The universe *is* the totality of everything that exists; what else could it be?" And so forth. Or else we can recognize that our human worlds, our languages and systems of symbols, are actually all our own constructions—that humans have always constructed their worlds out of just such categories and concepts—and that when these no longer effectively give order to experience and thought, it is not the time to reify them by insisting on their "objective reality." Rather, it is a time for reshaping our categories and reconstructing our world. If and as our categorial scheme, our conception of the world,

*As Ludwig Wittgenstein points out, if we did not trust the meanings of most of the terms of our common language, and did not trust our memories to make those meanings available to us, we could neither affirm nor doubt, neither think nor act. "If I do a calculation I believe, without any doubts, that the figures on the paper aren't switching of their own accord, and I also trust my memory the whole time, and trust it without any reservation . . . If I ask someone 'what colour do you see at the moment?', in order, that is, to learn what colour is there at the moment, I cannot at the same time question whether the person I ask understands English, whether he wants to take me in, whether my own memory is not leaving me in the lurch as to the names of colours, and so on . . . We teach a child 'that is your hand', not 'that is perhaps [or 'probably'] your hand'. That is how a child learns the innumerable language-games that are concerned with his hand . . . The fact that I use the word 'hand' and all the other words in my sentence without a second thought, indeed that I should stand before the abyss if I wanted so much as to try doubting their meanings—shews that absence of doubt belongs to the essence of the language-game." *On Certainty,* ed. G. E. M. Anscombe and G. H. von Wright (Oxford: Blackwell, 1969), secs. 337, 345, 374, 370.

begins to work better for us again, its reality and power and meaningfulness will once more seem obvious, and no impassioned assertion or defense of it by true believers will be required.

It may seem difficult to believe that any conceptual scheme or world-picture which is being deliberately criticized and reconstructed—in the way I am suggesting we must do today with our most fundamental religious ideas—could continue to have experience-forming power, particularly for those engaged in the activities of criticism and construction. Indeed, it may be argued, to worship at the shrine of a God, the understanding of which we ourselves have imaginatively constructed, is the crassest sort of idolatry. What is required now is the emphatic assertion that God *does* exist; Christ *is* God's only begotten son; the Bible *is* God's authoritative revelation; the church *is* God's institutional representative on earth—these claims all are "true," and it is the part of faith and of theology to "believe" them and proclaim them to the world. For a defensive mentality of this sort, it may seem that the first priority of faith is to insist that the meanings with which faith deals have explicit, objective referents to which they correspond in every important detail. From this point of view my claim that what is needed in this situation is thorough criticism and radical reconstruction of faith's basic categories may seem like a cop-out, a failure of nerve in which the central claims of faith are given up just at the moment when their firm affirmation is most needed; instead of accepting God's revelation from on high, I seem to be proposing—arrogantly, sinfully—that we should substitute fantasies of the human imagination.

Persons who take this sort of tack do not recognize the real significance of the cracks and strains in the Christian world-picture, which nearly everyone today feels to some degree. These show that, far from being an absolutely secure bastion of salvific Truth, the Christian perspective must be seen as but one among many others that have appeared in human history, a worldview with very distinct limitations and problems. As historical studies of biblical and Christian history show, this conceptual frame has grown up in a particular history as have all others, and it has been criticized, reshaped, and reformulated many times and in countless ways. Throughout this whole process, however, it has succeeded in giving form and meaning to the lives of many generations. If it is faltering today, therefore, that is neither a reason to abandon it nor simply to reaffirm it. It is, rather, a reason to search out how and why its fundamental categories have worked in the past, and to see whether reformulation of them in new ways today might enable them once again to become effective. If and as this occurs, their reality, significance, and independent power will once more become evident, as they give experience significant form and as life's meaning is apprehended in the terms they prescribe. I would like to present two sorts of argument on this point, one largely anthropological, the other more specifically theological.

First, the anthropological considerations. As we noted a moment ago, it is simply not true that concepts like "experience," "meaning," "self," "reality," "nature" lose their meaning [*sic*] and cannot be used when they are recognized as purely human constructs with highly problematical features. We are well aware that these concepts (along with all others available to us) have been created in the course of a long linguistic history by women and men seeking to understand and make sense of various dimensions of their lives. Moreover, although these particular concepts seem to us to designate "realities" [*sic*] of some sort, we must admit they are realities which we never directly perceive: however important they may be as points of reference in terms of which we appropriate our experience and seek to understand it, they clearly do not refer to specific "objects" somewhere out in the world. Many cultures, in fact, do not have these concepts at all; the notions of experience, meaning, self, reality, and the meanings [*sic*] which these hold for us today, are distinctly modern, and their historical development can be traced. Philosophers, poets, and others have long scrutinized these terms, criticizing them in various ways and reformulating them. In the future, doubtless, they will come to have meanings significantly different from those they now bear.

All of us are aware of these points, but they do not prevent us from using these concepts daily to make sense of our lives and to give order and structure to our world. We are quite capable, thus, of living in a world even while it is being reconstructed, and of ourselves participating in the reshaping of our concepts and categories at the very moment we are using them to order our experience and give it meaning.

Experience is always in this way dialectically interconnected with our reflection on it and our reconstruction of it. We take in the events of life and the objects of experience in terms of concepts and categories inherited from our culture, even though all the while we are actively participating in the remodeling and remaking of these very categories and concepts so they will better fit that experience—that is, so they will enable us better to anticipate its diverse features, to absorb their richness and fullness, and to direct our activities in response to them. Some of us, of course, are more sensitive than others to the lack of fit, to the confusions and distortions, of our symbols and concepts: these are the prophets, poets, and philosophers calling us to reexamine ourselves, see things in new ways, direct our lives down different paths. Most of us simply live out of the conceptual frames and systems of symbols inherited with our religion and culture, paying little attention to their peculiarities and problems until, perhaps, some tragic event occurs (as with Job) which racks us with pain and suffering; or the slow monotonous running down of life at last confronts us with the meaninglessness of it all; or a hopeless dilemma in which we find ourselves leads us to break down in despair. Then we realize how desperately we need a new faith, that is, a new frame of orientation, if we are to go on. Such a new frame is never simply spun out of thin air. It is always the product of rebuilding, transforming, reshaping the old categories—or those among them which still, to some extent, provide a way of grasping our situation—enabling them better to interpret life as we now experience it. This is a precarious and dangerous project, repairing and rebuilding the very boat which keeps us afloat. But of course it is even more dangerous simply to sit complacently in that boat as it sinks, or to oppose or otherwise obstruct those seeking to rebuild it. If it has gotten into waters which it cannot manage, something must be done.

Let us return now more directly to the theological issues with which we are here concerned. If "God" and "Christ" are taken as "symbols" or "categories" in a humanly constructed conceptual scheme (as I am suggesting here), how, one might ask, could anyone properly have faith in them? Must we not believe them to be *objective realities,* outside of and independent of us, if we are to commit ourselves to them? Indeed, would it not be idolatrous to commit ourselves to them while knowing them to be simply human imaginative constructs? In considering this issue it might be useful to distinguish three rather distinct moments or dimensions in the human consciousness or awareness of meaning. First, there is the *moment or sense of naive awareness* in which meaning seems to be simply there, something directly given and to be accepted. In this sort of consciousness our speech about, for example, the value and significance of God and Christ—or of democracy, justice, truth, America, et cetera—is taken to refer to objectively given *realities,* realities which certainly *exist,* are *there,* realities in terms of which life must be ordered. In most of our unreflective use of such symbols or concepts as these, their meaning is taken in this more or less "objective" way. It is hardly surprising, then, that in cultures that are largely tradition-bound, as well as with more or less unreflective individuals in all cultures, the objectivity of the whole network of meanings within which life is carried on is taken for granted.

Human consciousness, however, is capable of transcending in some degree the meanings within which it lives and of subjecting them to criticism and creative transformation when they do not seem to fit what we are experiencing. We must then, second, take note of what we can call the *critical moment* or dimension of consciousness in which our concepts and categories seem in some ways questionable and problematic. Sometimes this critical moment becomes sufficiently widespread and powerful to call into question large complexes of cultural meaning—for example, at the time of the destruction of Jerusalem and the exile to Babylon, many wondered whether the covenant with Yahweh had any meaning any longer; with the sophists (and Socrates) in ancient Greece many traditional values were questioned; since the Enlightenment critical attitudes and practices have been deliberately cultivated by some segments of modern culture. In situations like these it becomes apparent to many that, far from being simple representations of "objective realities" with which humans must come to terms, these structures of meaning are human creations; they are cultural artifacts which have grown up in a history and which can be transformed in further history. This conception of meaning as humanly created has been worked out systematically in modern times by such persons as Feuerbach, Marx, Nietzsche, James, Freud, Dewey, Foucault, Derrida, and others, and it has become very influential in the contemporary intellectual world. In many ways it has been destructive of the power of major symbols which for generations had provided significant orientation in the West. Since those symbols, instead of presenting "objective realities" with which humans must come to terms, are now seen (by many) to be human creations—perhaps even corrupt and destructive ones—we can take them or leave them as we choose; and we might well be the wiser simply to leave them behind.

It is important to recognize that human beings are not able to live entirely and exclusively within this critical moment or dimension of consciousness. Without some accepted conception of the world and of the human place within it—a symbolic frame of meaning for the orientation of life—we can neither think nor act. After critical consciousness appears on the scene with its destructive questions, therefore, it is necessary to make some response. Two distinctly different moves are available: (1) It is possible to confine our critical scrutiny and questioning to certain specific domains of meaning (for example, traditional religious symbols) while actually orienting our lives by some other meaning-complex(es)—perhaps a Marxist conceptual frame or a Freudian or positivist one—which are not themselves criticized in this radical way, and which are, thus, taken (more or less naively) to present the actual "realities" with which humans must come to terms. When this move is made, the sense of naive conviction of meaning (the first moment of consciousness just mentioned) returns in full force, but now that conviction is held with respect to a somewhat different symbolic frame. Or (2) we can move into and live out of a third stance, one rooted in what we shall call a *reflective moment* of consciousness. This moment includes awareness both that symbolic meaning is indispensable to human life and that every actual structure of meaning is humanly created and must be subjected regularly to scrutiny and criticism.

When abstractly formulated in this way, this stance may seem possible only for a few elite intellectuals; but that is a misunderstanding. The reflective moment of consciousness is as much a function of the dialectical structure of central idealizing symbols in our language and culture as it is of the degree of sophistication possessed by groups or individuals. Consider, for example, such symbols as "justice," "truth," and "God," all of which have fundamental orienting significance in modern cultures. It is characteristic of these symbols that they somehow escape every attempt to grasp or understand or practice their full meaning: no articulation of them can be regarded as adequate; no practice or institution developed in connection with them fully expresses that toward which they are directing us; every understanding and practice, thus, must be continually revised, reformulated, reconstructed in light of the (never fully realized) ideal which the symbol suggests. Symbols of this sort, it could be said, manifest a continual strain toward self-transcendence; this is a feature of great importance, since it keeps them (as well as lives oriented by them) open to new experience and to unanticipated possibilities. Such symbols present themselves as having power to draw us, our practices, and our social institutions, beyond where we now are, to bring us to deeper understanding and humaneness and thus to a more profound self-realization; this is one of the features that makes symbols like Truth, Justice, Equality, Freedom, God, and the like so attractive to men and women and gives them such cultural power. It is important to note that the values and meanings, to which symbols of this sort call us, continue to shine through them even when we are aware that every version of them is limited and inadequate: who does not feel real force in cries for *justice* or demands for *freedom* or *truth,* however problematical each of these notions may seem? Such idealizing symbols manifest their power to a critical consciousness as well as to more naive mentalities; and they often provide the basis for criticism of traditional practices and institutions.

This third reflective moment of consciousness, thus, including as it does awareness that all particular meanings are human constructions as well as a sense that such symbolic meaning can both draw humans forward and significantly constrain them, has great importance for orienting and for motivating human life. It is to this sort of consciousness, I suspect, that Paul Ricoeur is alluding when he speaks of a "second naiveté" within which life today must be carried on.[2] Ricoeur's expression, however, is somewhat misleading, for this reflective moment or stance is anything but naive: it involves a consciousness even more critical, in certain respects, than moment two (the moment of "criticism") which may nihilistically—and thus naively—suppose that humans can live without significant value- and meaning-commitments. It is out of a stance rooted in this third moment of consciousness, and with the desire to enhance the meaning sensed in this moment, that the constructive work of theology proceeds, in its attempt to put together a Christian conceptual frame which can make sense of contemporary experience and life and to which, therefore, we today can commit ourselves with integrity.

All human life, as we have noted, proceeds in face of profound mystery, and symbolic meaning is created by humans to give order and orientation to life in that situation. But our structures of meaning may function in quite diverse ways with respect to this ultimate mystery. In what I have called the moment or sense of "naive awareness" of meaning, the ultimate mystery of things tends to become obscured—or even to dissolve away—since the meanings carried in tradition are taken to represent "objective reality"; thus, we *know* how things ultimately are. Every fundamentalism, religious or secular, lives out of this kind of naive certainty. In contrast to this self-assurance, the second or "critical" moment or activity of consciousness arises out of a renewed awareness of the pervasiveness and inscrutability of mystery. Hence, in its criticism it calls into question the structures of meaning to which people are committed; and in so doing it easily becomes either a new dogmatism or else nihilistic. We should note, now, that although both these moments of consciousness express certain definite faith-commitments, neither is grounded in a deliberate or self-aware faith—for both know too much: the moment of naiveté supposes itself to know how things really are; the moment of criticism knows that we can never know this.

In contrast, the third or reflective moment of consciousness is connected with a kind of faith that is significantly aware of itself. For it involves commitment both to the meaning of our most profound orienting symbols as well as to the meaningfulness of our activities of criticizing and reconstructing these same symbols in face of the ultimate mystery of life: in a reflective consciousness of this sort we live out of a trust which enables us to continue acting creatively and constructively even though we do not know with finality who we are or where we are going. With such a faith—such a consciousness of the profound mystery of life combined with confidence in the possibility of living creatively within that mystery—life can go on, however problematic our particular conceptual frame may have become. Thus, it is possible to engage in criticism and reconstruction of our conceptual schemes, even while we are living and thinking within them. I shall argue that the symbols "God" and "Christ" (in the Christian categorial scheme) are intended to articulate the ultimate mysteriousness of things in a manner that facilitates this sort of creative faith or trust in women and men.

It is evident that my contention that it is both possible and desirable to engage in radical reconstruction of a conceptual scheme even while we are living and thinking within it has begun to move beyond general anthropological considerations—about the role of worldviews in human life and how they change—to more specifically theological concerns. I want now to sum up these remarks by considering in more explicitly theological terms the central issue with which we are here concerned: the fact that our lives unfold within a context of ultimate mystery which makes questionable all our symbols and ideas.

In western religious traditions the ultimate mystery, to which our limitations of understanding and knowledge call attention, has usually been given a name, *God;* and in affirmations that God is "infinite" or "absolute," "transcendent" or "ineffable," believers have reminded themselves that this one whom they worship must be understood, ultimately, to be mystery. The mysteriousness of life, thus, was not regarded as grounded simply in us and our limitations: with the idea of God (as traditionally understood) it became objectified and brought to a focus in the ultimate reality with which men and women felt they must come to terms. Speaking of God as mystery in this way, and of the ultimate mystery as God, is a highly dialectical point, however, that has important implications for our understanding of theology: it may lead, for example, to acknowledgment that all our theological ideas and images are (as I have often put it) human imaginative constructs; and this understanding may in turn enable us to develop a conception of God, as we shall see in our reconstruction later on, that resists the reifications to which we are prone. Let me expand briefly on this point.

On the one hand, the traditional image/concept "God" was intended to symbolize that—whatever it might be—which brings true human fulfillment; that is, in speaking of "God" women and men were seeking to attend to the mystery of reality in its aspect as source and ground of their being and their salvation, as that on which, therefore, they could rely absolutely. But, on the other hand, as genuinely mystery, God was taken to be beyond human knowledge and understanding. There is a profound tension here which has not often been clearly recognized. This notion of God's ultimate *mystery* implies (and requires) an acknowledgment of our *unknowing* with respect to God—an acknowledgment, that is to say, that we do not know how the images and metaphors in terms of which we conceive God apply, since they are always our own metaphors and images, infected with our limitations, interests, and biases; and we dare not, therefore, claim they have been directly revealed by God. Only in and with this acknowledgment does the symbol "God" turn us—by indirection—toward that ultimate source and context of our humanity which completely transcends us, our ideas, and our control. In this way, we can say, the ultimacy of the mystery ascribed to God means (paradoxically) that we acknowledge God as indeed *God* only to the extent that we recognize our theological concepts, symbols, and methods as our own imaginative creations.

The image/concept "God" is a humanly constructed symbol by means of which we (in western traditions) attempt to focus our consciousness on that ultimate resource of human being and fulfillment to which (we believe) we must relate ourselves if we are to become fully human, if we are fully to realize our potentialities. Theologians (and also ordinary worshippers) certainly exercise considerable freedom in deciding which metaphors and images they will emphasize in speaking of (and worshipping) God, and the theological tradition is full of criticism and debate on such questions. There is no doubt, then, that theology is a thoroughly human activity, employing human norms and criteria and directed toward specifically human objectives. But it is an activity involved in highly dialectical moves because of the complexity of its central symbol "God." The recognition that all our theological concepts and symbols are our own imaginative constructs is essential to this dialectic.

The difficult issues on which we are here attempting to focus are not of merely intellectual interest: they express a posture which has always been regarded as central to religious piety, namely repentance. Repentance is certainly a human act (or attitude), but it has the peculiar dialectical character of being an act not of self-assertion but of giving up, an act of renouncing our own claims rather than insisting upon them. This giving up (repentance) must include, I want to emphasize now, our claims to knowledge and certainty. If we try to overcome and control the mystery within which we live—through, for example, our supposed religious knowledge or practices—we sin against God, for with this stance we are in fact trying to make ourselves the ultimate disposers of our lives and destiny. We must, then, repent: we must turn around from this posture, which we all too easily take up, and move toward a recognition that our destiny is ultimately in God's hands not ours—that is, that it remains a mystery to us. Repentance for this order of sin is difficult for us, maybe impossible when we are hardened in our ways. It is, perhaps, only as we actually fail to accomplish our purposes—for example, our religious or theological purpose to "know God"—only as we are broken in our attempts to reach this goal, that "grace" may break through the mystery that establishes and sustains us, creating in us the new modality of existence which we call faith. Piety of the sort we are discussing here may or may not involve verbal prayer: to insist that it *must* would presuppose we know more about God—about the ultimate mystery—than we possibly can. But prayer in the sense of expressing ourselves in face of the mystery, of coming to full consciousness and intention, of deliberately giving ourselves over to that beyond the human which constitutes us as human, is certainly central.

With this emphasis on our faith in and dependence on what is ultimately mystery, I do not mean to suggest that we do not in many ways continue to create and sustain ourselves; we certainly do this, including through such religious activity as theological reflection. My contention that our religious symbolism is our own construction is intended to emphasize just this point: that we humans create the structures of meaning within which we come to dwell. But simultaneously (as I have just tried to show) this emphasis on our human creativity deepens our consciousness of the inscrutable mystery within which we live and which gives us our being as human. The forthright recognition that our theology is our own work, our own doing, can thus open us to what has traditionally been called God's grace and mercy. That is, by clearly indicating what is our own activity it indirectly opens us to that beyond the human sphere of knowledge and control, that which, ultimately, constitutes us as human and which (we may hope and believe) will further our humanization.

To the extent that Christians have insisted that certain formulas and practices known in the churches are alone saving for humans, they have expressed, unfortunately, a piety of law not gospel: the dialectic inherent in the concept of God seems to require an agnosticism, not a dogmatism, with regard to all such matters. Not a cynical agnosticism, of course, that is destructive of everything that humans believe in and need; but that agnosticism which indirectly opens us to what is beyond our world, to that which we do not yet know but which will be creative of our future. Faith is the "letting go" (Kierkegaard) of all attachments, including specifically and especially our religious and theological attachments, because it is just these idolatries which shield us from—and thus close us off from—that ultimate mystery in which both our being and our fulfillment are grounded.

The contention that our theology is always our own construction reminds us that there is a sphere which we humans can (and should) control, and that our theological work takes place within that sphere. But just this recognition raises indirectly the question about that which we do not control, that which we do not and cannot consciously or deliberately construct, the ultimate mystery which we (in faith) call "God." Traditional theology sought to express the insight that we are beyond our proper powers when attempting to speak of God by maintaining that what was called "God's revelation," that is, the biblical and traditional symbols, must be held inviolable to our criticism and reconstruction. But that was a wooden and misleading way of making the point; moreover, it was subject to demonic uses and it led to a heteronomy of religious tradition. In my view the dialectic actually at stake here is expressed more adequately in the understanding that all theology (including that in the Bible) is human imaginative construction. This conception straightforwardly expresses the religious awareness that gives rise to theological reflection: everything is ultimately in God's hands, that is, it is mystery—and just for this reason every expression of faith (including this one), since it is our own human construction, must be questioned and criticized.[3]

For the most part in these remarks I have been emphasizing the epistemological dimensions of the notion of mystery—that the concept of mystery tells us more about our *unknowing* than it does about some reality with which we stand in relation. But before we leave this issue, it is important to note that more is involved than that. When the ultimate mystery is construed as *God,* our finitude and our unknowing no longer carry simply negative connotations. For this construal implies the belief that the ultimate mystery is trustworthy, that in which we may properly place our faith. The sense of mystery often has an aesthetic dimension, as well as the epistemological one which I have emphasized: it may include awe and wonder as well as bafflement. But when the mystery is apprehended as *God,* it calls forth from us not only wonder and awe and bafflement but trust and confidence as well, and our attempts—as finite creatures in a mysterious world—to live out our lives in faith and in faithfulness are given new support. Here is the positive side.

My problem here is this. What is said here is certainly true; theology & scripture too are human constructions, I agree to criticism. If that is his point, then he is simply arguing against fundamentalism. But if he is also concerned to say something against Atheism and nihilism, he must say something more than neg. criticism of fundamentalism. His statements here do not appear simply as affirmations where more is to be said. They seem to be closure statements, denying other things that might also be said.

5. Mystery, Theology, and Conversation

I have been using the concept of mystery a good bit in the opening chapters of this book, and it is important, before we go any further, that we reflect explicitly on its meaning. It has often been suggested that the overall context within which theological work is carried on is one of mystery.[1] In my opinion, however, the radical implications of this for the understanding of theology itself are seldom taken as seriously as they should be; and this leads to dangerous misconceptions. I want to make explicit, therefore, what is intended when the concept of mystery is invoked in this book.

"Mystery" (as I use the word) does not refer to a direct perceptual experience of something, as do "darkness" (in a cellar room at night) or "dense fog" (when we can not see anything), or as words like "unclear" or "obscure" do when used of some distant object which we cannot discern well enough to identify with confidence. To be sure the word "mystery" sometimes conveys this aura of something—we know not what—being experienced; however, I want to focus attention on a different aspect of its meaning. "Mystery" has a fundamentally intellectual character, whatever its experiential overtones. It refers to bafflement of mind more than obscurity of perception. A mystery is something we find we cannot think clearly about, cannot get our minds around, cannot manage to grasp. If we say that "life confronts us as mystery," or "whether life has any meaning is a mystery," or "the fact that there is something not nothing is a mystery," we are speaking about intellectual bafflements. We are indicating that what we are dealing with here seems to be beyond what our minds can handle.

To begin theological reflection (as we have been doing here) by emphasizing the overall mystery which surrounds us, the mystery in which we live, is to stress, then, that what we will be dealing with is really at the very limits of our intellectual capacities. We will be concerning ourselves with profound puzzles, conundrums that we cannot solve and that we should not expect to solve, but which are of great import to us nevertheless. In my allusions to mystery thus far, therefore, I have been concerned more to prescribe an attitude we need to take toward what we will be doing than to describe some object (of experience). Since in our theological work we are undertaking something at the very limit of our powers—or even beyond our powers—we must be cautious at every point about what we suppose we are achieving; a question mark must be placed behind everything that is said. This does not mean that it is not worth saying, that it is just empty talk. (That would be one way of interpreting the assertion that it is ultimately mystery with which we will be dealing: Wittgenstein's "What we cannot speak about we must consign to silence.")[2] If I had wished to make that point, of course, I would never have written this large book. I do have some things to say, but I want these put into proper context. I want it understood from the outset how problematic all of this is, how uncertain; but however uncertain, these are matters worth attending to, worth trying to understand as well as we can. The word "mystery," even while indicating that the questions we are dealing with are beyond our comprehension, has a way of eliciting our attention and interest and respect. It suggests that despite our limitations with regard to these matters—indeed, perhaps precisely because of these limitations—they are of great import to us.

When the word "mystery" is thought of as descriptive of some object of theological awareness or knowledge, rather than as prescriptively applying to us and our attitudes, obscure claims for which no grounds can be offered may be made to seem theologically legitimate. Speakers or writers may claim they are in a position to "unveil" the mystery (as is sometimes said), allowing us to see what we cannot see—like a landscape after the fog has lifted, or a dark room after a light has been turned on. This way of speaking may lead us to suppose we are being let in on secrets hidden from others, "secrets known only to God." (The use of perceptual metaphors in this kind of talk encourages such confusions.) But to say, "It is a mystery" does not yet tell us anything specific about the subject matter we are seeking to grasp or understand. "Mystery" is, rather, a grammatical or linguistic operator by means of which we remind ourselves of something about ourselves: that at this point we are using our language in an unusual, limited, and potentially misleading way. The word "mystery," thus, is a warning to ourselves not to mistake what we are now doing for our ordinary ways of speaking and thinking. It calls our attention to certain special rules that must be followed in our use of language as we do theology: take special care; beware of what is being said; the speaker may be misleading you; you may be misleading yourself; especially if the subject addressed is of importance, attend to what is being said with critical sensitivity to its problematic character.[3] When we introduce the concept of mystery into our theological work, there is no suggestion whatsoever that we may now let down the bars of a thoroughly critical employment of our faculties; on the contrary, we are alerting ourselves to the necessity here to employ our critical capacities to their utmost.

I suggested in the preceding chapters that a major function of religions (and also of theologies) is to present human beings with visions of the whole of reality. That is, religions (and theologies) provide us with construals of the ultimate mystery within which human life transpires—construals which are sufficiently meaningful and intelligible to enable human beings to come to some significant understanding of themselves in relation to the enigmatic context within which their lives proceed, and which are sufficiently appealing to motivate attempts to live fruitfully and meaningfully within this context. This suggests two important questions to which we will need to give considerable attention in our theological reflection: (1) What holistic pattern or picture or concept should we adopt as the "best" ("right"? "true"?) construal of the mystery of things, and how is this to be ascertained? (2) Through what steps can we best construct our picture or conception of this whole?

Since all "parts" of a holistic vision are organically interrelated and interdependent—and there is, thus, no obvious "foundation" with which we can begin our activity of theological construction—there are an indefinite number of alternative paths which might be followed in theological work. Moreover, since what we will be constructing here is a construal of what we actually confront as ultimate mystery, we can never be certain that the path down which we choose to move, or some particular turn in the path which we choose to take, will not lead us away from, rather than toward, a "more adequate" understanding of human life and its problems. It must never, then, be claimed that the particular choices we are making in our theological construction are the only possible ones, or even the best possible. Our theological moves will necessarily be tentative and problematic. The most we will be able to do is attempt to assess each step along the way as carefully as possible—giving the best reasons we can for taking it, while granting there are other plausible ways in which we might proceed—and then move on in our constructive activity.

Acknowledging in this way the highly questionable character of theological work may seem to render it pointless: How could one ever have faith—a faith sufficient to sustain life—in terms defined by a vision as shaky as what can be produced through this sort of cautious theological construction in face of the ultimate mystery of things? Surely humans must have other, less speculative and shaky, possibilities of commitment available to them than those opened up by theological reflection, and they would do better to go with one of these. Our religious traditions have, no doubt, led us to have such expectations, especially because of their claims that what they have to offer has been revealed by God on high to be the true salvation of humanity from the deepest ills of life. However, even though virtually every religion has claimed to be making available to humans some ultimate Truth about human life, and has thereby been enabled to attract faithful—and often fanatical!—adherents, it is important to note that they have been able to do this only by downplaying the ultimate mystery within which we all live, that is, by claiming to *know* (in some significant sense) what the ultimate reality with which we have to do actually is (a point discussed in the previous chapter). And in so doing they have in fact falsified our actual human condition, often thereby becoming dangerous threats to human life and flourishing, rather than trustworthy guides. The only possible check against the monumental deceits which human religiosity works on our gullibility—and on our desire for certainty in a terrifying world—is the constant reminding of ourselves that it is indeed *mystery* with which we humans ultimately have to do; and therefore we dare not claim to know the right and the true, the good and the real, but must acknowledge that in these things we always proceed in faith, as we move forward through life into the uncertain future before us. Theological construction which at every point acknowledges its problematic and questionable character, while simultaneously inviting a commitment of faith to lead our lives in this particular way rather than that, expresses accurately our actual situation as finite (but thoughtful and in some measure free) beings in a vast enigmatic world. Precisely because of the mystery, we must engage in relentless theological criticism of our faith and its symbols; precisely because of the mystery, we must give a prominent place in our vision of reality to forthright acknowledgment of our ultimate unknowing; precisely because of the mystery, we must undertake disciplined but imaginative construction of a vision of the world to which we can give ourselves, in faith, with confidence. (Faith is a very complex matter, and it will take the full analysis of this book to explain; see especially Chapters 4, 9, 16–20, 22, 23, 29.)

In our theological work, thus, our every move will be one of faith. Our choice of some particular holistic vision—one which is sufficiently compelling, or at least inviting, to attract us to exploring it with care—is itself a beginning act of faith, of commitment, to a particular way of seeing the ultimate mystery with which we have to do. Our decision to pursue this particular path rather than that, as we seek to discern and to construct our vision in detail, is a further act of faith. Our choice to take each new step of theological construction, to follow each new turning of the path, as we seek to see better what this holistic vision really means for the way we live, involves more steps of faith, taken with the consciousness that we might also, at each point, turn some other way. As we shall see, the activity of thinking theologically consists of one step of faith after another, each new step elicited by hope that our movement down the path of theological construction will enable us better to discern the role and place of human life within the mystery that encompasses us.

Since theology is principally concerned with what is ultimately mystery—mystery about which no one can be an *authority*, with true or certain answers to the major questions—I suggest that the proper model for conceiving it is not the lecture (monologue); nor is it the text (for example, a book): it is, rather, *conversation*. We are all in this mystery together; and we need to question one another, criticize one another, make suggestions to one another, help one another. Each of us is in a unique position within the mystery, a position occupied by no one else; and each of us, therefore, may have some special contribution to make to our common task of coming to terms with life's mysteries.[4] It is imperative that the theological conversation be kept open to and inclusive of all human voices.

As finite beings we are always engaged in adapting ourselves to one another—that is, we are involved in the activity of continually adjusting the desires, intentions, motivations, actions of each of us to the others roundabout. This first-order political activity of continual adaptation to others is carried out, of course, in terms supplied by some frame of orientation, some language and tradition, which provides the patterns of meaning, the ideologies, within which we think and act. Since there is never full agreement, however, on what these ideologies are or should be, second-order political activities directed toward adjusting our various ways of understanding and thinking to one another are necessary. From a sociological point of view, we could say, theology is a second-order political activity of this sort, an activity of adjusting certain of our ideas about human life and the world to those of others, of thinking together about matters of ultimate importance. The full range of the political dimensions of theological work will be kept in view, however, only if our theological conversation is kept open to all interested parties; that is, only if considerations of position, prestige, and power are prevented from dominating our interactions. It has been a mistake in the Christian churches to think of theology as basically ideology rather than conversation, that is, to suppose that theology is essentially a body of truths which can be defined clearly and can be passed on from generation to generation, instead of an activity requiring continuous adjustment of the thinking of each of us to all the others with whom we are *ipso facto* thinking together. Ideological conceptions of theology both imply a denial that the issues of life and death are ultimately mysteries to us—since the ideology being promoted is presumed to give what are regarded as adequate answers to these questions—and also lead easily to uses of religious symbols and doctrines for alien purposes of political manipulation and power. In such moves the concept of mystery—which should function as a protection against claims to special knowledge by any and every individual and group—is itself often perverted into an instrument of domination.

Traditional conceptions of religious truth and its dissemination appear to have grown up in the context of fundamentally authoritarian relationships, in which the truth that is saving was something known to a teacher or prophet or guru, and he or she, then, communicated it to, or passed it over to, others who received and accepted it. This sort of unidirectional relationship or movement characterizes much traditional religious thinking and practice with respect to truth—consider the special authority given to sacred texts by readers and interpreters, and especially by religious communities; the importance of the activity of preaching to audiences (large or small) who remain basically hearers, recipients of the word; the authority given to traditional doctrine or teaching in many religious groups. In all these instances (and others that could be cited) religious truth appears to be understood on the model of *property:* it is a kind of possession owned by one party and thus not directly available to others, a possession which can be passed on or given over to others if the owner chooses so to do.

In the traditions heir to ancient Israel the authoritarian tendencies of this property-model of truth were enhanced even further by the belief that the saving truth known to and available within the tradition had been revealed by God; it was, thus, absolute and infallible, simply to be accepted by the faithful, never criticized or doubted. It is hardly surprising that, given these conceptions, elite groups which were believed to be the only ones in a position to interpret sacred texts and explain obscure ideas emerged and gained positions of prestige and authority. This in turn fostered hierarchical social patterns easily subject to abuse: religious knowledge and power were in the hands of the few, and the masses of ordinary people were expected simply to believe what they were told and to obey. And religious symbols and ideas (whether wittingly or not) became ideological instruments supporting these powerful, educated, well-to-do groups—largely male—in their exploitation of the weak, the unlearned, the poor—often female. Thus it has almost always been, even though these same religious symbols and ideas had resources which, from time to time, could (and did) inspire powerful prophetic criticism of social evils of every sort, sometimes fueling the passions of revolt and revolution.

These traditional hierarchical and authoritarian patterns of religious understanding and theological reflection are no longer acceptable today, not only because they flagrantly violate modern democratic conceptions and ideals, but also because they seriously compromise the understanding that (as I have been contending here) in religious myths and symbols, and in theological doctrines and reflection, we are dealing with matters of profound, ultimately unfathomable, mystery; the ultimate meaning of human life, the final truth about the world and our place within it, is simply not available to us humans. It is, therefore, human presumptuousness of the highest order for any individuals or groups to make claims to special knowledge on such matters: the concept of mystery—and, I would say, the concept of God, when God is understood to be the ultimate mystery with which we have to do—levels all human cognitive elites and all religious hierarchies with respect to these profound questions of life and death. The most desirable overall context, therefore, for dealing with our deepest religious and theological issues would be unrestricted interchange among all interested parties—that is, unrestricted dialogue among *all* individuals and groups wishing to pursue such matters. The best image I know for conceiving what theology ought to be is not, then, the exegesis of sacred texts or the arcane debates of learned intellectuals, nor is it meditation or reflection in the privacy of one's solitude (however important may be the contributions of each of these), but rather free-flowing, open, and unfettered conversation.

We can see more clearly just what is involved in this suggestion by contrasting a conversation with a lecture. In its very form a lecture expresses an essentially monolithic and finitistic conception of truth: it suggests that religious or theological knowledge can quite properly be presented by a single voice in continuous ongoing monologue, and that it can be brought to a satisfactory conclusion at a particular point in time. The model of conversation implies, in rather sharp contrast, that many voices, representing quite different sorts of experience and points of view, are required even to begin to articulate religious truth; and, indeed, that such truth demands a kind of open-endedness into an indefinite future (conversations are often simply broken off for extraneous reasons without being brought to any "conclusion"), and therefore that even a multiplicity of voices is not fully adequate to the task. In conversation every voice knows that it is not complete in itself, that its contribution is in response to, and therefore depends upon, the voice(s) that came before, and that other voices coming after will develop further, modify, criticize, qualify what has just been said. Bakhtin has put the point well:

> There is neither a first nor a last word and there are no limits to the dialogic context (it extends into the boundless past and the boundless future). Even *past* meanings, that is, those born in the dialogue of past centuries, can never be stable (finalized, ended once and for all)—they will always change (be renewed) in the process of subsequent, future development of the dialogue . . . Nothing is absolutely dead; every meaning will have its homecoming festival.[5]

Free-flowing conversation presupposes a consciousness of being but one participant in a larger developing yet open-ended pattern of many voices, each having its own integrity, none being reducible to any of the others; and it presupposes a willingness to be but one voice in this developing texture of words and ideas, with no desire to control the entire movement (as in a lecture or other monologue). When theological or religious truth is conceived in these pluralistic and dialogical terms, no single voice can lay claim to it, for each understands that only in the ongoing conversation as a whole is truth brought into being. In this model truth is never final or complete or unchanging: it develops and is transformed in unpredictable ways as the conversation proceeds.[6]

This model of theology is democratic, open, and public, a model which encourages criticism from new voices and insights from points of view previously not taken seriously. In the sort of conversation I am imagining here, all participants are accepted on equal terms: all are there to participate with the others in search of understanding and truth; none dare claim they alone possess final religious knowledge or insight; each wishes to contribute whatever possible from the richness of experience and the perspective on life which has come to him or her, and will be listened to respectfully and attentively; all expect to learn from the others through appropriating with appreciation what they have to offer, and through opening themselves willingly to probing questions and sharp criticism. Christian theology conducted with these sorts of attitudes and ground rules would, it could be hoped, become a thoroughly critical and yet significantly constructive examination and assessment of a range of conceptions and interpretations of Christian faith, and of the basic possibilities for addressing the great mysteries of life opened up by that faith. The exploration of strands and resources of the Christian tradition long unknown or ignored, which ongoing conversation of this sort would encourage, should provide theologians with new insights and understandings otherwise unavailable; and the large-scale reconception and reconstruction of central Christian symbols and concepts, which the problems facing humanity in today's world necessitate, would thus be greatly facilitated.

It may be that the only institutional context available in modern society for such open and unfettered theological conversation is to be found in our great liberal universities. The academy, of course, has always been an elite and exclusive institution. However, under the impact of egalitarian and democratic ideals, as well as Marxist, Foucaultian, and "liberation theology" criticism, some academic theologians appear to be becoming increasingly interested in transforming theology done in the academy into a conversation in which as wide a range of voices as possible is present in a free and open discussion of issues of fundamental human importance. Perhaps it is time to think of academic theology (in contrast with, for example, various denominational or liberation theologies) as having the special vocation of providing a setting within which the whole range of theological (as well as appropriate "nontheological") voices could be heard, a setting within which each would be respectfully listened to and could be engaged in serious conversation with voices from other (often conflicting) perspectives. One would hope for lively participation by biblical theologians as well as philosophical theologians, by historical theologians and moral theologians, black theologians and WASP theologians, feminist theologians and humanist a-theologians; by representatives of a variety of religious and cultural traditions, as well as sociologists and historians of religion, psychologists and anthropologists, physicists, biologists, poets, artists, and others with theological interests. In this interchange among many diverse voices, each with its own concerns, academic theology would also have its own particular "advocacy": namely, the maintenance of a free and open ongoing conversation, as inclusive as possible, on theological issues. Academic theology conceived in this way would be intrinsically pluralistic and public in character, in the sense that (a) it would recognize clearly the existence and legitimacy of a wide diversity of theological voices (including voices that are "nonacademic"); (b) it would facilitate serious conversation among these widely diverse positions, so that each could learn from the others; and (c) it would contribute (theological) concepts and theories to this ongoing conversation (for example, concepts of historicity and pluralism, as in this book) which would interpret and emphasize the importance of pluralistic conversation of this sort to the theological enterprise as a whole and to the wider public.[7]

I see my own work as one voice in this emerging wider theological conversation.* I make no claims that what is presented here is the last word on anything. It represents my present thinking on what I regard as central issues for Christian theology today, and I expect that what I say here not only will be subjected to criticism but will be superseded by other voices also occupied with these questions. Thus the theological conversation proceeds, taking up into itself what its various participants find important and interesting, but always making its way in new and unpredictable directions—creative, we hope—as the issues presented by contemporary life are addressed

*The "emerging conversation" of which Christian theologians today are a part is actually considerably wider than suggested thus far: it now includes, for many, dialogues with representatives of other religious traditions, as well as conversation among diverse Christian communities. Such a larger dialogue also, if it is to be effective, must be completely open and unconstrained, following many of the same sorts of ground rules suggested in the above paragraphs. I have discussed some of the theological issues involved in this wider inter-religious dialogue in "Religious Diversity, Historical Consciousness, and Christian Theology" in *The Myth of Christian Uniqueness,* ed. J. Hick and P. F. Knitter (Maryknoll, N.Y.: Orbis Books, 1987), and also in "Religious Diversity and Religious Truth," in *John Hick: A Festschrift,* ed. Arvind Sharma (London: Macmillan, forthcoming). The latter article moves considerably beyond the issues taken up in the present chapter and proposes a conception of religious truth as itself pluralistic and dialogical. That idea is also developed briefly in "Critical Theology as a University Discipline," mentioned in note 7 to this chapter.

from many different perspectives. (For a discussion of the creativity of the conversational process itself, see Chapter 19.)

Modern historical studies have shown that the growth and development of the theological tradition in the past have come about largely through what I am here calling "conversation"—that is, through internal dialogue and through reflection on and appropriation of ideas which originated outside of explicitly Christian circles. New religious truth, that is to say, has emerged from and developed—often in quite unexpected ways—within ongoing conversations among many different voices over many generations. Since religious truth is in this way a function of conversation, it should not surprise us to discover that the efforts made, from time to time, to freeze it into unalterable authoritative monolithic forms have always failed. The relentless forward movement of history into open and unexpected futures repeatedly discloses how fully the ultimate mysteries of life and death elude our every attempt to capture or control them in words, in theological reflection, in ritualistic practices; it reminds us again and again, in short, that theological work is always carried on by particular finite human beings, with their own particular limitations of vision, insight, and understanding and their own propensities to prejudice and self-interested falsification.

Claims to incorrigibility or absoluteness with respect to theological issues—either by individuals or groups—are, therefore, never appropriate. Theology is, and always has been, an ongoing conversation among a variety of voices, even though, through most of Christian history, it has been thought to consist largely in a somewhat esoteric discussion within a relatively small elite group of highly educated males. In view of the immensity of the issues we today face, often involving matters seldom (if ever) taken up in earlier periods, it is important that the theological conversation be kept as open as possible to new and previously unheard voices—to women, blacks, the poor, "third world" persons, representatives of other religious and secular traditions, and so on—however unfamiliar to "the theological tradition" may be the issues with which these voices are concerned and the dialects in which they speak and think. For only thus will our theological conversation begin to engage the full range of enormously complex religious problems which we today face. Only thus will we have some chance of coming to grips in a fruitful and redemptive way with the profound mysteries with which life today confronts us.

6. The Christian World-Picture (I): The Monotheistic Categorial Scheme

Human evolution from a largely animal mode of existence to a cultural and historical mode required the development of complex forms of symbolization, differentiated social and institutional arrangements, and patterns of concept, value, and ritual which could provide orientation, guidance, and motivation as the decisions and actions of women and men became increasingly deliberate and complex. In my brief sketch (Chapter 3) of the anthropological reasons for the emergence of religious traditions and worldviews within this overall development, I suggested that a major function of what we have come to regard as religious practices and ideas has been to provide a comprehensive framework of orientation which enables humans to gain some insight into and understanding of themselves, their most profound problems, and the sort of fulfillment or salvation that might be available to them. Hence, if we ask what human societies are *doing* when they create religious traditions, and what individuals are doing when they participate in them, we can answer that they are seeking to gain orientation in life and some measure of understanding of the human place in the world.[1]

Although I intend this as a general observation about the nature and function of human religious institutions and practices, it is particularly applicable to the symbol "God," with which we are here especially concerned. The idea of God has proved a remarkably effective focus or center, around which a wide range of experiential and conceptual materials could be ordered and integrated into a flexible and powerful picture of the world. Is it possible to discern a basic symbolic pattern that gives worldviews focused in the symbol "God" a distinctive structure? We can best answer this question by looking briefly at the emergence in ancient Israel of the dialectic of God-and-the-idols, culminating in the development of what H. R. Niebuhr has called "radical monotheism."[2] The symbolic emphases and patterns which developed there have had great historical impact, especially on western culture and thence on the rest of the world; and it is their potential for continuing vitality and relevance with which we are especially concerned in this book. If we can discern an overall pattern or structure characteristic of those worldviews (descendant from ancient Israel) in which the symbol "God" has been the central focus, and take note of some of the strengths of this sort of symbolic pattern as well as weaknesses and problems to which it gives rise, we will be in a better position to move forward with our own constructive project.

The origins of our inherited symbol "God" are to be found in ancient near eastern polytheism, a symbolic scheme built up on the basis of human experience of social interaction and social life. In polytheisms the important powers in the world with which humans must contend are pictured as a society of interacting persons. What happens to humans here on earth is a kind of fallout, often unpredictable, of the interactions and struggles and tensions among the goddesses and gods in heaven. The overarching world, thus, is not a great impersonal material process, as we today are inclined to think of it, but essentially a structure of acting and interacting agents.

Polytheistic (and other pluralistic) frames of orientation have certain important strengths, in comparison with monotheistic or monistic schemes: they keep human life open to the great diversity of powers and values in the world and in ourselves, open to all the richness of experience. But they have the disadvantage of giving little help in ordering and assessing all this multiplicity and fullness; and they do not provide a sufficiently unified interpretive framework to bring all the variety and richness of experience and life into intelligible patterns which will enable women and men to move toward meaningful freedom and responsibility. In schemes of this sort each of the gods (or principles or values) has a certain integrity and independence of its own, and when these are in tension or conflict with one another there is no obvious way to decide among them. Since there is no single high god or ultimate principle beyond all the others, providing unity and order to the world-picture as a whole and to the course of life and history, there is no clear criterion for deciding among competing values and obligations, and no focus for an overarching commitment or loyalty which can give integrity to selves and communities. The various values and powers impinging on humans can only be played off or balanced against one another, as they push or pull this way or that in a world always threatened with disintegration and chaos.

For communities and selves living within such frameworks, life is essentially a matter of reacting to this or that power or value or god; and a sense of genuine freedom—that sense of being able significantly to determine one's own course, one's own future—is not likely to be evoked. For freedom and creativity, self-determination and responsibility to become significant possibilities for humans, the world must have sufficient unity and order to give a certain regularity and predictability to life, and yet be open to and permeable by human decisions and actions. Monotheisms offer more promise than do polytheisms of providing a frame of orientation in which the world will be experienced in this way. Let us turn briefly, then, to the monotheism that emerged in ancient Israel.[3]

Israel's god, Yahweh, was apparently originally one of the many gods of the near eastern pantheon, probably especially associated with Mt. Sinai in the desert. However, this god started early to break through his (Yahweh is clearly male) accepted place in the polytheistic scheme. He soon succeeded in overpowering the gods of Egypt (at least so the Israelite storytellers have it) as well as those of Canaan, giving the Hebrew people a land of their own—at the expense, of course, of these other peoples and gods. So this was a god of unusual power, especially in warfare. The relationship of the Hebrews to him was also unusual. Instead of some supposedly eternal and unchangeable natural or cosmic connection, it was based upon a free covenant made between Yahweh and the Hebrew people at a particular time; from thenceforth he would be their god, and they would be his people. It is important that we take note of the significance of these two points, Yahweh's power and the covenant relationship between Yahweh and Israel.

I have already noted that from our first awareness of him Yahweh's power seems to grow. This continues through the subsequent centuries of devotion, struggle, and reflection, and eventually Yahweh is regarded as the very creator of the heavens and the earth and all their contents, including humans (Gen. 2:4ff). By the time of the exile, six hundred years after the exodus, Yahweh is believed to be the all-powerful lord of the universe who has created the world by the word of his mouth (Gen. 1), one whom Second Isaiah can proclaim as "the first and . . . the last; besides [whom] there is no god" (Isa. 44:6).

> I am Yahweh, and there is no other.
>   I form light and create darkness,
>   I make weal and create woe,
> I am Yahweh, who do all these things. . . .
>
> I made the earth,
>   and created man upon it;
>   it was my hands that stretched out the heavens,
>   and I commanded all their host (Isa. 45:6f, 12)

Yahweh's great and expansive power, first manifest at the exodus, now is understood as the sole power creating and governing the universe and moving it toward a glorious consummation. The universe, thus, is a personal order (as it was also in polytheism) shaped by divine decisions and actions, but here that order is unified by the purposes and acts of a single divine agent. Moreover, it is an order intended to provide an appropriate context for human life: men and women are conceived here as free and responsible agents, capable of entering into moral covenant with Yahweh and with one another. After telling us that God "created the heavens" and "formed the earth," Second Isaiah declares that "he did not create it a chaos, he formed it to be inhabited!" (45:18). The picture of the world being painted here is of a moral and personal order, established by a supreme creative and governing moral and personal agent to be the context within which finite moral and personal agents (created "in God's image") can meaningfully live, an order moving toward a glorious consummation in which God's creatures will participate.

This monotheistic world-picture orienting Israel's life provided answers to (at least) three important questions: it presented an image or conception of humanity, an interpretation of the context within which human life transpires, and a claim about the way human life was to be directed or oriented within this context. These matters were presented in and through the very structure of this worldview, a structure constituted by three fundamental symbols or categories in complex interrelationship with one another: humanity, the world, and God. (From this point on, since "God" is now being used as a proper name, replacing "Yahweh," I shall capitalize it.) Monotheistic world-pictures in the religions descendant from ancient Israel appear to be given their basic structure and character by the filling in and developing of the interrelations of these three categories.

God (in such worldviews) is the ultimate point of reference in terms of which all else is to be understood, the creator and governor of all that is. This means that the other two categories, humanity and the world, cannot be understood simply in terms of themselves, what they appear, intrinsically, to be. They gain their being and their meaning from their relationship to God, their place in God's purposes, and it is only in this connection that what they are, and what they should do and become, can be rightly grasped.

Humanity (the second category) stands in a special relationship to God. Like God, human beings have creative powers and are morally responsible: they were created "in God's image." They have the capacity to enter into covenant with God, therefore, aligning their wills and their activities with what God is doing in the world; through taking up this special relationship with God they realize such fulfillment as is open to them (what the tradition has called "salvation"), so they are effectively motivated to obey the divine will. As free and responsible beings, however, humans also have the power to move in directions not in accord with the divine will; and human life and history are in fact marked everywhere by the existence and effects of such counterproductive and self-destructive activity, institutions, and practices (sin). So the human relationship to God within history is one of absolute dependence at one level; but at another level there are autonomy and freedom of self-determination which make possible both the tensions of sin and rebellion and the unique fulfillment of covenant and communion, together with the promise of ultimate salvation.

The world, our third category, is the context within which human life transpires; it includes all creaturely existence. In the monotheistic perspectives which have developed historically from ancient Israel, human beings do not live simply suspended before their creator, as it were, in direct and continuous face-to-face interaction with God. The experience of men and women in the world could hardly have been made intelligible in such terms, for actual human life unfolds within the spatial and temporal context of a multitude of other creatures to which humans are also related and on which they depend for their existence and well-being in many ways.

All that we know or experience or can imagine can be given a place within this threefold categorial scheme; and what we ordinarily call "faith in God" is simply human life lived within the terms it prescribes: all experiencing and reflecting, all imagining and thinking, all deciding and acting take place within this threefold pattern.

The interpretation of human existence provided by this radical monotheism is attractive in many ways. It presents a picture of human beings as possessed of a significant measure of freedom and creativity, and as placed within a world where this can be exercised and meaningfully developed. Although older deterministic attitudes, stemming from fatalistic and polytheistic perspectives, have sometimes reasserted themselves in Christian history—in doctrines, for example, of double predestination by an all-powerful God—in principle the fundamentally moral conception of a covenanted relationship between God and humans was strongly resistive to such views; hence, in this tradition men and women have usually been understood to be moral agents who can take responsibility for their own lives and actions and can in significant respects determine their own destinies.

This conception of the human as having genuine agency and responsibility—as having some degree of freedom both from external determinism (by fate or the gods) and internal determinisms (by, for example, desires for food and sex, for power, prestige, and glory)—is achieved by the special place and character given to the central category of this worldview, *God*. God functions not simply as an external determining power impinging on humans from without, but also as a center or focus for the (internal) devotion and orientation of selves and communities. To the extent that women and men orient themselves on God (it is believed), they can reasonably hope for lives of genuine freedom and fulfillment; however, if they orient themselves largely in terms of other powers and values, they become enslaved and debilitated in idolatries. This is no mere doctrinaire point. Since God is visualized as a perfectly righteous and loving being, devotion and obedience encourage the disciplining of communities and individuals in terms of such moral qualities as righteousness, mercy, and faithfulness; thus, the qualities emphasized in the concept or picture of God tend to become replicated in these selves and communities, and morally responsible life and action become valued highly. Through providing a center for devotion conceived to be in a significant way "beyond" both humanity and the world, monotheisms of this sort are able to overcome the tendencies toward disorder and chaos characteristic of polytheistic or pluralistic worlds, without falling into a rigid determinism or fatalism; in this way, they both provide a place for, and tend to encourage, the historical development of responsible human freedom. A sense of confidence and well-being in life's struggles is fostered by the consciousness of God's continuous care and by hope for the future which God is bringing, and this is combined with belief in the importance to God of human life and work, men and women having been given "dominion" over the rest of creation (Gen. 1:26); all of this together produces strong incentives to order human existence in accord with what is taken to be the divine will. Thus, by devoting themselves to the God who transcends everything finite, men and women (in this monotheistic culture) have increasingly shaped themselves (over many generations) into morally responsible agents with powers of freedom and self-determination similar to God's—they have become formed, that is to say, "in God's image." It is not surprising, then, that highly dynamic communities and cultures—politically, artistically, morally, technologically, scientifically dynamic—grew up historically under the aegis of this frame of orientation, shaped by this understanding of life and the world.

It should also not surprise us, however, to discover that this conceptual framework, like all others that have thus far appeared in human history, has certain significant biases and blind spots that can prove—and, indeed, have proved—very destructive, both of human existence and of the environment in which we live. I would like to mention two matters in this connection, each of which is inherent in the basic categorial notions that constitute this conceptual frame. Neither of these two can be downplayed as merely a distortion or corruption which some minor adjustments can remedy; each represents a fundamental problem in the monotheistic categorial scheme itself, a problem with which any attempt at contemporary theological construction within the framework of radical monotheism must come to terms.

The first issue to consider here is the highly anthropocentric character of this world-picture. By this I do not mean to be recalling simply the well-known fact that, in the form in which this perspective originally developed, human existence was located spatially in the center of the universe and it was principally humans (in all of creation) with which God was concerned. Both of those points, perhaps, can be attributed to the "near-sightedness" which (naturally?) accompanied the gradually dawning consciousness of questions about humanity's place in the world; and they are matters that can be relatively easily corrected in light of modern knowledge of the immensity and complexity of the universe. What I do want to direct attention to is the contention (in this categorial scheme) that the originative and ultimate reality behind everything (God) is to be understood largely in terms of images and metaphors derived from and peculiar to *human* existence—indeed, *male* human existence: God is pictured as lord, king, creator, judge, father, and so on. The defining model on the basis of which the conception of God is built up is that of an *agent,* an actor, a notion which gains its distinctive meaning almost entirely in and through human exemplifications.[4] Moreover, human beings are given their fundamental definition not principally by their relatedness to the other creatures roundabout them, but by their unique relationship with the creator, to whom in their inmost spirit they are thought to be akin. Very literally, then, in this perspective, the world revolves around a humanlike—a manlike!—center, and the ultimate reality from which all else stems (God) is conceived in quasi-human terms. Nature (in the modern sense), with its enormous variety of modes of being and life all in complex structural interconnection, does not have a significance here in any way comparable to that of humanity, nor does it have any real integrity of its own; rather, it functions largely to provide stage setting and props for the central dramatic action which transpires between God and humans.[5] In view of this emphasis, it should not surprise us that it has become a rather popular theme with recent ecologically minded writers to attribute much of the pollution and destruction of the environment which we western humans have caused to attitudes fostered by this biblical monotheistic perspective.[6] This point is obviously well taken. The fundamental anthropocentrism of the frame of orientation which has informed most of western history must be thoroughly deconstructed if we are to put together a version of radical monotheism which can orient human life properly in the world as we today conceive it.

A second problem inherent in the conceptual apparatus of radical monotheism as we have received it is its hierarchical character: in this scheme there is an ultimate orderer—God—who determines all else from on high. It is important to recognize that such a way of imagining the fundamental order in the universe can easily have seriously repressive effects in human life, both in the religious attitudes it evokes and also in its social and political consequences. In Judaism, Christianity, and Islam God has usually been conceived in terms of monarchical and imperial models, as a sort of king or emperor; and sometimes God is depicted as a virtual despot who rules by arbitrary fiat. Such images tend to evoke a piety of utter submissiveness to the divine will. If they are not qualified by other images emphasizing God's righteousness and love, the fundamental attitude toward the divine being inculcated in the believer is one of cowering obsequious fear, rather than the sort of healthy self-respect from which free and creative responsible action can ensue. Such a religious stance, in relationship to such a God, has serious social and political consequences. It tends to produce what have been called "authoritarian personalities"[7] in a society structured by authoritarian patterns of order. In such a society power and knowledge are ordered so as to move from their source on high down through the hierarchical layers of society, each higher rank having authority over those below and the whole structure legitimated by the divine king ruling over all. Those who know (or believe they know) what God wills, have inside information on the ultimate ordering activity in the universe, and feel authorized, therefore, to carry out whatever course of action seems required to implement this. To "serve God" is to try with all the resources at one's disposal to impose this order on whoever or whatever appears disobedient or rebellious. So humans (both in the churches and out of them, but especially those with a strong "religious" self-consciousness), taking themselves to be the agents of God on earth, try to impose their ideas of right and good on others who disagree; and they work hard to "subdue" (Gen. 1:28) the natural environment within which we all must live—all of this motivated by a strong confidence that they are carrying out the will of the creator. Such motivations can be quite powerful, helping to produce highly disciplined and integrated self-structures, capable of effective well-organized purposive activity. But they are also very dangerous. For they can issue into demonic fanaticisms which willingly destroy all who disagree; they may serve to authorize highly repressive social and political arrangements in a racist or sexist or class society; and they can easily lead to the unthinking exploitation of the earth's natural resources.

Unlike polytheisms—in which there are a number of gods each representing different interests and values, and authorizing different sorts of claims on individuals and communities, thus serving to relativize one another[8]—a radically monotheistic frame of orientation includes nothing that can call into question or relativize the claims or demands believed to be made by *God.* (This is the point, of course, of Kierkegaard's famous interpretation of the Abraham/Isaac story.)[9] God's demands are absolute, and must be fulfilled to the letter—even if they go against custom, conscience, or reason. Monotheistic frames of orientation are thus especially susceptible to developing into fanaticisms. Any individuals or groups who believe they know what the absolute God requires feel themselves fully authorized to carry out the divine will—at whatever cost to themselves or others. Moreover, there is no argument, point, or position from which it is possible to obtain leverage over against such divinely commanded or authorized activities or institutions. The inquisition, crusades and other holy wars, burning or drowning of heretics, and the like are well-known examples of the consequences of such attitudes; Samuel's violent response to Saul for failing to murder Agag, king of the Amalekites (1 Sam. 15) is perhaps the classic model for this pattern of the human relationship to God. With respect to the issue of fanaticism polytheistic positions, it would appear, are always preferable to monotheisms—particularly monotheisms in which some men or women believe themselves, or are believed, to be especially authorized by God to know and to carry out the divine will.

There are two ways in which monotheisms can be protected against falling into such fanaticisms. (1) Moral limitations may be placed on what can qualify as divinely willed: if God is perceived to be a thoroughly moral being, whose will is always just and righteous, believers may see that *moral criteria* can quite properly be used for ascertaining whether or not a particular demand or claim is to be regarded as expressing the divine. (2) If God's absoluteness is conceived as always *calling into question* our human understandings and claims, and never as directly *authorizing* specific human contentions—that is, if God is conceived as the supreme relativizer of everything human, in particular as the relativizer of those who believe in God—then faith in God will function to constrain human fanaticisms rather than to legitimate them. Precisely these two considerations will be made central in our constructive work later in this book, in which we shall attempt to conceive God's activity as at once supremely humanizing and supremely relativizing.

There is little doubt that western monotheisms, whatever important goods they have contributed to human existence on earth, have also bred and reinforced some of the more horrible evils of history. It is no longer tolerable, therefore, to continue promoting monotheistic religious symbolism simply because it is our inherited tradition and is, for this reason, uncritically accepted as "true." If we are to advocate radical monotheism as a framework for orienting human life today, it will have to be in a carefully considered chastened form, one constructed with particular concern to guard against these abuses and corruptions to which in the past it has so often lent itself.

With these strengths and these dangers inherent in monotheistic modes of symbolism in mind, we are in a position to consider a provisional definition of our inherited concept of God. As we have seen, in the original form in which radical monotheism developed, God was both the creator and the savior of humanity and the world, that is, that reality in relationship to which humans gained both their being and their well-being. In our work we want to avoid (so far as possible) perpetuating uncritically those aspects of the monotheistic framework, and those particular models and images, which have had powerful corruptive and destructive consequences. At this point, therefore, I shall propose a rather formal definition, one which abstracts certain elements from the early mythic images of God but which will be given its actual content only as we proceed with our constructive theological work. As a provisional working definition I suggest that by "God" we mean that reality, *whatever it might be,* orientation on which evokes our human moral and creative powers (that is, our distinctively human powers), encouraging their development and enhancement by promising significant human fulfillment (salvation) in the future. (That it is our "moral and creative powers" which are "distinctively human" will be argued below, especially in Chapters 8–10.)

It is obvious that this definition, by picking up the early perception of God as the One who is both creator and savior of humankind, brings the conception of God into close connection with the idea of humanity. Moreover, the understanding of God is here tied to a definite conception of what human beings are or can be ("moral and creative" beings), and what, therefore, constitutes human "fulfillment." Every conception of God, of course, is logically interconnected with an anthropology of some sort; and this emphasis on moral responsibility, as we have seen, actually grew up historically in interconnection with the monotheism with which we are here working, and has not, thus, been arbitarily imposed. (It will be necessary to examine, as we proceed, whether and in what respects this particular understanding of the human remains justifiable today.) Aside from this specifically anthropological matter, however, our definition of God remains quite formal. God is said to be simply that, "whatever it might be," which grounds and enhances human existence and agency, thus bringing human fulfillment. This leaves completely open the concrete specification of who or what God is. A major part of our task will be to find a way, which will be intelligible and significant in light of modern experience and knowledge, to give some concreteness to the notion of that which grounds and enables the emergence and maturing of human moral agency and responsibility. In order to do that, we must examine in some detail our human existence itself. To this we will turn in Part II.

This definition suggests that, in the traditions stemming from ancient Israel, by "God" is meant an "X" which is positively or constructively related to human life and its problems: the True God (these traditions have insisted), in contrast to all idols, is the one who brings genuine salvation or liberation to women and men. This is the deepest existential reason for human interest in, search for, and devotion to God; and it provides an important criterion for distinguishing God from the idols. On the basis of this criterion we can assert that any kind of human devotion or activity, any institution or social order, which is oppressive or destructive of human beings must be regarded as idolatrous; it is not grounded upon faith in or obedience to what is intended by the word "God." Unfortunately, this criterion has not often been employed consistently. All too frequently it has been claimed that God is made known simply and directly by tradition (that is, the specific tradition accepted by the speaker), and no thought has been given to the possibility that this particular God-of-tradition may perhaps itself be an idol, and that worship of "Him" is in fact idolatry.

When the symbol "God" (understood as I am proposing here) functions correctly, humans are presented with a focus for worship and life to which they can devote themselves freely, a focus which will bring order to what otherwise might be a chaotic play of impacts upon them and impulses within them, a focus which will point them toward a promising future; and when the conception of God is given concrete specification by particular images and metaphors appropriate to this understanding, it provides criteria both for assessing our many desires and impulses, customs and institutions, and for disciplining them into integrated and productive selves and communities. If God, then, is given precedence over all other objects of affection, devotion, and loyalty, communities and selves have a focus which draws them toward responsible freedom, self-determination, and moral agency. A radical monotheism of this sort can thus help bring order and orientation into human affairs, not by imposing a rigidly determined scheme on life or by denying the great diversity of powers in the world, but by supplying a unifying center for human devotion and service.

In setting out this conception of monotheism, I am attempting to call attention to a symbolic structure which pervades (or is intended to pervade) the whole of life, among those peoples who have inherited ancient Israel's devotion to a single God. My contention is that their social, political, and economic institutions, family patterns, customs surrounding work and leisure, the stories they tell and the songs they sing, their personal and private practices of meditation and reflection—these all are in certain respects ordered and organized in relationship to this categorial pattern. The whole of life, both individual and social, is believed to come from God (the Creator) and believed to be subject to God's jurisdiction and ordering. Every object or event in the world, therefore, is experienced in terms of this categorial structure, and all human decisions, plans, and projects are conceived and worked out within this understanding of the world.

This does not mean, of course, that there is never any backsliding by those living within a monotheistic world-picture, or any misunderstanding or deliberately malicious breaking of what are believed to be God's ordinances. Obviously there has always been much of this, and the Bible and other historical records are full of stories of sin, idolatry, serving "false gods," and the like. But all these matters, also, were understood and interpreted in light of the demands of the covenant with the True God: sin and idolatry were defined (in the traditions which ultimately became normative) as violations of the relationship of humans to this True God. None of this, of course, was worked through without much social and political struggle—including suppression of some groups and their religious beliefs and practices, often for what we today would regard as unworthy reasons, for example, for short-term political gain, or to expand economic power, or to make war against national enemies, or to establish patriarchy as dominant socially and culturally. At this point, however, I am not passing judgment on the price that was paid as monotheistic patterns of life and thought were created but am interested, rather, in uncovering the basic pattern of the monotheism that emerged. For it is that pattern with which we shall be working here—all the while attempting to correct for the sorts of abuses and corruptions to which it is susceptible.

In making the point that monotheistic language articulates a world-picture structured by three principal categories (God, the world, and humanity), I do not mean to imply, of course, that all who believe in God are explicitly aware of this, and that they deliberately order themselves accordingly. For the most part believers simply devote themselves to God, worshipping God in church and synagogue, praying to God, understanding themselves as persons seeking to respond to God in their lives here in the world. The notion of a threefold categorial scheme underlying and expressing itself in and through the monotheistic world-picture is a twentieth-century way of trying to grasp and articulate the basic structure of this faith-world. If we can understand how its central categories function to provide orientation in life, we will be in a better position to reconceive them, as we seek to construct a meaningful and plausible monotheistic frame of orientation for today.

Implicit in the way the three monotheistic categories are formulated is one fundamental contention: that human existence gains its true definition, and thus finds its fulfillment, only through orientation on God. To the extent that we define ourselves or orient ourselves simply in terms of the world (or any of the many items within the world), we will be frustrated, stunted, diseased, ultimately destroyed, for all such attachments are idolatrous, and thus corruptive and destructive of human life. Obviously this is not the only way to see human existence, and we may wish to reject this whole conception of human life and its context either as false or as inappropriate to our human nature or to modern life. We may believe, for example, that humans are essentially pawns in the hands of unchanging cosmic forces, and thus find behavioristic interpretations of life more to our taste. Or some contemporary version of polytheism, which emphasizes the pluralism of our motives, desires, and experiences, and which decries all attempts to discipline the various impulses of life through the development of morally responsible selves and communities, may seem to provide a truer picture of human possibilities and fulfillment. These (and other) ways of viewing human life express perennial dimensions of human experience, and they will always be able to make credible cases for themselves. Radical monotheism is but one of a number of proposals for understanding our human situation in face of the mystery of things.

It is precisely because monotheism is totalitarian—that is, has implications for all dimensions of life, including what we might otherwise think of as secular domains—that it can have great unifying power and meaning; but, as we have observed, this also opens it to very serious forms of corruption and abuse. The threefold categorial scheme which characterizes radical monotheism is, then, of much more than merely intellectual interest. It provides the structure for widely influential forms of life which first began to take concrete shape in ancient Israel's customs, institutions, and lifestyles, and in the reflection of Israel's prophets and poets, historians and law-givers. Subsequently various versions of this structure became important in Israel's progeny (Judaism, Christianity, and Islam) and widely influential in western culture, with significant effects around the world. My notion of the "threefold categorial scheme" of radical monotheism, thus, is not intended to represent merely a particular set of beliefs or intellectual problems with which some men and women have concerned themselves; it is intended to call attention to a deep-lying structure that has given pattern, meaning of a very specific sort, and a distinctive character to a widespread and influential form of human personal, social, and cultural experience.

7. The Christian World-Picture (II): The Category of Christ

It would be useful to compare and contrast the ways in which Judaism, Islam, and Christianity have each worked out the threefold categorial structure of monotheism, but I have neither the competence nor the space to attempt that here. We shall concern ourselves in this chapter, therefore, with certain peculiarities of the specifically Christian version. Christian faith, life, and theology are distinguished from these other two traditions by the addition of a fourth category—Christ—to the basic monotheistic framework of interpretation. This category, moreover, is just as important in defining and articulating the Christian world-picture as are the other three. We must try to see how this is possible and what it means.

The significance of the category of Christ was expressed in classical Christianity by claims about his deity; that is, by the contention that Christ can properly be understood only as somehow identical with God, identical with that ultimate reality which is the source and ground of all else, and the contention that God cannot be properly understood apart from Christ. Such claims already appear in the New Testament; some representative examples:

> No one has ever seen God; the only Son, who is in the bosom of the Father, he has made him known. (John 1:18)

> I and the Father are one. (John 10:30)

> All things have been delivered to me by my Father; . . . no one knows the Father except the Son and any one to whom the Son chooses to reveal him. (Matt. 11:27)

> He is the image of the invisible God. (Col. 1:15)

Later on at Nicea (325 C.E.) the mythic language of these New Testament passages was given a hard metaphysical interpretation: Jesus Christ was said to be

> begotten of the Father uniquely . . . of the substance of the Father, God of God, Light of Light, true God of true God, begotten, not made [that is, not a creature, not part of the world, not subsumable under either the category "world" or the category "human"], consubstantial with the Father.[1]

We shall not take up here all the difficult metaphysical issues, including problems of sheer credibility, which this language raises. But it should be noted in passing that it also raises very severe theological problems: from the beginning Jews, and later on also Moslems, held that Christians, in their extravagant christological claims, were guilty of idolatry; that is, that in their talk about Christ they seriously confused and compromised the most fundamental of the monotheistic categories, *God.* (I think they were substantially correct on that point, but this is a matter which we cannot consider until later. I mention it here simply as an example of what might be learned by Christians if they gave more serious attention to the other great monotheisms.) I have brought up these mythical and heavily metaphysical formulations at this point to underline only one issue: from the very beginning Christians have insisted on the centrality and importance of what I have called the fourth category of the Christian world-picture, the category of Christ. It is this category in particular, we could say, that distinguishes and defines a perspective as "Christian."

In the modern period the centrality of this category for Christians has been underlined in another way. Some recent writers (for example, some of the "death of God" theologians and certain other Christian humanists) have given great weight to Christ even though they have become dubious about the continuing viability of the category of God. In effect this reduces the standard fourfold Christian categorial scheme to three and proposes a strikingly different worldview from Christian monotheism, a view structured by the categories "world," "humanity," and "Christ." Whatever the merits of such a position, it is interesting in this context because it shows that the significance of Christ for human orientation and self-understanding is not simply derivative from the symbol "God," that is, it does not depend on the Christian dogmatic claim about Christ's divinity; the category of Christ has its own intrinsic and independent meaning. And for this reason it has its own unique contribution to make to the Christian picture of the world, a contribution that cannot be reduced to or subsumed under any of the other three constitutive categories (God, world, human). It was the independent significance of this symbol for understanding human existence, the world, and God that led the early Christians to give Christ such a high place in their lives and their reflection. The deifying of Christ, thus, whether idolatrous or not, was an expression of the early sense of his unique and incomparable importance for human self-understanding and orientation. Christian faith through the centuries has concurred in this view; and for this reason I am suggesting that we have here a fourth category with as important a role to play in giving structure to the Christian perspective as the other three.

In the sort of theological analysis and construction I am proposing the point is to proceed as self-consciously and intelligibly as possible, as we examine and then put together the various pieces of a Christian understanding of God, humanity, and the world. If we are successful in our work, any intelligent interested persons should be able to follow the reasoning and understand the steps being taken. Theological construction, as we shall pursue it, is not "faith seeking understanding" (Anselm) in the narrow sense suggested by some who hold that a full commitment to Christian faith is necessary even to understand the issues involved in Christian theology (a claim often made in connection with authoritarian appeals to "revelation"). In the theological construction we are undertaking, we attempt first to locate the principal building blocks with which a religious (or "secular") position—a "faith"—is put together, and then we assemble these step by step so that at each point anyone can see clearly just why this particular claim has been made, why that position has been taken, in preference to others. Any interested persons, whatever their faith-commitments, should be able to understand and follow this activity of construction. By the end of our path the reader should be able to see both what a Christian worldview is and what it might mean to live within it—that is, the reasons why one might commit one's self to it, or against it.

Our constructive theological work will not, of course, be wholly successful; the problems we will be addressing are much too massive and intractable. It is, after all, the ultimate mystery of things with which—in and through the categories of God, world, humanity, and Christ—we are attempting to come to terms; and we should not, therefore, expect to succeed fully in discerning, articulating, and understanding all that is involved in them. But we must do the best we can, for (in a broader sense than just mentioned) theology is "faith seeking *understanding,*" and this means attempting to make intelligible to ourselves what faith in God can possibly mean in our time, what this way of grasping life and of living in the world comes to today. The very attempt to construct a Christian world-picture piece by piece will reveal to us, in a distinctive way, the nature and meaning of Christian faith. And that understanding, that intelligibility, will be open to all persons willing to and interested in pursuing it, whatever might be their present faith-commitments. Theology, like every other intellectual enterprise, should conceive itself not as concerned largely with private or esoteric ideas grounded on privileged presuppositions or claims but as a public activity.

Let us now attempt to see how "Christ" functions in the Christian categorial scheme; it does not play a structural role in precisely the same way as the other three categories, thus producing a four-sided worldview instead of a three-sided one. Its function, instead, is primarily to qualify in a definitive way the other categories, particularly the understandings of God and humanity. On the one hand, Christians have taken Jesus to be the perfect or normative or true expression of what humanity is and should be; on the other, he has been seen as the perfect, definitive, and final revelation of God. So normative understandings of both the human and God are gained (in the received Christian view) by reference to Christ. This equipollent double-sidedness of the significance of Christ was given dogmatic standing in the formula of Chalcedon (451 C.E.), where it was held that Christ has "two natures," divine and human, which are perfectly united and balanced. He is, thus, "perfect in Godhead . . . [and] perfect in humanness, truly God and truly human, . . . consubstantial with the Father in Godhead, and . . . consubstantial with us in humanness."[2]

It is not necessary for us to come to terms with all the difficult metaphysical and theological problems associated with these formulations in order to see the central conceptual point being made, a point accepted in virtually all subsequent Christian reflection and thinking: that it is not possible to understand what is meant by "Christ" without bringing in the concepts of God and humanity; but it is also not possible properly to understand either "God" or "humanity" without reference to Christ. There is a complex dialectical interdependence among these three symbols in Christian perspectives, and this has decisive impact on how each is understood. The categories of God and humanity are not left completely open to be interpreted simply in accord with their ordinary meanings; each is now qualified in important ways, for the norms for their proper understanding are to be found in Christ.

Let us look at the concept of God first. In the various religious traditions around the world all sorts of claims about divine powers, gods, goddesses, demons, and the like have been made; many sorts of religious experience (often supposed to be of God or the gods) have been reported historically—experiences of the holy, the awesome, the terrifying, experiences of grace and beatitude, of mystical union; in addition, philosophers have had wide differences of opinion as to what notions of ultimate reality or of God are adequate, or whether it is appropriate to speak of God at all. Although this great diversity of human experience and reflection is certainly to be acknowledged and consulted and learned from, for Christian thinking the definitive clue or key which brings it all into order has been *Christ;* "He is the image of the invisible God," as Colossians puts it. For Christian theology, that is to say, God has been understood as Christlike: God is not to be imagined as hateful, indifferent, or impersonal; rather, God is to be thought of as loving, forgiving, redemptive—as a *moral* reality, concerned with the personal being and fulfillment of men and women. "Christ," thus, has served as a criterion or model in terms of which the idea of God has been constructed. (The concrete content which the notion of Christ will be given in our theological construction here must remain an open question for the present; and it would be a mistake to assume that any simple identification with the man Jesus will prove satisfactory for our purposes. For discussion of these issues see Chapters 25 and 26.)

The conception of the human in Christian theology has similarly been concentrated and shaped by the symbol of Christ. Here also history confronts us with an extremely wide range of possibilities: from the no-self doctrine of Buddhism to highly egocentric forms of individualism and solipsism to social theories of persons-in-community; from highly spiritualistic notions that the soul alone is real, the body unimportant or an alien prison, to thoroughly materialistic conceptions; from rigid moralisms to nihilistic antinomianisms. Obviously not all the questions raised by these diverse views can be settled simply by looking at "Christ." But for the Christian perspective Christ has been taken as significantly defining or normative for deciding what the human really is, what the central human problems are, and what is to be understood as salvation for humans. Thus, exploitation or oppression of others, or excessive concern for personal pleasure or the fulfillment of one's own desires; cynical devaluing of the meaning of life, or indifference to human needs and suffering; prideful self-assertion, accompanied by the downgrading and humiliation of others—all these (and many other) human attitudes and forms of life and activity are called into question from a Christian point of view. In contrast, virtues like love, mercy, forgiveness, service to others above self, working toward reconciliation and community among humans, and the like are regarded as expressing the authentically human. In all of this, what is called "Christ" (whatever disagreements there may be about the specific content of this symbol) is believed to provide a model or normative picture of what human being really is and ought to be; and hence the understanding of human nature, its problems and its fulfillment, is to be worked out with reference to that model.

In giving some examples here of what it might mean to regard Christ as normative, I do not intend to prejudge the question of the concrete content or meaning to be given this symbol in our constructive program. Rather, my concern is to make a strictly conceptual and methodological point: that the distinctive mark of Christian perspectives (in contrast with other monotheisms) is to be found in the impact the symbol "Christ" has on the understanding of both God and the human. This is, of course, due to the close dialectical interdependence of these three categories in Christian conceptual schemes; and it means that the questions regarding how God and humanity are to be understood should always (in Christian theological work) be pursued with one eye on Christ, who is regarded (by Christian faith) as the key or clue to both.

I do not mean to suggest that in our work here we will take it for granted that Christ *is* the definitive revelation of God and the normative human being. These claims also can and should be carefully examined; certain of their features we may find acceptable, others unsatisfactory. At this point we are seeking only to get clear how Christian conceptual schemes have generally worked, what the Christian grammar has been, so that if in due course we wish to criticize or change these matters, we will know what we are doing and why we are doing it.

No one has succeeded in defining and developing the notions of God and the human entirely in terms of Christ. Karl Barth tried to follow this methodological procedure with more consistency than any one before him, but clearly he failed: he succeeded only in demonstrating that this is an impossible project. It is impossible because (1) in order to fill out the notions of God and of humanity, much *extra-Christic* material must be put together from experience, from reflection, and from a whole range of traditions; and (2) there is no agreement or certainty—or any way to arrive at agreement or certainty—on just what content the symbol "Christ" should be given: many alternative possibilities are plausible. Moreover, if the conceptions both of God and of humanity could be directly and completely derived from Christ, it would be *Christ* (not God) that would be the ultimate point of reference in the Christian scheme. But that has seldom if ever been claimed, even by Karl Barth; rather, these three terms have always stood in complex dialectical interconnection with one another. It remains an open question, then, to what extent the concept of God is to be defined with reference to Christ, to what extent it is to be defined on the basis of other considerations; and it is also an open question to what extent the human is to be defined by Christ, to what extent in terms of general human experience, or Freudian insights, or Marxist perspectives, or Buddhist understandings. In pointing out some of the interconnections of the principal terms of the Christian conceptual frame, I do not mean to be foreclosing any of these questions; I am simply trying here to make evident the complexity of this point of departure for the work of theological construction to which we shall shortly turn.

It must also be considered an open question whether we should adopt this Christian fourfold categorial scheme at all, as the one within which to carry on our reflection on life's deepest problems—and, indeed, within which to lead our lives. To proceed along this path involves a definite choice and commitment: to attempt to see the ultimate mysteries of human life in Christian terms rather than others, such as, for example, Buddhist or Marxist, and to organize our thinking and analyze our experience in this way rather than that. Such a move, if we make it, will be an important decision of faith which will shape significantly all that follows. Later on I will say more about this and other "steps of faith" which are involved in theological work; for now, however, before taking this particular step, we are trying to get clear just what it would mean, what sort of step it would be; that is, what is at stake in a decision to work within the Christian categorial pattern.

In our consideration of the way in which the symbol "Christ" modifies and affects the other monotheistic categories, nothing has been said thus far about its impact on the category of world; that impact is somewhat more indirect than with God and the human, but it is no less significant. The terms of the monotheistic categorial scheme are not independent of one another in such a way that we can modify decisively one or two of them without affecting the third; a change in any of these categories reverberates throughout the whole system, transforming and reshaping the entire perspective. The introduction, then, of the symbol of Christ, with its powerful effects on the notions of God and humanity, is bound also to affect the conception of the world. We can see this already in the thinking of the earliest Christians. Christ is not thought of merely as the man Jesus of Nazareth, nor even the savior of all humanity: he is said to be the agent of the creation of the world, one who is continuously active in the world, sustaining and supporting it. John, for example, identifies Christ as the very "*logos* [word or wisdom] of God" and declares that "all things were made through him, and without him was not anything made that was made" (1:3). In Colossians we read that "in him all things were created, in heaven and on earth, visible and invisible, . . . all things were created through him and for him. He is before all things, and in him all things hold together" (1:16–17).

To a modern ear these far-reaching claims sound very strange; but however implausible they might seem on their face, from the perspective of our conceptual analysis it is not difficult to see why they were made. If God (the ultimate point of reference in terms of which all else is to be understood) must be interpreted in the light of Christ, and if humanity gains its normative definition from Christ, then surely the concept of the *world*—God's creation, on the one hand, and the context within which human life falls, on the other—must also be significantly affected when the symbol "Christ" is introduced into the categorial pattern. The world must now be understood as the sort (a) which this kind of God (defined with reference to Christ) would create and sustain, and (b) which provides a suitable context for the support and sustenance of the mode of human existence of which Christ is the paradigm. Thus, the world may not be thought of as simply an impersonal material order, nor as a rigidly determined fatalistic order, nor as a chancy ramshackle structure about to disintegrate into chaos: it is to be seen as an order established by the loving God working out creative and redemptive purposes in and through the movement of history, an order which provides a proper context for the emergence and development of loving human beings living in faithful community with one another and with God. (Whether we today will still be able to meet fully the requirements of this desideratum cannot, of course, be determined until we are much further along in our theological reconstruction.) Humans do not, thus, live in an alien world; their souls, for example, should not be regarded as "imprisoned" in their bodies (Platonism and gnosticism), and salvation is not a kind of escape from this life and this flesh. The world is, rather (as viewed from within Christian perspectives), a proper context for human existence, sustentive of human beings and helping to evoke their highest potentialities (as represented by Christ). God has placed us in this world, and it is within this world that God is working toward our fulfillment. Putting this all in the more contemporary language we will be using later on, we can say that the world (in the Christian categorial scheme) is understood to be the context of our humanization, our being brought into full humanity; and the this-worldly social and historical processes in which we are immersed and from which we have emerged are the very processes through which that humanization—that divine creating of the human—is brought about.

These are momentous claims, and we may well want to question or dispute them. I am not now trying to argue their truth but rather am making a conceptual point about the dialectical interconnectedness of the principal terms of the Christian categorial scheme: introducing the symbol of Christ not only decisively affects the concepts of God and humanity; it also has powerful effects on the notion of the universe, the context of our experience and life. This raises very difficult problems for contemporary theology since the conception of the world held by most educated modern people (at least in the West) is quite different from that found in the Bible. Within the Bible's cosmological picture, for example, it is plausible to see the entire universe as pervaded by the personal purposive activity of a loving God; but this becomes quite difficult, perhaps impossible, with modern scientific and historical conceptions. Again, in the biblical cosmology it seems appropriate to picture humankind as the center and crown of all creation, but from a modern perspective such anthropocentrism seems ridiculous; indeed, as modern ecological awareness makes clear, in many respects it is pernicious and dangerous. In the face of these sorts of problems, we cannot but wonder whether the Christian God can be intelligibly regarded any longer as the ultimate point of reference for all that is. And what are we to make of Christian claims that the human is to be normatively defined by Christ? Have these not also become quite dubious, possibly absurd, in light of what Freud, Nietzsche, Darwin, Marx, and others have taught us? If modern understandings of the world put Christian views of its personal and humanizing character into question, then they also raise serious problems for Christian conceptions of God and of humanness: the Christian categorial scheme is a dialectically interconnected organic whole, and if any of its four terms no longer fit our experience and need reconception, that whole must be reconstructed.

Let me now sum up this preliminary consideration of the Christian categorial scheme. In providing an ultimate point of reference in terms of which all else is grasped, "God" serves as a powerful unifying category. All of life and the world is seen as fundamentally held together and meaningfully ordered, since it is understood as derivative from and in continuing connection with this single supreme reality. This way of conceiving unity and order, as we have noted, produces a pattern of hierarchy, a pattern with significant strengths but also giving rise to certain problems. The sense of connectedness and wholeness of experience and life, which this sort of frame encourages, fosters the development of selves and communities that are centered and well-ordered, capable of acting with some freedom and creativity. This is an important strength, in comparison with more pluralistic schemes which may not propose a center for life at all, and which depict a world full of tensions and even threatening to disintegrate, a world within which responsible action would be difficult. The disadvantage of such a well-ordered world, of course, is that it may fail to do justice to the chaotic aspects of life as well as to its diversity. Important dimensions of experience and of the world may thus be ignored, even suppressed. Moreover, groups and institutions that subscribe to this sort of hierarchical ordering can all too easily subvert this scheme to repressive or oppressive social and political purposes and policies, if they take themselves to be agents carrying out God's will on earth. Many examples of this are to be found in Christian history.

Monotheisms, however, do not present as suffocating a pattern of unity and order as straightforward *monisms,* in which every finite reality is conceived as a direct expression of the One, or as simply part of the all-encompassing Whole. In monotheisms each of God's creatures has a distinct sphere and integrity of its own; and therefore conceptions of creaturely freedom and creativity can be given a significant place. Moreover, the overarching sovereignty of God to which all creatures are subject implies a fundamental egalitarianism among the creatures; and this can provide a basis for social and political criticism and reform, even for revolution, and it has not infrequently been so employed. Nevertheless, historically it has proved much too easy to push monotheistically informed patterns of social organization in repressive directions; and some interpretations of the central symbol of God, particularly those strongly emphasizing the divine omnipotence, have often been dehumanizing. It should be clear, then, that if we decide to make the symbol "God" the central ordering category for our reflection, we are making a definite choice among alternatives, and it is not a completely innocent choice. It is a decision to attempt to see the world and human life in a particular way, a way that has important social and political consequences as well as intellectual implications. Theology has the responsibility of bringing all these matters to as clear consciousness as possible, so that the dehumanizing dangers they present can be discerned and guarded against; and the conceptual scheme will thus become an instrumentality of human salvation.

A decision to move in a monotheistic direction in our theological work does not in itself determine that we will be constructing a specifically *Christian* monotheism, that is, that we will give a distinctly normative significance to Jesus Christ in our understanding of God, humanity, and the world; if that is desired, a further decision will be required. There are many different ways in which the principal categories of a monotheistic framework can be developed, and some of these are ruled out if we decide to give normative significance to Christ; our understanding of what human life is all about and what is a truly "good life," as well as our conception of ultimate reality (God), will be significantly shaped by this choice. Once again, such a move has certain important positive features as well as some distinct disadvantages. On the positive side there is the challenge and the attractiveness of the man Jesus and the mode of life he epitomizes. Jesus exemplifies, and he requires of his followers, a style of life characterized by intense human concern—mercy, forgiveness, healing—certainly much needed in today's world.

There are also, however, some serious problems connected with giving decisive normative significance to the symbol of Christ. In part these derive from the fact that this symbol has traditionally been understood to refer almost exclusively to the man Jesus of Nazareth. Focusing so heavily on a single figure from an ancient story as paradigm of the human leads to a limited, and in some significant respects distorted, picture of human existence and its possibilities. Many feminists today, for example, have pointed out that at best Jesus can symbolize and represent the experience and reality of only half the human race; and a view that makes him normative for all helps to legitimate and reinforce patriarchal social and cultural practices and institutions, in this way contributing to the oppression of women. Beyond this, it has been argued that many of the central features of the story of Jesus—his personal example of not resisting his enemies but submitting to a martyr's death, his emphasizing humility and patience as important virtues, his injunction to his disciples to love and serve even their enemies though it bring them a cross—lend themselves easily to ideological uses by dominant groups attempting to keep others in subjection; and in fact they have often been so used in oppressing blacks and other poor or powerless people.

One must ask, therefore, whether this symbolic figure should continue to be given the importance he has had in the Christian categorial scheme. In our attempt to work out conceptions of humanity and God adequate for today, should Jesus be supplemented, or perhaps even supplanted, by other figures, other concrete images? In our constructive theological work it is important that we take into account the limitations of the Christ-symbol as it has been employed in the major Christian traditions, and that we correct for them. We need to recognize that, although this symbol presents in quite dramatic fashion certain important human possibilities, and thus can throw significant light on our understanding of God, humanity, and the world, it also ignores and tends to close off others. In the end we may conclude that just this selectivity is as much required of theology today as ever; but if so, this should be an explicit self-conscious judgment. Within the Christian categorial scheme Christ is not ultimate, God alone is; and we must be careful, therefore, that the symbol "Christ" is not employed in an idolatrous way. This has often occurred in the past, and intolerant Christian imperialisms as well as destructive fanaticisms have been the consequence.

At every point, as we move now to construct our picture of human life and the world, we will be making definite choices, attempting to view the world and the human in one particular way rather than in any number of others in which we might also be interested. Obviously my decision to employ Christian categories will seem more justifiable to those readers who think of themselves as Christian and who have some commitment to the Christian church; for it is an expression of *Christian* faith seeking understanding, and thus of the life of the church. However provisional this decision to work with the Christian categorial scheme may be, it at least means that (for the purposes of the argument of this book) readers will find it necessary right from the outset to take two important steps (at least imaginatively) into, or from within, Christian faith: they must be willing to attempt to see all of human life, indeed all of reality, (1) in its connection with God, and (2) in terms of the normative significance of Christ. This initial imaginative move does not mean, of course, that we have already made our decisions about how these two central symbols of Christian faith are to be understood; rather we are simply agreeing to make them fundamental categories in the conceptual scheme we shall attempt to construct. Whether such a move will really prove illuminating and persuasive, that is, whether we will in fact be able to give significant employment to these Christian categories as we seek to construct a viable contemporary understanding of human life and the world—and thus whether Christian faith can prove significant for us today—remains to be seen. It is this "experiment in thought" in which every contemporary Christian theology is engaged.

Part II

Constructing a Concept of the Human

It is a false dichotomy to think of Nature *and* Man. Mankind is that factor *in* Nature which exhibits in its most intense form the plasticity of Nature.

A. N. Whitehead

Freedom is given to man as every other creature is given its peculiar gift by God. It is his creaturely mode.

Karl Barth

. . much philosophical thought in the last century has been engaged with this problem[:] how to go beyond a notion of the self as the subject of a self-dependent will and bring to light its insertion in nature, our own and that which surrounds us, or in other terms, how to situate freedom?

Charles Taylor

8. Historicity and Biology

Christian outlooks on life and the world are given their fundamental character and structure by four principal categories: God, world, humanity, and Christ. The task of Christian theology today is thus to assess critically the viability and significance of this categorial scheme for ordering, interpreting, and orienting contemporary life, and to reconstruct it so that it will perform these functions as adequately as possible. This four-term categorial structure is an organic whole in which the principal terms are dialectically interrelated, each determining the others in certain crucial respects as well as being determined by them. Since it is obviously impossible to undertake analysis and reconstruction everywhere at once, we must begin our constructive theological work at one or another point and gradually move through all the categories, always keeping in mind their dialectical interconnection and interdependence.

The symbols "God" and "Christ" have in many respects become quite problematical for modern people, and this makes it difficult to see how one might initially approach the categorial structure through them; it is better to take up these two symbols somewhat later in our work, after we have begun to get our bearings. In contrast, the concepts of "world" and "human" find wide, and usually rather unquestioned, employment in current discourse and thinking (however philosophically questionable they may be in many respects); these two terms obviously make contact with features found in virtually every understanding or interpretation of human existence. It seems appropriate, then, to begin our reconstruction of the Christian categorial scheme with these two categories, and later to work back from them to the more difficult, less immediately intelligible, notions of God and Christ. All human understanding grounds itself on what is taken to be known or easily accessible, attempting from that point to come to grips with that which is darker and eludes comprehension. This is also the way in which we shall proceed in our constructive theological work.

If we turn to the notions of the human and the world, however, we still find ourselves confronted with serious problems. "World," in particular, including within itself (as it apparently does) *everything,* seems an especially vague and difficult notion with which to begin. We are left, then, with the category of the human as our point of entry into the Christian categorial scheme. Here it is at least *prima facie* clear about what we are attempting to speak: it is we ourselves; each of us is human, and we daily engage in interchange with many others whom we also acknowledge to be human. Since the referent of the category of the human is thus intuitively clear, it can provide us with a point of entry into the fourfold Christian categorial scheme.

This does not mean, however, that it is self-evident how we should proceed. A moment's reflection will show that the notion of the human is also quite indefinite, and there is little agreement on how it is to be understood. Are humans to be thought of as essentially very clever animals who have evolved to a high level of intelligence and are therefore capable of manipulating their environment in ways going far beyond the capabilities of any other animal? or should we conceive them as immortal souls, destined for communion with God? Are they essentially self-conscious egos or selves, self-constituted and self-sustaining? or are they to be thought of as finite manifestations of some pervasive world-spirit, a spark of the divine? Are they complicated pieces of matter, functions of and participant in the vast, lawful order of nature? or are they essentially free, moral agents, capable of setting their own course in life? Are they in some sense all of these? or, perhaps, none of these?

Each of these characterizations is an interpretation of what humans *really are;* it involves, thus, a definite claim about where we should begin our investigation of the human and how we should proceed. For example, if we take humans to be essentially "intelligent animals," we will see them as primarily complex biological organisms to be understood in relation to the rest of life; and the findings of so-called animal psychology may be regarded as the best point of departure for our understanding of human existence. In contrast, if we see humans as fundamentally "immortal souls," our primary interest will be in their eternal destiny, their place in the "spiritual world" and their relation to God. Again, if we believe humans to be essentially "moral agents," we will seek to understand them in terms of such qualities and relations as trust, loyalty, responsibility, freedom, dignity, and the like. My point is that each of these views is "theory-laden" (as is sometimes said): each contains within itself an understanding of what human nature is and thus predetermines what questions we will pursue in our investigation, what we will look for, what findings we will regard as important. Each of these views, and every other one that we might mention as well, highlights a certain aspect of the complex that is human reality; it seizes on that as the key or clue to the whole, and proposes to understand human life fundamentally in those terms. Although human reality is always before our eyes, so to speak, and is directly present in our experience—for we are it—it is so variegated and complex that there is no way for us directly and immediately to see *what* it is, what sort of reality or being it has.

It is, thus, not possible for us to grasp what human existence is directly, but only *reflectively*. Only as we "think back," as we remember and reflect on our experience and on what we have learned from others, especially as we reflect on the various interpretations (that is, the various *theories*) that have been suggested to us, do we gain a concept of the human. There is no way to get directly to human nature as such, to examine it and thus see what it is; every move we make will be in terms of some particular interpretation of the human and the procedures implied by that view. This is why there is so little communication and understanding among, for example, behavioral psychologists, Christian theologians, and philosophers of action, though each claims to be telling us what humans really are and do. Each begins with a set of presuppositions about what is important in human nature; each has a distinctive vocabulary and a distinctive method; and each works out a carefully elaborated position. But how these relate to one another, and which is valid and true, which misleading or false, there appears no way to say, since each approach seems justified in its own terms.

The several approaches to understanding human existence which I have thus far mentioned are all found in modern western culture; despite their diversity, in many respects they share, therefore, a common history and have common presuppositions. The problem of the starting point for our investigation becomes immeasurably complicated and deepened if we widen our vision now and attempt to take some account of the perspectives of other cultures, other religious traditions. In Buddhism or Hinduism, for example, with background for understanding provided by mythological frameworks and metaphysical reflection quite different from ours in the West, strikingly different conceptions of human existence have appeared. These have provided the terms in which hundreds of millions of people have lived out their lives, and they often throw light on possibilities and problems which have scarcely been noticed in the West. It is no longer justifiable, therefore, for us simply to assume that our western viewpoints by themselves provide us with everything we need to gain adequate understanding of human existence: western presuppositions about self or ego, and western emphases on rational power, on autonomy and on technological control, may be at the root of both our most serious environmental problems and our most intractable social and political problems. It would be foolish any longer simply to ignore the claims of other traditions that human existence should be understood in terms of quite different conceptual frameworks and perspectives than those familiar to us.

In addition to these difficult questions, and cutting sharply across them, feminist writers in recent years have been raising a further set of issues. It is becoming increasingly apparent that female experience in all cultures has been significantly different in many respects from male. But the importance of this for our general understanding of human existence has only recently been noticed; it was never appropriated philosophically or theologically, since in every society of which we know the principal explicit conceptions of human nature were articulated and systematically developed by members of a male elite who often ignored or disparaged or simply were not aware of significant features of female experience. So in all the familiar interpretations of the human, the experience and self-understandings of half the human race have not been taken into account.

The difficulty of getting beyond misleading or false conceptions of the human reality we are trying to investigate, to that reality itself, is no mere academic or methodological issue which, having noted, we can easily correct. For what we men and women are and do and what those others with whom we interact are and do is significantly affected by what we (and they) take ourselves to be and what our practices are. Our practices shape what we become and how we understand ourselves; and our understanding of what it is to be human affects significantly the way we interpret ourselves to ourselves and to others, and thus informs the way we act. If we acted in different ways, and held a different conception of ourselves, of what persons are, we would perceive different possibilities for ourselves and anticipate a different course of life; we would, thus, order our lives differently and act differently. In short, we would be different beings than we now are. Human nature (as we earlier noted) is not a kind of fixed objective reality that simply is what it is. It is always in part constituted by the practices of the women and men involved and by their understandings of human nature and destiny, of the meaning of life; human existence is diverse and pluralistic to very deep levels.

In investigations of the human, then, it is not possible to begin simply and directly with an object, human nature, which is to be examined and described just as it is: we always, in fact, begin with some particular conception or interpretation of the human—usually one we simply take for granted—and this guides our attempt to locate and understand what human reality is. If, now, we do not wish to proceed in a simply uncritical way in our theological reflection on human existence, with what interpretation should we begin? What conception is least likely to be seriously misleading and most likely to open us to the wide diversity and range of human life?

Our preliminary conception of the human should at least provide a way to understand and take account of the issues we have just been considering, that is, how diverse have been the manifestations of the human in history, and how various have been the interpretations of human life and its meaning. We should begin with a view, that is to say, which sees both *that* the human is no simple object which can be directly observed and described, and *why* it is not that sort of object—namely, because of its peculiarly complex makeup which includes and is partially constituted by its own practices and its interpretations of itself. A preliminary view or a starting position of this sort is, of course, itself an interpretation of human existence, and thus one view among many. But it is a view which from the outset provides space for virtually unlimited diversity and plurality. It should enable us, thus, to avoid foreclosing alternative interpretations too quickly; it should encourage us to remain open to what they are and what they claim, thus facilitating our learning from other perspectives, incorporating their insights into our own view.

Beginning in this way with an openness toward human diversity and pluralism is no mere academic desideratum, advanced for purely theoretical interests in a universal theory of the human: it has become a matter of great practical importance. Lack of serious attention to the extremely diverse ways of being human which have appeared in the course of human history has led to the assumption—not only by many theorists, but by most political leaders and ordinary people as well—that *our* mode of life, our institutions and practices, our attitudes and beliefs, are the normal and normative ones for human beings. What we do and are and believe are thus taken as the *standard* in terms of which the human is understood, and whatever deviates significantly from this standard—being less-than-human or anti-human—may justifiably be discriminated against, suppressed, even obliterated. Such evils as racism and sexism, classism and nationalism, with their innumerable forms of oppressiveness and dehumanization, all are expressions of ethnocentric biases and prejudices of this sort. Only gradually are we coming to see that, instead of shutting ourselves off from other points of view, other ways of life, other understandings of what it is to be human, we must learn to open ourselves to them, allowing our parochial provincialisms to be corrected by them, thus neutralizing their dangerous destructiveness. In our utterly pluralized world the threats of ecological collapse and nuclear disaster have made it clear that we must learn to live and work together on this planet or we will not survive at all. And to live together, we must learn to understand, appreciate, and respect the attitudes, practices, and beliefs of those who live and think very differently from ourselves. So it is indispensable that we find a way of bringing precisely the diversity of humankind into our very conception of the human.

We can begin to develop such a perspective by reflecting on this fact that in the course of history humans have created many different patterns of life and conceptions or interpretations of themselves, in this way giving rise to quite diverse forms of human being. In seeking to come to some understanding of themselves they have hit upon various alternative conceptions—animal, spirit, moral will, child of God, self, not-self, and so forth. In different historical settings around the globe they have adopted one or another of these and have then gradually, over time, shaped themselves according to that image. In this way they built into themselves (in the course of many generations) a special sort of relation to themselves—that is, their own attitude toward and conception of themselves, their self-understanding—and it is only out of and in terms of that relation to themselves that they are what they are and do what they do. As Kierkegaard put it, "The self is a relation which relates itself to its own self."[1] This distinctive kind of self-relation is involved in all our experience and all the other relationships in which we humans stand. The relationships of both persons and communities to realities other than themselves (whether human or nonhuman) are, then, never simple and direct:

$$H \rightarrow O$$

they are always a function of the prior self-relation within the human:

$$\overset{\circlearrowright}{H} \rightarrow O$$

It is in significant part through our own grasping of ourselves both as individuals and as groups—through our awareness of ourselves, that is, our relation to ourselves—that we human groups and individuals are what we are. And if that grasping, that consciousness, that self-relation, were something different, we would be different groups and different individuals who acted in different ways.

We are now in a position to understand at a deeper level a point made earlier, namely, that we can grasp human reality only *reflectively*, never directly in perception. Our perception of all human realities (persons, communities, institutions, cultural artifacts)—what we see in these and how we see them—is never in fact immediate or straightforward; it is always shaped by our ideas, our interpretations, our understanding of what we are and do and can be, that is, by our relation to ourselves. Human perceptions are always affected by the "feedback loop" of self-relatedness with which human groups and individuals grasp and understand themselves. In and through this act of grasping ourselves, interpreting and understanding ourselves, we become not merely something grasped and understood, but something understood *in this particular way* rather than that—as "souls," or "clever animals," or "morally responsible selves," as Americans, blacks, females, Christians. Thus, the very acts of grasping and understanding ourselves shape us in particular ways; and the human process of self-creation moves one step further. This process of ever-developing self-creation through self-interpretation (as well as other modes of self-relation) can continue indefinitely, both in individuals and in cultures at large; or it can be arbitrarily halted at some point by, for example, dogmatic insistence that one particular conception of the human is *the* true one, and then the forcing of all further experience and reflection into that mold.

We will try to get a firmer grip on this complex set of issues later on. For now we simply note provisionally that persons and communities are (to our best knowledge today) modes of reality that grasp and shape and create themselves in and through historical processes. The great religious and cultural traditions of humankind are the major processes through which humans apprehended and shaped and reshaped themselves by means of certain practices and according to certain patterns or images in terms of which they understood themselves. The name which I propose to use for this process of grasping and understanding, of shaping and creating, through which a culture gradually defines and develops itself in the course of its own history, is "historicity." Humans are in a special way *historical,* beings who create and shape and come to know and understand themselves in and through unfolding historical processes. If we understand human reality as in this way radically and profoundly historical, we will be able to take all the varieties of humanity, and of the understanding of the human, which have emerged in the long history of women and men on earth, with full seriousness.

We begin, then, with the conception of human reality as fundamentally historical, with the conception of human historicity. This is a notion which includes within itself, but more precisely specifies and refines, what I discussed in an earlier chapter as the "sociocultural" side of human existence. The conception of historicity has not been arbitrarily selected from among the many first-order interpretive notions which might have been chosen; it is intended to take account of the full variety and richness of the conceptions of human being known to us. I do not claim that this is the only possible conception appropriate for initiating the sort of study we are undertaking; but I do hold that only with the help of some such view can we move our starting point from a largely arbitrary choice or preference or prejudice for one view rather than others to a position rationally arguable. Reasons can certainly be given for taking humans to be essentially clever animals, or moral wills, or very complex cybernetic mechanisms, or creative spirits, but each such position is defined over against the others and thus demands reducing them to itself. The notion of historicity which I am proposing here is not in that way exclusive but is rather inclusive, for it makes sensitivity to and interest in precisely this variety in the conceptions of human existence a central concern. As I have thus far sketched it, of course, the notion of historicity by itself is far from complete or sufficient; it will need to be filled out and added to in a number of ways, including drawing on the other conceptions available to us—but, just because of its openness to these others, it is an appropriate place for us to begin.

I do not mean by this to suggest that the notion of historicity should simply be uncritically accepted as true. Every claim is philosophically questionable in principle, as Descartes held with his methodological doubt; I am not disputing that theoretical point. But in practice we must begin every investigation (including doubting) at some particular point. If we did not accept certain conceptual assumptions—for example, about what it is to think; about what a question is and what it is for; about the possibility of formulating our questions in symbols, in words; about the possibility of manipulating these symbolic forms according to certain legitimate logical patterns (which can be distinguished from fallacious or false patterns of reasoning); and so forth—we could not even doubt, or formulate a doubt, or know what a doubt is, or understand what we are doing when we are doubting. So, although in principle everything can be doubted, in practice it cannot. We always begin our investigations with a complex structure of presuppositions and assumptions which we take for granted; and our doubting and questioning and exploring proceeds from there. Actually, the practice of systematic questioning and doubting appears only in complex reflective cultures, and only in certain locations within these; it is not a universal human practice. In some cultural situations it is not even a possibility. It presupposes social and economic institutions and conditions which free some persons from concerning themselves with much of the ordinary business of life, so they can engage in systematic reflection; and it presupposes the existence of traditions of reflection and critical questioning in which those persons can be educated, so they can pursue critical reflection effectively. In the modern West the great universities (along with a few other institutions) provide such contexts for sustained and open inquiry, and our society allows a certain amount of free time to teachers and students and researchers to pursue such activities.

I do not propose here to sketch a full picture of the assumptions and presuppositions on the basis of which modern inquiry proceeds. What is important is that we take note of certain of the particular assumptions with which we are beginning this inquiry into the human, and that we attempt to see, and to agree, that these are reasonable and appropriate and can thus serve as a point of departure for our constructive moves. Obviously, without such a relatively agreed—and, in that sense, noncontroversial—starting point, we could not get under way at all. One of the assumptions on the basis of which we will proceed I have just been outlining: that human existence is in a fundamental and quite special way *historical.* It is important now for us to see a bit more of what is involved in this claim.

I can put the matter most strongly, perhaps, in this way: humans have a power of creativity, a power to transform their inherited conditions of existence, which is unique among all living beings of which we know. Humans have produced a whole new order of reality—culture, the symbolical world, the order of meaning—which they have superimposed on the natural order into which they were born, and they have made this artificial world their home. Of course, all living beings are able to process information, and animals are able to communicate with one another and to rearrange their natural environment so that it will be more suitable to sustain them (by building nests, storing food, and the like). Humans, however, have gone far beyond all others in constructing an entire artificial world which does much more than simply meet their biological needs: it introduces a wholly new realm of being, the symbolical order, the order of meaning (what we shall later call the order of "spirit"), and this has in turn generated in men and women new desires, interests, and needs which go far beyond strict biological utility, and sometimes even contradict it.

Thus, for example, in every society of which we know women and men have developed interests in form and color and sound *for their own sakes* (not merely for their biological usefulness), and accordingly they have spent years, indeed generations, training themselves in skills which would enable them to create strikingly beautiful works of art—from the carvings and paintings in the caves of Spain and southern France ten thousand years ago to Jackson Pollock, from the intricate rhythms beaten out on a single drum to Stravinsky's *Rite of Spring.* Humans have developed an enormous interest in language, not just to communicate and to express their social interdependence more effectively, but *for its own sake:* they take delight in poetic forms of expression, they have worked out elaborate grammars to enable them to see more clearly the structures of their languages and how to use them most effectively, and they have created diverse literary forms to better express and communicate the different aspects of human experience. In connection with this interest in language and symbolism humans have created ideal values—truth, beauty, freedom, justice—and they have often developed a passionate interest in these, working out magnificent philosophical systems to interpret their meaning, and sometimes becoming so passionately attached to them that they have been willing to forgo their most basic biological drives and needs because of their loyalty to these ideals. "Give me liberty or give me death," cried Patrick Henry; "It is better to suffer injustice than to inflict it," declared Socrates; "Love your enemies," said Jesus. Bloody wars and revolutions have been fought with slogans like "liberty, equality, fraternity."

The change from strictly biological life into cultural life has been an immense and unprecedented one. It has, in fact, included in its wake a transformation of the whole face of the earth, as women and men have cultivated fields and constructed roads and factories and, above all, built cities. In addition to all of this, men and women, unlike members of any other species, have from early on asked about human life itself: What is the meaning of human existence? What sort of beings are we humans? What are we here for? Why must we die? Is death the end, or is there some destiny for us beyond this world? And humans everywhere have generated religions—pictures or interpretations of themselves, of the world in which they have found themselves, and of the ultimate reality or God in relation to which all else has its meaning.

In and through this culture-creating activity (as we have been noting) human life has become radically diverse in its manifestations and pluralistic in its most fundamental structures; it has become pervaded with symbolic meaning at every point, and this has made it possible for women and men to become self-conscious and self-directing in important ways. Humans, thus, have emerged from the strictly biological order into a cultural or spiritual order in which they are able (to some extent) to set their own goals, to create and serve new values and meanings, to give life forms which they themselves choose. And now in recent years our cultural development has reached a point where genetic manipulation has become possible for humans. That is, we can now transform in significant ways even the biological foundations of human life; and ultimately we may be able to bring about our own evolution into a new and somewhat different species. With and in *Homo sapiens,* that is to say, life (as a strictly biological process) has begun significantly to transcend itself: it has moved in certain crucial ways beyond blind evolutionary processes governed by natural selection, the survival of the fittest, to a process which is in certain respects self-directing, a process in which goals and objectives for life and its further evolution can be deliberately set from within.

This acknowledgment of the importance of our unique powers of creativity and transcendence must not tempt us to lose sight of the fact that we remain a part of the complex web of life here on earth: we are related to all other forms of life and through them and with them to inorganic being as well. We are but one tiny moment of that great ecosystem which is the earth, and it is in turn but a moment of the system which is the universe as a whole. Apart from certain delicate balances of matter and life and energy, which brought us into being and which continue to sustain us, we would never have existed at all, nor could we continue to exist for another moment.

That we are made from the dust of the earth (Gen. 2:7; 3:19) was already known to the writers of Genesis in the Old Testament (about 950 B.C.E.);

and many primal peoples have been aware of our relatedness to the rest of life, especially to animals—the widespread feeling of a reverence for life, and such practices as totemism, show this clearly. Despite this consciousness, however, as human civilization developed to relatively high levels in the valleys of the Nile and the Euphrates and the Indus, the *distinctiveness* of the human over against other forms of life increasingly impressed itself on men and women. As a way of understanding and interpreting this distinctiveness, they developed religious and philosophical conceptions of the *soul,* a distinct nonmaterial kind of reality taken to be the very heart of our humanness. According to this conception, human beings—at first, perhaps, only the rulers of a society—were thought of as an entirely different order of reality than animals and plants, certainly than matter: they were "spiritual" beings, gods or descendants of gods. Theories of this sort were, of course, not universally accepted, but they became dominant in Indian culture and in the West, where what was regarded as our distinctively spiritual nature became accepted as what we essentially are. In the West it was believed that our immortal souls linked us to God in a way not true of any other animal, that we had had the divine spirit breathed into our nostrils (Gen. 2:7), that we had been made in the very "image of God" (1:27). Our distinctiveness set us apart, then, from all other forms of finite being, as especially connected with the divine and thus unique.

This notion was developed in many different ways in western history, but with Descartes, perhaps, it took its sharpest conceptual form, a thoroughgoing dualism. Humans alone, Descartes held, have minds (or souls); all other beings are simply collocations of matter. Even animals are only very complex mechanisms, and thus totally different in their essential constitution from men and women. This sharp dualism of spirit and matter, soul and body—with antecedents all the way back through gnostic traditions to early Greek and Hindu religious practices and reflection, and still existing today in some corners of contemporary culture particularly influenced by religious ideologies and traditions—began to break down in the nineteenth-century West, partly because of its sheer unintelligibility. In the radical view of Descartes mind and body were metaphysically so different from each other that it was incomprehensible how they could in any way interrelate. And yet it was obvious that both were intimately involved with each other in every human act, every experience. Not until a new perspective developed could the problems connected with this dualism be resolved.

Partly because of a growing interest in and study of the variety of living beings, including attempts to classify them carefully and show their relationships to one another, the concept of "life" began to receive increasing attention. Living beings had both physical and mental features. Perhaps life could be understood as in some way comprehensive of both mind and body, a reality more fundamental or primordial than either; "mind" and "body" could then be regarded as abstractions, not independent substances in the manner of Descartes.

The emergence of the new conception of "organism" helped to make possible such a wider, more comprehensive notion of life. Organisms are not structured either according to simple mechanical principles (that is, as matter was believed organized) or according to logical ones (as mind was thought to be); neither strictly external relations (one billiard ball striking another and making it move) nor relations of logical deducibility seemed able to interpret the kinds of interconnection and mutual interdependence among the various organs within a living being. Instead, a new and complex conception of "purposiveness without purpose," as Kant put it,[2] was required. Though many organisms (for example, plants) could not be said to have conscious purposes, they were organized in such a way as to achieve certain ends such as nourishment and reproduction. The notion of "internal relations," that is, the conception of a mutual interconnectedness and interdependence of the several parts or organs of an organism so that each presupposes all the others as they together make their distinctive contributions to the harmonious functioning of the whole, provided a way to think this distinctive complexity of living beings. (This conception of internal relations was actually pioneered in theological reflection centuries earlier, when the notion of *perichoresis* or *circumincessio* was developed in the attempt to think through the interconnectedness of the three persons of the trinity.) Thus, a new and distinctive conception of reality as organic, that is, ordered in terms of internal relations of interdependence rather than the linear notions of logic or of mechanical succession, gradually emerged; and a way to overcome the incomprehensible notion of reality as fundamentally dualistic—composed of two distinct and utterly independent substances, mind and matter—was at hand.

When Darwin came along in 1859 and showed an evolutionary interconnectedness of all forms of life including the human, this was but the capstone to an intellectual development challenging the dualism of "soul" and "body," "mind" and "matter," which had been under way for some time. It meant that humans could no longer be understood as made of different "stuff" from other living beings, as earlier ideas of "soul" (or "mind") had suggested: human beings have evolved out of lower forms of life and remain in many respects closely connected to them as well as dependent upon them. Humans must be understood, then, as fundamentally *animals,* that is to say, as living beings, as but one branch on the great tree of life—even though we may want to go on to say that they are "rational animals" (as Aristotle put it), or "symbolical animals" (to use Cassirer's phrase), or, as I have been suggesting, animals with "historicity."

I do not mean in this discussion to prejudge the question whether humans cannot also be interpreted in some sense as, say, "immortal souls." What I am suggesting is that a traditional notion of that sort does not provide us with a good place to begin our interpretation of the human today. The phrase "immortal soul" no longer conveys clear or agreed meaning, and to many it seems not only archaic and obscure but nonsensical; it certainly does not express a common starting point that we can all take for granted as we begin our thinking together. Rather, I suggest, we will come much closer to articulating the fundamental assumptions about the nature of the human which are widely accepted today if we speak of our interconnectedness and interdependence with all other forms of life (on the one hand), and of our cultural creativity in history, producing a thoroughly cultural form of existence (on the other)—if we speak of ourselves, that is to say, as what I shall call "biohistorical" beings. We are given our life by—and we continue to be sustained by—the great evolving ecosystem of life on planet Earth; but we humans have ourselves transformed that life into diverse forms of historical existence, and it is this our historicity which, above all, gives our existence its distinctively human character. If we ultimately want to say something about "immortal souls" or an "eternal destiny" or the "infinite value of the human spirit," it must be with this particular living being in mind—this biohistorical being—emergent from and dependent on lower forms of life, but transcending these through its creation of culture in history.

It is this complex developmental reality which (for most educated westerners) the word "human" commonly designates today. If we look backward and downward through the biological foundations of our being, and through the various tiers of life and complex crystalline forms from which they evolved, we come ultimately to the fundamental structures of energy and matter underlying and composing our universe; if we look outward and upward through the historical realities of culture and consciousness and creativity, which have evolved out of and become superimposed on those foundations and which make our existence distinctively *human,* we find ourselves immersed in and aspiring toward realms of value and meaning—Truth, Beauty, Goodness. Any religious or theological interpretation of our humanity, if it is to be intelligible to us today, must make sense of this complex open-ended developing process that we are—rooted in the earth, but aspiring to the heavens above—and of the qualities of life and being that we have in and through this process. For this is the way we who live this biohistorical process, and who are aware of ourselves as moments within this biohistorical process, today experience and understand ourselves.

It must be acknowledged that it is quite possible to deny the desirability of beginning our anthropological construction with this notion. One might hold, for example, that because ancient religious traditions teach that we are "immortal souls," radically distinct from all other creatures, we ought to begin with that conception; or one might claim on the basis of certain esoteric experiences of so-called higher regions of consciousness that our "spiritual" reality (believed by some to be our true nature) is utterly distinct from any material base; or, from another point of view, someone might insist that we begin our investigation with the acknowledgment that *Homo sapiens* is simply one more very clever animal, to be understood entirely in biological terms. There is no way to prevent people from choosing any view they please, and then insisting that we must work in the terms it specifies; nor is there any reason to try. But views of the sort I have just mentioned always demand acceptance of claims that are arbitrary and authoritarian as seen from the standpoint of our modern pluralized human experience. I contend that our thinking about the human today should be grounded on our modern awareness that we are culture-creating beings, on the one hand, that our existence is in significant respects humanly created and thus *historical* through and through; and that we are part of the interconnectedness of all life and all being in the vast evolutionary ecosystem, on the other. One can make claims for the desirability of a different approach from this biohistorical one, on the basis of ancient religious traditions or special esoteric experiences or particular scientific theories, but not on the basis of the common experience and understanding of life and culture which have become pervasive in modernity. Such other claims, therefore, always presuppose (in contemporary debates) an appeal to one or another alleged authority—divine revelation, or special so-called spiritual experiences, or the very particular claims of one or another science; and to arbitrarily begin with any of these would be to make our starting point authoritarian, not democratic or common. It is, of course, quite possible to work out an authoritarian philosophical or theological position, if one chooses. But we are not undertaking that sort of theological program here: we want to work, as far as possible, from within widely accepted contemporary assumptions.

In other historical periods it was generally assumed that theological work would begin with the acceptance of an authoritative divine revelation; and for other purposes it may be quite appropriate to take for granted certain very particular scientific theories. In those situations such moves are not arbitrary or heteronomous but rather an expression of the actual cultural experience and life of a whole people, or of the accepted practice in certain scientific pursuits; and in those contexts they are legitimate and proper moves. But, as we have seen in our earlier consideration of problems of theological method, such fundamentally parochial, uncritical, or authoritarian procedures are not appropriate for theological work today; a much more open and democratic approach is called for.

Our task, then, is to attempt to understand better, and in due course to understand theologically, what we "biohistorical beings" are and what it means to be a biohistorical being, to live out of this sort of self-consciousness with this sort of self-understanding. This preliminary characterization provides us with a point of departure from which we can proceed with our larger attempt to construct an understanding of the human for today. The concept "biohistorical" takes up into and includes within itself the notion of historicity (which we saw was helpful in ensuring the openness of our work to diverse conceptions of the human which have appeared in history); and it overcomes some of the tendencies toward abstractness and vagueness in that notion by lodging our historicity firmly in the concrete process of evolving life, which has given birth to humankind and therewith to history on this planet.

9. Humanity in the World

The categorial scheme that gives Christian life and thought their structure is a symbolic pattern ordered by four principal terms: God, Christ, humanity, world. Since there is little agreement today about the meaning of the first two members of this scheme, God and Christ—or even about whether they can any longer be regarded as sufficiently relevant to the conditions of modern life to continue providing significant orientation for women and men—I have suggested that we begin our theological explorations with the latter two, humanity and world. These concepts obviously continue to order human experience and activities in the most fundamental way, and they remain indispensable for reflection and self-understanding.

In the last chapter I suggested that the characterization "biohistorical" holds together and sums up reasonably well what many today, at least in the West, understand humans to be. Central to this notion is the contention that humanity cannot be understood simply in and of itself but only in relation to its context, the whole complex system of life which has gradually evolved on earth; humankind is emergent from other forms of life, and it continues to be sustained by the web of life as a whole. This complex web of life, moreover, has emerged within a very particular context of material energies and other conditions here on earth which constitute and sustain it; and the earth's own character and being are determined largely by its situatedness in the solar system and ultimately in the steadily expanding universe. We humans exist really as point-instants in a vast, complex ecosystem, hundreds of millions of light-years across and billions of years old. Humanity, thus, cannot be thought of as a distinct and independent reality, separable from the world; it must be thought of as essentially in the world, part of the ecosystem within which it emerged. Our initial reflections on the concept of humanity have brought us necessarily and inevitably to consideration of the concept of the world.

Formally and abstractly the term "world" means simply the structured whole of all that is. In this definition the phrase "all that is" is intended to indicate the all-inclusiveness which the concept "world" (or "universe") suggests: nothing is left out of the world; there is nothing that is not a part or feature or dimension of the world. But the concept "world" does not hold this totality before us simply as a kind of additive sum of innumerable separate individual things, a huge heap of objects. As the phrase "structured whole" suggests, the world is taken to be an ordered and unified reality, that within which everything has a place. The world is a *uni*verse, not a chaos nor an additive heap; it is a "structured whole."

As Immanuel Kant saw, human thought would be impossible without the concept of world (or something like it). For if the mind had no such notion, it could not hold all the ideas and experiences and things and events, with which it must deal, together in a way that would enable us effectively to focus attention on them and relate them to one another, to reflect on them and think them and gain some understanding of them in their relations to one another. Furthermore, without such a notion it would be impossible for us to act. To act is to fit oneself effectively and significantly into the pattern or structure of events and objects in which one finds oneself, for example to go out the door; in a context of sheer chaos (if such a situation can even be imagined) we could not take even one step (there would be no door through which to exit, no walls containing us, no floor on which we were standing). Thus, our reflection and action always presuppose contexts of pattern and order. For most practical purposes these are of indefinite and changing boundaries and of variable structure. The conception of the world, now, is the notion of the overall context within which all living and acting go on, the overarching context of all the changing day-to-day contexts of our lives, and thus the pervasive underlying order and structure of things, always taken to be in certain fundamental respects knowable (and known), something on which we can rely.

This was just as true for earlier generations who thought of the world in the "three-story" terms of heaven and earth and hell, or who thought of the earth as a flat disk floating on primeval waters, as it is for us with our Copernican and modern Einsteinian views. It was true of Plato's world, constructed in the Receptacle by the demiurge according to patterns among the eternal Forms; of Sankara's world of Advaita Vedanta in which only Brahman is truly real, all the patterns of events and objects found in ordinary experience being simply *maya* (illusion), due to our *avidya* (ignorance); and of Nagarjuna's Buddhist world in which everything is ultimately *sunya* (empty). In each of these instances, however much they may differ in fundamental conception and in details, we find a picture or conception of the overall context of human life, that is, of the world. The fact that there are so many widely different—indeed, contradictory—conceptions of the "structured whole" which provides the context of human life raises, of course, questions about them all. It suggests that, although it is necessary for humans to have some concept of world, in order to attain a degree of orientation in life, there is no way to establish that the particular notion which any of us holds corresponds closely to what is the case. Rather, the real context of our lives (as I have been arguing) is mystery. And it remains mystery even when we suppose we know something of its structure or pattern.

Without our pictures or conceptions of the world we would have no way to orient ourselves in face of this mystery. These products of the human imaginative attempt to grasp the overarching context of our living and acting are indispensable to us, but we are not in a position to declare them true (in any metaphysical sense). The most we can say is that we find a particular picture or understanding of the world—usually the one we have inherited and have imbibed as we acquired our native language—persuasive and attractive, able (apparently) to give some measure of significant order to our experience and activities. For this reason we commit ourselves to it and live out our lives in terms of the pattern with which it provides us. Such commitment is based (implicitly) on faith (something not often recognized). It is because of such faith (in what we have been taught) that our lives—no matter who we are, no matter what position we take—have the overall order and meaning which they do. It is faith, thus, coupled with the imagination's creation of frames of orientation—pictures or conceptions of the world—that enables men and women to live with, and in, the ultimate mystery that life and reality are to us.

Increasingly, the underlying faith for many in our time is informed by the conception of the world as a universal ecosystem which provides the context for all of life, including all human life. How this context is to be understood theologically is a central issue to which we shall have to give a good bit of attention. But that it is this sort of world with which we today must concern ourselves—and not, for example, the "heaven and earth" of Genesis 1 (or some other simplistic notion)—seems undeniable.

The notion of ecosystem alone, however—of an organic structure of interdependent parts—does not by itself adequately characterize the modern view: it is an *evolutionary* ecosystem in terms of which we think today, a structure moving and developing in time. We are able to trace this process of development back fifteen billion years or so—a number unimaginable by us but conceivable in terms of our modern time scale. The whole universe (as we think of it) appears to have been in process from that primordial "big bang" onward. In the course of this great development, in at least one corner of the universe (possibly in other places as well), appeared the physical and chemical conditions without which life could not have emerged. Gradually, over billions of years, countless species appeared and evolved. Many died out in the course of time; some reached a stable equilibrium with their environment, enabling them to persist in substantially identical form for hundreds of millions of years; others continued to evolve and develop. Among some of the latter, mammals appeared, and then eventually humans. With the appearance of humanity, however, evolving life reached a new and especially significant moment: it had produced a creature which in due course would itself be able to create. And as language and culture were gradually created over the course of time, this creature began to reorder its own life according to its artificially produced patterns of action, of images and ideas, of institutions, ultimately undertaking to reconstruct the face of the earth by means of its technology. The world which we must seek to understand theologically is precisely this whole evolving and developing ecosystem.

We can now see that the two terms of the Christian categorial scheme which we set out to explore initially, "human" and "world," cannot—logically cannot—be conceived independently of each other (though this has often been overlooked in traditional Christian thinking as well as in much modern reflection); they belong to each other, and they complement each other. We cannot understand human reality (in modern terms) apart from the world within which it emerges; but we cannot understand the universe in which we live, either, apart from the evolutionary process through which it has moved, a process which has resulted in the appearance of multitudes of forms of life, some of which are so intricately ordered as to be self-conscious, self-directing, deliberate creators of an entirely new mode of being, *culture*.[1] In our modern conceptual frame the concepts "world" and "human," thus, belong to each other, and they must be understood in much closer dialectical interconnection than theologians have usually supposed. This intrinsic interconnection of world and human is one of the most fundamental conceptual presuppositions of our modern experience and knowledge. It is into relationship with this complex dialectic that the symbols "God" and "Christ" must be brought, if the Christian categorial scheme is to become truly intelligible and meaningful for us today.

Most educated persons in the West today take for granted some such understanding of the world and the human as I have been sketching here, though it probably does not inform all spheres of their experience and action; an understanding of this sort is, that is to say, accepted in the basic faith with which the mystery of life is approached by moderns. We will be examining in some detail this faith that underlies and helps to make possible modern views of life and the world in due course (especially in Part III); and in the course of this examination we will come to see that "faith" is not a single big leap which we either make or do not make, in which we either swallow certain claims whole or else totally reject them: it can be broken

[margin note: Human + world are correlative terms]

down into a number of steps which it is helpful to distinguish from one another. Careful examination of these steps will enable us to ask at each point whether we want to make this particular commitment or not, whether we find this move illuminating or would prefer to go down some other road. I have just called attention to one such faith-move, the (typically contemporary) commitment to seeing humans as closely bound up with the lower forms of life from which we emerged in the course of evolution and on which we continue to depend, the commitment to seeing us as interdependent with the vast ecosystem that is the world as a whole. In due course we shall see how this commitment can be amplified and developed—through further steps of faith—in such a way as to render it open to interpretation in close connection with the other two fundamental symbols of the Christian categorial scheme.

I do not have the competence to trace in detail the course of biological evolution which produced mammals and then hominoids, but we do need to look briefly at the point at which humans evolved out of the wider family of hominoids. Here I will be following Clifford Geertz's summary description in *The Interpretation of Cultures.*[2] The most interesting and important point for us to note is Geertz's discussion of the overlap between the beginnings of human culture (that is, the origins of history) and the final stages of human biological evolution. Apparently *Australopithecus* three or four million years ago was already beginning to use tools and weapons of a sort, choppers and hammers made from rocks; this creature had, however, a brain only one-third the size of ours.[3] Erect stature, a more thumb-dominated hand (which could manipulate tools), and expansion of the brain to its present size all thus came after the beginnings of cultural activity.[4] This means that in certain respects the growth of culture—including an increasingly flexible and complex language, new forms of social organization (such as a division of labor which enabled males to engage in hunting long distances from home, while females gathered food locally and cared for the young), increasing use of tools, and so on—itself shaped the biological development of the predecessors of *Homo sapiens* over some millions of years. So the biological organism that finally developed as human was "both a cultural and a biological product,"[5] and our present biological organisms, if left simply to themselves, would be incomplete and could not function. As Geertz sums up the matter: "We are . . . incomplete or unfinished animals who complete or finish ourselves through culture—and not through culture in general but through highly particular forms of it: Dobuan and Javanese, Hopi and Italian, upper-class and lower-class, academic and commercial."[6]

Thus our culture—the roles we learn, the language we speak, the skills we acquire, the ideologies we accept, the values we cherish—is an indispensable feature of our nature as humans. Without the particular culture which has formed us in a quite specific way, we would not exist as human at all—though of course it is also true that we might just as well have been formed in some very different way, by a quite different cultural context. There are diverse forms of humanity, then, many different sorts of human nature, as various and variegated as the plurality of human cultures and subcultures. The only thing that is common to us all is our basic biological structure—a structure of great plasticity, open to a wide range of patterns of development, requiring external programming by a culture in order to function. Our capacity for language, for symbol-using and symbol-making, is innate; but our capacity for English, for speaking and thinking and experiencing in this particular way, is acquired. And with it we also acquire a particular way of being human—particular ways of seeing and understanding ourselves, particular likes and dislikes, particular possibilities of thinking and experiencing, particular conceptions of the meaning of human life and of the nature of the world in which we live.

This cultural in-building of our human nature means (as I suggested earlier) that our humanity is created as much by history as by biological evolution. To be sure, the possibility of there being humans at all resulted from a process of evolution through some billions of years; but the actual emergence of distinctively *human* beings came about through historicocultural processes which helped to push the development of *Homo sapiens* in surprising but decisively important directions. We are, then, all the way down to our deepest roots as humans not simply biological beings, animals; we are biohistorical beings, and it is our historicity that gives our existence its distinctively human character.

This radically historical character of humanity, because it opens up such a wide variety of possibilities for human realization, presents (as we have already noted) some serious problems for our attempts to conceptualize the human. One major problem can be tagged with the well-known label "historical relativism." According to this conception, since all customs, practices, institutions, ideas, and values of a society have developed in and through the history in which that society came to be, they are relative to that history and that society in every respect; they have their significance and meaning and validity there (and only there), not in other societies that have gone through different histories and developed their own distinctive customs, institutions, and values. All humans probably come from one original genetic stock, evolving from Australopithecus through millions of years. In the course of this long time-span, however, and particularly during the last thirty thousand years or so, they migrated over the face of the earth, settling down in extremely various living conditions, from the tropics to arctic cold, from deserts to rain forests, from rugged mountains to rolling prairies to seacoasts. Very often they lived in isolation from other groups of women and men for many generations. Consequently, these different human groups developed a great variety of patterns of life, distinctive languages and social institutions, and sharply contrasting religious beliefs and practices, as they sought to adapt themselves to the climatic, topographical, and other conditions of their diverse locations. Hence, many different cultures developed in history, each with a certain appropriateness to the setting in which it emerged. There would appear to be no basis, then, for making universal or absolute claims for the particular practices or beliefs or institutions of any such traditions, though of course these have often been made even for some of the most isolated and peculiar ideas and practices. The values, meanings, and truths of each society are relative to the cultural setting in which they emerged, and they should not be regarded as binding or valid beyond that context.

Such relativistic contentions raise difficult problems for theology, for theologians have ordinarily thought they were working with some sort of ultimate Truth—truth about the world in which we women and men live; truth about the ultimate reality with which we have to do, *God;* and truth about human existence, about the norms and standards which should order human living and acting and which should measure human fulfillment. As we have noted, the claim that there is one (and only one) ultimate point of reference in terms of which all reality should be understood, a single ultimate ordering principle, is part of the very meaning of the symbol "God"; and the symbol "Christ" makes claims to being the one decisive key or clue to that ultimate reality, as well as to the proper understanding of human existence. However, if the entire Christian categorial scheme is simply a culturally relative product of one particular historical stream, these claims about the universal significance of God and Christ seem seriously undercut. At most, as Ernst Troeltsch suggested in the first quarter of this century,[7] Christianity may present itself as the (an) appropriate form of life for humanity in the West; but other lifestyles, other religious practices and beliefs, developed in and relative to the cultures of India or China or Africa, should be regarded as valid and proper in those places. No one conception of the world or of humanity can justifiably claim universal significance or validity.

It was no doubt reasonable and appropriate to understand human historicity in this relativistic way during the early part of the twentieth century, when Troeltsch was writing. One of the greatest achievements of the nineteenth century—sometimes called "the century of history"—was the discovery of the thoroughly historical character of human existence; and this new understanding impressed itself deeply on the minds of many at the turn of the century. Furthermore, this was a time of growing realization that the cultures of India, China, and the West were each distinctive and unique, each having its own special magnificence, power, and meaning, and each, therefore, quite properly claiming a right to its own integrity, its own lifestyles, values, institutions, religious traditions. Each was an impressive human achievement. By what right, then, was the West, with its imperialism and colonialism, destroying these other great civilizations, swallowing them up as it imposed its own political, economic, technological, and religious patterns on them? It was time to recognize and affirm the thoroughly pluralistic character of human life.

However valid and proper such conclusions about cultural relativism may have been (or seemed) in the first half of the twentieth century, they are no longer an adequate interpretation of the significance of our historicity, nor are they especially relevant to the present state of world history. On the one hand, the idea that the several great civilizations which have appeared in history are relatively monolithic structures has broken down in our growing awareness of the distinctiveness of the many smaller groups and subcultures of which each is composed. These often exhibit lifestyles, social and moral practices, value preferences, religious beliefs and attitudes, and even institutional structures, directly counter to the dominant patterns which had been thought of as defining and normative for the larger culture of which they are part. Thus, the internal pluralism of the great cultural and religious traditions is becoming increasingly recognized; and the supposed normativity of dominant values and practices for all groups in a culture seems now somewhat arbitrary and questionable. In this respect the sense of relativity in everything cultural has deepened even further. On the other hand, in the latter part of the twentieth century it is becoming apparent that the several great streams of civilization, each of which earlier had seemed to exist in relative independence from the others with its own quite proper integrity, are now rapidly flowing together and mingling with one another. What had been several quite distinct histories is today becoming one history, one world, one overarching universal civilization—doubtless with many subdivisions, many unique local colors and smells, many distinctive local practices, institutions, and traditions, but all interconnected and interrelated in the on-moving all-inclusive tide of human history.

The rise of the multinational corporation and of international banking are witness to the rapidly growing economic interdependence of different parts of the globe; the development of modern methods of warfare, including such practices as satellite monitoring of the armaments of other nations, but above all the stockpiling of nuclear weaponry which can annihilate not only an enemy but human life as a whole, has made the old patterns of national sovereignty obsolete; modern instantaneous communication makes us daily aware that crises and catastrophes on the other side of the globe affect us all; and the increasing interchange and travel of people everywhere has brought first-hand awareness of exotic cultural practices and unusual religious beliefs to almost everyone, if not through one's own personal travel then because one has met and come to know persons from other lands. In

America and Europe a vast new consciousness of eastern religious traditions is manifest everywhere. This opens up new possibilities for those who wish to savor the novel and the exotic, and it also brings about a new self-consciousness of the distinctiveness, both in strengths and in problems, of our own western cultural and religious practices and beliefs. However rich and pluriform this increasingly universal human civilization may be, it is really impossible to imagine it falling apart again into sharply distinct and different, relatively independent cultures. We are moving very rapidly toward one world: that is the great historical fact of our time, and our religious practices and theological reflection must adapt themselves to it.

We may not like this. We may think that modernization and unification of the cultures around the globe will result in irreplaceable losses in human value and meaning, those meanings and values associated with the older ways of life, the traditional artistic styles and religious beliefs, the established communal and institutional patterns. This is undoubtedly true, as modern China and India and Africa bear witness; but it seems to be inevitable, as these societies also show. It is no longer possible to turn back. The period when an attitude of relativistic appreciation and toleration of the several great civilizations was appropriate, each being granted its own integrity and autonomy in its proper place, has proved to be only an interlude. As human consciousness everywhere has increasingly begun to move beyond the parochial bounds of the particular civilization which had previously nourished it, and awareness of the beauty, value, and meaning of quite alien cultures has become widespread, a threshold into intercultural consciousness has been crossed by many; and a dynamism of intercultural interaction, which cannot any longer be reversed, has opened up. It is a dynamism not to be stopped short of a vast, worldwide, pluriform, single human civilization—unless ecological disaster or nuclear catastrophe prevents this. Human history is once more becoming one, and our theological analysis and construction today must be done in light of that fact. We must strive once again, therefore, for genuinely *universal* conceptions of the human, for genuinely universal conceptions of the context of human life (that is, of the world), and for genuinely universal conceptions or symbols of that which can or does make possible responsible human life and flourishing (that is, religious symbolizations). But as we seek to develop these conceptions, we must at the same time find a way to give full recognition to the significance of the pluralities and relativities and particularities of human life, both among the great cultural and religious traditions and within them, in a way that earlier supposedly universal notions of humanity, the world, and God did not.

My suggestion that it is once again possible and appropriate to attempt to formulate universal human values and truth does not imply a repudiation of the understanding that we humans are thoroughly historical beings; it is not a proposal that we move back to static-structural conceptions of humanity and develop notions of permanent truth and value on the basis of some concept of unchanging human nature or some doctrine of eternal "natural law." On the contrary, I am suggesting that we move one step further forward in our understanding of the significance of precisely our historicity. For it is the unfolding of history itself that has brought us to this new quest for a unity and universality in contemporary human existence, not a belated realization of the implications of our supposedly universal and permanent human "nature." The process of human cultural creativity which had for hundreds of generations flowed through many relatively isolated channels, often in directions contrary to one another, has now, with the growing interdependence of all human life in the limited space available on earth, brought the various separated segments of humanity back into relation once again. It is the onward movement of history itself, then, which has brought us to a position that demands a new universal vision of the human, a vision which now will take fully into account the enormous diversity of human life. Happily, recent historical developments suggest that just such a new vision may be in the making. Thus, the understanding that historical change is fundamental to our human mode of being is in no way negated or overcome by this call for a new truly universal and open conception of the human. On the contrary, it is precisely our *historicity* that is being expressed in it and realized through it: the central question to which we are addressing ourselves continues to be, What is the actual historical situation in which we are living, and what demands does it place upon us? We must have values and ideas and institutions which are relevant in this situation—and thus *relative* to this situation—if we are to survive as human beings. For, as we have recently come to realize, human survival is really at stake here: we may be about to obliterate ourselves. Historical relativity, thus, is neither forgotten nor surpassed in our new search for universally valid values and truth; rather, it is our cultural and religious *parochialism* that is being destroyed. The nihilistic consequences of the earlier forms of relativism are being overcome, as we are opened to the new worldwide humanity of which we all are part and to which we must contribute.

Let us go back now and collect our thoughts. We are engaged in trying to get clear our conception of the human, our understanding, that is to say, of what sort of beings we men and women are. This turns out to be a complicated matter. It has become clear that we cannot come to an understanding of what humans are simply by looking at individual persons, or even particular groups or societies, hoping thereby to discover their needs and their capacities, their structure and their activities, and thus to put together a conception of the human. Individual men and women and the various human groups and societies are all members of a particular species of life and are complexly related to all other living beings, on the one hand; and they have grown up gaining their individuality and uniqueness in particular social and cultural settings which have formed and shaped them into these particular personalities and groups, on the other hand. So it is not really possible adequately to grasp what human beings are by simply and directly observing them: we will understand them aright only when we see them as inseparably bound up with the vast human biohistorical process of which they are part. All human existence—that is, the existence of every individual woman and man, every community and society—is constituted fundamentally by this interlocked biology and history, and it is in terms of this biohistorical process that our humanness must be conceived. That is, humanness is not a property which belongs simply and directly to each one of us as an individual, or even to the society of which we are a part; it exists, rather, only as this very complex process of development (going back some millions of years) in which, in the last ten thousand years or so, strictly biological evolution and change have been greatly overshadowed by the historical cumulation of cultural change. At first the process of historical development, in many diverse cultural settings around the globe, was quite slow; but with the advent of civilization and the invention of writing it accelerated in a number of different centers where the several different civilizations each developed distinct traditions. In the past two or three centuries the diverse and relatively independent civilizations which grew up in the course of human history have become increasingly open to one another; and now, especially since World War II, we have been moving rapidly toward a single intraconnected human civilization. What this will look like if it actually comes to be, no one can say; but that there are now enormous momentums in this direction seems hardly disputable.

According to this reading of history, humanity today is being asked to give up the parochial patterns which have characterized it ever since the Stone Age and to take on a new universal form. This is a demand which today's historical situation apparently places upon contemporary humanity as a whole. This does not mean, of course, that all women and men are prepared to acknowledge this demand, or are even aware of it; the exigencies of many local situations make it virtually impossible for such a consciousness to develop in innumerable cases. But those of us who have become aware of this movement of our history toward a new unifiedness and a new universality can hardly help feeling drawn (or driven) to orient ourselves, not simply by the particular values and customs, institutions and forms of life, characteristic of our own parochial traditions, but instead by a *global consciousness*. We feel a demand upon ourselves to move beyond our limited loyalties to American, western, or Christian consciousness and institutions and traditions into a universal human consciousness, and into social and cultural forms appropriate to that.

What might such a universal consciousness be? How should it be conceived? how defined? What institutions would best express it? what attitudes, motivations, practices, ideals promote it? None of this is clear, yet obviously these are among the most important questions facing men and women today; and we shall be concerned with them throughout the remainder of this book.

In my view precisely these sorts of issues are the proper business of theology. The creation of worldviews, of conceptions of the human, of symbols to focus human work and worship, has always been central to religious activity; and theology grew up as the need for careful criticism and systematic reconstruction of all these became apparent. As we have seen, in the course of human history innumerable religious visions have been produced, each having some appropriateness to its own situation, to the needs of women and men for meaning and orientation in that place and time; each, thus, having a significant justification and integrity. To the extent that a particular world-picture provided adequate orientation—so that life could go on, and men and women found meaning in their activities, and some sense of who they were and what they should do—the religious tradition survived and developed. To the extent that it failed to provide adequate orientation and motivation for survival and growth, the perspective either died and was replaced by some other—as happened in many great and small religious changes in history—or poets and seers and prophets appeared, persons who were able to criticize and transform the tradition so that it could adapt itself better to the circumstances it had to address. The latter, of course, is what happened with those great religious traditions, such as the Hebraic, Hindu, Zoroastrian, which developed relatively continuously over many generations from ancient times to the present. Sometimes, in a moment of crisis and creativity in a great tradition, what had begun as a movement of reformation and transformation of older patterns turned into the birth of a significantly new and distinct vision of human existence in the world, as with Christianity, Buddhism, and Islam. Once established as distinctive symbolic frames of orientation within their own communities, these perspectives also went through long histories of development and transformation as new conditions arose to which they had to adapt.

Humankind today is confronting a similar historical moment of crisis and possibility: we live increasingly in a single "global village," and we are faced now with ecological and nuclear calamities that could destroy us all. A demand is thus placed upon all the great religious—and secular—traditions today to reconsider the symbolic structures within and through which they have grasped and interpreted human life and the world, to see whether it is possible to uncover or create symbols and practices and institutions suitable to the new age into which we are rapidly moving, that is, structures that will enable us truly to *live* in this new age, creatively and fruitfully, and not destroy ourselves utterly. This is a daunting assignment, perhaps an impossible one. But to provide orientation for life in this way, through creating appropriate and meaningful sociocultural dimensions of human existence, has always been the part of religion; and the criticism and reconstruction of religious symbols in order to facilitate this, however ambitious and difficult, has always (in the West) been a central feature of theological work (though seldom acknowledged as such). It is, therefore, quite appropriate that theologians address themselves to this task today, in face of the new historical situation into which humanity has moved.

In our reflections thus far we have, in fact, already moved a good distance down this path. The attempt to formulate our understanding of religion and theology in terms of an overview of biological evolution and human history is itself an important step in our effort to get oriented properly in the world in which we today take ourselves to be living. Thus, the very framing of our theological problems in the way I have proposed has resulted in an initial (however provisional) sketch of a symbolic map of our world, and of ourselves within that world. We have already begun (that is to say) theological reconstruction, particularly of the categories of the human and the world.

We may, in fact, have moved somewhat further toward the formulation of a symbolical frame for contemporary understanding and life than has thus far been apparent. Early in this chapter I pointed out that today's concepts of the human and the world are dialectically interconnected with each other. Each implies and presupposes the other; neither can be understood properly apart from the other. This means, however, that the world—that vast ecosystem in process of evolutionary development—cannot be understood simply and fully in physical and biological terms: for it has shown itself to be a physicobiological reality that has the very significant potentiality of evolving into a *historical* process; a process, that is to say, of symbolical and cultural development. It is a process within which the deliberate creation of institutions and patterns of life and systems of value can occur, a process within which living creatures can gradually gain the ability to direct and order their lives according to values and goals which they themselves posit. The universe is a place within which self-ordering, self-determination, and freedom can emerge—and then develop to the point where they are able in some degree to transform the world itself. In the course of our exploration of the concept of the human, thus, unexpected and fascinating accretions to and transformations of the concept of the world have occurred. The world turns out to be the very matrix within which life and history, and ultimately consciousness and freedom, meaning and value, truth and goodness, are born.

In later chapters we shall be directly concerned with the significance of this fact. But before we turn to that, we must examine further the new historical situation into which humanity is moving: in particular, I want to argue that it has opened up a quite distinctive way to construct a normative concept of the human, a concept especially appropriate for today's world. To that issue we now turn.

10. Toward a Normative Concept of the Human

It is not possible to find a completely neutral or unquestionable starting point for theological construction; in this book I have proposed that we begin with the category of the human, and that we provisionally characterize humans as "biohistorical" beings, since this label sums up central dimensions of the way human beings are conceived today (at least in the West). We noted earlier (Chapter 8) that any conception of the human with which we decided to begin our work would have normative implications in the sense that it would significantly affect the way we would pursue our study of human beings—what we took to be important about them, what questions we asked, what would count as evidence in our research, and so on. We must now explore further this normative dimension of the concept. Humans (like any other living beings) can be crippled or ill or deficient in various ways. An important function of our conception of the human is, thus, to provide criteria for distinguishing what we call "healthy" functioning from sickness or disease, "normal" behavior (or attitudes, or social relationships) from abnormal, "wholeness" in contrast with various deficiencies. These criteria are used, of course, in our understanding of ourselves as well as others; thus, the particular concept of the human which we employ carries an imperative force for us, exerting pressure on us—and through us on those others whose humanness we also understand in its terms, and with whom we interact accordingly—to meet the standards implicit in it and to order our lives (including our social institutions and public practices) accordingly. (This normative dimension of our thinking—implicit in all our concepts—will be discussed in more detail later; see especially Chapter 13.) We have seen that there are many diverse modes and varieties of human existence and of conceptions of the human. Each makes its own normative claims; each expresses itself in certain specific human ideals. We need to ask ourselves now, What are the norms implicit in the conception of humans as biohistorical beings? What reasons can be offered for accepting these as appropriate for assessing and ordering human existence today (in preference to others which might be proposed)?

It should be clear that the understanding of what is normative for men and women will always have to stand in close relationship to the conception of what humans actually are, what our human nature is. The question of the normative arises because human nature, as we have seen, is very elastic and can actualize itself in quite diverse ways. To the extent that we are aware of these different possibilities, we can exercise some choice among them, molding and shaping ourselves and our societies in one way rather than another, moving in this direction rather than that. The question about normative caninity does not arise for dogs, nor does the question of normative oakness arise for maturing acorns or seedlings. This question can arise only for beings who are self-conscious—that is, who have images of themselves and ideals for themselves, and can judge themselves in terms of these images and ideals—and who are aware that they have some measure of freedom to shape themselves and direct their own future course; and that they can and must, thus, take responsibility for themselves and their actions. From this point of view the philosophical cliché that there is no interdependence between "is" and "ought," between "facts" and "values," is simply and clearly false. There can be an "ought" only for certain sorts of beings (that is, only for certain kinds of "is-ness"). Oughtness belongs to and is an expression of, or characteristic of, only certain types of existence, namely those for whom the circle of self-reflexiveness (briefly considered in Chapter 8) is constitutive—those who are, therefore, self-conscious, who take up attitudes toward themselves and are capable of acting on themselves, and who are thus able to take responsibility for themselves.

Another way of putting this is to say that the question of the normative, of oughtness, of the distinction of right from wrong, belongs to and is characteristic of beings with historicity, historical beings (as contrasted with those whose resources are exclusively biological). Beings who are shaped by the historical processes of cultural development, and who are capable in turn of shaping and reshaping those cultural processes and institutions, unavoidably confront questions like: What direction should we go now? What should we do? What is our next step? When the awareness that it is we humans who have created, and continue to create, culture—and it is we, therefore, who must take full responsibility for the directions in which it is moving—grows to the point that it has reached in modern times, these questions become sweeping and somewhat overwhelming: Toward what visions of human existence should we—communities as well as individuals, indeed humanity as a whole—be moving today? In what direction should human history be going? Which way should we—should *I*—try to nudge it?

Once we see that it is only within this sort of existential (or ontological) context—that is, the context of human history and culture—that the questions about norms and values and ideals arise, and that it is within this sort of context alone that they have meaning and are relevant, we have taken a long step toward resolution of the question whether there can be general standards or norms in terms of which the human as such can be judged, the question of the normatively human. Like language, norms and standards—not this or that specific moral rule or cultural value, but the necessity to have values and rules—belong to our humanity as such, to our self-consciousness and our capacity to, in some measure, take responsibility for ourselves; they are central features of the historical dimension(s) of our human existence. Whatever, therefore, facilitates the proper functioning of this normative dimension of our being in fact helps to constitute and to sustain our humanness as such; it has—and should have—normative force for us. Let us, then, attempt a formulation of the norms inherent in our humanness, those norms connected directly with the fact that we are beings for whom the peculiarly reflexive features of self-consciousness and the capacity to take some responsibility for ourselves are central.

I want to make five points in this connection. The first is a general remark reaffirming the intimate interconnection of the historical aspects of our being with the significance of normativeness for us, and suggesting that what is properly normative for humans is connected directly, therefore, with our historicity. The next three represent a more detailed specification and elaboration of what it means to take our historicity in this way, as itself having normative significance. The last returns this whole discussion to our full biohistorical being, setting this consideration of the normative significance of our historicity in its larger context.

1. That which most sharply distinguishes human beings from other forms of life, I have argued, is their historicity, their having been shaped by and their having some control over the processes of historical change and development. This implies that an optimal realization of our biohistorical being will depend in an important way upon an optimal realization of our historicity. (What that optimality can be and how it is to be determined will be specified somewhat in the following points.)

2. It is clear that historical existence—that is, history and historicity—would not be possible without the maintenance of delicate balances between order and freedom, continuity and creativity. The maintenance of such balances (as we shall see in more detail later) in communal institutions and practices, and in individual agents and their actions, is what can be called "responsible" ordering and acting. An optimal realization of human historicity in any particular concrete situation, therefore, can occur only to the extent that communities and selves are able and willing to take significant

responsibility for their institutions, practices, and actions (however differently such responsibility may be understood in different sociocultural and historical contexts).

3. It is important that the exercise of our historicity in responsible ordering and action, shaping not only our own communities and selves but future history and thus future humanity as well, continues to grow through the increase of well-ordered freedom in individuals and societies. The enormous growth of human technological power in recent centuries, culminating now in the power to destroy all of humankind along with many other species of life, means that only as humans gain the ability to take greater responsibility for the effects of their actions on both the environment and the ongoing movement and direction of history and culture is there much possibility that they will survive at all (let alone flourish).

4. Our historicity, especially with respect to our capacity to take responsibility for ourselves and for the direction history is going, depends on a relatively high degree of self-consciousness and on a proper orienting of that consciousness (again, precisely what these can be and how they are to be determined in different situations and for different persons remain open questions). The functioning of our historicity depends significantly, that is to say, on our awareness of who we are and what our real possibilities in life are, as well as on the existence of practices and institutions that facilitate this functioning. There are imperatives, then, both toward adequate knowledge of our historicity and its significance and also toward certain patterns of societal organization and practices.

5. Our historicity cannot function optimally, of course, unless it is working harmoniously with its biological base (which, in turn, it significantly qualifies); and only if that biological base is itself functioning well. Taking responsibility for ourselves as historical beings must ultimately include, therefore, taking significant responsibility for the wider organic and physical networks of which we are part. (We shall turn more directly to an examination of this fifth set of issues from Chapter 14 on.)

These norms of the human, as thus far sketched, are quite formal; and in that respect they violate the very concern for historicity which I am trying to express here. To state the overarching norm, for example, as an imperative toward the "optimal realization of our historicity" is to leave this central point in much too abstract a form. This norm, as we must actually invoke it, is concerned with the optimal realization of human historicity in the many diverse particular contexts in which humans today live: what is "optimal" for one sociohistorical situation or natural setting will be quite different from what is "optimal" in other significantly different contexts. "Historicity" means that the historico-natural context itself shapes our understanding of what is required of us. For example, although one particular feature of the (contemporary) historical context with which we are especially concerned in this book—namely our becoming a single interconnected worldwide humanity—may shape the way in which the notion of "optimal realization of our historicity" is understood by my readers, in many other sociohistorical contexts today this would carry virtually no weight, other problems being felt as much more urgent. The conception of us humans as fundamentally historical beings has itself developed in a particular historical context (among intellectuals in the modern West); as with all other such conceptions, therefore, it will be seen as having meaning, significance, and truth, principally within that context. The extent to which it will be taken seriously into account in other situations will depend very much on those situations themselves.

A similar comment must be made about my fourth point, that such an optimal development of our historicity presupposes the emergence of knowledge that we are historical beings, and this requires a "relatively high degree of self-consciousness." Once again, the level of self-consciousness, as well as the kind of self-consciousness which we have about our historicity, depends largely on the particular historical situation within which we find ourselves. Certainly not everyone in the world at this moment needs to understand himself or herself explicitly as "a historical being"; the mode and degree of consciousness of this fact which are appropriate to different local situations differ greatly—precisely such differences are implied in the claim that we are shaped by and relative to our immediate historical context. This norm of historical self-consciousness, therefore, will be specified rather differently for those who increasingly have the power to affect humanity as a whole, and hence must learn how to take responsibility for humanity as a whole, than for those with (for example) a newly emerging consciousness of their own oppression—itself an important mode of historical consciousness—those with whom liberation theologies have been especially concerned. (The moral implications of these sorts of differences will be taken up later, especially in Chapters 13–15.)

These considerations also affect my third point about the necessity of developing "well-ordered freedom in individuals and societies." As it stands here, this is simply a formal prescription, and the way it is to be articulated in different social contexts, positions of power and leadership, and the like, is left quite vague. It clearly demands, however, a bias toward egalitarianism—that is, toward freedom and responsibility for all, regardless of race, class, gender, or other specifics: our historicity as such provides no basis for giving normative significance to distinctions of this sort. We will look at all these issues in more concrete and specific detail when I sketch briefly the ethics implicit in these notions.

Thus, given our modern understanding of humans as biohistorical beings—beings who have emerged within, but whose very existence as historical drastically qualifies, the biological process of evolution—several distinct norms for assessing different forms of human life and orienting their future directions can be stated: the central norm is our historicity itself (apart from which the issue of normativity would never arise); and this, then, can be further specified as involving responsibility, self-understanding, well-ordered freedom, and concern for the organic and physical world to which we belong. As historical, self-conscious, culture-creating, and in some respects self-determining beings, humans must decide what they are to be, how they should shape and order and orient their lives, toward what sort of future they will work in this world in which they find themselves; and these norms should help us address those questions.

I am not claiming, of course, that all men and women have thought of themselves as free and creative, as able to shape and determine their own future and their children's future. In some cultures ideas of this sort have not appeared or have been downplayed; and in most cultures they have been deemphasized for women. Thus, the forms in which experience has come to many individuals and groups in history have often inhibited these notes from coming to consciousness. In ancient Hebrew culture, as well as in Persia, Greece, and China, among others, the sense of genuine human power and responsibility became especially strong. And from our modern standpoint, which sees the great variety of cultures, religions, and societies which the human spirit has produced, we can hardly avoid thinking of that spirit as possessing great freedom and creative power; it is difficult, therefore (for those of us who are aware of these matters), to evade a sense of the necessity for both societies and individuals to take significant responsibility for themselves and their world. We are well aware that what humans decide today—this is especially, and most frighteningly, evident in the realms of international politics and ecological concern—will shape future generations, will even determine whether there will be any future generations.

In face of the enormity of human power today, there would seem to be only two real possibilities for biohistorical beings like us—and one of these turns out not to be an actual possibility at all: either we attempt to damp down and still our self-consciousness and our sense of accountability, moving back toward the innocence and simplicity of the animal life from which we emerged, or we attempt to take responsibility for the historical situation in which we today live. The first of these alternatives, however, is not a real possibility for us: the biological foundations of our human nature have been so drastically altered by cultural activity over some millions of years that we could no longer survive simply as animals. Without externally imposed cultural or symbolical programming our central nervous systems would be too open and unstructured to be able properly to direct life. It is no longer possible then—biologically possible—to turn the clock back to an unhistorical mode of existence.

This impossibility to move back to a less accountable form of life is made clear in the most dramatic way by the fact that we are living in the nuclear age. The gradually cumulating growth of human power over our long history has now come to a point at which we are able to destroy all human civilization, together with many other forms of life on earth. Our international political arrangements have put this power into the hands of nations competing with one another; and our moral and religious commitments and values and suspicions—especially in the fundamentalistic versions appearing in many places around the globe—focus our energies and interests on these diverse and warring political and cultural fragments of humanity, rather than on the well-being of humanity as a whole. So our moralities and our religions and our value-loyalties, instead of facilitating some sort of salvation from the evils that confront us, tend to increase the possibilities of disastrous wars. It will not be possible to avoid these, it seems clear, unless we humans take up our full responsibilities and act in behalf of humanity-as-a-whole—and the environment on earth which makes all life possible—rather than according to the demands of our present social, political, and religious arrangements and commitments.

We must, that is to say, move toward making ourselves more accountable for life on earth, not less; that implies that we must move toward a more universal human consciousness, not backward toward more limited and parochial cultural, religious, and political commitments. And we must make these moves quickly, or it will be all over for us humans. The possibility is no longer open for us to live a more "natural," less historicized, life: human history has moved past the point of no return in this regard. The only real possibility open to us is to move further forward in our historical development, attempting to realize our historicity in such a way as to facilitate ongoing life on earth. We are "condemned to be free" (Sartre), and we must make the best of that.

The claim made by some, that in large-scale "philosophy of history" issues of this sort we have no valid criteria for differentiating better from worse choices, appears to me to be incorrect—though of course we can assert it and attempt to base our lives on it. Such a conclusion may be drawn from either of two rather different kinds of argument. One of these places emphasis on the enormous variety of human forms of life and religious perspective, each with its own values and standards: since all human judgments and decisions are rooted in one or another such frame of orientation, it is claimed, they will inevitably be arbitrary and self-serving, and there is no way to overcome this. Hence there are no legitimate grounds for holding any particular choice to be better than the others, and we are led toward a thoroughgoing cultural relativism, on the verge of becoming completely nihilistic. The other alternative, although agreeing that it is not possible to make *rational* choices about such fundamental issues, avoids this distressing consequence by maintaining that ultimate truth resides in one particular form of human life, in one particular religious or cultural or political tradition; happily, as advocates of this alternative usually claim, this favored tradition is the one to which they are committed. A claim of this sort seems implicit in the position of those who simply accept unquestioningly the religious and cultural traditions they have inherited, living out their lives in the conviction that here goodness and truth are to be found. But it also finds expression in the convictions of otherwise sophisticated and thoughtful people who have been known to utter such phrases as "My country right or wrong," "Outside the church there is no salvation," "Faith is believing in spite of all evidence to the contrary," "We will remain loyal to our leader (or to the party, or to our cause, or to our nation) regardless of what is demanded of us."

In my view, however, neither of these positions—the relativistic/nihilistic understanding of the variety of religious and cultural perspectives, or unquestioning loyalty to a particular tradition, even if it lead to fanaticism—is justifiable any longer now that we are aware that it is we humans who have created this culturally plural world, and that we now may be about to destroy ourselves. Both presuppose a historical situation that no longer obtains: a situation in which orientation in life is believed to be adequately provided by one or another *particular cultural tradition.* In the one case all such particular traditions are regarded as equally arbitrary and ungrounded, so there is no satisfactory basis for choosing among them; in the other case it is believed that one particular tradition alone has saving truth and all others are to be ignored—or opposed, defeated, or destroyed (as in crusading forms of Christianity, Marxism, liberalism, Islam). In earlier historical periods, when the plurality of incommensurable cultural and religious traditions—each with its own independent resources and integrity—seemed to be an unalterable fact about human existence, such positions as these may have been justified. But we no longer live in that sort of situation. We live now in a time when these diverse cultural streams are flowing back together once again to form one universal history. And one multiform but increasingly interlocked humanity—bound together in part by the threat of mutual annihilation—is beginning to appear, as the enormous variety of human customs and life-patterns, institutions and ideologies, steadily interact with and transform one another. It is an intraconnected and intralocking political and cultural and religious world in which we live today, and in which future generations will increasingly live; and neither we nor they can avoid this development, if a disaster does not prevent it. All who are reading this book, I suspect, are aware of these facts at some level of their being. It is important now that we attempt to order and shape and orient our lives in terms of this new global self-consciousness; for this is the situation in which (so far as we can see) humanity is now living.

I can sum up the matter like this: For those of us for whom a global consciousness is beginning to take hold, *all particular and thus parochial religious and cultural and philosophical traditions are now outmoded and superseded to the extent that they cannot give an adequate or illuminating interpretation of our new historical situation, these new sociocultural facts about human life.* For such traditions no longer provide an interpretation of our actual human existence, of our situation in the world as we today are aware of it. And thus they cannot provide adequate orientation for (our) human life: the road map with which they supply us is not of the actual terrain through which we take ourselves to be passing; and we dare no longer live our lives simply on the basis of these inherited patterns and values and norms, whether these were supplied by our own cherished traditions or have some other source.

But of course we cannot simply dispense with tradition either. For we are bio*historical* beings, sociocultural beings, and everything about us, including all our ideas and values, our standards and norms, our ways of living and patterns of action, have been shaped by and in the culture within which we have emerged; that is, by tradition. Without such historicocultural shaping we would have no form at all; we would not even be. So we must move forward, becoming as aware as possible of the traditions which have shaped us and of their limitations and strengths, adopting from them whatever we can and adapting them to the new circumstances in which we find ourselves, as we seek to reshape them—imaginatively to reconstruct them—so they can better provide orientation for the new world into which we are moving. And of course we must also be open to learn whatever we can from those other traditions, those other religious and secular ways of ordering and understanding human life in the world, with which we increasingly come into contact.

This way of orienting ourselves—in terms of our historicity, and thus with reference to the historical situation in which we find ourselves and the demands it places upon us to take responsibility for the future—is increasingly the way in which many women and men worldwide are coming to think and act; but it stands in a special relation to western religious and cultural traditions. The latter fact, of course, does not make it either right or wrong, true or false. But it is not mere ethnocentrism, I think, to assert that the crisis of modernization and development, through which all the great civilizations of the world are now passing, is a consequence of, and part of the process of, the westernization which has been going on in those cultures for some time. In many earlier periods the West (and its antecedent cultures) borrowed from and learned from other civilizations; now political and economic institutions, technology and science, as well as traditions in the arts and religion, which first developed into their modern form in the West, are spreading throughout the rest of the world. China, for example, with the inspiration and organization of its Marxist revolution, is trying to industrialize rapidly: both the Marxism and the industrialization are imports from the West. They involve a thorough reordering of traditional patterns of life and traditional modes of social organization, as well as many other traditional practices and beliefs, however much ancient Chinese motifs may shine through and continue to influence the styles of life and the institutional forms that are taking shape there. India, also, is attempting desperately to modernize and industrialize, in this case in and through democratic political institutions. Once again, the influence of the West—especially of the British, who were in India for two hundred years as a colonial power and who left their mark everywhere—is apparent at every point, not least in the fact that English continues to be a very important medium of communication, especially in India's great cities. Similar processes are going on in Africa; and Latin America (though closely connected with the West for many generations) is also now in the midst of fierce struggles to modernize politically, socially, and industrially. Japan has become thoroughly modernized, and has addressed some of the problems of contemporary industrial society more effectively than any western nation; but this did not happen without the convulsion of World War II, in which central religious and political patterns and traditions were given up as western political and economic institutions were adopted.

What is becoming worldwide here is not simply one or another western cultural pattern, institution, or practice, but, above all, western presuppositions about and attitudes toward history and human historicity: that all of us—all human beings—belong to one vast historical movement, and that it is possible for us to become conscious of our historical situation and increasingly to take responsibility for our future. However tragic may be the destruction and loss of important traditional forms of life and patterns of value and meaning in these ancient civilizations, they are no longer simply living out of, and in terms defined by, inherited cultural patterns, social institutions, and religious traditions, floating wherever the stream of history carries them. Increasingly they are moving self-consciously and deliberately to build social and cultural institutions which will make it possible, as they hope, to meet the essential needs of their people more satisfactorily and to bring greater fulfillment and meaning into their lives. People worldwide are beginning, that is to say—both socioculturally and as individuals—to take charge of their lives in new ways, attempting to transform them in accordance with deliberately posited goals, which, they hope, will enable greater human fulfillment in life than would a continuation of the older practices and ideas.

In India, for example, conceptions like karma and reincarnation were used for millennia in ways which reinforced a largely static social structure, the so-called caste system. People were taught that their present situation was the irrevocable and just consequence of their behavior in previous lives. Since the cosmos was so ordered that nothing could be done about this, they could only resign themselves to their condition and their fate. According to widespread interpretations of the concept of *maya* the things of this life and this world are all illusory anyhow, so what happens here is of no great importance. In this way the status quo was fully legitimated by central religious symbols, and to those living within this symbolic world any attempts of women and men themselves to change things significantly would be irrational; it would be working against the very grain of the universe. Long ago Buddhism emerged in India in part as a revolt against such thinking, but it was ultimately swallowed up once again by the older traditions, and it continued to develop and flourish only in other lands. However, the ancient Indian patterns seem at last to be changing significantly. Notions like karma, for example, as interpreted by modern leaders like Vivekenanda, Aurobindo, Radhakrishnan, and Gandhi, have quite different implications than were traditionally emphasized: if the conditions of our present life are the just consequence of our actions in the past, then it should also be true that our present actions will have significant consequences for the future. Thus, the paralyzing fatalism of the older view can be replaced with a stress on the importance of present decisions and actions; and an emphasis on taking responsibility for the future emerges. Instead of legitimating the status quo, the concept of karma begins to imply the importance of transforming the patterns and practices of this present life, including social and economic and political conditions and institutions. For Gandhi and others human injustice and oppression were seen, thus, as terrible evils which must be overcome. Now even in remote villages many of the poor and the oppressed are beginning to think in terms of some sort of upward mobility, for their children if not for themselves, a notion that would have been unimaginable in older India.[1] Thus, religious and moral assumptions and values that have oriented India for thousands of years seem now to be changing. Time and history and the things of this life have been given new significance; and it is becoming important to take greater responsibility for the world in which we live, transforming it into a more habitable human home. The problems of India, of course, remain massive; but a demand for change is widespread in India today, and that is itself an incalculable spiritual gain.

A growing awareness of human historicity and a correspondingly increasing sense of responsibility are rapidly becoming significant marks of the human around the globe (though of course other ways of understanding human nature also remain strong, and it is not really clear just how consequential these new developments will be). This changing conception of human nature brings along with it, as we might expect, changing standards and criteria in terms of which persons and societies assess what they ought to do, how they should order their lives and their communities. For human historicity to come to full fruition (we have noted) it is necessary to move toward orders of free and responsible persons who live in meaningful and just communal relations with one another; only in this way do all begin to take effective charge of their history(s). Thus, conceptual ideals for both individuals and communities—ideals articulated in notions like freedom, justice, responsibility, good order, equality, and the like—are all implicit in many of the movements now gaining momentum around the globe. (In the next four chapters I shall present a detailed analysis and argument in support of these somewhat broad and sweeping claims about the moral ideals and values implicit in the notion of historicity.) It should surprise no one, therefore, that there are revolutionary tensions of many sorts in Latin America, Africa, India, China, the Middle East, and elsewhere. The historical power of this transformative movement of the human spirit has been demonstrated most recently by the dramatic events in Eastern Europe.

The ideals of liberal democracy and of socialism, as well as of some versions of Christianity, appear to represent preliminary (western) formulations of this conception of the universally human which is now struggling to come into being worldwide. These earlier conceptions, however, were usually formulated in static-structural and highly individualistic rather than socio-historical terms. They emphasized an eternal human essence (the "soul," or the "human spirit," or "reason") present in each individual and always and everywhere the same; and it was on the basis of these beliefs about individual persons that democratic practices and institutions were advocated as universally valid. Instead of grounding their humanism on our historicity—our openness and undefinedness as individuals, our historically developing power to create the new and to take responsibility for our world and our future—these movements spoke of "unchanging truths," "eternal values," and "natural rights," all based on the particular content and character of this universal human essence which was believed present in every person. An understanding of human historicity which could overcome this individualistic bias of much western thinking did not become available until the last century or so, and only since World War II has the import of this for the question of universal humanness become visible.

Christian faith has long spoken of universal history, and before Christianity had appeared on the scene ancient Israel had already adumbrated the notion. But the Christian interpretation of history (like the Jewish and the Muslim), though making universal claims, in fact remained very parochial. Christians saw *their own history* as the universal and true history of all humankind, and *their own God* as the driving force behind all of history, the God of the universe. By the same token, of course, other histories, other religions, other gods were regarded as pagan, heathen, false, wrong, ultimately to be destroyed. The idea of a single universal history, grounded in the universal foundation of all that is, was certainly present in the Christian tradition, but it was present in an abstract and warped form.

The conception of salvation-history which is still widely held in Christian circles continues to follow essentially this line: The God of the universe, the creator of the heavens and the earth, chose one particular people (Israel, the descendants of Abraham) to be God's own people; over a period of about two thousand years God then interacted with this people in a special way, finally entering directly into their history and culture in the person of the man Jesus. This man was destined to become the cultic lord of a new offshoot of Judaism, the Christian church; and since that time God's principal relations with humanity have been carried on through this unique figure, Jesus—"God's only son"—and the institution founded on faith in him, the church. Ultimately this particular historical stream—from Abraham to the present living church—will take up into itself all other religious and cultural traditions so that finally "at the name of Jesus every knee [will] bow, in heaven and on earth and under the earth, and every tongue confess that Jesus Christ is Lord" (Phil. 2:10–11). Many, perhaps most, Christians still think in these terms. It is in many ways a powerfully attractive picture of universal history, though very ethnocentric: a story that comes to its climax with the triumph of the Christian faith and the Christian God, and above all the triumph of Jesus and the church.

This parochial concept of salvation-history, however, served as a womb within which ideas of a truly universal history and historicity could be conceived and developed. But for these conceptions to be born into their full reality and meaning, the womb had to be left behind as too narrow and constricting. We are today living through that birth and its after-shocks. There is much that can be taken over from the prenatal past, especially the understandings of human existence as historical and of universal history as the context of human life, the shape of the world in which we live. But we no longer dare conceive the universal simply in terms of ourselves—our beliefs, our traditions, even our God. Rather, the other way around: we must learn to see our traditions, our beliefs, our God, in terms of the universal world-process of which we all are part. Our way of thinking (whether Christian or Jewish or something else), our beliefs and practices, our religious traditions with their conception of God, all emerged in the great cosmic evolutionary-historical process which is the context of all life and being, and thus of all human existence. Their emergence, however contingent, was no mere historical accident, and it certainly should not be regarded as unimportant: it was part of the development through which humans (at least those of us in the West) became conscious of the world-process that is the home of all of us, and conscious of our distinctiveness as human beings within that process—the process through which our modern self-consciousness, self-understanding, self-responsibility emerged. The movement (around the globe) from biological evolution to historical process, and from historical process to historical consciousness and ultimately to historical accountability, is not insignificant or trivial; it is a momentously important historical development, the ultimate significance of which, and the full metaphysical implications of which, are still far from clear. But a very grand notion may seem to be intimated here: in and with this development (so far as we can see) the world-process itself—or a certain dimension of it—was beginning to become conscious of itself and beginning to take a new sort of responsibility for itself.

With respect to that intimation, more will have to be said later, but we must take note of one important point now. Although it may strike many of us today as parochial and narrow to continue to speak of Jehovah (or Yahweh) as the creator of the world and the absolute lord of history, we should observe that faith in one God and the understanding of human life as caught up in a single unified historical movement were born together in human consciousness and culture; each facilitated the other's coming into being, and in some sense each seems to belong to the other. Belief in the activity of one God made it possible to see the chaos of human social experience as a unified and patterned historical development within which all human beings—and more specifically Israel and (later) the church—had distinctive roles to play. This sense of a significant part for humans within the overall movement of cosmic history facilitated a vision of human life as fundamentally historical in character, and it simultaneously provided a powerful motivation to work toward the realization of God's historical purposes. The conception of one God, creator of the world and working in it toward certain historical ends, thus proved to be a highly dynamic notion, for it provided a center or focus for a kind of devotion which could evoke in human beings a new sense of selfhood and of moral responsibility and creativity; the enormous dynamism of western culture undoubtedly owes much to this inheritance. The Hebraic notion of God has meant that historical creativity and dynamism—in contrast with any number of other features of human experience which became highlighted in other cultures—were grasped in the West as the clue or key to the ultimate Reality with which we humans have to do and thus to human existence itself; and the context of human life, that is, the world, came to be seen as essentially historical in character, as a process of cumulating creative events. Thus a coherent picture of human existence, the world, and God as all fundamentally historical realities gradually emerged.

If we follow out the implications of this interconnection of the ideas of the human, the cosmic, and God, we will see why the traditional notion of Jehovah or Yahweh has today come to seem so parochial and unsatisfactory: though it fits the rather exclusivistic Hebraic and early Christian perspectives on history, it does not correspond well with our modern understanding of the significance of the diversity of human historical development around the globe. It has become increasingly difficult to accept the idea that the God belonging in a special way to our particular history, *our* God, should continue to be believed, in a fantastic parochialism, to be the lord of the universe. Rather, it would seem, God should be thought of as that ultimate (quasi-historical) reality, whatever it might be, underlying and working through the whole cosmic evolutionary-historical process that provides the actual context of our lives and of which our lives are part—that reality, thus, toward which our lives must in fact be oriented, if we are to be in effective rapport with the actual cosmic-historical movement in which we live.

Our analysis of the concepts of the human and the world, the conceptual points with which we began this attempt to develop a contemporary version of the fourfold Christian categorial scheme, is now bringing us directly into touch with the other two categories, God and Christ. The conception of the human which we have been gradually developing—involving notions of historicity, self-consciousness, and moral accountability—though not itself explicitly Christian, is, as we have been observing just now, in close contact with certain Christian claims, and grew up in interconnection with them. It is particularly dependent on the historicism of Christian experience, culture, and tradition. In light of this one cannot help wondering—in today's world, in which it appears that it is just these sorts of historical processes that bring into being, sustain, and further develop humankind—whether the ultimate metaphysical reality with which we have to do should not also be understood somehow in historical or historicist terms. Clearly, such a view of reality would not, as such, involve an explicitly Christian conception of God; but it would be coming within range of the Christian vision of the world. These matters will have to be explored further in due course; before that can be done, however, a fuller examination of the historical and moral character of human existence must be undertaken.

The normative implications of our biohistorical conception of the human which I have been sketching in this chapter have been worked out largely in terms of western presuppositions and ideas about history and historicity. These notions properly understood, I have contended, can illuminate and effectively interpret the great diversity of human civilizations, religions, and forms of life; and in this chapter I have argued that for just this reason they provide a significant basis for developing normative conceptions of human existence for the present historical period. This is, of course, a momentous claim, and it can easily be attacked as just one more expression of western ethnocentrism.

I suspect that those who are most likely to feel the parochialism and other limitations of the conceptions I have set forth here, and who are, therefore, in the best position to develop significant countervailing evidence and arguments, will be representatives of nonwestern religious, cultural, and philosophical traditions. There are, in such contexts, many thoughtful persons with styles of life and reflection—with structures of self and society, value orientations, perspectives on life and the world—significantly different from those of modern educated westerners. I would especially welcome responses to my anthropological proposals from such persons, precisely because of the significance I give to human religious and cultural diversity: only through ongoing open and comprehensive dialogue across religious and cultural lines are we likely to find a way beyond the parochialism of each of our traditions to a conception of humanity—and to norms for human life today—appropriate to both our pluralism and our interdependence in today's world. If my proposals help to stimulate counter-proposals from other perspectives on these fundamental anthropological, philosophical, and religious questions, it will be to the advantage of us all. For in today's pluralistic world, what is most needed is a breakthrough from monolithic monocultural patterns of practice and thinking to dialogical practices, conceptions, and institutions. However much my biohistorical proposals for conceiving human being and human normativity aspire to universality, I make no claims to be sketching here some final or ultimate truth about human being and well-being: the context of mystery within which all theological work proceeds renders such presumptuousness entirely inappropriate (see Chapters 4 and 5). My voice is but one in the ongoing human dialogue about these matters, and the most for which I dare hope is that it will make some contribution to that larger conversation as it wends its way into the future.[2]

I have been trying to show that the conception of human historicity is able to interpret sympathetically and explain intelligibly precisely the diversity of human history and existence; indeed, it is just because of that interpretive and explanatory power that I am advocating it here. If, however, this claim can be shown to be seriously misleading or false, its normative usefulness must, of course, also be called into question. Evidence or arguments, therefore, that bear directly on this issue are to be welcomed, for they can only help advance our overall understanding of the human reality which we are.

11. Agency and Self-Reflexiveness as Sociohistorically Constituted

Humans have brought into being a mode or form of reality—the world of culture, or rather, a large assortment of very diverse cultural worlds—which did not exist before them, and which, so far as we know, could not exist apart from them. Prolific cultural creativity seems, from a contemporary vantage point, to be a central feature of human existence, sharply distinguishing human life from every other form of which we are aware. Further reflection, now, on this power of creativity, this capacity to bring into being reality which did not and could not exist independently of human activity, can serve as a convenient point with which to carry forward our constructive theological anthropology.

The major cultural structures which humans have created in the course of history—languages, customs, political and economic practices and institutions, patterns of reflection and understanding, complexes of meaning and value, and so on—were seldom if ever direct products of deliberate human intention; but they were not created independently of human action either. They certainly did not come into being just "accidentally" or by chance, as the Colorado River, for example, carved out the Grand Canyon, simply as the natural consequence of water running downhill for millions of years. Nor were these cultural structures produced as a simple and direct expression of innate drives and instincts, like the building of nests by birds or dams by beavers, a sort of behavior that follows virtually unchanging patterns for thousands or even millions of years. Human culture is something quite different: it is a growing, changing, developing reality, produced by human activity itself, as new practices appear, new styles of life emerge, new institutions are created. Even such a basic physiological activity as eating is done very differently around the globe by humans (in contrast with other animals), and what is considered edible in different cultures varies enormously. Obviously something more is involved in producing these patterns than mere expression of instincts leading to the satisfaction of basic biological needs.

This "more" is connected with, though not entirely explainable by, what in its fully developed form we call *intention.* Humans are always trying to *do* something in and through their activity; that is, they have purposes and goals which they are trying to realize. Only at certain levels (for example, in such fundamental body functions as breathing or the beating of the heart, or in so-called reflex actions) is human activity a straightforward expression of biological mechanisms or a simple and direct response to external stimuli; and under certain circumstances, sometimes including special sorts of training, it is possible to alter even these patterns consciously and deliberately. Humans have learned to set purposes for themselves which include wider interests than the merely biological, and nearly all their activity is directed at least in part by these wider purposes—for example, painting a picture or weaving a piece of cloth, winning a war against a neighboring people or celebrating a good harvest with thanks to God, preparing a tastier meal or making love with one's spouse. Human life, both individual and communal, has become pervaded with culturally defined objectives and goals. Work toward those goals is sometimes very concentrated and intense, involving great effort; at other times it may be casual, easily interrupted, almost uncaring. But in almost every activity in which they are involved women and men have some end in view; they are trying to *do* something or other—even if it is only to relax or take a nap.

Every culture is a structure of extraordinarily complex and diverse purposive activities and relationships of this sort; and human culture as a whole is created in connection with this purposive activity. This all began, of course, on a small scale and in quite simple ways, perhaps some millions of years ago when human life—or rather, proto-human life—was much more like that of other higher animals: biological needs were satisfied in simpler, less elaborate ways than now, and "purposes" distinct from biological drives could probably not be identified. In the course of many generations, however, as humans—gradually becoming aware that some ways of procuring food, or of protecting themselves from the cold and from enemies, or of organizing social life, were more effective or successful than others—began increasingly to take this into account in ordering their activities. That is, a more *intentional* sort of selection (connected with but not to be simply identified with "natural" selection) of patterns of activity and modes of social organization slowly began to develop, and so in different tribes different patterns of culture were built up. Every example of human existence of which we know bears the imprint of these humanly invented and shaped cultural patterns; in a significant respect, thus, it is a product of human creativity, of women and men trying to *do* something. As we shall see later, however, the creation of culture has involved more than this; there is a serendipitous creativity working through our human activities that goes far beyond anything directly intended by human agents (see Chapter 19).

Our biohistorical mode of existence cannot be easily broken down into parts which reveal how it was constructed or created, and I certainly am not competent to attempt any such analysis. It will be useful for our purposes, however, to explore briefly the "intentional" component in cultural creation and activity. What is it to "do something" (intentionally)? What is involved in setting a goal for ourselves and seeking to attain it, in having an intention or purpose and seeking to realize it? Our everyday lives are filled with decisions and intentions and actions, large and small—from getting dressed in the morning and going jogging, to carrying through programs of work or study which may require years to complete—but we do not often reflect on the operations and structures which these common ingredients of experience involve. Even the simplest sorts of everyday choices presuppose exceedingly complex biological, social, and psychological cybernetic networks; and choice turns out not to be simple at all.

In this connection we may note first that if we are to choose one particular course of action from among two (or more) that confront us, we must have some way of holding the different alternatives before our minds so that we can examine and compare and evaluate them, eventually deciding to reject one and accept the other (to "decide" means literally to "cut off"). Alternative actions, of course, can never be present to us in fact, that is, as deeds which have already been done and which therefore can be examined and assessed: the point of decision is to be able to make our evaluation and choice before the fact, so that our assessments and decision can determine our course of action, not merely reflect it. How is this possible? In an act of choice our projected deeds are present to us "in imagination,"[1] that is, as deeds envisaged but not yet performed; the deeds are present to our minds symbolically though not actually. By means of images, words, and other signs we "hold" the projected deeds "before our minds," thus enabling us to consider their significant features—that is, those features which particularly interest or concern us—and on the basis of this consideration we make our decision. The image or the pattern of words "stands for" (as we say)—it "means" or refers us to—the deed which we are considering: our power of symbolization enables us to examine the projected deed before we do it, that is, without actually doing it. It is important to note that this power of symbolization is not a kind of natural capacity (which each of us has as a private or solitary individual) to survey every possible action; rather, the types and patterns of symbols, which are available to us in our culture and with which our minds become stocked from infancy on, determine in important respects the range of decisions that are open to us, and thus the sorts of actions that are feasible.

Although we often make what we take to be our own individual choices, the whole structure of choice by which and within which we live is a social reality, largely shaped by our particular cultural heritage. We will examine the significance of this matter in more detail a little later.

Our powers of imagination and symbolization make possible a great deal more than the mere envisaging of acts prior to their performance; at every point, as we proceed to carry a decision through into action, these powers are employed, though not as self-consciously and deliberately as when we set ourselves to make an explicit decision. Our imaginatively envisaged act now comes to serve as the pattern or plan by means of which we guide our acting; and it is the standard by which we implicitly judge, as we proceed, how effectively we are performing the act. When envisaged act_2 is chosen (over envisaged act_1) as the one to be performed, act_2 (symbolized in and guided toward its goal by what we call our "intention," what we intend to do) begins to take form in our action. Were there no such symbolic dimension to our acts (whatever be the mechanism of elaborate circuits in the nervous system that makes this possible) we would not be able to say at some point, "I failed to do what I intended," and then move to repair the error; nor would it occur to us to ask forgiveness of one offended, or, recognizing our failure, simply to go on to the next task; nor could we say, "I am doing now (or I have done) exactly what I intended." An act, thus, is a bodily motion that is informed from within by its own symbolical standard or plan (intention) to which (as it is being performed) it is made to conform. Like a self-guiding missile, every act has built into it a cybernetic mechanism which continuously corrects deviations and points us more accurately toward the target.

It would not, however, be possible to adjust the action according to the intended plan, or, perhaps to reformulate the plan in light of new data now coming in, unless the agent (the person acting) possessed—in addition to powers of imagination, symbolization, and decision—the capacity to *sense* what is going on roundabout him or her, what are the various objects in the field of action, and precisely where the target is to be found. This sensing mechanism, if it is to do its job, cannot consist merely of some general receptive equipment which discerns all motions, events, and objects in the field of action; such a picture of the total environment would simply confuse us and be useless. Rather, the sensing mechanism must be focusable, so to speak, and it must itself be guided by the intention which is being expressed in the act; for only in this way will the objects and events which are sensed be pertinent to the action being undertaken, and only in this way will relevant data about those objects and events be fed back. This focusing of our sensory apparatus in terms of our intentions is what we call "attention," the power to perceive, to attend to, to focus on certain features of our environment while ignoring others that do not bear directly on what we are attempting to do. For example, in the act of driving a car our attention is highly focused so that we take note of such things as red lights, other moving vehicles, automobile horns, and the like, while most of the objects in our environment are ignored completely: we fail to perceive them because they are not relevant to what we are attempting to do. Indeed, if we did take note of much else going on in our environment, we could not drive effectively; we would be so utterly overwhelmed by the variety and complexity of data coming in that we would be unable to carry through our intention. The phenomenon of attention, thus, involves another complex feedback operation guided by our intention, an operation without which the simplest act would not be possible.

A diagram will make clearer the structure of action as I am elaborating it here (see Figure 1). In the moment before decision, the agent envisages symbolically several alternatives—act_1, act_2, act_3. Act_2 is chosen, thus setting the *intention* which is to be carried out. But for this intention to be realized,

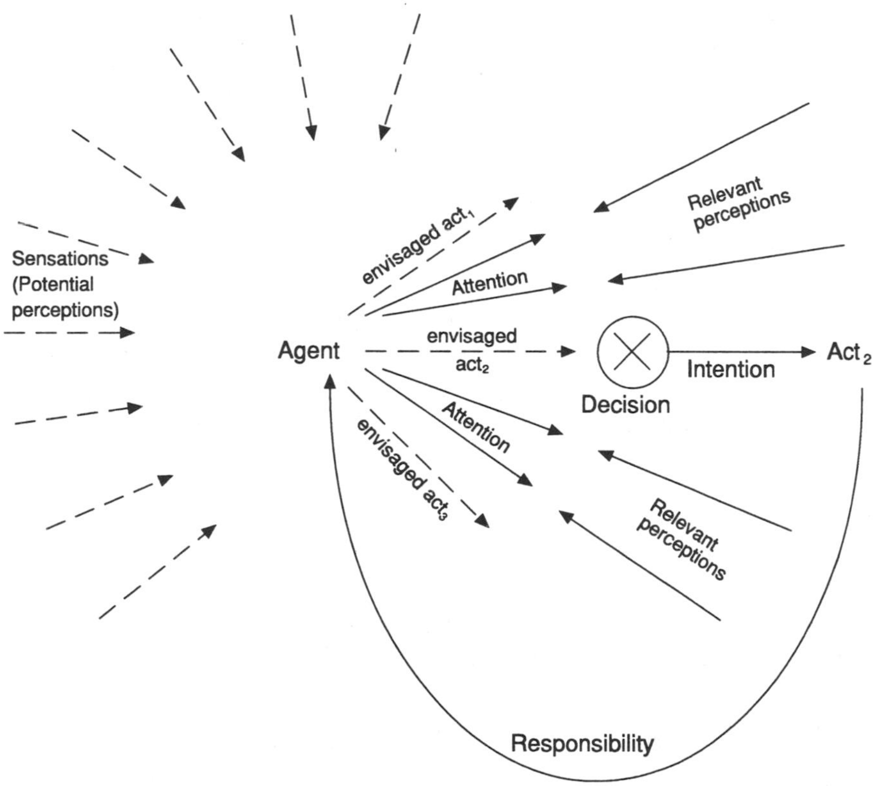

Figure 1

it is important that from among the masses of sensory data physically available to the agent, *attention* be paid only to perceptions relevant to the intended act; many other sensa impinging on the organism, thus, will remain completely unnoticed, and the agent will be able to perform act_2. This brief and oversimplified analysis shows how signs, making present to the mind what is not present in actuality, inform our actions at every point. Symbolization is required for decision (envisaging different alternatives); it is required by intention (to guide our acting); and it is required in attention (to focus our sensory equipment so we will perceive what is relevant to our goal).

Of course our abilities to intend and attend are not purely and simply symbolical. Without the foundation of a highly complex nervous system, which is itself but one part of a biological organism able to be conditioned, trained, and disciplined, these activities would not be possible at all. Intention and attention have their analogues in forms of life less complex than *Homo sapiens*. A hungry dog, for example, seeks food. That is, a dog can focus its powers on the particular goal of finding food and eating; something similar to "intention" seems to be involved here. And in this focused activity the dog tends to perceive for the most part (that is, "pays attention to") only what contributes to this end. A cat, showing great powers of "concentrated attention," is capable of stalking its prey for hours. Many animals, thus, have behavioral capacities similar to those which are taken up into what, in human beings, become intention and attention. But there is a very important difference: animals pursue goals which have been *set for them* directly by their organic needs and instincts, that is, by nature (or perhaps, in the case of domesticated animals, by their trainers). Humans, however, pursue (along with such "natural" goals) *artificial* objectives, that is, goals learned from their culture, objectives which humans (in creating culture) have themselves created (in some sense), and which they may (at least in some cases) freely decide to pursue or not to pursue. Humans, thus, are capable of choosing a wide range of goals other than those imposed by nature, goals which they represent to themselves in signs and symbols—words, images, diagrams—as they direct their own activity. In this respect humans are agents in a way that other animals are not: they can intend and attend *deliberately,* and not only as a function of biological need or impulse.

Only one who is able to carry through, more or less automatically, these functions—imagining, symbolizing, deciding, intending, attending—is able to act. Since only such an agent can *deliberately* do what he or she does, only such a one is held *responsible* for the acts performed. (However, even here there are distinct analogues in animal behavior: we hold a dog which has been housebroken "responsible," as we might say, if it soils the living room carpet.) What are we doing when we hold persons "responsible" for what they do? We are making a further symbolical reflexive move which binds agent/decision/intention/attention/act all together in a new larger unity, and the act performed now becomes attributed to the agent (see Figure 1 for diagrammatic representation of this). The agent is now regarded, and regards herself or himself, as the dynamic origin or source of the act, without which the act would not have occurred at all; and for this reason the agent is held accountable for that act. Here the peculiar character of human consciousness which we noted earlier—that it relates itself to itself, that it is self-reflexive in a unique and important way—again appears. We shall have to inspect this more closely soon.

Obviously the movement through which we attribute responsibility is of a higher logical order than the previous cybernetic relationships which we have noted (intention, attention, et cetera), for it presupposes all of these and it extends their meaning. To be an agent, it now appears, is not merely to be one who can do something: it is to be one who is held accountable for what he or she does, and who holds herself or himself accountable. This deeper understanding is now fed back into the self-awareness of the agent when further acts are envisaged. The agent now knows that it is not enough to think of oneself as simply choosing between envisaged alternatives: one must recognize that one will be accountable for the choice that is made and accountable for the way in which the act is carried out, and this accountability is now also factored into the process of decisionmaking. Hence, further choices will be made, intentions advanced, and actions performed, in light of the question whether one wants to be held accountable for these—and this constitutes another feedback loop in the self-reflexiveness of the agent. A new and more complex level of symbolization and self-consciousness has begun to pervade the entire process, a level which deepens significantly the sense of what it is to be an agent, what is involved in decision and action. What is emerging here is *moral* agency: it is now necessary to find ways of assessing the sorts of acts for which one is willing to be held accountable, distinguishing them from those for which one does not wish to take responsibility. In this way an entirely new question arises: the question about standards and norms which will define responsible conduct for us and can thus provide guidance in our deciding and acting, that is, the question about what we call moral standards and values, moral rules and norms. The possibility—and the necessity—of making distinctions between moral and immoral, good and bad, right and wrong action has emerged.

Later we shall have to examine in some detail what these distinctions involve. For now we simply take note of the complexity of consciousness and symbolization that is required—with increasingly complicated feedback loops taking up into themselves simpler loops—for what we call "morality" to appear in human existence; a moral agent is an exceedingly complex sort of self-reflexive being. It is also important to note that we have uncovered an essential interconnectedness between morality and action in our analysis here. Morality is not a more or less independent sphere of human life with which one may concern oneself if one chooses, or which one may disregard if one prefers: the moral dimension of life is a cybernetic extension of, and a further symbolic complexification and sophistication of, our existence as actors; it is an intelligible, and quite important, development in beings capable of deciding and acting, and thus taking responsibility for themselves. It is not surprising, therefore, that it has appeared—in some form or other, and to some extent—in all cultures of which we have knowledge.

I have been briefly sketching here some of the basic symbolic cybernetic structures involved in action, whether in very simple decisions or in comprehensive long-range programs involving many interconnected purposes. (As we proceed we shall see that this picture will have to be complicated a great deal more.) To the extent that deciding and acting is a feature of the daily life of women and men everywhere, patterns similar to the sort I have sketched must be present in persons of every culture. This does not mean, of course, that all women and men have been able to actualize their agency to the same degree. Some, because of the cultural patterns or the social structures in which they participate, or the psychological pressures under which they must live, or a lack of adequate education and training, are able to express and exercise their potential for action only in quite limited ways, perhaps only in the relatively small decisions required in everyday living. Others in significantly different contexts may have the opportunity to make decisions which have far-reaching consequences, not only for themselves but for many others as well, even for whole societies. But in all these cases, whether humble or great in consequence, an important threshold has been crossed, that threshold which closes the circuit that introduces *accountability* into the feedback system. When we cross this threshold, we become responsible participants in and bearers of humanity, and thus enter into relationships truly and fully human.*

For sociological, psychological, physiological, and other reasons, some persons have the opportunity to fulfill their potential for agency to a much greater extent than others, who may be, for example, members of an oppressed or repressed class or nationality, race or sex. Contemporary liberation theologies have called for the overthrow of the oppressive social structures which prevent such persons from fully exercising their capacity to take responsibility for themselves and their lives, from becoming more truly free.

*It is important that we conceive humanness in terms of "crossing a specific threshold" rather than in terms of the *degree* of agency or power that a person (or class or race or gender or community) possesses and can exercise. To do the latter would mean that different persons and groups differ in the degree to which they are human: those in a position to make only small decisions with limited consequences would be considered human to only a limited degree—perhaps less than fully human, subhuman creatures—in comparison with those of great power and responsibility. Slave and caste societies in past and present have always tended toward these sorts of distinctions.

The premise of all such calls is, of course, that our agency, as I have been arguing here, is a central feature of our humanity. With respect to the issues raised by liberation movements, thus, it is not human agency as such (human power, human self-consciousness and creativity) that is the central social and religious problem that requires attention: it is, rather, the unequal and oppressive distribution and exercise of human agency which must be overcome. Of great importance in the assessment of institutional and other social and psychological structures, as well as of all actions, policies, and programs, is the degree to which they inhibit or prevent—or enhance and reinforce—the exercise of agency and responsibility by all men and women. As we shall see, it is issues of this sort with which the moral dimension of human existence is centrally concerned.

Our consideration of the complex operations required to make possible the simplest sorts of decision and action has put us into a position from which we can start to examine more directly what I have called the "self-reflexiveness" characteristic of human existence. Self-reflexiveness operates at many levels, and these are interdependent in different ways. It would be a mistake, therefore, to assume that there is one proper place to begin an analysis of human existence—by looking at decision and action, for example, as we have been doing—and that all else can then be set out in linear fashion following from this beginning point. We are dealing here with organic relations of interdependence, not with simple relations of cause and effect. Our analysis thus far, therefore, should be considered only a doorway into the complexities we need to examine. Important matters that we have not yet taken up have, in fact, been presupposed in the brief sketch of decision and action with which we have just been occupied.

The self-reflexive relations involved in the consciousness humans have of themselves, in their ability to act with purposefulness or deliberation, in their capacity to hold themselves responsible for their own action, cannot be understood in terms of the ordinary model of relationship, according to which two or more individual objects are considered to be related to one another externally, as are A, B, C, and D in the following diagram:

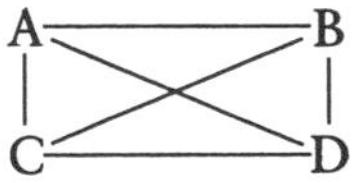

Selves and communities in their self-consciousness or self-responsibility, in contrast to such external relations, are turned back on themselves:

Whenever we say (or think), "I know who I am," or "We know what we are doing," or "We are aware of what's happening to us," or "I intend to keep my promise," we are performing self-reflexive acts of this sort; or, we might say, we are expressing in speech—and in this way further building up—certain cybernetic structures of self-relatedness.

It is important to note that it is first-person words ("I," "we," "myself," "ourselves") that are used in such expressions. These words have a peculiar character: they can (ordinarily) be used by speakers or agents only to refer to themselves as the speaker or agent.[2] That is, these words have self-reflexiveness built into them: to say "I" is to refer to oneself, to invoke one's own self-relatedness; to say "we" similarly invokes the internal self-relatedness of a group. If we did not have such self-relatedness, we could not say "I" or "we." But the matter is more complicated than that: if we English-language speakers did not have words like "I" or "we," we would not have the sort of self-consciousness we do—that is, we could not have developed the high degree of internal self-relatedness in which we daily live. For it is in learning to say "I" and "we" that we begin to construct ourselves as an "I" or a "we," thus becoming aware of ourselves as agents (whether individual or group) capable of acting and taking responsibility for our actions. In languages which do not employ first-person pronouns in the way English does (along with other European languages), significantly different sorts of "self-awareness" emerge.[3]

The internal self-relatingness of the "I" and the "we," thus, help to constitute the sort of acting we have here been discussing. But this internal self-relatingness does not suffice by itself to constitute agency: in order to act, an "I" or a "we" must be able to project itself beyond its present situation into the future; it must be capable of moving intentionally and deliberately into the external world. Agency thus presupposes and expresses relatedness to what is outside or beyond the self or community just as definitely as internal self-relatedness. External self-projection and internal self-relatedness are two interdependent dimensions of the structure of agents; our words "I" and "we" both refer us to and help to constitute this double-sided structure.

In the West a powerful sense of individuality, of the significance of the individual ego, has developed particularly during the last several centuries—especially among males. Since it is precisely such highly centered and active males who have produced most of the (published) philosophical reflection on human existence, it is hardly surprising that in western writing the "I" (the individual self) has become widely accepted as the very locus of our humanity: to be human is to be an individual human being, an individual self/subject/actor. Through a long history our religious and cultural traditions have cultivated and developed this sense of humanity as located essentially in the individual. Christian religious practices and beliefs, emphasizing God's special care for each individual, taken together with the doctrine that each of us is an "immortal soul," early set western thinking on this course. These historical trends culminated ultimately in the atomistic individualism of modern political and industrial societies, and in the "epistemological turn" of modern philosophy where everything we can know or understand is thought to be based on the experience of the individual subject, the "I," which became (with Descartes) the one indubitable metaphysical foundation for all philosophical reflection ("I think, therefore *I* am").[4] For modern western consciousness, thus, the other personal pronouns, and what they signify, have seemed to many to be logically derivative from this indubitable "I." "You," "he," and "she" all refer to the sorts of beings who can say "I"—that is, beings who are agents: they each must be understood as essentially an "I." Similarly with "we," a term which is often taken to express simply the solidarity of a community of "I's." (In contrast with these personal pronouns, the word "it" has a much more general significance which does not imply or directly presuppose the complex self-reflexive structure of the "I.")

This way of thinking, however persuasive it may have seemed for a time in the West, is quite misleading. In some other cultures (for example, Japan), and also (as is now being claimed) among women in western cultures, the importance of being an independent and autonomous ego/agent has not been stressed in the way it has among white western males. Here a sense of *relatedness to others,* of "we," has seemed more primordial than "I."[5] If one reflects on these matters, one can see that the "I," with its emphasis on the autonomous ego, is in fact an abstraction, an exaggerated reification of something that can actually exist only within certain complex patterns of interrelationship with other selves. It is to the *community of selves in interaction* that we must look for the actual locus of the human, not the individual self, the ego. No individual selves could exist without a community which gave birth to them and continued to sustain them—not least through providing them with language, that medium of signs which (as we have been observing) is an indispensable ingredient of individual selfhood and agency. Thus, although a close examination of the "I," the individual agent, may disclose to us certain features (under a microscope, as it were) of what we humans are, it would be a mistake to take this abstraction as itself presenting us with the human. Human existence is fundamentally social in character, not individual, and the complexities to which "we," "they," and "you" point cannot be understood as simply the consequence of putting a number of autonomous ego-selves together in various combinations. (For this reason, in the preceding paragraphs, I consistently paired "I" and "we" in my discussion of first-person reflexivity, instead of treating the "I" alone as the primordial example of agency.)

All the personal pronouns taken together—"you," "he," "she," "we," "they" (in their various declensions) as well as "I"—are required to articulate the human for us fully in modern English. (In other linguistic worlds, somewhat different patterns—often more complex than this—are found necessary.)[6] And these are all logically interrelated with one another and interdependent in such a way that no one of them—certainly not the "I"—can be regarded as the foundation of all the others. It is in connection with this whole complex of personal pronouns, and what they signify, that our sense (in English) of what the human is—and thus the reality of the human—is given to us. I shall focus for a time now on the "I" (even though this oversimplifies matters considerably), because this will enable us to see in more sharply etched lines certain important characteristics of the peculiarly distinctive power which we humans have (in the course of a long historical development) increasingly come to possess: the power to act and create, a power that has produced a magnificent efflorescence of cultures and in so doing has created widely diverse forms of human existence. Most of what I have to say here would apply—with appropriate modifications—to communal forms of agency (the "we") as well as to individual forms (the "I"), but in order to simplify my presentation, I shall not attempt to show that here.

Up to this point we have considered the self-reflexive structure of the "I" only with respect to the ability of the self to act, that is, to project itself into the future, to move out into the world in order to transform certain of its features. But this picture is much too simple. It tells us nothing about the resources on which agents draw in setting purposes and then carrying them through in action; thus far action has been described as though an agent started simply from Ground Zero, creating projects *ex nihilo*—obviously a misleading abstraction. We can consider an agent's resources conveniently under two headings: experience and power. The ever-growing resource of our experience provides us with ways of understanding each new situation as we confront it; we imagine alternative courses of action which are now open to us on the basis of what we have experienced in the past, and we make our choice among these alternatives "in the light of our experience." But experience is not all that is required for deliberate action. We must also have resources of power, the ability to do things, to bring about actual effects in the world. Each of these types of resource involves further self-reflexive dimensions within the agent.

The mode of self-reflexiveness we have considered thus far—action proper, including taking responsibility for oneself and one's act—is an expression of the self's ability to move ahead-of-itself, as it were, the ability to project itself into the future and to bind that future back onto itself (cf. Heidegger). The modes of self-reflexiveness involved in the self's ability to draw on resources of experience and of power, however, have to do principally with the other two modalities of time, past and present. It is our ability to *remember the past*—that is, to make certain features of the past present to ourselves in memory—that provides the reservoir of experience on which we draw as we project ourselves into the future through action. And it is our ability to control our own bodies *in the present*—for example, to make our arms and legs move in the ways we intend—that provides us with resources of power to effect our intentions; for our bodies are living organisms with appetites, drives, and other dynamisms that can bring about physical changes in the world. Thus, our little word "I" indicates not only the self's relating itself to itself with respect to the future (the self-reflexiveness involved in action and responsibility) but also its relating itself to itself with respect to the past (memory, including experience, education, training, et cetera) and to the present (control of the body). We can diagram this triple self-reflexiveness of the "I" as shown in Figure 2. Without these three quite distinct sorts of feedback, each complexly involved with the other two, there could be no human agency, historicity, and creativity as we know them.[7]

It would be possible to sketch in a simplified way the structure of cybernetic relations involved in memory and body control (cf. the outline of the structure of action in Figure 1, with its interconnections of decision, intention, attention, perception, responsibility), but that sort of detail is not necessary for our purposes. I shall confine myself therefore to summarizing briefly the resources made available to agents through memory and bodiliness.

There are two points I would like to make about memory. First, memory provides the reservoir of symbols (language, images, et cetera) required by conscious experience and action. Although many of our images may be

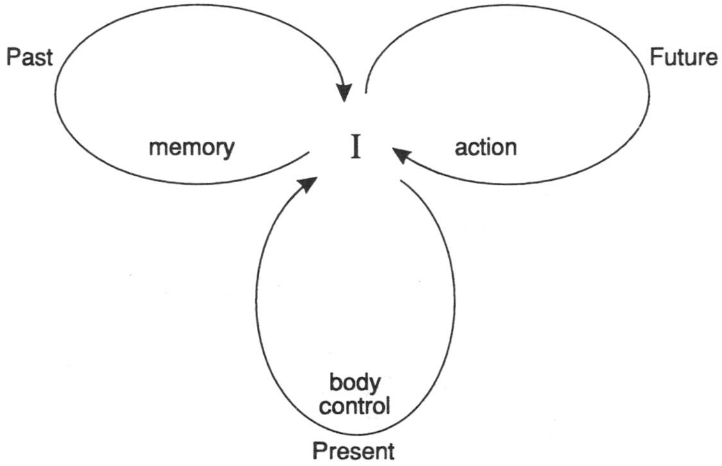

Figure 2

private, the language we learn from childhood is a complexly ordered system of public symbols continuously employed by the imagination to shape and order and classify experience, and to project alternative futures. The individual "I" (with its subjectivity and privacy) could not exist at all apart from this context of symbols within which it emerges and which gives it specific structure and otherwise helps nourish and sustain it. The infant's inability to perform deliberately intended free acts is due quite as much to its lack of an ordered system of symbols as to the absence of well-developed motor skills. Both of these require years of learning and training, years of socialization. This brings me to my second point about memory. It is in connection with the long-term training and learning through which every child goes, that a reservoir of conscious experience is built up, a reservoir without which we would not be able to enter upon the responsibilities of adult life. Experience provides us with the material out of which we imaginatively envisage possible courses of action, and through experience we gradually develop criteria for evaluating such envisaged acts in comparison with one another. In experience we learn what is possible in action and what impossible, what consequences will follow from one course, what from another. All this is gradually stored up in memory. But, as anyone watching an infant slowly gaining some control over its body and particularly over the power to speak can see, it is only in consequence of a long drawn-out process that a mature, well-experienced, linguistic being with a well-stocked memory can appear on the scene, ready and able to take responsibility for itself in free and deliberate action.

No such action would be possible, of course, were we not embodied beings with appetites, drives, desires—that is, living beings with energies of many sorts organized into patterns that serve the organism, beings capable of bringing about changes in the physical world roundabout us, and thus able to act with some effect. Our bodies are well-coordinated physical structures which provide us with at least four distinct sorts of resources without which human experience and action would be impossible: (1) a sensory apparatus, which continuously feeds in data about what is occurring in our environment; (2) instrumentalities for moving in the world and in this way effecting various changes—for example, arms and legs, and the muscular and neural structures which make possible their operation; (3) a continuous welling-up of dynamism and energy (so long as life goes on), as the organism seeks to meet its basic needs for sustenance, sex, sleep, shelter, and so on; (4) a complex system for coordinating, ordering, and interconnecting all of this—the central nervous system. All animals possess these functions in some degree; humans have them in a sufficiently developed and well-organized form to support the high-order symbolic functions involved in memory, imagination, and linguistic behavior.

As memory and imagination, emerging slowly with experience, become coordinated with the organism's growing ensemble of habits and motor skills, deliberate action gradually begins to become possible. But, as examples like learning to hit a tennis ball or to play the piano show, our bodies do not become particularly effective instrumentalities of our acts until they are under well-disciplined control. Human agency is, thus, much more complicated than our initial analysis of decision and action suggested. Acts never begin simply *de novo,* in the moment of present decision. All decisions and acts emerge as expressions of the organism's fundamental dynamisms—these having become modified and transformed in experience ("sublimated" and/or "repressed," to use Freud's terminology) through culturally guided discipline and learning. And they are always shaped and informed by that past out of which they have come, and by the physical drives and needs of that organism which they (in part) express.

The "I," thus, the self-conscious agent (once it has emerged), is a very complex cybernetic structure which transcends itself in three directions simultaneously, binding each of these back into itself. It is "ahead-of-itself," as it projects itself into the future and binds that future to itself; it is "behind itself," as it carries with it its past (now no longer existent) in the form of memory, training, and habits; and it "interpenetrates itself" with discipline and control, as it increasingly permeates its bodily activity with skills and practices which would otherwise be absent. Thus the organism comes to function in new and significantly creative ways.

This picture, however, is still seriously misleading. I have been speaking as though the "I" were a kind of commander on the bridge of a ship: orders are shouted and levers are pulled to make the body move this way or that; charts are checked to see where the ship has been in the past and to plot its course for the future; everything is under the commander's control. Such an image portrays the life of the self in a way reminiscent of the mind-body dualism (of which Descartes is the classical representative) in which the self is a kind of amalgam of two distinctly different sorts of reality: mental (ideas, intentions, decisions, et cetera), and physical (a mechanical system of ropes, pulleys, levers, and the like which can move one another this way and that). But this dualistic sort of thinking makes human action—in which physical motions are internally informed by decisions and intentions—completely unintelligible. There is simply no way to conceive how *ideas* can pull levers or push buttons, that is, have mechanical effects. The unity and effectiveness of an act cannot be understood if we break it down into components which are in this way utterly distinct from one another and cannot be related to one another. Acts become intelligible only if they are understood as the expressions of beings which are themselves already organized into highly complex patterns of structure and activity: agency, that is to say, is a capacity that can be developed only by living organisms of a highly specialized sort.

The "I" emerges into consciousness and intentionality as a feature of a physical organism that is already going somewhere, already on its own course, satisfying its needs and desires, seeking to nourish itself, to grow through its life-cycle, to reproduce itself so that its species will survive. At birth an infant has no conscious, deliberately chosen intentions of its own; its life is governed entirely by the blind drives and needs of an organism striving to live and grow. It is only slowly, over many years, that this blind organic behavior becomes interpenetrated with and transformed into the deliberate, self-conscious purposiveness of genuine agency. Consciousness has its origins in the organism's physical awareness of need—for food, warmth, a dry diaper. One could say, then, that a person's coming to self-consciousness is in the first instance simply the body's own coming to awareness of itself; and this body-consciousness always remains as an indispensable dimension of our self-consciousness. Consciousness emerges—that is, the "I" emerges—riding on the back, as it were, of a dynamic, striving organism, already in motion toward the realization of its own objectives of nutrition, comfort, reproduction, and the like. As the organism becomes aware of its dynamisms by learning to direct them to some extent, to take charge of them, it gradually begins to become aware of itself, begins to acquire the self-reflexiveness characteristic of an "I"; in connection with this what would otherwise be simply "behavior" is transformed into intentional *action*. Underlying and energizing this action, however, there always remain drives, movements, needs of the self below the level of consciousness, concealed from its awareness. To the extent that the behavior of the organism proceeds out of such unrecognized or unknown drives and desires, the "I" is not in control; indeed, no "agent" (in the sense in which we have been using the word) is involved, nor is there "action" (properly speaking), only organic striving.*

To the extent that the behavior of the organism is redirected and refocused with the emergence of the "I," the organic drives and desires are being rechanneled. That is, they are no longer being allowed to proceed immediately to satisfaction; they are being in some measure repressed and delayed, forced to realize themselves in new "unnatural" ways. It would be difficult to understand how a self with the power to discipline, thwart, and

*On this whole set of issues, Freud's analysis has been seminal for much modern reflection. Freud saw that the "ego" (the English mistranslation of what Freud had himself referred to simply as the "I"—*das Ich*) is basically the coming to self-consciousness and some measure of control over what would otherwise have remained submerged and unconscious, the "id" (English mistranslation of what Freud called simply the "it"—*das Es*). Much, thus, that impels me, that drives my movements and actions, remains dark and hidden, the unconscious striving of the organism. But at some points intentionality, consciousness, deliberate control and thus responsible action, emerge. For discussion of the serious consequences of the many mistranslations of Freudian terms in the official English editions of his works, see Bruno Bettelheim, *Freud and Man's Soul* (New York: Knopf, 1982).

sublimate those primal drives in this way could ever have emerged, if nothing but the animal desires of the organism had been involved during these transformative processes. However, the emerging self is connected not only with its own body: it always stands in another set of relations as well, to other much more fully developed selves. And these other selves (usually the child's parents) demand of it behavior shaped according to patterns which they externally impose, in place of the simple and direct satisfaction of the infant organism's desires: regular feeding (not simply on demand), toilet training, and so on. And thus the infant learns to adapt to socially imposed patterns of behavior, learns to redirect its energies and dynamisms in socially approved ways. This internalization of sociocultural patterns Freud called the construction of a "superego." Thus the ego, the "I," the agent, emerges at the point of intersection between the sociocultural and the biological. Its roots are in both spheres, and its life and possibilities draw on both sets of resources.

Our picture of the agent has now been complicated once more in a very decisive way. It has become abundantly clear how misleading it is to think of selves as though they were simply extrapolations or developments of individual organisms: selves are sociocultural products, the result of complex patterns of interaction between the infant organism and the adult persons caring for it. In consequence of this social interaction further feedback channels, of a sort different from any we have yet considered, are created and become constitutive of the self. Without these socially imposed patterns and symbolic structures, the "I," the agent-self, could never come into existence at all. One is not born an "I"; nor is selfhood acquired through a more or less autonomous process of growth—like an acorn becoming an oak—in which the full potential present in the seed from the beginning needs only to unfold. One becomes an agent-self through becoming a participating member of a community of persons. That is, it is through complex processes of interpersonal interaction, including internalizing many social rituals and a complex role system, as well as learning a language, that agency—freedom—is gradually evoked as a child emerges into personhood.

This fundamentally social character of our selfhood—indeed, of our very humanity—implies that the historical emergence of humans from animality into humanity should not be thought of as having occurred in a day, as it were. It came about over many generations through a long slow process during which what had previously been strictly biological behavior was gradually qualified by the increasing complexity of the social order and its growing system of symbols. These developments in turn led to the further transformation and complexification of the biological structures which carried them (as we saw in Chapter 9), making possible the emergence of a truly "biohistorical" being. In and through all of this, human behavior was not only becoming increasingly complex; a new mode of being, created by men and women, was gradually being brought into the world: *culture,* a system of symbols and artifacts and new patterns of living and acting, was gradually becoming superimposed on nature. It is important that we recognize that this does not involve merely introducing something alongside what had already existed. Human social organization, symbolization, artifacturing, and the development of new skills and activities are all interlaced with one another and interdependent. So through this expanding process one species of the genus *Homo* was in fact transforming itself from a mere animal into a cultural and historical being, was moving from animality into humanity. What had been to this point blind biological evolution was turning into history, and human beings (properly so called) were coming on the scene.

Action (as a distinctive form of behavior) and agent-selves (capable of deliberative and responsible acts) appeared on earth as a consequence of this development of increasingly complex patterns of sociocultural life. What had begun as packs or hordes of clever animals gradually became tribes, with social functions increasingly differentiated and specialized, as various skills (in hunting, weaving, building, growing and preparing food, healing diseases, making war, and the like) each began to develop its own practitioners with special traditions to guide them. Forms of apprenticeship and education appeared, and some became specialists in one skill, others in another. To make all this possible, it was necessary to invent increasingly complex forms of social organization, that is, means of coordinating and relating these various groups to one another, so they would all work together harmoniously for the sake of the whole tribe. And so further specializations came into being with the development of forms of political organization which could maintain and enhance the social order and could provide means of settling disputes among members of the tribe. It is clear that by this time behavior had developed to a level rather far removed from the merely instinctual and biological, though at every point it was grounded in this. When new problems were encountered, the possibility for women and men to make more or less deliberate choices among alternatives became increasingly open: they were becoming agents, actors, beings who could in some measure shape their own destinies.

None of this could have occurred without a vast increase in the modes and possibilities of symbolization; but language was also growing all the while, into a highly flexible instrument for expressing, articulating, and specifying many of the facets of life. It had to be capable of articulating the various operations and phases of each of the different skills and vocations maintained by the group, so that each new generation could be taught the lore accumulated during past experience, thus building on its predecessors instead of relearning everything from scratch. This required not only the invention of various technical terms but the creation of a grammar and syntax which would enable clarity and precision in communication. This was not all that was needed: the relatively complex forms of social organization now being utilized laid their own special requirements on the language. Formulating the various political, social, and personal problems and concerns arising within the increasingly complex interpersonal structure of the tribe necessitated further technical terms defining the various statuses and roles and their relations to one another and making it possible to articulate ways of handling tensions and other difficulties. Thus, precursors of political, moral, and legal terminology appeared, and the basic grammatical and syntactical structure of the language had to be made capable of carrying all this freight also. Clearly, human life, even at what might seem to us a very primitive level of culture, required a highly developed language with a capacity for articulating a great variety of details of experience and possibilities for action.

From a very early time on, thus, human existence has been structured largely in socially developed linguistic and ritualistic terms, and the world and the self have been ordered and organized symbolically. An important threshold had been crossed: with the creation of a relatively large vocabulary, it became possible to express things in a variety of ways, and humans found themselves able to *choose* one articulation in preference to another. When a question is posed or a comment is made, the answer is seldom simply automatic; rather, the person chooses (in some sense) to respond in this way rather than that, to say these words and not those, to express this mood or feeling but to leave that other undisclosed. Thus, as symbolism comes to interpenetrate every level and dimension of experience, new powers of memory and imagination, and new opportunities for decision and action, open up for humans. *Freedom* has entered upon the scene.[8]

What we call "freedom" is not the property of an atomic individual, something possessed by selves independently of their relations with others; "action" is not behavior performed by solitary agents who simply do what they choose. Rather, freedom—action—is a function of a certain level, complexity, and type of sociocultural organization. It is fundamentally a social reality, and only secondarily and derivatively a capacity or property of individuals. In a very primitive, simple society, still quite near the animal level of existence, there would be little that approximated what we ordinarily call action (or freedom); and it would hardly be appropriate to characterize members of such a society as agent-selves. In contrast, in complex societies like our own with elaborate patterns of roles, women and men may have open to them such vocational choices as physician, taxi driver, social worker, farmer, minister, salesperson, plumber, teacher, and so on; but this is possible only because there are institutional structures which support these many roles and educational programs (forms of training) which prepare persons for them. Or, to take a simpler example: it is possible to choose to go to the movies for the evening instead of reading a book only because our society presents us with these opportunities. In other settings neither of these possibilities would be open to us—though others, not available to us here, would be. Virtually every sort of activity in which we engage is in some respects a function of socially defined possibilities that become open to us through processes of socialization and learning which begin in infancy and continue through the rest of life. My action, thus, is never simply *my* individual doing: it is always a function of my appropriation of roles—and of the possibilities within those roles—as made available to me by my society. Doubtless we each perform these roles in our own unique way—and sometimes we significantly transform the role in so doing—but for the most part we play the role as socially defined: one simply cannot play first base if one insists on spending most of one's time out in left field.

In general, the possibilities of agency in a society increase as the differentiation and complexity of the society increase. There would seem to be, however, a point of diminishing returns where differentiation has gone so far that it is no longer possible to maintain social order, and the society breaks down. With bureaucratization (as in modern society) such rigid rules and role definitions may develop that the exercise of real spontaneity and freedom is hardly possible, and selves become stunted and eventually destroyed. Or persons may become fragmented as they seek to respond to the enormous variety of demands made on them by the unrelated bureaucratic institutions and processes among which they must move, nowhere finding a context which can sustain the whole person and within which, therefore, they can become (or be) integrated selves. In situations of these sorts the networks of interdependence in the society have become so complex and heavy that, instead of facilitating and enhancing freedom of action, they make it increasingly difficult. For there to be free and responsible action in a society there must be sufficient differentiation to make possible significant choices combined with the kind of ordering and interdependence that facilitates the emergence of integrated selves, capable of spontaneity and creativity.

Similar sorts of things can be said with respect to language; for freedom is also a function of the level, complexity, and types of symbolization available in a culture. With very simple languages few symbolical alternatives are presented to the speaker and the range of choices is narrow. Highly complex languages like English, however, consisting of half a million words or more with countless grammatically and syntactically correct ways of combining them, present one with almost infinite possibilities. The subtlest dimensions of experience can be discriminated, attended to, and related to one another in many combinations and permutations; an immense variety of styles of life and possibilities for life can be envisaged; and activities of the most complex and far-reaching sort can be planned and executed. The types, possibilities, and extent of our freedom of thought, imagination, and action are heavily dependent on the structures and the flexibility of the language in terms of which we do our experiencing, imagining, and thinking.

Here also we can say that in general the possibilities of freedom, awareness, and creativity increase in proportion to the variety and scope of articulation available in the language; but here also a point of diminishing returns can be reached. When the variety of ways in which we can apprehend, articulate, and assess alternatives becomes too great for us to manage—many alternatives seeming attractive and significant in their own right, with no way to choose among them—we may be rendered immobile instead of enabled to think and act with freedom and creativity. In a pluralistic culture like ours, with very diverse traditions of value and meaning competing with one another for our attention and allegiance, the symbolic abundance with which we are surrounded, instead of enhancing our creativity and freedom, may undermine them.

I have been attempting to show in this analysis that patterns of social organization and of symbolization are directly constitutive of our selfhood and agency: without certain levels of sociocultural differentiation and complexity, agent-selves could not exist. Human beings cannot, then, be properly conceived as essentially separate and autonomous individuals, as we all too often suppose. They are, rather, persons-in-community, a form of reality that emerges in and through historical processes, a new order of being which can exist only within a highly complex sociocultural system.

If this analysis is correct, the customs, roles, and institutions of a society, and its ways of speaking, thinking, and valuing, have decisive effects on the sorts of selves that can emerge there, on what they can do and how they will understand themselves. For example, in a society in which blacks and women are assigned certain roles regarded as undignified and commonplace, while being excluded from other "more important" positions reserved largely for white males, it is hardly surprising that whites and males would come to think of themselves as superior; and pressures would be strong on more oppressed groups, which acquired their valuations and self-understandings from the same society, to think of themselves as less worthy, less valuable, inferior. Moreover, since it is biological characteristics (skin color, sex) that externally distinguish these groups from one another, the respective positions in which they find themselves and the valuations and self-understandings that go with these may themselves seem to be biologically grounded. In a society in which such conclusions are drawn, biology is destiny, with significantly different sorts of opportunity and different degrees of freedom open to these different biological groupings. Historically, most societies have tended to regard what were in fact their own social definitions of such matters as being rooted in the nature of things, thus giving a metaphysical or religious authorization to the society's own hierarchical valuations and institutions. It is only recently that we have come to realize that all matters of social status and role, valuation and dignity, are socially created, not biologically determined. This opens up the possibility of much more egalitarian societies in the future than have obtained in the past.

From this vantage point it becomes clear that such moral and religious matters as standards of right and wrong and conceptions of God and salvation cannot be properly understood apart from the social and historical context in which they have emerged and which they reflect and reinforce. Moral and religious ideas are not universal truths, applicable always and everywhere; nor are they optional or dispensable matters, which individuals can "believe" if they so choose or reject if they like. They are intrinsic and important features of the sociocultural process, without which human life would have neither order nor stability nor meaning. But for just this reason they need to be continuously scrutinized and evaluated (like all other sociocultural structures and processes), and criteria need to be developed for reconstructing them so they will more adequately fulfill their function(s). These are all, of course, central issues for a constructive theology.

12. Subjectivity, Experience, and Freedom

We have been examining what might be called the "objective" preconditions for agency, for human action and freedom: (a) there must be cybernetic structures within individuals which make possible the complex sorts of feedback required for memory, imagination, interconnection among the drives and dynamisms of the organism, intention, attention, and of course acting itself; (b) there must be equally complex cybernetic structures in the society within which these individuals emerge and act—that is, complexes of roles, statuses, institutions, forms of symbolization—providing the society both with a stable order and with dynamisms of its own. Neither of these, as we have seen, could emerge and develop independently of the other; they are intimately interconnected. If acting is to be possible at all, both *self* and *society* must be complex systems, and these two must be interconnected and coordinated with each other.[1] However, the presence of two complex interrelated systems in interaction with each other—like two computers with their circuits interconnected, so they will affect each other in various ways—is not all that is required for action (in the sense in which we are interested in it) to be possible. In addition to these objective conditions, certain "subjective" ones must also be met. Acts are performed by conscious subjects who are aware of what they are doing and who deliberately formulate their goals and objectives, subjects who think of themselves, as well as those with whom they are interacting, as responsible agents. How should we understand this feature of agency?

The complex structures in self and society which we have been examining make possible a special kind of subjectivity in human beings which we call "experience." All forms of animal life—and particularly the higher forms—have some sort of "subjectivity" or "awareness." They have receptors that enable them to attend to certain features of their environment and to sense whether these are threatening (and thus to be fought in anger or fled in fear) or to be desired (and thus to be approached with a certain enthusiasm and satisfaction, as with food or a mate). Awareness of this kind does not consist merely in fixating on an object, as a plant turns toward the sun; it includes the presence within the organism of feelings appropriate to the object and correlated with it, feelings which help to motivate behavior in relation to that particular object. However, although the animal *has* such feelings, it is not conscious of them *as* feelings; nor is it conscious of their appropriateness (or inappropriateness) to certain objects in the environment or of their connections with its behavior. This more complex sort of awareness, which I am here calling "consciousness," emerges only for the linguistic animal—the human person—who is able to *objectify* for herself or himself these "inner states" by means of words which name them.

Certain of our words enable us to focus attention on our subjective states as such; and this in turn makes it possible for us to compare and contrast them with one another, to discern that they are *ours* (as distinguished from some other person's), and so on. Thus, because we have words like "joy," "pain," and "sadness"—and not only the feelings of joy and pain and sadness—we are able to identify each of these and attend to them in a number of different ways. We can, for example, imagine joy or sadness in moments when we are not feeling them—that is, when no external object or preceding experience is stimulating us to have just these feelings—by symbolizing them for ourselves with the appropriate word. Again, when we are feeling joyous, we can and do recognize it as "joy"; indeed, we seldom (if ever) feel joy without some such recognition. The feelings of humans, we could say, are "broken loose" from the strict organic-biological connections to which they are bound in other animals, and they acquire a kind of independence and life of their own. Thus, we may come to think of ourselves as beings with an "inner life" that is not simply a mirror of, or in correlation with, what is happening in our external environment. This way of thinking (and thus of experiencing)—quite problematic in certain respects, as Wittgenstein and others have shown,[2] but also very important for understanding modern western conceptions of agency, freedom, and responsibility—has become possible because of certain important developments in western history.* For convenience I shall continue to use this language here in my attempt to sketch an understanding of human subjectivity, experience, and freedom; but we must be careful not to be misled by the metaphors we will be using. However

*Identifying and understanding these matters with the aid of metaphors of "inwardness," though very prominent in modern western culture, has not been characteristic of many other societies. Augustine's work especially influenced this development in the West, but it was not until the modern period that the conditions were right for this way of speaking and thinking—and thus of experiencing—to become pervasive throughout the culture. See Charles Taylor, *Sources of the Self* (Cambridge, Mass.: Harvard University Press, 1989), chs. 6–11.

important our "inner life" may be to our modern (western) self-understanding, we dare not forget that it is essentially a linguistic construction and thus a *historical* reality, a construction which might well have developed in other quite different directions, given other historical circumstances.

The consciousness of our inner life, the ability to distinguish the "subjective" or "inward" from what we regard as "external"—to focus on it, reflect on it, come to some understanding of it as a structure or flux of "feelings," "wishings," "moods," "desires," "memories," "hopes," et cetera—is made possible largely by certain specific linguistic patterns and practices. And it is language also, as we observed in the last chapter, that enables (or even leads) us to be aware of ourselves as the "owners" of (the ones who possess) all these complex inner states—in distinction from those mere *things* "outside of" or "beyond" ourselves which are not believed to be able to "feel from within." Our first person singular words—"I," "me," "mine"—enable us to attend to ourselves as subjects of experience, actors, agents, selves; they are, as we have seen, vehicles through which we come to self-consciousness. It is hardly surprising, in view of the internal self-referential complexity of these words, that it takes a baby two years or more to learn to say "I": this is one of the most difficult and important steps through which persons must go in attaining the sort of self-consciousness characteristic of our culture.[3]

"I," of course, as we have been observing, is far from a simple word; and consciousness of "I" includes much more than simply consciousness of our inner states, or consciousness of ourselves as subjects of those states. It includes, for example, consciousness of our bodies ("I am six feet tall") and also awareness of our special relatedness to other persons; consciousness of "I" and of "you" grow up together, as Martin Buber and others have emphasized. Moreover, none of these modalities of speech which focus on individuals could emerge apart from complex interconnection with our consciousness of "we" and of "they," our awareness of our communal connectedness with those with whom we are in close interaction, as distinguished from those others with whom our relations are more casual and distant. Along with this growing linguistic facility and emerging consciousness of humans in the modalities of first, second, and third persons, an awareness of the significant difference between persons and things—between those with whom we interact and communicate in full reciprocity and those other "objects" with which this is not possible—early appears.

This enormous complexity of interconnections in experience, shaped and appropriated and interpreted in diverse ways through the elaborate structures of symbolic meaning which have come to inform it (in quite various ways in different human cultures), is gradually internalized as one learns to say "I"—that is, learns what it means to be an "I" of this particular sex and race and class in this particular culture—and thus emerges into self-consciousness.

These complex structures of meaning (our words) are not learned simply abstractly and by rote, of course, as one might attempt to acquire the vocabulary of a foreign language. From the beginning they are directly interconnected with the most fundamental biological needs and feelings of human beings—for example, of mother and child for each other. These meanings are, in fact, just these very organic states and connections, but now transposed into a new key by being articulated in speech and in this way emerging into consciousness. As examples like that of Helen Keller show quite clearly, it is speech, or some direct substitute for vocal speech in those physiologically incapable of it, that makes full self-consciousness possible.

Kant has argued (along with many subsequent writers) that such self-consciousness—awareness of oneself as subject of one's own experiencing—is an indispensable ingredient of what we (in the West) call "experience," that is, it is a central dimension of what the word "experience" means (to us). Apart from the human acquisition of language, clearly, experience (as contrasted with mere animal awareness) could never have developed, and the emergence from animality of (what appears to us to be) distinctively human life would never have occurred. Of course, language informs our experience in many ways additional to making possible self-consciousness. In language the items and objects of experience, their dimensions and qualities, are named and otherwise articulated, thus enabling us to focus on them in perception, attend to them, compare and contrast them with one another and otherwise express their relations and interconnections, come to understand them as part of the *world,* as belonging to that structured whole within which we live and act. Every dimension and region of consciousness and experience is in this way permeated with and structured by language. This is not to say, of course, that our experience is made up only of words. We experience objects, persons, ourselves, our feelings, all the many things of which our world is composed; but we experience all these things as articulated in, colored, and structured by the language we speak. Whenever we are aware of something, it is of *this particular something* as distinct from *those others* (those others of which I am not in this instant directly conscious but from which my language separates it out and distinguishes it for me): I am aware that it is my *cat* I am stroking now (as contrasted with dogs and mosquitoes, days of the week and the number two, feelings of joy and the institution of marriage); or I am aware in this moment of the dark in the middle of the night and my inability to see anything (in contrast with the daylight of my usual waking experience); or I sense just now a certain underlying but obscure despair in which I live (instead of hope or faith or peace); or my conviction that nirvana is the true and proper goal of all human life comes to mind (in contrast with my awareness of the ceaseless activity and struggle and pain in which we all are daily involved). Unlike the nonlinguistic awareness of other animals, the language we humans have internalized provides us with those patterns of meaning (to which we are not in this instant attending but) which serve as a background in contrast to which each particular meaning gains its distinctness and clarity. Though our language remains almost entirely unspoken in any particular moment, it nevertheless functions as the fundamental ordering principle of experience, helping (by implicit contrasts and comparisons) to focus our interest, our attention, and our commitments.

An agent-self, thus, is not merely a cybernetic mechanism operating within a cybernetic social system. An agent is a self-conscious subject, an "I," a mode of being not only aware of the various features and dimensions of the world in which I am acting at this moment, but also implicitly aware of myself and my immediate feelings, desires, wishes, moods, attitudes. Beyond that, of course, there is much more (not just now being attended to): my knowledge that I have certain abilities and skills and lack others; that some people like me and others despise me; that I have hopes and dreams for myself and those I love and that there may be difficulties in realizing some of these aspirations; that I have had some successes in the past as well as failures; that I am responsible for what I have done and what I am, indeed guilty for my more egregious blunders as well as, perhaps, for the kind of person I have become; and so on. Above all, I am aware in every situation (to a greater or lesser degree, as we shall see later) that I am acting—both *that* I am acting, and that it is *I* who am acting: I must decide what to do; I must assess the situation in which I am acting; I must carry through my act; I am responsible for what I am doing.

Despite this sense of responsibility for what I attempt and what I do, I often become conscious of how tenuous and fragmentary are my powers to act. My action is a projection, a movement into the future, a future which is still indeterminate and which I must help to determine. But there are many other forces which will also shape this future; I may be aware of some of these, but of most I am only dimly conscious, and about many I know nothing at all. How, then, can I decide what is the fitting and appropriate act, the right thing to do, in this situation? How can I determine the goals toward which I should be working, and the most effective way of achieving them? Much about our action, particularly our more important acts, always remains obscure, vague, and in doubt. And yet we cannot avoid moving, acting, deciding; and we cannot avoid taking responsibility for our action. Our past experience has taught each of us how frail and weak and mistaken and blundering we often are in our action, yet we continue to act. We are on an inexorable conveyor belt which forever moves us forward into an unknown future, and we must take responsibility for our part in that future. It is hardly surprising, then, that in many, perhaps all, situations of difficult decision we find ourselves anxious, fearful, wishing to escape, not knowing which way to turn, often trying desperately to avoid acting and taking responsibility.

Of course, the degree of our self-consciousness about all these features of our acting differs enormously at different times and for different persons. In some moments we are quite aware of ourselves as agents who must take full responsibility for what we are doing; at other moments this awareness fades into the background. And some persons, perhaps because of unusual circumstances of class or role or education, may be much more conscious of themselves as agents than others. They are, thus, able to take, or attempt to take, greater responsibility for themselves and their actions than others who have not had such opportunities and consequently have not had the experience of agency which those opportunities afforded. Agency and responsibility—and our sense of agency and responsibility—are not qualities of life that are either fully present or entirely absent: they vary greatly in strength and significance from moment to moment, from person to person, from group to group, from social situation to social situation, from culture to culture, from historical period to historical period. But no individual person or social group, no culture or class or gender or race or historical period is ever entirely devoid of all possibilities for responsible action; nor is any human being ever in a position to take full responsibility for every feature of the future into which she or he is moving. This consciousness of our finitude (from which we never escape) sharply distinguishes us from, and simultaneously provides the basis for, one of the traditional images of God: God seen as the absolutely omniscient and omnipotent one, the one who can and does both know and determine every detail of every future.

From this perspective the ultimate symbol of our human lack of power and control with respect to the future, and our unavoidable movement into the future, may well be *death*. All animals die, but only we humans (the self-conscious animals) are *aware* that we must die—aware, that is to say, that although we always must face a future, one day that future will be gone; aware that although we seemingly must always be projecting, planning, deciding, moving, one day all these projects and motions will be cut off in mid-air, unfinished, incomplete, never to be realized; aware that one day we too will be gone forever, that we will no longer be conscious biohistorical selves, able to appreciate and enjoy our small achievements, to remember moments of joy and happiness, to hope for new and rich experiences of meaning, fulfillment, peace. The great religions have all sought to minister to and interpret the awareness of human finitude that is connected with death. They have developed various mythologies (that is, frameworks of meaning) in terms of which humans could understand this feature of their situation in the world and accept it, could continue to live and act in this life even in face of death. And they have created rituals which provided modes of symbolic action through which participating communities and selves could feel in harmony or at one with those ultimate Powers which sustain and support human life, thus being strengthened in their efforts to live with the suffering and evil that befell them, to face whatever threats of death and destruction life confronted them.

It should be evident that not every mode of interpretation and form of action (together with the subjective moods, attitudes, and beliefs with which these are connected) will be equally conducive to the emergence and exercise of responsible agency within a society or by an individual. The mood of despair or hopelessness, for example—the feeling and belief that there are no truly significant possibilities open to us, the sense that the world is closing in on us and it is impossible to do anything to stop it, that all effort will be to no avail—may render individuals and whole communities completely unable to act. Again, certain sorts of anxieties or fears, accompanied perhaps by beliefs about extreme forms of punishment which will be inflicted upon those who fail, may so upset people that they misperceive the situation in which they find themselves, misjudge what they could do, make bad decisions, and are unable to execute their decisions successfully. A deep sense of guilt—feelings of enormous responsibility for the evil we have wrought in the past, accompanied by self-condemnation and self-hatred because of what we have done and what we have become—may so fixate all our energies on ourselves as to make it impossible for us to turn toward the outside world in action: we are unwilling to take the chance of acting once again and thus moving further into perdition, further deepening our guilt. Or, to take a quite different sort of example, our conception of our place in society, of the roles we are expected to play, may lead us to suppose that certain possibilities, though open to some persons, are not open to us. Or again, our sense of satisfaction with ourselves and our life, our feelings of comfort and ease, may be such that we do not find ourselves motivated to act: we prefer to float easily and lazily down the stream rather than undertake any heavy responsibilities. There are many other psychological, sociocultural, and ideational conditions—deep fears, unrealistic fantasies, oedipal problems, particular self-images, fixations, attachments, compulsions, valuations of various sorts—which may interfere with our capacity to act, warping and inhibiting it or blocking it altogether.

In contrast with these (subjective) conditions which negatively affect action, there are other patterns of belief and feeling which tend to encourage it. For example, attitudes of hope about the future (in contrast with despair) lead men and women to look for possibilities which might otherwise be missed, and to strive to realize those possibilities. Self-confidence with respect to our understanding of what is to be done and our capacity to do it facilitates our moving with sureness and skill. A sense of the significance of the projected activity, and a dissatisfaction with the way things now are, helps to motivate us to act speedily and with effect. Love and respect for others may motivate us to do certain things for their sakes; and awareness that we are loved and accepted by our fellows—that they are ready to support and help us, and that they will forgive our failures and blunders—helps to free us to act in situations of great difficulty. Self-knowledge about these fears and doubts and repressions, these loves and hates, about the complexity of our feelings toward and relations with our associates and with others roundabout is also essential if our actions are to be free of hidden compulsions and prejudices that undermine their effectiveness.

Much more could be said about the conditions that enable and facilitate responsible action in contrast with those which inhibit or block it, but perhaps this is enough to make the point. Human action (as I am developing the concept here) becomes possible only within contexts of instrumentalities and circumstances of the most extraordinary complexity: cybernetic patterns in self and society, and the necessary physiological and physical supports for these; learned patterns of behavior and symbolical facility, together with corresponding social customs, roles, and institutions; and a proper configuration of subjective feelings and moods, attitudes and beliefs—all of these must be in place and properly tensed and balanced and attuned to each other. With this complexity before us we are in a position to draw together our analysis of human agency by considering what it means to speak of human groups and individuals as *free,* as in a significant sense self-determining.

It should be clear by now that it would be a mistake to regard free acts (acts thought of as freely chosen) as simply *spontaneous* in origin, that is, as coming from nowhere, just beginning on their own; the image of spontaneity, often appearing in discussions of human freedom, can be very misleading. A better metaphor is that of *emergence.* Free action emerges out of ongoing processes of activity and striving in an organism, and ongoing sociocultural processes: it is the (gradually emerging) power to guide and order these processes consciously and deliberately (to some extent), to turn them in directions they would not otherwise go. Dynamisms are already present and working in these processes when free agency comes on the scene, and these are presupposed as the matter and power to which the agent gives a distinctive form and direction.

This emergence of free agency is no sudden event—as if, when a certain complexity of organic and social behavior is reached, a threshold is crossed and suddenly freedom is there. Freedom is, rather, a gradual emergent, made possible as several conditions are (concomitantly) realized. Thus, as certain linguistic resources are developed and complex forms of symbolization appear, it becomes possible to envisage certain sorts of potential actions with increasing sharpness and accuracy, and the possibility of comparing and choosing among alternatives arises. This could occur, of course, only after humanity itself had progressed through a long cultural-historical development; language, of the complexity that is required here, was not born in a day. Both the bare possibility of free action and its scope and range, thus, are a function of the historico-cultural process: in certain cultural situations these remain minimal; in others, which supply the necessary patterns of social differentiation and organization together with appropriate resources for symbolization, these may become highly developed. Further (given the necessary sociocultural context), as appropriate behavioral habits and patterns of symbolization, together with the requisite motor skills, are formed in the individual, possibilities for acting, which would not otherwise have been available, begin to appear. As one severely disciplines one's fingers and learns to read music, for example, one gradually becomes able to play the piano—and the possibility of *choosing* to play Chopin thus opens before one. All such choices, of course, become possible only on the basis of a growing reservoir of experience in both communities and individuals. We are able to be aware of the possibilities latent in the several alternatives confronting us because we have experienced similar things in the past; hence, we can now compare the alternatives and decide which we would prefer to actualize on this occasion. Certain subjective conditions, as we have seen, must also be met: communities and selves able to maintain a significant sense of self-identity, self-value, and self-understanding—and thus able to develop and carry through manageable projects without too much disruption—must have emerged. (To the extent that communities or selves are "driven," as we say—that is, virtually controlled—by compulsions and complexes and prejudices, by hates, fears, anxieties, and other such passions, they are unable to act "freely.") Psychological studies suggest that childhood environments in which love, acceptance, trust, and loyalty are experienced (note: these are all *moral* qualities) are most conducive to the development of free and creative and responsible agent-selves; contexts of rejection, neglect, and hatred frequently bring forth warped and stunted selves, often incapable of effective and responsible action. Thus, even in its most intensely subjective and personal dimensions, freedom is not a quality belonging simply to individuals as discrete individuals: it is interpersonal and social in its origins, and it requires an appropriate social and interpersonal context for its continuing nurturance and its exercise.

Action (freedom) is a gradual modification over many generations of what had originally been simply organic patterns of behavior into patterns largely humanly created and thus susceptible (to some extent) of being deliberately chosen. Since our action is always an expression (in part) of its organic base, as well as of the habitual and customary patterns characteristic of earlier stages of social development and the modes of symbolization made possible by the linguistic resources available to us, it never becomes "totally" or "absolutely" free (whatever that might mean). It always remains a modification or qualification of previously existing appetites, habits, and customs over which some degree of deliberate control has been attained. Freedom, then, and its correlative, responsibility, are always matters of degree: it is a mistake to think (as the old determinism debate posed the question) that we humans are either free or not free, that there is some kind of pure or absolute freedom which we either possess or do not possess. In every society some persons are more free than others, at least in certain respects; and every person is more free in some situations than in others—more aware of what he or she is doing, more competent to achieve it, more effective in bringing it about. In some relationships I am freer than in others; with respect to certain tasks I am freer than with others. My "freedom" has to do with the degree to which I am the agent—I have significant control—of my own behavior, and this varies greatly from situation to situation. In some situations I may be so bound up with anxiety or guilt, or so "self-conscious" (as we sometimes say), that I am scarcely able to act at all; in others, when I am with persons who accept and love me, I may feel free "to be myself." My freedom, thus, belongs as much to my context, to the relationships in which I stand, as it does to me. It is simply not possible everywhere and always to be open and spontaneous in speech and action. If I am an accomplished pianist, I am free to express myself through playing Beethoven or Chopin; if I do not have this skill, I do not have this freedom, and correspondingly, I am not as responsible for what I do when I sit at the piano.

Thus, freedom is not a kind of metaphysical quality which we either believe in or don't—and if we are Freudians or Marxists or Calvinists, we don't, because we know about unconscious psychological processes or hidden economic determinants or God's all-powerful will. Rather, the term "freedom" refers to that which distinguishes human *action* from mere behavior; it points to those situations and those respects in which we are in some significant degree *agents,* not merely organisms; it indicates the fact that we in certain respects have control over what we do, and that we can therefore take responsibility for it and be held accountable for it. Although in different societies the degrees and possibilities of freedom may vary greatly among persons of different sexes or races or classes, or according to the social situations in which they find themselves, from the point of view being sketched here all (normal) human beings—male or female, black or white, wealthy or poor—have crossed the basic threshold into free and responsible agency.

This insight into human nature—that freedom is a distinctive and important mark of our humanity, but that there are great disparities in the degrees to which different humans, or groups of humans, are enabled to exercise their freedom—informs and motivates the great liberation movements today. The several "liberation theologies," taking up the Marxist emphasis on the inequality with which social structures and cultural practices distribute power (and thus freedom) among different social groups, have insisted that the "good news" about which Christians speak must include liberation from the various sorts of repression and bondage under which the poor, people of color, and women have been forced to live; only thus can such persons realize their full humanity, and precisely this is promised them in the Christian message that God is bringing salvation from every form of bondage. (Cf. Paul: "For freedom Christ has set us free; stand fast therefore, and do not submit again to a yoke of slavery," Gal. 5:1.) In this emphasis on human freedom the liberation theologies are at one with many other modern movements as well as with certain historic Christian themes. Both Freud and Marx, for example, far from being simple undialectical determinists as is sometimes suggested, devoted their lives to enlarging the scope of human freedom: they sought to deepen our awareness of, and thus to increase our human control over, determinants of our conduct of which we had not previously known. They helped to move into consciousness forces of which women and men had hitherto been "unconscious," in this way making possible some measure of control over them. Just this enlarging of human freedom, enabling men and women to become in a deeper and fuller sense the agents of their own behavior, is what psychoanalysis, as well as the class struggle, is all about.

We are now in a position to expand and deepen a bit further our conception of freedom. Thus far I have been using the idea of deliberate choice among alternative possibilities as the principal metaphor for developing the notion of freedom, but (however important and impressive this may be) it does not yet show clearly the full reaches of our freedom: more significant than our ability to choose among various alternatives confronting us moment by moment is our power to act upon, and to transform, ourselves. All forms of self-discipline, of training the self to do something or be something—reading, studying, developing a skill, practicing various sorts of exercises, meditating—involve a self's actions on itself. (Note once again the circle of self-reflexiveness that is presupposed and activated here.) Such activities are intended to modify the self, to transform it into an agent with possibilities of action and being different from those that presently obtain. Activities like these (in which we are constantly engaged), introducing further cybernetic complications into our picture, involve feedback of the agent directly on its own agency. If my discussion up to this point has suggested that agency, however complicated its internal machinery, is a fundamentally static structure, we can now see that this is quite misleading: an agent is, rather, a living process, a process continuously engaged in transformation of itself (opening up new and different possibilities of action for itself) as well as engaged in transformation of external realities. Through this power of deliberately acting upon ourselves in such a way as to change ourselves into different persons, we take responsibility not only for our particular choices and actions but for our very selfhood, for what we ourselves are and what we become.

We began our consideration of human agency by looking at ordinary everyday human choice, but our analysis has carried us, by its own inner logic, into profoundly moral, even religious, issues: questions about self-acceptance, responsibility, guilt, self-discipline, the meaning of life. Morality and religion, we can now see, are not peripheral matters superimposed on our basic human existence, matters which we can take or leave as we choose: they emerge unavoidably out of what is near the very center of our humanity, namely our agency, that we are in some measure free. Beginning with the next chapter we shall undertake to explore what this involves in more detail.

To be free agents (in the sense I have given to that term here) does not, of course, mean that we are free of external actions upon us; these also decisively determine us. Our selfhood, I have argued, emerges in contexts of, and superimposes itself upon, our bodiliness and our past histories, and these shape and determine it in many respects. Apart from this particular facticity, which defines the particular being that I am, I would be nothing at all; I would have no distinctive character or individuality. However, my facticity by itself, my being acted upon from beyond my self-conscious selfhood—whether by unconscious drives and desires or by God—could not bring me across the threshold from animality into humanity. It is as we each become an "I," as we learn to speak and become aware of and learn to accept and to take responsibility for ourselves, that we transcend ordinary animality and enter into full humanness. For this reason it seems to me a mistake, which blurs and tends to conceal what is distinctive and unique about human existence, to attempt to understand the human simply in terms of such notions as animality or bodiliness, on the one hand, or "absolute dependence" and determination by external powers (whether God or material energies and forces), on the other. None of these concepts (with the possible exception of the idea of God, very carefully interpreted) can, without great pulling and stretching, take up into itself and explicate the peculiar self-reflexive structures of the "we" and the "I," the power of communities and selves to relate themselves to themselves and thus to develop some measure of autonomy and self-direction. To all such deterministic theories we can say: it is only self-reflexive agents, after all, who could create these deterministic theories themselves (whether naturalistic or religious); the very existence of such theories, therefore, is their own disproof, so far as they claim to interpret that which is distinctively human but do not give a satisfactory account of the "we" and the "I." Even creating and advocating such theories as these, is always experienced as *our own doing,* and is thus not interpretable in deterministic terms, for the logic of "our own doing" is not one of *external* determination—no matter how we might feel about this, or what theories might seem to us to have the greatest plausibility in other respects.[4]

In emphasizing in this way the appropriateness of a term like "freedom" for characterizing the distinctiveness of our humanity, I am not making a primarily psychological point—that we humans *feel* free in our action. Rather, I am making an ontic and empirical one: I am suggesting that humans *are* in fact free (in a certain very fundamental sense), however we may feel about it. (Doubtless, as pointed out earlier, our feelings have considerable effect on the degree of freedom which we may be able to exercise in any given situation—some feelings being conducive to our freedom and others inhibitive—but that is a different issue.) What I have been calling "freedom," as we have seen, emerges within a complex configuration of conditions within which men and women come to have some measure of power to shape their own existence and destiny: it is, therefore, their *being free* to do and to be certain things (within this context) that leads to their "feeling" or belief that they are significantly free; not the reverse. Our freedom is at heart an aspect of our human self-reflexiveness: that is, of our having learned to relate ourselves both to those others with whom we are interacting and to ourselves as well, of our having learned to make decisions and take actions which relate us to the world in which we are living.

13. The Interpenetration of Action with Reflection

We began our consideration of human existence by taking note of the enormous diversity of human life, and of cultural and religious traditions, throughout history; and I argued that any understanding of the human adequate for today's world must take into account this diversity. In recent chapters I have suggested that the conception of humans as essentially creative—as persons-in-community who can act, who can take responsibility for themselves and their communities and who are in this sense free and creative agents—can provide us with a helpful way to understand this. According to this interpretation the great historical realities which we call "cultures," the matrices within which successive generations of humans are formed and out of which they grow, are themselves regarded as created by preceding generations of communities and individuals. As each of these varied cultural matrices takes on its own distinctive character in the course of history, distinguishing it significantly from others around the globe, diverse shapes and forms and qualities of human existence are brought into being, and the many forms of humanness of which we today are so aware are created. This approach, thus, provides a way to account for and interpret human life in all its diversity. Moreover, it is an interpretation which (as we saw in Chapter 10), in its emphasis on the centrality of historicity in human existence, provides the basis for proposing a normative account of the human; an account, that is, of the conditions that must be met for human life to continue and to flourish in its distinctly *human* character. In this chapter and the next we shall explore in some detail the way in which the normative dimension of our historicity gives rise to structures of morality and ethics.

Norms and standards of several different sorts are of especial importance for agential beings—beings who can and must act—for central to action is setting purposes and carrying them through, making decisions and choices.

If individuals and communities must set goals and objectives for themselves, they need guidelines and standards and criteria to assist them in identifying and evaluating the most important issues that lie before them. All societies, for this reason, have developed systems of morality—rules and norms of many different kinds, character models, social ideals, and so on—which provide members of the society, and the society as a whole, with guidance on major questions that must be faced in life. And all societies have developed religions—pictures or conceptions of the world, and of the human place within that world, together with rituals and other symbolic modes of action by means of which women and men could participate in and fully identify themselves with this world, thus orienting themselves in life and acquiring motivation to address life's major problems.

These facts raise some important questions: Do some systems of moral norms and values, and some religious conceptions and practices, encourage the emergence of human creativity, freedom, and responsibility more than others, thus more effectively facilitating the realization of our distinctively human potentialities? If so, can these be identified? Does the normative dimension of our historicity provide us with a means for assessing the diverse moral and religious conceptions that have grown up around the globe, thus putting us into a position to appropriate more intelligently and fully those which facilitate human flourishing and fulfillment? Each of the great religious and moral traditions, of course, proposes its own understanding of what brings genuine "salvation" or "liberation" to women and men, and in this way gives its answers to these questions. A major issue which presents itself to constructive theology today would seem to be, thus: How should we assess these many and diverse perspectives and claims which confront us? Is it possible or appropriate to attempt to choose among them? and if so, how? Or should we try to develop an overall position which goes in significant respects beyond all these conceptions inherited from the past? Translating these questions into the terms of Christian theology: In view of this complex of issues, how should we today distinguish *God* from the many idols in our world? How should we construct a valid image/concept of God for our day? In our utterly diverse and conflicted world, what should be the unifying focus for human devotion, work, commitment, worship?

To begin to address these issues more directly, we must return to our analysis of human action and carry it further. Human actions are deliberate movements, movements intended by agents in their efforts to achieve certain objectives which they have set for themselves. Action thus always has an ideational dimension or element to it: intentions, thinking, ideas are taken up into it. We need to pay some attention, now, to the way in which thinking or reflection comes to interpenetrate, and thus to shape or affect, action. I shall, therefore, attempt to unpack more fully some of the patterns of self-

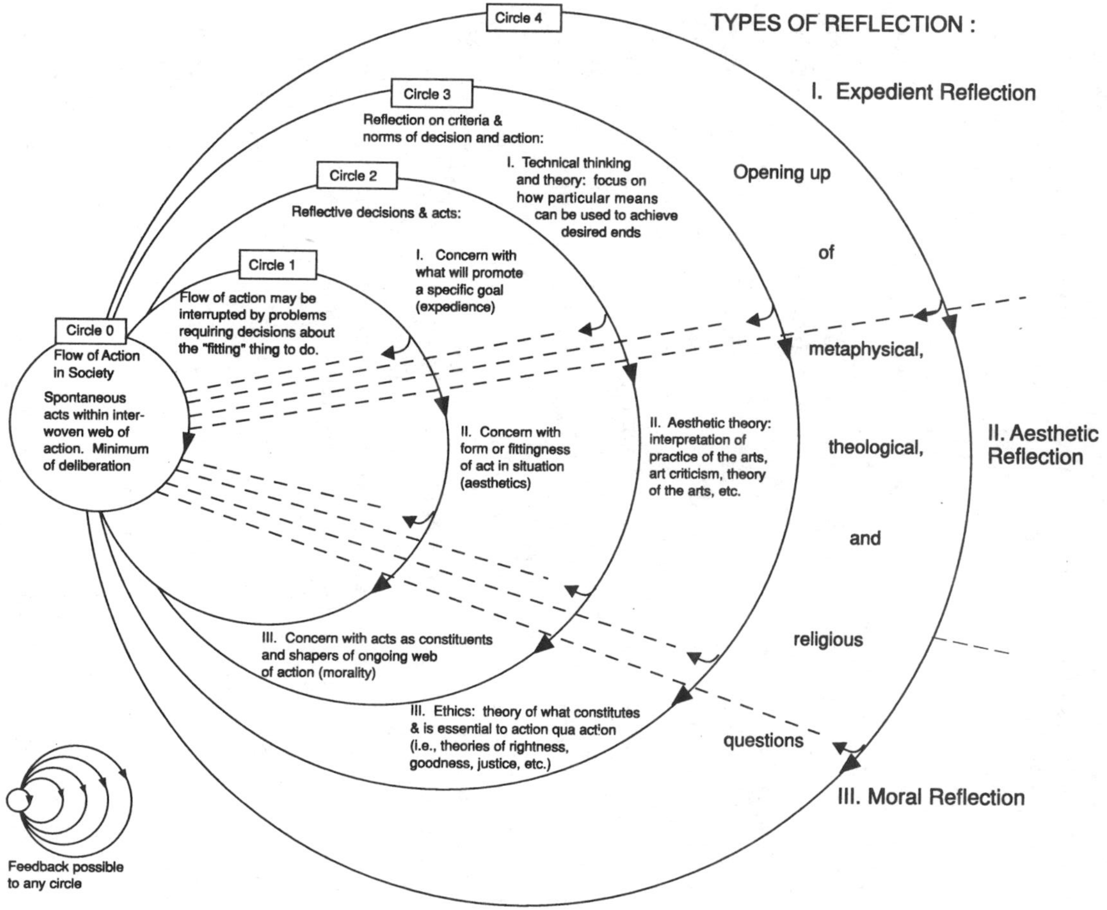
TYPES OF REFLECTION :
I. Expedient Reflection
II. Aesthetic Reflection
III. Moral Reflection
Circle 4
Circle 3
Reflection on criteria & norms of decision and action:
I. Technical thinking and theory: focus on how particular means can be used to achieve desired ends
II. Aesthetic theory: interpretation of practice of the arts, art criticism, theory of the arts, etc.
III. Ethics: theory of what constitutes & is essential to action qua action (i.e., theories of rightness, goodness, justice, etc.)
Circle 2
Reflective decisions & acts:
I. Concern with what will promote a specific goal (expedience)
II. Concern with form or fittingness of act in situation (aesthetics)
III. Concern with acts as constituents and shapers of ongoing web of action (morality)
Circle 1
Flow of action may be interrupted by problems requiring decisions about the "fitting" thing to do.
Circle 0
Flow of Action in Society
Spontaneous acts within inter-woven web of action. Minimum of deliberation
Opening up
of
metaphysical,
theological,
and
religious
questions
Feedback possible to any circle

Figure 3 Interrelationship of action and reflection

reflexivity which (can) get built up in the exercise of human agency, focusing particularly on the way in which *moral consciousness* (as it is called in the West) has emerged and comes to permeate action.

It is helpful in this connection to think in terms of a pattern of increasingly complex feedback loops, beginning with a small, relatively simple circle of what is sometimes called "spontaneous behavior," and moving outward to wider circles of increasing self-consciousness, intentionality, and reflexiveness (see Figure 3). Human motives and actions become transformed and complexified as consciousness of their ramifications deepens, and as reflection thus is increasingly made to impinge on, interpenetrate, and shape further action.[1] We may conveniently distinguish five circles of increasing internal complexity, beginning with the relative simplicity of mere "behaving"—moving with an absolute minimum of reflectiveness or deliberateness—and proceeding through stages to the broadest kind of metaphysical generalization or abstraction, what may be regarded as almost "pure thinking" or pure linguistic activity, with a minimum of physical moving to *do* something. What we will see, as we develop our pattern of feedback loops, is the way in which different sorts of reflective consciousness emerge quite naturally out of action and also redound back upon action, thus transforming it in significant ways; we will also see that moral and ethical consciousness in particular (as distinguished from other sorts of reflexivity) has a special connection with what is central or essential to action, a connection with action per se, as I shall put it. This does not mean that the only significant dimension of action is the moral: there are indispensable "aesthetic" and "expedient" components as well, and these will also be given a place in our overall scheme. Indeed, we will come to our understanding of the moral dimension of action, and of the special significance of that dimension, precisely by seeing its distinctiveness over against these other components.

The analysis I wish to present here can be followed more easily with the aid of a diagram which displays visually the points I want to make. Figure 3 is intended to show the increasing complexity created in action as consciousness interpenetrates it in deeper and deeper respects (from Circle 0 to Circle 4). We shall begin our analysis with Circle 0 of the figure and gradually work through the several positions of increasing reflexiveness.

Circle 0

It is important to observe at the outset that no deliberate human act begins simply from scratch, with someone just deciding arbitrarily to do something that has no connection at all with what has been going on before; every act (as we have noted) appears within a social context which is itself an elaborate structure of ongoing action. Many institutional arrangements and patterns of behavior which enable a society to maintain and advance itself were worked out long before and have become operational: at any given time in the life of a society procedures for attaining important objectives and goals are always already being carried out; specific roles have been differentiated and statuses have been assigned; the society is engaged in a complex pattern of activities, and this provides the matrix within which every new self emerges, gradually learning to act as a member of that society. In this sense society, with its complex of customs, institutions, and ideologies, is always prior to the individual person; it is the necessary condition for there being any individual persons at all. And the ongoing structure of action within the society is always prior to, and provides the matrix for, every individual act performed by a member of that society. Figure 3 expresses this point by showing all acts and all reflection as emergent out of, and modifications of, the ongoing "Flow of Action" in the society (Circle 0). To the extent that this flow of activity simply follows established patterns without encountering serious difficulties or problems, it remains largely unreflective and in that sense spontaneous. Probably most of what any of us does in the course of an ordinary day is of this largely habitual sort, a participation in patterns of action which we earlier took over from the society in which we live. It is this complex of patterns and habits, then, that serves as the foundation or matrix out of which our more individualized acts emerge and on which they continue to depend.

I have designated this circle of spontaneous or unreflective action "0" because from certain points of view it may not be considered *action* (properly so called) at all. In this sort of activity we are not making deliberate choices with respect to what is done; we simply move spontaneously to carry out already established patterns of behavior. To the extent that deliberateness and choice are taken to be indispensable marks which distinguish an *act* from other sorts of behavior, it may seem incorrect to include these underlying patterns of custom and habit as species of action. To draw that conclusion, however, would be misleading. On the one hand, as we have noted, the structures of customary and habitual behavior were themselves built up partly in consequence of deliberate intentions and choices of previous generations, so this sort of behavior cannot be regarded as simply "instinctive" or "natural." On the other hand, it is clear that though we are here concerned with acts performed "spontaneously" or "without thinking," we nevertheless often hold ourselves responsible for them, and we sometimes regard them as worthy of praise or blame; even though such acts may not be deliberate (in the usual sense), we regard them as *our own doing,* something for which we are quite properly held accountable.

Most of our ordinary speaking and acting and moving about in the world, carrying out the routine tasks of life, is of this largely spontaneous unreflective sort which I have designated Circle 0; this is the limiting case of action properly so called. Behavior of a human organism below this level—reflexes, behavior in a trance, "unconscious" behavior, and so on—lies off the chart, and we will not give it further consideration here.[2] For our purposes, thus, it is with Circle 0 that the distinctively human—action, historically shaped and formed behavior, historicity—begins to manifest itself; and it may also be here, where what has been historically created and formed has become spontaneous (that is, "second nature"), that the highest form of the human which we can imagine is to be found.[3] But the latter is a question to which we can return only somewhat later, when our project of imaginatively constructing a conception or vision of humanity in the world under God has been more fully articulated.

Circle 1

The most obvious example of *deliberative* behavior—what some might regard as the prime mark of action properly so called—is to be found in *decision.* Decision is necessitated (in communities as well as individuals) when the ongoing flow of action is interrupted by some problem, and we are faced with alternative possibilities for action among which we must choose. We find ourselves able to move in any of several directions, the direction that we go depending on our choice. In the moment of decision, thus, we become aware both of our responsibility to act and of our responsibility for the action that we take, in a way that is not true of Circle 0—although, as I suggested, we may hold ourselves responsible *retrospectively* for (at least some of) our spontaneous or unthinking acts. In decision, however, we hold ourselves responsible *prospectively,* that is, before the act is performed. The moment of decision thus involves a significantly greater awareness of our own responsibility for our action than was true of Circle 0: the act of deciding is itself a direct taking of responsibility in a significant way.

These two circles, of course, actually shade off into each other (though that is not shown in Figure 3), and no sharp line can be drawn between them. In a conversation do I *decide* what I shall say, or do I simply speak spontaneously? If I am overly careful about my remarks, and take too long deliberating over what to say, my hearers may suspect that I am trying to conceal something or play a role instead of directly and spontaneously opening myself to them. And yet, there are points at which we do deliberately "choose our words," sometimes with considerable care, lest we be misunderstood. Similarly with other kinds of action: though it is not difficult to see that deliberate decision is something quite different from simple spontaneity, it is also obvious that no sharp line can be drawn between them. As we shall see, the movement from Circle 1 to Circle 2 is similarly without any sharp breaks.

What is involved in the direct or immediate choices characteristic of Circle 1? The metaphor of the "fitting" is particularly apt for interpreting this sort of decision that does not require us to undertake deliberate reflection (something to be considered in connection with Circle 2): we simply do what seems to us most fitting in that situation.[4] Imagine a small child with a set of pegs of various shapes which are to be put into the appropriate holes in a board. Only the triangular peg will "fit" into the triangular hole, the square peg into the square hole, and so on. The child is confronted with a simple problem of decision: Which peg fits into which hole? Many everyday examples of this sort of decision can be given: we decide to put on an overcoat before going out into a winter storm, or we decide to lie down and take a nap in late afternoon when we are sleepy, simply because these seem to be fitting things to do under these circumstances. Actions are called forth by particular situations in which something needs to be done; until it is done, something is lacking in the complex structure of action/interaction in which we are living. We seek, therefore, to fit our action into the situation in such a way that the need will be met, the lack supplied, the hole properly filled. Agents exist in situations of living interaction with other agents, within a society that is a structure of such continuous interpersonal interaction. It is when this complex web makes a demand on us to act that we act. When someone puts a question to me, or issues a command, or confronts me in need, a demand for action that "fits" in this situation is laid upon me. Which peg will fit into this hole? Which of the alternative possibilities before me (including turning my back on the demand confronting me) should I try to actualize? What is the fitting thing to do here?

To respond immediately and spontaneously, without awareness or consideration of any alternatives, is to operate within Circle 0; to be vaguely aware of possible alternatives, but to pass quickly over this one and that as inappropriate and choose another as the fitting thing to do, is to act within Circle 1, simple decision; to hesitate for a moment as I cast about for some maxim or general rule to guide my choice among the alternatives is to respond *reflectively,* that is, to move to Circle 2 (which we shall take up in a moment).

This sort of immediate and direct judgment-and-decision about the "fitting" thing to do is largely aesthetic; that is, it is grounded in our intuitions of balance, appropriateness, harmony, even beauty. We have an immediate sense of what the conversation—or other interpersonal interaction—requires, so that its harmony, contrast, meaning, grace, beauty, direction will be extended and, if possible, enhanced; and we seek, in our own move, to contribute accordingly. Like a painter who is trying to decide whether it would be better to deepen that red spot or to cover it with some other color, we usually make our decisions about what to do next in the steady flow of life on the basis of our judgment about what fits best in this particular situation. Without this aesthetic or intuitive sense of what is going on in the processes of interaction in which we are engaged, and what would contribute to their furtherance, action as we know it would be impossible; we would be capable only of blundering about clumsily.

Circle 2

The human sensitivity to the fitting (expressed particularly in Circle 1) underlies and grounds the interpenetration of action with the several types of reflection that come into view in wider circles of agential consciousness. In Circle 2, distinctions among the expedient, the aesthetic, and the moral dimensions or modalities of action emerge; and it is only when this degree of consciousness is reached, therefore, that explicit concerns about these matters arise. This does not mean that the issue of fittingness is now left behind; rather, it becomes complicated by new and distinctive considerations, and thus the "fitting" itself becomes transformed (in the more complex circles) into something more comprehensive, self conscious, and nuanced. There are situations in which we find ourselves unwilling or unable to make an immediate intuitive decision about the fitting thing to do; so we step back for a moment to *reflect* on the matter. It will be useful for our purposes here to distinguish three distinct sorts of deliberation and reflection which may be undertaken at this point, concerning questions of expediency, of aesthetics, and of morality. Let us consider expediency first.

Perhaps the most common first move that we make when we encounter a problem is to remind ourselves of what it is that we are trying to do. If we can get our objective clear, and see what is hindering us from achieving it, we may be able to ascertain what needs to be done in order to resolve the difficulty. I decide to leave the room that I am in, but when I get to the door, I discover that it is stuck. What should I do? Perhaps if I give it a good hard kick it will open and I can be on my way. This sort of reflection and decision I refer to as "expedient," because it is concerned only with the immediate end that I am pursuing (in this case, getting through the door and on my way). No other considerations are taken into account, such as, for example, about the form or style of the act I wish to perform (Is this an aesthetically pleasing act, one that is intended to be harmonious with its setting?); or about its moral quality (Would it be right to do this?). The only question I entertain is, How can I get through this door quickly? Many of the decisions that we make every day are concerned, like this, simply with expediency; and there is nothing wrong with that. If we stopped to ask about aesthetic or moral considerations every time we took a step, we would never get anything done.

A strong interest in expediency, reflecting as it does a central dimension in our acting (that we are attempting to do something) is, thus, quite legitimate.

The expedient dimension of action, when developed and expanded through deliberation and reflection on the many sorts of things we humans wish to do, produces the wide range of skills and crafts found in every culture. Crafts are essentially elaborate structures of rules and practices for achieving certain objectives, elaborate systems of maxims and habits of expedience which guide the work of the craftsperson. There are, of course, many such complexes of maxim and habit and skill which are not the property of any specific craft because they must be learned by all of us; acquiring these is part of the basic process of socialization and enculturation in our society—how to speak the common language; how to hold a fork while eating; how to drive a car; and so forth. In the modern era this concern with means-ends relationships, and the corresponding reflection on the most effective techniques for achieving certain ends, has been developed to a high degree of self-consciousness, becoming a distinct major sector of civilization that we call "technology." Modern technology has (as is well known) given rise to enormous new problems for human beings: with its single-minded focus on expediency, it now so dominates the whole of human life that it may destroy us all. In its origins, however, technology was innocent enough: it is simply an extended elaboration and development of one of the central characteristics of action, that we are seeking to attain some end or objective.

Action is not constituted solely by means-ends relationships, however; it also always has a form or style. We have noted that in acting we seek to do the fitting or appropriate thing in the specific situation in which we find ourselves. It is not surprising, then, that we humans attend to, reflect on, seek to shape, refine, and elaborate this dimension of action as well as means-ends relationships. The child's attempts to draw a's and b's with more accuracy and smoothness when learning to write, the golfer's attention to proper form in swinging the club, the dancer's incessant practice directed toward moving with perfect ease and grace—all of these are examples of attending to the *form* of action. This kind of concern—clearly distinct from attention to what the act is *for* (its objective or goal) or whether it is *right* (its moral quality)—is directed to the way in which the act is being performed: whether with grace and style and balance, how smoothly and beautifully it fits into the situation, and so on.

Much of the artistic and aesthetic side of human life develops out of attention to this dimension of action. Important traditions—what we call "the arts"—have grown up around, and have further cultivated, our interests in matters of form and harmony, beauty and fittingness. As these became distinctive spheres of culture, they in turn generated further reflection, producing theories of the arts, of music, of beauty, art criticism, and so forth, all concerned with the aesthetic side of human living. It has been in part a growing reawakening of these concerns, after prolonged attention in the West to largely utilitarian goals, that has given rise to increasing criticism of the way in which modern technology has been destroying the beauty of our environment, creating ugliness and pollution instead. Surely, the critics say, there is a better way—that is, a more fitting way, a way more harmonious with the world we live in and with the true needs and the overall quality of human life—to realize our objectives. Such criticism of the concentration on expediency in our culture is certainly valid and important; but it is equally important to note that it is essentially *aesthetic* in character and should not be confused with *moral* critique (as it often is).

In what, then, does properly *moral* reflection and criticism consist? What further question—distinct from questions about the goal or objectives of an act and questions about its form or fittingness (about expediency and about aesthetics)—can be asked of action? We can also concern ourselves, I suggest, with what we could call the act *qua* its being an *act,* that is, *qua* its being a free and responsible expression or movement of an agent. Earlier we noted the complex structures of society and selfhood which must be in place before there can be action properly so called at all, and without which it could not continue to be sustained—social networks of differentiated roles and statuses, institutions, behavioral patterns, linguistic and ideological traditions, on the one hand; and on the other, complex feedback networks (in individuals) of body control, behavioral habits and skills, linguistic facility, mental training and discipline. Every new act performed will have its effect upon, and will make its contribution to, this complex interconnected web indispensable to action. Agents—whether individuals or communities—are, of course, quite as responsible for these wider consequences of their acts as for the immediate objectives or goals intended (expediency) or the way in which the acts are performed (fittingness). As we have seen, it is through the growth of human agency over many generations that the networks making action possible have been created; and it is only through the responsible exercise of further human agency that these will be sustained and further developed. When we ask the distinctively *moral* question—Is it *right* to do that?—we are asking about this quality of the act as *responsible doing,* that is, about the quality of the act *qua* its being precisely an *act.* This is something significantly different from asking whether the act is "expedient" or whether it "fits" well within its immediate context. Here we are asking about such things as: Is the intention expressed in the act a *responsible* one, that is, does it take into account all that should be taken into account in connection with this act? Has the act been carried through in a responsible way? Is the agent (whether a self, a community, or a nation) acting responsibly in performing this act? In posing questions like these, moral reflection and criticism raise more fundamental and far-reaching issues than either expedient or aesthetic reflection, for here action in its distinctive character as free and responsible doing by selves and communities is being scrutinized.

These assertions, of course, remain to be justified; and that can be accomplished only by examining the functions which morality, and moral language, perform in our common life. (I shall endeavor to set forth such an examination in the remainder of this chapter, and shall sketch out an ethics appropriate to it in the next.) The label "moral" is generally applied in our society to certain rules that it is claimed should govern our behavior, to virtues and vices said to distinguish persons who are "moral" from those who are not, to ideal norms or values like justice and equality in terms of which we judge social institutions and practices, and so on. What have these to do with action-as-such? There are, of course, many theories of morality, and my claim about the unique interconnection of morality and action has perhaps not often been so explicitly made.[5] What argument can be given for it? I propose to address these questions by developing this sketch of the interpenetration of reflection and action further, incorporating an analysis of morality into it. That is, I wish now to show how specifically moral issues, in a distinctive form of reflection found in Circle 2 consciousness, emerge out of, and bear back upon, the more primal circles of action we examined earlier in this chapter (Circles 0 and 1).

As we have been noting, acts are complex connecting links between agents, on the one hand, and the sociocultural situation(s) in which the agents are acting, on the other; and both the larger society and the agents acting within it are complex cybernetic structures. Moreover, virtually all acts serve a variety of ends or objectives, some far removed from the immediate situation and others not even known to the agent or to anyone else. So an act is seldom a matter of simply fitting one piece of a jigsaw puzzle into its appropriate place, leaving everything else unaltered. It is an expression of an agent, but it also brings about certain alterations within the agent; it fits into a sociocultural nexus but it also transforms that nexus into something new and different, something calling for further acts by this agent and others. In short, a particular act is a living link in a number of chains of connection: some of these run outward in a variety of directions throughout the society; some penetrate backward into the depths of the agent's own character; all involve projections and guesses about an indeterminate and unknown future. *And we who are about to make our decision and perform the act are vaguely aware of all these matters.* Of course, in many of the trivial decisions we make, these wider effects and more general characteristics of our actions are relatively unimportant, and they remain largely unnoticed. But with our weightier choices we may feel impelled to make some judgments about this more far-reaching, though much less determinate, significance of what we are about to do. This awareness of and concern with the ramifications of our action on the action-network itself, both in our society and in our selves, is the root of the third distinctive sort of reflection on action, what we call *moral* reflection.

The movement from spontaneous action and direct decision (Circles 0 and 1) to specifically moral reflection on action (Circle 2) gradually developed in the long course of human history as concepts and categories were created which focused on and helped to call attention (in various ways in different cultural and religious settings) to what was required for free and responsible action. As I have indicated, all three dimensions of action which become visible within Circle 2 consciousness—expedient, aesthetic, and moral—are present implicitly in Circles 1 and 0; that is, our interest in the "fitting" thing to do in these less self-conscious circles includes an implicit awareness that we are indeed trying to *do* something as well as an intuitive sense of the meaning and importance of the interpersonal network within which we live and are acting and which nourishes our very being. But it is not until Circle 2 consciousness that each of these becomes sufficiently differentiated from the others to be attended to independently and thus developed in terms of its own intrinsic significance and integrity. The attainment of this degree of self-consciousness—accompanying the historical appearance of distinctive arts and crafts and skills—represented, of course, an enormous gain for human creative potential. It was a gain, however, which exacted a price; for concentration of attention, interest, and effort on one thing means diverting them from something else. So what had been unified and whole in the more primal stages and circles of consciousness (0, 1) now (in Circle 2) becomes broken apart and distributed to different moments of time, different members of the community, different social groups and classes (or castes), even to different genders and races.

In simpler societies than our own, where members of most communities live in more or less continuous face-to-face relation with one another, this differentiation of function occurs within the context of a relatively integrated communal whole, so the several dimensions of responsible human life and action remain in significant interconnection and interdependence with each other. But in large urban populations, and especially in highly differentiated and pluralistic mass societies like those of modernity, the independent development of each of these dimensions may go so far as to destroy their effective interaction with and relativizing of the others. Thus, we today have a civilization with an uncontrolled technological sector threatening us all; with art created simply "for art's sake"; with a "high wall" between religion, on the one hand, and politics and economics, on the other; with females confined largely to "the domestic sphere" or lower-level service functions, and "public life" and managerial assignments largely the prerogative of males; and so on.

In all this differentiation, specialization, and development, whole segments of a society may lose sight of the significance of the moral dimension of human life and action, or may regard it as important only in the relatively private sphere of personal relations. Since, however, the function of the moral dimension is to protect and enhance the conditions indispensable to the development of free and responsible action throughout human life, it should come as no surprise that we are now discovering that the very foundations of our society have become badly eroded, and our civilization—indeed possibly the entirety of human life—may now be about to self-destruct. Given the enormous confusions today about morality and its fundamental human significance, it is urgent that we gain a clearer understanding of the important functions of moral language and concerns, so that we can more directly address these dangers now confronting us.

The movement of consciousness to Circle 2, as I have suggested—whether concerned with issues of expediency, fittingness, or morality—is reflective; it involves an appeal to maxims or rules or practices (transmitted in our cultural and religious traditions) which can give guidance as persons or communities make decisions about what to do in case of certain quite specific problems. In the case of the moral dimension of consciousness this movement seems to go in three distinct directions, toward searching out rules or maxims for ascertaining the "right" thing to do in a given situation, toward inquiring into the moral characters of agents, and toward making judgments about the social context or situation as a whole in terms of pertinent social ideals. Each of these moves of emerging moral consciousness is a step toward greater or more explicit rationality in the human awareness of action: it expresses an attempt to grasp action in terms of wider or more general principles, bringing greater universality into our understanding. This is a movement which in our knowledge of action resembles the movement from *per*ception to *con*ception in our spectating knowledge. Our moral concepts, as we shall see, can be understood as *action concepts:* they enable us to focus and reflect upon those features of action without which it would not be free and responsible doing. They direct our attention to that which (in a perceived act, agent, or situation) has import for us *qua* our being actors, that is, *qua* our responsible doing.

Consider the way in which such ordinary perceptual concepts as "table" function. This concept enables us to distinguish certain objects (percepts) from others, instantly discerning the meaning they have for us and their usefulness to us. It furnishes us with what we could call criteria of *tableness;* and we use these criteria to identify something as a "table" when we see it, or, in certain circumstances, to identify something that can be used as a table when no actual table is available (for example, we may choose a large flat rock as our "table" when we are picnicking in the wilds). The concept "table" contains within itself a number of subconcepts—"writing table," "dining table," "lamp table," et cetera—each with specialized criteria important for particular purposes. Concepts of this sort function normatively as well as descriptively: by means of the criteria with which they provide us, we make judgments as to whether a particular writing table is "well built" or "well designed" (that is, can function adequately or only marginally as a writing table), whether it needs extensive repairs or is so dilapidated as no longer to be usable, and so on. Spectating concepts of this sort are employed constantly. Some, like "jump" and "run," "laugh" and "cry," identify and classify forms of behavior simply as *behavior* (that is, without respect to questions about responsible action, questions about our powers of self-determination); others, like "effectiveness," "success," and "energy use," though often used with reference to "acts," direct our attention primarily to considerations of expediency; still others, such as "grace," "style," "harmony," "fittingness," identify aesthetic qualities. All of these are to be distinguished from the action concepts with which we are especially concerned now—that is, moral concepts—though they function in similar ways in certain respects.

Concepts like "honesty," "stealing," "courage," "justice," "loyalty," "equal rights," and the like, in contrast with those just mentioned, focus attention specifically on the respects in which *free and responsible doing* is expressed in the acts, agents, and social situations to which they are applied.[6] These moral concepts, thus, enable us to discern the meaning and significance of what we are experiencing and doing with respect specifically to our concern to be responsible agents in the fields of action within which we are operating. In a way similar to our spectating concepts, our moral concepts provide us with criteria for assessing the diverse features of various instances of agency, comparing them with one another, judging their importance: "Bill is loyal in a way not true of Jack"; "It is unjust for the poor to be taxed as heavily as the rich"; "A 'little white lie' is really not dishonest in the way a malicious falsehood is"; and so on. It is obvious in examples like these that our moral concepts are functioning normatively (as well as descriptively); what is not so obvious, perhaps, is that this normative functioning (as with our spectating concepts) follows naturally and directly from their being abstracted out of the flow of experience and action and then generalized so as to apply to a wide range of instances. In contrast with our spectating concepts, however, the normativeness of our moral concepts provides us with criteria by means of which we judge human behavior (including our own) not simply as *behavior* (as with some of the concepts mentioned above), but as free and responsible doing. These concepts thus apply directly to *us* in a particular way (and not only to objects external to us): we use them to focus attention on, and help us control, our own action, what we are doing, what we are responsible for; and for this reason we *feel* their normativeness in a personal subjective way. Since we judge our own selves and acts in terms of these moral concepts, they exercise a direct constraint upon us and our activities.

Moral concepts call attention to features bearing on what we can call the "moral quality" of acts, agents, and situations. For example, consider the concept of "truth" as used in the moral injunction to "tell the truth." The word "truth" here is not intended to call attention simply to what fits easily or well into the situation at hand—the truth may be embarrassing or insulting; nor is "truth" necessarily a way to gain our immediate objectives at this moment—a lie might be much more effective for that purpose. "Truth" refers here to a certain desirable quality of speech-acts, namely, that what is uttered be trustworthy, that it may safely be believed by the hearer (irrespective of its apparent fittingness or the consequences which might ensue). When we say that it is *right* to tell the truth and *wrong* to lie, we are declaring that it is important for speech-acts to possess this particular quality of trustworthiness. Why is this the case? The answer to that question can be very simple and straightforward: if what we say proves not to be trustworthy, the network of interpersonal trust on which effective communication among men and women depends will be weakened a bit; and with each new failure of trust, it moves further toward complete breakdown. Similar considerations hold for other moral injunctions such as "Keep your promises!" "Act justly!" and the like. The moral concepts employed in maxims of this sort all focus on the quality of our acts as such, that is, their quality as *responsible doing;* and this focus provides us with a distinct, and very significant, way of examining and criticizing our activity, and of bringing an important kind of consistency and order into it. As we shall see when we move to "ethical" reflection in Circle 3, this is a consistency and order that is absolutely essential if the fragile social fabric of human life as we know it is to be maintained—certainly if it is to develop to higher levels of complexity and meaningfulness.

Moral constraints are laid upon us by the society within which we emerge into selfhood, as we internalize the language and the patterns of action of that society. Often, therefore, they are not felt to be directly connected with the immediate situation of action (as are expedient and aesthetic constraints) but to be imposed from without. For this reason moral constraints are frequently interpreted as *commands* or *imperatives* to which we ought to submit (but which we may, if we choose, resist); and it is not surprising that it is sometimes claimed that they have been heteronomously imposed. This way of putting the issue is misleading, however, for the moral concepts we use—which give our moral experience its distinct character and specifications—are, after all, *our own concepts,* carried in the very language and mores that *we ourselves* speak and practice: these are *our* norms in terms of which we do our own judging, not someone else's; these are our own yardsticks. The authority of morality, therefore, is not in any simple way heteronomous; it is grounded on our own usage and practices.[7] Our moral terms and concepts enable us to see with specificity and detail just what is involved in *responsible* doing, that is, what is involved in action in its fullest and deepest sense. (In Chapter 14 I shall spell out these contentions in more concrete terms with reference to Kant's analysis of morality.)

In a pluralistic culture such as ours there are many tensions and conflicts among the moral concepts available to us. From the perspective of some of these concepts others may appear particularly heteronomous, externally imposed—compare, for example, "justice" and "freedom" (and their implied emphasis on "self-realization") with "law and order" (connected closely with the sense of duty and discipline). Tensions of this sort are probably present even in relatively monolithic cultures. The very processes of abstraction and generalization through which our moral concepts are created lead necessarily to emphasis on one feature of action and experience at the expense of those others which the concept does not highlight: there seem to be intrinsic and ineradicable tensions between the implications of "freedom" and "equality," for example, or "truth-telling" and "love" (to the extent that the latter involves concern for another's feelings). Thus it appears that the very movement toward a deeper self-awareness and rationality in our agency and of our agency—through the development of moral language and consciousness (Circle 2)—gives rise to new problems and irrationalities. In a pluralistic society, of course, many of these ambiguities and tensions in the available moral language become magnified into outright contradictions. It becomes necessary for us to move, then, to a broader and more comprehensive reflective circle than that of morality (Circle 2), namely that of ethics (Circle 3), in order to examine, reflect upon, and come to some understanding of these enormously complicated issues. (We have, in fact, already made just such a move in the interpretation of morality that I have begun to sketch here. It is time, therefore, that we turn directly to Circle 3 consciousness, so we can see more clearly just what is involved in this move.)

Circle 3

In ethics we seek both to come to an understanding of our moral categories and concepts and to inquire into their justification. This brings us into a position from which we can assess the competing claims in our moral language (Circle 2) and begin to find a way to address these tensions deliberately, instead of remaining victim to the cultural pressures and conflicts to which they give rise. Through moving to a more comprehensive circle of consciousness (Circle 3) and creating "meta-concepts" in terms of which our moral concepts (Circle 2) can themselves be examined, interpreted, and evaluated, we gain some degree of rational control over their conflictive relationships and patterns. Ethicists seek to develop fundamental "principles" from which our customary moral concepts can be shown to derive. If such principles can be uncovered, we are enabled to see which usages and practices are justified and which misleading, which are overemphasized and which neglected, et cetera. The search for and the attempt to formulate ethical principles necessitates the creation of notions of sufficient generality to rationalize and bring some order into the more or less chaotic patterns of moral concepts, rules, and practices governing behavior in our culture. It is, thus, an attempt to gain fuller understanding of action, and thus further rationality in our action, through developing language and concepts within which we can assess and reconstruct our (Circle 2) moral language.*

When I say that in ethical reflection we move to more comprehensive concepts and principles from which traditional moral rules, virtues, and the like can be "derived," I do not mean that we will be turning now to some supposedly universal principles found in our reason. In views of that sort reason appears to be thought of as a kind of independent storehouse of truth; and ethical reflection becomes essentially a matter of uncovering and articulating those moral principles—universally true, binding on all women and men—which reason makes available to us. Many ethicists have argued in this way, particularly so-called intuitionists and rationalists, who have often held that such notions as "rightness," "goodness," and "justice" are valid and true for all times and places; and the business of ethics is to intuit and formulate that truth, showing its significance for human life. My use of the word "rational" here is quite different from that, much less imposing: I mean by this word to refer simply to our powers of symbolization, our powers to abstract, generalize, criticize, and evaluate. "Reason" is the name we use for our capacity to move imaginatively (by means of signs and symbols) beyond the givens of an immediate situation, comparing these (in terms of common elements, similarities and differences, and so on) with others; it refers to our ability to create (symbolic) standards and criteria for assessing what confronts us, and to imaginatively develop (symbolic) plans and programs for reorganizing or reconstructing aspects of this world in which we find our-

*There is a similar movement in our spectating knowledge from "common sense" experiential concepts (corresponding to Circle 2) to a correction and revision of these through more general ones developed in scientific laws and theories (Circle 3). For example, though our ordinary language still preserves the perceptually based belief that "the sun rises in the morning," we have all come to accept on theoretical grounds that in fact the sun does not go around the earth at all in the way suggested by this expression, but that the earth is itself round, is rotating on its own axis, and is in orbit around the sun.

selves. Thus, I do not understand our reason to be a kind of reservoir or bank from which our moral rules and principles can be withdrawn as needed; it is, rather, simply our critical capacity to discern, assess, and revise. The source of our concepts, rules, and principles is nothing else than the creativity involved in this very symbolizing activity itself: the activity of abstracting an element from the immediately given (through representing it symbolically) while simultaneously significantly transforming this symbolical abstraction through generalizing it to wider contexts.

This is an activity which begins (tacitly) already in Circle 1, with its intuitive sense of what is "fitting" in the immediate situation; but it becomes increasingly explicit and self-conscious as we become aware of wider, less obvious considerations which must be taken into account in action. Our every action, for example (as we have noted), has many effects reaching beyond the immediate goal posited in it, effects on the whole complex network of action; and it is shortsighted, therefore, to confine ourselves only to matters of expediency or immediate fittingness. The intuitive sense of these wider ramifications of action has led in every culture to the creation (through abstraction and generalization) of something like our (western) moral rules, concepts, ideals (Circle 2); as new contingencies force the examination, criticism, and reformulation of these customary patterns of (moral) thinking and acting, consciousness continues to widen and deepen (and in that sense it becomes further rationalized) as conceptions and principles of wider generality and more universal import are sought and gradually articulated (Circle 3). What occurs here is not unlike what happens as our spectating knowledge grows into science: reason does not function as a storehouse containing truths about the world which scientists gradually uncover; it is rather simply our capacity to create concepts and principles of wider and wider generality. Similarly with our moral consciousness: reflection on the moral dimensions (Circle 2) of our institutions, customs, and patterns of action and thought leads to the formulation (in Circle 3) of principles of increasing generality intended to interpret what is going on in all of these, thus enabling us to introduce greater order, meaning, and rationality into them. In Chapter 14 I will outline (briefly) an ethics that sums up and draws together these various issues, further illuminating our action and historicity. We will, thus, move from the analytical-critical mode of Circle 3 consciousness (which we have been exercising in the latter part of this chapter) to a more explicitly constructive mode; and I will attempt to articulate more systematically the ethics of action and historicity which has occasionally begun to come into view in these pages.[8]

14. An Ecological Ethic

It will not be possible here to set out a full ethical position; that would require much more space than would be appropriate in a book such as this. Nor will it be possible to analyze and assess, in terms of the schemata I am developing in this work, the various ethical theories which have appeared in western philosophy and theology.* I will, however, develop my own position in part by indicating some of its connections to that of the classical ethicist whose work (despite significant problems in it) seems most sensitive to distinctions

*It would be illuminating in many ways to undertake such an examination of major ethical proposals. For example, it would be possible to show quickly (with the aid of distinctions made in the last chapter) that simple teleological theories (such as hedonistic utilitarianism) essentially reduce action to goal-directed behavior (that is, attention is paid almost exclusively to what I have called the dimension of "expediency"). It would not be difficult to show that many of the problems which the critics of modern utilitarianisms have uncovered result from this narrow reductionistic approach. The great classical teleologist Aristotle, in contrast, took a much broader (if less consistent and systematic) approach; he is not, therefore, subject to the same criticism. Although Aristotle held that all action is undertaken with happiness as its ultimate objective, he also held that unless one seeks virtue for its own sake, true happiness will never be reached. Aristotle saw, thus, that the moral quality of acts *(rightness)* and the moral character of agents are as irreducible and important as the goal being sought in action. Acts must be done, he said, "at the right times, with reference to the right objects, towards the right people, with the right motive, and in the right way" (*Nicomachean Ethics,* II, 6). Aristotle thought, however, that virtue had this importance because unvirtuous acts lead to unhappiness, that is, he understood ethics to be fundamentally teleological, with the ultimate goal of human action (happiness) being the ground of morality; he did not take seriously enough the fact that sometimes happiness can be promoted by morally wrong policies and actions (for example, through breaking a promise) and that virtue often goes unrewarded. As our schema of action and morality suggests, the independent importance of virtue and rightness (which Aristotle seems, inconsistently, to have affirmed) requires us to recognize that these have a ground distinct from the goal-directedness of human activity. The failure of teleological theories of ethics to note this point leaves them incomplete and misleading in their understanding of both human action and morality.

I have been attempting to make—a philosopher to whom I am deeply indebted in many ways—Immanuel Kant.

Kant saw that behavior done from a sense of obligation or duty has a different *quality* than behavior that simply expresses inclination or desire. Indeed, duty may require us to go against all our inclinations: this is why moral struggle is sometimes so difficult. According to Kant, a moral act is one deliberately willed because it is the *right* thing to do, regardless of our likes or dislikes. Morality is possible and actual, therefore, only because human *willing* is possible and actual; it is bound up with the voluntariness or freedom which (as we have been observing) is the distinctive mark of human acting and is to be contrasted with mere physical behaving or moving.[1] Kant is very clear that the moral dimension of acts is to be sharply distinguished from the telic dimension; his carefully drawn distinction between "hypothetical imperatives" (derived from particular goals being sought) and the "categorical imperative" (which is unconditional) is in fact the classical locus for this fundamental point.[2]

A moral act, according to Kant, is one done in accord with the categorical imperative. The first version of the imperative which Kant presents in elucidating this point is the one commonly regarded as most fundamental for him: "Act only according to that maxim by which you can at the same time will that it should become a universal law."[3] Kant is suggesting here that the principle which is operative in all moral rules is universalizability. Truth-telling, for example, in sharp contrast with the incoherent and parasitic character of lying, is universalizable; and it is thus self-sufficient, self-sustaining, and self-propagating. It is because of the basic self-contradictoriness of an act of lying, in Kant's view, that our reason has developed a moral rule prohibiting it. Similar analyses of other moral rules (for example, against stealing, committing suicide, disloyalty, and the like) show that each of them protects us against significantly incoherent or self-contradictory action. Putting this in the terms of my analysis here, we can say that for Kant what customary morality (Circle 2) does is work toward the rationality of human action by formulating maxims and rules against the various tendencies of our wishes and desires to lead us in irrational directions. That is its importance, and that accounts for the categorical character of its imperatives: morality is nothing else than our own *reason* commanding us to act rationally.

I want to draw a slightly different point from Kant's analysis. He is certainly correct in pointing out the basic incoherence of such acts as lying and stealing; but, in my view, it is not simply this incoherence (that is, mere formal inconsistency) that our moral rules are to ward off, but rather the utter irrationality of acting in ways that undermine or tend to destroy the very social fabric that makes all distinctly human life (and action) possible.

The regular practice of telling the truth (as we noted in Chapter 13) is required to create, maintain, and enhance the context of trust without which neither lying nor truth-telling could exist at all, that is, without which there could be no significant interaction—not even simple conversation—among women and men.[4] Every lie, moreover, although parasitic on this context of trust, actually helps to undermine it. The importance of our moral rules then, I want to emphasize, is not only that they protect us against incoherence in our actions, but that they are guides to the sorts of action which are required to sustain the social, interpersonal, and intrapersonal feedback networks without which human historical existence could not continue. Action that violates these guides introduces into the social fabric momentums moving human existence toward its own self-destruction, while right actions help to keep open the possibilities of further action, and thus have a fecundity for further action. Morality, thus, is concerned at its heart with matters bearing directly on human survival; it supports and strengthens human beings in their agency, in their basic historicity.

This brings us to a second important point in Kant's analysis: he uses his concept of the categorical imperative not only to clarify our understanding of moral *acts,* and the rules and maxims which are supposed to govern them; his exposition is also directed toward illuminating our existence as *agents,* as the doers of these acts, as persons. The unique status—Kant calls it "dignity"—of human agency is addressed by Kant in the second and third versions of the categorical imperative. The second version reads like this: "Act so that you treat humanity, whether in your own person or in that of another, always as an end and never as a means only."[5] That is, persons—as free and responsible agents, and thus in important respects self-determining and with projects of their own—should never be dealt with as mere "things," mere instruments for the purposes of others; they are always entitled to special respect. This widely known version of the categorical imperative expresses Kant's profound awareness of the distinctiveness of human beings as bearers of reason and moral responsibility, and the unique dignity that these confer.[6]

Translating these ideas into the terms of our analysis, we can say that Kant is here addressing the moral significance of the fact that actions cannot be properly understood simply in and by themselves but are living connective links between agents: only attitudes and action that respect the freedom and responsibility of all those others that they touch—in that way helping to enhance their agency—may, therefore, be regarded as morally *right;* whatever is inhibitive or destructive of such freedom and responsibility is wrong. That is to say, right is here again understood as that which helps to sustain and to enhance the moral fabric which makes all action possible—but now this matter is considered with respect to the persons who, in an important way, themselves constitute that fabric. When interpreted in this way, it becomes clear that the second version of the imperative is really addressed to the same underlying issue as the first, except that now this is expressed with respect to those persons affected by my act rather than in terms of the (moral) quality of the act itself. In both cases the central issue is the maintenance and enhancement of the quality of the social fabric without which responsible and free action could not continue. The fecundity of a community or society for ongoing human existence and action is what morality seeks to protect.

The third version of the categorical imperative—bringing in "the idea of every rational being as making universal law . . . as self-legislative and only for this reason as being subject to the law"[7]—articulates further Kant's view of the basis of human dignity, and provides a transition to his notion of a "realm of ends" (which we will take up in a moment). Agents (persons) are in a significant sense self-determining (Kant's word is "autonomous."):[8] we are the ones who *do* actions and are accountable for them; we are not mere slaves of passion or desire, or of other agents. But we are truly free and responsible (that is, agents) only to the extent and in the respects that we legislate for ourselves truly universal laws, and act in accord with those laws; that is, only as we take responsibility for universal concerns, not merely our own immediate interests or desires.

Here again the Kantian point translates easily and directly into the terms we have been developing: right action is that which maintains and enhances the moral fabric which is its context. Now, however, attention is focused directly on the nature of the agent who is acting (instead of on the act itself, or on the persons affected by it). The complex socio-moral fabric which makes action possible has itself been created by the exercise of human agency, and it can be sustained and developed further only by the continuing exercise of free and responsible action by selves and communities ("self-legislating" wills). It is as important, thus, that we make ourselves accountable to our own agency as it is that we address the other moral issues we have considered. These all belong to one another; they are diverse but interconnected constituents of a single complex whole. The third version of the categorical imperative (interpreted in this way) addresses the same underlying issue as the previous two, this time with respect to the agents who are doing the acting.

With the several dimensions that constitute the complex whole which makes action possible now before us, we turn to Kant's conception of that whole itself. This is expressed in what is sometimes called the fourth version of the categorical imperative (though Kant himself never uses precisely that language): always act as a member of a "realm of ends"![9] That is (putting it in our terms): always act in consideration of the fact that you are a member of a community in which each person is expected to act and interact with the others responsibly, thus mutually supporting and helping to enhance the complex social fabric that makes possible the freedom and responsibility of all.[10] Action is right if it helps to support and build up this complex socio-moral structure (the "realm of ends"); it is wrong if in any way it undermines or otherwise weakens it. Kant is well aware that the social practices and institutions, norms and values, which have made it possible for humans to begin to take responsibility for themselves and their world were created slowly and painfully in a long historical process;[11] and they remain fragile, always in danger of self-destructing. But he believes, also, that his own time is a critical moment in which men and women are becoming aware of their freedom and their responsibilities in a new way, and thus humanity is now in a position to move out of its "adolescence": the task now confronting women and men is to take upon themselves the full responsibilities which fall to them as they come into their majority.[12]

Kant's ethic, thus, is worked out with a specific philosophy of history in mind. He understands that only within the context of certain sorts of social institutions, practices, and expectations is free and responsible action cultivated and encouraged; and these social preconditions can emerge only through very particular historical developments over long periods of time. It is possible, thus, to connect his views directly with a historicistic understanding of moral responsibility and freedom (though he might well find such a linkage surprising), an understanding in which the essential priority of history and society over the individual is recognized, but in which it is also recognized that the flowering of human history is to be seen in the emergence of free and responsible women and men in well-ordered communities of peace and justice. When Kant's injunction to act as a member of a "realm of ends" is put together with his ideas about the historical development of moral communities, we have the rudiments of a holistic picture which ties the several dimensions of action together into a coherent interlocking and interdependent historically developing process. The "fourth version" of the categorical imperative, thus, addresses once more the same basic issue as the other three, except that this is formulated now with respect to the encompassing whole within which are included all the conditions required to make action possible: morality is concerned with the maintenance and enhancement of that historically developing whole, and with its fecundity for the future.

According to the interpretation I am suggesting here, Kant's several versions of the categorical imperative (far from being independent unrelated principles, as some interpreters have claimed) each express an aspect of the same fundamental point (as Kant himself believed);[13] and taken together they contain the rudiments of a full theory of (the moral character of) action. For this theory (when made explicit), moral *rightness*—that is, the principle underlying our moral rules, virtues, social ideals, et cetera—is whatever supports and enhances the web of action, making possible its fecundity for further action. Right action, thus, is that which (a) is in accord with duty and thus consistent with itself at the deepest level; (b) treats agents as *agents,* that is, as "ends in themselves," responsible persons, not as means only; and (c) supports the social fabric of interacting agents (the "realm of ends").

In Chapter 13 I pointed out that all action depends on intuitive aesthetic sensitivities (Circle 1) to what is the fitting thing to do in a given situation. The emergence of explicit moral consciousness (in Circles 2 and 3), we can now see, in no way negates this sense of the importance of acting "fittingly" in the situation in which we find ourselves; rather, it broadens and deepens it. The actual situation within which we must attempt to do the fitting thing is now no longer confined to what immediately confronts us; rather, it shades off imperceptibly into the larger sociohistorical order of which we are part, that order which sustains free and responsible behavior among the women and men with whom we interact, the "realm of ends" within which we live. This is the matrix of our distinctively human mode of existence, and thus of all our acting; and the overriding concern to which moral consciousness is directed is that we do what is fitting within this larger context. Even though a particular action might seem to us aesthetically satisfying and in that sense the "fitting" thing to do in the immediate situation, we can now see that if it is not *morally* fitting, it is not fitting at all; for it is then destructive of (continuing) action, and thus (ultimately) destructive of human existence itself. In making this point I do not mean to suggest that our intuitive sense of fittingness needs to be replaced by considerations first introduced by (Circle 2) morality. Rather, the other way around: since our original intuitions of fittingness in Circle 1 already include social and moral sensitivities (which in Circle 2 develop into more self-consciously moral considerations), our moral concerns should not be interpreted as heteronomous superimpositions on the "simple, natural feelings" we experience in Circles 0 and 1, but rather as articulating, explicating, and widening our primal sense of what is fitting.

In western philosophical traditions morality and ethics have often been understood as essentially rational activity, the "rational side" of the self attempting to take charge of more intuitive "emotional" tendencies, which were often seen as sub-moral (cf. Kant). This represents, in my view, a misleading interpretation of the matter, perhaps due at least in part to the fact that our reflective literature on ethics was produced almost entirely by elite male thinkers with a very strong sense of their own rationality and freedom: conscious of themselves as fundamentally autonomous individuals, they understood ethics to derive from the ability of humans to transcend rationally the practices, ideologies, and customs of their own society in their pursuit of the True and the Good. From this point of view the human moral problem may well have appeared to be essentially an individualistic affair: it has to do with the decisions an individual makes, the difficulties "he" surmounts, the degree of rationality "he" achieves in "his" acts, and so forth. Although the social situation in which the individual acts was often acknowledged in moral reflection, it easily slipped from the center of attention. There is some evidence that the sense of social dependence and interconnectedness present in early human life is often significantly weakened by the socializing practices to which males in western society are subjected,[14] and in particular by educational practices directed toward developing strong individual egos with a sense of their own autonomy and rationality. Given these circumstances it is hardly surprising that the traditions of ethical reflection produced by figures of this sort often took for granted conceptions of rationality, objectivity, and individual autonomy which do not take serious account of the social and historical embeddedness of human existence, action, and reflection.[15] Traditional philosophical and theological conceptions of the human, particularly interpretations of the moral and religious dimensions of life, have nearly always been significantly flawed by this bias, and today it is important to offer suitable correctives for it.

Issues of this sort have increasingly come into view recently, largely because of the growing theoretical articulateness of blacks and women, representatives of groups that heretofore have not heavily participated in or contributed to the development of western philosophical and theological reflection. It is becoming clear that the special social and historical circumstances within which these groups have had to find their way have facilitated the development of sensitivities and perspectives which now can be seen to be of great social importance. On the one hand, these groups have been oppressed in significant ways, and thus the pressure of the social context on the individual has been felt directly and powerfully: through circumscribing the modes of action and styles of life open to members of such groups; through restricting their efforts to take full responsibility for themselves; through limiting and skewing in various ways their moral possibilities. On the other hand, the necessity for persons in such groups to band together in order to protect themselves against encroachments of all sorts by powerful oppressing classes and individuals has helped to induce a strong sense of social relatedness, of connectedness and interdependence, among them. Thus, in contrast to the situations within which the highly educated, rational, relatively autonomous white males who have produced our ethical traditions were formed, here a strong consciousness of the significance of the social dimensions of human moral existence could more easily emerge and develop.[16] Although it may be the case that for males in our society the demands of social responsibility are largely perceived through the rationalizing and generalizing that are made possible by our moral concepts and customs (Circle 2) and by ethical reflection (Circle 3), for females, blacks, and other oppressed groups socialization processes apparently facilitate a deepening and widening of the primal intuitive sense of social dependence and interconnectedness, rather than weakening it and damping it down (as often with white males). For an ethical theory (such as the present one) which interprets morality as an expression of human awareness (intuitive as well as rationally developed) of the sociohistorical conditions that make possible all action, the cultivation of social sensitivity and situational consciousness in all human beings—in contrast with a focus on the production of autonomous egos, however "morally responsible"—is of great importance.

To sum up the argument to this point: morality (Circle 2) is not something heteronomously imposed on decision and action (Circles 1 and 0), a special sort of action in which we engage when we pay attention to certain moral rules. Rather, it should be seen as action taking fuller account of its own complex cybernetic character, whether this occurs intuitively or through a more reflective moral consciousness: it is action of a higher degree, action fructifying further action, action having become more fully responsible and thus more fully and truly *action.* And ethics (Circle 3) should not be regarded as free-standing theory concerning the ideals and values, the rightness and the goodness, that men and women ought to seek if they wish to be moral: it should be seen, rather, as broad and comprehensive *theory of action,* as analysis and exposition of what is required for action to be fully responsible and thus self-sustaining, for action to continue to provide the conditions making possible further action instead of lapsing back into mere impulse, instinct, or reflex, mere behavior. This means that ethics (theory) and action (practice) are intimately involved with each other, and they mutually shape each other. Action must necessarily have a self-aware and reflective dimension, leading eventually to ethics; and ethics is nothing else than this dimension of self-awareness, self-reflectiveness, self-criticism in action now carried to a high degree of self-consciousness.

This conception of morality and ethics can be conveniently tied together and summarized in terms of three basic commandments. Each of these corresponds to one (or two) of the several circles of consciousness which we have been exploring, and together they show how morality and action intrinsically belong to each other.

It is through action that human social life, culture, and history—which we have taken to be the most distinctive marks of the human—have all been created; action is, thus, an indispensable component of our historicity, and thus of our humanity. Nevertheless, for human individuals and communities it is to some degree a matter of choice whether they will act or not, whether they will take responsibility for themselves and their communities. For it is possible for us simply to float, to exist, to allow our individual and societal lives to be carried this way or that by whichever winds are blowing. That is, we can live largely in Circle 0, our lives essentially determined by patterns already in play, taking virtually no responsibility for ourselves or our world, not even entering the arena where morality is a significant factor. The *first commandment* addresses this threshold of the distinctively human, exhorting us to take possession of our humanity. It is addressed to both communities and individuals: *Act! Take responsibility for yourselves!* In light of this commandment we can see that the primal sort of human vice is not really deliberate vice at all, but rather the state of unawareness and unconcern about the potentialities and significance of agency in human existence: to simply live out our inherited patterns of custom and habit with virtually no consciousness that anything can be done, or needs to be done, with these; to live in what Tillich (and others) have called "dreaming innocence."[17] Movement over the threshold into action properly so-called (that is, from Circle 0 to Circle 1) is both the presupposition of morality and the actual beginning of moral awareness. The command thus to move from an amoral or nonmoral level of existence to the moral makes explicit the pressure on us to take up our responsibilities as human beings. It articulates the threshold of human societal, cultural, and personal life: it is imperative that we appropriate our humanity, that we take on the responsibilities of being human.

Our western languages, we should note, contrast the "moral" not only with the "nonmoral" (or "amoral") but also with the "*im*moral"; and this second contrast is quite different in its implications from the first. With it we are brought well into the sphere of morality and ethics. How does this second contrast arise? When we are confronted with a decision for which we are willing to take responsibility (Circles 1 and 2), we find that several alternatives are nearly always open to us. Some we may regard as *immoral,* others as more clearly moral. In this situation we are not confronted with the choice whether to act at all (the issue focused on in the first commandment), but rather with a decision between right acts (and attitudes) and wrong. The contrast with which we are concerned here, thus, is *within* action, not between action and a mode of behavior not truly intentional.

How is this to be understood? I have suggested that right action is that which sustains the moral fabric and thus supports, enhances, and helps to fructify further action; wrong action is that which undermines and weakens the moral fabric, thus threatening future action. Our various moral rules and catalogs of virtues are important to us because they point to the conditions without which responsible human life could not be maintained.* And our

*In contrast, what are called "vices" or "sins" (cowardice, gluttony, treachery, et cetera) are either traits of non-agents, or actions or traits which work toward the destruction of the moral fabric sustaining action. (Cowardice, for example, is the inability to act in face of danger; and a glutton is one so overcome with the desire for food and drink as not to be able to control his or her behavior; treachery, however, is dealing with persons or communities in a deliberately destructive way that serves one's own purposes, after offering friendship and loyalty.)

social ideals (of justice, law, equality, freedom, et cetera) indicate features of the wider community and society without which significant freedom of action, and thus responsible action, would be impossible. The meaning of all these moral considerations, thus, is connected with the support, strengthening, and enhancement of (responsible) action. From this point of view morality is to be seen as an extension or extrapolation of action itself, a cybernetic complexification within action which results from growing consciousness of the conditions required for responsible human life to be sustained. Action, as it increasingly takes responsibility for itself, develops distinctions between right and wrong; and thus moral consciousness comes on the scene.

With these considerations in mind, the first commandment (simply to *act*) appears exceedingly vague. For distinctively human life to emerge and develop, more specification of what is required in and by action is needed. We can formulate this further specification in terms of a *second commandment: So act, that your action will sustain and strengthen the moral fabric!* That is, *Act morally!*

Moral action (as here interpreted) requires us (a) to be responsible and deliberate in our actions (cf. Kant: Act from duty!); (b) to respect the freedom and integrity of all persons affected by our action (cf. Kant: Treat persons as ends in themselves, not as means only!); and (c) to work at all times toward strengthening the moral fabric of communal life (cf. Kant: Act as a member of the realm of ends!). The corresponding (second) level of vice or immorality is any activity that works destructively in these respects—a characterization that, as we have seen, accords well with widely held beliefs that such actions as lying, stealing, and murder, as well as oppressive social and political institutions, inequities of opportunity, gross economic inequalities, and the like, are all morally wrong. The implications of this second commandment for educational institutions and practices, for questions of medical ethics, for race and gender issues, for matters of public policy in every sphere, as well as for intimate interpersonal relations and other private concerns, could all be drawn out had we the space here to develop a full ethics. The second commandment provides a normative point of reference for thinking through the moral issues at stake in the wide range of problems which confront women and men today.*

*Serious problems arise if the first moral imperative (act! take responsibility for yourself! take possession of your humanity!) is confused with the second (where the distinction between the moral and the immoral first arises), or if their proper order is not observed. For the second commandment presupposes the first: to demand "moral" behavior (Circle 2) of persons who are scarcely able to maintain themselves as genuine agents (Circle 1) is not utterly meaningless; but it may be counterproductive, destructive of these very persons instead of supportive, and thus demonic. This is the insight that lies behind the contention of some liberation theologians and ethicists that the first and most important thing which blacks and women and other oppressed peoples must do is assert themselves—that is, take responsibility for their own

The moral meaning of slavery now becomes clear: it is the systematic, institutionalized prohibiting or otherwise preventing of some members of a society from taking up full responsibility for themselves. Obviously (from the point of view of our analysis here), a major imperative for all in such a society who have achieved some measure of responsible freedom and therefore are subject to the commandment to act morally, is to help break the bondage of such slaves, of all those deprived of their full selfhood. For the deprived themselves, however, the most fundamental commandment remains the first: take responsibility for yourselves! reach for your freedom! claim your full humanity!

Let us move one step further now in our consideration of the notion of responsible (that is, moral) action. Most of our action falls within Circles 0 and 1 (that is, it occurs immediately, intuitively, without much reflection) not in Circle 2. And that is as it should be: if we stopped to reflect before our every move, we would get nothing done at all. The mark of moral maturity, then, is not to attempt always to act with deliberate moral consciousness (Circle 2), but rather to be sensitive to those moments when it is important that pertinent moral considerations be brought to mind, when it is necessary to move from Circle 1 to Circle 2. Moral maturity is the ability to sense when moral concerns are threatened with violation, and then deliberately to bring them into play. (In this respect, as is often suggested, moral awareness begins in a negative or restrictive consciousness, what is often referred to as "the voice of conscience.") Even when we move into Circle 2 consciousness, it must be noted, moral considerations are not always the ones to which attention is (or should be) given. A woodworker, for example, in trying to determine how to make a difficult joint, or an architect attempting to design a building appropriate for a location of difficult and peculiar topography, will be engaging in much Circle 2 reflection about how to act; but in these cases it would not normally be moral considerations to which attention was being paid. Indeed, it would usually be intrusive to raise moral issues here, more disruptive of the possibility of acting effectively and responsibly than enhancive of it (unless, of course, the projected plan were in some way injurious of others, or dishonest, or in some other respect morally questionable).

Is morality, then, essentially limiting and restrictive in character, with no positive meaning of its own? This is certainly not the case according to the

---

condition and destiny instead of simply accepting the roles thrust upon them by the socially powerful. This contention is fundamentally correct; in some cases, therefore, explosive activity, destructive of the standing order, may be necessary before reconciliation and integration and meaningful cooperation can occur. To become an agent is the primal task confronted by every person, a task presupposed by all others.

interpretation I am setting out here. The whole point of my analysis has been to emphasize the positive character of our moral concerns, that they are directed toward building up and enhancing the possibilities of (responsible) action, directed toward helping to make possible the creation of a just society and a meaningful culture.* When we are aware of this positive meaning of morality, the enhancement of the moral web of action within which we live itself becomes a goal to be deliberately pursued. This does not mean, of course, that morality is now placed constantly at the center of our attention: as we have noted, expedient and aesthetic interests must also continue to be given their appropriate places. The proper balancing and arrangement of these various constituents of action, and the degree of attention to be devoted to each, will vary in accordance with individual talents, our vocational, family, and other social roles, special commitments we have made, and so on. Action is always a delicate art of sensing what is going on in the situation in which one finds oneself, discerning what moves are demanded in that situation and are appropriate to it, and then fitting one's own actions into the situation with sensitivity and skill. Temptations, conflicts, tensions are the very stuff within which this living movement is immersed, and of which its deliberations are composed. No set of rules or principles (moral or otherwise) can take away from us this continuous demand to sense and to decide for ourselves just what we should do in each new situation. Nor can any ethical reflection or theory resolve these sorts of tensions and dilemmas with which the fluid and complex situations in which we live daily confront us; what morality and ethics can do is enable us to understand better what is really at stake in our action, in this way assisting us to act with greater sensitivity, intelligence, and responsibility.

Awareness of the expedient and aesthetic dimensions of action is more immediate, and thus generally somewhat stronger in its power to motivate, than is moral consciousness. Our needs for food, shelter, sex, social recognition, our desires for comfort, pleasure, excitement, security, and the like, all impress themselves upon us directly; expedient concerns of these sorts are constantly demanding our attention. It is similar with aesthetic considera-

*Though we may first become aware of moral issues in the essentially negative consciousness that we ought *not* to do something, reflection (Circle 3) reveals (as I have argued) that this negative consciousness is rooted in the positive intuition of the importance of sustaining and enhancing the web of action, the fabric of communal life. Moral consciousness may seem, however, essentially negative and restrictive (and thus something to be resented and resisted) until awareness of its positive meaning emerges; and this emergence may for many occur only through a movement to ethical reflection of some sort (Circle 3). For this reason moral consciousness which remains entirely within Circle 2 is often experienced as heteronomous. Such morality is usually practiced in legalistic ("moralistic") ways (by those who subscribe to it), or ignored or rejected (by those who see morality as essentially an alien constraint on what they want to do) except when it seems prudential.

tions: if we act clumsily, unfittingly, abrasively, we soon enough feel the inappropriateness of what we are doing, either through the response of others to us—restricting and restraining us in various ways, inflicting punishment or pain upon us through ridicule, disapproval, social pressures, and the like—or through our own direct experience of pain or discomfort, as we lunge blindly into a thorn bush, or hit our finger (instead of the intended nail) with the hammer in our hand. Our feedback machinery, thus, alerts us continually to the effectiveness (or ineffectiveness) with which we are taking account of the expedient and aesthetic dimensions of action. When we turn to moral awareness, however, the issues become more complex. Moral considerations often do not so easily and automatically attract our attention and interest, nor can they be so straightforwardly defined and addressed. Frequently, thus, they do not even come into consciousness; or if they do, we may deliberately ignore them.[18] It is hardly surprising, then, that the moral dimensions of life, though absolutely indispensable to human flourishing—indeed to our very survival—are often seriously neglected, by communities and societies as a whole as well as by individuals. It is the particular vocation of ethics to call attention to these wide-ranging issues, and to act as educator to society regarding their complexity and importance, deepening our sensitivity to what is required to create and maintain a truly humane world. In this way ethics also has its own distinctive role to play in the maintenance and enhancement of responsible human life. This fact may lead us to formulate a *third commandment: Act with ethical sensitivity and consciousness!* Make sure that you know what you are doing and why you are doing it! Keep yourself and your community aware of the complexity, difficulty, and subtlety of the situation of action, and attempt always to take these matters into account!

These three commandments—1. Act (don't just coast)! 2. Act morally (that is, so as to sustain the moral fabric and enhance future action)! 3. Act ethically (that is, with awareness of the wider meaning and significance of what you are doing)!—correspond, respectively, with Circles 0/1, 2, and 3 of the action-morality schema with which we have been working throughout this chapter and the last. Each command calls attention to a moment that is indispensable to fully responsible action in our complex interconnected world today; taken together they express the increasing interpenetration of human life and activities by morally reflective self-consciousness. To act responsibly is the principal demand laid upon us as moral beings, whether individuals or communities; if the distinctive mark of our humanness is indeed that we are agents, creators of history and culture, the deepest claim upon us is to take up the full responsibilities of our humanity, to become truly humane—and thus, at last, fully human.

We can sum up this entire theory of action and morality by noting how the conception of freedom has now been further expanded and transformed. At the beginning of our reflections on human agency, freedom was treated as essentially synonymous with action, that is, with the simple power to set objectives for ourselves and carry them out: we seemed to be free to the extent that we were able to do what we wanted to do. From the perspective of that understanding, morality could only appear as essentially a constraint upon us, a constriction of our power to act, a kind of bondage. Morality, it seemed, often prevents us from doing what we really want to do; and when it has been internalized, it can only produce a self divided against itself (as a long line of writers from the apostle Paul to Sigmund Freud have argued).

The analysis of morality which I have given, however, is intended to expand, and ultimately to contradict, precisely that (not uncommon) understanding: I have tried to show that morality is not essentially an external constraint upon individuals and communities; on the contrary, it is a cybernetic extension or development of their freedom. From the perspective that we have now reached, the earlier notion of freedom—as a kind of simple self-realization—appears shortsighted and inadequate; if it were followed consistently, selves and societies would destroy themselves in the chaos of their interactions, as everyone sought to do his or her own thing without regard for others. Human existence would be, as Hobbes so well put it, "a war of every man against every man," and life could only be "solitary, poor, nasty, brutish, and short."[19] Freedom and agency, from the vantage point we have now reached, are seen to be much more complicated matters than they at first seemed; a wider set of considerations must be taken into account if they are to sustain themselves and not simply self-destruct. We could say that the result of our investigations has been to bring us to a more *ecological* understanding of freedom: we now see that in our actions we must take into account (so far as we can) *all* that we are doing, long-range ramifications as well as immediate consequences (expedience). From the standpoint of this wider, more dialectical conception of freedom, our earlier definition seems thin and deficient. Merely to possess the power to realize our immediate desires is no significant freedom at all; it is, in fact, to live in bondage, enslaved to desire. True freedom is a much more impressive matter than that: it is the power to lift our humanity beyond mere desire to a new and significantly different mode of existing, to live as responsible members in communities of freely interacting persons.

A few pages back I pointed out that the movement into moral consciousness does not entail forsaking or overriding our intuitive concerns about the "fitting," but is rather a significant further development of these concerns, taking into account wider, more far-reaching considerations. With morality we do not attend simply to what is fitting in the immediate situation, but rather to what is fitting within the overall web of action within which we are living and which sustains us as free agents. Ultimately, thus (as we noted), there is a significant convergence of the moral and the aesthetic dimensions of action.

We can now see a similar convergence between moral and expedient considerations. As long as expediency is interpreted as having to do largely with the immediate goal of our actions (as in our original definition), there will be, of course, conflicts between the expedient and the moral: the price of keeping my promises or telling the truth may sometimes be high, and quite impractical. However, as our analysis has unfolded, we have come to see that morality is actually concerned with what is required to sustain human historico-cultural existence, human life as truly *human.* When seen in this light, morality turns out to be a thoroughly practical matter: it has to do with the very survival and well-being of human existence as such, the survival of women and men as free and responsible agents. Is there any more practical goal for which we might be working than such survival? We can see here, thus, a kind of convergence of the moral dimension of action with what we earlier called the "expedient"—but only (as with the convergence of the moral and the aesthetic) when "expedient" is not understood simply in terms of the immediate situation, and when "survival" is not understood simply biologically; in short, only if we think of a very long-range expediency, a kind of ultimate prudence. If it is the survival of our *humanity* of which we are speaking, of ourselves as free and responsible persons in humane communities, then the aesthetic and the prudential and the moral all three ultimately converge. What had seemed in Circles 2 and 3 to split into three distinct dimensions, can come together once again in a wider, more comprehensive circle: a vision of human society and culture in which the practical, the aesthetic, and the moral all find their proper place in a truly harmonious and meaningful ordering of life. Such a fully humane personal and social order is not, of course, at hand; it exists only in our eschatological dreams, our dreams of that ultimate human—and humane—world to which all of us are called to give ourselves.

Dreams of this sort suggest that ultimately our freedom need not mean (as many have claimed) that humans have become permanently alienated from the natural order which gave them birth.[20] If our freedom ever reaches its potential (in the proper dialectical interconnection of our various powers) and we are enabled to act with a fully ecological self-consciousness, women and men should find themselves able to fit more smoothly and effectively into the natural environment which is the setting for their lives and their activities. And it may become possible at last for humans to feel truly at home in their world. We are, of course, very far from realizing this eschatological dream of human fulfillment, but we have tasted enough of human agency and freedom, and we know enough about what constitutes human responsibility, to have some sense of what it might mean to live as members of such a community of truly free persons, perfectly at home in the world. It was an early version of a vision of this sort that was expressed in the ancient metaphor of the coming "kingdom of God"; Jesus—and many others for the last two thousand years—have prayed that that kingdom might come "on earth as it is in heaven."

15. The Corruption of Historicity: Freedom and Evil

Our analysis of human action and cultural creativity, morality and ethics, has suggested that these are all dialectically interconnected: that which distinguishes human existence from other forms of life—what we have characterized as "historicity" and "agency"—slowly develops over many generations as a web of action, morality, and the wider culture gradually builds up. Action generates within itself (in each historical context within which it appears) certain distinctive but indispensable normative requirements ("morality"). If this contention is correct, the violation of these requirements will exact a heavy price: corrosion of the complex socio-moral web apart from which human life is not possible, and ultimately destruction of individual and communal human existence. Violation of the moral conditions essential to sustain free and responsible action opens a Pandora's box almost impossible to close, and complex patterns of evil arise. These patterns of evil—though historically created and always taking historically distinct shapes—often become structural elements of the prevailing forms of human life. Such unfortunate developments are not unintelligible, I want to point out, given the conceptions of historicity and history with which we have been working here. In this chapter I shall present an interpretation of how and why certain major forms of evil become such powerful fixtures in human affairs. (Later on, especially in the latter part of Chapter 21 and in Chapter 24, the interpretation of evil developed here will be brought into direct connection with the symbol "God"; and, in Chapter 26, with the symbol "Christ.")

An adequate discussion of the question of evil in human existence would require, first of all, a comparative examination of the concept "evil" itself, to ascertain whether in all (or most) other cultures and religions around the globe there are similar concepts employed to identify and represent dimensions of life so negative and so destructive that they must be utterly repudiated. Only after careful analysis of the diverse concepts uncovered in such a study, to see the various ways in which these negative matters have been defined and understood by women and men in different social and historical contexts, would we be in a position to make some assessment of our western ways of understanding these matters; and thus be in a position to develop a general conception of "the corruption of historicity." To my knowledge, this kind of comparative study is not yet available to us; in any case, I am clearly not in a position to make the sort of comparative judgments required to justify universalistic claims about these important issues. Nevertheless, something must be said here: a major reason for developing a general anthropological position is to get some purchase on the deep problems of human life, so they can be appropriately and effectively addressed. Much more will need to be said about these matters as we proceed in later chapters to our construction of conceptions of God and Christ—the principal normative symbols in Christian perspectives; but it is possible at this point to draw from our analysis of human historicity and agency some notions about why and how "evil" emerges in human affairs, why and how our historicity becomes corrupted. Analyses by recent theologians and others have suggested that anxiety and guilt as experienced by individual human beings, and social oppression and disorder as these appear in many communities and in society as a whole, develop into perduring structures, in the human psyche and in social institutions, from which many other evils spring. I shall attempt to show that the action/morality/ethics cybernetic pattern which I have outlined in Chapters 11 to 14 suggests a way to understand structures of these sorts as the consequence of unfortunate, but not entirely surprising, historical developments.

Let us begin by reminding ourselves of the three basic commandments with which (in Chapter 14) the action/morality interconnections were tied together and summarized: Act! Act *morally!* Act *ethically!* We must ask ourselves now, What consequences follow when we violate these imperatives? If it is correct that self and society are interconnected and correlated with each other in the complex dialectical ways I have suggested, we would expect to find that violations of these commandments will have deleterious consequences both psychically and socially.

The first imperative has to do with our task (as individuals and communities) of taking up our agency and our responsibility, our task of becoming and maintaining ourselves as agents. I would like to suggest now that in *individuals* the inability or failure (either occasionally or in much of their lives) to take up the burdens of agency and responsibility often manifests itself in a sense of anxiousness, a sense of having little power to do things effectively, a fear of losing their fragile centeredness and going to pieces. And in *society at large* it may easily manifest itself in patterns of oppression and/or slavery; that is, in social orders in which positions of power are used by some in ways that prevent others from realizing and exercising their potential for taking responsibility for themselves, their potential for historicity and freedom. Let us first look briefly at the issue of individual failure (or inability) and its manifestation in anxiety, and then we will turn to the social dimension of this problem.

Psychoanalysts and others often make a distinction between fear and anxiety.[1] Whereas fear is connected with the awareness of a specific object perceived as a threat, anxiety arises when we have a sense of being in some way endangered but find ourselves unable to identify any threatening object. The difference between fear and anxiety, thus, is largely conceptual, having to do more with the object (or lack of object) present to consciousness than with the distinctiveness of the subjective feelings being experienced; the latter shade off into each other. When I am aware of what it is that threatens me and of how I am being threatened, I am able to respond in some way—by flight, by defending myself, by obtaining the right medicine, by buying fire insurance, et cetera. However, if I sense danger but have no idea of its source, if I have a vague but strong apprehension that something terrible is going to happen but cannot imagine what it will be, the problem is of a different order: I am rendered powerless; I have no way to deal with the situation. Theologians like Reinhold Niebuhr and Paul Tillich, heavily dependent on Kierkegaard,[2] have argued that this strong sense of apprehension and concern characteristic of anxiety is inherent in human existence since all humans are at once finite and free, limited in many ways and yet essentially responsible for themselves and their world. "Anxiety is finitude, experienced as one's own finitude,"[3] as Tillich put it. Given this powerful sense of unease and threat in the substratum of all human consciousness, it is hardly surprising that sin and evil of many different degrees and kinds continually erupt into human life and action everywhere.

I am not inclined to make such universalistic claims about anxiety or sinfulness (as we know these in the West)—my emphasis on human historicity and historical diversity clearly precludes that—but it is not my intention here to debate the pros and cons of these and other theological and psychological interpretations. My interest, rather, is in connecting this discussion of what is obviously an important dimension of human consciousness and experience (at least in the modern West) with the conceptions of selfhood, agency, and historicity that I have been constructing in the past several chapters. I have argued that an important component of the consciousness of being an "I," a self, is the awareness of being able to act, an awareness of having the power to bring about certain effects, to (in some measure) take control of oneself and the situation in which one finds oneself. It is worth noting now that the "anxiety" we have just been discussing appears to be precisely the opposite of this sort of consciousness: it is the (disconcerting) sense of *not* being in control, of our *in*ability to act in response to our sense of danger. When life goes on fairly smoothly, we are not much troubled by the vague sense of risk and endangerment around the fringes of our consciousness; in fact this mild level of anxiety probably has significant survival value for us, since it helps keep us alert in a world where the unexpected may occur with little or no warning. Attacks of *neurotic* anxiety, however, are another matter, for far from assisting the self in coping with dangers, they interfere with effective action. We might say, in fact, that intense anxiety of this sort is not merely a sense of the self's inability; it is much more than that, the self's awareness that it is going to pieces, falling apart, disintegrating. Awareness of being an "I," an ego, an actor, is the awareness of being together, of being "centered" sufficiently to focus one's energies to *do* things; a powerful anxiety attack, in contrast, is the awareness that one is losing centeredness and becoming utterly unable to cope. Herbert Fingarette has expressed the point well: "Anxiety, the peculiarly central threat to the ego, *is* ego-disorganization . . . [Where] the tendency toward psychic organization . . . operates successfully we speak of ego [of 'I']; where it is threatened with central failure, we speak of anxiety. Ego and anxiety are the opposite faces of the same coin."[4]

We have seen that to become an "I," an agent, is a task to be performed; since this task is never fully completed, one must continually work at maintaining oneself as an ego. The first commandment is to *perform this task,* to *act,* to take responsibility for oneself, to be an "I." The experience of strong feelings of anxiety, we can now see, is our awareness (at some level) of failing at this task, our sense of slipping back into non-agency, losing our center, coming apart. If we recognize (as I have been arguing throughout) that the self is not a kind of *thing* which we simply are or possess, but is instead a consciousness that gradually grows within us as our sense of centeredness develops in and through our learning to act—first in relation to others in the family, and later through taking roles in a wider community—then we can see that neurotic anxiety is not simply a disease or malfunctioning of what is essentially an ongoing self but is rather the very falling apart, the disintegration, of the self itself. Anxiety is, thus, the consequence and expression of, and the consciousness of, failure to carry out the first commandment.

From this point of view the continuous pressure of an undercurrent of anxiety (in which most of us live most of the time) is to be interpreted as a subliminal awareness—despite my knowledge that I am *I,* and that I can do certain things—that I may fail to maintain myself as "I," I may not succeed in my efforts adequately to take responsibility for myself. Anxiety and ego ("I") are dialectical opposites: they exist in ongoing tension with each other, each presupposing—and yet opposing—the other. These two distinct yet dialectically interconnected types of consciousness have very different significations: the presence of one signifies our success in keeping the first commandment; the presence of the other, our failure. Our sense of agency, of "I," is actually, thus, quite ambiguous: it always carries with it symptoms of its own potential disintegration.

We have only begun to touch on the dialectical complexity of human self-consciousness. As human existence becomes increasingly shaped by creative action (self-directing freedom), moral sensitivities may begin to come into focus (as we have noted), and a distinctly normative dimension of existence and consciousness ("morality") may gradually emerge and take its place along with concerns for expediency and fittingness. An "I," we saw, can come into being only within a community of "I's" who are acting and interacting with one another. That is, persons can take up the burden and satisfaction of acting, can begin to take responsibility for themselves, only by becoming responsive participants in a community of agents, thus beginning to live in accountability to others (at least in some respects):[5] the first imperative (Act!) thus gives rise to the second (Act morally!). But this means that anxiety does not exist in a "pure" form (as I have thus far been describing it), for failure to be the "I" which potentially I might be—to take responsibility for myself—is never simply a private matter: it also involves falling short of my obligations to those others who existed before me and brought me into being through interacting with me. I fail my friends as well as myself when I do not become, or remain, a responsible person; and the awareness of this *social* dimension of my failure also manifests itself in my consciousness—as guilt. Anxiety is usually mixed with guilt—with my awareness that I have betrayed those ties of trust and loyalty and love which brought me into being and which were growing reciprocally between myself and the others surrounding me, and that I am responsible for this betrayal: it is *I* who have done this; I am the guilty one. Failure to take responsibility for myself, to be an "I," is not, then, merely a violation of the first commandment; it involves violation of the second as well.

An increasingly convoluted consciousness thus begins to develop. On the one hand I feel that I am unable properly to act, to take responsibility for myself (anxiety); on the other hand I feel responsible for precisely this failure, not only to myself but also to those others with whom I had begun to interact (guilt). And so now the feedback loops of Circles 1 and 2—or rather, deficiencies in those feedback loops—come to interpenetrate each other in increasingly complex ways. I may begin to feel guilty (Circle 2) about the way my unmanageable anxiety (Circle 1) interferes with my responsible interaction with others; thus my sense of guiltiness comes to interpenetrate my feeling of anxiousness. But there is also a movement in the other direction: I begin to feel increasingly anxious (Circle 1) about my failures to keep faith with others (Circle 2), anxious about whether they will continue to trust and be loyal to me despite my betrayals; and I become anxious about the very guilt that I feel over these betrayals, fearful that this sense of guilt is itself further destroying me, interfering with my ability to act responsibly. Anxiety and guilt thus feed on each other, further weakening the ability of the self to interact freely and responsibly with others (Circle 2), and thus further weakening the "I" itself, the ability to act (Circle 1). The possibilities of growing deterioration—through an increasing dialectical interpenetration of anxiety and guilt into each other—are endless. Psychiatric archives are full of examples; and theological psychologists like Kierkegaard and Dostoyevsky and Kafka have described in detail the ingenious kinds of obscene self-destruction of this sort in which men and women engage.

We shall not explore further here this interpretation of the emergence of destructive evils within the individual self; it will be more illuminating to turn to its societal analogue. In what ways may the failure to fulfill the imperatives arising in Circles 1 and 2 manifest itself in social structures and relationships? It must be emphasized that in taking up this question we are not leaving the problems of individuals behind; rather, we are concerning ourselves with further complexities of the patterns that we have already begun to discern. The societal analogue to the complex interplay between failure to become an effective agent-self (Circle 1) and failure to be morally responsible to others (Circle 2)—between anxiety and guilt—is what Hegel articulated as the master/slave dialectic.[6]

"Slaves"—that is, socially oppressed persons and groups—are those who are prevented from realizing their inner drive or impulsion to *act,* to take responsibility for themselves by becoming full agent-selves, because of societal constraints which they cannot overcome. And "masters" are those oppressive groups and individuals who have the ability and power to act effectively (Circle 1), and who, moreover, act to maintain and strengthen the established social order, thus helping to make continuing agency possible (Circle 2)—in this respect their action is "moral" and "responsible" in a certain sense, at least in their own eyes—and yet it is *immoral* "moral action" in which they engage. For it fails to treat some of the individuals and groups with whom they are interacting as themselves *agents* (as "ends" and not simply as "means"); it is, in fact, action directed (at least in part) toward preventing these others from becoming full agent-selves, directed toward keeping them "under control." In this respect it is the opposite of truly *moral* action (as I have interpreted it here). This sort of action is, thus, profoundly incoherent, simultaneously moral and immoral: it is directed toward maintaining the social fabric which makes action in the society possible, yet it works to undermine precisely the moral dimensions of that fabric. Virtually all historical societies of which we know manifest this dialectic of oppressive and oppressed groups, masters and slaves, those who take responsibility for society as a whole (Circle 2), guiding it and directing it, but who do so in such a way as to make it difficult or impossible for others to realize their potential to become free self-directing agents (Circle 1). In consequence, in most societies there are ongoing class and caste struggles which manifest themselves in profound tensions between oppressors and oppressed, and which sometimes erupt into the violence of revolution and war.

The concrete expressions of these tensions and struggles over issues of political power, property, wealth, prestige, race, gender, and so on have been widely discussed; and it is unnecessary for us to explore them here. The important point for us to note is that the dialectical interpenetration of Circles 1 and 2 which develops in connection with the struggles to attain selfhood and moral responsibility is not to be understood as simply a privatistic issue concerning essentially subjective matters (anxiety, guilt), an issue of concern principally to individuals; this interpenetration manifests itself just as surely in the objective structures of societies—in institutions and customs, statuses and roles and ideologies—as in the self-structures and consciousness of individual persons. Failure to meet the requirements laid down in the first and second commandments generates tensions which threaten to blow societies apart; and it spawns societal patterns and institutional arrangements which make it impossible for the selves formed and nurtured in these societies to become truly free and responsible. In their relations and interactions with others they nearly always find themselves either in positions of some vulnerability or weakness, with significant constraints upon their potential to act (that is, among the oppressed); or in positions of significant prestige, privilege, and power (oppressors), actively engaged in constricting and constraining others; or in some complex combination of these. As one might expect, warped social and institutional conditions and relationships of these sorts ramify in various ways throughout the society, and in particular within the dynamic dialectic of anxiety and guilt which we have already briefly noted.

The weight of the whole social structure only serves to deepen the anxiety of the weak and the oppressed regarding their inability to act with effectiveness; and it may give rise to desires to rise up and seek to overcome, or even destroy, those whom they perceive to be oppressing them—and thus to further feelings of guilt. The powerful, on the other hand, live with anxieties about the impermanence of the social order which gives them position and privilege, and sometimes with guilt about their treatment of those who serve them. These forms of anxiety and guilt, moreover, themselves become institutionalized in the class structure—in behavioral practices, in patterns of etiquette and courtesy, in the stories that are told, the myths that are believed, the social roles that are inculcated: "A woman's place is in the home!" "In America anyone can succeed if they really try!" "Blacks should know their place!" "The poor you will always have with you!" So what in a just and free society would develop as a sense of respect for others becomes instead, among the oppressed, obsequiousness before powerful "superiors"; and what might have grown into the honest dignity of free and responsible selfhood and agency becomes, in oppressors, the social power to exploit, conferred by wealth and position. And feelings of anxiety and guilt, instead of functioning as symptoms (an "early warning system") which aid in the discernment of significant threats to selves and their moral responsibilities—so that the delicate cybernetic balances of responsible selfhood and responsible social interaction in a responsibly ordered society can be maintained and enhanced—now become levers helping to reinforce precisely these power-driven social relations of obsequiousness and exploitation. Instead of cybernetic patterns in self and society which could sustain selves and open up possibilities of free agency, patterns of deterioration and degeneration develop, always threatening major breakdowns, or explosions into revolution and war. Thus further rounds of anxiety and guilt are generated; and so on and on.

We cannot here explore further these complex dialectical relations between self and society, and between Circles 1 and 2, as revealed in the failures to keep the first and second commandments. (For the significant bearing of the symbol "God"—when it is available—on these issues, see Chapters 21, 22 and 24.) I want instead to extend this consideration of the complicated ways in which historicity becomes corrupted (through misuse of such freedom as develops within it), to some remarks about Circle 3 consciousness and action. The third moral imperative directed to both individuals and societies is: Act *ethically!* that is, with as full knowledge and self-consciousness about what you are doing as you can muster. In situations of personal and social moral failure of the sort we have been considering, what happens to this commandment? Unfortunately, the wider consciousness represented by ethics (Circle 3)—in and through which men and women seek to further clarify and illuminate the action/morality situation in which they find themselves (Circles 1 and 2), thus helping to facilitate the growth of freedom and historicity—may now move in a direction opposite to that expected for Circle 3, thus corrupting the situation further.

Within individuals, where anxiety and guilt often become compelling, a powerful "false consciousness" (Nietzsche, Sartre) may develop as "rationalizations" (Freud) are worked out by men and women seeking to justify their behavior and attitudes to themselves and to others. On the one hand, they persuade themselves that they and their activities measure up well against "reasonable" standards of goodness, value, humanity; on the other, they argue that those standards which they fail to meet are, for the most part, largely "unrealistic" sentimental ideals, false values which "practical" persons are wise to ignore. All of us know how adept we are at excusing ourselves and putting the best possible face on our behavior, how convinced we are that *our* ideals are the ones that are proper and true, and those who disagree with us are clearly in error. If we are ingenious enough and energetic enough and so inclined, we may spin out wide-ranging philosophical notions, or perhaps a social psychology or a political theory, which show clearly that our failures to live and act in fully responsible ways (as prescribed by the second and third commandments) are entirely justified, that our own egocentrism, aggressiveness, and self-protectiveness are precisely what is natural and proper for human beings.

Within communities and societies which become corrupted, the wider consciousness of Circle 3 manifests itself in the form of "ideologies" (Marx). Instead of a theory of society and persons which enables us to understand why the social and institutional dimensions of life must be ordered so as to enhance the freedom of all participants, and how this can be achieved, we get ideologies of the "master race" or of "black inferiority" to justify the subordination of some groups in society to others; or ideologies which declare American democracy and western culture superior to other social and cultural patterns, thus justifying American attempts to continue dominating and exploiting the rest of the world; or ideologies which prescribe child-rearing and other domestic activities as "natural" for women, with business and politics the "proper" domain of men; or ideologies which proclaim the Christian Church to be a "divinely ordained" institution, in contrast with other institutions and religions; or ideologies which denounce Jews as "Christ-killers," or, from the other side, which proclaim the Jews to be God's "chosen people"; or ideologies which insist that only certain "experts" ("technocrats")—whether psychiatrists or Pentagon officials, university professors or other "intellectuals"—are capable of judging what is right and good for all the people, and should therefore be empowered to make major decisions about policies and practices for society as a whole; and so on and on. In this way, Circle 3 consciousness—which should provide clarification and illumination of the basic personal, social, and moral issues in a culture—becomes subverted to justifying the existing power-relations in the society. And in so doing it helps to further entrench those unjust patterns: whites and males come to believe that they are in fact superior in certain ways to blacks and females, and (sadly) females and blacks also come to accept this; Christians and Americans believe they have the right—indeed the duty!—to impose themselves and their ideas, their institutions and their practices, on the rest of the world; and most of us in academia are pleased when another professor goes to Washington, because we believe he or she really can do better than the "bureaucrats" now there.

These various ideologies and forms of false consciousness interpenetrate in innumerable ways the patterns of social differentiation and struggle between oppressed persons and groups and their oppressors, and they permeate also the layers of anxiety and guilt pervading the consciousness of individuals; they thus complicate further the patterns of evil which we have already noted. Entire philosophies and psychologies are developed to justify the most egoistic, self-serving forms of behavior; and sciences of sociology and economics, politics and law, explain and legitimate utterly corrupt social practices and institutions. And so the dialectical interpenetration of these various corrosive and corruptive powers moves ever deeper.

In modern technologically developed societies, with television regularly used by those with money and power to spread seductive images and slogans everywhere, the increasing momentum of deterioration and breakdown may become almost impossible to halt. We may at this moment be witnessing an example of this in the United States. In the 1980s and early 1990s leadership willing to address the major problems of American society has almost completely disappeared. And so the growing "underclass" of poverty and despair, together with the widening gap between rich and poor; rapidly increasing homelessness and illiteracy, drug addiction and crime; unwillingness to give up immediate gratifications in order to address major long-range problems such as environmental issues, the increasingly serious demographic and economic plight of "third-world" peoples, the development of renewable sources of energy, maintenance of the nation's essential infrastructures, provision for adequate education and medical facilities for all—all these problems and many more continue to fester and multiply. In the presidential campaign of 1988 the public seemed to be completely unwilling to entertain any serious discussion of matters of this sort, either domestic or international. What has happened since then—especially including the diversion of attention from the serious domestic problems in the United States by the war with Iraq—has done little to quiet the fear that the moral illness of this society may have become irreversible.

The problems to which the corruption of human historicity have given rise are by no means limited to the United States. In the other "most developed" countries many similar sorts of social and moral deterioration are to be found, and it has become a serious question whether western social, political, and economic institutions will be able to manage the sorts of issues which they now confront. Economic power is becoming concentrated in the hands of great uncontrolled conglomerates which willingly exploit for their own gain whatever they contact; the exceeding instability of the international economic system leads to roller-coaster movements from boom to bust in various parts of the world; and inadequate means of distribution leave some peoples in a virtually permanent condition of starvation. Our democratic political structures, which have promised the greatest degree of self-determination for individuals together with systems of checks and balances intended to guard against tyranny, seem unable to provide adequate leadership to address the long-range problems of modernity; and it is becoming obvious to all that our much vaunted high standard of living in the West and our technological success in transforming the face of the earth have been bought at the price of enormous exploitation of the earth's energy resources. Moreover, we have been poisoning other basic resources needed for the sustenance of all life (water, the atmosphere, the food chain, et cetera), so now we are threatened with irreversible ecological disaster. And, of course, we have all lived for years under the threat of a breakdown of international political arrangements (or of some absurdly simple misunderstanding or technical accident) which could result in a nuclear holocaust destroying all civilization, perhaps all human life. It is hardly surprising that the ordinary anxieties and guilts which seemingly accompany most finite historicity and freedom have become magnified in our time to a pervasive underlying sense of meaninglessness and hopelessness about the human condition and the human future. For good reason our time has been picked out by W. H. Auden as in a special sense an "age of anxiety."

Add now to these exceedingly complex difficulties in which the so-called most developed countries find themselves, the enormous new political and economic problems faced by Eastern Europe and the former U.S.S.R. And then, of course, there are the massive struggles in which the "third world" is engaged as it tries to modernize and industrialize in great haste. Seeing the chaotic conditions in the "first" and "second" worlds, these peoples cannot but ask themselves what sort of modernization can really make sense for them. What mix of institutions and practices learned from the "more developed" countries (democracy? socialism? modern medicine? mass industrialization? the "green revolution"?) should they adopt, and how should this be combined with their own traditional religious and cultural patterns? How can they achieve the total transformation of life which modernization demands, without so destroying their own customs and institutions, traditions and values, as to lose themselves entirely—their sense of who they are, what they stand for, how they live? These issues become especially poignant when the major thrust of certain important emphases and values of their central religious and cultural traditions seems to go directly counter to what is required for modernization—as, for example, in India. Since for most of its history life in India could not easily be changed, the only way many could survive was through learning to accept the status quo; traditional values and patterns of thinking like those represented by the idea of karma, therefore—the ways of living and acting which they inculcated, and the structures of selfhood and the social institutions which they helped to create and form—in fact helped to make it possible for life in India to go on for many generations. Now, however, precisely these same social and character structures, and the traditional conception of what human life in the world is and should be (at least for the lower castes) work against the formation of the sorts of habits and customs, character types and institutional patterns, that seem required for India's modernization. The very form of the human—as defined by ideals and values in the deepest strata of much Indian religious feeling and conviction, and thus expressed in the major institutions that give order to life as well as in widely practiced rituals and widely accepted myths—all seem to require radical transformation.

But this is to ask people to give up their very being, their sense of identity, their conception of who they are and of what it is that enables them to be what they are—that is, it requires them to give up their history, their very historicity—in order to live in a different world than the one they have regarded for generations as the real world, to change their whole sense of self and their most basic intuitions of what is proper and right and good in life. The central notion which I have stressed so much in these chapters—that we are fundamentally historical beings, and are given our very reality as persons by the history from which we come—teaches us that we cannot forsake our past without destroying our very selfhood. Here, in the necessity to modernize felt by many traditional societies, it would seem, the demands of today's new historical situation—demands placed upon them by, and to be realized through, their historicity (in one sense)—themselves require the forsaking of that very historicity (in another sense). The problems faced by those of us living in the West, nourished by the cultural and religious traditions which originally gave birth to modernity, seem in many ways minor beside the inner tensions and conflicts faced in such third-world countries.

Comparative judgments of that sort, however, are really not very illuminating. The central point with which we must come to terms is this: whether in the West or in more traditional societies, the processes of modernization (into which the development of our historicity and agency has brought us) now confront us with dilemmas that seem to be increasingly unmanageable by us, dilemmas which can eventuate not only in the extinction of various cultural traditions but in the annihilation of humankind itself. Our historicity, that which gives us our distinctiveness among all living beings, has proved to be a mixed blessing. But it is no longer possible to retreat into non-historical, non-agential modes of being (as we have seen): human life has become so thoroughly historicized that such moves backward into a simpler form of animality are inconceivable. We must, then, attempt to take responsibility for this situation in which we find ourselves, no matter how great its complexity and incomprehensibility. We have no choice but to move forward into a further widening and deepening of our historicity, and of the agency and responsibility which it makes possible.

There are further frightening problems. We will, for example, soon have to decide what kind of beings we should seek to become in the future, into what sorts of beings we should seek to transform ourselves. The most obvious point where this question is beginning to make itself felt is in recent developments in biology. We can now conceive the possibility of bringing about changes in the very genetic basis of human life, and we shall soon need to decide whether we want to do that. If so, in what directions should the biological substructure of human existence be moved? Should we think of our desired future as some sort of continuation or extension of the historical existence which is now ours? Or would some other mode of being, something above or beyond historicity, be more desirable? Can we even imagine a transhistorical mode of human existence? Would it be a form of life "beyond freedom and dignity," to use B. F. Skinner's famous phrase?—an existence in which we were conditioned or programmed in such a way as to function perfectly, without anxiety, stress, guilt, failures, crime, insanity; in short, without the enormous human problems which we have just been noting? If we could make the necessary genetic modifications to bring off a mode of existence of that sort, would that really be a gain? or a tremendous loss? Are anxiety, guilt, failure, the threat of meaninglessness inseparable from the powers of creativity and freedom which make responsible historical existence possible? and is self-responsible historicity, with all its problems, more desirable than a perfectly programmed life, well tuned and adjusted, in a society without major issues that need to be addressed?

It is difficult to know how to answer such questions, or even to grasp what they mean. We have no concepts for thinking clearly about what we are here trying to conceive. The imaginative works of science-fiction writers may provide some suggestions, but it is difficult to know what should be taken seriously there and what is just fantasy. The old religious dreams about a heaven in which human life goes on in a perfected form, without any problems or difficulties, express the attempts of earlier generations to imagine a form of human existence beyond historicity; but the fundamental absurdities and incoherences of all such pictures simply confirm the difficulty (or impossibility?) for humans either to conceive or imagine a genuinely transhistorical mode of existence. This might seem to argue that in posing questions of this sort we have simply moved beyond our depth, and that we should, therefore, not bother ourselves with them. But that option is really not available to us, for the possibilities of actually changing the biological base of human life are clearly opening before us, and we shall have to make decisions about these matters soon. The human movement through a long history into historicity has always been a movement into the unknown; it has often involved fearful dangers and has resulted in tragic losses. To be historical beings means to take risks in face of unknown futures. Who is in a position to say that gaining some degree of genetic control over human evolution is not an appropriate next step in the development of our humanity, a next major move forward toward our fuller humanization? Our evolving into historical beings in the first place involved massive evolutionary modifications in the central nervous system and the brain, the development of the hand, the change to an upright posture, and the like. Why suppose these biological modifications are now completed? Clearly, we are in fact ill-adapted in many ways. We have bodies which gained their fundamental form and capacities during the long period when humans lived in small packs or hordes, the form of their life shaped largely by activities like hunting and food-gathering. But modern civilization is far removed from those sorts of patterns; historical changes in human existence have far outstripped the biological evolution which produced the physical organisms undergirding our existence. If it is becoming possible now to more directly adapt the biological organisms of future generations to match the character and strains of modern life, why not attempt it? Would this not be an important—even necessary—extension of the whole evolutionary-historical development which has produced humanity?

How can we come to grips with issues like these? It is clear that the problems we are here contemplating move us far beyond ordinary moral questions to the most fundamental religious and metaphysical issues: What sort of beings are we, in the last analysis? What is the real nature of the process, or the complex of processes, that has produced us? Where is that process going? What are its possibilities? What is our role or place within it? What are the ultimate parameters within which we live? In the past theologians dealt with these sorts of issues largely on the basis of tradition. They assumed that in the Bible and in traditional Christian teaching the basic nature and character of human existence, of the world we live in, and of the ultimate reality with which we must come to terms, was correctly depicted: God is the creator/lord of the universe; humans, created in the "image of God" as the apex of God's creative work, have been given a certain "dominion" (Gen. 1:28) over the rest of creation which they must exercise within the context of the ultimate purposes which God is working out through history; eventually, as history is brought to its consummation, God will bring us to "salvation," a life of perfect fulfillment in the "kingdom of God." For a constructive theology, however, such direct reliance on ancient tradition for answers to the most fundamental metaphysical questions about life, death, and ultimate reality is not acceptable. This would amount simply to taking over uncritically a conception of the world and an understanding of the human which was worked out by earlier generations. No doubt there is much to learn from the many millennia of reflection on these matters, but we dare not forget that traditional ideas and pictures regarding all such matters are human constructs quite as much as any views which we might develop; on issues as important as these, we must ourselves take full responsibility for the conclusions to which we come.

This is, of course, the issue on which we have been working throughout this book: we have been trying to get our bearings in the world, as that world is known to us modern human beings. In this way, we hope we will come to see more clearly who we really are, what we are doing in the world and what we should be doing, what are the parameters within which we must live and work. Our sense of historicity and agency—our awareness that, having come out of a past which has significantly shaped and formed us but in which we began to take responsibility for ourselves, we must now act appropriately and effectively in this present, as we move inexorably into what seems such an opaque future—requires us to create imaginatively the most adequate symbolic pictures of the world within which we live that we can, so that we can orient ourselves effectively in our living and acting. In modern times our imaginative vision of the world extrapolates far beyond our local experience on earth to a conception of a universe hundreds of millions of light-years across and billions of years old; and human life on earth has itself become completely transformed from the patterns within which it originated through the cultural and technological inventiveness of women and men. Given this modern awareness of the enormous power which we have to remake the environment in which we live, and (now very recently) even to recreate ourselves genetically—taken together with our knowledge of the complex, devious, exceedingly destructive patterns of evil that corrupt our historicity and creativity at every point—how shall we today conceive the context, the whole, within which our human life falls and with which we are in continuous interaction? and how shall we understand our real human possibilities within that context? What imaginative vision of human life in the world can most effectively provide orientation for our lives today? In Parts III and IV of this book we shall attempt to address these issues. Before we can begin to undertake the massive constructive work which that will require, however, we need to ask ourselves more directly (in light of the understanding of human historicity and its corruption to which we have come) about the meaning and functions of religion in human life. To that we turn in the next chapter.

16. Historicity and Religion

In earlier chapters I have suggested that what we today call religion had its beginnings during the emergence of humankind from animality into sociocultural modes of existence—modes which humans themselves created over many generations, as they sought to come to terms with the physical and historical contingencies that bore down upon them. Religion gradually became differentiated from the rest of culture and was institutionalized—with distinctive rituals and myths and other traditions, with specialized personnel (shamans and priests, gurus and prophets and healers, and so on), with particular claims on the society as a whole and the men and women who constituted it. Today we can see that what was developing as "religion" was a sphere of culture within and through which humans would seek and find orientation for life in the world, together with motivation for living and acting in accordance with this orientation—that is, would gain, and gradually formulate, a sense of the *meaning* of human existence.[1] The forms and practices and institutions of human religiousness have been exceedingly diverse, but it is not necessary for our purposes here to present either a phenomenology of religion or a detailed interpretation of its meaning and significance for human history and life generally. We do need to note, however—as a conclusion to the anthropological section of our theological construction and a transition to our consideration of the wider categories of the world and God (dealing with the *context* of human life)—just what is involved in this turn to what are generally regarded as more specifically "religious" matters.

In the anthropology I have been developing in these pages attention has been focused particularly on human historicity. I have tried to show that this notion is useful descriptively in helping us comprehend the enormous diversity of human life; and that it provides a basis for developing a normative conception of the human, in connection with which criteria and standards can be generated for identifying and addressing major problems. The concept of historicity also enables us to understand to some extent the pernicious self-destructiveness and corruption into which human existence seems (always?) to fall: our historicity itself (as we saw in Chapter 15) easily becomes corrupted, moving into convoluted spirals of self-destructiveness and evil from which women and men find it difficult to extricate themselves; and the possibilities for free and creative address of life's problems diminish rapidly, as the ability to take significant responsibility for life dissipates.

In our consideration of human historicity thus far, we have confined ourselves largely to the human by itself (so to speak), devoting only brief attention to the wider cosmic context which has given birth to human existence and continues to impinge upon it in many ways. This was done intentionally since it is impossible to examine and (re)construct all major features of a holistic world-picture at once. From the beginning I emphasized, however, that the human is but one component in Christian and other monotheistic categorial schemes, a component that cannot be properly understood independently of the other categories. It is important now, if we are to understand human historicity aright, that we see it in its interconnectedness with the wider cosmic context within which it appears. This is not only a methodological necessity of the approach we are following here: in today's ecologically self-conscious world it is a material requirement as well, laid on us by our awareness of the situatedness of human existence in the natural order and the disastrous consequences that follow from lack of responsible attention to this.

What we today identify as *religious* symbol-systems have largely provided human beings with their interpretations of the whole of reality in which they live as well as of the ultimate powers and other realities with which they have to do. Although the various religions have presented quite diverse construals of the mystery within which human existence transpires, they have usually succeeded in setting out a picture sufficiently intelligible and meaningful to enable the men and women in a particular time and place to (a) come to some significant understanding of themselves in relation to the context within which they found themselves, and (b) live out their lives (more or less) fruitfully and meaningfully within that context. It was a people's religion that gave them a sense of solidarity as a group, uniting them in common cause and a common sense of meaning (Durkheim). The symbol-system and the ritualistic practices of the religion helped fuse the biological energies of the people with their deeply felt bonds of social and interpersonal connectedness, focusing their consciousness and their activities in terms defined by a particular "center of value" (H. R. Niebuhr)[2] or complex of values and meanings. The religion of a people, thus, not only provided them with meaningful orientation in life (as I have suggested frequently here): it simultaneously evoked powerful motivations and loyalties that energized and directed their common life.

For an interpretation of human existence that emphasizes historicity, matters of this sort are obviously important. Our ability to take responsibility for ourselves—that is, to act in ways that maintain and enhance our historicity—depends upon our possessing both (a) knowledge of the world within which we live, of ourselves as actors in this world, and of the problems and the possibilities which confront us, and (b) motivation to live and act responsibly, even though we encounter formidable difficulties. The various religions, through developing powerful symbol-systems combined with significant patterns of life and action (rules and rituals), were able to create contexts within which human beings could live and act in what seemed to them meaningful and fruitful ways. By making available to women and men the deepest levels of the symbolic and ritualistic resources of their society, the religions have enabled them to look upon and to experience what they were doing and what they were living through as worthwhile, as worth committing themselves to sufficiently to make significant sacrifices should they be required—in short, as enabling them to see their activities as "meaningful." In this book, therefore, I use the words "religious" and "religion" (however complicated this all becomes when we consider a culture as "secular" as our own) to designate these underlying resources of meaning and ritual that inform and fund the ongoing living and dying in a culture as a whole.[3]

For most persons in most societies most of the time the affairs and problems of everyday life can be satisfactorily negotiated in terms of the ordinary patterns of meaning and action internalized from infancy on. There are, however, occasions when questions about whether life is worth the struggle, whether it makes sense to continue trying to live responsibly within the order in which one finds oneself, whether life really has significant meaning or is just an absurd scene of pain and suffering, may erupt powerfully. Here the religious myths and practices of a society, drawing on and expressing its deepest symbolic resources, become especially important. The myths present an interpretation of the overall context of human life—of the world and God (or the gods and other divine powers)—in terms of which human existence, whatever its pain and suffering and tragedy, is seen to have significant meaning; and the rituals and other religio-moral practices and rules offer forms of action through which meaningful participation in this symbolic world is facilitated. Because religious worlds in this way encourage, indeed require, active commitment and participation, they come to possess a strong sense of reality for those living within them, providing a context within which most of the more difficult crises of life can be faced. This contrasts sharply with the world-pictures created, for example, by the metaphysical or scientific imagination, which, however intriguing and persuasive intellectually, always seem somehow bloodless and abstract, presenting us with theoretical and speculative ideas of observers or spectators rather than the hard realities of the world within which we must actually live. Since the religious myths and rituals of a culture provide resources for the daily living and dying of human beings, they are able—with far greater success than most metaphysical or scientific theories—to attract the wholehearted allegiance of women and men. The deep and broad reserves of meaning which they make available "back up" the ongoing meaningfulness of everyday life and provide resources for times of profound personal and cultural tragedy. (Further discussion of some of these matters, with particular reference to the institutional dimensions of religion and the ambiguous situation of the churches in modern culture, will be found in Chapter 28.)

It is, perhaps, in situations of human extremity that the turn to specifically religious meaning most often occurs. We should not be surprised, therefore, to find that traditional religious consciousness and praxis have often focused more on our human powerlessness in the world—our suffering and illnesses, ignorance and failures, disasters and death—than on our freedom and creativity and achievements; and that (to explain and interpret these matters) notions of fate and karma and predestination, of the all-pervasiveness of suffering or sin, of the devil and other powers of evil, of creatureliness and finitude, and the like have been fashioned. The cold, hard reality of death—the experienced deaths of loved ones, and anticipation of and reflection on one's own death—everywhere seems to have impressed men and women with a strong sense of the ultimate powerlessness of humans in the world. Among the earliest religious practices of which we know are those concerned with death;[4] and the mythic resources of virtually every religion attempt to address the problem of death in some way (often with promises of life after death). Death is the outstanding symbol of the speciousness of human power; it suggests that, in the last analysis, we are more sufferers than actors, more at the disposal of external powers than the determiners of our own destiny. Together with birth, death symbolizes vividly the fact that our lives are always bounded by powers that call them forth and then also cut them off; we do not control our coming into being, nor can we avoid eventually departing. Birth and death display dramatically, thus, the extent to which our agency, our ability to act—whatever distinctive human powers it may represent—exists only within limits set from beyond itself, and cannot be rightly understood simply in terms of itself: our existence is determined radically, not only in past and future but in every present as well, from beyond the human sphere. We are not our own. This situatedness of human existence with respect to the powers that create, shape, sustain, and finally cut it off has (as is well known) been a central theme in all the great religious traditions. Each proposes its own distinctive interpretation of these matters;

in each we see an impressive attempt of the human imagination to come to terms with this fundamental condition of human existence.

It is important to note at this point that nothing quite like our modern notion of historicity—human existence understood as produced and decisively formed by past historical developments, and yet as having significant freedom to shape and take responsibility for the future—emerged as a central theme in any of the major religious traditions. In ancient Israel a distinctive sense of human responsibility gradually developed, and this prepared the way in important respects for this modern notion. And the idea of karma, which became so influential in the religions to which ancient India gave birth, contained elements which might have grown into something like the concept of historicity (though in fact karma actually functioned much more like the notion of fate, and it was not until quite recently that these other possibilities in it have come clearly into view). For millennia, of course, there have been critics of traditional religious pictures of the world and of the attempts of humans beings to interact with the various supposedly divine and other powers in life. Very few of these saw, however, that since all of these images and ideas—as well as our very notions of reality and truth—are products of the human imagination,[5] it is not only possible for humans to take greater responsibility for them, but important and right so to do. Precisely this (as we have seen) is what is implied by our modern idea of historicity, with its understanding that it was we humans who in the past created the culture which has in turn created us today; and that we must now, therefore, take responsibility for the future into which we are moving.

It is not possible here, and I do not have the competence, to present a phenomenological description of the various symbolic worlds which have appeared in the different religious traditions. That would be an interesting and important project in the philosophy of religion; and it would put us into a position to see better how these various schemes have actually functioned—what sorts of possibilities they each opened for humans and what sorts they closed off—thus enabling us, perhaps, to make comparative assessments on some issues of import.[6] As we have seen, the concept of historicity developed in this volume provides us with criteria for identifying major human problems; these criteria should also be useful in assessing the respects in which the various extant religious orientations and world-pictures have been appropriate and helpful in human efforts to address those problems.

This brief discussion of human religiousness may help us understand why the questions to which our examination of human historicity has now brought us—How should we today conceive the overall context within which human existence falls? What conception of the world in which we live would enable us best to come to terms with the central problems and evils which confront contemporary human life, including the fragility and dangerous deterioration of our historicity itself?—are of a sort which have not ordinarily been posed (explicitly) in the past. Each culture inherited (in its religious and other traditions) what were taken to be adequate world-pictures and conceptions; so questions of this sort simply did not arise. Past practice gives us little guidance, then, on just how we should move to address these matters.

The sorts of issues to which I am trying to call attention here can be posed more clearly if we reflect briefly on the following question: Is it possible for us (deliberately) to construct a picture or conception of the context of human life (as we understand this today) which will function *religiously* for us, that is, which will both orient us with respect to the issues that require our most urgent attention and motivate and energize us to address those issues? This question immediately raises several others: What holistic pattern or picture or concept should we today adopt as the "best" ("right"? "truest"? "most helpful"?) construal of the ultimate mystery of things? What conception or picture of the world do we need today as we attempt to identify and address the major evils and problems with which we must come to terms? What steps should we follow in order to construct this sort of vision of the overall context of human life?

Despite a wide modern consensus that humankind has emerged out of "lower" forms of life in the course of an evolutionary development on earth over many millennia, and could not exist apart from the whole web of life which continues to nourish and sustain it, it is not at all clear just how human historical existence is to be understood within this setting. For although human history has emerged within nature, and the natural order in all its mystery continues to remain its context, human beings—over the many millennia of their developing historicity—have acquired much knowledge about this natural world in which they live and also about their own constitution and possibilities; and this has given them very considerable powers over their immediate environment and over the physical and biological (as well as the sociocultural and psychological) conditions of their existence. So human beings, and the further course of human history, are no longer simply at the disposal of the natural order and the natural powers which brought them forth, in the way they were ten millennia ago: in and through their knowledge humans have gained some measure of transcendence over the nature of which they are part; and with their developing practices and skills, emerging in modernity into enormously powerful technologies, they have utterly transformed the face of the earth, even beginning to push beyond it into outer space. How, then, are we to understand the human qua human, qua historical being, in its context within nature? On the one hand, in its transcendence of the natural order within which it emerged, humanity today is obviously radically different from any other living creature; on the other hand, in its continuing "absolute dependence" (Schleiermacher) on the web of life from which and within which it emerged, it is of the same substance as the rest of life. And correlatively, what do these remarkable facts mean for our understanding of the world of nature itself? What does the fact that this sort of being—with self-consciousness, freedom, and the ability to take responsibility for itself—has emerged within this world tell us about the natural order, the powers and possibilities of nature?[7] As far back as we can trace, humans have wondered about their paradoxical position in the natural order: even the most primitive totemism provides its devotees with mythical interpretations of their relations to other creatures and their place in the world, and also with ritualistic procedures for enacting these matters (that is, for acting appropriately with respect to them). The most abstruse metaphysical theories are similarly attempts of highly sophisticated men and women to understand better the "real" context of human life, so that its meaning within that context can be rightly discerned.[8] In Parts III and IV of this book (to which we are now about to move), I shall attempt to address these religio-metaphysical issues in terms appropriate to contemporary thinking.

Since in moving to these questions we are beginning to address religious issues of the most fundamental sort, it should not surprise us to discover that much will prove to be obscure and baffling; as I have emphasized throughout, the deepest religious issues are always shrouded in mystery. How should we respond to this ultimate mysteriousness of things when we come up against it directly in this way? It is important to recognize that it is not just flat inscrutable mystery that we face here, mystery about which we can say nothing else than that we are utterly baffled by it; for this is not the way in which we are confronted. It is possible for us, in fact, to specify with some precision certain features of the mystery, and why we come up against it at just this particular point. In the earlier chapters of Part II I suggested that we are able to say a good bit about the "biohistorical" character of human existence: we run up against mystery now, when, on closer scrutiny, we see that the actual relation of the human to its context—the relation of the "historical" to the "bio"—is not as straightforward and intelligible as it at first may have seemed. The possibilities for purposive action, creativity, freedom, responsibility, reflectiveness, and thought, and the modalities of experience that have opened up in human existence, go so far beyond anything found in the forms of life from which humankind emerged that the question of whether or how this emergence can itself be understood becomes a serious issue. We shall have to give a good bit of attention to that question in Part III. We should note here, however, that in and with this problem we are in fact brought face to face with one of the ways in which the larger metaphysical/religious question about the place of human existence in the world—the meaning (or total lack of meaning) of human life in the ultimate scheme of things—today confronts us. What we will be attempting to address here, that is to say, will be a version of the profoundly existential mystery which has provoked—and also nourished—much human religious activity and reflection over the centuries.

It is unnecessary to repeat at this point what was said earlier (especially in Chapters 4 and 5) about the indissolubility of this mystery of the ultimate Whole of which we—and all else that we can know or imagine—are part (or whether it is even appropriate to think of this widest context of our lives as a "whole"). We are clearly beyond our depth here. And yet the questions will not go away. For we who live and think, experience and act, continually in terms of purposes and meanings, values and significances, cannot help but wonder—especially in moments of crisis or calamity or suffering, or of overwhelming tedium and boredom—what kind of sense it all makes, whether it makes any sense at all. In face of this ultimate mystery the various religions (and in modernity, quasi-religions like Marxism and humanism) have presented a variety of visions of the Whole within which human life falls, each providing its own interpretation of the meaning (or lack of meaning—which is also a meaning) of human existence, each thus suggesting how life should be understood and lived. We need to ask ourselves now whether it is possible, in full consciousness of the inscrutability of this mystery, for us to set about deliberately to construct a vision of the overall context of human life which is appropriate to our existence today—with its wide range of knowledges and technologies, and its enormous ecological, political, social, psychological, moral, and religious problems—a vision which will provide us with effective orientation in life and the world, as we seek to identify and address those issues which most require our attention and energies. Should we undertake a project as utterly daunting as this? Or would it be better to drop this idea entirely, as pretentious and absurd? But can we really afford *not* to make an attempt to understand, as best we can, the full complexity of the problematic situation in which humanity today finds itself? How else could we live and act responsibly in today's world?

Answers to questions of this sort cannot be given in the abstract. Only by working much further into this project itself—to see better what is actually involved in it, and what ways of addressing the issues suggest themselves—will we be in a position to make informed judgments on them. At this point it is well to remind ourselves again how the pictures and conceptions of the world which we find in the various religions were themselves originally created and developed. It is true, of course, that it was not by the kind of deliberate, self-conscious imaginative construction that I am proposing here. And yet what actually happened, though it extended over many generations of a long history instead of being worked out in a few chapters of a single book, was not all that different in certain crucial respects from what I am suggesting that we undertake.

Every religious tradition of which we know grew up over many generations in connection with the basic activities and experience of everyday living and dying—the continuous adaptation to and coping with the conditions and contingencies of life—of particular women and men in particular times and places. As they sought to address the issues that confronted them, they drew upon the resources of knowledge and wisdom and skill made available to them through traditions and practices passed on from earlier generations; but they also used their own inventiveness and ingenuity to come to terms with new and unexpected difficulties and problems. Each new generation thus added (sometimes only slightly, sometimes quite significantly) to the traditions it had inherited, deepening and enriching and refining them in response to the new circumstances which it confronted. Over the course of time, in each growing tradition, certain modes of thinking and acting, of meditation and practice, proved increasingly helpful in diagnosing and defining some of the more difficult problems and ills faced by the society, thus making available treatments and remedies that were healing and in other ways effective. These modes of understanding and praxis became, in due course, honored and respected and preferred to others—regarded as good and right and true, to be followed if the men and women of the society were to survive the terrors and evils of life in the threatening world roundabout. Out of these complexes of images and ideas and practices—including pictures and conceptions of the wider world which encompassed human life, as well as beliefs and disciplines that addressed day-to-day problems—what we today call the society's "religion" emerged among the growing patterns of specialization and institutionalization that were appearing in the culture. The world-pictures which became central to the religion were, of course, the ones which had grown up in the culture at large over many generations, as women and men sought to imagine—and thus better understand and come to terms with—the sort of world in which they lived; they were at first not in any way specifically or distinctly "religious" in our modern sense (which so sharply contrasts the "religious" with the "secular"). These human images and ideas of the world have always been the product of human imaginings in face of the wide range of problems confronted in life, the "imaginative construction" of pictures which made some sense of life by setting it in a wider and deeper context, thus facilitating (more or less) effective address of the problems which it posed.

The difference between my proposal (that we now undertake the construction of a plausible modern picture or conception of the world) and the processes which produced the great religious world-pictures of the past does not, then, lie in my claim that the major human problems we today confront require us to engage in "imaginative construction" of an appropriate world-picture (drawing on whatever wisdom, insights, knowledges, and practices are available in our culture). It was through just this kind of activity—however unselfconsciously engaged in—that the various religious traditions were originally produced and continually creatively modified over the centuries (by prophets, priests, poets, philosophers, theologians, and many others) as new contingencies and problems arose. My proposal differs only in its suggestion that we today are in a position to make this human religious constructivity more self-conscious, self-critical, and deliberate than has been possible previously; and that it would be, therefore, both obscurantist and irresponsible not to do so. In this volume I attempt to reconstruct the Christian categorial scheme in ways that will enable it (I hope) more effectively to orient life and reflection in face of some of the major problems confronting humankind today. As I have acknowledged throughout, the method of imaginative construction which I propose offers no final solutions to our theological (and other) problems: it is, however, a disciplined attempt to attack the issues we face—including the issue of how the world is to be understood, and with reference to what symbolic scheme(s) life should be oriented—as responsibly as I can. Further reflective and constructive work by others in the future will, no doubt, modify in decisive ways what I suggest here. This is to be expected, given the historical character of all our human work; and it has been the fate of every serious religious proposal or contention ever advanced.

Part III

Constructing a Concept of the Context of Human Existence: The World

Two things fill the mind with ever new and increasing admiration and awe, the oftener and more steadily they are reflected on: the starry heavens above me and the moral law within me.

Immanuel Kant

It must be remembered that the object of the world of ideas as a whole is not the portrayal of reality—this would be an utterly impossible task—but rather to provide us with an instrument for finding our way about more easily in this world.

Hans Vaihinger

Faith is our attitude toward reality as a whole, reason our attitude towards its details as distinct and separate from each other.

R. G. Collingwood

17. Small Steps of Faith

In earlier sections of this work I suggested that humans can best be characterized as biohistorical beings, beings with historicity—that is, beings who have been in important respects created by history, and who in turn create further history. Over many millennia humans have created cultures, languages, social institutions, and these in turn have become the molds which formed each new generation, transforming and developing the animality with which human life begins into the historicity within which beings with self-consciousness, with some measure of freedom and purposive creativity, with some ability to take responsibility for themselves and their societies could emerge. Now we must ask ourselves: given all of this, how should we move to construct a picture or conception of the larger context within which our lives fall which will enable us to understand better (a) what we humans are and (b) what we can and should do in the world in which we find ourselves? What distinctive features would such a conception of the world have; and through what steps do we need to move to construct this conception? Then, with our picture of the world and our understanding of ourselves as biohistorical beings more or less in place, how should we move on to construct a conception of God for today? This last question is the most important of all, for it is in terms of the symbol "God" that our western languages and cultures most fully and profoundly represent to us that which is ultimately Real, True, Good. "God" is the name, thus, of that to which we can give ourselves and our lives without reservation, the proper object of our unqualified devotion, that in terms of which human life in the world can most properly be oriented. Clearly our conception of God cannot be developed independently of our understanding of the world; but neither can our conception of the world be constructed completely independently of our understanding of God—if it is indeed our intention ultimately to sketch a *theocentric* world-picture. At a number of points in Part III, therefore, we will be engaged quite as much in the deconstructing and reconstructing of the concept of God as in working out a conception of the world. These two tasks must be carried out in tandem with each other.[1]

There are four considerations which we will need to keep in mind as we proceed: (a) It is the ultimate mystery within which human life falls with which we are dealing here at every point; we are, thus, attempting to address questions which will finally prove to be beyond our grasp. What we say will need to be expressed cautiously and with reservations. (b) Despite these problems (as I have argued in Part II) we have good reasons to believe that we have some fairly reliable knowledge about ourselves, about what it is to be human—for example, that we are biohistorical beings with some measure of freedom, some powers of imagination and creativity, et cetera. (c) We also believe we know some things about our world—the commonsense knowledge which enables us to get along from day to day; the vast stores of scientific and historical knowledge accumulated during recent centuries; the awareness that our world is of the sort that has given birth to, and continues to sustain, processes of life, including such highly complex forms as we ourselves. (d) All of this will need to be brought into relationship with what the symbol "God" has meant in our religious traditions: that "X" (whatever it may now prove to be) which we can properly take as that to which we should give our unqualified devotion and service. In Part II I sketched the understanding of the human with which we will be working throughout the remainder of this volume; now in Part III we must take up the questions raised for theological construction by modern conceptions of the world. In Part IV we shall build on Parts II and III as we move on to address directly the most difficult task of all those confronting contemporary theologians: the construction of a conception of God appropriate for today.

For contemporary women and men the question of the concept of the world (cosmology) has become very complex. It is clear that we humans have in many ways dramatically transformed our environment, the context within which we live, from the order of nature within which we originally emerged. The world in which we live, thus, cannot be conceived any longer simply as a given structure which women and men must accept precisely as it is. In many respects it is plastic to our interests and purposes; we have the freedom and power to make it into something that it at present is not. To what extent do we have such freedom and power? To what extent are we constrained by orders and powers completely beyond our control? And in what respects *should* we attempt to transform further the world in which we live, and the structure of human existence itself? All these questions require address if we are to be properly oriented in life today.

What moves should we make to address these issues? Is there any way to make a valid, or at least usable, assessment or decision about the nature of the world in which we live? How can we deal with deep and obscure metaphysical questions of this sort? It may seem that in the constructive work on human existence sketched in Part II certain important metaphysical decisions about the world have already been made (at least implicitly) and that these underlie what we have done thus far—for example, I may seem to have taken for granted that the modern "common creation story" (as Sallie McFague has called it),[2] according to which we live in an evolutionary-historical universe, a universe ever moving forward toward an open-ended future, is metaphysical truth. To draw that conclusion, however, would be a mistake. It is certainly the case that for any overall world-picture to be plausible and intelligible today, it must meet certain stipulations implied by our anthropological and cosmological reflections. There must be, for example, a significant place in this world for the kind of evolutionary-historical development which is so central to our modern thinking about the universe and humanity's place within it. Moreover, the world will have to be conceived in such a way as to allow for an understanding of what we have called human historicity; that is, it cannot be a tight, fully determined and determinate structure, but must be one in which there is sufficient openness or looseness to allow a certain ongoing creativity which ultimately may produce agents capable of purposes, decisions, and actions, agents to some extent free and responsible. But these stipulations can be accommodated in a number of ways; they do not, as such, commit us to one particular overarching worldview. What they demand is that any conception of the world which we adopt must provide a background for and help make sense of (a) modern scientific knowledge (or theories) about the developmental character of the universe in which we live, and about the origins of human life; and (b) the biohistorical conception of the human (including the normatively human) which sums up our contemporary understanding of human being.

Up to this point we have not directly faced questions about the metaphysical reality of the world, and about the meaning of human life within this ultimate reality. For most people throughout most of history (as we have noted) religious myths have provided answers to whatever ultimate questions were posed; and it has been the terms supplied by these myths, therefore, that have defined the overall context within which men and women have lived out their lives. In our project here, however, we do not want to take over uncritically the mythic patterns (whether ancient or modern) which are available to us. Instead we shall attempt to construct a conception of the world (and of God) appropriate to the knowledges we have available and to the problems with which we humans today must contend. As we shall see, there are a number of alternative positions open to us when we face these extremely general and abstract questions about the ultimate nature of things. Since no coercive reasons can be given for adopting any one of these,[3] in order to move forward we shall have to make some choices. Whichever direction we move will, then, involve what some have called "leaps of faith." I think this kind of dramatic talk is misleading, however, and I would prefer to speak of a number of "small steps" of faith that we must take as we build up our picture of the world and of God.

At this point some might suggest that the wiser move would be to remain completely agnostic on all such issues. This suggestion takes seriously the insight that human life and its cosmic context are ultimately inscrutable mysteries to us. Since we have no way of dissolving these mysteries, we had best simply acknowledge them and then get on with our day-to-day life as best we can. Let us, then, deal with the concrete problems of life as they arise, putting all these obscure and impossible metaphysical questions out of mind lest they distract us from the business at hand, or otherwise confuse or mislead us. This appears to be the advice given in some forms of Buddhism; the Buddha himself is reputed to have counseled against getting tied up in metaphysical pursuits.[4] It is also the way that modern positivism has often seemed to go. There is no question that this alternative should always be kept in mind, as we look at the complexity and the difficulties of the metaphysical issues that confront us.

It is doubtful, however, that it is really possible to suspend judgment completely on these questions about what we humans really are, what kind of world we live in, whether human existence has any meaning in the cosmic scheme of things. Can we in fact address our human problems, even decide what are the most important problems to which we should be attending, without making (or presupposing) *some* judgments on metaphysical questions like these? Is it really possible to presuppose nothing at all regarding what is finally real, and what place humans have in the real scheme of things (whether we acknowledge this or not)? Both ancient Buddhism and modern positivism seem in fact to make certain assumptions about these matters:[5] Buddhism sees all reality as an ever-changing flux, with human life regarded as essentially *duhkha,* or suffering; and most positivists, though making metaphysical disclaimers, seem to take it for granted that we live in a fundamentally materialistic order, with human life an accidental evolutionary development on earth. In both these cases, morever, the suggestions about how life should be ordered appear to be fully consistent with these *metaphysical* assumptions; they clearly influence the practical advice and actual lifestyles which are generated by these positions. Even in these cases, then, it is doubtful that we are presented with a thoroughgoing metaphysical agnosticism. Certainly it is possible speculatively—that is, in our reflection and thinking—to remain skeptical or agnostic about these so-called ultimate questions; but when we must *act,* for example with respect to the needs and problems of another human being, or in connection with the massive human social problems that confront us today, or with regard to the pollution of our environment or the possibility of nuclear war, we have to make choices about what is important and what is less significant or unessential. And this cannot be done without making some judgments (at least implicitly) about what is really going on in our world, what is really the case with human beings and the world.

It seems both prudential and more candid, then, to deal with these assumptions about reality, these metaphysical questions, as openly and explicitly as we can. In that way we will at least be made aware of some of the presuppositions underlying our thoughts and actions, and will be able to assess, to some extent, their validity or desirability; the claims and points of view which we may have unconsciously picked up from this or that tradition will then not be left entirely unexamined and uncriticized.

Whether we actually move toward making some self-conscious metaphysical judgments, as I am advocating here—rather than leaving these matters at the level of (largely implicit) presuppositions—must remain, of course, a matter of choice (once we have become aware of this issue). There seem to be three alternatives that are open to us at this point, none of them susceptible to a fully coercive argument. First, we may, if we wish, choose to follow the positivistic/agnostic option, and simply not pursue these matters further. Second, we can take up what might be considered an essentially dogmatic position (no invidiousness intended), accepting the teachings of one or another religious or secular tradition as giving us the truth about human life and the world, and proceeding to order our lives accordingly. (In actual practice, as I suggested a moment ago and also earlier in Chapter 4, most attempts to remain thoroughly agnostic on these matters in fact issue in a dogmatic position, though perhaps quite unconsciously.) Third, we can decide to go down a more reflective religious/metaphysical road, seeking to think self-consciously and deliberately about these ultimate religious and metaphysical questions, searching for a position that seems plausible and justifiable.

At this point, with this choice before us, we have arrived at an important fork in the road with respect to our theological work. Though the picture of the world and of human life which has thus far been presented in this book as typically modern has obviously been my own construction, it is a construction that claims to be based upon a summing up and pulling together of widely accepted "factual knowledge" drawn from the physical and social sciences and from history. However, as I noted when beginning to sketch these themes (see, for example, Chapter 8), they rest on important presuppositions about the nature of knowledge, how it is acquired and how tested, and about human life and the world—presuppositions which we moderns largely take for granted (that is, which we accept on faith) but which have by no means been always and everywhere accepted. Since our objective in those preliminary anthropological investigations was to construct an understanding of humanity that would be intelligible in contemporary terms—that is, that would be in significant positive relationship to modern widely accepted knowledges—I chose at that point not to engage in criticism of those presuppositions or of the knowledges based on them, but instead accepted them as providing a reasonable point of entry into our theological work. Now, however, as we begin to consider specifically metaphysical issues, we can no longer take for granted all these presuppositions. Certain of them will need to be explored (however briefly), or we must decide deliberately to ignore the whole metaphysical question. Many thoughtful persons, as we have already noted, do not regard it as either necessary or wise to spend time on issues of this sort; and those who are prepared to look at them are very far from agreement about them. We will not be able here to work our way through long and elaborate formal metaphysical arguments—that would take us far beyond the scope of a book of this sort, leading us into many technical questions—but I will propose that we make some decisions about certain broad metaphysical issues that bear directly on how we understand human existence. It will not be possible any longer, therefore, for us to claim that our procedure is based on a widely accepted modern faith-consensus. Rather, we will be looking at alternatives, none of which have overwhelming arguments supporting them; and we will be making choices among these. As we shall see, these metaphysical choices will articulate—and also help to make possible—some "steps of faith" which lead ultimately to a conception of God to which, as I believe, moderns can commit themselves with integrity.

Faith in God involves a number of important—and controversial—metaphysical claims, that is, claims about how things really are and what human life is all about. Therefore, any thoroughgoing agnostic response to all metaphysical questions—a refusal to take any position at all on the place of humanity within the cosmic scheme of things—is clearly a rejection from the outset of all moves toward constructing an understanding of reality in which God has a significant place. It must be granted, however, that a metaphysical agnosticism of this sort does not necessarily close the door on every significantly "Christian" orientation on human life and the world. There are perspectives which give Jesus Christ centrality in their understanding of what human life is all about, what is good and meaningful and true in human affairs, but which prefer not to make any significant claims about God. One can, for example, regard Jesus as an exemplary human being—indeed, as a model or standard of what is truly human and humane—and can seek to orient one's life in terms of love of neighbor and enemy, without taking up any particular position on the nature of ultimate reality or the question of God. It is not surprising, then, that some forms of Christian humanism—such as the recent so-called "God is dead" theology—have explicitly held Jesus in high regard but have been negative or agnostic about God. One need not, of course, be as explicit and blatant about this matter as this; one can, for instance, continue to use the symbol "God" rather freely without seriously concerning oneself about its implications for one's understanding of life and the world. It is not essential, then, in order to orient one's life in largely Christian terms—including use of the symbol "God"—to make a move beyond metaphysical agnosticism. But it is necessary to make such a move if one wishes to develop a *theology* (whether Christian or other)—that is, a carefully thought through understanding of God, and of the meaning of God for contemporary life; for talk about God claims to be talk about what is ultimately important, ultimately real, in human affairs. Hence, to move forward with a constructive theology, we must be willing to take the risk—in face of the ultimate mystery of life—of making some hard decisions about the important and the real.

One way we might go here would be to follow a straightforwardly *dogmatic* approach: to simply affirm (what are regarded as) traditional Christian claims (or some other claims) regarding who or what God (ultimate reality) is; and go on from there. If, however, we resist this kind of dogmatic approach (which assumes it already knows the answers to these difficult and controversial questions and therefore need not enter into any investigation of them), our decision to move toward exploration of certain metaphysical issues pertinent to theology can be regarded as a first or beginning step toward a more self-critical faith.

We will discover, as we move along this path, that faith in God is not really a matter of a single gigantic "leap" into trust in or belief in God, as Kierkegaard (and many others have) maintained. It is built up, rather, out of a number of metaphysical moves and claims which, when they cumulate into a full-blown understanding of reality, and of the human place in this reality, constitute a theocentric world-picture. We noted much earlier in this volume that the program of theological construction in which we are engaged rests on certain commitments: on the one hand we committed ourselves to taking seriously the modern scientific understanding of the cosmos as an evolutionary ecosystem, with humanity emerging and having its place within that system (see Chapter 8); on the other, we committed ourselves to seeking, or at least to exploring the possibility of, orientation for human life in the terms specified by the Christian categorial scheme, which gives a central place to the categories of God and Christ in addition to those of humanity and the world (see Chapter 7). We have devoted a good bit of time to considering the respects in which the first prong of this double act of faith—this double commitment—itself provides us with a beginning orientation for life in the modern world, through enabling us to develop a picture of human existence and its situatedness within its context. Now we shall begin to explore what is involved in the second prong of that initial commitment, as we seek to see how the Christian categorial scheme bears on the overall comprehensive frame of orientation we are attempting to develop. What would a Christian framework for today look like and why might we be justified in employing it for life-orientation? To address these issues we shall examine one by one several further "small steps of faith" suggested by the Christian categorial scheme—steps which, when taken together, will constitute a contemporary version of that scheme—attempting to take into account the alternatives or options which confront us at each of these points. Thus, we should be able to ascertain how far we are willing to commit ourselves along the path that leads to a Christian theological frame of orientation for today, to a symbolic world in which God and Christ play decisive roles in orienting life.

The first such further step of faith, the first decision to be made on this path, is the one we have just now been considering: do we wish to commit ourselves to the possibility and the desirability of attempting to think through (at least in a rudimentary way) our position on some aspects of the ultimate questions about life, death, and reality? Or do we prefer to remain agnostic or positivistic on these issues, or to accept uncritically the dogmatic claims of some religion or philosophy? When I say this is a "first step," it should be understood that I do not mean this in a psychological or genetic sense, that before people can believe in God they must believe in the legitimacy and importance of metaphysics. That would be absurd: most persons who believe in God have given little or no thought to the metaphysical issues with which we shall concern ourselves. Rather, I am speaking here of a first step in an ordered activity of theological construction. In the movement in which we are now engaged—a movement from what we have considered to be largely factually given matters (our sketch of the modern understanding of human life as transpiring within the evolutionary ecosystem here on earth) to the wider, more comprehensive metaphysical issues on which faith takes positions—this is the first step we shall take. It is an appropriate first step because it deals with the most basic presupposition of all further theological construction, namely, that it is plausible and desirable that we commit ourselves to examining pertinent metaphysical issues.

It is important to be completely clear that this is a step of *faith,* a free decision to go forward with this commitment because of our interest in exploring the meaning which God might have for us today, not a decision in any way forced upon us by "scientific" or other "objective" evidence or argument. In taking this step we are beginning a movement *of* faith, and *toward* faith, in God; we are not at the beginning of some sort of rational "proof" of the existence of God, or even at the beginning of an argument intended to persuade us to believe in God. The human stance toward God from beginning to end is one of faith in face of the ultimate mystery of life; and what we are attempting to do here is bring into view and examine some of the major components of this sort of faith. Hence, this decision to begin an exploration of certain metaphysical questions is properly understood as a step of faith, not of rational argument.

If we are prepared now to make such a first step—to take up these matters—what beginning options does it open for us? This is a large and difficult question. We must remember that our exploration here is not to be grounded primarily in a speculative interest in the question of what is ultimately real but rather in the practical interest of finding orientation for life in face of the problems and evils of modernity—and in the hope that the central Christian symbols may provide us with such orientation. We will not, therefore, attempt to sketch out a full metaphysics or cosmology here, but will confine ourselves to exploring those metaphysical questions that (a) are bound up with, or will lead us toward, the symbols of "God" and "Christ," and (b) are important for providing orientation for men and women in face of the problems and evils of the modern world. Which metaphysical questions are these? How shall we decide which issues to investigate?

Three dialectically interconnected considerations will guide our explorations: (a) the understanding of the sort of beings we humans are, and of our place in the world, already reached in the earlier chapters of this book; (b) our sense of the way "God" and "Christ" function in the Christian categorial scheme (as sketched in a preliminary way in Chapters 6 and 7); and (c) our intuitions and insights (probably more or less uncriticized at this point) of the deepest problems and evils with which men and women around the globe must today contend. We humans need symbolic orientation in life, unlike any other animals, because we are moral beings who must take responsibility for our lives and actions. The Christian faith claims to provide such orientation by proposing a categorial scheme in which "God" and "Christ" are fundamental symbols: "God" is the name given to that reality which grounds, makes possible, and calls forth all that exists—including, of course, beings with historicity and freedom, such as ourselves; and "Christ" is at once the premier image of the normatively human and an indispensable link to this God. On the one hand, then, we need to explore what must be said about the cosmos (the world) if freedom, historicity, and responsibility are to be intelligible; on the other, we must ask what sort of orientation—in face of the major problems and evils which seem evident to us today—can be provided to us biohistorical beings in this sort of world by the symbols "God" and "Christ."

We can begin to see what is involved here by getting clearer in mind certain characteristics of the symbol "God." Let us take note briefly of some features of this symbol as it originally developed (under the name "Yahweh") in the traditions of Israel. The Israelites became acquainted with Yahweh as the one who had brought them out of Egypt and given them the land of Canaan as a homeland. That is, Yahweh was first known as a reality which upset structures of social and political domination and exploitation, bringing about the liberation of those who had been enslaved.[6] This movement into freedom was originally understood in an objectifying mythic way, as brought about by a particular divine being who acted to bring Israel's release from captivity. But we need not suppose that the most important point of this early story has to do with the *existence* of this mythic being; rather, it is concerned with the actuality of historical liberative power in the world, transforming the situation of these slaves.

What is this power, and why is this situation different from any other breaking-loose from captivity which took place in antiquity? There must have been many similar master-slave struggles: what peculiar significance does this one have? We must note that (whatever may have been going on in other such cases) here the struggle was not understood (in the texts which became influential in ancient Israel and its religious descendants) as simply one more attempt of an enslaved people to gain freedom. For the initiative and the effective power in this struggle were not seen as simply and directly an expression of the desires of some slaves: it was Yahweh who called the people out of Egypt and who empowered them in their struggle with Pharaoh. That is, the slaves objectified their desire for liberation into the mythic god Yahweh, in this way attributing the historical movement toward liberation to something other and greater than themselves and their own immediate desires: it was the notion of a liberating power, or spirit, working within and through history that was emphasized. In this mythic account, thus, a *cosmic* ground and source of the movement toward liberation is posited; the movement is not due simply to the human desire to be free.

This "step of faith" of the ancient Hebrews is one in which we may or may not wish to join. Its importance from the point of view of our work here is that it suggests understanding the human dynamism toward freedom in a metaphysically more fundamental way than simply through attributing it to human discomfort and pain (though of course such basic human feelings are also involved). Human liberty, self-determination, a people's ability to take responsibility for their own social order, to create their own history, are here displayed—by the objectifying and mythic language that attributes their empowering to Yahweh—as having an extra-human grounding. Thus it became possible to focus on and attend to precisely these dimensions of human being—in the form, now, of their mythic objectification into the idea of God (a point on which Feuerbach was to concentrate much later)—giving these central importance in the interest and activities of the people. That is, through their conception of God the early Israelites were enabled to begin to imagine—and thus to create—a picture of a world in which these motifs (liberty, self-determination, ability to take responsibility) had centrality and metaphysical grounding.

This world (this picture of the world) gradually unfolded (that is, was *created*) in the course of Israel's history; in hindsight we can see that its significance involved much more than the mere liberation of a few slaves. The prophets and the lawmakers of Israel came to see Yahweh as one who was particularly concerned with the oppressed and the downtrodden: for just this reason, special care was to be taken of the widow and the sick and the stranger in the land. So notions of social justice, and of the solidarity and equality of all members of society with one another, developed out of (or at least came to be authorized by) the conception of Yahweh the liberator; and justice, righteousness, mercy, and the like were understood to be required of humans. In the further articulation of this picture God is seen increasingly as that X (whatever it might be) which calls forth and undergirds and enhances human existence as *moral* (that is, as concerned with taking responsibility for others as well as oneself). At first, of course, this sense of solidarity and morality was applied largely to Israel (though we should not forget the emphasis on duties to the stranger). But by the time of the prophet Amos (middle of the eighth century B.C.E.) it was becoming clear (at least to some) that God's activity and morality must be of much wider significance than this. This theme gets further development in Habakkuk, Jonah, and others, and as Israel comes to understand itself to have a mission to all humankind (suggested in the "call of Abraham," Gen. 12:1–3; in the "servant songs" of Second Isaiah; and elsewhere).

As Yahweh gradually emerged from being a God bound only to the Hebrews and became the creator of the heavens and the earth, the mythic objectification of liberative activity in the symbol "Yahweh" made possible a growing consciousness of the universality of the demands of morality. And thus morality, freedom, responsibility—what was to become historicity—became understood as grounded in that which is at the foundation of all that exists. The focus of human life and action in this way became significantly enlarged beyond narrowly human concerns to the reality which underlies the world as a whole; and the possibility of profound human concern for that wider world (however anthropocentrically conceived at this point) was thus opened up and encouraged. Mythic developments of this sort should not be regarded as mere epiphenomena of the human, and they certainly should not be seen as limited in significance to only one human cultural stream: they clearly bear a much wider—potentially universal—import. We must note, however, that it is not the mythic objectification as such that is important; it is, rather, the conception, which is beginning to be formulated in and through that objectification, of the cosmic grounding of certain features of human moral and historical existence.

These reflections could be carried much further, but here I shall take them only one more step. The creation of this vision of a "moral universe" under Yahweh's governance gave rise to the enormously difficult problem of theodicy: why is there evil in a world governed by a just God? Prophets like Jeremiah found their own sufferings difficult or impossible to understand; and in Job, Habakkuk, and the meditations on the "suffering servant" the articulation of these sorts of issues was extended in new ways. In due course reflection on these matters led to further deepening of the understanding both of morality and of its metaphysical grounding (though the problems themselves remained unresolved). When Jesus of Nazareth appeared on the scene (much later, of course), his teaching, ministry, and death—as interpreted in light of themes suggested by the "servant songs" of Second Isaiah—impressed themselves deeply on the minds of a small group of followers. The radicality of Jesus' emphasis on forgiveness, love, healing, and service, rather than lordship or domination, provided a way to understand his own suffering and death: these were vicarious, undertaken for others, even though they led to Jesus' personal loss of the strong sense of God's care which had empowered his ministry (cf. Mk. 15:34). Thus, radical mercy and forgiveness, self-sacrifice and love even of enemies, came to be given their own special cosmic (theological) significance and grounding within the new communities of love, freedom, and responsibility that were born through Jesus' ministry and became central to the Christian vision.

It is not likely that any of this would have occurred without the mythic and narrative form in which it was all originally conceived. But (I must emphasize again) this objectifying form is not the really important matter for us to focus on: as we shall see in due course, God need not (indeed, should not) be understood as a particular object, being, or person in some way over against the world. Rather, that to which we should here direct our attention is the faith-claim about this extra-human activity which gives us our humanity, which enables us to be human—that to which, therefore, we must give ourselves if humanity is to find a fitting way to live in the world, and is thus to realize its potential.

These brief remarks provide us with some guidance for the theologico-metaphysical construction which we are now about to undertake. We shall attempt to develop a conception of the world and that which is ultimate which focuses attention on that reality (or those realities) that ground and sustain us as human, that is, as beings with historicity, freedom, and responsibility. We are undertaking these metaphysical explorations and construction for the purpose of gaining more adequate orientation in life for today—that is, orientation *for us humans,* as we seek to find our proper place in the world. A conception of the world which abstracted from the fact and significance of the existence of humanity (as do many modern cosmologies), however valuable it might be for certain (scientific or philosophical) purposes, would be of little direct help in our project of providing significant orientation for human beings—just as little help as a conception of the world out of touch with contemporary scientific reflection. We will not, then, be seeking here to develop a picture simply of "reality as such," if that is taken to mean reality without attention to our distinctively human presence in it: it is reality as providing a foundation for, and continuing sustenance for, human existence that we are seeking to understand and to articulate. But it must be equally emphasized that we are not interested here in simply projecting a human fantasy onto the cosmos, painting a picture of what we would like to believe is true, but for which there is little or no justification and which could only, thus, be misleading in life.

The metaphysical task which we are undertaking has important practical implications for the everyday lives, and the exceedingly difficult problems, of women and men today. If in and through these metaphysical explorations we are successful in developing a picture of the world which illuminates our human position within it, and which, therefore, enables us to say something about that which grounds and calls forth human—and (we can properly hope) humane and ecologically responsible—existence (as we understand these matters today), we will be well on our way toward constructing a contemporary conception of God—the real God who is in fact our creator, sustainer, and redeemer, and thus the God whom we today can and should worship and serve with unqualified devotion, respect, and love.

18. Cosmic Visions and Human Meaning

The first "small step of faith" in our construction of an understanding of God for today was the decision to enter the metaphysical arena and take upon ourselves the responsibility for making judgments and claims about what, from a human perspective, may properly be regarded as of ultimate importance and reality. In making that step we rejected both the positivist insistence that humans should attempt to ignore or avoid all metaphysical issues, attending instead simply to the "practical" tasks involved in meeting the problems of everyday life; and also the dogmatic position that what is ultimately important to humans is already known (in this or that tradition), and that therefore it is unnecessary, or perhaps even a serious mistake, to seek guidance for human life by engaging in inquiries of a metaphysical sort. With the rejection of those alternatives, we made the small step of affirming our faith that certain sorts of metaphysical exploration are worth undertaking in connection with our move toward a contemporary understanding of God. We are now in a position to proceed to a second step involving the consideration of some very general metaphysical questions in the background of the basic cosmological and theological issues with which we are concerned.

There are many ways in which we might frame the principal metaphysical questions which the Christian categorial scheme raises, and I shall not try to sort them all out. What we are interested in here is developing a world-picture or understanding of the world which can make intelligible our own existence as free historical beings, beings capable of taking significant responsibility for ourselves, and which can thus provide us with helpful orientation for dealing with the issues posed by contemporary life. Let us turn our attention to two major questions about the world in which we live, questions on which we need to make decisions. The first is a formal one, about the metaphysical significance of *time,* of temporality; the second is a material question regarding the metaphysical ultimacy of such things as purpose, meaning, will, consciousness—what we can refer to collectively as *spirit.* As we shall see, these questions are interconnected, and we shall, therefore, take them up in relation to each other. Our way of dealing with these two issues will set the stage for our further cosmological work, and thus will constitute a second small step of faith (or toward faith) in God.

The first question—about time—may be framed in terms of the following alternative: Should we conceive the evolutionary-historical development here on earth (which has given rise to human existence) (a) as transpiring within *an eternal structure* of things which follows essentially the same patterns forever, that is, as set within parameters or limits determined by some eternal, unchanging order? or (b) as a part, and expression of, *a cosmic evolutionary-historical process* that characterizes or pervades all reality? If we take the first alternative, processes of evolution and history of the sort to which we found it necessary to pay so much attention in developing our understanding of human existence do not have ultimate metaphysical significance; and they should not be taken as providing significant clues to what is ultimately real. These events and processes (as well as all others) should be understood to occur within limits and according to patterns set by cosmic structures or orders that cannot in any way be violated, transcended, or transformed. In its ultimate structure the universe is not fundamentally evolutionary or open-ended; rather, it simply is what it is, always and forever the same. Doubtless the processes going on within the universe occasionally throw up unique events or developments—as they have, for example, on earth—but the cycles of endless change are like a vast system of wheels spinning on forever, always moving yet always the same in their fundamental patterns. On this view our human existence—what we humans are and what we can be and do—is to be regarded as essentially a kind of cosmic accident of merely local interest in our corner of the world. Our evolutionary-historical development is simply one more or less accidental phase of the eternal spin.

This sort of interpretation of the ultimate context of human life (a not uncommon one) is reminiscent of the ancient astrological and religious conceptions of life as taking place within a system of great cosmic cycles, each lasting many thousands of years, a pattern common to much Hindu, Buddhist, and Greek thinking. Human life goes on within a fundamentally unchanging cosmic order. Within this overall picture, the details of life may be thought of either as fully determined in all respects (as in certain types of fatalism) or, in conceptions of a looser sort, as somewhat chancy, open, and even free. In either case, however, according to this view it is *structure* that is the metaphysical ultimate, not process or change. The basic question about human existence becomes, therefore, whether we should orient ourselves in terms of the local earthly changes and developments in history, with all the insecurities and anxieties these tend to promote; or whether, recognizing that none of these have any final or ultimate meaning, we should orient ourselves primarily with reference to the fundamental, eternal, unchanging structure of things, an immovable rock of ultimate security. Given the enormous problems which our historicity raises for us, the answer might well seem obvious.

The other great metaphysical frame which we have inherited from antiquity does not attempt to understand ultimate reality in terms of a (supposedly) eternal structure underlying everything, but instead sees historical development in time as central. In this view change is more fundamental than structure: all structures come into being in the course of time and eventually pass away again in time. This perspective reached its most influential early articulation in ancient Israel, where the world-process (God's activity) was seen as having a beginning, as going through several stages of historical development in which God's purposes were gradually being worked out, and as ultimately reaching a consummation or goal when God's purposes would be realized. In this scheme the structures and cycles of the cosmos are not permanent or eternal; they come into being through God's creative activity in time. While human life has a proximate setting within the context of natural processes, and itself involves repeated cycles of birth, growth, death, and decay, its ultimate meaning is to be seen within the wider context of God's unfolding purposes.

Our earlier conclusion (in Part II), that human existence is evolutionary-historical, in no way settled the religious and metaphysical issues about the ultimate context of human life posed by the option now before us. Whether women and men should orient themselves in terms of reality conceived on the model of *natural structure* or on the model of *evolutionary-historical development* is left entirely undetermined by that discussion. If, however, we are to be able realistically and effectively to tackle the fundamental religious questions of what we humans should seek to make of our humanity, what goals we should posit for human life, what we should attempt to do here in the history in which we find ourselves, we must make some attempt to address this issue. Answers to these religious questions will depend, in part, on the answer we give to this question about the metaphysical significance of time.

In the past (as we have noted) it has been religious myths, world-pictures, and worldviews which have provided a sense of the ultimate context within which human life transpires and in terms of which, therefore, its real meaning can be grasped. And there has been a great divide among human civilizations between these two fundamentally distinct perspectives: those which have taken structure/order/being as primary, an emphasis characteristic of most of human religious history (including especially "eastern" religious traditions, but also Greece); and those which have taken history/change/process/development as primary, essentially the descendants of ancient Israel (Judaism, Christianity, Islam, but also Marxism, and modern secular humanism with its confidence in historical progress).[1] The central religious problem, then, for most of humankind, has been: How can we come into and maintain a secure relationship with that which is absolutely stable, dependable, unmoving—that is, the ultimate order of things, the ground of all being—thus giving us security, assurance, in face of what Eliade has called the "terror of history"?[2]

But in ancient Israel religious development took a different direction. Change and movement, the historical process itself, became valued as meaningful, since Yahweh was understood to be at work within it moving the world toward a goal of significance to human beings. As the prophet Micah put it:

> It shall come to pass in the latter days
> that the mountain of the house of the Lord
> shall be established as the highest of the mountains . . .
> and [people] shall beat their swords into plowshares,
> and their spears into pruning hooks;
> nation shall not lift up sword against nation,
> neither shall they learn war any more;
> but they shall sit every man under his vine and under his fig tree,
> and none shall make them afraid;
> for the mouth of the Lord of hosts has spoken. (4:1, 3–4)

Sometimes this vision of the overcoming of all strife and terror in God's world was extended from its human setting to include all living creatures. For example, in the familiar words of Isaiah:

> The wolf shall dwell with the lamb,
> and the leopard shall lie down with the kid,
> and the calf and the lion and the fatling together . . .
> They shall not hurt or destroy
> in all my holy mountain;
> for the earth shall be full of the knowledge of the Lord
> as the waters cover the sea. (11:6–9)

Later on Second Isaiah restates this vision of the glorious time to come within the context of his expectation that Yahweh is about to "create new heavens and a new earth" (65:17), that is, the basic structures of the cosmos itself are to be transformed as history comes to its consummation.

We have, then, two quite different religious visions, each providing an interpretation of human existence and its meaning in terms of a distinct conception of the ultimate scheme of things. According to one, time, temporality, presents an enormous threat to all things good and significant to humans—to dissolve them away, to dissipate them, finally to destroy them; but an ultimate stability and peace in face of this threat are available to humans if they connect themselves and their lives securely to the unmoved and unmoving eternal order of being which grounds all that is. According to the other, far from being an ultimate threat to human well-being, time is the vehicle of salvation. This forward-looking positive valuation of time became especially powerful in the early Christian era; Paul put it this way:

> I consider that the sufferings of this present time are not worth comparing with the glory that is to be revealed to us. . . . the creation itself will be set free from its bondage to decay and obtain the glorious liberty of the children of God. . . . we ourselves, who have the first fruits of the Spirit, groan inwardly as we wait for adoption as sons, the redemption of our bodies. For in this hope we were saved. (Rom. 8:18, 21, 23–24a)

In the one case, thus, the movement through time is a threat and an evil, something to be avoided and, if possible, overcome. In the other, the movement through time is positively valued, a good, because through it the kingdom of God and thus the final fulfillment for humanity (and, indeed, creation as a whole) is being ushered in. These two conceptions of the significance of time imply two radically different understandings of human existence, two quite different proposals about how humans should orient themselves in life. They are based on sharply different assessments of the nature of the world in which we live and of what is going on in that world. How should we choose between them? Which one is correct?

It is my contention that this is a misleading way to pose the issue, for it confronts us with an unanswerable question. How could we humans ever ascertain the ultimate nature of the universe with respect to such an issue as this? Here once again we are up against the problem which both underlies and forever baffles all human pursuit of orientation in life, the ultimately inscrutable mystery of things. There is no possible way to settle questions of this sort: we simply do not have access to the universe-as-a-whole, enabling us to ascertain its ultimate character.

Our idea of the universe is not, in fact, a fundamentally *empirical* one at all, based chiefly on careful examinations and experiments; it is a creation of the human imagination. Here we sit, on our second-rate planet rotating around a third-rate sun in some obscure corner of one of millions of galaxies, trying to picture to ourselves what this vast complex of processes and orders, within which human experience and life falls, is like. As far back in history as we can trace, humans have tried to picture to themselves this whole, this totality, within which they live. They have imagined it in many different ways; and they have developed these imaginings in a number of different directions in the great religious and cultural traditions. In this respect our modern views of the world are no different from any others: they also are magnificent products of the human imagination, constructing a picture of the world. Our modern picture, most of us believe, takes into account many of the details of life and experience that were unknown to earlier generations—the velocity of light and the red-shift in the spectrum of certain lights in the heavens, the relativity of all measurements of time, the conservation and the convertability of matter and energy, the complex atomic structure of matter, the evolution of life over many millennia here on earth, the ecological interdependence of all living forms and the threats to all of this posed by human pollution of the environment, depletion of resources, and destruction of other species; and so on. All of these are conceptions grounded on certain discriminable differences experienced here on earth, and then extrapolated speculatively by magnificent imaginative acts into the vision of a universe billions of years old and hundreds of millions of light-years across. No one has ever moved back through these billions of years in time, to see whether presently observed patterns obtained then; nor can we move out hundreds of millions of light years in space, to see whether the regularities we observe here on earth hold there as well. This whole picture of the world is the product of human imaginative construction. Even such a familiar reality as the sun is not known directly and immediately in experience for what it is; what we take it to be is constructed imaginatively on the basis of experienced patterns of light and heat here on earth. Today we explain these to ourselves in terms of a theory about a fiery star burning away in the skies, but most other peoples and cultures have not understood the sun in this distinctly modern way at all.

I am not suggesting there is any reason to doubt the existence and the reality of the sun, or, for that matter, of the most distant stars, or quasars, or "black holes." I am simply pointing out that all that we know about any of these is a result of human imaginative construction, on the basis of a very close and highly systematic scrutiny of a wide range of clues that we find in our experience here on earth.[3] The human imagination is a magnificent instrument indeed: all our knowledge depends on it; and since our experience is always heavily shaped by what we think we know, it also is significantly constituted by the activity of the imagination. Doubtless our knowledge, experience, and reflection on these matters are all "objective" in the sense that they are intended to be not merely about ourselves but about the objects and structure of the world which environs us; but what we take all this to be and to mean is inevitably the result of our own imaginative construction, and it should not claim to be anything more. If we were different sorts of beings, with different experiential capacities and different powers of imagination, we would be constructing quite different universes than we presently do.

Once we acknowledge this heavily anthropic character of all our experiencing, imagining, and thinking about the universe in which we live, and thus of all our cosmological and metaphysical notions, we are in a position to look in a fresh way at the issues we have just been examining. Clearly there is no strictly "objective" way to address the ultimate metaphysical questions about the real or true nature of the universe and our place in that universe: we have only our various imaginings to work with. Even the idea of a "universe," as we have just seen, is our own imaginative construction based on clues we think we find in our experience here on earth. Of course, we will want to examine critically, and test experientially and experimentally in every way we can, these imaginings and these clues. But we will never be able to check out our conception or vision of the world against what we might call "the universe itself," in the way we might check out, say, our image of George Bush by the actual George Bush, or our notion of Times Square on a Saturday night by going there, or our beliefs about the properties of water by carefully examining it. That sort of direct access to the universe-as-universe is simply not available to us. We always live and work *within* a particular cosmic vision, and the only sort of testing open to us is from within the perspective which that vision supplies. This means we are never in a position to choose our cosmic vision on the basis of careful examination of several alternatives, thus reaching the conclusion that one in particular is true (in the sense that it corresponds reasonably well to the "real universe"); rather, we carry on our lives within a particular cosmic vision (usually the one we have inherited) simply because it seems to make sense of life here on earth.[4] As long as that continues, we are not much disposed toward radically questioning it or exchanging it for some other.

It is not that our acceptance or consent to the world-picture within which we are living and thinking is completely arbitrary, as though we could live within any myth we liked: significant dimensions of our experience (those, for example, which are so intensely scrutinized in the modern sciences) reveal patterns of order which it would be stupid for us to ignore or deny. In this respect, Rudolf Bultmann is correct in speaking of a "scientific worldview" which most moderns take for granted[5] (even though, strictly speaking, science as such—as a cognitive and imaginative activity and method—is not committed to a particular metaphysical scheme). But whatever understanding of the cosmos we accept, it will be a creation by humans here on earth, humans imaginatively constructing a picture of the world which makes sense of their experience, their life. We engage in such constructive activity to provide ourselves with better orientation in life and the world. We need to see and to know what the world is like, so we can better comport ourselves within it; we need to know "how things are" so we can effectively adapt ourselves to them, or transform them for our own purposes, thus facilitating human flourishing in life.

Given these facts, what sort of cosmic vision should we construct in our theological search for orientation in life? To what conception of the world should we commit ourselves? Two points are worth noting in this connection: (1) Since it is orientation for human beings *in the world* that we are seeking, we need a picture or map of the world (and of ourselves as part of the world) which will enable us to find our way about with some success; which will help us identify the major obstacles or problems with which we must come to terms; and which, so far as possible, will prove of assistance in addressing these issues. (2) Since it is orientation *for human beings* in the world that we are seeking, we want a picture or map which takes into account our specifically human needs, capacities, and opportunities; which assists us in making judgments about what sorts of policies and actions are right and what sorts wrong for human beings, what is good and what evil for us men and women; which enables us to see what kind of "flourishing" might be available to and appropriate for us humans, and how such flourishing could be sustained. It should be a vision of human life and the world, in short, which can facilitate and promote human existence within the actual ecosystem within which we live; in this respect our metaphysical/theological construction will necessarily be anthropocentric in its purpose and in its emphases. (Theology, we might note here, concerned as it is with what has traditionally been called "salvation" for humans, in this way makes explicit and deliberate some of the anthropic presuppositions which science and metaphysics, in their quest for what they may suppose to be purely "objective" knowledge, usually leave unacknowledged or even attempt to conceal.) It is true, of course, that no metaphysical conception or world-picture could provide adequate orientation for human existence if it did not attend as carefully and completely as possible to the actual place of human life in the world as we today understand these matters; in this respect, therefore, our theological construction must be as "scientifically objective" and as "hardheaded" as we can make it.[6]

Before we return to our question about the significance of time and temporality, let us turn briefly to the second metaphysical issue posed for this chapter: should we take *spirit*—the symbolic order of meaning and purpose—to have fundamental metaphysical importance, or should we seek to understand reality in essentially *materialistic* terms?[7] Obviously, we must move with great care in examining this issue. One of the most powerful accusations which many critics bring against traditional religious beliefs is that they are largely rather naive expressions of a simple sort of "wishful thinking" about a "heavenly father" (a "divine spirit") who cares for all our present needs and will provide us with "pie in the sky, by and by." We should not, however, adopt any particular cosmic vision simply because it seems to make life more attractive, and in that way enhances the human sense of fulfillment: with terms like "world" or "cosmos" we intend to refer to the actual, factual context of human life; and in many respects this is not what we might wish it to be. Nevertheless, we should not make the opposite mistake of many materialistic critics of religious views (Marx, Haeckel, Freud, Monod) who hold that only anthropomorphizing dreamers could suppose that spirit and meaning and purpose are more than epiphenomenal: the universe is really a thoroughly mechanistic material order. In fact, as we have just seen, we are in no position to say what the universe "really is." That must remain ultimate mystery to us, every claim about the universe (including materialism) being a human imaginative vision. The question we should be putting to ourselves, thus, is this: Which of the several visions of reality available to us most adequately interprets all the wideness and richness of human life in our ecologically ordered world? That is, which gives the most adequate account of all the dimensions of experience, and of the complexity of our situatedness within the web of life on earth? It is by no means easy to answer this question.

In order to grasp what is involved in constructing a religio-metaphysical position for today, it is important that we recognize that all the terms with which we do our metaphysical or cosmological thinking—matter, mechanism, life, mind, spirit, history, et cetera—are employed metaphorically when we use them in metaphysical reflection. The original and basic meaning of these words is found in ordinary experience: for example, our experience of material stuff (rocks, earth, et cetera) which we bump up against and which resists our pushing or penetrating; our experience of machines (bicycles, clocks, and the like) in which the parts are so fitted together and mechanically coordinated as to function smoothly; our experience of living things like plants and animals; and so on. It is in connection with everyday experiences of these sorts that concepts like matter, mechanism, and life gain their basic meanings, which, in due course, are then refined and otherwise developed. When these concepts are made to do metaphysical or cosmological work, they are extended far beyond these ordinary uses and are employed to characterize, or at least to throw light on, what is taken to be the ultimate nature of things; that is, they are used metaphorically. Obviously, very different pictures of the universe as a whole will be created, depending on which of these various metaphors—matter, machine, life, history, et cetera—we make central in our metaphysical reflection and construction.[8]

The notions of matter and machine, for example, if taken strictly, are very limited in their capacity to make intelligible the totality of human experience; for much in our world is quite different from matter and machinery. In order to interpret this richness and diversity, therefore, it becomes necessary (in materialistic perspectives) to introduce into the overall conceptual scheme such notions as "emergence" or "evolution." "Emergence" is the idea—the word literally means to come forth, or arise out of, or come into view—that more complex or "higher" forms of being somehow appear or "emerge" in certain contexts of material energies. When the conditions are just right, a "threshold" is crossed, as it is often put (again note the highly metaphorical character of this notion), and a new mode of reality appears: "life" emerges out of "matter"; "consciousness" emerges within "life"; and so forth. Each new modality has different properties, different patterns of organization, above all different potentialities, than those found in the mode from which it emerged. Metaphors such as "emergence" and "crossing a threshold" suggest that the world is so constituted that under certain conditions new and unexpected forms, forms which are novel and perhaps unprecedented, may come into being. This, however, seems to imply that the world is not to be understood simply as an unchanging structure of endlessly repeated patterns; on the contrary, it is an order in which things that previously did not exist can *come to be,* an order in which the *new* can happen in the course of time, a world in which significant *creativity* occurs. In evolutionary processes emergence is piled on emergence, creativity on creativity. Hence, for perspectives employing these concepts "time's arrow" appears to be irreversible; and the cosmos (even within materialistic perspectives, as generally understood today) must be conceived as in some sense evolutionary or developmental in character.[9]

As I argued in Part II, it is within the mode of reality or experience which we ordinarily call *history* that our most distinctively human concerns and interests have their locus, not in the material order which underlies history and from which it emerged and evolved. It is, for example, because we are radically historical beings (that is, beings with historicity), that we find it necessary to search for means to orient ourselves in life, in order to take responsibility for ourselves; and it is always in terms of historical meanings and values (that is, symbolic patterns which have developed in history) that we gain whatever orientation we ultimately come to have. Even thoroughgoing materialisms are essentially structures of meanings and symbols—not simply collections of physical noises and marks on paper—which have been created (by humans) in the course of history and which have been intentionally placed in particular configurations or patterns believed to be useful for the orientation or guidance of human life in the world; materialisms themselves are, thus, at once products and examples of *spirit,* in the (empirical) sense in which I am using that word here.

These observations bring us into a position from which we can rejoin our earlier reflections on the significance of time, as we formulate—in a way important for our theological purposes—the difference between materialistic and spiritualistic understandings of the world and of human life. Materialistic views appear to be attempts to understand everything in terms of the supposed *beginnings* or *foundations* of the cosmic evolutionary process, to understand it in connection with that *from* which it seems to have come; in contrast, in views which emphasize spirit or history, the overall process is understood in terms of the point *to* which it has come, that is, in terms of what has emerged and evolved in its course, the *complex forms which have been created in and through it.* It should not surprise us to realize that an understanding which grasps human life largely in connection with the material order out of which evolution seems to have sprung will incline us to see ourselves not so much in terms of the uniqueness and special meaning of the human spirit as in connection with that which we have in common with everything else. Such a view tends, thus, to be reductionistic, and it may well have the effect of dampening our spirits and discouraging our hopes for the future. That is, a main effect of a materialistic orientation, with its structural thinking and its inclination to regard physical being as the ultimate reality with which we have to do, is to discount the significance of the facts of emergence and evolution, the significance of creativity and of time. Such a view, instead of facilitating our orientation as self-conscious human beings through portraying as intelligible and meaningful that which is unique about conscious life in history, tends to downgrade the significance of all this and thus to undercut human work and human efforts to take responsibility.

There are two principal functions, I suggested a few pages back, which a theological understanding of the world today must perform: (1) It must make the structure, the development, and the contents of the universe, as we now understand these matters, intelligible to us. (2) It must do this in such a way as to provide orientation for human life; since human existence is historical in character, this means it must facilitate our abilities to take historical responsibility for ourselves and our world. As we have just seen, it is difficult for a materialistic cosmic vision (which gives preeminent metaphysical importance to what are regarded as the permanent structural features of the world) to give a positive significance to the specifically historical dimensions of human life (that is, those dimensions which give it its distinctively human character); for this reason, such a view can hardly (without significant modification) provide adequate orientation for the further development of, and the enhancement or fulfillment of, what is distinctively human about our existence, namely our historicity.

This serious defect of the materialistic/structural type of cosmology suggests the advantages of constructing our cosmic vision from the other end, so to speak; that is, in terms of the significance of the fact that life and history have emerged within the world, and have been sufficiently sustained and supported to enable them to develop to levels of great complexity, finally producing (in history) beings who are self-conscious and self-directing. Such an approach is fully consistent with the facts known to us, that is, that the universe is an evolutionary ecosystem in which life and history have appeared; it satisfies, thus, the first criterion of the adequacy of a cosmic view, that it must do justice to the facts (as we know them). Moreover, this second approach takes account of the further fact that when life evolves to stages within which historical beings emerge, symbolic frameworks for orientation and motivation become necessary. For humans—being products of the evolutionary/historical developments on earth and unable to exist apart from them—adequate orientation and motivation for ongoing life can be provided only by a world-picture in which both the evolution of the web of life on earth and human historical activity within that web are seen to have a significant place. That is to say, any picture of the world intended to provide humans with orientation for life, and with motivation for addressing responsibly the complex problems with which life today faces us, will need to portray the temporal developments within which we live and to which our activities contribute as in some important way meaningful. The universe will need to be seen as a reality which not only gives birth to self-conscious historical beings (beings for whom issues of meaning are central) but also continues to sustain them, giving them opportunity to flourish; if human life is to be grasped as having what can properly be called a "place" in the world, the universe will need to be thought of as in some sense actually facilitating or promoting historical existence.

In a perspective of this sort our human work, our taking responsibility for ourselves in history, will be seen as part of a wider cosmic process which has for many millennia been creating new and more complex orders of being and meaning (at least here on earth). And our own human creativity, our striving to bring into being new values and meanings—through working for greater justice, equality, and freedom; through attacking all manner of social and personal evils; through creating new cultural forms; through responsibly caring for the ecosystem which has given us our being—will all be seen as part of an ongoing cosmic process. In this vision our human work is not simply for ourselves: we are contributing to the creative transformation of the web of life on earth. And thus our historicity—that which gives humanity its special distinctiveness in the world—comes to have a metaphysical significance all its own. This vision of the metaphysical context of human existence as an ongoing process of evolutionary and historical development clearly satisfies our second criterion for an adequate worldview as well as the first: it provides a framework for orienting human life which can help motivate men and women toward the finest—the most humane and ecologically responsible—sorts of historical achievement; by giving our historical work a measure of cosmic significance, it thus encourages further realization of our historicity. We have here, then, a contemporary demythologized version of what Paul expressed so powerfully in traditional mythic idiom when he said, "we are labourers together with God" (1 Cor. 3:9 KJV).

Each of the sketches of the character of the universe that I have been discussing here—one emphasizing physical structure and order, the other evolutionary and historical development—can do justice to the basic facts about the world which we moderns think we know: that within it life has evolved and historical existence gradually emerged, eventually developing to a high level of complexity and meaning. Each of these basic outlines presents an interpretation of the ultimate mystery of things, a proposal about how the world should be understood. It is important to note, however, that they give quite different assessments to the meaning of these facts (on which they are otherwise in agreement); that is, they give different assessments to what these facts can and should mean to us human beings. And they lead, therefore, to significantly different understandings of the meaning of human existence itself, the meaning of our historicity and our involvement in historical struggles. This divide between the two interpretations of the ultimate mystery is momentous: one could say that this is a major fork in the road, where two different faiths about the real character of the mystery draw apart and go their separate ways. We need to recognize that whichever way we go on this decision about the ultimate nature of things, it will be a decision of faith. To opt for the view that ultimate reality is physical structure and nothing more is to take up a faith-stance which will make it quite difficult eventually to affirm the reality of God; to opt, however, for the metaphysical significance of the evolutionary-historical process is to make a second small step toward faith (or of faith) in God. It is, thus, to take a second important step along our path of theological construction. For theistic faith today—at least for faith in the God who began to come into view in Israel's history, and who (as Christians see it) became decisively known in and through Jesus Christ—it is important that the evolutionary-historical process be seen as metaphysically meaningful; human existence and activity as part of that process then also have (potential) metaphysical significance, and the proper home for humanity can be seen to be this historically developing cosmos.

In the biblical traditions, God was spoken of as the creator both of the world and of us humans within the world; and it was said that we were placed here in expression of God's purposes both for us and for the world at large. God's purposes for us were taken by faith to be good (that is, good for us humans—they were humanizing, humane); and God was working toward the ultimate salvation of women and men from the evils, the dehumanizing and inhumane powers, in life; was working, thus, toward our ultimate fulfillment, the realization of our full humanity. It would take a good many more steps of faith to arrive at such a familiar and consoling conception of God as this traditional one, and the probability is that we will not be able to travel that entire path; but it should not be too difficult to see that the metaphysical decision between the two alternative proposals about the ultimate mystery of things which we are now considering involves a significant step toward, or away from, what faith in God has meant for the orientation of human life.[10]

I have not argued here that faith in God (or faith that human life and its projects have some ultimate significance) is true, and that other sorts of faith are false; nor have I argued the reverse. We have not moved far enough in our theological construction, as yet, even to see whether it is possible to develop a plausible conception of God for today. I have simply tried to show that the *facts* of our world, and of human life in the world, are interpretable in terms of a conception of reality—a construal of the ultimate mystery—either as supporting and sustaining our human history and historicity or as not supporting, not sustaining them. Either metaphysical vision is plausible; they both seem equally well grounded. One of these visions, however, through affirming the meaning of the human and the historical, opens the door to our proceeding further in the project of constructing a concept of God for today. The other makes all such talk extremely difficult, if not impossible; for it makes all talk of God—that is, all talk of the ultimate mystery as significantly sustentive of the human, as in some sense "humane"—simply unintelligible. In our subsequent work we shall be building on the vision which enables us to see our evolving and developing world as a meaningful evolutionary-historical process, a world within which it is possible to proceed toward specifically theological construction.

I want to emphasize again that this move forward must be clearly acknowledged as a *decision* on our part, a decision of faith (and toward faith) in face of the ultimate mystery of life; no coercive metaphysical argument or proof can be devised to give it grounding. If we make this decision, however, we are in a position to move toward a third step of faith which we must now begin to explore.

19. Serendipitous Creativity

We have seen that the vast ecosystem which is the universe is susceptible of metaphysical interpretations with two quite different sorts of emphases: (a) in terms which give priority to what appears to be its foundational structure, patterns of matter or material energies, with developmental processes given a secondary or derivative status; or (b) in terms which give greater weight to its processive dimensions, including the emergence and evolution of life and history, with structural patterns regarded as of secondary importance (at least for theological—that is, human-orienting—purposes). The first option tends toward a materialistic kind of reductionism of all higher and more complex forms of being, life, and meaning; the second leads toward emphasis on a continuous creativity displayed in the world, a coming-into-being of increasing complexity, value, and meaning (including ultimately a form of reality directly engaged in deliberate creative activity of its own). Each of these interpretations appears to account for "the facts" as presently known to us; but they lead to quite different metaphysical (and religious) pictures of the world and to quite different conceptions of the meaning of the world for us humans. Since the emphasis on creativity and development in the second interpretation can provide a meaningful grounding for human historical activities and projects, it seems to promise orientation in the world better suited to our historicity, which we have taken to be the distinctive mark of our humanness; so I suggested that we opt for this way of thinking about the universe. A coercive argument for the ultimate metaphysical truth of this conception cannot, of course, be given (as we have noted); our decision here, thus, is to be understood as a second step of and toward faith (in God).

We are now ready to move on to a third step of faith and of theological construction. This step will be made as we consider a number of important questions: What further implications can be drawn from the fact that the universe is the sort of reality that gives rise to evolutionary processes of life, and ultimately to history? Can any particular significance be seen in the fact that out of what seem initially to be blind purposeless processes there eventually emerge beings with consciousness of this world and these processes, indeed with self-consciousness; beings with capacities to act deliberately and purposefully within the ongoing temporal movement, and to take responsibility for some aspects of the future course of that movement?

In order to see what is at stake in these questions, we need to examine more closely the uniqueness of human historical existence, and the significance of that uniqueness. History and historicity emerged within the order of reality that we call "life," but they cannot (as we have seen) be understood simply in terms of ordinary biological notions such as nutrition, metabolism, reproduction, and the like. They include and depend upon the appearance of modalities of being which in important respects transcend the strictly biological and signal the emergence of a new "cultural" dimension of reality with patterns of existence ordered largely symbolically: consciousness and (especially) self-consciousness; deliberate creative activity, including activity that is self-creative; moral responsibility; religious, philosophical, artistic, and scientific reflectiveness, imagination and symbolization; and so on. Within the historical modes of being that began to appear on earth, the rate of change and development through time gradually but increasingly accelerated, eventually becoming far more rapid than in biological evolution. We humans are substantially the same biologically as we were fifteen to thirty thousand years ago, but historically and culturally we are almost completely transformed; and we seem to be continuing to change ever more rapidly. The emergence of history within life and out of life shows that the cosmic process (as we know it) is capable of giving rise to forms of organization considerably more complex and open than those fully describable and comprehensible in strictly biological terms.

These cultural/historical dimensions of our existence have deeply affected what we take ourselves to be—indeed, they are an essential precondition of our "taking ourselves to be" anything at all. Our consciousness of ourselves, our sense of who or what we humans are, our sense of identity—these are all made possible by our historicity and are decisively shaped by the specific historico-cultural context within which we emerge into consciousness. It is our culture, particularly our religious, artistic, literary, and philosophical (and more recently our scientific) traditions, that supplies us with the very categories in terms of which we imagine or conceive ourselves as human—immortal soul, rational animal, member of the wolf totem, emptiness, social self, individual ego, et cetera. And our particular social situatedness within our culture supplies each of us with the basic concepts that give us our individual self-understanding—peasant, craftsperson, or priest; prophet or healer, teacher or student; doctor, lawyer, merchant; divine king with rights over all, slave who is less than human; and so forth. Thus, our self-consciousness is (as we have noted in earlier chapters) largely culturally and socially defined and formed; it is neither biologically determined nor significantly explicable biologically (except, perhaps, to a certain extent with respect to gender). History and historicity clearly cannot be understood simply in terms of biology: they represent a distinct order of reality which must be understood in terms of its own qualities and characteristics. The new modes of organization and new forms of activity which they involve mean that the irrevocable cosmic movement into the future is no longer one that is completely blind and purposeless; it has become deliberate in certain respects, intentional, permeated with meaning.

Whether human historical life will long survive, we do not know; there are many grave warning signs suggesting it may be approaching its end. But that there is a significant distinctiveness about historical modalities of being and order hardly seems controvertible; and it is really somewhat absurd—even comical—for us to refuse to consider our own modality of being as a clue of some significance for our construction of a concept of the world, simply because we are not aware of any other empirical beings who possess our sort of creative historicity. For the theological position which we are beginning to articulate here—a position intended to orient the existence of us humans within the world—our mode of being will be regarded as a matter of considerable significance, a clue or sign of the possibilities and qualities of the creativity manifest within the cosmic process.[1]

Let me make this point in another way. Freud argued that all human ideals, values, meanings are rooted in biological needs or urges, of which they are the sublimation and transformation. Freud's point is often used in reductionistic arguments, in which it may be held, for example, that all love is really simply lust, supposed fear of God is actually fear of one's father, all cultural and artistic productivity is just suppressed sexuality, and the like. But if these sorts of connections actually obtain, as Freud claimed, then a reverse argument is just as plausible as this reductionistic one, as Paul Ricoeur has pointed out.[2] These linkages suggest that what in its biological foundations is simply sexual desire can be transmuted and developed (through historical processes) into profound love for other human beings, a love that includes appreciation of those others as persons, respect for their integrity, rejoicing in the value and meaning of their presence; the awareness one has as a child of physical helplessness vis-à-vis one's parents can grow into a reflective understanding of the problems and the meaning of human finitude; and the vital powers of the human physical organism can be put, not only by a Beethoven or an Einstein but by all of us, into the service of values like beauty and truth. Though human existence is grounded in the biological order, grounded on our structural biological capacities, in many of its historical manifestations it reaches toward, and attempts to create and to serve, a quite different order of reality: what I am calling "spirit." And this aspiration or striving of the human toward spirit is just as important an empirical fact about us as our biological grounding. Moreover, there is surely considerable justification for regarding this movement and striving (which we experience in ourselves and see in the humanity all around us) as having some significant relationship to "how things really are," as providing a clue, that is to say, to the ultimate mysteries with which we humans have to do.

We can summarize this point briefly in this way. If one holds that the fundamental reality in the world is matter, and believes that bare matter has no potentiality in itself for becoming something other than itself but always remains mere matter, it is difficult to see how one can avoid acknowledging there must also be some sort of *creative activity* in the universe which cannot be simply identified with or reduced to bare matter—the creativity manifest (for example) in the evolutionary development of life. To make this point one need not postulate a creative *power* working in some way behind and through the evolutionary process to move it to higher and more complex levels—a kind of *élan vital* or a being called "God"; it may well be (as most evolutionary biologists hold) that random variations in genetic processes, combined with the "natural selection" that is brought about as organisms adapt to various kinds of adverse conditions in their environment, provide a sufficient causal explanation for the emergence of increasingly complex forms of life, and ultimately of historical processes and modes of being.[3] But whatever the character of these causal processes, it is undeniable that through them genuinely *new* forms of life have come into being in the course of time; and in that sense a significant *creativity* is manifest in the universe (at least here on earth). As we shall see in due course, this provides a metaphysical opening for the development of a conception of God.

The symbol "God" has signified more powerfully than any other in the West that what we are calling "spirit" has an ultimate metaphysical significance. Indeed, according to the traditional doctrine of creation, spirit—or some sort of spiritual or quasi-spiritual reality—is the ultimate metaphysical grounding of all that is (direct identification of God with spirit is explicit in the familiar Johannine text, "God is spirit, and those who worship him must worship in spirit and truth," John 4:24). But such grandiose claims as these for spirit carry us much further down the road than we have thus far traveled. For now the most we can affirm is that there are reasonable grounds for thinking that significant creativity occurs in the cosmos, and for interpreting the emergence of historicity and spirit as a manifestation of that creativity. It is certainly possible to refuse to take the step toward faith in God which committing oneself to this way of seeing the world and the ultimate mystery of things involves; and there are many today who prefer such reticence. But it is important to recognize that if we choose to conclude that human life on its cultural and spiritual side has no metaphysical grounding, we are taking a long step toward seeing the world in nihilistic terms, that is, toward living with an underlying metaphysical despair about all human and humane values, hopes, and projects. Thus, this third step toward faith (or of faith), which may enable us to see the human project with all its hopes and aspirations as significantly grounded in ultimate reality, is an important one.

The concept of creativity (as thus far presented) remains very abstract: how can we make it more concrete and intelligible? It will be helpful at this point to sketch briefly—by reflecting on different features of human action and history—two distinct models of creativity. The first is drawn from ordinary life and is known to all: it is based on our everyday experience of being persons who act and who experience the actions of other persons, those features of experience that lead us to think of individual human beings as agents or selves. The second model will be developed through reflection on the sort of historical action and creativity that comes into view in connection with our modern knowledge of history as a long cumulating process of human working and purposing, and which (over many millennia) has utterly transformed human existence through producing increasingly complex patterns of culture, social institutions, language, constellations of value and meaning; let us call this broad-ranging creativity manifest in the historical process as a whole "the serendipity of history." The conception of God central to the formative western traditions, as we shall see, was based largely on the first model—the human self or agent—drawing upon widely known modes of experience and action. I shall propose, however, a conception of God which draws upon the serendipity of history for its principal model.

In the Bible God is portrayed as a self-aware, all-knowing, all-powerful, free agent. God has purposes and acts to realize those purposes. The world is understood to be the product of deliberate, self-conscious, creative activity by God, an activity culminating in God's creation of humanity, a finite being made in God's own image (Gen. 1:26–27). This conception of God is clearly constructed on the model of the human purposive agent, capable of self-conscious creative work. Just as a carpenter may say, "Let there be a house," and then set about to build one, or a painter may say, "Let there be a portrait," and produce one, so "God said, 'Let there be light'; and there was light" (1:3). "Let there be heavens and an earth; let there be living creatures on the earth," and so forth. The entire universe and all the creatures in it are here portrayed as the products of God's direct creative acts. In a similar way the movements of history and the developments of human life and culture within history are all conceived as grounded directly in God's providential activity: they are the product of God's decisions and purposes for the creatures, which are gradually being worked out. In due course the historical movement will reach the goals which God posited for it from the beginning, and this will bring history to its climax and conclusion. The model underlying all such talk is obviously human purposive action. When this model is used in this way to construct a world-picture, we are presented with a unidirectional historical development in which the appearance of human beings on earth is a significant high point, and the unfolding of human history a major theme.

Several points should be noted about this way of interpreting the creativity manifest in the cosmic evolutionary-historical process. In the first place, when the model for God is the human agent, the most fundamental reality is not taken to be a basically material order, or even a living organism or process of evolutionary development: it is seen, rather, as like a human self; and this has meant historically that God was thought of as a self-conscious and self-directing spirit. It is through the activity of this quasi-personal reality that all other forms of being, including material beings, have come to exist. We humans, thus (in this scheme), far from being aliens in an impersonal or inhuman world, are regarded as having been created in the very image of that which is the origin and foundation of all that is; by virtue of those features of our nature that we call "spirit," we have a special metaphysical rapport with God, a rapport not shared by any other creature.

For this reason, secondly, it should not surprise us to discover that the relationship of humans to God is portrayed as significantly similar to those which obtain between finite persons—the most meaningful sort of relationship that we experience. It can be a relationship of love and trust and loyalty, but it will be damaged badly by malice, hatred, and unfaithfulness; above all, it lives in and through communication with the other party (this is why prayer is so important for the religious life, when God is conceived in these terms).

As this scheme is worked out further, God becomes understood not only as an agent with vast powers but—and this is my third point—as a personal being, who loves us humans and cares for us; God has purposes for each of our lives, and is working toward their realization. So not only human life as a whole, but each of our individual lives as well, is seen to have a significant place in the divine scheme, and thus its own unique meaning. Because God has special tasks for each of us to perform, our work, also, is more than merely humanly significant; it is of importance to the very creator of the universe. In the Christian texts presenting this notion, God's personal interest in each of us is expressed in very powerful metaphors: "even the hairs of your head are all numbered" (Mt. 10:30); not a sparrow falls "to the ground without your Father's will . . . [and] you are of more value than many sparrows" (10:29, 31); "there is joy before the angels of God over one sinner who repents" (Lk. 15:10), like a father's joy over the return of his prodigal son (15:11–32). All such imagery underlines the profound personal meaning which every moment of our lives, and our every act and attitude, comes to have within this world-picture.

We should note, in the fourth place, that such striking imagery as this, used to depict the underlying reality from which we have sprung and with which we are in continuing connection, evokes from men and women a powerful affective response—to love God, to serve God, to trust God, to commit ourselves without qualification to God's will for us. Thus, this imagery significantly affects the ordering of human life, shaping the principal configurations of meaning and value which believers employ to orient themselves. The conception of the perfectly loving/faithful/just God becomes now the model and standard by which women and men are to measure themselves: they also should be perfectly loving and faithful and just. Communities and selves devoted to this God, thus, seek to make themselves over in terms of the norms and criteria generated by this imagery. And notions of responsible selfhood, and of loving and forgiving interpersonal relations, become social and cultural ideals and standards in those societies devoted to this God. In these ways, as humans develop a conception of the ultimate ordering principles in the universe as suggested by the model of the human agent *writ large,* they are led to a significant and powerful world-picture, one which orients individual existence toward free, responsible, and loving selfhood, and communal existence toward justice, equal respect for all persons, and peace. It is not difficult to see why the central symbol which has been built up in this way, "God," has been so attractive and powerful in the West for such a long time.

There are, however, serious problems with this symbolism. The conception of the all-powerful cosmic agent can easily become, for example, a notion of an essentially authoritarian tyrant, one who is arbitrary and unjust in the exercise of omnipotence; and in fact God has often been conceived in this way in traditional Christianity—as one who (in Paul's words) "has mercy upon whomever he wills, and . . . hardens the heart of whomever he wills" (Rom. 9:18), one who arbitrarily predestines some to salvation and others to damnation. This image of God, as the terrifying all-powerful ruler of the world, can be as evocative and compelling in its effects as the more humane portrait I just sketched; but in this case what are evoked from worshippers, as they shape themselves in accord with the divine model, are patterns of arbitrariness and the quest for tyrannical power, and relentless determination to work one's own will without regard for the feelings or integrity of others. Unfortunate drives toward dominating and domineering of this sort have often appeared in western religiosity. The very effectiveness of the traditional western conception of God in ordering and orienting human life—projecting, as it did, a powerful image of self-conscious, dynamic agency—has enabled this notion (and the world-picture generated in connection with it) to become, when the wrong images and concepts fill it out, exceedingly destructive and dangerous. (As we shall note in a moment, this makes it especially problematic in today's world.)

A second problem with this traditional notion of God is of a more specifically metaphysical sort: the world-picture generated in connection with it is fundamentally dualistic and is thus difficult to reconcile with major strands of contemporary thinking. In the tradition the defining image of God (the notion which provided the basic understanding of God's metaphysical status) was *creator*—creator of the heavens and the earth, creator of all things visible and invisible. This notion implies a fundamental duality in reality, a cleavage between God (the source of all that is) and God's creation (the world and all its contents); a duality between that which is underived and ultimate (God), and all that is derivative and finite (the created world). Since the world is something God has produced and continues to work upon, God is conceived as, so to speak, "outside" or "other than" the world, as human potters and poets are outside and other than the pots and poems which they create and shape. For many today this sort of dualism is no longer plausible, or even intelligible. Our modern concept of the universe, as we have seen, is of a self-contained intradependent whole, an evolutionary ecosystem in which all parts develop in complex interrelationship with one another; not an essentially dualistic order with all real dynamism and productivity found on one side, and the other relegated essentially to receptiveness and passivity. Indeed, the idea of a God who is "outside" the universe is scarcely thinkable today: the universe is all there is, and all spatial relations are found within it; what can it possibly mean to speak of something *outside* it? And how are we to think of the universe in its entirety as somehow the direct result of external purposive activity? It is possible, of course, to verbally affirm these things (on the authority of the Bible, or the words of Jesus, or on some other basis); but it is quite doubtful that we can really *think* them—that is, that we can make clear to ourselves and to others just what it is that we are trying to say with this language. For these images and this model simply do not fit together with the scientific and quasi-scientific ways of thinking about the universe that have become so largely constitutive of experience today.

A third difficulty with the traditional notion of God has to do with its heavy dependence on the model of the agent-self: this model presupposes that selfhood or agency can be conceived as freestanding, as metaphysically self-subsistent and self-explanatory; but everything we know today about persons suggests that they could neither come into being, nor continue to exist, independently of long and complex cosmic, biological, and historical processes. Agency and selfhood are to be understood and explained as an outcome of evolutionary and historical developments and could not exist apart from a complex ecosystem—not the reverse, the latter being explained and understood by reference to the activity of some aboriginal cosmic self or agent. In this respect, also, the traditional conception of God stands in massive incoherence with modern patterns of knowledge (however valid and appropriate it may have seemed in earlier periods).

To these serious problems regarding the basic intelligibility of this notion, we may add a fourth difficulty with the traditional conception of God: there do not seem to be any compelling reasons any longer which can be cited in its favor—except, of course, that it has been traditionally held. Indeed, it is not clear just what might count as a reason for speaking of the existence and nature of some being—a cosmic agent—who exists on the other side of a metaphysical divide as absolute as that supposed to obtain between the creator and creation. What could there be in the finite order (which includes everything to which we creatures have direct access) that could count as evidence for some reality that is utterly other than everything finite? As Karl Barth frequently argued: though there may be a way from God the creator to us, there can certainly be no road from our finite experience and knowledge, where all is contingent, limited, and incomplete, to an unconditionally necessary being, infinite and absolute. It is significant that the so-called arguments for the existence of (this) God are usually persuasive only to those who already believe in the God portrayed in tradition; those with no such prior commitments find these arguments singularly unconvincing.

This traditional conception of God, moreover, has not only become increasingly implausible to many moderns; perhaps the most important objection to it is that in today's world it has become very dangerous religiously. The dualistic world-picture to which it belongs and which it also authorizes portrays God as an absolutely authoritarian figure of utter omnipotence, a figure conceived to be beyond human reason and thus metaphysically protected from human critical assessment. This God of unquestionable authority has often been taken by believers as authorizing and legitimating highly destructive forms of human activity—"holy" wars, persecutions, inquisitions, crusades, torture. Symbols and worldviews that can be used to encourage and support policies and behavior of this sort—along with the social, political, and economic institutions of dominating power which facilitate such behavior and policies—are simply too dangerous in a world in which humans possess utterly destructive powers. Any world-picture appropriate and useful for orienting human life today—as we seek to address our unprecedented problems—must be constructed in a way that diminishes the likelihood of such dangerous abuses.[4]

Despite these many shortcomings, however, it is clear that the traditional western conception of God, based on the model of the self-conscious and dynamic human agent, has been (and still is in many quarters) of great effectiveness in the ordering and orienting of human life. The world-picture which accompanies this notion portrays the universe as a kind of teleological historical process, moving from a beginning through important stages of development to an end or goal of profoundly human and humane meaning. Whatever problems there may be with the overall intelligibility of this picture, it does provide a framework capable of interpreting the cosmic and historical processes of which we are aware; and many may prefer to opt for the more traditional agent-God portrayed here rather than move to the process-God which I shall present in this book. For even today, despite its problematic features, this world-picture continues to function in important ways, not only among the traditionally pious but also in shaping values and ideals and goals in society at large. In later chapters we will examine more fully the respects in which the traditional symbol "God" continues to perform important orienting functions for human life in our world; and we shall take these into account as we construct a conception intended to overcome or to avoid major shortcomings of this notion.

In view of the very considerable difficulties we have just noted, I suggest that for our third step of faith—our interpretation of the creativity manifest in the world—instead of moving now to a conception of God modeled on the human agent, we explore the possibilities of employing the second model I mentioned above, a model based on the creative development in history of human culture as a whole. This model, I shall try to show, is better fitted to interpret the cosmic creativity with which we are here concerned, and it does not suffer from the defects noted in the concept of the cosmic agent; it can, thus, provide a more intelligible and persuasive basis for our construction of a contemporary conception of God.

It is what I call "the serendipity of history" that I wish to examine now. With this name I mean to focus attention on that tendency in historical processes and events to produce more than was intended by the women and men acting in and through them, the tendency to outrun human expectations and purposes. Although the movements of history are shaped in many ways by human decisions and actions, much more is going on in them than simply the realization of deliberate human intentions. Columbus was looking for an easier way to get to India, but what he did was "discover" America. A group of Dutch settlers founded New Amsterdam in 1625, but in their wildest dreams they could not have foreseen the modern New York City which was to grow out of their colony. The Magna Charta was signed in 1215 by King John to guarantee certain feudal rights to some nobles, but in due course it became a significant foundation for the development of English constitutional liberties and modern Anglo-Saxon democracy. The invention of movable type by Johannes Gutenberg made possible completely unanticipated developments in modern culture through making the printed word available to almost everyone. And so on. Many events, which might seem rather small and insignificant when they occur, turn out to have far-reaching unforeseen consequences, sometimes transforming the course of history in quite unexpected ways.

Often these unexpected consequences are not happy. The Versailles Treaty, for example, was deliberately fashioned to prevent defeated Germany from ever again becoming a dangerous power; it proved to be a major factor in the rise of the Nazis, who succeeded in bringing most of Europe into World War II just a generation after the conclusion of the first great war. The modern penitentiary, invented early in American history as an institution with individual penitential cells which were to induce remorse in criminals and lead to their conversion to a new and productive life, has become a major breeding place for crime, with solitary confinement one of its most inhuman features. Henry Ford's assembly line, producing cars cheaply enough so that every family could own one, has resulted in a complete transformation of both the American countryside and modern lifestyles; and now we have enormous problems growing out of our high mobility—from the breakdown of the family to the pollution of the air in our cities to the "greenhouse effect" in the upper atmosphere; and our unwillingness to give up our instant mobility to everywhere has made us into free-spending energy-wasters, heavily dependent on oil from the Middle East and consequently deeply involved in middle eastern politics and wars. And so on. It is clear that historical decisions and actions, originally of largely local interest or significance, have a way of snowballing far beyond the expectations or intentions of anyone, sometimes coming to affect the entire human world.

This enormous, often rapid, expansion of effects seems characteristic particularly of historical actions and events, and we need to understand it—at least initially—in specifically historical terms. It is certainly not to be accounted for largely in terms of natural physical or chemical processes, nor is it to be understood as essentially an expression of biological instincts or drives (though all these are also involved in their own way, of course); rather, it is human decisions and actions (nearly always intending something quite different), women and men trying to do something, humans positing goals which they then seek to achieve, that (usually) set these great historical momentums into motion. History unfolds in quite surprising ways and quite unexpected directions—both good and evil—as it gradually produces the vast network of folkways, institutions, languages, ideologies, values, practices. The historical order of being which we call "culture" is created, with its manifold institutions and structures of meaning, its complex patterns of goods and values—but also its enormous tensions and its momentums toward destructiveness, including oppression, corruption, war, even human self-annihilation. The great literary symbol of this outworking of human creativity is Frankenstein's monster; the great factual symbol is the discovery of ways to harness the energy of the atom. The creations of the human imagination with the greatest potential for good, it seems, always threaten to get out of control and to bring about enormous destructiveness and evil.

This capacity or feature of history, to produce vastly more than we human inventors and creators and purposers expected or intended is what I call the "serendipity of history." Most of what we men and women count as goods peculiar to human existence have resulted from this serendipity: our complex institutional structures and divisions of labor; our intricate languages, making possible highly nuanced modalities of experience, consciousness, and self-consciousness; our very historicity, and hence our capacities for creativity and for taking responsibility for ourselves and our future; in short, all that is truly distinctive about our humanity—our humanness itself, the distinctly "spiritual" dimensions of our existence, our capacities for humaneness.

To see better what is involved in this serendipitous creativity manifest in historical processes, let us examine briefly a micro-example of it, the creativity that sometimes occurs in and through ordinary conversation.[5] A conversation, it should be noted, is not simply an interchange of discrete "acts," in which each agent is attempting to realize a particular goal. Though in each remark the speaker is attempting to say something that is fitting at that moment, what happens in a conversation cannot be understood simply as the summing up of all these individual actions. Often the interchange comes to have "a life of its own" (as we say), and it may well go in directions no one had anticipated and lead to new insights and ideas which none of the participants had thought of before. (These may be exciting and happy developments; or they may sometimes be quite tragic, ending in the bitter enmity of hitherto friends.) Let us see if we can unpack somewhat the way in which this serendipitous creativity in conversation comes about.

It is important to note the mix of determinateness and indeterminacy which is characteristic of every word used and each speech made in a conversation. Every word in a language has, of course, certain fairly definite meanings and uses; but these actually shade off into one another, and into a rather indefinite penumbra of meaning which surrounds each word. The various participants in a conversation understand one another because of the relative determinateness of meaning of each word spoken—a meaning made even more definite by the particular context (in the sentence, in the ongoing conversation, in the private and the common experience of the participants) in which the word is used at this particular moment. But the penumbra of connotations and indeterminacy surrounding each word's relative determinateness of meaning, taken together with the diverse kinds of experience and history undergone by each participant in the conversation, make it inevitable that each hearer will grasp and attend to something slightly different from the others, and sometimes significantly different from what the speaker had intended. Thus different responses are called forth from the different hearers, and the conversation proceeds down pathways not expected by the original speaker or by any of the others. An intervention by speaker B moves the conversation in a way that A had not intended; and a succeeding intervention by C moves down a slightly different path, not anticipated by either A or B, so that when A responds again, it will be with a comment not directly continuous with his or her earlier remark, one which takes into account what B and C have unexpectedly said. And thus the path of the conversation as a whole, though definitely continuous, is not a direct working out of the original intention which A (or anyone else) was attempting to express.

If this pattern of conversation is allowed to proceed for a while, it may depart substantially from the subject matter of A's original remark, going down quite unexpected pathways that none of the participants have followed before. Sometimes, in an exciting conversation of this sort where new ideas seem continuously to be bursting forth, the participants are "carried away" by the flow of the conversation itself, which has come to have a seeming intention of its own. These can be moments of high "spirit" for human beings, even of "ecstasy"; they are moments in which the creativity of the social process is being directly experienced. This social experience, in which a spirit of the group comes alive and takes over, does not mean that the individuals cease to act as free agents in their own right: they each contribute to the conversation out of their own freedom, not under some external compulsion. And yet that freedom is led beyond anything any of them could have deliberately "decided" to think or to say on their own; it is a moment of creativity which the group process itself makes possible.

The experience of being "carried away" by the group process without losing one's own freedom also sometimes occurs in playing an intense game, say of basketball or tennis, where the expertness of the players and their knowledge and love of the game so take over that none of them simply and directly thinks out what he or she is doing; each simply "plays the game," that is, plays whatever the game requires to the best of his or her ability.[6] It may also be found in musical performance—not only in a quartet or orchestra, which may become melded into one voice, as it were—but also in a private performance where the Chopin polonaise seems to "take over" the pianist, though without in any way compromising the pianist's own freedom and creativity. But these examples involve the playing out of previously prescribed patterns; they, thus, do not display the same potential for creativity—for bringing into being the truly *new*—which spontaneous conversation does.

The important point to observe here is that a conversation proceeds with a certain independence from the explicit intentions of the individual speakers, and yet each of their individual contributions has an essential place within it. Moreover, in the course of the conversation new insights or meanings appear which, though not directly intended by any of the speakers, may prove of great importance to them; indeed these may become of greater interest than what they themselves originally had in mind with their own contributions. Thus, the ongoing conversation maintains a close connection with the speakers' interests, desires, and needs, although the speakers themselves may often not be directly aware of all this until it comes out in the conversation itself (so-called unconscious intentions getting expressed in quite unexpected ways). The experience of the conversation may, moreover, be so unforgettable as to meld the several speakers into a group which lives and develops for a long time, shaping and reshaping the individual lives of its members in the future in ways none could have anticipated during the original exchange. The important point to note in all this is that the individuals feel their freedom and creativity *extended* by this participation in the social process, not in any significant way diminished. (Of course, this is a highly idealized description of conversation: most of our ordinary conversations are interrupted or broken in many different ways and do not carry us away to this extent, and thus what I am here calling the "spirit" of the group usually does not take over so fully from the individuals making it up.)

What happens here among three or four or five people in an intense conversation provides us with a model which can throw light on the serendipitous creativity of cultural history. In larger historical developments there are many individual acts directly expressing individual intentions and objectives, as well as the actions of various communities, institutions, and other social bodies in relation to one another. Each of these belongs to ongoing "conversations" of actions and reactions in which the act is understood and interpreted rather differently than the original agents had intended (because of the vagueness of the penumbra of meanings and connotations it expresses); and it is responded to, therefore, in unexpected ways, and itself calls forth further new and unexpected responses. In the course of this exchange of actions and reactions major social institutions and practices may be created and developed in ways which no one had anticipated or desired, ways which are, nevertheless, significantly bound up with the intentions and interests of many. Thus, there is significant continuity of historical development both within individual communities and in the interactions of communities with their neighbors. But, as the historical process moves on, much is created quite unexpectedly, some for good and some for ill but all of it the serendipitous product of human actions directed toward ends far less grand than those which actually work themselves out.

This account of creativity (as it appears in the historical process) is similar in certain important respects to the creativity manifest in the emergence of new species through biological natural selection (as understood in contemporary evolutionary theory). According to Ernst Mayr, "Evolutionary change in every generation is a two-step process: the production of genetically unique new individuals and the selection of the progenitors of the next generation."[7] In the first step of this process new genetic combinations come into being; in the second stage (in which so-called natural selection occurs) it is determined whether these new emergents are able to adapt more (or less) successfully—than earlier (or other rival) forms—to the environment in which they appear. Most new emergents simply become extinct, either quickly or after a relatively short period; only a few adapt themselves more successfully than earlier forms, and thus survive and perhaps flourish. But such successful adaptation, and the consequent emergence of new species, Mayr points out, "is an important driving force in macroevolution."[8]

With this in mind, if we return again to our interpretation of historical process, we can see that a similar sort of "natural selection" seems to be at work there.[9] In most cases (as with our example of conversation) the historical consequences of a moment of creativity in human interactions are virtually negligible, and they soon disappear from view. Occasionally, however, something appears with unusual potential to adapt well within the immediate situation; it is, therefore, picked up, amplified and developed in various ways, and becomes a significant factor in the further movement of history. Even successful adaptation in the immediate situation indicates little, of course, about the long-range survivability or significance of the new practice, idea, or attitude: it may be of great positive significance, contributing to the growth and flourishing of the society in which it appears; or it may prove—in a generation or two, or perhaps only after some hundreds, or even thousands, of years—to be dangerously destructive. Human institutions, practices, and beliefs that were exceedingly useful and meaningful in one period of history may become, in a later historical context, unable to function effectively—that is, to adapt to the new conditions—thus contributing to the downfall of the very civilization which they had, for such a long time, helped to sustain. Our own time appears to be a case in point: certain long-valued practices and institutions and patterns of belief are becoming obsolete and no longer functional, and it is imperative, therefore, that we find new ways to think and act and to organize our world. My attempt in this book to explore the possibility of constructing new and more relevant conceptions of God is only one small example of current efforts to address the varied aspects of this massive problem which today confronts humanity.

The notion of the "serendipity of history," I am suggesting, provides an illuminating way for faith (in a third step now) to conceive the creativity manifest in the historical process—a creativity which often brings into being what appear (from human and humane perspectives) to be horrifying evils, as well as great goods. It must be acknowledged, of course, that—because of the powerful symbolism (in our religious traditions) of an agent-God whose purposive activity underlay and ordered major historical movements—a much more explicitly teleological notion of these movements (than I am suggesting here) has usually been set forth in the interpretations of history that have informed most western consciousness. But precisely this picture of a powerful teleological movement dominating the overall historical process has become quite problematical in the twentieth century.[10] The more open and even random notion of the serendipity of history seems more accurately to represent much that occurs as the historical process unfolds. Furthermore, as the analogy between the serendipity of history and such biological conceptual complexes as mutation/natural selection suggests, this idea of serendipitous creativity can also be utilized in interpreting the evolutionary development of life here on earth; it can even be extended to cover the enormous expansion and complexification of the physical universe (from the "big bang" onward) which preceded that evolution and was the condition of its possibility. It seems possible, thus, to speak of the whole vast cosmic process as manifesting (in certain respects) serendipitous creativity. It is a process that has often produced much more than one would have expected, given previously prevailing circumstances, indeed, more than might have seemed possible—even moving eventually, in certain of its dimensions, toward the creation of history and historicity.

Of course, no sort of proof can be provided that the universe in its entirety is a serendipitously creative movement; as we have seen, we simply do not have independent access to the universe as such, enabling us to check the adequacy and appropriateness of this (or any other similar) concept. In this connection we should not forget that even concepts like "the universe in its entirety" or "the universe as such" are our own imaginative constructs; and we have no way of directly testing their validity either. They are, however, indispensable to us: without concepts of this sort we could not organize and bring into overall order the exceedingly diverse and complex contents of our experience and reflection, as we seek to attend to the ultimate mystery of things. Our concept of the cosmos as permeated by serendipitous creativity (as we shall see) can be quite useful in helping to orient human existence today; and it will prove suggestive as we seek to reconceive "God" in a manner consonant with modern knowledge. I propose, therefore, that as our third step of faith (and toward faith) we agree to think of the overarching context of human life—the universe—as a serendipitously creative process or movement. If we take this step, we will be conceiving the universe in a way that enables us to attend particularly to the significance of its being the creative source not only of the continuing context and sustaining environment without which our human existence would not be possible, but of the richness and fullness of our existence itself.

We would probably not be inclined to think of the great cosmic order of matter and energy—which is perhaps what first comes to mind when we use our word "universe"—as serendipitous (in the munificent sense that I have just now been developing), were we not being particularly attentive to the mystery of life's appearing here on earth. An extraordinary combination of physical and chemical conditions, quite precisely ordered in a very particular way, was required to make possible the emergence of this new form of being.[11] The order of life has proved to have quite remarkable properties and possibilities which could not have been predicted or guessed simply on the basis of the ordinary physical and chemical characteristics of energy and matter: it was an order that would give rise to the great evolutionary march upward from the primeval slime, a march serendipitous at every step. In due course, moreover, this cosmic serendipitous creativity brought into being even human historico-cultural existence.

In interpreting the world, in all its diversity, grandeur, and richness, as the expression of serendipitous creativity at every point, we put into place the first building block of a conception of God for today. Much more remains to be done, however, before we will be in a position to construct a notion of God capable of providing significant orientation for women and men within the complexities and details of contemporary life. Our next step of faith will help us fill in and specify somewhat further our picture of the world—our construal of the ultimate mystery of things; it will put us into a position from which we can turn directly to our project of constructing a new conception of God.

20. Directional Movements in a Serendipitous Universe

I have been sketching a picture of a serendipitous universe as the overarching context of human existence, a universe manifesting a creativity that expresses itself in many different ways, including the emergence of life on earth and its evolution into increasingly complex forms of many sorts, eventually producing human beings on one of its lines. Our human historical mode of reality, however, is in significant respects also a product of the activity of men and women, as they have created culture and developed symbolical worlds to orient themselves. It is important to distinguish it from all other forms of life not only (1) because it is our own, one which we must understand well if we are to realize our potentialities and to order our activities more responsibly on earth, but also (2) because it is in fact qualitatively distinct from all other forms of life known to us. Through our historicity we have gained power to alter the earth and the living beings on it in far-reaching ways. Though our historicity is easily corruptible, as we have seen (Chapter 15), and can be expressed in enormous destructiveness, it also, happily, enables us to gain some understanding of our situation in the world; and this—together with the serendipity of the evolutionary-historical process as a whole—provides (perhaps) some grounds for hope that we may in due course learn to use our power responsibly, for the well-being of all creatures on earth. We men and women are the only living beings (so far as we know) who can deliberately and self-consciously set purposes for themselves, and can deliberately and self-consciously work toward realization of those purposes. That is to say, in and through and with us, activity that is straightforwardly intentional—explicitly teleological activity—becomes operational within the world. We have begun here to explore what this implies not only about ourselves but about the evolutionary process which has brought us forth, and ultimately about the world.

To move further now in addressing these issues, let us examine more carefully some important characteristics of the evolutionary process. First, there is the fact that movement in and through time, as we trace it through the long history of the universe and particularly through the evolution of life on earth, seems to be irreversible and in this respect unidirectional. That is, although many whirls and eddies and detours appear in the cosmic and evolutionary development, and many cycles of night and day, of seasonal changes, and of birth, growth, and decay are to be found here on earth, there seems to be through all of this an essentially continuous movement onward toward new forms, toward unprecedented developments—not simply patterns which forever repeat themselves. Moreover, these developments, to the extent that they involve the appearance of new evolutionary lines (that is, new species), each have specific potentialities for further movement in some directions but not in others. Such tendencies, as Ernst Mayr says, "are the necessary consequence of the unity of the genotype which greatly constrains evolutionary potential."[1] To the extent that an evolutionary tendency enables a new species to adapt to its environment more successfully than its predecessors, a certain momentum of development in a particular direction may be set up; and increasingly effective adaptation may appear over successive generations, leading to the emergence of further new species. Such developments are visible, however, only to a retrospective view, and there is no reason (from a biological perspective) to suppose that the process is actually directed, somehow, toward some specific goal. Processes of natural selection, it appears, can of themselves bring about directional movements along the various lines down which life evolves; and thus time as a whole, in biological evolution, seems to take on an increasingly linear and directional character.[2] This becomes evident also from another side: when living forms become extinct, as many if not all eventually do, they do not reappear at some later point, but are forever left behind. Cosmic time, then, to the extent that it is to be understood in light of evolutionary processes continually branching out and developing in many different directions, is (in certain respects) irreversible, creative of the new, and in that sense unidirectional and linear.

Second, evolutionary development here on earth has not stayed on a level plane. From our human standpoint, well aware that highly complex species have emerged on (at least some) evolutionary lines, directional movements toward what we cannot but regard as "higher" forms may appear;[3] and on one line (our own) this has given rise to what is actually a new order of reality: history. We must be very careful about what we say at this point. It is not that the evolution of life has been a sort of straight-line development, up from the primeval slime to humanity. Obviously, that is a misleading image: evolutionary developments (as we have been observing) have gone in many different directions. Most of these lines have died out, although some have achieved a basic equilibrium with their environment and thus become stabilized. Moreover, it is not evident that the human form is as biologically viable as are, for example, some insects. So from a strictly biological point of view (which emphasizes survival, perpetuation of the species), there is little reason to think that human life is the most successful product of the evolutionary process. However, in our analysis here we are not taking a strictly biological point of view: we are concerned rather with our distinctly *human* need—as historical beings—to find a way to orient ourselves in life and the world. For us the fact that history and historicity have emerged within (or out of) the order we call "life" is, obviously, of great significance. For it has been precisely with these developments that our very humanness has come into being.

As we noted earlier (Chapter 9), history and historicity did not appear suddenly on earth simply as the last stage of a strictly biological process: it was only after many millennia of a gradually emerging *historical* mode of development (to be distinguished from, though it was interwoven with, further biological evolution) that human existence as we now think of it came on the scene. We humans are, thus, quite as much a product of long and complex historical and cultural developments (going in significantly different directions in different parts of the world) as of evolutionary biological processes. Moreover, it is only from the particular *historical* standpoint of late modernity that this biological-historical movement eventuating in contemporary humankind has become perceptible. As we look back now, over this gradually cumulating evolutionary and historical development, the outlines of a kind of cosmic "trajectory" moving toward the creation of beings with significant historical powers, beings with historicity, may begin to come into view. (There are, no doubt, many other cosmic "trajectories" as well, moving in quite different directions.) It is important to be clear that (in keeping with our observations thus far about biological evolution) neither the "creative advances" nor the "directionality" visible in this trajectory need be attributed to some causative power pushing evolution and history forward toward a particular goal. But however that may be, from where we stand—with our anthropic interests and modern values—it would be strange indeed were we not to affirm the forward movement of this trajectory as *good,* to be valued (at least by us). And in connection with this, we may well wonder whether there might not be some sort of movement or tendency in the ultimate nature of things which encourages the emergence of ever higher and more complex forms of being (even though there is, of course, no strictly *scientific* warrant for such a notion).

If we take an affirmative position on these questions, we do not need to view the long upward march visible in our line of the evolutionary process as due entirely to chance, whatever role chance genetic variations and other physical and biological conditions of extremely low probability might have played in its occurrence. The trajectory eventuating in the creation of human historical existence could be seen, rather—in a fourth step of faith—as a significant expression of the serendipitous creativity manifest in the cosmos as a whole; and thus the appearance of human modes of being in the world would be properly regarded not as a metaphysical surd but rather as grounded in the ultimate nature of things, in the ultimate mystery. Such a view clearly requires an act of faith that goes beyond the general affirmation of pervasive creativity in the universe (our third step). This is not, however, as uncommon among intellectuals these days as one might at first suppose. All speculation about, and search for, intelligent life in other parts of the universe rests on precisely this assumption that there is something in the world which is everywhere pressing toward what we have been calling "historicity"; and we may, therefore, if we search long enough and carefully enough, eventually uncover some signs of this highly complex form of life in regions far removed from planet Earth. Whence the particular trajectory culminating in historicity on our planet will move in the future, we do not, of course, know—perhaps toward the opening of ever new possibilities for human beings, as we increasingly take responsibility for our lives and our future; perhaps going beyond humanity and historicity altogether, however difficult it may be to image what that might be; perhaps coming to an end in the total destruction of human life.

From the point of view which we are here exploring, the universe displays (at certain points in the evolutionary process) directional movements, trajectories which—when viewed retrospectively from our late-twentieth-century standpoint—seem in some respects proto-teleological. Moreover, with the emergence of historical modes of being, genuinely teleological patterns appear in the world, as human intentionality, consciousness, and purposive action begin to become effective.[4] Thus, just as physical energies and vital dynamisms in individual human beings gradually become sublimated and transformed through processes of socialization and enculturation into strivings of and toward spirit (see Chapter 19), so also cosmic trajectories, which have their origins in what seem to be mere physical movement or vibration, may (in some instances) gradually develop increasing directionality, ultimately creating a context within which deliberate purposive activity can emerge.[5] To the extent that we are able to regard the existence of us humans, of our historical and purposive mode of being, as a significant clue to or sign of the direction of at least one important trajectory on which the serendipitous creativity working through all things is moving, we begin to discern a metaphysical grounding for the human spirit—for its aspirations, projects, and prospects—in the ultimate mystery. Talk of this sort, of course, is often scornfully rejected. If we choose to read the evidence positively, however, we move one step further toward an understanding of human existence as having significant meaning in the cosmic scheme of things—that is, one step further toward faith in God.

We are engaged here in building a worldview, in imaginatively putting together a picture of the world and of human existence in terms of which we can gain orientation for life and self-understanding, a picture, therefore, to which we can commit ourselves. The steps along this path of theological construction are all questionable: significant leaps of imagination, going well beyond the direct evidence before us, are required; and firm commitments of will, to orient our lives in terms of these imaginative constructs, are demanded. Matters of faith, of course, are never matters of certainty; they always involve a willingness to make leaps and take on commitments. However, in traditional religious communities (and in more traditional theological work) the precise character and extent of these imaginatively grounded commitments and loyalties was somewhat obscured; for the basic framework which made it possible to understand the world and human life to be "under God" was taken for granted, simply accepted from tradition. Hence, questions about the components of this frame were never raised. One committed oneself (in one's believing) to the whole framework of interpretation; and life was lived as much as possible in the terms it defined and prescribed—or perhaps in rebellion against those terms, but never independently of them. In contrast to this traditional theological stance and approach, here we are trying to see how a contemporary theistic interpretive frame might be put together, what presuppositions it would take for granted and build upon, and what steps would be required to deliberately construct it. Instead of arbitrarily taking over from tradition an entire conceptual scheme constructed by earlier generations (one just as much a product of imaginative creativity as ours will be), we are trying deliberately and self-consciously to construct a modern theocentric frame. That is, we are trying to put together a way of seeing human life and the world (as we today understand these) which gives centrality to what we can properly call "God", a picture within which such notions as "God" and "God's revelation" and "God's salvific activity" are conceptually possible and important.

As a result of our procedure, what has traditionally appeared to be one large leap of faith—a single act of both appropriating and committing oneself to the (already completed) traditional framework of interpretation (which we are asked simply to take or leave)—here gets broken down into a number of smaller steps and commitments. With each of these we are called on to decide whether to accept the proposed construct; and in each case we have the liberty to refuse this invitation and to decide to construe our world, and our lives within that world, in some other way. Faith in God, thus, reveals itself in our analysis to be not a single monolithic either/or: one believes in God or one doesn't. On the contrary, such faith turns out to be a very complex matter, made up of many components, including particular conceptions of humanity and of the world. (And for this reason it can be broken down into a number of subsidiary decisions, in each of which we could move in several different directions.) The task of theological construction is the task of putting together a succession of steps which will finally culminate in what we can meaningfully regard as faith in God. At the end of the road we will not so much be called upon to make a single all-encompassing dramatic leap of faith as to reconfirm the path of small steps toward faith along which we have traveled.

So far we have identified four such steps on the way to faith in God (see Figure 4 for a diagrammatic presentation of these steps in the context of the overall program of theological construction set out in Parts III and IV). The first was the decision to go beyond the bare facts of contemporary scientific, historical, and commonsense knowledge about humanity and the world we live in, taking a position on the metaphysical issue of what is real, what is truly important for human beings; in thus moving beyond positivism and agnosticism, dogmatism and naive realism, we committed ourselves to engaging in reflection upon metaphysical issues and making some metaphysical judgments. Second was the decision whether to think of the universe as essentially a static, stable, unchanging, material structure, in which all process and development are ultimately ineffectual and thus without enduring meaning; or to think of it as fundamentally an evolutionary-developmental process, in which biological, historical, and other changes can be seen as having lasting effects and some sort of metaphysical significance. The latter alternative is the one most open to the notion of significant creativity manifesting itself within the world and the processes of its development, and is thus a step toward the conception of God. This does not mean, of course, that it is not possible to develop a religious position based on a metaphysics of unchanging structure: if one thinks of worldwide religious history, this other alternative has been the one more frequently followed. But in those traditions (particularly influential in western history) for whom the monotheistic God of ancient Israel became significant, change and history came to have great metaphysical import. With this in mind, third, we asked ourselves whether the course of biological evolution on earth, including the emergence of our own human historical mode of being, could properly be regarded as a significant clue to the ultimate mystery of things. If so, we would be in a position, perhaps, to begin thinking and speaking of a kind of serendipitous creativity pervading the cosmos, bringing into existence new modalities of being in and through temporal evolutionary processes. Further reflection on the emergence of human historicity through long evolutionary and historical processes has brought us now to a fourth step of faith (and toward faith): Should we regard the gradual historical emergence and development of

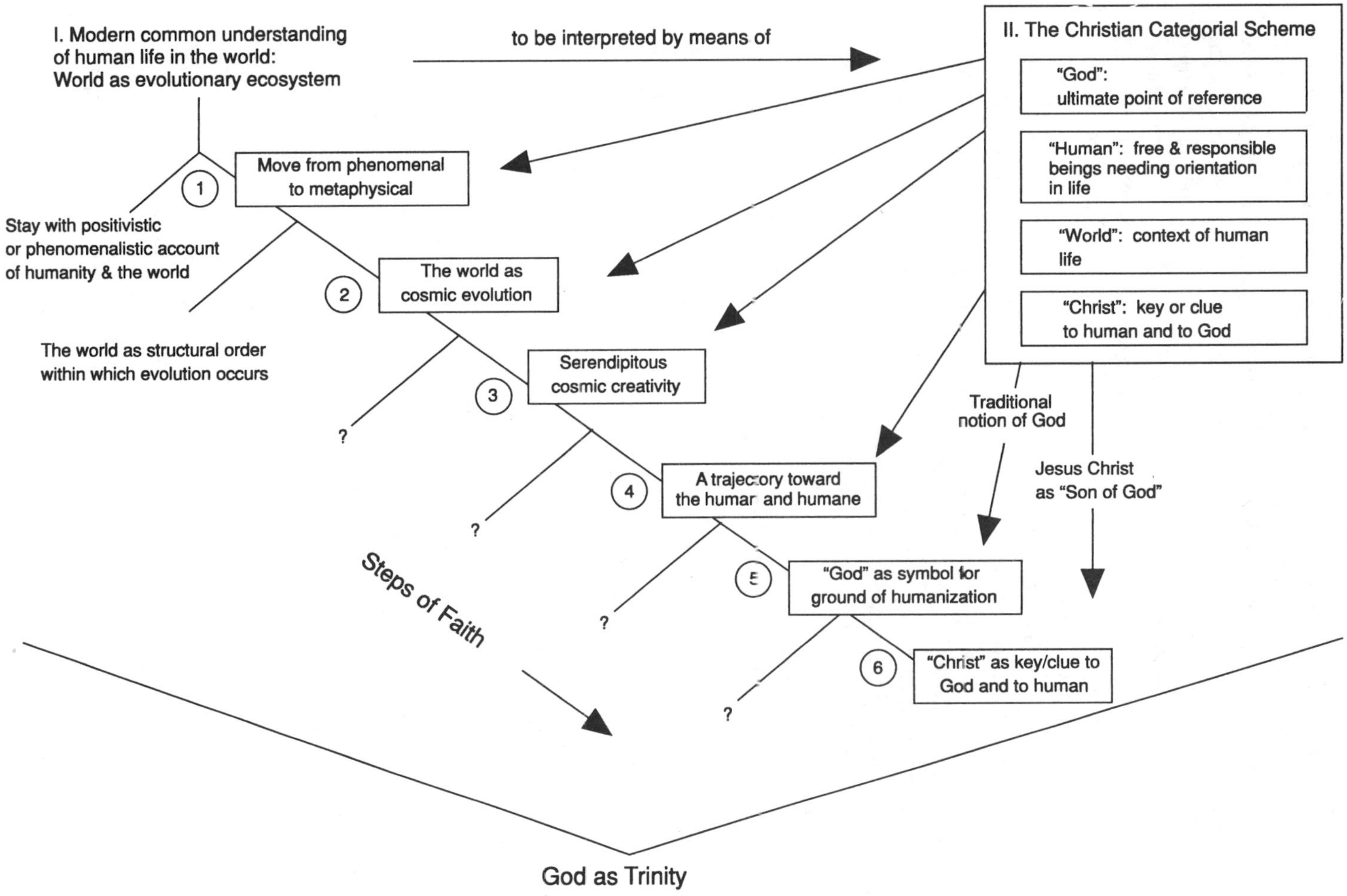

Figure 4 Christian theological construction: "small steps" of faith leading to a modern understanding of God

humanity in the world as an integral part of a larger trajectory grounded in this creativity of the ultimate mystery?

The notion of cosmic trajectories, as thus far sketched, remains very abstract, scarcely more than a schema; before we can make this fourth faith-decision and thus move our theological construction one step further, it is important to see more clearly what it means. Let us consider some models based upon certain features of biological evolution, on the one hand, and historical development, on the other, to see whether either of these can further illumine this matter. Consider first a model drawn from evolution. In the evolutionary process (as we have seen) there are movements in many different directions, often proceeding toward greater complexity. Apparently without any previsioning of what was going on, without any deliberate or conscious purposive activity directed toward this or that end, a vast development has unfolded with an irreversible (and in that respect unidirectional) movement along many distinct evolutionary lines. This suggests one possible way to view the serendipitous creativity in the world: it produces a complex cosmic evolutionary development branching off in many different directions, one of which has eventuated in the creation of human historical existence.

This picture, however, really throws very little light on what we are here seeking to understand: that human existence—shot through with deliberate purposiveness, self-directedness, and self-awareness—has emerged in the course of this development. Can we understand characteristics like these as simple straightforward products of processes and patterns of organization acknowledged to be totally blind? Although processes and events up to the emergence of self-conscious and self-directive activities and movements can certainly be understood in largely evolutionary-biological terms, it is hard to see how specifically *historical* developments of this sort, including above all the emergence of historicity, are much illuminated by recourse to biological explanations. If we are to gain any real understanding of the cosmic trajectory which has given rise to precisely those features of human existence in which we are most interested, the biological account of evolutionary development will need to be significantly supplemented. Let us turn, then, to concepts constructed to enable us better to grasp and interpret the distinctive characteristics of the *historical* process, to see whether these can suggest a model adequate for understanding the emergence of history and historicity on one of the trajectories generated in course of the evolution of life.

Two different ways of conceiving the cumulating historical process have dominated modern western reflection, one based on the idea of progress, the other on the notion of historical relativism; neither of these conceptions, however, is particularly useful for our purposes. The idea of progress proved attractive to nineteenth-century writers, who were among the first to become fully aware of history as a unique mode of reality. Looking back over the human past, they believed they saw steady historical progress from human beginnings in quite primitive stages of culture, through the great civilizations of the Middle East and India and China, and then Greece and Rome, to the rise of western civilization; the latter, it seemed, was increasingly leaving all these others behind. Doubtless throughout this long historical development there were many tensions and problems, many setbacks and even catastrophes; but gradually the difficulties of human historical and cultural life, which had destroyed earlier civilizations or left them in a kind of static atrophy, were being overcome, and the powerful dynamic of historical progress was increasingly concentrating itself in the West—that is, in a civilization created largely by Christians (especially, in the modern period, by Protestants) and dominated by whites (especially males).

This highly ethnocentric, raciocentric, and gendercentric interpretation of world history was, of course, not simply created out of whole cloth by eighteenth- and nineteenth-century European chauvinists; it had its origins many centuries earlier in the sacred texts which had long nourished western religious consciousness. The Yahwistic historians whose work became a central strand in the Hebrew scriptures, the eighth-century prophets, the Deuteronomic historians, the Jewish post-exilic writers, all contributed to the concept of a "chosen people," through whom God's purposes were being worked out in a special way; and this notion was picked up by the early Christians and made a central feature of the church's self-understanding. This was above all a historical or historicist self-understanding, grounded on a conception of the world, and particularly of human existence in the world, as a historical movement toward the realization of God's purposes. The church saw itself as a central vehicle of God's working in history: it was the New Israel in and through which all human history was being brought to its consummation. This has been a common theme all the way from Irenaeus and Montanus through Augustine and Joachim of Flora down to Jonathan Edwards and many contemporary traditional Christians. Little wonder that the modern West has been dominated by a powerful ethnocentric historical consciousness; and that, human nature being what it is, this has expressed itself in chauvinistic views of historical progress, even though, as western culture has become increasingly secularized, the religious mythology which gave birth to these ideas has been rapidly falling away.

One major way, thus, of interpreting the serendipitous development of human institutions and culture through history has been in the teleological terms of the conception of progress. In the modern period this became a kind of metaphysics of history glorifying the creative powers of the human spirit (one thinks especially of Condorcet and Hegel here, but also of Auguste Comte, Karl Marx, and the many humanist successors of these important writers). The doctrine of progress was basically a secularized version of the notion of divine providence, which for earlier generations had made a teleological movement of history seem both intelligible and plausible.[6] An interpretation of evolution/history of this sort would, of course, provide one way to understand the trajectory culminating in human existence as we know it; unfortunately, however, this kind of metaphysical conception is no longer plausible either biologically or historically.

We have already acknowledged the difficulties today with straightforward teleological interpretations of biological evolution; for most twentieth-century thinkers such views of history seem equally dubious. On the one hand, the institutions and values and magnificent cultural creativity of all the great human civilizations are now increasingly taken to be explicable as responses of the human spirit to various challenges of life; on the other hand, the massive problems and failures of western civilization, from World War I down to the contemporary ecological crisis and the threat of nuclear annihilation, have become obvious. The interpretation of the human story as a unified movement of historical progress culminating in western civilization now seems utterly ethnocentric and imperialistic—and quite implausible. So, in place of this unified overall teleological movement, history has become understood by many in largely relativistic terms: each of the several great civilizations is seen as a product of significant creative activity, but these various creative developments have moved in diverse directions. Each distinct line seems to have an integrity of its own, and each must be appreciated, therefore, in its own terms, its right to continuing historical existence being acknowledged. A relativistic view of this sort certainly expresses the serendipitous creativity manifest in the world; but it does not help us address the question with which we are at this point concerned: How are we to understand the fact that within the biological process of evolution has appeared a distinctive trajectory eventuating in the emergence of this pluralistic history and historicity? Relativistic modes of interpretation (as we shall see in a moment) simply replicate on the historical level a pluralizing pattern similar to that found in the biological order. In no way do they illuminate the peculiar *singularity* which we find in the very emergence of history, in each of the many diverse paths along which historical developments have moved, and especially now, as these paths are converging once again into an exceedingly complex, but *single,* global process.

The interpretation of human cultural plurality along relativistic lines seemed plausible during the first half of the twentieth century (as I noted in Chapter 9), but we now find ourselves in a rather different historical situation: human history, which had seemed for many generations to be divided into more or less independent traditions, is becoming a single interconnected whole. Unlike the evolution of life, which seems destined to continue indefinitely throwing up new forms that move down distinctly different lines of development, the several great lines of human cultural history appear to be converging once again. Much of the impetus toward this new development originally came from the West (with its political, economic, cultural, and religious imperialism and colonialism); but this can no longer mean for us (as it did for many in the nineteenth century) that there is any simple pattern of progress in history toward western modernity, with earlier civilizations left behind to stagnate or die. For, contrary to that view, those other great civilizations seem to be coming back to life again, modernizing in their own ways, making distinctive places for themselves in the world-historical process that is now unfolding; and the unquestioned historical preeminence of the West appears to be fading. These cultures are playing roles in part defined by the unique histories which have produced each of them, but also in part determined by the forces of modernity that are now bringing us all together into "one world." The histories of the various cultures appear to be converging into one great historical stream, moving onward we know not quite where—possibly toward the total annihilation of the human species and much of the rest of life on earth; possibly toward a technocratic totalitarianism; but also possibly, we may dare to hope, toward a more humane and just world where the wretched of the earth may gain some fulfillment in life.

This great new vision of one world, of a humanity unified in a single multiplex history, is itself a manifestation of the serendipity of history and a quite unexpected development: emerging out of the enormous diversity of human cultures, modes of life, ways of being human, the unforeseen possibility of a new humanity is opening before our eyes, a humanity in which each of these distinctive cultures will have its own unique role to play, contributing special values and meanings to the new world now being created. No one is yet able to describe in any detail what this new world (if indeed it comes) will look like; even its broadest outlines are difficult to imagine. But it is evident that in recent decades human history has taken some important turns that open up new possibilities which the concept of historical relativism did not envision at all.

In relativistic interpretations historical trajectories are treated according to a pattern similar in important respects to that of biological evolution. Evolution, as a cumulating creative process producing many different forms of life—all of them complexly interrelated and interdependent but each with its own integrity and its own distinctive qualities and character—cannot properly be understood as a singular development moving in only one direction; it has flowered down many different lines. When human history is interpreted in terms of the idea of cultural relativism, a similar pattern is displayed: one sees the many strange and wondrous forms of human life that have appeared in the course of time, and it seems evident that each of these should be appreciated in its own right. None should be regarded as "truer" or "more valid" than the others, with the right (to use the words of Genesis 1:28) to "subdue" them and gain "dominion" over them; each should be allowed to coexist alongside the others, in its own integrity and to the best of its ability. This pattern of interpretation appears to be clearly warranted in the case of biological evolution, where new developments are made possible by the appearance of new species, each of which, on a trajectory of its own, can reproduce its own kind but can almost never breed with others, however symbiotically their life-cycles may become intertwined. In human history, however, the movement into increasing diversity has been of a quite different sort. It has been essentially historical and cultural in character rather than genetic; and this means that it has always remained possible for separated and distinct peoples, each with their own unique ways of being human, to meld themselves together again (when historical circumstances demanded this) into a single society, fully capable of reproducing itself both biologically and culturally. When diversity is cultural and historical rather than biological, the several different groupings retain the ability to adopt institutions, ways of behaving, systems of value and meaning, from one another; and to adapt their ways of living and acting to one another, mixing and uniting what had been separate and distinct into new creative syntheses. Virtually none of this is conceivable with the biological model.

These facts, quite important for our understanding of the overall sweep of human history, are seldom taken fully into account by advocates of historical relativism. Now, however, on the basis of our historical knowledge of the enormous diversity found in the human past and our perception of movements in the present overcoming the separation and isolation of different peoples from each other, we are in a position to see that, despite all this diversity, human history has actually always been a single intraconnected stream moving forward. The basic unity of this stream, and the unidirectional character of its overall empirical movement, were not, of course, clearly visible to human eyes and minds until quite recently (though the idea of a forward movement in history—not necessarily a continuous progress—has been, of course, affirmed in much western religious thinking from ancient Israel to the present). There have been many side-eddies, many whirlpools and detours, many breakdowns and collapses and reversals, but none of these has been powerful enough to permanently arrest the surging forward-movement which carries all human existence, and all styles of culture, with it: human history, it seems, is really a single vast, complex, irreversible process.

One of the latest expressions of this forward-moving trajectory of human history—with its serendipitous creativity always bringing into being the new and unexpected—is this dream of a new humanity living on a new ecologically ordered earth. The entirety of human history, with its many diverse details, is here taken up into a grand vision of the movement of humankind into this new hoped-for future—a contemporary version of the Christian expectation and prayer that God's kingdom would "come on earth as it is in heaven" (Mt. 6:10). For us today, of course, there can be no guarantee of such an outcome: as we have seen, the serendipitous creativity of the historical process expresses itself in what appear—to our human perspectives, especially those shaped by humane concerns—to be horrifying evils, as well as great goods. Nevertheless, if the appearance of human life on earth—the appearance of historical modalities of being—can be regarded as a significant clue to at least some features of the ongoing cosmic process (as the idea of a trajectory toward the human and the humane suggests), there may be some grounds for hope.

Neither the idea of progress nor the notion of historical relativism provides us with a satisfactory way to interpret the sort of trajectory manifest here: human history is too open a movement, with too many unanticipated developments and unexpected surprises, for the progress view; it is too unified and interconnected, even unidirectional in its overall unfolding, for historical relativism. How, then, should we characterize this trajectory on which the human has been created, this emergence of history and historicity from biological evolution? Let us return to the two basic ideas in terms of which we have organized our reflections on evolution and history thus far: (a) the notion of cosmic serendipitous creativity which (b) expresses itself through trajectories of various sorts extending through longer and shorter stretches of time. When these two notions are taken together, they point up rather well, I think, the character of our historical existence as a process which is in many respects directional—even quasi-teleological—but which has a creativity working within it that remains deeply mysterious to us. The notion of serendipitous creativity taken simply by itself is too open and random to illumine satisfactorily either the full significance of the emergence of historical forms of order out of biological or the overall movement of human history, with its diverse streams converging once again (after many millennia) into a single ongoing and developing process. However, to use the idea of teleology to interpret this development is to suggest a process too unswervingly and unqualifiedly goal-oriented to be plausible any longer (this is a major problem with nineteenth-century notions of progress, as well as with traditional conceptions of the sovereignty of God). In this respect the somewhat vaguer and simpler notion of trajectories (directional movements) has significant advantages for a contemporary understanding of the world. These two concepts taken together, I suggest (note the similarity here to the "two-step process" characteristic of evolutionary change in biology; see Chapter 19), can generate a way of conceiving the evolutionary-historical world within which we can meaningfully consider how human life should be oriented today.

Brief mention of five points will indicate how this is so. First, this approach provides a conceptual frame within which we can characterize quite accurately, and unify into an overall vision, what seems actually to have happened, so far as we know, in the course of both cosmic evolution and human history. Second, it gives a significant, but not dominant, place and meaning to the distinctive character of human life and history within this cosmic process. Therefore, third, it can be the basis for developing general principles of interpretation in terms of which communities (and individuals within those communities) can attempt to grasp and understand both the biological context of their lives and the historical developments through which they are living, thus orienting themselves in a manner which should encourage taking responsible roles with respect to this context and these developments. Fourth, it is an approach which, because of the significance it gives to humanistic and humane values within the cosmic order as a whole, can provide a ground for hope (though not certainty) about the future—a hope about the direction of human history and about the possible development of a new humanity living in a new age. Finally, fifth, a hope with a cosmic grounding of this sort—even though carrying much less assurance than traditional religious expectations of the coming of God's kingdom—can help to motivate women and men to devote their lives to bringing about this more humane world to which we all aspire.

Here, then, are the rudiments of a conception of the world, a cosmic vision, which can focus and provide orientation for religiously committed communal and personal lives, a focus and orientation in important respects similar to—though much more reserved than—that provided by the traditional Christian myths. In this conception we employ thoroughly contemporary understandings of human existence and the world—modern myths—framed in such a way as both to orient human life significantly and to motivate it toward fulfillment of its tendencies toward full historicity, toward taking full responsibility for itself, its future, and its world. This frame of orientation or vision of reality is not, of course, in any way forced on us: it can be appropriated (as we have seen) only by means of our own personal decisions, our own acts of faith; it will provide orientation for us only as we decide to commit ourselves to it, ordering our lives and building our futures in the terms it prescribes. What is required of us here is not, however, one gigantic leap of faith to a position disconnected from all historical and scientific evidences—as belief in the more traditional religious frame of reference, with its agent-God, today demands—but rather a succession of smaller steps of faith, for each of which there is some justification but no conclusive argument.

When we come to understand that the frame of orientation in terms of which we live—whatever it may be—is unavoidably a product of human imaginative construction and thus far from incorrigible, our commitment will quite properly be in certain respects tentative. Though such a frame can never justifiably claim to be indubitable, it need not, however, seem so unsubstantiated or absurd, so unconnected with our experience, life, and knowledge as to appear arbitrary or unreal or "merely imaginary": the kind of deliberate imaginative construction we have been undertaking here is an attempt to put together a picture of human existence and the world (an overarching myth or story) with which we can in fact identify. Since it makes sense of our experience and is deeply informed by modern knowledges, it provides a basis for orientation in the world which can be trusted; it is a vision which can meaningfully focus our long-range commitments and guide our actions. What is asked of us now is whether we are prepared (in a fourth step of faith) to affirm this vision of human existence as emerging on, and being sustained by, an evolutionary-historical trajectory grounded in the serendipitous creativity at work in the world. If we are so prepared, we have before us the basic outline of a world-picture in terms of which we can meaningfully and responsibly order our lives today, and we are thus in a position to move to a fifth step of faith: explicit construction of a conception of God. It should not be difficult to guess where in this world-picture we will pick up threads to continue our constructive work. It is the concept of serendipitous cosmic processes—a serendipity within which the overflowingness or creativity in things can come to manifest a kind of directionality in its evolutionary and historical trajectories—that will serve as the necessary opening for our construction of a concept of God for today.

The principal concepts and experiences with which we have worked here, I want to point out, are similar in important respects to those which provided the inspiration and stimulus for the originary historical creation of the image/concept of God: these were a sense of grace (serendipity) and of promise (directionality) working in and through the events of Israel's history. It was above all a conviction about the meaning of a new historical situation (the escape of a group of slaves from Egypt) with the new possibilities this opened up, the new demands this laid on the Hebrew people, and the expectation which this created of a truly good life that was to be theirs in the future—that is, it was the conviction that the history in which they were participating was really going someplace that would be meaningful and fulfilling for them—that inspired the mythopoetic creation of that great historical figure Yahweh, the creator of the world and the mover of all history. We have noted problems with that particular expression of the religious imagination, and we shall have to examine some of these more closely as we proceed further; it is unlikely we will want to move down precisely the same paths in our imaginative construction of a conception of God for today as did the poets and prophets of ancient Israel. But it is an encouragement for our project that, despite the enormous dissimilarity between modern and ancient understandings of humanity and of the world, we have been able to locate and describe experiential and conceptual dimensions of the human situation today which show it to be in significant respects analogous to that within which the conception of God was originally born.

This is not the place to begin spelling out the concept of God which we will be developing here, but I would like to call attention to one further point: that we now have before us the ingredients for a specifically *trinitarian* view. (This is somewhat surprising, when one considers that our analysis of human existence in the world up to this point has not in any way been intentionally guided by trinitarian considerations or themes.) The main metaphysical features of the world-picture we have been sketching could be summed up in this way:

1. The overflowingness or serendipity or creativity which seemingly expresses itself in and through everything that exists is to be understood as an appropriate construal of the ultimate mystery which grounds all reality, that point farthest back, beyond which we have no way of moving in our reflection. It would be a fairly simple and direct metaphysical extrapolation to see not only the evolution of life and the development of history but *all that is* as having its originary source and foundation in this munificent creativity. Such a conception would be a contemporary version of the traditional view that God, in the person of the transcendent almighty creator—the "first person" of the trinity—is the source and foundation of all that is.

2. As we have noted, the particular structures and concreteness of human life and the world cannot be properly understood simply by vague references to this overflowing fountain of creativity. This is a universe of very specific modes of order and meaning; and the particular structure and orderliness in things, without which the meaning and purposefulness of human life would be inconceivable, was also (for the early Christian thinkers) to be understood as grounded significantly in God. So to metaphors like "source" and "foundation" and "creator" they found it necessary in conceiving God to add "order," "logos," "word," "wisdom," and the like; and, indeed, it was this "second person" in the divine reality (as they conceived this matter) that they held to be the very agent "through" whom or "in" whom all things were created (John 1:3; Col. 1:16). Our notion of "directional movements" in the cosmic processes, including a trajectory toward the authentically human or humane (that is, toward that which, in the Christian categorial scheme, "Christ" signifies)—movements grounded in the ultimate creativity working in and through all things and manifesting increasingly complex forms of order—is significantly similar to the "second person" of the trinity in its function and in its relation to the primordial creativity.

3. As we have observed, this directionality manifested in the creativity of

the ultimate mystery of things has come to significant fruition (for us humans at least) with the emergence of *historicity* within the evolutionary-historical process, that is, with the appearance within the created order of modes of *subjectivity* which are themselves free and creative in important ways. In some respects this development can (as the tradition put it) be thought of as exemplifying the very "image of God"—that is, as showing forth (in an appropriately finite way) the divine creativity itself. Working directly, then, within the cosmic process as a whole—and, through history, in-forming the human spirit in a special way—is the divine spirit itself, the "third person" of the trinity; so ongoing human life, with all its complex structures of purposiveness, meaning, and value, and its struggles toward a greater humanization and humaneness (along with all the rest of reality) is to be seen as expressing the immediate and continuous presence of the divine creative activity.

I cannot at this point work out the implications of this trinitarian pattern, just beginning to emerge in our attempt to construct a contemporary understanding of humanity, the world, and God. (Further elaboration will be found in Chapter 27.) We are only at the beginnings of our systematic analysis and (re)construction of the concept of God, and it is not possible as yet to see whether these trinitarian intimations will prove plausible and illuminating. But it seemed worthwhile, at this juncture, at least to take note of the way in which our anthropological and cosmological reflections connect up with these central Christian contentions about God: that the ultimate reality with which we humans have to do, that toward which and in terms of which life must be oriented if it is to realize its deepest potentialities, must be understood as at once (a) the ultimate creativity which is behind and working through all things, that creativity (b) which expresses itself in the modes and patterns of order in the world, including the trajectories which constitute our world and lives as human, that creativity (c) which is, therefore, present and working within all reality, and is significantly manifest and experienced within human history and the human spirit.

Part IV

Constructing a Concept of an Ultimate Point of Reference: God

In our traditions the term "God" is the symbol of ultimate values and meanings in all of their dimensions. It connotes an absolute claim on our loyalty. It bespeaks a primacy of trust, and a priority within the ordering of our commitments. It points the direction of a greatness of fulfillment. It signifies a richness of resources of the living of life at its depths. It suggests the enshrinement of our common and ecological life. It proclaims an adequate object of worship. It symbolizes a transcendent and inexhaustible meaning that forever eludes our grasp.

Bernard Loomer

God is love.

1 John 4

God . . . is the eternal process.

G. W. F. Hegel

. . . we ought to speak of God. We are human, however, and so cannot speak of God. We ought therefore to recognize both our obligation and our inability and by that very recognition give God the glory.

Karl Barth

21. Functions of the Symbol "God"

We have before us now an interpretation of humanity and the world which is intelligible in relation to modern scientific and historical knowledge, and which leaves some openness, some space, within which we can develop an image/concept of God for today. In Chapter 6 we noted that in monotheistic religious traditions world-pictures with a threefold categorial structure—humanity/world/God—characteristically develop. Since the symbol "God" has become so problematical in contemporary culture, I suggested early on that we begin our construction of a contemporary version of the Christian perspective with the categories of humanity and the world, both of which necessarily have an important place in all frameworks intended to provide orientation for life. Part II of this book was devoted to developing a conception of the human as biohistorical reality; and Part III to sketching (through four distinct steps of faith) a conception of the world as an evolutionary-historical process permeated by serendipitous creativity. With our conceptions of humanity and the world now in place, we are in a position to move on to direct consideration of the symbol "God," in the course of which we shall take our fifth step of faith. Following this we will explore the ways in which the symbol "Christ" can qualify the definitions and understandings of humanity, God, and the world with which we have been working; this will bring us to our sixth and final step: to faith in God understood in specifically Christian terms.

The notion of God which we have inherited was not, of course, originally produced through a process of systematic theological construction of the sort we are attempting here; rather it grew up in connection with a picture of the world that developed in the ancient Near East, a picture in which a sharp distinction was made (at least in Israel) between "creation" and "the creator"—or (as it was put later) between "this world" (in which we humans live) and an "other world" (the locus of the realities of most importance to life), or between "nature" and "supernature." In dualistic frameworks of this sort "otherworldly" or "supernatural" beings like gods and angels and demons hold sway over much that goes on in human affairs; and it is important, therefore, that humans learn as much as possible about these beings, and that they maintain positive and satisfactory relations with them. Many religious schemes betray dualistic patterns like this: one thinks, for instance, of the sharp distinction in Hinduism between Brahman (ultimate reality) and *maya* (the world of illusion in which we humans live); and of Plato's distinction of the world of the Forms from the world of everyday life. In ancient Hebrew religion God, the ultimate reality with which humans have to do, the creator of the world and the lord of history, lives in the heavens above and rules the creatures from there. In a symbolic scheme of this sort we humans, living here on earth, have no direct access to or experience of the "other world," of heaven; and all our ideas about it, therefore, must be based on a kind of extrapolation from our earthly experience. It is not surprising, then, that the gods and demons and other supernatural beings are usually depicted in quite anthropomorphic terms, and the various sorts of otherworldly power are imagined on analogy with the well-known powers of this world. As Rudolf Bultmann put it in his classic paper on demythologizing: this sort of mythology involves "the use of imagery to express the otherworldly in terms of this world and the divine in terms of human life, the other side in terms of this side."[1]

This dualistic way of thinking dominated the minds of the ancient Israelites who produced the Old Testament. They made use of a wide range of earthly metaphors in putting together their idea of God—"light," "rock of salvation," "spirit" (that is, breath or wind), "mighty warrior," "Most High," "Holy One," "shepherd," et cetera—but two images in particular largely came to define the basic notion of deity which emerged in that culture: "lord" (or "king") and "creator." When people prayed to Yahweh, it was to the creator/lord that they prayed; when they lived in "fear" of God, it was the creator/lord whom they feared. Many other metaphors and images were used to qualify and amplify and fill in the conception of God, but it was the creator/lord who was the subject—the reality—of which all these other characterizations were predicated. The notion of God as *the Lord* became so dominating in culture and consciousness that in the Septuagint, the early Greek translation of the Hebrew Bible, the tetragrammaton *YHWH* (God's name, so holy it was no longer permissible to utter) was regularly rendered as *kyrios,* "the Lord"; and this practice has also been followed in many subsequent translations, including the Revised Standard Version and the New English Bible. Thus, the phrase "the Lord" is used repeatedly in the biblical texts of most readers to refer to the chief character or actor in the biblical story; and in the thinking and prayers of many believers "God" and "the Lord" are virtually synonymous terms.

In the New Testament (and the subsequent Christian era) a third defining metaphor, "father"—which seems often to have been on Jesus' lips—gained prominence similar to that of "creator" and "lord." But there is no question that the one whom Jesus called "father" was also the creator/lord; indeed, the notion of father has intrinsic connections with the other two ideas (a father is both the progenitor of his children and, at least in much premodern practice, the ruler of his family and household). In the early church there was some debate as to whether the "father of Jesus Christ" was the same being as the creator of the world and lord of history. Gnostic Christians often denied this, and the followers of Marcion (almost half the church in the late second century) claimed that the creator/lord of Jewish belief (who ruled this evil world) and the father of Jesus Christ (who was the savior from this world) were two quite distinct gods. Eventually, however, this ditheism was rejected as heresy, and the church officially affirmed a fully monotheistic understanding of God. The first article of the so-called Apostles' Creed made it unmistakably clear that the Christian father-God and the Jewish creator/lord of the world were one: "I believe in God the Father, Almighty Maker of heaven and earth." God had become identified as creator/lord/father, maker of all and ruler over all.

I will not here provide a detailed analysis of these three principal metaphors that have largely defined the Christian image/concept of God,[2] but it is important for us to take note of some of the motifs that are highlighted when God is conceived in the terms they provide.

1. Absolutely central to the traditional notion of God, as constructed with the help of these metaphors, is the idea of God's *transcendence* of the world, God's radical otherness from all creatures; it is the metaphor of "creator" that most decisively makes this point. God is not to be confused with any other being or any other order of reality: everything other than God is created reality, finite being, it is in the world; God exists, however, in utter independence, over and above the world, transcendent. God brought the world into being; without God's activity no finite orders of reality would exist at all. God rules over and ultimately controls the world and all that is in it. But God does not need the world or anything else in order to exist: God has *aseity.* So God in Godself (as creator of all) is entirely transcendent of—wholly different from—the world and all the creatures within it. The creator/creation distinction which is foundational for the traditional conception of God makes a sharp dualism between God and the world inescapable.

2. When developed in this way, these metaphors emphasize the absoluteness of God's power. Without immense power God would not have utter independence from everything else, nor would God have the capacity to create and rule over this entire magnificent universe. God must be thought of as the source of all power in the world, all power both to *be* and to *do* (including the power which humans possess to choose freely and to create).

Since all creaturely power is derivative from God's, God can quite properly be said to be all-powerful, omnipotent. God alone thus is absolute: God is awe-inspiring, terrifying, glorious!

3. God's power is not to be conceived as mere blind force; on the contrary, it is *personal* power. God is a self-conscious being with purposes and intentions; and in acting God carries these through deliberately and self-consciously. All three of the central constitutive images (creator, lord, and father) are based on human models which emphasize intentionality and self-consciousness. Since all nature is under the control of the divine will, even powerful seemingly blind catastrophic events—earthquakes, thunderstorms, volcanic eruptions—must be understood as expressing God's purposive activity. The decisions and purposes of God are worked out in many ways, sometimes through moving the minds and hearts of humans—an Abraham or a Moses, an Egyptian Pharaoh or a Cyrus of Persia, a Nicodemus or a Saul of Tarsus—sometimes through earthquake or storm, sometimes by simply uttering the almighty creative word, "Let there be light." In all of this God's power is personal and purposive, like that of a human artisan able to make what he or she decides to make, like that of a ruler with control over a people and a territory.

4. The creator/lord/father is thus the source and sustainer of all that makes human life and well-being possible, and the source of life itself. Women and men live out their lives at God's pleasure and in continuous interrelation with what God has done and is doing for them; and their proper response to all of this is gratitude and praise for all God's gifts. Since the creator/lord/father cares for all creatures, particularly for those made in the divine image—men and women—it is quite appropriate for humans to pray to God, to call on God in their hour of need. As a loving father cares for the sons and daughters he has brought into the world, so God also seeks always to bring "his" children to wholeness, fulfillment, salvation. It is both possible and appropriate—indeed, it is the supreme blessedness open to women and men in this life—to enter into personal relationship with their heavenly father. This image/concept of one who is not only transcendent, omnipotent, and glorious but also loving, merciful, and forgiving—the creator/lord/father—is the core notion out of which most western thinking about God has evolved and to which it always returns for nourishment.

This conception of God, however, has become problematic for many moderns. Although it sets out what many might want to believe about human life and its ultimate foundations, persuasive arguments available today count heavily against it. (Some of these were noted in Chapter 19; others will be taken up as we proceed.) A widely influential interpretation found in contemporary psychological theory suggests that this whole picture is essentially a projection—onto the cold and cruel world of adult human life—of deep childhood wishes for a loving parent who will always be there, always caring for one no matter what the difficulty or crisis. That the world is a place where every hair on our heads is numbered (Mt. 10:30) by someone who keeps track of such things; that not even a sparrow falls to the ground without our heavenly father knowing and willing it (10:29), seems today simply incredible to many. The massive evils experienced in the twentieth century—the terrible suffering, destruction, and death in two world wars, the deliberate murder of millions of human beings in death camps, the stockpiling of weapons which threaten a nuclear catastrophe that could bring human history to an end—present overpowering counter-evidence to the myth of the God who cares for each person in even the tiniest details of life. The meaningless horrors and death suffered by six million Jews (supposedly God's "chosen people") under the Nazis have become perhaps the ultimate symbol for the stark incredibility of this old comforting dream of a loving father in heaven who protects his children against all evils. If there really is a God, and if we are to continue to have faith in God, we will need to understand these matters in rather different terms from those suggested by the defining metaphors of the tradition.

When one adds to these problems of credibility the growing awareness today that Christianity itself, including its way of symbolizing the human and the world, may be an important root of some of the evils of modernity—western (and Christian) imperialism, certainly partly produced by the powerful sense in Christian faith of a unique divine authorization guaranteeing the superiority of Christianity over other religions (and cultures); Christian sexism and racism; the powerful thrust toward exploitation of the environment provided by the belief that humans are to have "dominion" (Gen. 1:28) over the earth; and so on—we are forced to ask some new hard questions about Christian faith, practices, and institutions. These questions require us to engage in close examination of the symbols and ideas that have traditionally informed this faith and these practices: Have the image/concepts of God and Christ (as these have been received and understood)—somehow contributed significantly to these evils? How could Christian practices, attitudes, and ideas have led to such horrors? What has gone wrong here?

What we know (or think that we know) about the world in which we live suggests a picture very different from the one purveyed in Christian tradition; indeed, it makes the traditional picture, I suggest, literally unthinkable by us, unintelligible (though of course we can still *assert* it). To try to think the idea of a divine super-Self *outside of* or beyond the universe (which is hundreds of millions of light years across) boggles the mind; moreover, trying to resolve this problem by thinking in terms of a divine Spirit or Self moving immanently *within* the universe (obviously a considerable transformation of the traditional mythic picture) is no easier. So other metaphors for

God, supposedly more compatible with modern notions of the world, may be proposed in the attempt to save something of the original meaning: ground of being, first cause, creative event, power, life, a vague "cosmic love." All of these present watered-down versions of the meaning carried by the picture of the creator/lord/father; they are masks for this great conception on which they secretly draw and which gives them their religious power. What is needed today is not one more camouflage of the old mythic notion but rather a new conception of God, one that resonates more directly with our modern experience and understanding of the world.

Obviously, we can not address this problem satisfactorily by simply attaching the name "God" arbitrarily to some aspect of our modern cosmic scheme which may seem to be a plausible candidate for it; we must be able to give good reasons for regarding precisely this as God. What sort of reasons might these be? The identification and elaboration of some feature or dimension of modern life or experience as *God* will be justified only if it can be shown to perform functions which (a) are reasonably similar to (at least some of) those attributed to God in the traditional picture of the creator/lord/father, and (b) are today still important, or even indispensable, to human life. That is, our new conception must have sufficient continuity with what "God" has meant in the past to warrant our use of the name; and we must also be able to show that God (as conceived in this way) will contribute significantly to guiding and orienting human life today. It is necessary, therefore, for us to examine the traditional picture in which western God-talk originated, and which continues to nourish it, (a) to see how the conception of the transcendent creator/lord/father has functioned to order and orient human existence and (b) to see if we can construct a conception of God for today capable of performing similar functions (at least those which we think are still important). Only careful attention to both these matters will entitle us to use the name "God" with respect to something in our modern world-picture.[3]

We cannot here, of course, inspect all functions and meanings of the image/concept "God" during its more than four thousand years' history; that would take massive investigations for which I have neither the space nor the competence. But it is not necessary for us to work with all this variety of historical detail, for our principal interest is in coming to an understanding of how this notion has functioned in the threefold monotheistic categorial scheme (world/humanity/God) of which it is a principal term (see Chapter 6). Just what does the category "God" do in this scheme? What does it add to, and how does it otherwise qualify, the categories "world" and "humanity," thus giving the monotheistic framework its distinctive character? To put this in other words: for those living within this world-picture, how did the creator/lord/father provide significant meaning and orientation for life? The image/concept of God did not serve merely to answer such speculative questions as, Where did the world come from? or, Is there an ultimate power behind everything, and if so, what is it? What else, then, did it do? My summary answer to these questions is this: For those living within a theocentric worldview, *the name "God" was believed to focus human devotion and service on that which would bring human fulfillment (salvation).* For this reason it was given a central place in consciousness, devotion, and service, providing overall orientation and guidance for human life. For this reason also (for those with faith) God provided a kind of ultimate security in life, profound consolation in moments of deep sadness, healing in situations of despair. God, that is to say, was regarded as that reality—and the symbol "God" was therefore taken to express that complex meaning—to which each person must give herself or himself, and on which communities must orient themselves, if human life is to gain wholeness, meaning, salvation.

What sort of symbol or concept—what kind of focusing of the mind—is needed to orient men and women in life today?* The concept of the universe taken by itself, of the evolutionary-historical process as a whole, cannot provide this, nor can the notion of the ultimate mystery of things. The one presents us with such enormously complex patterns and such a multiplicity of detail that it can scarcely be grasped by our limited minds; the other is so vague and amorphous in its meaning that it can tell us nothing specific about what we should be or do. Moreover, since both of these notions are intended (each in its own way) to be inclusive of everything, neither can provide us with clear norms or criteria for making choices; for decisions always involve giving preference to some things over others—to some possibilities, some forms of life, some persons or loyalties or causes. Neither the concept of mystery nor the concept of the world can be of much help, then, in guiding our day-to-day decisions or providing direction for our lives as a whole. What we need is a symbol which draws upon both our understanding of the world and our awareness of the ultimate mystery of things in a way that holds before our minds in sharp synoptic focus what is essential for the orientation

*It is through creating synoptic foci that our minds grasp the various qualities and dimensions of experience in usable ways; this is how concepts work. For example, the concept "chair" enables us to hold together in a focus or unity a wide range of experienced objects-of-a-certain-sort-to-be-sat-upon, so that we can attend to and act with reference to this particular feature of those objects. Similarly, the concept "table" holds together and focuses in a unity that miscellaneous group of flat-topped objects on which we write and on which we usually place the food we wish to eat, which provide convenient stands for lamps, vases with flowers, and so on. And the concept "furniture" unifies in a wider, more comprehensive focus tables and chairs and many other (but not all) of the often-used objects in a home or office. Concepts like "house," "street," "business district," "footrace," "amoeba," "light-year," and the like all are similar sorts of synoptic foci useful for ordering and organizing our experience and activities; and they are themselves all grasped in wider synoptic unities with the aid of more comprehensive concepts.

and guidance of life. Such a symbol will have a double bearing: (a) on those dimensions of the serendipitous evolutionary-historical process to which we need to attend as we seek to identify and address the major problems and evils with which life today confronts us, which can assist us, thus, in the practical decisions of day-to-day life as well as provide us with overall orientation in today's world; and (b) on the questionableness, the problematic character of all our attempts to provide ourselves with adequate orientation in life, the danger of giving ourselves over too completely and uncritically to our values and meanings and conceptions of life and the world, all of which we finite humans have ourselves constructed.

The image/concept of God—properly reconstructed—can provide both these desiderata. For this symbol, more than any other in our western languages, has always been understood to represent, on the one hand, that which gives us humans our being and continues to sustain us in being, which heals our diseases and brings us salvation from evil, that in relation to which women and men finally find fulfillment; but that which, on the other hand, must ultimately be acknowledged as mystery. By means of the symbol "God" humans hold together before their minds—in a complex of powerfully evocative images and concepts—those values and meanings, criteria and norms, which they believe will orient them in the world and motivate them to address their most pressing problems, while simultaneously alerting them to the questionableness and necessary tentativeness of all their this-worldly commitments. In traditional Christian faith the simplest, most untutored mind was able to focus these sorts of concerns with the aid of images like creator, lord, and father; and the most sophisticated and learned philosophers or scientists could do so as well. In the monotheistic categorial scheme the symbol "God" provided a center for consciousness, devotion, and service, which drew all the diversity and multiplicity of life—indeed, of the entire world-process—together into a coherent pattern or order or unity in terms of which the concrete decisions of daily life could be made. This symbol today calls us to seek out and consciously attend to that which, in the evolutionary and historical processes that provide the context of human existence (as we understand it), gives us our humanity and will draw us on to a more authentic humanness.

To be persons, beings with historicity (as we have seen), is to be capable of setting goals and ideals for ourselves—capable of imagining what might or could be the case, though it is not now the case—and then judging ourselves and our activities in terms of these goals and setting ourselves to realize them; that is, it is to take an active part in the creation of the future world and our future selves. Humanity evolved beyond its animal origins as it grew into self-consciousness and gradually acquired the ability to participate in its own further development, creating practices and imagining ideal-

* This is appeal to the cultural despisers. After talking about the Xian God in negative terms; 305 here he describes God functionally in positive terms.

ized conceptions which communities and individuals could employ to order their lives. Many sorts of symbolical focusing and ordering of human life have appeared in the enormously variegated cultural and religious traditions that women and men have created; which of these would be most appropriate for today? In view of the historical character of human existence, it should be clear that concepts and images—foci of attention and devotion—which tend toward a freezing of further human development, which lead to the creation of rigid unchangeable patterns of selfhood and social structure and thus stultify further humanization, are undesirable. In contrast, images and concepts which orient and order human life in ways that open up our possibilities for realizing more fully the human and the humane—which augment human powers of creativity and freedom and the capacity to take responsibility for ourselves and our world—encourage the development of free and responsible women and men; that is, they contribute to our further humanization, and thus to the forward movement of the human evolutionary-historical trajectory.

With these considerations in mind, we can see the importance of the emergence of the image/concept of God in ancient Israel. This was a symbol that (a) provided a sharp and distinct focus for human consciousness, devotion, and activity, a focus which (b) through orienting humans on an image of powerful moral agency outside themselves (God) drew them beyond themselves toward higher reaches of freedom, self-understanding, responsibility, historicity. Thus devotion to God has been significantly humanizing (though it has also been, as we have seen, in many respects problematical). If God is appropriately reconceived today, I shall attempt to show, such devotion can continue to promote the development of humanness and humaneness within history, and thus a fuller and truer historicity. The symbol "God" can provide a powerful focus for human consciousness and devotion, helping to orient human life toward realizing the potentialities latent in our historicity.

I want to elaborate this point further under three headings. First, because of its anthropomorphic and anthropocentric features, this symbol provides a vision of the human and the humane—of justice, righteousness, love, et cetera—which can function normatively in the reflection and action of men and women, and in the ideologies and institutions to which they devote themselves. Second, these humanizing ideas and ideals help to generate interpretations of the ongoing events and movements of history that bear on issues of further humanization and humanness. Third, because the symbol "God" has normative significance (on the one hand) and makes ontological claims (on the other), it can perform important relativizing functions in human life: in signifying the ultimate mystery of things, that which underlies and expresses itself through the entire world-process and is of importance far beyond the merely human sphere, it provides a point of reference in terms of which all human values, meanings, concepts, judgments, activities, practices and institutions can be called into question, assessed and reconstructed. In what follows I shall develop my interpretation of the image/concept "God" as a unifying orienting focus for human life, by elaborating these three distinct but interconnected dimensions of its meaning.

Let us turn first to the way in which this symbol provides a normative image of the human and the humane. Consider again for a moment the imagery of the creator/lord/father, within which the symbol "God" was born. These central constitutive metaphors are all human characterizations or titles, and it is not surprising, therefore, that the conception of God has almost always had a decidedly anthropomorphic cast: God is depicted as a powerful agent who makes decisions and performs actions, working out purposes in the world; God creates, God rules over the creation, God loves and cares for all the creatures; God is faithful and true, merciful and forgiving, just and righteous, kind and long-suffering. God appears, thus, as a kind of personification or actualization of a configuration of idealized human virtues, powers, activities, and roles. Because God is taken to be the very actuality of what in human affairs is much to be desired but rarely found, the image or conception of God functions as a kind of standard—or even a sort of "role model"—in terms of which women and men can and do measure themselves, discerning their inadequacies, failures, corruptions and also setting their goals and assessing their achievements. But since God is seen, of course, as the *perfect* realization of these desired human qualities, exemplifying them at a cosmic level (as the creator and lord of the universe), humans inevitably see themselves as falling far short of what is here depicted. Nevertheless, orienting themselves in relation to the symbol "God" has meant that life was ordered (in some significant sense) in accord with these meanings and values which the divine being exemplifies in perfection. Since God is righteous, just, merciful, faithful, true, and the like—in short, a morally responsible being—serious devotion to God gives impetus to the formation of humans who are also morally sensitive and concerned to be morally responsible.

Values of many sorts continually attract the attention of men and women, claiming their commitment and loyalty: family, nation, truth, pleasure, power, work, political causes, beauty, health, charismatic leaders, sex, sports, ideologies, physical discipline or indulgence, and many more.[4] Particular moments—or major segments—of life may be oriented in terms of one or more of this immense variety of fascinating objects which come to human attention. The attraction in diverse directions of incompatible values may threaten on occasion to pull a community or person to pieces; intemperate subservience to particular values may enslave and ultimately destroy them. In contrast with all such "idolatrous" attachments, however, the symbol

"God" presents a focus for orientation which claims to bring true fulfillment and meaning to human life. It sums up, unifies, and represents in a personification what are taken to be the highest and most indispensable human ideals and values, setting these before the minds of men and women in what seems an almost visible standard for measuring human realization, an image/concept capable of attracting devotion and loyalty which can order and continuously transform individuals and societies toward fuller realization of their humanity. To love God is to be wholly devoted to the meanings and values mediated through this image; to serve God's will is to attempt to realize in life and action all that is required by such devotion and love. Thus, the symbol "God" helps form both the wider society and the individual women and men making it up, inculcating within them values and virtues that facilitate moral sensitivity and responsibility—matters important (as we have seen in Part II) for the further development of human freedom and historicity.

Devotion and action oriented by the symbol "God" have not been restricted in their effects to the raising of human moral consciousness; they have also given rise to a significant consciousness of history, as the distinctive order or context within which human existence has its being and life—and this brings us to the second dimension of the symbol's meaning. Yahweh was a powerful historical agent, working steadily in and through social and political events to bring the movement of history to its consummation. In order to recognize and understand what was really going on in the sociopolitical world roundabout, therefore, one had to know God, and to know what God was doing in and through these historical events. In this perspective human life does not exist within an utterly impersonal or amoral universe: rather, this world is a moral and historical one in which divine purposes for humanity and the rest of creation are being worked out in time. The historical movements and developments in which human life is immersed, thus, have a deeper meaning than appears on the surface, a significance deriving from the purposes that God is working out through them: the actions of the Egyptian pharaoh and the king of Assyria, as the prophets proclaimed, were actually expressions and bearers of the cosmic intentions and decisions of the One who is sovereign lord over all creation. If one knows who Yahweh is, then, and what Yahweh's purposes in history are, one will understand something of the real meaning of these historical movements. Since Yahweh is a moral being (righteous, faithful, merciful, just) who is working toward human salvation, one can rest assured that what is transpiring historically will be of benefit to humans. In this way, in addition to providing an image or picture of the qualities of life and selfhood toward which humans should aspire, devotion to God also facilitates a specific interpretation of the historical context within which human existence falls. It is up to human beings to try to discern within history those movements working toward the transformation of existence into that truly humane order imaged as the coming "kingdom of God"; in aligning themselves with these movements women and men realize the potential of their humanity. As they thus increasingly shape themselves and their institutions in accord with the direction in which God is moving history, their lives and customs and practices all become oriented more and more in moral and historical terms. Devotion to God thus helps catalyze the emergence and development of communities and individuals with historical consciousness and with significant motivation toward morally responsible existence and action.

This anthropomorphic and anthropocentric side of the image/concept of God, however—this quasi-human dimension which makes God intelligible to humans in certain respects and which attracts their devotion and loyalty—stands in powerful dialectical tension with another motif in the creator/lord/father, a motif resulting from the projection of these images onto a cosmic screen encompassing all the vastness and depths and mysteriousness of life and being: as creator of all that is, as lord over all and father of all, God is ultimately beyond all human comprehension or understanding. Thus, the inscrutable mysteries which men and women inevitably come up against when pondering the hard questions of life and death and the world become (in this world-picture) assimilated to the divine reality; and the creator/lord/father turns out not to be so easily and directly intelligible as the language I have been using may have suggested. God becomes seen, rather, as the utterly transcendent one, all-powerful and all-knowing, Alpha and Omega, ultimate Mystery. God is one who "builds" and "plants" but who also "plucks up" and "breaks down," "destroys" and "overthrows," as Jeremiah noted (1:10), the relativizer of everything human and finite—and this is a third important dimension of our symbol's functional meaning. In transcending all things human, indeed all things finite (as the creator and lord of the entire finite order), God is radically independent of all human striving and desiring—certainly no product of mere fantasies and wishes—and yet it is only in relation to God that humans can flourish.

This idea of God's radical transcendence was expressed traditionally not only in the images of God as creator of the earth, lord of history, and judge of the world but also in such ideas as God's eternity, absoluteness, and aseity. In all these images and conceptions God's *otherness* from and radical *independence* of the human and everything else finite is emphasized. God is not to be understood as in any sense our tool or device, to be used for our advantage or as we please. We are God's servants, not God ours. We must submit ourselves to the order which God imposes; God is not subject to our arranging and ordering.

This dimension of the image/concept of God addresses the need for a center of orientation and devotion which is not a mere extrapolation of human desires and wishes—one which is, that is to say, in some sense significantly "outside" or "beyond" everything human. As finite beings seeking security and satisfaction, men and women all too easily make themselves the center of life, rearranging all else so that it conforms, as far as possible, with their own wishes. Relationships within the finite order are all characterized by reciprocity and mutual interdependence, and this makes it possible for self-conscious beings to deal with other finite realities in ways directed toward the fulfillment of their own desires, using these others to which they are related as "means only" rather than treating them as "ends in themselves" (Kant). The narcissism of individual egos seems inevitably to lead to corruption of these finite relationships, and the ethnocentrism of communities and the anthropocentrism of the species lead to warfare among peoples and to exploitation of the environment. In recent years we have become particularly aware of problems of this sort in connection with the ecological and nuclear crises: the organization of human economic life into institutions geared to satisfying human needs and wants (for example), and of political life into nation-states, prevents us from directing our concerns and energies toward the larger world beyond our human-centered interests, and working for the common good of all creatures. What is needed to break through this curved-in character of human existence is a center and focus of meaning which can draw us out of our preoccupation with ourselves and our own wishes, our social groups and their parochial interests and biases, our anthropocentrism. The image/concept of a God radically "objective" to human beings, entirely independent of all our desires and not susceptible to any remaking or reshaping in accord with our wishes, that which we can in no way control, has traditionally performed this function. Devotion to such a God is able to overcome the warfare of a thousand idolatrous interests and desires, opening human existence to meanings and values and patterns of order otherwise beyond reach. (The symbol "God," of course, is not the only human imaginative construct capable of such deparochializing and universalizing effects; in other traditions symbols like "Brahman" or "sunyatta" have performed similar functions.)

Both the sense of transcendent otherness, supplied by the imagery of a *cosmic* creator/lord/father, and the sense of relatedness and similarity fostered by the anthropomorphism of these metaphors, made indispensable contributions to the image/concept of God which we have inherited. If this symbol (in some reconstructed form) is to continue to focus orientation and devotion, it will have to be attractive to us, promising significant meaning and fulfillment for us, something we identify with enough for it to arouse our interest and compel our attention. But simultaneously, to draw us *beyond ourselves* it must not be simply a kind of extrapolation or extension of what we already are (with our little idolatries and petty loyalties, our narrowness of interest and vision, our self-centeredness, and our anthropocentrism) but must refer us to that which is truly *other* than we, different from us, mysterious, ultimately beyond our ken. These two central motifs—God's "humaneness" and God's "absoluteness," the Savior who fulfills our needs and the Relativizer of all our present loyalties, ideas, and interests—when held together in a single unified symbol, provide a powerful focus for orienting human life toward an increasing realization of our historicity and thus our humanity.

There is, it should be noted, a considerable tension between these two motifs, a tension which gives the symbol "God" much of its power and effectiveness, but which is also a source of instability that may lead it to disintegrate or become dangerously destructive. If a proper balance is not maintained between the two motifs, either God loses attractiveness and power as a center for devotion, or the devotees of this lopsided God may themselves become twisted and warped.

Consider, for example, the consequences of overemphasis on God's absoluteness at the expense of God's humaneness. This may lead to a dissolution of God's attractiveness as a center for devotion. In the West this has happened in two ways. On the one hand, overemphasis on God's tyrannical omnipotence has so offended sensitive and thoughtful humanists (J. S. Mill, Bertrand Russell, Albert Camus) that they have found it impossible to worship or believe. The horrendous evils to be found in human society, especially as these have come into clear view in the twentieth century, suggest that any God actually responsible for this state of affairs must be a monster. If God is indeed omnipotent, the one whose will is being realized in human history, God is not one whom we should serve but rather one whom we should loathe and despise and against whom we should struggle with all our strength. Worship of an arbitrary and cruel being of this sort can evoke harsh and authoritarian attitudes and actions from devotees, attitudes similar to those attributed to God, and thus can contribute significantly to the worsening of the human condition. Of course devotion to such a God of overwhelming power (as the history of Calvinism shows) may also become a source of great dynamism in human affairs, as men and women seek above all else to carry out the will of the Almighty; and some historians have argued that much of the energy and goal-directedness of modern western culture can be traced to the worship of this all-powerful and terrifying despot. But a dynamism not qualified and restricted by humane concerns is always dangerous and destructive; and in recent years we have begun to awaken to the rape of other peoples and of the environment which western civilization, too much devoted to such a God, has consummated. Thus, the motif of God's absoluteness, developed one-sidedly in terms of the notion of God's overwhelming power, may become very destructive, and is rightly resisted by thoughtful humanistic critics.

In this respect (as we noted in Chapter 6) monotheistic frames of orientation may prove considerably more dangerous than polytheistic ones. In polytheisms the various gods, each representing different interests and values, serve to relativize one another; in a radically monotheistic frame of orientation, however, God's demands are absolute, and must be fulfilled to the letter—even if they go against custom, conscience, or reason. Any individuals or groups who believe they know what the absolute God requires feel themselves fully authorized to carry out the divine will—at whatever cost to themselves or others; and there is no point, no position, no argument from which to obtain leverage against such divinely commanded or authorized activities or institutions.

There are, however (as we also observed), two features of classical monotheism which, if properly invoked and emphasized, can be used to protect against such fanatical uses: (1) The conception of God as a thoroughly *moral* being, one who is in all respects just and righteous; if this side of the creator/lord/father is kept clearly in view, it will seem reasonable and appropriate to use our moral intuitions and values as criteria for discerning whether or not a particular demand or claim is of God. (2) Awareness that it is always blasphemous presumption to appeal to God's absoluteness for authorization and legitimation of our own human ideas and practices. As we proceed with our construction of a concept of the humanizing and relativizing God appropriate for today, we shall build upon both these points.

In rather sharp contrast with this dangerous rendering of the motif of God's absoluteness, the notion of transcendence is sometimes developed with an extreme emphasis on God's mysteriousness and unknowability, God's wholly-otherness. This sort of interpretation has also occurred in the West, and it has had the consequence for many of reducing God to a completely unknown "X," the ultimate Mystery which bounds all our experience and knowledge but which we can never grasp or understand. Such a totally abstract God, one emptied of all content and meaning, eventually becomes perceived, however, as one essentially irrelevant to the day-to-day concerns of human life, and thus one which can safely be ignored or neglected. Much modern agnosticism and religious indifference are an expression of this profound loss in meaning and significance of the symbol "God." God has become something of which we can in no way take serious account, and which, therefore, we need no longer take seriously into account.

It is also possible to overbalance the tension in the idea of God in the direction of God's humaneness—at the expense of God's absoluteness—and this has equally deleterious effects. A God without transcendence and otherness is a God without independence of the human, a God who is simply our creature, the extension of our own wishes and desires. A focus for worship of this sort may be in many ways attractive to us (as the personification of all that we want) and we may be quite willing to serve such a God devotedly. But in the end this kind of worship is self-stultifying. Not only can such a God easily be exposed as simple projection and wish-fulfillment (Xenophanes, Feuerbach, Nietzsche, Freud), a product of self-deceit and of cowardly unwillingness to face the hard facts of life; but this God also proves to be as fickle and changing as its devotees, and is capable, finally, of maintaining only sentimental interest. A God who gives easy divine approval to *our* projects, and is the means for legitimating and even sanctifying what we already are and believe, places on us too little tension to draw us out of ourselves, out of our fixed habits and attitudes and ideas. A symbol of this sort easily functions ideologically, helping to shore up race and class and gender interests, thus supporting unjust social institutions and practices. Instead of providing critical leverage which would facilitate persons' and communities' coming to significant awareness of their shortcomings, failures, and perversions (cf. the traditional idea of the "judgment" of God), this sort of God blinds and corrupts the consciences of worshippers, deepening tensions and divisions in society rather than helping to heal them. Since every society, and every group within society, tends to divinize its own desires and needs, a multitude of these henotheistic gods appears, each at war with the others and each promising salvation to its devotees. In this way, far from providing a center of devotion which draws humanity, with its petty distinctions and divisions, into increasingly wider communities, the symbol of God breaks down into a plethora of little gods, each reflecting but sanctifying the interests of its worshippers and thus each contributing further to the chaos and warfare in human affairs. Our gods become constructed too much in the image of our particular style of humanness. (Fuller analysis of these issues is presented in Chapter 15 and Chapter 24.)

Thus, the image/concept of God, with its origins in the traditional picture of the creator/lord/father, is structured by a complex inner dialectic between motifs of humaneness and of absoluteness, motifs suggesting that God both fulfills all our deepest needs and simultaneously relativizes all our values, ideas, and activities. Orientation on God is orientation both on an idealized picture of the human—not humanity as it is, but as it might and should be—and at the same time on that power or creativity which underlies all that is and all that happens, which is continuously expressing itself in and through the movements of cosmic and human history, the ultimate mystery of things. The symbol "God" promises to draw communities and individuals out of and beyond their petty loyalties and parochial visions of ethno-, self-, and anthropocenteredness, placing them in effective relationship to what is really happening in the world, the direction history is actually moving.

We are now in a position to consider whether this symbol can bring our modern picture of the world to a focus capable of significantly orienting human life today. The world, I have suggested, is a serendipitous process that has produced a variety of trajectories, one of which has brought into being the historical order and which may be continuing on in further creativity. This trajectory (on which humanity finds itself) appears to be at least one significant direction in which the cosmic process is moving, and we humans are being drawn beyond our present condition and order by this ongoing creative movement. However, if we fail to respond appropriately to the historical and ecological forces now impinging upon us, we may not even survive. *God,* I now propose, is to be understood as the underlying reality (whatever it may be)—the ultimate mystery—expressing itself throughout the universe and thus also in this evolutionary-historical trajectory (of particular interest to us humans) which has produced humankind. It should be obvious that if a theological understanding of this sort is to be persuasive in the light of modern conceptions of nature and history, we will have to thoroughly qualify and transform the traditional image/concept of the creator/lord/father, since it does not fit well with our modern thinking about evolution and history. It is important, on the one hand, that we develop a conception not so easily susceptible to the dangers of anthropomorphism as the traditional symbol (with its tendencies toward arbitrary authoritarianism and despotism, its sexism, its openness to both pietistic and political abuses); and, on the other hand, we must be able to show the appropriateness of our reconstructed symbol for effectively orienting human existence in the biohistorical context within which we now take ourselves to be living. A reconstructed concept of God of this sort is what I shall present here.

In this interpretation the anthropomorphisms which our traditions have ascribed to God—essentially idealized human characteristics—are transmuted into an idealized conception of human historicity; and this is taken to be the key in terms of which the direction of the cosmic-historical trajectory on which we find ourselves should be understood. These anthropomorphic dimensions of the symbol "God," however, must be limited and constricted by the motif of "absoluteness" or "transcendence" (as we have seen): in our conception this is expressed in the insistence that the ultimate meaning of this whole cosmic process—where it is going, and what its ground is—will always remain beyond us. In this reconstruction the ultimate reality from which we come is taken to be neither a simple fantasy of ours nor something that we can manipulate or control, make or remake as we choose: God is a reality genuinely distinct from us and all our imaginings, that which—quite apart from our own doing—has given us our being as humans and continues to nurture and sustain us, that without which we would not exist at all. The symbol "God," thus (as we shall construct it), will hold these two motifs—God's connection with our humanness and our struggle for humaneness (the vision of a cosmic-historical trajectory moving toward a more idealized historicity), and God's "transcendence" of everything human (the irreducible mystery of things)—together in a manner that will enable us to understand and respond to this ultimate ground, source, and directionality in the cosmic process as that which creates and sustains our humanity and undergirds our further humanization. Devotion to God here is significantly humanizing because it promotes orientation on that which (a) draws us beyond what we presently are toward an existence more truly humane and better attuned to the environment in which we live, and (b) helps break our parochial and destructive idolatries, enabling us to become centered on the cosmic-historical movement which has actually given us our being and is drawing us toward greater humaneness and ecological sensitivity.

Before we develop these ideas further we should note the importance of this double-sidedness of the symbol "God" (humaneness and absoluteness, cosmic humanizing activity and relativizing activity) for our understanding of evil, the question of the fundamental distortions or corruptions into which human existence can and does fall (see Chapter 15). As I argued in Part II, communities and selves must today be conceived as essentially processes of development, as tasks to be performed rather than self-subsistent fully defined "beings" or "natures" which simply are what they are. That is, we are always in process of *becoming human,* never fully and completely human; each of us is a moment within wider processes of humanization. Some, particularly in oppressed groups, or who are otherwise severely handicapped or held down, may be prevented from realizing, or find it impossible to realize, the full potentialities of their humanity; others are enabled to achieve a high degree of freedom and self-understanding, and they often have large opportunities to take responsibility for themselves and their world. Most of us fall somewhere between these extremes. When our humanity is conceived in this way there are two obvious types of evil to which we are subject: those evils connected with our falling short of achieving our full humanity, and those bound up with our overshooting the mark. The two major motifs constituting the symbol "God"—humanizing activity and relativizing activity—correspond to these two types of evil; together they signify divine activity (cosmic and historical) working to overcome them both.

One severe handicap to our full humanization derives from the failure of the cultural and religious models and ideals made available to us in our particular society (or our subgroup within the larger society) to present an adequate vision of what it is to be human, of what we should be striving to become. We need images and conceptions of what the human truly is, some way of holding before ourselves what we can and ought to become, if we are to order our lives toward full humanization. The anthropomorphic side of the symbol "God," with its cluster of images and concepts of humanness and humaneness and its presentation of the divine activity as a trajectory moving toward a truly humane order in human affairs, will (if properly developed) supply this: God's activity in history and nature will be thought of as working toward justice, righteousness, merciful and loving communities, ecological sensitivity, and so forth; and the image/concept of God will thus continue to serve as a standard or norm of humaneness and ecological concern and will suggest that our own efforts to work toward and build a humane order are undergirded by extra-human cosmic and historical movements and tendencies. In this way, this symbol works against those evils connected with our falling short of realizing our potential for freedom, self-understanding, and self-responsibility in communities of justice and peace in an ecologically well-ordered world, thus drawing us on toward a deeper humanness.

The other major emphasis of the symbol "God"—relativizing activity—functions in just the opposite way. As men and women acquire some measure of self-consciousness, freedom, and the ability to take responsibility for themselves and the future, they gain significant power in the world. But power centered in particular selves and communities can easily become—and almost always does become—self-centered power, power directed toward ordering ourselves and everything around us in terms of our own needs and desires and wishes. In short, we make ourselves, our social groupings (class, race, gender, nation) and our projects into our gods. And thus our activities (both communal and individual) become destructive, sometimes even demonic, instead of furthering the humanizing of all men and women and the developing of an ecologically well-ordered context for human (and other) life. The motif of God's absoluteness—of God as a center beyond the human which relativizes all our ideas and desires, all our activities and projects, mores and institutions—stands over against these tendencies toward hubris and self-idolatry. With respect to this motif, we can say, to believe in God, to worship God, is to seek to orient our selves, our communities, and our activities on this center outside ourselves and our little world, that is, on those powers creative and sustentive not only of humanity but of all that is. The two central motifs in the idea of God thus stand over against the two major sorts of evil, or possibilities for evil, inherent in our human historical mode of existence—failing to realize fully our humanity, and treating our human existence as an absolute end-in-itself.

In the position I am sketching in this book, the creative power at work throughout the universe—what I have called the serendipitous cosmic process—is regarded as grounding both the cosmic context of human life and also the emergence of humanity and humaneness in the course of biological evolution and historical development. There are good reasons (as we have been seeing) for introducing the venerable name "God" to symbolize this whole grand process. This symbol performs, and holds together, a number of functions which are important to the proper orienting of human life in the world as we know it today, all of them to some extent visible in the ancient imagery of the creator/lord/father, which initially gave it content. These include: first, giving profound meaning to human life and its tasks—summed up here in the concepts of humanizing, historicity, and humaneness, all taken to be grounded in the divine creative activity; second, providing believers with a means of identifying and interpreting what is of central importance to human existence in both the natural world and the historical developments roundabout them, through seeing the trajectory toward humanization and historicity as God's activity; third, relativizing, and thus providing critical leverage upon, every aspect of our pictures of humanity, the world, and God, through emphasizing that these all are grounded beyond what is visible to and imaginable by us—that is, in the ultimate transcendent mystery, in the God whom "no one has ever seen" (John 1:18). If the symbol "God" is interpreted as identifying and holding together in one the ultimate mystery of things and the serendipitous creativity at work in the world (particularly as it has expressed itself in the evolutionary-historical trajectory on which humankind has appeared, and in our interconnection with the web of life that environs us), it can continue to provide an appropriate focus for human devotion, meditation, and service.

With the image/concept of God, we humans attempt to symbolize that which grounds our humanity, that which makes possible our very existence even while driving us, or drawing us, beyond what we now are. On the one hand, thus, the word "God" stands for something *objectively there,* a reality over against us that exists whether we are aware of it or not: we did not make ourselves; we were created by cosmic evolutionary and historical processes on which we depend absolutely for our being. On the other hand, however, the word "God" functions as a symbol within our minds, in our self-consciousness as beings who are not entirely made from without but who significantly contribute to our own creation, shaping and forming ourselves in accordance with images and symbols to which we are devoted. This self-making through devotion to idealizing images is central to our historicity and significantly distinguishes us from all other animals. Our distinctive humanness, therefore—our humanity as such—is (in significant part) grounded on those symbols and practices, or complexes of symbols and practices, which open us toward our world and encourage us to take responsibility for it as well as for ourselves. A great variety of symbols (in the many different religious and cultural traditions humans have created) have, in varying ways and degrees, had their distinctive effects on human formation—symbols like freedom, Brahman, nature, power, justice, Torah, dharma, democracy, truth, nirvana, Shiva, reason, love, Yahweh, and many others. Not many of these, however, combine and hold together in one—in the powerfully effective manner of the symbol "God"—the functions of both humanization and relativization. As a focus of devotion, this unifying symbol can bring order and meaning into the whole of life, providing values which facilitate the assessing, disciplining, and transforming of both communities and individual selves. Thus, precisely through its functioning *subjectively* in and through our minds—as a focus for consciousness, devotion, loyalty, sacrifice—the symbol "God" has important *objective* effects, becoming a powerful incentive toward and support for the emergence of full historicity in individuals and communities, in this way contributing to God's continuing historical activity.

22. Reconstructing the Concept of God

In our culture "God" is the name ordinarily used to designate that reality (whatever it may be) which grounds and undergirds all that exists, including us humans; that reality which provides us humans with such fulfillment or salvation as we may find; that reality toward which we must turn, therefore, if we would flourish. According to contemporary scientific and historical understanding (as interpreted in this book) what create and sustain human life are the serendipitous evolutionary and historical processes which provide its context; it is with these processes, therefore, that a theological perspective for today should connect what it calls "God." The name "God" can take up and hold together these vast and complex processes in a distinctive and powerful symbol that accents their meaning for human existence. As we men and women seek to order our lives and our activities in terms of this vision of human existence situated among many other realities in a vast ecosystem, the symbol "God" can focus our consciousness, devotion, and work, thus providing orientation and direction for the concrete everyday decisions and actions of life.

The symbol "God" has always functioned in this way, as the focus for a worldview. In the world-picture in which this symbol originated, for example, however much God's radical independence and self-subsistence were emphasized, God was not portrayed as a being which humans encountered directly in its solitary splendor, a being to be understood entirely in and by itself: on the contrary, a central biblical theme was that no one ever has direct or immediate contact with or experience of God. Even Moses, through whom God is said to have made Godself known decisively, was not allowed to see God's "face," we are told, but only God's "back" (Ex. 33:23), for no one can see "[God's] face . . . and live" (33:20). This inaccessibility of God is a theme that is frequently repeated; for example, Job, in the midst of his tribulations, seeks God for an explanation, but God is nowhere to be found:

"Lo, he passes by me, and I see him not; he moves on, but I do not perceive him . . . Behold, I go forward, but he is not there; and backward, but I cannot perceive him; on the left hand I seek him, but I cannot behold him; I turn to the right hand, but I cannot see him" (9:11; 23:8–9). In the Fourth Gospel (1:18) and again in 1 John (4:12), we are told that "No one has ever seen God." For the biblical traditions in the main, God is simply not the sort of reality that is available to direct observation or experience.[1] For the most part subsequent theological reflection has taken this same line: it has held that all knowledge of God is analogical or symbolical; that is, it is never unmediated or direct but is based on likenesses drawn from ordinary objects of experience.

The idea of God, thus, should not be regarded as epistemically similar to the idea of a perceptual object (for example, a table or a person or a mountain); it is not based on direct human perceptions of God. Rather it is constructed imaginatively in the mind, built up on the basis of analogies, metaphors, and models thought to be appropriate. These models and metaphors perform their distinctively theological functions by giving specific content to the idea; the mind combines them into a symbol that holds together, fills out, and interprets an overall picture of the world which can take up into itself in a meaningful way the manifoldness of what we humans take to be our direct and immediate experience. Each of the constitutive metaphors of the traditional image/concept of God (creator, lord, father) is a *relational* term; these metaphors thus identify and characterize God not primarily in terms of some meaning which God has in Godself, but rather in terms of God's relatedness to and significance for the world of human experience. The Bible opens, for example, with God depicted as the source and ground of the entire finite order of reality ("the heavens and the earth"). Then, having made the universe and all its contents, God is portrayed throughout the rest of the Bible as ruling over the creation, bringing it ever forward toward the realization of the righteous purposes which will constitute it as a perfect "kingdom." In due course expectations develop that this will be a community of peace, justice, and love, where wolves will dwell peacefully with lambs, and children will play with what are now experienced as poisonous snakes, but none "shall . . . hurt or destroy in all [of God's] holy mountain" (as Isaiah, for example, sees it) "for the earth shall be full of the knowledge of the Lord" (Isa. 11:6–9). What we have here is a picture of the world—the context within which human life appears and flourishes—as coming from God, as pervaded by God's continuous activity, and as moving toward the fulfillment of God's benevolent purposes. But God in Godself is never directly available within this world as an object of experience and knowledge; what are available are *memories* of what (it is believed that) God has done in the past, and *hopes* for what God shall yet do (given the faith, the confidence, that God continues to work in the world). Human experience is always grasped and interpreted in terms of images, categories, and concepts derived from the past and carried in language and memory, and so here also: the understanding of all reality as "under God," acquired in Israel's history, provides the interpretive grid which gives present experience and future hopes their basic shape and deepest meaning.

That is, God-talk has developed here, not on the basis of direct perceptions or experiences of the divine being itself, but rather in connection with a *world-picture* (constructed by the human imagination over many generations) in which the creator/lord/father is taken to be the dominant active power. Within this world, human life is experienced as coming from someplace (God's prior creative and governing actions) and going someplace (toward the realization of God's perfect kingdom). Hence, the meaning of life is sustained and nourished by (a) memories of what happened to the forebears of presently living believers (in the conviction that God was actively working with them) and (b) hopes for what shall yet occur, as God overcomes the sorrows of present life and brings the movements of history to their culmination. For those living within this world-picture (constituted largely by memory and hope), the joys and sorrows of present life are experienced and understood as expressions of the ever-present activity of the living God, the origin of life and its ultimate goal. The image/concept "God" is the great symbolic focus with the aid of which believers' imaginations bind everything together into a meaningful whole within which all life's vicissitudes have a proper place and significance. The meaning which the notion of the creator/lord/father has, thus, should not be understood to derive from the encounters women and men have had from time to time with a particular *something*—a something which we also might encounter "face to face" sometime; it derives, rather, from its employment as the principal symbolic center and focus binding together an entire world-picture. The creator/lord/father was a focus for human devotion, meditation, and service to which women and men could give themselves without reservation.

This focus took up into itself and pinpointed in a dramatic image/concept the whole structure of meaning which this world-picture provided for the understanding and interpretation of human life. It enabled believers to see (a) what the real structure, the actual character of the world is—namely God's creation; (b) what the movements of history mean—they are the working out of God's purposes; (c) what place human life has within the cosmic scheme of things—as the very "image of God," men and women are made for communion and covenant with one another and with God, and human experience has its meaning as these covenants are fulfilled and that communion is realized; (d) what aspirations and hopes women and men may legitimately have—to participate in the kingdom God is creating; and

(e) what humans ought to do here and now—obediently follow God's will, as made known through the law and the prophets (and later, through Jesus Christ). Since this whole world-picture was brought into focus and held together by the symbol "God" ("Yahweh") it is not difficult to understand why devotion and service to God were held to be the principal concerns of human life. And conversely, since the symbol "God" acquired its meaning not in and through itself, as it were, but as the center and focus for an all-encompassing world-picture, devotion to God and service to God were taken to consist in nothing else than living and acting in terms of the patterns and structures of meaning which this picture itself provided.

This world-picture, I have suggested several times, is essentially *dualistic:* it employs materials drawn from our human experience within this world to speak of an *other* world; and in so doing it presents to humans who are on *this* side of the great divide in reality, what it is important that they know about the *other* side. We have already noted a number of problems connected with this dualistic way of speaking (see, for example, Chapter 19); we must now consider one more: it is fundamentally incoherent, leading us to suppose we know something(s) which we cannot possibly know. This idea of an "other world" or "other side"—the idea of a Most Important Reality outside this world in which we live and have our experience—leads us to imagine and speak of things which, though totally inaccessible to us, we nevertheless come to believe we know a good bit about. In the biblical stories and poems and laws, we are told much about God, and about what God does; but of course the only basis we have for this information is the stories and poems and laws themselves—these mythic materials created by the human imagination thousands of years ago. Rudolf Bultmann's proposal that we demythologize materials of this sort, dropping their time-bound details in order to get at their profound existential significance,[2] really does not address the fundamental issue which they pose; for he seems to retain the basic idea of the "other side"—another reality outside this life, this world of our experience—which is more important than anything on "this side" since it is the real foundation of life and its meaning. That is, he retains the fundamentally *dualistic* presupposition on which the traditional understanding of God and the world is founded (though he wishes to drop many of the more incredible details of particular stories). It is, however, precisely this dualism itself that is the most problematic feature of this product of the human imagination.

In the present attempt at theological construction I am proposing that we go much further in our reconception than did Bultmann, and that we refrain from postulating an "other side" or "other world" at all. There seems no good reason for such a postulate—except that that is the way these ancient myths, regarded as authoritative in our religious traditions, spoke. I maintain that since we now regard such stories—including the dualistic way in which they present the context of human life—as products of the human imagination, we should today undertake to do our own imagining; but we should do it in a critical fashion unavailable to the ancient prophets and poets, a fashion informed and disciplined by modern scientific and historical knowledge and philosophical reflection. In particular we should, in our attempt to construct conceptions and pictures of humanity, the world, and God, try to speak only in terms of *this world,* of the realities of *this life*—making as clear as possible the respects in which what we say has a firm basis in our experience and knowledge, as well as the respects in which it is an imaginative elaboration and interpretation. In all of this, of course, it is important that we keep in view the fact that our "knowledge" of this world in which we live, and all the realities within it, always shades off into ultimate mystery, into an ultimate unknowing (see Chapters 4 and 5). In developing the concept of mystery in the way I do, I am seeking to retain what is valid in dualistic ways of thinking, without falling into their fallacies.

There is a significant feature of this dualism running through all Christian teaching—between God and the world, or this world and the other world, or nature and supernature, or this life and the afterlife—of which we should take note at this point. These dualities are all ways of signifying that what is normative may not be reduced to the given; that is, that it is important there always be a basis for criticizing any given human situation with a view to transforming it into something more and better. A certain duality is intrinsically connected with any understanding of human existence that gives a significant place to human creative activity, and to the importance, therefore, of (moral and other) standards for judging the present situation and for guiding human activities which are intended to transform it into a better order. In traditional Christianity this point was made through the two-world theory in which reference to the "other world" or to the "afterlife" provided an Archimedean point for critically examining this world and this life, and thus for orienting human existence to something better. Visions of "heaven," the "kingdom of God," a perfect "supernatural" order, were imaginings of what a transformed human existence and a transformed world would be like (where "the lion lies down with the lamb"), and these could then serve as bases both for criticism and for human aspirations for this life. Conceptions of this sort have grounded much of the dynamism in western culture, with its hopes of creating a better world for humans to live in.

The problem with this kind of (metaphysical) dualism is that it is based on a reification of the "other world," and this has become incredible for us today. The secular solution to this problem is to say that this world is all there is, and therefore we must simply live within it as best we can. But this means that criticism grounded in a transcendent reference point is given up, and all we have to go on are our own standards, criteria, and dreams. Here either cultural relativism undermines our confidence or we adopt an imperialistic attitude toward normative visions differing from our own, seeking to assimilate, dominate, or destroy them. Neither of these responses can provide a satisfactory framework for contemporary human life. What is needed is a nonreified version of the normative, a version according to which it is never expected that life "on earth" will perfectly conform to the ideal—there will always be room for criticism and further transformation (this note is taken over from the traditional dualism)—and so there will always be a tension toward change; but at the same time it is not held that the perfect or ideal "exists" somehow or somewhere "outside" or "beyond" the world (a notion no longer credible).

The conception of God as an "ultimate point of reference" which we imaginatively construct can fulfill these requirements. The most fundamental duality in traditional faith was that between God and the world, creator and creation. This duality, however, when taken in an absolute sense, becomes so abstract as to be almost empty of meaning—for (as we noted in Chapter 21) if God is thought of as indeed "wholly other" from anything we know or experience, the notion of God finally loses all content. All traditional faith, therefore, has softened and mediated this absolute contrast (a) by giving some particular (usually anthropomorphic) content to the notion of God (creator, father, king, et cetera), and (b) by thinking of God as existing in a context which was in fact conceived largely in (this-)worldly terms: it was an *other* world but a world nonetheless, a *super*nature, a place where we could live an *after*life. Thus, although transcendence of and otherness from this world were asserted, connection to human existence and meaning for human life were not lost. If we think of the secondary dualisms (other world, afterlife, et cetera) and the anthropomorphism of the concept of God as functioning largely to fill out and thus make more vivid and certain the meaning of the primary duality of God and the world, we will understand why these notions were reified (this was really the only way human consciousness could conceive such matters at the time these conceptions were being developed); and we will also understand that we no longer need continue to reify them—providing there is another way to take care of these functions. The conception of theology advocated here, as concerned with the imaginative construction of an ultimate point of reference, can accomplish this.

On the one hand, with this conception we are clearly working with a notion of transcendence, for everything (else) must be understood in relation to the (imagined) ultimate point of reference; this notion does not refer to something "in" the world or a part of the world. Thus the primary and ultimate duality of God and the world is here expressed (without reification). On the other hand, the content of the notion of God, how we conceive God (as ultimately relativizing and humanizing, for example) and God's relations to the world and to humanity, are all recognized as our imaginative constructions—as our own quite human attempts to grasp ourselves in connection not only with the this-worldly context of our lives but in relation to that "X" by means of which we can criticize everything in this world and gain leverage to transform it. To recognize all this as our own imaginative construction is to refuse to reify it; to understand, however, that it is an "ultimate point of reference" for all that exists to which we are seeking imaginatively to relate ourselves here, is to think of this "X" (to which we are directing ourselves) as transcending everything in our world of experience and knowledge. If we can avoid reifying our ultimate point of reference, it will not become frozen into a reality unrelatable to new circumstances as they arise, but should remain flexible and revisable, allowing it to be appropriately transformed as new circumstances arise in human life. In short, it is not a static reified God from out of the past which drives this conception but the notion of the "living God." Thus (in our theologizing today), we are enabled to maintain continuing relevance to every new situation (as was intended with the notion of the "living God") without postulating some "world" beyond this world, or some "primordial being," as the "place" where the normatively human resides. In this scheme the duality between idealities or limiting ideas (created by the imagination to facilitate making the judgments necessitated by human historical existence) and the actual, factual empirical world takes the place of the mythical or metaphysical dualism inherited from tradition.

The dualistic world-picture which we find in the Bible and much of Christian tradition is no longer viable (I have argued) without fundamental qualifications, since it does not accurately describe or meaningfully interpret either the actual world in which we today take ourselves to be living or much of our experience in this world. Moreover, it seductively intimates that it can unveil for us features of the ultimate mysteries of life which otherwise must remain hidden from our view, and that it can make known to us the ultimate reality with which we humans have to do. Although this world-picture may well continue to represent to us a beautiful poetic expression of the meaning of human life, it remains, nevertheless, quite unclear how it bears on the world in which we now take ourselves to live, how it can directly inform our actual lives today. Hence, we need to redraw our theological pictures of the world and of the human so they describe the actual world we are living in as well as our understanding of ourselves. And we must also redraw our picture of God, if we are to continue to see God as the proper focus for our devotion, reflection, and service in this world daily experienced. I have proposed the notion of serendipitous cosmic evolution and history as a way to characterize in modern terms the world which provides the context of our lives; we must move forward now—in a fifth step of faith and toward faith—to the construction of a conception of God which can provide significant focal images and concepts for understanding ourselves and our situation in this modern cosmos.

Let us return first to the images of creator and lord, to see in what ways they can be related to our modern conceptions. Through a long evolutionary process the world-system of which we are part gave birth to life; eventually humanity emerged, with its potential for cumulating historical development and its capacity to take responsibility for the future. What is of most direct importance to human beings in all of this, of course, was the appearance of an evolutionary-historical trajectory or movement giving rise to humanity. Directional movement appears to be an intrinsic expression of the serendipitous creativity working through all things; and the course which cosmic evolution and history have taken need not, therefore, be thought of as simply a metaphysical accident or surd. The metaphors "creator" and "lord" emphasize this point and go on further to suggest that this directionality is the expression of some sort of intentionality or purposiveness at work in these broader cosmic and historical movements—a consideration of great import when the question of the meaning of human existence is at stake. The picture of God creating the world and governing history, we could say, thus presents in a kind of poetic way the meaning of what has actually transpired here. It is hardly surprising that, to the extent that the cosmic process as a whole seemed to the biblical people to be "going somewhere," they symbolized and focused their understanding of this with the image of a cosmic maker and purposer who had set certain goals and was working to achieve them. The only locus of outright intentional or purposive activity known to humans is, after all, humans: we men and women regularly make decisions, set goals for ourselves, and work toward their realization. Purposive activity, thus, as we directly experience it, is always grounded in a self or community, in a *purposer;* and these images express well this sense that life and history are moving forward toward goals of importance to human beings. All the multifarious events, processes, and activities in the world of human experience are now seen to be held together, focused, and interpreted by purposes in the mind of the creator and lord of the world.

It is not necessary for this idea of the creator and lord to be reified (as has often occurred in our religious traditions) for it to be useful in symbolizing and focusing the vast cosmic movement of which we today are aware; that is, we do not need to think in terms of some "cosmic person" out there somewhere, who at some point in time envisaged creating the world and working in it in certain specific ways, and then proceeded to do so (though we can, of course, imagine things in that literalistic way if we choose). Reification, as we shall see shortly, is at the root of many of the problems in traditional God-talk, and I shall be presenting arguments against it. What the symbols "creator" and "lord" signify is the conviction that the directional movement(s) which we discern in the cosmos are not to be thought of as simply accidental happenstances but rather as grounded in the ultimate nature of things; for they have been "created by"—that is, produced or brought about by—the creativity underlying and at work in all things. To be devoted to God the *creator* is to be devoted to that ultimate reality—that ultimate mystery—which expresses itself in and through all that exists, including the evolutionary and historical development of the ecosystem that has given birth to us and to many other creatures. And to seek "to do the will" of God the *lord* is to seek to fit one's life appropriately into the forward movement of the evolutionary-historical trajectory within which we humans find ourselves to be living. That is, devotion to the "creator/lord" today consists in the attempt to live in rapport with the movements of life and history that provide the actual context of our human existence; it is to attempt to be in tune with what we discern as the nature of things, to live and to work "with the grain" of the universe as apprehended in our part of it. These metaphors and images out of which the traditional notion of God was constructed need not, then, be given up completely to accommodate our modern understanding of the world; but, if we continue to use them, they should be interpreted as essentially poetic metaphors, not ontological models or concepts. If we are to understand what they can properly signify today (that is to say), it is important that we do not reify them.

What is "reification"? It is taking the content of a symbol (or image or word) to be a proper description or exact representation of a particular reality or being; in Kant's apt phrase, it is "treating our thoughts as things."[3] We reify the symbols "creator" and "lord" and "father" when we take them to mean that God *really is* a creator/lord/father. (The literal meaning of the word "reify" is simply "to make into a thing.")

It is useful, I think, to distinguish between "reifying" and "referring." From the point of view of faith such symbols as "creator" and "lord" *refer* to something "real"—for us today this is the evolutionary and historical processes which produced us. We take these processes to be real, and it is to these realities that we today should understand ourselves to be referring when we use these theological symbols. This means, however, that our traditional theological symbols by themselves do not enable us to grasp precisely *what* it is to which we are actually referring here; and that we dare not, therefore, attempt to answer this question simply through reification of these symbols, that is, through taking them to refer to some particular being or person who could quite properly be characterized as a "creator" and "lord." In our theological reconstruction (as we have seen) that to which these terms actually refer must be understood in much vaguer and more abstract terms, perhaps something like "those evolutionary and historical processes creating, sustaining, and enhancing our humanity"; our terms "lord" and "creator," thus, function as *metaphors* for us, not as concepts. To regard a metaphor as *referring* (without reifying it) is to take it as indicating something real, something in some way significantly related to the metaphor's imagery (so that it can justifiably be said to "symbolize" or "represent" the reality concerned), but it is not to regard this reality as a straightforward exemplification or instantiation of the content or imagery of the metaphor. The metaphor functions, thus, to help focus our attention on certain features of the reality in which we are interested, but it is not an adequate concept of that reality.[4] To understand our theological language as largely metaphorical in this way is to acknowledge (implicitly) that what is *really there* remains a mystery to us: it is something only dimly intimated in our symbols, never fully grasped. To speak of this mystery as "creative" or as "governing" is to give it an interpretation that highlights certain aspects of our world and our experience in a way which can help orient men and women in life; but we really do not know precisely what it is in the world-process to which these metaphors refer. Faith believes *that* they refer, but to what they refer remains in many respects mystery.

Reification began early in religious history. It has never been easy for humans to distinguish clearly the mental images and concepts important to them from actual objects in the world; and it is not surprising, therefore, that from early on the creator/lord/father was taken to be an objectively existing powerful agent-self, a supernatural character. In the Bible God stands behind and governs all that exists. In this picture it is apparently the autonomous free agent, the "I" (ego) existing alone in its solitude, that is the core model on the basis of which the image/concept of God has been constructed. When Moses, in a very early story, asks the voice from the burning bush, "Who are you? What is your name?" the answer that comes back is, "I AM; I AM WHO I AM" (Ex. 3:13–14). God is identified here as the great "I AM," an ego-agent *par excellence,* sheer unrestricted agential power. Given this model, it is not surprising that God has often been conceived as an all-powerful tyrant, a terrifying arbitrary force before whom women and men can only bow in awe and fear.

Let us recall at this point a conclusion to which we came in the course of our examination of human agency and selfhood in Part II: that all autonomous agential power of which we know actually emerges only within a social network, within a moral context which brings it into being and continues to sustain it, and which provides an ongoing context for action. In that analysis I suggested that we deceive ourselves if we suppose that we can conceive an absolutely *individual* agent: the autonomy and agential power of an individual have meaning—and, indeed, can have existence—only in a social context. This means that the very heart of our received image/concept of God is based on a misleading abstraction and reification of the human experience of individual selfhood and agency, which is then projected onto a cosmic screen. It should not surprise us to discover that a concept of God built up on this false and misleading model of the autonomous agent[5] leads to distortions, inadequacies, and corruptions of many sorts; indeed, it is precisely out of this conception of God as the all-powerful *individual ego* that the highly destructive tyrannical side of God-talk developed in the religions descendant from ancient Israel. If the image/concept of God is to symbolize and call our attention to the structures and processes that actually provide support for human being and well-being, human agency and morality (as we understand these matters today), God will have to be understood as a profoundly *social* reality. The idea of God as essentially an autonomous ego—utterly distinct from and independent of all other agents—not only is unintelligible in itself; it provides an inappropriate model for human life today, and it can, thus, only prove increasingly destructive in today's world.

As long as it was not understood that this whole world-picture, with God as the center and focus for all human devotion and activity, was a creation of the human imagination (like all other world-pictures), it was difficult to avoid objectifying and reifying these received images and concepts of God; even today one may feel disinclined to oppose theologically, or decisively to modify, this way of thinking about God as an arbitrary, imperial potentate, a solitary eminence existing "somewhere" in glorious transcendence of all else. It is a serious mistake, however, to take the symbol "God" in this objectifying and reifying way, for (as we have seen) this symbol is actually but one feature of a larger mythic map of reality. The function of all such world-pictures or maps is to provide orientation in life and the world for women and men, for beings constituted by historicity; and the adequacy and effectiveness of such conceptual frames is to be assessed in terms of the respects in which and the degree to which they enhance human agency for all. To the extent that our received traditions about God—however deeply rooted they may be—are inadequate to or destructive of human life and the environment within which it has emerged and by which it is sustained, it is theologically requisite that we transform or eliminate them; for our objective must be to formulate a conception of God which is appropriate to focus human devotion and orientation in today's world.

As we give up literalization and reification of the traditional imagery and concepts, some things dear to traditional pieties will be undermined. God will no longer be pictured or conceived as a personal being in the heavens above who "before the foundation of the world" (Eph. 1:4; 1 Pet. 1:20; Rev. 13:8; et cetera) devised a detailed divine plan that included a special place and task for each of us; and we will no longer, therefore, be able to imagine ourselves as in direct personal interaction with this divine being, as we seek to learn and do "his" will. Much of the intensely personalistic flavor of the relationship of individuals to God, which traditional piety cultivated and enjoyed, we can now see was the product of a rather literalistic reading of the metaphors which dominated the tradition. For the reconstruction I am suggesting here, it will no longer be appropriate to expect and to long for a relationship of this sort—or to despair when it is absent or has become incomprehensible (for example, in experiences of tragedy or evil, including the massive evils of the twentieth century). Our experiences of personal warmth and meaning have their real grounding in our actual interpersonal relations on the human level, with other men and women; and (as we shall observe in a moment) it will be in and through these relationships that we will come to realize whatever personal relation with God—with the reality which (ultimately) has created us as human—is possible for us and appropriate to us.

It should not be thought that this radically de-reified conception of the love of God—both God's love for us and our love for God—is a far-fetched new idea. A similar understanding is already present in early Christian sources, though it has not frequently been given as central and defining a place as I am proposing. In 1 John, for example, after pointing out that "No man has ever seen God" (4:12)—that is, that humans do not have direct or unmediated personal relationships with God—the writer goes on to declare that it is in our "love [for] one another, [that] God abides in us and his love is perfected in us." Indeed, this love of humans for one another is presented here as the very criterion of the presence of God's spirit and God's love: "By this," the writer says, "we know that we abide in him and he in us" (4:13). To underline this claim that the love of God is indivisible from love of our fellow humans, the writer states emphatically: "If any one says, 'I love God,' and hates his brother, he is a liar; for he who does not love his brother whom he has seen, cannot love God whom he has not seen" (4:20). Thus, our personal relation with the ultimate reality with which we have to do—God—is to be found most fundamentally in and through our *interpersonal* relationships with our fellow humans. From the anthropological perspective developed in this volume, this is not difficult to understand: after all, it is in and through interpersonal relationships that we are created as human in the first place, and that we continue to be sustained; obviously, it is precisely here, then, that the creative and sustentive activity of God—with respect to our distinctive humanness and our humaneness—is in fact mediated to us.

To the extent that the traditional images of God have suggested otherwise—that, for example, it is more important for human beings to have a direct personal relationship with God than with our fellow humans—they have been extremely misleading, indeed oftentimes destructive, as a great deal of human brutality, terror, murder, and war bears witness. All too often, among persons who considered themselves Christian, activities of this sort were undertaken in obedience to what was believed to be explicitly "commanded" by God—with very little consideration of whether they were an expression of genuine love for those women and men directly affected. In recent years we have become aware of the way in which such reified imagery has promoted and helped to sustain racist and sexist oppression. "God," thought of as white and male, has been the ultimate symbol legitimating and sanctifying white-dominated social institutions and customs and practices, as well as male domination over every area of life.

This religious symbolism has had repressive and oppressive power of this sort not so much because of its particular content as because that content was reified: God was taken to be *in actual fact* a kind of creator/lord/father "out there" who really established—consciously willed and deliberately created—the patterns of order governing life here on earth. With such views of the metaphysical ordering of things, authoritarian (and thus oppressive) social patterns are almost inevitable. Everything changes, however, once we de-reify this cosmic picture. We come to see that our religious symbolism is not valid in its own right, but only to the extent that it represents, and thus reinforces, those cosmic and historical tendencies and forces which are moving us toward further humanization, toward a more humane and ecologically sustainable order—that is, which are promoting what was called (in the tradition) human "salvation." Many have doubts today that the old metaphors of creator, lord, and father, so heavily invested with patterns of male dominance in society and culture, are any longer usable. They may be right: no one who is aware of these problems can avoid facing that question. What I am trying to show here, however, is that the problems which these metaphors pose arise primarily from their reification and the excessive authority with which this reification invests them, rather than simply from their content. If God is conceived as that reality working through the actual humanizing and relativizing cosmic and historical powers which give us our humanity, we are provided with a means for criticizing and reinterpreting these symbols; and they may thus still be able to perform salvific functions.

This view not only offers some protection against important symbolic abuses; it goes a long way toward addressing one of the most intractable issues with which theologians have had to deal, the problem of theodicy, the justification of God in view of the massive evil in the world. This problem arises because God, understood as the creator/lord/father of all that exists, has often been portrayed as in direct personal control of all that happens. God planned the course which historical events take, and if impossible difficulties arise for the faithful, it can be hoped (according to traditional piety) that God will perform a miracle which will lift them out of their misery. A literalistic understanding of the images in terms of which God is conceived obviously lies behind such views as these; and it is hardly surprising that the piety which accompanies them often finds itself in difficulties, since the expectations it generates are so frequently disappointed. The so-called problem of theodicy is actually rooted in the same literalism as this piety: if God is an all-powerful, all-knowing, absolutely righteous and merciful Person, why are there such horrible evils—enormous misery, injustice, suffering—in the world? Why would a good God ever have made such an evil order? Why has God not straightened it up long since? These questions are already posed in the Hebrew Bible—by Habakkuk, Job, Ecclesiastes, and some of the Psalms—and they have come up repeatedly since, in the conversations of Jesus, in the reflection of Paul and John, and in much subsequent theology and philosophy, as well as in the meditations of many ordinary women and men. Traditional piety has often attempted to put these questions down by retreating into the inscrutable mystery of the divine will, even while desperately holding on to faith despite powerfully negative experiential evidence: "Though he slay me, yet will I trust in him" (Job 13:15 KJV). This is a wonderfully moving sentiment which has comforted many suffering individuals. But "after Auschwitz," as Richard Rubenstein and many others have argued,[6] it seems bland and weak; the massive human suffering already witnessed in the twentieth century, and which may be outdone by what is still to come, renders highly problematic all such traditional pieties and arguments.

Reification of the traditional image/concept of God is the deepest root of this problem. Everyone agrees that a just and merciful *human* king or father would do everything in his power to protect his subjects or children from meaningless evils and sufferings: it seems appropriate, therefore, to assume that so must it also be (indeed, many times more so) with our creator/lord/father in heaven. If these traditional metaphors are taken at all literalistically, this conclusion surely follows; and the problems which it poses are insoluble. However, if we de-reify our understanding of God, all these problems fall away: the images of creator and lord and father are not, then, regarded as concepts from which we can deduce rather specific ideas of omnipotence, omniscience, goodness, and the like, and on the basis of which we can legitimately imagine God to be governing the earthly order in accord with detailed divine plans for history, including even highly particularized miraculous acts of intervention. This language does not, after all, adequately identify or describe the evolutionary-historical trajectory which has in fact brought humanity into the world and which continues to ground and sustain it, and in relation to which, therefore, contemporary faith needs to define and understand itself. For the perspective we are working out here, the difficulties encountered in life are to be understood as arising largely out of the complexity of the patterns of nature and history in which we are living—

with a good deal of human bungling and malevolence added to the mix; they are not a direct intentional expression of some "will" thought to be divine. (This conception of "the problem of evil" will be more fully worked out in Chapter 24.)

According to this (more contemporary) picture of human-life-in-the-world, it is a mistake to suppose that everything which happens to men and women is somehow a direct expression of a specific intention of God. Rather, each event is but one small piece of the ongoing massive and complex movements in the nature/history ecosystem; and particular events and developments are to be understood and explained, therefore, largely in terms of the (more or less) local contexts in which they occur. This means that the various "evils" of human existence must be analyzed and understood with reference to their empirical causes, the particular historical developments or natural events which brought them about; they should not be seen as the expression of some single universal evil condition—sin, estrangement from the divine creator/lord/father, rebellion against the divine will—which is regarded as the root of all misery and suffering. And our attack on the evils of life will consist in the attempt (1) to identify the major human problems found in the world today—poverty, disease, oppression, racism, sexism, war, injustice, inhumanity, meaninglessness, destruction of the ecosystem, and so on—and (2) to ameliorate these as much as possible through modifying or radically transforming the institutions and ideologies and practices that are their proximate conditions and causes. As we shall see in due course, there is still a proper place for talk about sin and alienation from God, but now these notions will have a more general, and less highly personalized, meaning: they symbolize our failing to live and act in harmony with the basic ecological and historical trajectories which have created human existence, and which alone are capable of continuing to sustain and enhance it—rather than serving as explanations for some deep feelings of shame and guilt before a personal creator/lord/father whom we believe we have offended and whose forgiveness and justification we desperately need.

I have been suggesting in these remarks both some of the positive uses of the metaphors which have traditionally constituted the image/concept of God, and also some of the difficulties these metaphors pose when they are reified. It is obvious that it would be a serious mistake to continue defining the symbol "God" largely in the terms they provide: these metaphors need to be complemented and supplemented by others which significantly qualify them and balance some of their misleading emphases. If we decide to continue using personalistic/anthropomorphic metaphors like creator and lord in our worship and reflection—despite their tendency to induce misleading or even false expectations about God's direct personal involvement in all the problems and difficulties which afflict each of us as individuals (as well as our society as a whole)—we will want to add other less traditional ones that bring out features of our interpersonal and social life which these neglect, for example, mother, friend, lover.[7] It is also important deliberately to use naturalistic metaphors in our thinking and worship—nature, world-process, life, ecosystem, evolution, and the like—which emphasize our embeddedness in the natural order and remind us of our interconnection with and dependence on the vast and complex ecological network which provides the context for our existence. And more abstract metaphysical concepts and metaphors, such as ultimate reality, being, eternity, transcendence, the One and the All, which bring out in a special way God's universality and ultimacy, have important functions to perform in both theological reflection and personal meditation. Above all, a central place should be given to the concept of *mystery,* which reminds us how limited, incomplete, and inadequate are all our religious convictions and theological concepts, how much they need continual criticism and revision, how little justified we are in taking dogmatic positions on the ultimate questions of life and death. This symbol, when properly employed, is the best protection we have against our tendencies continually to reify our thinking about God.

Thus far in our analysis of the creator/lord/father symbolism, most of our attention has been devoted to the metaphors of creator and lord; we have not yet looked closely at the notion "father," so central for Christian faith. In many ways this is the most difficult of the principal traditional metaphors to deal with today, because of its intensely personalistic overtones, on the one hand, and the sexism and paternalism which it implies, on the other. Is it appropriate to continue using this metaphor to symbolize the relatively impersonal cosmic evolutionary-historical process we have been discussing? If it is not, does that not imply that there is really very little significant contact left between the symbol "God" (as we are reconstructing it here) and the central themes of Christian faith?

Here we must be very careful. In the traditional image/concept of God, which was initially constituted primarily by the metaphors of creator and lord, the metaphor "father" (or "parent") serves as an important qualifier. The earlier images (as we have seen) together symbolized the creative and purposive power believed to be at the foundation of the world and working within the world; but the metaphor "father" emphasizes a further distinctive note: the divine activity is moving history toward a *humane order,* God is working toward patterns of life which will make possible human fulfillment. The world and history are ordered, that is to say, not by an arbitrary divine will that works its way however it pleases: rather, the trajectory of evolution and history (as we are calling it) is moving toward human salvation, toward providing a context and ordering of human life which will fulfill the personal, moral, and spiritual values toward which we humans, in our best moments, aspire—much as loving parents seek fulfillment and happiness for their children, and attempt to arrange the period of the children's growth and development so these will come about.

According to widely accepted developmental and psychiatric theories, contexts of love, care, and trust (usually provided by the immediate family) are required if human infants are to develop into free and responsible and loving persons. Familial and communal contexts pervaded by hatred and malevolence, arbitrariness and instability, despair and guilt, tend to produce warped selves with paranoid self-understandings that inhibit free and responsible relationships to other persons; but contexts that are well ordered but open, in which there is peace and joy and love, promote the formation of free and responsible and loving women and men. If the creation of persons able to take full responsibility for themselves and the world in which they are living and acting depends on social contexts most clearly typified by families with genuinely caring and loving parenting figures, it should not surprise us that the ultimate symbol for that which grounds and creates our humanness has been drawn from parenting: God is thought of as a father and/or mother. But God is not just any father or mother: God is a loving parent, just yet merciful and forgiving, working toward the full maturity and freedom of us children. The symbol "God" obviously must include certain highly personalistic dimensions, if it is to bring into unified focus all the major cosmic, historical, and interpersonal forces or powers which ground our humanity, which bring us into being and draw us on toward full realization: virtually the only concrete symbolism which can express some of the most important features of what is involved here is parental, the images of mothering and fathering. We are *social selves,* literally; it is in and through our *interpersonal relationships* with our parents (or parent surrogates) and siblings—and not simply by virtue of our genetic connection with them—that our selfhood is created, that we *qua our humanness* are brought into being.

To speak of God as "father" or "mother" is to acknowledge the importance of these familial interpersonal relations in the creation of free selves and loving communities, and to affirm that this indispensable condition for our becoming fully human is itself grounded in the ultimate nature of things. These parenting metaphors, thus, symbolize forthrightly a central dimension of the meaning which the image/concept of God is meant to convey: faith's conviction that the existence of human moral and spiritual values and virtues—mercy and love and justice; trust and loyalty; beauty, goodness, and truth—is not a metaphysical accident but is grounded in the overflowing creativity of the cosmic process. For faith in God our striving for humane values and a thoroughly humane order is not to be taken as a merely human enterprise; these struggles are, so to say, important to God, and they are to be understood as an expression of God's activity in the world. Our deepest human aspirations, therefore, are not alien to this ecological-historical order into which we have been born: the world in which we live is a humane-seeking order (in certain significant respects), and we can give ourselves wholeheartedly to responsible life and work within it.

The struggle for humane order in the world has not, of course, been easy. It has moved forward only very slowly through the many millennia of human history; and perhaps only in the last two or three thousand years has the vision of a truly humane existence gradually come into view. Given this vision, however, and the conviction that our struggles and hopes to become fully human and humane are grounded in the serendipitous creativity working in and through all things—in God—we can say of the cosmic evolutionary and historical process which has brought forth human life on earth (paraphrasing Job): "Though it slay us—as individuals, even as whole communities—yet will we trust in it." For we believe and hope that the cosmic trajectory which has brought us into being is drawing us onward toward a humane ordering of life—the coming "kingdom of God" in a "new heaven and new earth," as our religious traditions envisioned it; and we shall, therefore, commit ourselves willingly to whatever is required to enable communities of genuine love and peace, truth and justice, to come into being. Since these indispensable interpersonal and social dimensions of the evolutionary-historical trajectory in which we humans "live and move and have our being" (Acts 17:28) are most effectively symbolized and evoked by such metaphors as "father" and "mother," these continue to be appropriate when thinking and speaking of God—if properly de-reified for a contemporary faith-stance. When such metaphors are used, however, it is important to make clear that it is only within our interpersonal relations with women and men here on earth that God's "fatherliness" and "motherliness," God's "sisterliness" and "brotherliness," are experienceable*—as we receive our humanity from others and are able to offer the gift of humanity to them in return (cf. Mt. 25:31–46).

For faith today the symbol "God," if not narrowly or one-sidedly construed, can express—in a more effective way than any other symbol available to those of us heir to western religious traditions—the profound meaning of the situatedness of human life in the world. Because of the unique power and significance it has acquired in a long history of religious meditation and

*For Jesus (and many of his followers in the past) the word "father" was apparently employed in connection with a sense (or experience) of intense, intimate, personal relationship with God. Though for many such claims generated experiences that have been among the most precious features of the Christian life, for others the disappointed expectations to which they gave rise often led to deep inconsolable despair. Expectations and experiences of both these sorts appear, from today's standpoint, to have been grounded largely on the widespread reification of the personal metaphors so prominent in traditional Christianity.

worship, of religious experience and life, this symbol can focus our attention and devotion and lives on those dimensions of the ecological and historical order in which we live that facilitate our moving further toward responsive and responsible human-life-in-the-world—toward attaining our full humanity. Let us turn directly, then, to the question of what faith in this God looks like and means; that is the subject of the next chapter.

23. Faith in God (I)

With our outline of the concept of God largely in place, we are in a position, at long last, to say something about the way in which faith in God may be understood theologically; this will complete our consideration of the fifth step toward faith, and of faith, in God. Up to this point not very much has been said in these chapters about the subjective side of human religiousness. This is because, as I argued in Part II, human subjectivity remains largely inchoate until, in the course of the development of a person from infancy through childhood into maturity, it is given a specific shape and character by the language and culture and patterns of social interaction which are internalized as the self is created. In every culture there are basic patterns of value and meaning, imagery and concepts, which provide pictures and interpretations of human life and its place in the world—what I have called "symbolic frames of orientation"—and it is in terms of these that persons and communities come to understand themselves and to shape and guide their activities. It is the task of theology, as I have argued here, to bring to consciousness these symbolic patterns (whether "religious" or "secular"), to critically examine them, and to reconstruct them in ways which will enable them to function more effectively in face of the problems of contemporary life. Since it is the pattern of Christian categories and symbols which gives Christian subjectivities (that is, the loyalties and commitments and faiths of Christian persons and communities) their basic structure, we have had to hold in suspense the question about what faith in God can be or mean today, until we could sketch out an appropriate conception of the God who is to be the object of that faith.

The subjective posture which has guided our work thus far has been quite open: it was informed largely by a sense of awe in face of the ultimate mystery of things, profound gratitude for the gift of humanness in all its diversity, acceptance of modern understandings of the universe and the human, and a desire to explore the possibility of orienting life today in Christian terms. Now, however—after moving through a number of steps of faith and toward faith—we are in a position to specify in a preliminary way what we may today properly call "faith in God," and to ask whether we are prepared to commit ourselves in such faith. It should be noted, however, that what we will be describing at this point is not yet specifically "Christian" faith: that will have to await our examination and reconstruction of the symbol "Christ." Here we shall consider what theocentric faith can be, in light of our construction of the concept of God thus far.

The very idea of "faith in God" grew up within the conceptual framework in which God-talk (as understood in western religious traditions) had its origins. God was thought of as a quasi-person (the creator/lord/father who ruled the world), and *faith* in God, therefore, was in many respects like faith in another (very powerful) person: it was trust in God, confidence in God's dependability and God's benevolence toward us humans, belief that God's objectives for the human community would be accomplished and God's commitments to us humans would be kept since God was utterly powerful and utterly trustworthy, and that therefore we men and women could place ourselves and our future in God's hands without reservation. We must ask ourselves now, however: What can faith in God mean when God is no longer conceived primarily in terms of the personalistic and political metaphors of the tradition, but rather as the serendipitous movement which we discern in the cosmic evolutionary and historical processes that have created human existence? And what can faith in God mean when it is recognized that all of these images and ideas of ourselves and of the world and of God (both ancient and modern) are our own imaginative constructs?

At various points in my analysis thus far I have tried to explain and interpret what traditional faith has been and what it has meant, and why it has been significant and effective in human lives; but to some it may seem that this very analysis and interpretation has, for those who accept it, undercut the possibility of further faith. For it appears to display all such faiths as strictly *human* activities that give our lives a certain sort of meaning, and it interprets all our religious ideas as created by our own minds. A major point has been to show that our God-talk was not acquired through direct self-conscious interactions with a cosmic being, God, as the tradition has often suggested, but instead has been built up—like all other mythic and metaphysical frames for understanding human existence and its context—by the creativity of the human imagination. In the case of finite objects of knowledge—persons and trees, tables and houses and cities, languages and cultures, planet Earth and the solar system—our concepts are developed in connection with direct perceptions, experiences of *something there:* a "reality" that seems "given" to experience from "beyond us," a something "X" out there which gives our idea its powerful sense of realness, of objectivity, of referring to that which actually *exists*. It is this perceptual dimension of experience that provides the basis for our standard notion of knowledge as dealing with something "objectively real," something that can be "directly experienced." Given this customary model of knowledge it is hardly surprising that we find ourselves suspicious about any ideas which cannot be in some way experientially or experimentally tested: they may well be, as we say, simply figments of our imaginations, not to be regarded as mediating anything "real."

With respect to the issues with which we are concerned here, however, this is a gross oversimplification. Our overarching world-picture or frame of orientation can never be something "given" directly in and to experience like an ordinary object of knowledge: for it provides the background structure and patterning *within which* our particular experiences occur; it represents to us, we might say, that Whole (sometimes called "the universe") which is thought of as "containing" within itself all the objects, events, and processes of experience—as well as the *subjects* of experience, we ourselves—and which cannot, therefore, be directly identified with any particular experience or thing. Since this all-encompassing Whole is never directly encountered as such in experience, our concepts of it—including our mythic world-pictures and our notions of ultimate reality—are not built up on the basis of direct percepts or abstractions from experience (as are our notions of particular finite objects).[1] Rather, this conceptual and/or imagistic frame is created by the human imagination as a kind of map with places for all the objects and events of experience; and it is able, thus, to make intelligible (at least in some minimal way) our actual experiences, enabling us to live out our lives in reasonably satisfactory fashion. To that extent there is always an experiential check on this map: as is well known, the experiences and the reflection which occur in certain historical periods sometimes render the world-pictures and the world-conceptions of previous or other cultural epochs obsolete, completely incredible.

This is what happened, for example, to the picture of the "three-story" universe held by biblical writers (as well as many others): it simply became incredible to modern people. It was replaced long ago by a Copernican and Newtonian world; and that too has been undermined in many ways and is in process of being replaced by what has been called "the modern scientific worldview"—a world of vast galaxies in a universe of dimensions beyond our imagining, a world of infinitely small energy-particles in exceedingly complex continuous interaction. A rather different history is apparently being played out by the ancient Greek understanding of the world as a great living organism, with all parts interrelated and intersupportive, a view which almost died out with the rise of modern science during recent western history. Natural science was for several centuries largely dominated by mechanistic and materialistic conceptions of the world, conceptions partly fostered by the Christian understanding of all created reality as an artifact from the hand of the creator-God—a kind of object (or structure of objects), that is to say, entirely determined from without, an object with no inner spontaneity or vitality of its own. Today, however, such pictures of the universe no longer seem plausible, and scientific reflection is moving to ecological, evolutionary, and holistic systems theories—a return to something in certain respects like the ancient Greek view.

It is clear that ongoing experience and reflection are capable of effecting enormous changes in our world-pictures and our metaphysical conceptions. That is, experience can *disconfirm* features of our most comprehensive images and concepts, as Karl Popper has argued,[2] even though it cannot directly confirm them; it exercises an ongoing negative check on our conceptual and imagistic frames of orientation. Experience is not, however, their direct source and ground: as we have seen, the world-pictures in terms of which we live and act and think are essentially products of the imagination, which pulls the pieces and fragments of experience together into plausible patterns and ultimately some sort of whole. Many such comprehensive patterns have been created in the course of history, and frequently they have succeeded in demonstrating their effectiveness in organizing and interpreting human life for centuries and even millennia. Each of these pictures or conceptions has seemed plausible to those living within it, interpreting themselves and their experience in terms of it. Since talk about God is a particular feature characteristic of one group of these quite diverse worldviews, there is no *prima facie* reason to regard it as either more or less adequately grounded in *reality* than any of the others. How, with such an understanding, can one place one's faith in God? On this view does not all faith finally boil down to a completely arbitrary fideism, in which we simply believe—or decide to believe—even though there are no grounds for doing so? I think the issues posed by this line of argument are misleading; several things need to be said.

We need to remind ourselves first that although we can (if we wish) refuse to formally pursue ultimate metaphysical and religious questions—about the basic shape of the world, about the nature of the ultimate reality with which we have to do, about the place of human beings within the world (as I granted in Chapter 17)—it is impossible to avoid the powerful influence of our (implicit) metaphysical convictions and postulates on our experience and action, as some skeptics and positivists might like us to believe.[3] Though from a purely speculative point of view this might seem plausible, in actual practice it cannot be done, for profound convictions about the world and human life are integrally bound up with the most basic patterns of our everyday lives;[4] they bear directly on the way in which we conduct our lives, on the goals for which we strive, on how we treat other men and women, on what we value as important and what we regard as misleading or insignificant. What I *do,* what I am willing to commit myself to, how I regard myself and other humans, are all directly affected by the (mythological and/or metaphysical) frame of orientation in terms of which I have my experience and understand myself and my world. To suppose that we can avoid committing ourselves to, or being influenced by, one or another world-picture or metaphysical conception simply by refusing to take an explicit position on these issues, or by ignoring them, is to delude ourselves. The question about the frame of orientation within which we live and act is one, thus, which it is important that we directly face. It should be faced, that is, if we are seriously interested in attempting to take as full responsibility as we can for our lives, our actions, and our most basic beliefs. Those who understand our capacity to take responsibility for ourselves and our world to be central to our very humanness, central to the historicity that distinguishes us human beings as human, will see this as a fundamentally *moral* issue: we are morally obliged to take as direct responsibility for our basic beliefs and our faith as we can.

It is important to remember here that the primary reason that humans generate world-pictures, whether mythological or metaphysical, is not because of their insatiable speculative curiosity about "how things are" (though that no doubt sometimes becomes an important secondary motive). The reason is much more fundamental to ongoing human life than that: a picture of the world is indispensable to our ability to *act* in the world. To act we must have some sense of the situation within which we are moving, some awareness of the contours of the world (both natural and social) within which we are attempting to act; we need some sort of map to guide our planning and decisions. Our world-pictures, our metaphysical notions and religious symbols (as we have seen), provide us with ways of seeing and understanding the context in which we live as well as our own place, as humans, within that context. Moreover, it is not the case that all such frames of orientation are on an equal footing, that all choices among them are arbitrary. Some of the world-pictures and conceptual frames which women and men have created in the long course of human history have helped to reinforce the general sense of, and the possibilities for, human agency and responsibility, while others have tended to obscure or weaken these features of human historicity, especially for some groups such as women and the poor. Clearly (as I have argued repeatedly in this book), those which tend to facilitate the optimal development of these central dimensions of our humanness for all members of society, and which portray the world and the human place in the world in ways that enhance the growth and enrichment and responsible exercise of the potentialities of all, are preferable; they are preferable, that is, if we humans really are biohistorical beings whose continuing existence depends upon our moving intelligently and responsibly in the world in which we find ourselves. A universe pictured as significantly sustentive and supportive of human moral and cultural concerns, as manifesting forces drawing us humans on toward a more fully humane existence, tends to evoke from women and men efforts to take responsibility for themselves and their lives. Such a world-picture—centered in a just, righteous, and loving God—was developed in a powerful form, as we have seen, in ancient Israel.

Throughout these chapters I have been arguing that there is an alternative to the mythic dualism which underlies this traditional understanding of God, one that can be framed in strictly this-worldly terms: it builds on the idea of serendipitous creativity pervasive throughout the universe, on the one hand, and the notion of significant directional movements or trajectories—which appear in the patterns of evolutionary-historical development that we observe here on earth—on the other. According to this view God is not thought of as some being outside the world but rather as a particular form of creativity and ordering going on within the world, namely that serendipitous ordering which has given rise (among other things) to the evolution of life on planet Earth and the emergence of human beings, and which continues to sustain us and to move us toward a more profound humanization. If we agree to live and work and think within this framework, we will be able to continue to speak of God, and of faith in God, without postulating or implying some extra being "out there" somewhere "beyond the world." And faith (or belief) in God will be interpreted essentially as commitment, in face of the ultimate mystery of life, to this reality central to this particular vision of the world (rather than as assent to some quite dubious propositions about some cosmic person, as it so often is).

In two recent books, *Belief and History* and *Faith and Belief*,[5] W. C. Smith presents illuminating studies of what the words "belief" and "faith" (and their Latin, Greek, and Aramaic cognates) have meant historically in biblical and other religious contexts. He shows conclusively, I think, that until the last two centuries these words were used primarily to express one's basic commitment in life, to acknowledge that one was giving oneself wholeheartedly to a particular cause or way of life or activity; they were virtually never used (as they usually are today) to suggest that the statement we are now making, though personally important to us, is perhaps somewhat doubtful. Thus, for example, to say, "I believe in God the Father, almighty Creator of heaven and earth . . ." meant that *I commit myself* to God the Father, or to the cause of God the Father, not, "I am of the opinion that there is a being called 'God the Father.'" This older use of the word "belief" is still extant. For example, one might say, "I believe in classical education," or "I believe in jogging five miles each day," or "I believe in democracy."[6] In such affirmations we are saying that we have made a particular commitment, and we intend to keep it. Something like this, according to Smith, is what was involved in traditional affirmations of belief in God. This, however, is no longer the most common understanding of the word "belief," as Smith shows. Instead of expressing a serious commitment of the self, it now is usually understood in contrast with the meanings of the words "know" and "knowledge," and their strong claim that something is the case: to "believe" something to be true, in contrast with "knowing" it to be true, means to hold it as a personal opinion, an opinion which cannot be adequately verified and which is, therefore, somewhat uncertain. When the ancient creeds, and other religious claims, are understood in terms of this modern concept of belief, serious confusions and misunderstandings arise. Smith argues, therefore, that thc word "bclief" should no longer be used to translate these Greek and Latin (and even Old English) texts; nor should the word "faith" be regarded as more or less equivalent to "belief" (as is often suggested in current English-language use). Words such as "acknowledge" or "commitment" should be used instead, for it is primarily an act or stance of a community or a self that is being expressed in these religious affirmations rather than a claim about what is the case.

This point seems to me correct. The question is not so much, What propositions regarding the world should we hold to be true?—a question to which, as we have seen, no conclusive answer is possible—but rather, In view of the ultimate mystery of life to what vision or conception of human existence and its context should I commit myself? To what understanding of the world and the human am I prepared to devote myself? For what values and meanings will I give my life? To say, "I believe in God," is (on the one hand) to acknowledge the ultimate mystery of things, but (on the other) to commit myself to the reality and significance of that which the image/concept of God personifies and symbolizes—moral and personal values such as loyalty, honesty, integrity, freedom, self-sacrifice, love, responsible action, et cetera, and the serendipitous creativity which underlies and expresses itself in these (as well as much else). That is, it is to express my intention to take fully into account, in the ordering of my life, both the mystery of life and the world and the significance and place of the moral/personal/humane within life and the world. To believe in God, thus, is to commit oneself to a particular way of ordering one's life and action:[7] it is to devote oneself (according to the interpretation worked out in this volume) to working toward a fully humane world within the ecological constraints here on planet Earth, while standing in piety and awe before the profound mysteries of existence. On this view the symbol "God" refers us not to a particular existent being within or beyond the world, but rather to that trajectory of cosmic and historical forces which, having emerged out of the ultimate mystery of things, is moving us toward a more truly humane and ecologically responsible mode of existence: it is *that* to which I commit myself; it is that which I will serve with my life.

If we no longer take the name "God" to refer to a literally existent being, why continue to use it? Why not just speak of "cosmic and historical forces" working toward humanization and ecological order? The symbol "God" has served as a focus for worship and for orientation in life for many centuries. In focusing our attention and devotion with the aid of this symbol, thus, we are associating ourselves with those many generations of women and men—and those ancient religious communities—for whom it similarly evoked and focused commitments to a humane and responsible ordering of life. We make clear (both to ourselves and to others) that we do not regard ourselves as a generation basically disconnected from our forebears; we see ourselves rather as participants in an ongoing history and community—a historical trajectory—the values and priorities and commitments of which have shaped our own, and from which, in fact, most of our beliefs about the importance of the personal and the humane and the responsible have come. The principal focus for devotion and loyalty avowed by this ancient community from which we come and of which we also are part was God. When we commit ourselves to God today, we acknowledge all this by accepting the central symbol of this community as our own, and by confessing our desire to associate ourselves with this history and to enhance its strength in the modern world—as we all move onward into a future which seems likely to be increasingly dominated by anti-human and anti-ecological values and styles of life. It seems doubtful there will ever be a worldwide community, cutting across all classes, races, and conditions of women and men, which is grounded on and committed to the idea of "cosmic and historical forces" working toward humanization and ecological responsibility; that conception is much too abstract and intellectual to be able to generate universal interest and support. To commit ourselves to *God,* however, is to express just such a stance and loyalty by means of a symbol which is capable of drawing together and unifying persons of differing degrees of sophistication in all walks of life.

When we use the symbol "God" (and not just the concepts of "cosmic and historical forces"), our attention and understanding are focused in a particular and distinctive way: "God," as a proper name, does not lead us to think in terms of a miscellany of forces that somehow accidentally combined so as to throw up human existence on this planet some time in the past; instead it focuses our minds so they will grasp as significantly unified and of existential import to us what we might otherwise take to be simply diverse processes and powers. What justification can be offered for this sort of focusing of our attention and understanding? Human selves—with their historicity, consciousness, and freedom—are (as we have seen) centered beings, beings that can *act.* As nearly as we can tell, this centeredness did not simply appear completely unaccountably one day, but rather came about through a gradually cumulating biological/historical process. The creativity which produced us expressed itself, that is to say, through an evolutionary-historical trajectory in which both directionality and centeredness seem to have steadily increased; and in due course an organism was produced which was capable of sustaining symbolic activities of sufficient complexity to make possible self-consciousness and responsible action. When we use the name "God" now, to identify this trajectory, we are led to focus our attention and interest on this movement of increasing unifiedness and directionality that has brought into being human historicity; and we affirm the groundedness of this trajectory in the serendipitous creativity at work in the nature of things. (This affirmation represents, as we have noted, a significant step of faith.)

Bringing "God" into our considerations here does not commit us to the existence of some additional *being* (either in the world or beyond the world) from which these evolutionary forces proceed, any more than speaking of selfhood (for example) commits us to an additional "something" alongside the body, which brings about our bodily movements. Rather, what we are doing by employing the name "God" is attending to the significance (for us human beings) of the *unity* and *direction* which gradually developed in this particular evolutionary-historical trajectory (features which were to evolve later, when human life actually emerged, into what we call "purposive activity" or "intentionality"): these cosmic forces and movements were gradually becoming ordered in such a way that humanness could come forth from them. What they eventually collectively produced was not a simple perpetuation of their own seeming multiplicity but rather the sort of unified or centered beings which we men and women are. "God" (with its accent on that which grounds our humanness) is the principal word available in our language for focusing our minds on this growing unity of *directedness toward the human,* which faith (in its retrospective perusal of the trajectory which has produced us) discerns and affirms amid all the enormous diversity of cosmic powers and movements; "God" holds together in one these (seemingly disparate) cosmic and historical powers and forces which produce human existence with its unique centeredness. To deny any such directionality within the diversity of cosmic forces—and thus to affirm that human existence in its most distinctive features has no significant cosmic or metaphysical grounding—is to deny God's reality; to affirm this directionality, however—that there is some tension toward humanity and humaneness in the cosmic order itself is to confess the reality of God.

We introduce the name "God," then, not simply to designate the collection of disparate cosmic powers that have produced us, but to direct attention to the mysteriously increasing unity and directionality of these powers in the trajectory which has created human existence. In the use of the word "God" no claim to knowledge of how and why this all came about is being made.

On the contrary, precisely the *mystery* in it all is being accented: for here, in and through this evolutionary-historical trajectory, the ultimate mystery of things appears to be disclosing a human- and humane-affirming quality—at least so the faith that celebrates this as a manifestation of *God's* reality affirms. Without the special emphases of the symbol "God," attention to the cosmic order would provide us with little to orient our distinctively human interests and concerns and nothing to focus our devotion and activities. This symbol, through enabling us to see this vast, diverse cosmic process as significantly ordered (in certain respects) toward the creation and sustenance of the human and the humane (that is, toward what our religious traditions called "spirit" and "salvation"), lifts out of this cosmic diversity a particular focus for human work and devotion.* It is a focus which will help orient human existence toward the cultivation of precisely those values and concerns and practices that can bring about, in both us and our world, a richer and more profound humanness and humaneness.[8]

In addition to symbolizing for us the momentums toward humanization and the humane in the cosmic process, the image/concept of God also (as we have seen) *relativizes* everything about us and our world. This symbol underlines the fact that in every respect we—our lives and our world—are grounded in and founded upon something beyond and other than ourselves and our activities, a serendipitous creativity which has brought us into being and which ultimately sets the terms within which we must live out our lives. It steadily reminds us, thus, that our ideas (including our ideas of the world as evolutionary and historical), our values, and our standards must never be taken as ultimate or final: everything we know or believe, indeed everything about us, is called into question by the ultimate mystery—*God*—which

*Our traditional western *substantival* patterns of thinking and speaking lead us to expect proper names to designate particular "somethings" with distinct boundaries separating them from other "things"; when dealing with historical events and processes, however, we understand perfectly well that such sharp boundaries cannot be drawn, and the names we use are, for the most part, heuristic devices that may be somewhat arbitrary: Did World War II have its beginnings in Hitler's invasion of Poland or Czechoslovakia? or must we trace it back to earlier actions of the Nazis, and perhaps even to the Germany of the Twenties, to the Versailles Treaty, and ultimately to World War I? Though no sharp lines can be drawn at any of these points, and arguments can be given for a whole range of answers to these questions, this does not interfere with our using the proper name "World War II" quite intelligibly and comprehensibly in many different contexts; in fact, it is difficult to see how we could think or speak clearly about human life and experience in the twentieth century without using this name (or some equivalent). Similarly, since what we are concerned with in our theological world-picture here is a particular configuration of cosmic, evolutionary, and historical *processes* and *events,* there is no (linguistic or logical) reason why we should not use an appropriate proper name to lift these up, hold them together, and bring them into focus for us. There is no better word in our modern languages than "God" for designating precisely the especial importance of this particular configuration of processes and events to us human beings, as we seek to orient ourselves in what we today take to be the real context of our lives.

relativizes all else. In this way the symbol "God" continuously calls our attention to the danger of idolatry: the danger of devoting or committing ourselves without reservation to anything which we ourselves have made, have thought, have believed. Devotion to God as ultimate reality, as the ultimate mystery of being and value, is not, therefore, simply devotion to what we now know or believe to be true and good and beautiful: it is, rather, a posture of opening ourselves to being drawn out from where we now are to new levels of insight, action, and being, levels which we cannot now even imagine. The symbol "God," with its mythic overtones of mystery and transcendence, can perform functions like this which more strictly conceptual language cannot achieve, thus helping order and reorder our lives in ways and respects unavailable to more abstract ideas. From a pragmatic point of view, therefore—that is, from a point of view interested in the actual reordering of human affairs in a more humane and ecologically responsible direction—it can be both meaningful and important to employ it; always, of course, with discrimination and care. By providing a principal focus for communal and personal devotion, service, and overall orientation, the image/concept of God contributes directly to the promotion of humanization, making its own distinctive contribution to forwarding the cosmic tendencies toward the human and the humane.

There can be no humanization or humanness apart from active participation by the women and men involved: within the evolutionary-historical process which will ultimately produce human beings there must, then, develop a *subjective* dimension—commitments, devotion, loyalties, and decisions of concrete men and women—if it is indeed to be actual humanness (historicity with subjectivity and freedom) which here comes into being. Religious practices, institutions, and ideas everywhere contributed significantly to this development of subjectivity; and the appearance of practices and institutions in connection with the idea of God—as that to which we can and should be devoted without reservation—became central to the whole process of humanization as it worked itself out in ancient Israel and the several cultures strongly influenced by Israel's religious consciousness. Thus, the imaginative construction of the idea of God (at first, perhaps, as a "mighty warrior"), and its ongoing criticism and reformulation by prophets and poets, lawmakers and judges, philosophers and theologians, became a significant (subjective) feature of the historical and cosmic movement toward humanness and humaneness. In human imaginative and critical activities of this sort, we can say, the cosmic tension toward the human began to express itself *within* human consciousness and culture, that is, within the selves and minds and devotion and activities of actual women and men in living communities. In the "Abrahamic" religious traditions, it has been (at least in significant part) in and through the construction and reconstruction of God-talk (and, of course, many other related institutions and practices) that humans have become aware of who they were, of what was really going on in the world roundabout, and of the role they were to play in all of this.

With these considerations in mind we can make contact (once again) with certain more traditional theological claims. There is a sense in which we can say that in and through the emergence of God-talk (faith in God)—that is, in and through the emergence of an awareness in humanity of a cosmic grounding that has given rise to and continues to undergird our humanness—the cosmic tension toward humanization was beginning (so to speak) to communicate itself to humankind. Without the development of God-talk we would not have been led to think about the world in just these ways, or to orient our selves and our communities in these terms (one remembers in this connection the enormous diversity of religious understandings of life and the world). Thus, in and through the human imaginative activity of constructing ideas and images of God over many generations, God could be said to be making Godself known to humankind: in and through the emergence and development of God-talk the cosmic serendipitous creativity active in the evolutionary-historical trajectory toward humanization has gradually been "revealing" itself to us. We are moving here into a position from which we can freshly assess traditional claims about divine revelation, the use of metaphors like "speaker" and "revealer" in connection with God.

We must be careful here, of course, that we do not reify the notion of God as speaker—as though God utters actual human words (in Hebrew or English or some other language) which we could hear; or magically, by a kind of mental telepathy, transfers words and thoughts into our minds. Such a literal cosmic speaker is no more thinkable than a literal cosmic lord or father. And yet, if there really is a cosmic tension toward humaneness, toward the creation and flourishing of the human, and if our conscious intentional participation in this process of humanization is indispensable to it, then certain developments which come about *within* human consciousness and culture—within human intentionality and institutions and practices—will themselves quite properly be understood as expressions of this tension, as a communicating (as it were) of the meaning of this process of humanization in which we live and move and have our being to those of us who live within it. This is the essential point that was being made when (in our religious traditions) it was said that human faith, devotion, and reflection should all be understood as responses to God's (prevenient) activity, God's "revelation."[9]

It is important at this point, where we are dealing with some of the most anthropomorphic features of the tradition, that we remind ourselves once again that in all of this it is ultimately *mystery* with which we have to do; and to mistake our own imaginative constructs for that mystery is to fall into self-idolatry. One of the most important features of the notion of theology as imaginative construction is that it demands that we clearly distinguish our ideas—especially when we speak of God—from the mysteries to which we intend them to refer. This helps keep us honest in our theological work on the one hand; and it acknowledges, on the other, the full independence of God from what we may think or say. In reminding ourselves of God's mystery we allow God in God's concrete actuality to be whatever God is, quite apart from our symbolizations; in this respect the concept of mystery, just because of its conceptual emptiness and openness, most directly forces upon us what it means to confess God's *reality,* to confess the God that is truly *God,* the ultimate reality which is not to be confused with any of our "imaginative constructions."

With these reflections in mind let us look briefly again at the traditional claims about salvation-history and revelation-history—the developing story of Abraham, Moses, the prophets, Jesus, and so on. How should this story be interpreted today, when we must also give proper consideration to many other histories, the significance of which Christian theology has seldom acknowledged—histories of India, China, and Africa, of women, of Native Americans, of despised heretics? In and through all of these (we will want to insist today) God—the powers working toward humanization and humaneness—was also making Godself known in distinctive and important ways.

There is one respect, however, in which the Bible retains a unique place in the global perspective which is now becoming ours: it was in and through the traditions reported in the Bible that our image/concept of God was itself originally created and developed; it was the biblical traditions that taught us to see human historical events and developments in the terms suggested by this particular image/concept—that is, as an expression of the purposes and activity of *God,* indeed as the vehicle of God's revelation. These traditions, in an unparalleled way, encouraged the development of a form of human existence in which history and historicity were given centrality, and God was understood to be involved in this history and historicity.* All of our talk

*Because of its emphasis on history and historicity the Bible will always remain a crucial document of both our growing human self-understanding and our developing understanding of God. Traditionally the Bible's significance has been based on the claim that it is, or contains, unique divine revelation and therefore is the ultimate authority for theology and for faith. As we have seen, however, it is no longer appropriate to proceed in this authoritarian way in theology, claiming divine authorization for what we now must understand to be one particular tradition of human beliefs and practices. Rather, the significance of the Bible should today be assessed on essentially humanistic grounds: what role has it actually played in the emergence of human self-definition and self-understanding and self-transformation in the process we have been calling "humanization"?

about God, thus—whether as creator/lord/father or as serendipitous creativity manifesting itself in evolutionary and historical trajectories—is dependent in a unique way upon this tradition for its shape and content: the basic monotheistic symbolic pattern acquired its fundamental defining form here.

In this tradition (as we have been observing) God is spoken of in terms of such metaphors as love and care and self-communication—not taken in some abstract or idealized sense, as something going on "up in heaven," but rather in the concrete empirical sense of God giving Godself in and through the actual historical events in which men and women live and move. The nondualistic reconception of monotheism which I am proposing in this book grows out of a radicalization of these this-worldly historicistic motifs. (Later on, as we shall see, this conception of God's historical self-giving and self-revelation will also provide a basis for understanding how and why specifically Christian claims can qualify and modify the picture which has been sketched up to this point.) Since the locus of God's reality is not in some transcendent "otherworld" but rather in the actual evolutionary and historical processes and developments through which human life has come into being in this world, we must take with seriousness the histories of all peoples—not only to understand what sort of beings we humans are, but also to understand who or what God is, and what God's reality means for our human situation today. From this vantage point, the religious ethnocentrism which has been so prominent throughout Christian history turns out to be but one more form of idolatry, one more pretentious human attempt to domesticate and control the ultimate mystery, instead of to live before it and within it in awe and faith. If our conception of God—however precious and important it may be to us—does not call itself into question on such points as these, does not relativize itself, it is not properly a conception of *God.*

We are in a position now to take our fifth step of faith toward God, a step that simultaneously becomes faith *in* God. That is, we are now at the point where we can say both what we mean by the symbol "God" and whether we are prepared to commit ourselves to this God. The symbol "God" signifies that ultimate mystery in which all those cosmic and historical processes and powers—which, in concert, have given rise to humanity-in-the-world, which continue to sustain and support our existence, and which lead (or drive) us forward toward a fuller humanization, a more profound humaneness—are unified and held together. God is, thus, that on which we must be focused (whether we choose to call this reality "God" or not), and to which we must be devoted, if we are to flourish as creatures in this ecologically ordered world. From this point of view God is quite properly regarded both as our "creator" and as our "redeemer" or "savior": it is God, and God alone, who is our proper object of worship and the proper center of orientation for our work and our lives. This understanding of God—taken together with the conceptions of humanity and the world worked out in Parts II and III—provides us with the basic elements of a theocentric perspective on life and the world, a theocentric world-picture for today.

The symbol "God," as I have been trying to present it here, has a complex dialectical tension built into its very center: it can point us toward that which is utterly beyond us, that ultimate mystery which we neither comprehend nor can control; but the symbol itself, of course, is something present to us, something that we know—and for just this reason it is not to be straightforwardly identified with that ultimate mystery to which it points. When this dialectic in the symbol "God" is allowed to function properly, God is allowed to be *God;* and we are enabled to enter into a relationship of genuine piety toward God. As we shall observe in Chapter 24, to the extent that we try significantly to control this mystery—for example, through particular favored theological ideas or religious practices—we become idolaters who *sin* against God; for we are then trying to make ourselves the ultimate disposers of human life. And for this we must always repent, acknowledging that our destiny is really in God's hands: it is, finally, mystery. Then, perhaps, the possibility is opened up for a grace from beyond us to burst in with the gift of genuine faith.

Some would, no doubt, want to argue that proper and responsible theological reflection on the meaning of the symbol "God" requires us to take much more literally (than I have in these chapters) the traditional religious language about a cosmic Person. I really do not have serious objections to this contention, so long as we can agree that this sort of characterization is not to be regarded as an unquestionable premise which every believer and every theologian must accept, but is seen to be a debatable theological issue. One of the advantages of the functional employment of the symbol "God" which I have been advocating here is that it opens us to a wide range of ways of thinking about that on which we may rely unconditionally, and to which, therefore, we should devote ourselves. For those willing to understand the symbol in this functional way it can *unite* in significant respects (instead of divide) those who confess faith in God. For it will be employed to direct our attention, devotion, and service toward that which gives us our common humanity (God as creator) and that which helps us overcome the diseases, perversions, and other barriers which threaten to obstruct or destroy that humanity (God as redeemer, savior). Although the particulars of these realities and processes may be conceived in diverse ways, it will be understood that those who profess "faith in God" in fact mean to be committing themselves not simply to their own ideas of God but rather to that reality *whatever it might be* which draws us on toward full and responsible humanness.*

I have been arguing here that the most adequate way to conceive God today is in terms of the "personality producing activities" going on within the universe (to use Shailer Mathews's phrase),[10] on the one hand—the activities which have brought humanity into being and which continue to sustain us as responsible members of responsible communities—and the ultimate mystery of things, on the other; and I have tried to specify to some extent these cosmic and historical conditions that make possible our historicity. I have also argued that what we devote ourselves to (that is, which symbols and concepts focus our devotion and energies, and thus provide orientation in our lives) has important effects on our personhood and our communal life, on their enhancement or their diminishment with respect to freedom and responsibility, peace and justice, and a sense of meaningfulness

*This functional approach to the meaning of the symbol "God" is especially valuable for pastors and others who must deal in their congregations with a wide spectrum of beliefs. Although pastors need to be clear about who or what they themselves understand God to be—and they have a responsibility to educate their congregations on this issue—their work is not primarily analysis of the meaning of God-talk or propagating a particular theory about God. It consists, rather, in helping people orient their lives and deal with their problems from a perspective of commitment to God. This involves, above all, *using* the language and symbolism of faith (as distinct from analyzing or reconstructing that language, as a theologian must do) in such activities as leading public worship, counseling individuals with problems, administering the affairs of a congregation, and the like. If pastors employ this language with circumspection and intelligence (that is, with theological sophistication), they can reasonably hope and expect that members of the congregation (and the pastor as well!) will—through their participation in this actual use of the language of faith—get a sense of what it is like for this language to serve as the framework within which living and thinking and acting are understood; and in due course, perhaps, it will become the primary framework within which they understand themselves and their lives. When one's objective is to learn a language, the most important thing is to put it into use, not to take apart its fundamental symbols, proposing various new alternatives. Such activities would be, in this context, counter-productive; and for this reason in much pastoral work it is inappropriate to engage in the sort of theological analysis and reconception with which we have been occupied here.

This does not mean, of course, that pastors can afford simply to ignore the theological task. There are many occasions when they are obliged not simply to call upon God in prayer but to attempt to explain who or what God is; and it is certainly important that, as leaders of congregations, they understand, and are able to interpret to their congregation and others, what can properly be meant today by the religious symbolism they are using. So ministers must themselves be theologians of some competence and imagination, and they must be prepared to engage in theological analysis, interpretation, and reconstruction—both for the sake of their own understanding of their vocation and also in the educational dimensions of their work. Though consideration of the kind of methodological problems we have taken up in this book is not appropriate in sermons, prayers, or other liturgical acts (where the intention is to evoke attitudes of devotion and faithfulness to God) it is essential that it be carried on in the pastor's study and classroom, if those liturgical activities are to continue to be truly meaningful and edifying for those who participate in them.

and fulfillment. When the symbol "God" is understood not simply in terms of the specific content which the tradition gave it (based on reification of the creator/lord/father imagery), but rather in terms of the evolutionary-historical trajectory which has in fact brought human life into being and continues to sustain it, there is really no question about whether God "exists." The correct question is, rather, who or what is *God?* that is, what reality (or configuration of realities) in fact gives us our being as human and draws us on toward more profound humanization? When the question is refocused in this way, it becomes clear that God is the ultimate reality with which we humans in fact have to do. There should be little question, then, that faith in God, commitment to God—if interpreted along the lines proposed here—is a matter of fundamental importance.

In summary: to say, "I believe in God," is to say, "I commit myself to God; I intend to devote myself to that reality, that ultimate mystery, which brings us men and women to full humanization, to salvation; and thus I join myself in community with those countless generations who also confessed their most fundamental commitment in these words."

Let us now look back briefly once again at Part II of this book, where the idea of the human as biohistorical reality was initially proposed and sketched. Our examination and construction (in Parts III and IV) of concepts of the world and of God has put us into a somewhat different position than we occupied when we were working out that conception of the human; and it is important that we take note of the consequences this has for our understanding of human existence and the human condition. Our notion of historicity was developed, in the first instance, largely phenomenologically, in the effort to understand and interpret human being simply as it shows itself to us: we humans appear to be a biological form which has evolved into a culture-creating—and thus a history-creating and self-creating—mode of being. I suggested that, although the forms which this biohistorical being has taken in history have been quite various, it is nevertheless possible to define certain very general norms in terms of which these forms can be judged with respect to their capacity to sustain ongoing biohistorical life and enable it to flourish and develop further. Thus, a definite morality and ethics were shown to be implicit in our historicity. All this was worked out in essentially *naturalistic* terms, that is, without making any particular metaphysical claims either about humanity or about goodness, value, and meaning.

Although this approach enabled us to bring into view much that is important about human being, it left completely open larger questions about the way in which the wider cosmic—indeed, metaphysical—context within which human existence falls may affect it, and may also affect our understanding of it. We can now see that in that initial sketch of human being we were assuming that we could adequately discern most of what we needed to know without raising these larger questions. In Parts III and IV we have explored this assumption in some detail; and I have attempted to show that, although it appears to be possible for many humans to live out their lives without engaging much in explicit cosmological, metaphysical, or theological reflection, the way in which they picture and understand the overarching context within which they live and work in fact deeply affects their conception of themselves and how they should comport themselves in the world. In particular, I have argued that our sense of what we are doing in the world—of the meaningfulness of life and of our concerns and projects—is transformed in important ways and immeasurably deepened if we are able to see these matters as significantly grounded in the serendipitous creativity at work in all things.

Let us remind ourselves of two points in this connection. First, such an awareness—such a faith—provides a sense that humans are not utterly alone in the world, struggling to sustain forms of life for which there is no wider support than their own labors. Projects and activities that are significantly grounded in the ultimate creativity at work in the world have a larger and deeper meaning than their merely human significance, and a sense of participation in that meaning can provide sustenance and support in times of tragedy and crisis. Determination to live and act fittingly and responsibly, even at great cost to oneself, is thus strengthened; and motivation to continue the struggle even against enormous odds is deepened. In western religious traditions the symbol "God" has functioned to give this sort of metaphysical and religious depth to life, thus making available profound resources of energy and meaning for addressing life's burdens and struggles. Faith in God, it is clear, can provide responsible historicity with a grounding which the narrowly anthropological interpretation of Part II was unable to give it; and the likelihood is thereby increased that we will take seriously the demands made upon us as biohistorical beings.

Second, precisely this widening and deepening of our understanding of human historical existence means that certain important constraints and restraints are now placed upon it. No longer is it permissible to understand responsible life and action in largely anthropocentric terms. It now becomes imperative that we ask about the wider cosmic context within which human life falls: What direction is the evolutionary-historical trajectory, of which we are part, moving? How do we best fit our own projects and activities into that wider and more fundamental movement? Are corrections and transformations—perhaps quite drastic ones—required in our ways of thinking, living, and acting? In short, what is *God* doing in our world today, and how can we fit our actions into God's overarching activity which is their context?[11] Responsible historical existence—if understood as being grounded in the ultimate nature of things, the creativity at work throughout the world—not only takes on much deeper significance than was possible in our anthropological reflections of Part II; it simultaneously experiences itself as relativized and constrained by the wider and deeper context within which it falls, in a way not apparent in that earlier discussion. In this larger understanding of human historicity, life must at all points be lived in awe and respect before the ultimate mystery of things. But now this mystery is apprehended as profoundly humanizing as well as relativizing; it is a mystery, therefore, that can be loved as well as feared, a mystery within which we can feel "at home."

24. Sin and Evil

With the basic outline of a theocentric worldview for today before us, we are now in a position to develop further, and draw together, our consideration of those enormously problematic features of life often discussed as "the problem of evil." We will build here on notions set out in Chapters 15, 21, and 22, and push them to a deeper level. Our theocentric interpretive scheme is intended to assist us in identifying and coming to understand the principal "evils" with which we men and women must grapple; if it cannot do that, it will, in fact, fail as a frame of orientation—the main purpose for which we have been constructing it.

The concept of *evil,* as Spinoza suggests,[1] was originally—and perhaps is still primarily—an anthropocentric one: it refers (in the first instance) to what is destructive of, or threatens to destroy, human existence or well-being, what can make human fulfillment impossible. A few ordinary examples will make evident this anthropocentric character of the concept. Consider, for instance, earthquakes. If we think of earthquakes entirely without regard to their consequences for living beings, that is, as simply rapid changes in the structure of the surface of the earth, there seems to be no reason to describe them as either "good" or "evil": these terms do not properly apply in this sort of context. Earthquakes are pronounced *evil* when they cause great suffering and are enormously destructive of life—preeminently human life, but by extension other forms of life as well; that is, it is from the point of view of human life (or life more generally) that they are characterized as an evil. Consider another kind of natural catastrophe such as a forest fire: this also is not an evil simply in and of itself, but only to the extent that the forest is of *value* to some animate creatures, or to the extent that the fire is destructive of such creatures. It is not entirely clear linguistically whether a forest fire that destroyed only plant life should be regarded as an evil or not: indeed, we sometimes hear it said that such fires are often "good" in that they help to clear out the dead brush, thus making possible new growth. The word "evil" seems to be invoked largely when extensive pain or suffering is caused[2] (that is, in situations in which animal life is significantly involved); and it ordinarily finds its major application with respect to humans, beings who are consciously purposive and who look on the destruction of their projects and activities with terror and despair.

Although the concept of evil is closely connected with human interests, in the related notion of *sin* transcendence of the anthropocentrism of evil by wider theocentric concerns begins to emerge. For sin is defined essentially with reference to *God*—God's will and God's purposes (in the traditional understanding)—rather than human beings: it is that which goes counter to God's activity, actions, and attitudes, a form of behavior of which (so far as we know) only humans are capable. Thus, with the concept of sin the fulcrum moves from human attitudes, intentions, and actions to the wider context within which human existence falls; and this makes it possible to call into question the anthropocentrism underlying the concept of evil—a move that would be difficult apart from an understanding of human life as situated in an extra-human context of meaningful activity. When the symbol "God" is invoked in understanding human existence, precisely such contextualizing and thus relativizing occurs; for central to the meaning of this symbol from the Old Testament period on has been the conception of powerful purposive activity at work within the cosmic and historical processes that have brought human life—including its intentionality—into being, and that continue to sustain it.

This issue of the fundamental anthropocentrism (not to mention ethnocentrism and egocentrism) of much of our ordinary thinking and speaking of evil is put into an interesting light by the emerging understanding of the ecological crisis which we today face. Is our concern about what we are doing to our environment due principally to our human interests in survival? or is there some extra-human point of reference in terms of which our unrestrained looting and polluting of planet Earth can properly be judged *evil?* If we are now beginning to wonder whether the latter might be the case—whether our ecological concerns might signal something of more importance than mere human interests—we are moving in the direction which the concept of God symbolizes. What we are beginning to sense here is the reality and the importance (in its own right) of the wider web of being and life which provides human existence with its context. As we learn to transcend our largely utilitarian interests in making judgments on ecological matters, thus, we begin to move toward what I have been identifying as God.

I would like to expand upon these points now with a fuller exposition of the understanding of evil made possible by the picture of God, humanity, and the world which we have been constructing. The evils of human life are commonly said (by philosophers and theologians) to fall into two major classes, natural evil and moral evil. This classification, however, is not very satisfactory. In the first place, the anthropocentric motifs implicit in the concept of "natural evil" make it very problematic today (as we shall see in a moment). Secondly, the theocentric concept of *sin* cannot be properly understood as a form of either natural or moral evil; we will need a third notion, "theological evil," to interpret it adequately. However, the common distinction between natural and moral evil provides us with a convenient point of departure for considering these matters, so we shall begin by examining it.

The term "natural evil" is ordinarily used to refer to all those sorts of catastrophe or malfunction, difficulty or constriction, in human affairs which appear to be grounded simply and straightforwardly in the natural order within which we live, and which often make life a painful and miserable struggle—for example, natural catastrophes such as volcanic eruptions, earthquakes, or prolonged droughts, diseases and horrifying birth defects (for which humans are not themselves responsible), death. Sometimes events and processes of these sorts are immediately destructive of human life and human projects; sometimes they are slowly erosive. But however that may be, they are called "natural" evils because they are regarded as features of the natural order which are simply given, features for which humans are in no way responsible. In this respect these sorts of evil stand in sharp contrast with those evils which humans themselves bring about and for which they can quite properly be held accountable, so-called moral evils.

It is a dialectical question, however, whether it is really appropriate to regard the adversities with which the natural order confronts us—even quite extreme ones—as (without qualification) "evil." For it is precisely these same constricting conditions in life that have pushed or driven humanity toward agency and historicity, toward attempting to take some control over the situation in which we find ourselves, reordering it so that it will better sustain human existence. The mixture of adversity and difficulty with openness and indeterminacy, in the patterns of natural order here on planet Earth, has provided a context without which it would be difficult to imagine how agents with significant degrees of freedom, agents able to take responsibility for themselves, could have emerged. So the adverse features of nature are responsible, in part, for the development—in and through a long history—of our historicity, our very humanity. (Those committed to a theocentric understanding of the world will not regard this as merely an accidental matter: it seems too closely interconnected with the evolutionary-historical trajectory which in due course brought forth humanity.) But if these natural conditions are seen in that light, is it really appropriate to designate them as straightforwardly "evil"? Is the very idea of "natural evil" perhaps a misunderstanding? Since it is precisely this context of order, adversity, and difficulty that grounds the very possibility of our being human, we must conclude that the notion of "natural evil" represents at the very least a gross oversimplification.

The use of such an ambiguous concept is not only misleading; it can also be in its own way destructive. "Evil," as we have noted, is an essentially anthropocentric notion. The very concept of "natural evil," therefore, leads us to focus attention on (what we regard as) nature's indifference toward and destructiveness of our human interests and concerns—while we (all too often) overlook our human destructiveness of nature. That is, it leads us to regard nature as our adversary, as something to be overcome, mastered—just the sort of anthropocentric attitude that has led (in part) to the present ecological crisis. Whatever may be the difficulties and problems of our situatedness in the natural order, it is a mistake, in my opinion, to continue to think of these in the simplistic anthropocentric way suggested by the concept of natural evil. (The concept of sin, as we shall see later in this chapter, is better fitted than this notion to bring out the dialectical complexity of our relationship to that which grounds our human existence.)

Let us move our investigation, then, directly to the human realm, with its purposive action and moral responsibility, its concern with meaning and value. This brings us to what has traditionally been called "moral evil," the evil for which we humans are (partially or solely) accountable. The concept of evil in its originary sense (I have suggested) has to do with that which threatens or is destructive of human life and the meaning of human life. It is obvious that humans participate in and are responsible for much that bears on these matters; and an enormous literature has developed on problems of personal and social disorganization and disintegration, poverty, overpopulation, oppression, cruelty, rage, prejudice, discrimination, despair, the meaninglessness of life, political and economic inequalities, disease, and so on. We cannot, of course, go into the complexities of these issues here; the most we can do is consider briefly the respects and degrees in which women and men are responsible for such matters. To begin to get a grip on this aspect of evil, let us call to mind the interpretation of human responsibility (as a central feature of our historicity) which was worked out in Part II of this book.

In Chapters 13 and 14 I set out an analysis of action, freedom, and responsibility which interpreted these as of varying degrees of complexity. There is, first of all, the simple awareness that *we are acting* (as distinguished from being moved by forces impinging upon us), a consciousness most strongly felt as we make decisions among alternative possibilities and set objectives for ourselves; secondly (and more complexly), there is action with concern for moral values, norms, and rules (which are developed, more or less unconsciously, in every society to protect and strengthen the encompassing social fabric of interactions, customs, and institutions), without which neither individual nor collective action would be possible; thirdly, there are the highly reflective modes of consciousness ("ethics") and action that set themselves deliberately toward the careful scrutiny, assessment, and reconstruction of human action and its sociocultural context. (For a diagrammatic representation of these differing degrees and modes of consciousness and action, see Figure 3 in Chapter 13.) Moreover, each of these modalities (as we saw in Chapter 15) has its own characteristic forms of debility, failure, and corruption; and these all complexly intermix to produce highly convoluted patterns of evil in human society and culture, selfhood and consciousness—for all of which humans are (in varying ways and degrees) accountable. This schema of ever-widening degrees of consciousness of, and responsibility for, what action involves and requires—as well as what undercuts and eventually destroys this central feature of our historicity—suggests that what we call "moral evil" (that destructiveness of the human for which we humans ourselves are accountable) is an exceedingly complex matter. Let us see, now, what light the theocentric framework for understanding human existence (which we have been developing in Part IV) can throw on this.

All moral standards, values, norms, and practices have been, as we have repeatedly noted, humanly created through long and complicated histories. As such, they are in many ways confused, misguided, ineffective, weak, distorted, oppressive, corrupted—as well as life enhancing. Moral standards, thus, often tend to encourage and legitimate attitudes and practices which are actually destructive of women and men in many ways, constricting rather than enhancing their historicity. In short (as we noted in Chapter 15), our moral sensitivities and values, practices and institutions, are themselves (nearly always) morally evil in certain respects; and this deepens and complicates our problems immeasurably. If the very norms in terms of which we make our judgments about right and wrong, good and evil, cannot be trusted, if our consciences are themselves corrupt, we appear to be trapped in (evil) patterns of action and thinking from which there is no escape. Is there any way to address situations of this sort, or is this the point at which we must finally despair of human possibilities and seek rescue in some supernatural salvation? Christian speakers and writers have often claimed that it is precisely here, where moral law and moral consciousness show themselves unable to resolve our deepest human dilemmas and can even be seen to contribute to them, that the Gospel speaks a word about divine forgiveness and salvation from on high—and, *mirabile dictu,* we are saved!

This sort of short-circuit, however, is misleading, and it seriously obscures the significant illumination which theological symbols are capable of bringing to this situation. Though historically a direct move of this sort—from the impossible moral dilemmas of life to their religious interpretation and solution—has undoubtedly often been made, modern understandings of religious symbolism suggest that, if we are to discern correctly what is actually going on in the turn to religion, we must take into account something which this traditional view conceals. As we have seen, our religious symbolisms—quite as much as our moral and philosophical ideas—are themselves human creations. All of these are expressions of the human imagination attempting to develop wider frameworks within which human existence in the world can be more profoundly grasped and more adequately assessed (see Figure 3, Circle 4), thus facilitating better understanding of the increasingly complicated problems of human life, and providing orientation in face of those problems. These frameworks and perspectives are often used to justify or sanctify a society's practices and institutions, thus rendering them less open to change (even when such rigidity may be disastrous); but they also are able to move men and women beyond ordinary moral consciousness and practices to a more reflective and critical posture, and to forms of symbolism and practice which can sustain and support this.

Reflective consciousness of the sort I have in mind here arises out of dissatisfaction with the quality of human life as it is defined and informed by the accepted moral rules, by the understandings of virtue and vice and of various ideals and values, and by the regnant social patterns, institutions, and ideologies. Whatever might be the immediate occasion for the appearance of such dissatisfaction—some historical or natural catastrophe, the experience of oppression or injustice or other suffering, an unusual sensitivity to the social and moral evils roundabout (as with the prophets of ancient Israel), awareness of distinctly different forms of life to be found in neighboring cultures, or any number of other things—it gives rise to reflection about what is wrong with present practices and ways of thinking and what might be done about them. In this situation a mind with philosophical propensities may seek for criteria in terms of which current practices, institutions, and habits of mind can be assessed and judged; out of such reflection what we call "ethics" has developed, and along with it utopian visions of societies imagined as truly well-ordered are sometimes projected. A more religious consciousness may advocate and undertake certain special disciplines (prayer, fasting, pilgrimage, et cetera), and it may meditate on the meaning(s) of the deeper symbols known to it—the symbols in terms of which the women and men of its world have come to understand themselves, the universe in which they live, and the ultimate reality(s) or power(s) on which human being and well-being are believed to depend—searching for some salvation from the evils which have become so destructive. In either case the consequence may be a movement of the imagination sufficiently beyond the prevailing patterns of life and thought to provide a standpoint from which new possibilities can be envisioned and the old ways pertinently criticized. Thus the oppressiveness, corruption, and meaninglessness into which human sociocultural life so often falls do not necessarily bring humans into a cul-de-sac (as traditional Christian law/gospel dichotomies often too hastily suggested): if a truly reflective and imaginative consciousness emerges (whether "religious" or "ethical"), it may become possible for movements of moral or religious transformation, or even revolution, to get under way. When this happens, humans begin to assume responsibility for the moral evils in their world in a new double sense: (a) by acknowledging that it is humans themselves who have created these evils, and that they are not the irremediable outworking of some unalterable predestination or fate, written into the nature of things, which must simply be accepted; and (b) by beginning to address these evils through transforming the social, cultural, and personal orders within which they have appeared.

Even this highly critical, reflective, and imaginative consciousness, however—since it is but one more expression of human creativity (human historicity) with all its frailty, faults, and fallibility—can not effect a full escape from the morasses of evil which we humans create. Indeed (as we noted in Chapter 15), the movement to this wider circle of reflectiveness may itself further accentuate and deepen certain dimensions of the moral evils permeating human life. Instead of gaining new insight into the problems confronting them, men and women—whether members of sophisticated elite groups or of oppressed classes—may become even more blind to the evils roundabout them because of their growing "false consciousness" and their creation of "ideologies." Their corrupt constructs of ideas, values, and ideals prevent them from seeing what is really happening in their world (to themselves as well as to others) and what they themselves are doing, and also enable them to justify themselves and their practices, and to legitimate—as necessary and correct social arrangements and patterns of life—the evils in which they are involved. One thinks in this connection of the philosophical, religious, and supposedly scientific explanations and justifications—all of them products of highly reflective consciousness and creativity—that have been offered for slavery, poverty, disease, ignorance, class and caste structures, race and gender discrimination, wars, and on and on. The movement into reflective consciousness, though essential if women and men are to take full responsibility for the moral evil in which they are immersed, does not ensure that the deepest evils of human life will be addressed; it may actually help to draw both communities and individuals even deeper into the mire of self-destruction, making it more difficult to discern proper responsibilities and to address them.

A theocentric understanding of the human condition can significantly illuminate this profound ambiguity of human reflective consciousness. The symbol "God," of course (as we have seen), even though it both encourages our full humanization while simultaneously calling us into question, is itself susceptible to the serious sorts of abuse and corruption we have just been noting. When God is thought of essentially as the King of the Universe, as the very source of all right and good which in principle cannot be conceived ever to be in the wrong, there are no human norms or standards which can be invoked to assess or call into question what is believed to be God's will for a particular situation. What (by human standards) might be reckoned as intolerable injustice or cruelty may now seem to be what God requires; and any doubts we might have about this are credited to our lack of faith, our frailty, our sin. With such a "teleological suspension of the ethical" (Kierkegaard),[3] men and women may be led to carry out the worst imaginable atrocities, and to find acceptable the most dehumanizing sorts of social arrangements, because they believe these have been authorized—even commanded!—by God.[4] The important point for us to note here, however, is that these dangerous ambiguities in the symbol "God" have not gone unnoticed in the theological tradition; indeed, they have given rise to reflection that directly illumines all the highly dialectical forms of evil that seem to permeate human symbolization, understanding, and action of even the most conscientious and thoughtful sort. The notion of *sin* in particular, what we may call "theological evil," throws significant light on corrupted uses of the symbol "God" (as well as other high-level all-encompassing symbols, values, or meanings).

The concept of sin resembles the notion of natural evil in its focus on our relation to that which grounds human being and well-being; but its theocentric orientation gives it a distinctly different character. The anthropocentrism implicit in the idea of natural evil (as we have seen) leads to profound ambiguities in our understanding of, and attitudes toward, nature; however, when it becomes possible to orient human life on a center which transcends both us and nature—God—this anthropocentrism is overcome in a distinctive way: for our sinfulness (that is, the corruption, deterioration, malfunctioning of our relation to that ultimate mystery which grounds our being and well-being) is here taken to be something for which we humans are solely responsible (in this respect the concept of theological evil is more like that of moral evil). The symbol "God" was originally produced (I have suggested) in and through the need of human moral agency and consciousness (human historicity) to find an adequate religio-metaphysical grounding in terms of which to orient itself. With the generation of this symbol human consciousness was enabled to move to a new center that brought with it significant new possibilities, among them that of breaking loose from the anthropocentrism which had thus far dominated it. But precisely in this opening of a distinctly different orientation for human self-understanding and life, the symbol "God" simultaneously raises the specter (as we have just been noting) of even deeper layers of evil: it is with respect to the latter dialectical development that the concept of sin offers significant illumination.

In Genesis 3:4 the serpent uses the following words to tempt Eve with the fruit of the forbidden tree: "when you eat of [this fruit]," the serpent says, "your eyes will be opened, and you will be like God, knowing good and evil." The fall of humankind, that is to say, occurs when men and women come to suppose they know what only God can know, what is truly good and what is evil. This ancient story enshrines many profound insights. One of the most important is that the knowledge of good and evil belongs to God, not to us; that is, that the ultimate norms, values, and meanings of life always escape us, remaining a matter of profound mystery. To suppose that we know them is to *sin*—to fall away from God, the very ground of our humanity, thus falling away also from ourselves.

This story brings out one of the most important motifs implicit in the symbol "God." The idea of God carries with it very strong implications about our human finitude—particularly our limitations with regard to good and evil, what we should be and what we should do. To posit God, to believe in God, to commit ourselves to God, is to acknowledge that we are not absolute, not autonomous: we are finite, limited, subject to error, failure, self-delusion, corruption; and therefore our willing, our agency, our defining of what we should be and do, our ideas of right and wrong, must always be regarded as questionable. In this respect theocentric faith portrays the human condition quite differently than do most humanisms and naturalisms. For the latter, since humans are taken to be the only agents in the world, the only beings capable of making decisions and performing intentional acts, the grounding for the criteria which guide our decisions and purposes is necessarily located in our own human existence—our deep intuitions into and conceptions of good and evil, of right and wrong, and our reflection on such matters. As Protagoras put it, "Humans are the measure of all things": the world lies before us to dispose of as we please. Of course, not entirely as we please: it puts pressures upon us which we must recognize and respect. (Quite recently we have become aware that these include much more severe environmental constraints than had previously been supposed.) We dare not, then, simply follow every impulse and desire; we must act judiciously and prudently if we are to survive and to lead reasonably agreeable lives. But in all of this, it is we humans who determine the criteria which will govern our action, we who make the judgments about good and evil, right and wrong. We—our needs, our desires, our best wisdom, our deepest insights—provide the measure (for us) of all things.

The symbol "God," in sharp contrast to this human-centeredness to which we seem so naturally inclined, enables and requires us to put all this in question: there are standards of truth, of justice, of right and wrong which go beyond those known to us, standards to which our human criteria and judgments must themselves ultimately be conformed, standards before which we inevitably fall short—standards enshrouded within the ultimate mystery to which our word "God" points. To trust (or believe in) *God* is to place ourselves, finally, at the disposal of this all-encompassing mystery instead of relying with such assurance on our own sensitivities, ideas, and powers of reflection. That is, it is to hope and expect to be led or drawn *beyond* our own present insights to deeper, more profound understandings; and to recognize that to confuse our own ideas and insights with what is ultimately right and true is to fall into sin, to put ourselves in the place of God, to suppose that we "know good and evil."

The notion of God is one of the most complexly dialectical of all human ideas. On the one hand, it is clearly *our* idea: we humans created it; we shaped and refined it in the course of history; and we continue to criticize and reconstruct it in our prophetic visions and our theologies. On the other hand, this is the idea of that which is beyond the reach of our highest thought, our loftiest aspiration, our most profound insight, our deepest intuition; it is in fact a *limiting idea*, an idea which cannot be thought simply or directly but only indirectly as that which limits, relativizes, calls into question, all that we are and do, experience and think. In the traditional mythology this dimension of the notion of God was expressed in the image of God as *judge*—the judge of all the earth, who, at the "last judgment," would make the final discrimination between good and evil, right and wrong, the wheat and the chaff, the sheep and the goats. This image, of course, had its place within the wider context provided by the defining conception of God as creator/lord/father—God seen as source of the world and source of all creativity in the world, One always working to transform the world into fuller realization of the divine purposes, One therefore ever leading and drawing women and men to new levels of insight, deeper levels of understanding, better ways of living.

It is important that we recognize that in both its anthropomorphic dualistic form and in our biohistorical version, the symbol "God"—though referring us to that beyond all our human conceptions, and thus ultimate mystery—nevertheless remains one of our conceptions. When this symbol functions properly (and we sense the profound dialectic which it expresses) it induces within us a deep humility: for it continuously reminds us that we must *call into question* all our own actions, decisions, judgments, standards, criteria. We must acknowledge the possibility, even the likelihood, that we are mistaken, in the wrong; and we must repent, thereby opening ourselves to other ways of thinking and acting, and opening ourselves to those others expressing alternative perspectives and modes of life—even those who differ sharply with our views, our values, our judgments; indeed even our "enemies" (Mt. 5:43–48; Lk. 6:27–36). God is the God of all creation, One who is working in and through all creatures along trajectories the ultimate destination of which is beyond our discernment. And we dare never confuse our own finite, limited, relative objectives, values, and insights with the directions in which God is moving or with God's activities. We must do and be, of course, whatever we must do and be, striving for the right as best we can—but always qualifying our tendencies to absolutize our selves and our values and our projects, no matter how important or right they may seem to us, in our consciousness that we are, after all, not "like God, knowing good and evil" in any absolute or final sense.

When the idea of God functions in this way, tempering and moderating our self-understandings, our objectives, and our ways of acting, while simultaneously holding out to us the hope for continuing growth in insight, it relativizes radically our own moral and ethical understanding (and the self-righteousness often accompanying this); thus it can help to reduce the tensions and strife in the web of action within which we live by opening our eyes to the meaning and importance of positions taken and actions performed by those opposing us. That is, it facilitates our looking beyond our limited landscape to wider movements and goals of concern to humanity as a whole, even to all creation (so far as that is known to us). And we begin, thus, to become devoted not simply to this or that particular cause or being, limited and relative as it is, but to (in the words of Jonathan Edwards) "being in general":[5] the tendency (largely remaining implicit in the biohistorical morality and ethics sketched in Chapters 13 and 14) to move toward the widest, most comprehensive possible ecology now comes to have an explicit symbolic focus. In this way, the image/concept of God serves not only as a symbol referring us to the ontological grounding of our historicity: it becomes in addition an effective force working to overcome and redeem the evil in human affairs—the evils of narrow-mindedness, self-centeredness, ethnocentrism, anthropocentrism, idolatry. When this power inherent in the image/concept "God" is apprehended with faith in the "forgiveness and love" of God—that is, living trust in those cosmic and historical powers believed to be moving toward a more humane and ecologically responsible order—this symbol itself becomes a significant historical force pressing toward our further humanization, encouraging the establishment and strengthening of communities of love and peace and justice in an ecologically sustainable world.

All this is lost, however, even reversed, if the highly dialectical character of the notion of God is not sensed or is forgotten. For the idea of God always does remain, after all, *our* idea: we have created it, we criticize and transform it, we know what it is and means. And so we may—especially if we are among those with explicitly "religious" commitments—easily come to suppose "God's truth" to be a particular content that *we know* instead of a symbol to remind us that we do not in fact possess ultimate truth; and we may take "God's righteous will" to have commanded that we do this or that particular thing, or to be an explanation of this or that particular event or social practice or institution, rather than a symbol intended to remind us that there is a "will" and a "righteousness" (a cosmic trajectory of which we are part) which stands over and above our every judgment and act, calling them into question, showing their limitations and relativity—and thus drawing us beyond what we have come to take for granted. When these things happen the idea of God has become the vehicle of our own particular human interests—our American interests in a crusade against communism; the interests of our church in speaking with authority on such matters as pacifism or revolution, abortion or liberation; the interests of our class, or race, or gender; and so on—and we have fallen from moral evil into *sin,* into theological evil, supposing we are "like God, knowing good and evil." In this sort of move we are well on the way to what is called in the New Testament the sin against the Holy Spirit, that sin for which there is said to be no forgiveness (Mk. 3:28–29)—that is, the sin with respect to which the symbol "God" no longer has significant redemptive effect.[6]

What was called in our religious traditions "God's forgiveness" is the breaking open of the traps of self-righteousness, anxiety, and guilt, of social oppression and the exploitation of others, into which our human failures so often bring us, by the recognition or awareness that even in its most irresponsible and destructive features our humanly constructed world is not, after all, final and irrevocable. "God's forgiveness" means that there are always countervailing forces in history and the world working toward humanization, the building of community, the fructification of freedom and historicity, the overcoming of our human-centeredness. (The advent of the nuclear age, however, raises the question whether now there may not be another sort of sin for which there is no forgiveness.) We are not, then, irremediably caught up in unbreakable webs of anxiety, guilt, and sin: as long as we live, possibilities of beginning to act again with some measure of freedom and creativity continue to open before us. Though we may be unaware of the particular countervailing forces bringing this about, the biohistorical trajectory which has brought us into being continues to move toward a balanced ecological order among all creatures—an order which on the human level is expressed in the hope and striving for communities of peace, justice, and well-being for all.

In speaking of sin, of the depths of evil into which human historicity can all too easily degenerate, I have been describing the opposite of faith. For faith is simply the acknowledgment of God as *God,* the acknowledgment that we "are not [our] own" (1 Cor. 6:19). Even in our agency, our taking responsibility for ourselves, we are both energized by and acting in response to that cosmic biohistorical reality that evokes agency, freedom, and love from us, that reality which is thus our creator and redeemer, the source and perfecter of our humanity. Faith is the centering of our lives, our selves, our actions in this God. The emergence of humanity from animality would not have been possible without the development of centered selves and communities, selves and communities able to act. A great danger of such centered communities and selves, of course, is that they all too easily become self-centered and ethnocentric: that they act for their own aggrandizement, their own increase of power and freedom at the expense of other creatures, thus setting up tensions which threaten to destroy the web of life and action. According to a theocentric understanding of life and the world, for communities and selves to become truly free and loving they must find a center of devotion outside themselves, the center of a circle which is comprehensive enough, universal enough, to include not only all humans, or all living beings, but all that is. It is toward such a universal center that the symbol "God" is intended to point us. Faith in God, thus—the displacement of every anthropocentrism, the opposite of sin—is the orientation in and through which persons and communities can come to their true realization, their full historicity. For it is that faith which orients men and women within the universal community which is inclusive of all being, the universal ecological order created, sustained, and moved onward into the future by the action and love of God.

In this analysis I have emphasized two principal sorts of evil, moral and theological, both of them embedded in the complex webs of culture and life which human creativity, action, and reflection have helped shape. We humans clearly are responsible for both these types of evil; and only as we take up this responsibility will we be able to begin addressing these evils effectively. (The idea of natural evil, with all its inherent ambiguities and confusions, now no longer seems particularly helpful; the issues it is intended to address—problems arising from the complexities of our relationship to that which grounds our being and well-being—are treated more subtly through our de-anthropomorphized conception of God, on the one hand, and through our concept of theological evil, with its illumination of the depths of our anthropo-, ethno- and egocentrisms, on the other.) Our notion of the widening circles of agential consciousness enables us to discern some outlines of the webs of moral evil within which we daily live; and the concept of theological evil (sin) gives new depth to our understanding both of the evils for which we humans are responsible and of the ways in which we corrupt and subvert our own attempts to attack these evils. The several types of moral evil all remain in place in our theological framework, but now they acquire the deeper meaning carried by the concept of *sin:* they have set up trajectories which disrupt the wider ecological order as well as human life, thus becoming destructive of life at large and, indeed, of the very order of creation; and many of our efforts—themselves corrupted—to address these problems only succeed in complicating matters further. Defined as it is with reference to the ultimate mystery of life, the notion of sin thus opens a perspective which both can sensitize us to the subtlest, and most profound, forms of human self-deception, corruption, and destructiveness (even those based on misuse of the symbol "God") and can bring clearly into view the larger meaning of our human disruption and destruction of the ecosystem which environs us—the most disordering aspect of the evils for which we humans are responsible. Our awakening sense of the ecological destruction we humans are working in the world—an evil the full horror of which is most powerfully symbolized by the image of catastrophic nuclear war—provides a new context for grasping the significance of what it means to sin against God and God's activity.

Throughout the preceding chapters I interpreted the wider context within which human existence falls almost entirely in terms of the forward movement of the evolutionary-historical trajectory which has brought human life into being, which continues to sustain it, and which is drawing us on toward a richer and fuller humanization. We can now see that that picture was much too simplistic: our lives are in fact colored and warped, pushed and pulled in many directions by the patterns and momentums of sin and evil in the midst of which we are born and within which we daily live and work. Our personal and social practices, our ways of thinking and acting, our customs and institutions, our values and ideals—indeed, our very selves—are all permeated to deep levels by these anti-divine forces of corrosion and corruption and destruction. So we are far from riding on a straight-line trajectory toward more humane and well-ordered patterns of human existence: we live, rather, in the midst of tensions and powers pushing and pulling us in very diverse directions. Many of these are momentums of destructiveness, of evil and sin; some, however, offer us hopes that a better future for human beings, on a better-ordered earth, may still be possible—if we, and others, give ourselves and our lives over to what they demand of us. Faith in God, we can now see, is no matter of simple belief in some overarching trajectory carrying us forward willy-nilly toward a wonderful new order of human fulfillment and meaning. It consists, rather, in (a) our discernment that there are in our world some movements and momentums toward a more humane and ecologically sustainable order of life for women and men, (b) our living in the hope that these are the visible evidences of a deeply grounded trajectory along which human history is moving and may continue to move, and (c) our committing ourselves and our lives without reservation to this hope and the possibilities it opens up for us and the rest of life on earth. And it requires that we do all we can to help break the power of those momentums of evil which corrupt our common life, our selves, and our world. Faith, thus, is essentially an ongoing struggle with the sin and evil in ourselves and our world, as we give ourselves over as fully as we can to that trajectory—however dimly discerned—which beckons us toward a more humane society in a well-ordered world.

25. A Wider Christology

The conception of God which I have been sketching in this book maintains continuity with the creator/lord/father imagery of the Christian tradition, but with the insistence that it be de-reified. This we attempted to accomplish (a) through emphasizing that the underlying meaning of these images for our understanding of God can be captured in the twin motifs of humanization and relativization, and (b) through proposing certain other quite different sorts of images and concepts as important additions to and correctives of the traditional symbolism. Thus we constructed an image/concept of God which can serve as a unifying focus for contemporary life. It is a focus which can assist us today in attending to, and orienting ourselves with reference to, that serendipitous creativity manifest in and through all that is; more particularly, it focuses us on that creativity as it expresses itself in and through the evolutionary-historical trajectory that has produced us men and women, with our longing and struggling for truly humane forms of life—what was spoken of in our religious traditions as the coming of the kingdom of God, where all women and men shall "sit under their vines and their fig trees, and no one shall make them afraid" (Micah 4:4, paraphrased).

To assent to this analysis and interpretation, which connects the symbol "God" with the serendipitous evolutionary-historical movement that has produced human existence and is now drawing us toward making it more truly humane, was, I suggested, to take a fifth step of faith—a step in which the process of theological construction which we have been following at last breaks through into faith in God. I have given some reasons why I think this is a significant and important step to take. To some (I hope) they have been persuasive; to others they will not have been. The movement of theological construction through several steps of faith is always free, never logically or otherwise coercive (as I have said from the beginning); and in our work here it will remain free to the end.

We are now in a position to consider a sixth step of faith (our last): whether to introduce the symbol "Christ" as a major interpretive category into our theistic world-picture. I have suggested that Christian perspectives on life and the world are defined and structured by their employment of four major categories: God/world/humanity/Christ. We have examined closely only the first three of these thus far, and we must ask ourselves now, Does the category of Christ add anything truly fundamental to the world-picture we have been sketching? or is its contribution to be regarded as secondary and derivative, and thus not properly *categorial* in status? In traditional Christian faith and theology "Christ" is said to be of absolutely decisive significance for understanding both who or what God is and what human life is all about. It is asserted that Jesus Christ is at once the definitive revelation of God (the very "image of the invisible God," Col. 1:15) and also the normative or perfect human (one "made like his brethren in every respect, . . . tempted as we are, yet without sinning," Hebr. 2:17, 4:15). This double significance of Christ was given dogmatic definition in the formula of Chalcedon (451), where he is said to be "perfect in Godhead . . . [and] perfect in humanness, truly God and truly human, . . . consubstantial with the Father in Godhead, and . . . consubstantial with us in humanness, . . . two natures . . . in one Person."[1] The question now is: What can we make of this double-sided claim today? Does it have important bearing on the theocentric world-picture we have been working out? Should Christ still be viewed as in some way providing the definitive revelation of God and the normative image of the human? I think it may be possible to give an affirmative answer to these questions; we shall take them up as we explore now a sixth step of faith.

The symbol "God" refers to the ultimate reality with which we humans have to do; today, I have argued, this should be understood as that cosmic serendipitous creativity which manifests itself in the evolutionary-historical trajectory that has brought humanity into being and continues to sustain it in being. In this conception, although the actual relationship between God and humanity is clearly asymmetrical, our *concepts* of humanity and of God are logically linked with each other: our idea of God includes within itself implicit reference to the human, and our understanding of humanity influences our notion of God. If we frame our thinking and speaking of the ultimate in terms of *God,* we will be affirming not only that the universe in which we live has room for such beings as persons and communities, and for such values as truth and creativity, beauty and excellence, justice and freedom, love and friendship; but that these matters of profound human concern have an ultimate metaphysical grounding and significance. I have acknowledged that this is not the only possible way to see the world and humanity-in-the-world, but it is a plausible way. When we invoke the name of God (instead of, for example, matter, or power, or emptiness, or Brahman), we affirm an intimate interconnection between what we take to be ultimate and our deepest human concerns.

To see our conceptions of God and the human as significantly interconnected in this way is to take up a proto-Christian stance. For central to Christian faith has been the claim that at one particular point in human history (in connection with the man Jesus) we are given a paradigm for understanding both what God is and what the human is. I want now to examine this christological claim, to see in what ways it might illumine, amplify, and qualify the general position on God, humanity, and the world which we have been constructing. As I suggested earlier (in Chapter 7), introducing the term "Christ" does not require us to think in terms of a fourth principal "being" or "reality" to be added to the three which provide the basic framework of a monotheistic world-picture; rather, it demands that we radically qualify, even redefine, these three—particularly our understandings of God and of the human. What does this mean for our project?

In making this move, it is important to acknowledge immediately, we are taking up issues of interest and concern particularly to *Christian* faith; that is, a further step of faith is involved here. There is no obvious or *prima facie* reason why, if we are seeking to understand God, humanity, and the world, we should move now to a consideration of Jesus and the early Christian movement rather than, for example, to Socrates or Buddha or Gandhi; to Napoleon, Einstein, Beethoven, or F.D.R.; to the Communist Party or the Hare Krishna movement or the Society of Free Thinkers; or to any other of a thousand possible figures or groups; or to none of these. The movement to Jesus and the early church arises out of specifically Christian claims and Christian interests; and it is only because we already stand (in some sense) within the wider reaches of Christian faith—or at least within hearing of the Christian proclamation—that we might be inclined to explore this question at all. Of course, everyone who has grown up in western culture is in certain respects within hearing of the Christian proclamation. (This is true of many in other cultures as well.) For in western literature, music, and art there are many allusions and references to the Christ-figure; Christmas and Easter are major holidays known to everyone; Christian values are frequently expressed and reflected on and criticized; and the Christian churches are still prominent institutions in society. Moreover, all western thinking about God is permeated by Judeo-Christian motifs. Even those strongly opposed to Christian views cannot avoid understanding themselves in terms of them: as Paul Tillich, for example, pointed out, Nietzsche's "Anti-Christ" is defined and intelligible only with reference to the Christ against which it is posited.[2] What I want to do at this point is bring to the forefront of our consciousness this background melody that weaves in and out of all western culture, seeking to see its relation to the schema of humanity/world/God which we have been developing. To facilitate this I shall (1) discuss some of the terms and concepts within which traditional christological reflection was framed, and (2) show how these notions both relate to, and yet have importantly different implications from, the position we have thus far developed.

The Christian doctrine of the incarnation, together with the notion of salvation-history, can provide a point of entry for our reflections. I wish to present an interpretation of these notions which will help to illuminate, and will further deepen, our theocentric world-picture. To that end we shall explore the respects in which it might be intelligible and fruitful to think of God as in a special and unique sense *present* ("incarnate" or embodied) in the events surrounding and including Jesus of Nazareth. I put the matter this way, referring to the events "surrounding and including" Jesus, in order to distinguish the christological position that I shall develop from the talk, often found in the tradition, of God being simply and straightforwardly *in Jesus* (or *one with Jesus*). Christians have typically thought of God as incarnate exclusively in the man Jesus; and the man Jesus is, therefore, sometimes spoken of as the "God-man," as having "two natures" (a "divine" and a "human"), and the like. As a result, traditional christological reflection has been focused on such questions as: How can we think of this particular human being as divine? In what sense is Jesus the unique "son of God"? What are we to make of the claim that Jesus came back to life after his death, and is now "sitting at the right hand" of God the Father almighty? How can this man who died on a cross be thought of as the "head" of the church in which (nearly) all Christians have participated in the past two thousand years? And so on. These are quite peculiar claims, scarcely thinkable of a human being. I would like to point out here some aspects of what the Christian community seems to be saying (or implying) with some of this language.

Christian faith has been characterized from its beginnings by a deep ambivalence symbolized by the cross of Jesus, on the one hand, and by Jesus' resurrection, on the other.[3] The cross, standing as it does for Jesus' suffering, self-sacrifice, death, meant that for Christianity suffering would be seen as of central importance to human life, indeed as the very vehicle of human salvation. As Isaiah 53, which was appropriated early by Christians to interpret the meaning of Jesus' crucifixion, put it: "he was wounded for our transgressions, he was bruised for our iniquities; upon him was the chastisement that made us whole, and with his stripes we are healed" (53:5). Enormous human suffering, thus, even if brought on by crimes for which humans are clearly responsible, like torture and murder, is not simply evil: it may become, vicariously, an instrument of the redemption and transformation of others. The powerful Christian incentives toward self-giving, toward service of the weak, the poor, the unfortunate, toward self-sacrifice for others' well-being, which have always been central to the Christian ethic, are all rooted in this motif—symbolized by the cross—of the value and meaning of suffering for others. And the characteristic heroic figures of Christian history have not been those who exercised the magnificence of worldly power, but those, like Francis of Assisi or John Woolman or Mother Teresa, whose lives showed forth the virtues of patience, humility, kindness, and long-suffering; or those, like Albert Schweitzer or Martin Luther King, who gave up much, perhaps even their lives, in the service of others.

But Christian faith has not been focused simply on self-giving, as exemplified above all in Jesus' crucifixion. It has always had a strong motif of triumphalism also, and this was symbolized above all by the resurrection of Jesus. As the traditional story portrays it, Jesus' sacrifice was not for nothing: in the end he was exalted to the right hand of God the Father. And the sacrifices and self-giving of the faithful in this world will not be for nothing either: in the end they will receive their heavenly reward, the gift of eternal life in God's everlasting kingdom. When this prospect of eternal blessedness is coupled (as it often has been) with the expectation that some sort of everlasting torment in hell will be the ultimate fate of those who ignore or go counter to Christian teaching and practice, it clearly becomes a matter of simple self-interest to follow the Christian way in this world; for any cost or unhappiness one may experience in this life will be amply recompensed in the next. Thus, what at first seemed (in the traditional Christian symbolism) to be a motif of absolute self-sacrifice for others turns out on closer inspection to be, all too often, merely an expression of prudence—given the sort of cosmic order in which we are said to live, an order ruled by a divine king and judge who will mete out eternal rewards and punishments at the end of life or the end of time.

This reading of the Christian symbolism of death and resurrection, though somewhat crass, is far from unwarranted: it is directly rooted in the early Christian proclamation of the meaning of Jesus' crucifixion and what was called his resurrection. Paul expresses the ambivalence well in a familiar passage in Philippians 2. After reminding us that Jesus, though "in the form of God," took upon himself the "form of a servant" and then humbled himself even further to suffer death on a cross (2:6–8), Paul proudly declares that just because of this self-giving and self-humbling "God has highly exalted him," giving him a "name which is above every name, [so] that at the name of Jesus every knee should bow, in heaven and on earth and under the earth, and every tongue confess that Jesus Christ is Lord, to the glory of God the Father" (2:9–11).

Such use of the symbolism of cross and resurrection not only drew the sting from the Christian motif of absolute self-sacrifice by transforming it into ultimate prudence and self-aggrandizement; it also laid the foundations for later Christian imperialism. It meant, as Christians came to believe from near the beginning, that Jesus was really the only one through whom God's grace and salvation were mediated to men and women: "there is salvation in no one else," as Peter put it according to a speech reported in Acts, "for there is no other name under heaven given among men by which we must be saved" (4:12). The true way of salvation for all humanity, then, was known only to the followers of Jesus. Symbols and doctrines were soon developed to express this unique significance of Jesus, interpreting him not simply as God's messiah but as God's unique son, the Logos of God, the second person of the divine trinity; and in due course these increasingly exalted christological conceptions were reified and absolutized. This had important consequences for the meaning of Christian faith and the life of the Christian community; for it seemed to imply that the keys to all human fulfillment and salvation had been placed exclusively in the hands of the church (cf. Mt. 16:18–19). It is hardly surprising that with this sort of exalted self-interpretation the church would eventually become corrupted into crusades against the infidels and inquisitorial tortures and executions of heretics; and that it would ultimately give its blessing to western imperialism, and to the exploitation and enslavement of non-Christian peoples and cultures around the globe. The central christological symbols that emerged in the primitive church have been used, and are still being used, to authorize evils of this sort. It is important that we see that Christian symbolism must bear some responsibility for this fact.

I want now, however, to point out that this highly problematic character of these traditional christological symbols is not directly rooted in the story of Jesus itself (though that may raise problems of its own); it derives, rather, from the overarching symbolical frame within which and in terms of which that story was interpreted. Thinking of the ultimate context of human life (including the Jesus-story) in terms of the symbolism of God as creator/lord/father (the traditional conception of God which we have been examining) was what made possible, perhaps inevitable, the development of this triumphalistic christology. This suggests, however, that if we reconceive God along the lines I have proposed in this book, a thorough reconstruction of the understanding of Christ may also be necessitated. I shall attempt to show that such a new understanding will significantly affect our interpretation of God and of humanity, and will throw a distinctive light on some of the major problems we today face.

As we have seen, in the faith of Israel which provided the background and context within which the early Christian movement arose, God was conceived largely in terms of quasi-personal images, and the world was a quasi-political order in and through which the divine creator-king was working out "his" purposes through history; it was expected that history would reach its consummation as those purposes were realized. Within this faith-world Jesus appeared, preaching that this long-expected end of history was now at hand; and Jesus' followers thought of him as the Messiah who was going to inaugurate the divine kingdom on earth. After his unexpected death, they came to believe that he would soon return with heavenly hosts to overthrow all the evil powers resisting the divine will and would establish a new age of perfect peace and happiness. But none of this occurred in the way expected; and in due course Christians came to think of Jesus as God's unique son, enthroned at the right hand of God the father, ruling the world from on high. The faithful, after death, would join him there in his heavenly kingdom.

The point I want to make here is that this overall interpretation is largely a further development of the inherited dualistic imagery in which the universe is depicted as a political order ruled from on high by a divine king. As we have seen, within this world-picture human life is understood in terms of such metaphors as loyalty toward, trust in, and love for the king and the order he has established (or is establishing). In various ways, the early Christians claimed, fellowship between the king and his subjects on earth has become disrupted and corrupted, but because of the sacrifice now of the king's son, the divine order is being reestablished and it is possible once again to live in faithful communion with the lord of the universe. One need only enter into the community of those who acknowledge Jesus as Lord, accepting this overall picture of the world and the human place within it—that is, one need only become a faithful member of the church—to find salvation from the evils of a world gone astray and a new life in communion with Christ, and through Christ with God. On this interpretation the meaning of Jesus' ministry, suffering, and death (the historical core of the christology which became dominant in the church) is to be found in the role that these play in this grand drama of the salvation of humankind, which the creator-king is bringing about from on high.

It is not difficult to see how and why those committed to this picture often became chauvinistic and imperialistic champions of the divine king and his son Jesus Christ, willing to fight to the death their adversaries here on earth. With this mythicizing of the Jesus-story, it became easy to lose sight of what (to us) must seem to be the most obvious import of his suffering and death: they showed the real weakness of Jesus in this world, on the one hand, a weakness rooted in his unwillingness to use the means and methods of compulsive power to achieve his objectives; and, on the other, his great inner strength, sufficient to enable him to sacrifice himself even to his enemies. And the crucifixion came to be seen instead as but one phase of the powerful working of salvation by God from on high; it was a phase, moreover, which was almost immediately superseded and replaced by Jesus' triumphal resurrection. In and through the crucifixion/resurrection all evil powers on earth and under the earth—including even physical death—were being decisively overcome by the divine omnipotence.

The Christian tradition presents us, thus, with a deeply ambiguous christology. On the one side there is the picture of Jesus giving himself to others in service and healing, preaching and teaching that women and men should love and respect even their enemies, should do good to those who curse them, should become servants of all; and finally coming to a climax in the suffering and complete sacrifice of himself in crucifixion. On the other side there is the picture of Jesus the Christ, sitting at the right hand of God the Father almighty, moving history with omnipotent power toward its divinely set consummation, a consummation which will include glorification and heavenly reward for all the Christian faithful. With such sharply distinct—even contradictory—motifs bound together in the church's christological symbolism, it is not difficult to understand why Christian history has spawned such diverse and inconsistent emphases and movements and institutional patterns, each attempting in its own way to hold together in a dialectical vision these tensions and contradictions. It is not difficult to understand either—human nature being what it is—why in most Christian movements most of the time the triumphalistic motif, with its promise of heavenly (or even earthly) reward, became the dominant one, the motif of service and self-sacrifice sometimes being almost lost to sight. With such ambiguous symbolism at the heart of Christian faith, quite diverse interpretations could each be given a certain plausibility; and almost any kind of institutional structure, social practice, or political program could be provided with religious legitimation. The possibilities for corrupt and dehumanizing uses of Christian symbols were always present—and they have often, unfortunately, found expression. Yet at the same time this highly tensive christological core of Christian faith has been a seedbed nurturing deeper awareness of and appreciation for the dignity and meaning of human persons: it has instilled in many believers revulsion against injustice and other forms of inhumanity and inspired creative movements toward more humane social institutions and practices.

The traditional christology was, thus, an amalgam in which the tragic story of Jesus' ministry and death was interpreted in terms of, and thus combined with, the conception of God known to the earliest believers: God the all-powerful creator/lord/father of humankind and the world. A contemporary christology will also be an amalgam, but of a different sort. It will similarly require examination and appropriation of the story of Jesus, but this time the latter will be combined with a contemporary understanding of God—in our case, the understanding of God in terms of the serendipitous creativity working through the evolutionary-historical process. If the story of Jesus, when so interpreted, provides significant insight into and orientation for today's human life and problems, christology can and should continue to have an important place in our theological reflection and our religious devotion; if not, it should be allowed to fall away so that we can come to terms with the issues with which the world today actually confronts us.

Historians are agreed that we possess little reliable information about the man Jesus of Nazareth. He was apparently an itinerant preacher and healer in first-century Palestine who believed that the kingdom of God was beginning to break into human history, bringing history to its end; his own healings of suffering and sickness, and his forgiveness of sins, were dramatic signs of the kingdom's coming. In his teaching Jesus emphasized the importance both of love to God and love to one's neighbors, and he gave this twofold love a very radical meaning: it requires, for instance, repeatedly forgiving the offenses of others against us (we should forgive another "seventy times seven," he told Peter, according to Matthew 18:22), going out of our way to help suffering fellow humans (as the story of "the good Samaritan" suggests, Luke 10:29–37), always turning "the other cheek" and going "the second mile" (Mt. 5:39, 41), and all of this not only with friends but with enemies as well (Mt. 5:43–47). Jesus did not expect the wealthy and the powerful to respond to his call: "It is easier for a camel to go through the eye of a needle," he said, "than for a rich man to enter the Kingdom of God" (Mk. 10:25); and he did not hesitate to bless the poor, "for yours is the Kingdom of God" (Lk. 6:20), and to call down woes on the rich and powerful and self-satisfied (Lk. 6:24–26; Mt. 23:13–38). The life to which Jesus called his followers involved a reversal of ordinary political and social standards, where power over others is reckoned as signifying one's importance and serving others is regarded as demeaning: "whoever would be great among you must be your servant," he said, and "whoever would be first among you must be slave of all" (Mk. 10:43–44). This radicalization of moral demands by Jesus, and this reversing of ordinary standards of significance or greatness, was brought into sharp and unforgettable focus by the final events of his life: he refused to defend or protect himself against his enemies, accepting meekly their whips and curses and finally suffering a violent death at their hands. Since the cross epitomized so well all that Jesus did and taught and stood for, it very early became a major symbol for Christian faith, signifying self-giving, suffering, and ultimate sacrifice for others.

This sums up what we know of Jesus. What should we make of this today? That is, does this story of Jesus bear in some important way on our understanding of God and of the human? Let us look briefly at some New Testament texts which speak of Christ and of salvation. We shall find a more complex situation than is often supposed: these texts do not in fact refer exclusively to the man Jesus of Nazareth.[4] Sometimes "Christ" signifies

Jesus—especially in the phrases "Jesus Christ" or "Christ Jesus"—but at other times it can be better understood if we take it as signifying the whole complex web of saving and revelatory events within which early Christians found themselves; for it was in and through this whole complex of events (not the man Jesus alone) that they had come to realize their new relation to God. Consider, for example, the familiar affirmation in 2 Corinthians 5:17: "if any one is in Christ, he is a new creation." Clearly, the writer here is not speaking simply of the man Jesus of Nazareth, an ordinary flesh-and-blood human being: What could it mean to speak of being "in" the man Jesus? Something else must be intended. The transformation and recreation of which Paul speaks here had been brought about in and through complex sets of interpersonal relationships—doubtless in significant ways connected with the man Jesus, but certainly not confined to him. It would seem appropriate, then, to view this whole complex transformative reality within which believers knew themselves to be living—including especially the Christian community, where the gospel of God's forgiving love was heard and was participated in sacramentally through the powerfully salvific bread and wine—as that with which the term "Christ" here should be connected. This interpretation fits well with what follows in Paul's text. It would hardly be intelligible to hold that when he goes on to say, "In Christ God was reconciling the world to himself" (2 Cor. 5:19n), he means that the relationship of the entire world to God had somehow changed "in" the man from Nazareth. How, then, should we interpret this statement? It appears, once again, that we must look to this complex of events and new relationships that grew up in and around this man, if we are to understand what it might mean to affirm that God was acting transformatively. In general, thus, in passages like this "Christ" seems to signify the new order of relationships among humans and between humans and God which began to come into being in connection with Jesus and developed further after his death and resurrection. When Paul says in Galatians that "There is neither Jew nor Greek, there is neither slave nor free, there is neither male nor female; for you are all one in Christ Jesus" (3:28), he surely does not mean that all Christians are somehow one in the man Jesus of Nazareth. He means rather, I suggest, that within the new order of relationships with God and with each other initiated through the ministry and death of the man Jesus, they have all become intimately bound together. To say God is incarnate in Christ, then, is not to say simply and directly that God is incarnate in Jesus; rather, God is incarnate in that larger, more complex human reality, surrounding and including and following upon the man Jesus: the new Christian community, with its spirit of love and freedom, of mutual sharing and forgiveness of one another. It is in this new order of interpersonal relationships that the incarnation of God is to be found.

We cannot pursue this wider interpretation of Christ through the entire

New Testament (and I am not competent to do so), but I think we would find that it is applicable to and illuminating of a number of obscure passages. Thus, when the writer to the Colossians speaks of God delivering us "from the dominion of darkness" and transferring us to "the kingdom of his beloved Son" (1:13), he is pointing us to this new order of relationships into which God has brought believers, not to some arcane kingdom of the man Jesus. And when he goes on to say that this "Son" (Christ) is the "image of the invisible God, the first-born of all creation . . . [in whom] all things were created, in heaven and on earth, visible and invisible" (1:15–16), he does not seem to be characterizing the man Jesus so much as suggesting that what is incarnate in Christ is nothing less than the divine creativity itself; that is, what is to be seen in the new pattern of personal/social relationships surrounding and including the man Jesus is the image (or picture or expression) of what we have spoken of as the mysterious serendipitous creativity at work throughout the world. To take one more familiar text: in the prologue to the Fourth Gospel we are told that the creative power of God (here called the "Logos") "became flesh" in Jesus (1:14); but it is clear that John does not consider this creative power to be limited to what this man from Nazareth did or could do: he is speaking here, rather, of that through which "all things were made" (1:3). Later on, when John employs the image of the vine giving life to its branches, he hardly intends us to think that if we "abide" (15:4–10) in the man Jesus we will be in proper relationship to God and therefore "bear much fruit"; that would be scarcely intelligible. But we can understand perfectly well what is being said here if we interpret it as meaning that we must abide in the new interpersonal reality that came into being in connection with the man Jesus, the new spirit expressed in his action and teachings and now incarnated in the communities of his followers.

I do not deny that many texts in the New Testament suggest that the name "Christ" is virtually interchangeable with "Jesus"; and this view has certainly been dominant in most of Christian history: the "incarnation" of God has been understood almost always as referring exclusively to God's unique presence in the divine man Jesus. Legends like the "virgin birth" narratives in Matthew and Luke have encouraged this notion. These stories present an especially literalistic and crude interpretation of the incarnation, suggesting that it had a temporal beginning with the direct impregnation of the mother of Jesus by the Holy Spirit from on high (Mt. 1:18; Lk. 1:35): thus, like a Greek demigod, Jesus was born of a human mother and a divine father. Here the incarnation of God is identified decisively and completely with the individual man Jesus. This interpretation appears further confirmed in texts like John 1:14–18, and in John 3:16 Jesus is directly identified as God's "only begotten Son" (KJV). Moreover, the early creeds also make this point; and at Chalcedon in 451 these mythopoetic expressions were finally all reified into metaphysical fact, with the resultant dogma binding on all Christians: Jesus, though one person, actually had two natures, a divine and a human; he possessed perfect and full deity as well as perfect and full humanity. Thus, the crucified man from Nazareth was one and the same person as the divine Lord Jesus Christ, the central focus of Christian worship, loyalty, and discipleship.

It should be noted, however, that this did not mean that Jesus the man *is* God *simpliciter,* without qualification. It was well known that according to the New Testament Jesus clearly distinguished himself from God: he prayed to God; he looked forward to the coming of God's kingdom, of which, he said, "no one knows [the day], not even the angels in heaven, nor the Son, but only the Father" (Mk. 13:32); when someone addressed him as "Good Teacher," he rejected the title with the words, "Why do you call me good? No one is good but God alone" (Mk. 10:17–18). In the New Testament Jesus is obviously not identified in any simple way with God the Father in heaven, the all-powerful creator of the heavens and the earth; he is portrayed as one man among others, living under and serving the Lord of the world. And yet it is clear that God is regarded as present in Jesus and Jesus' activities in some unique sense not true of any other creature. How is this very subtle distinction from God yet oneness with God to be understood? The formulation finally officially adopted by the church, and subsequently regarded as binding on Christians, was highly paradoxical: Jesus Christ was declared to be

> in two natures without confusion, without change, without division, without separation—the difference of the natures being by no means taken away because of the union, but rather the distinctive character of each nature being preserved, and [each] combining in one Person and *hypostasis*—not divided or separated into two Persons, but one and the same Son and only-begotten God, Word, Lord Jesus Christ.[5]

Christians have taken it to be quite proper, then, to worship God in Jesus; and one could worship Jesus himself without falling into idolatry. And yet God the Father is not to be simply and straightforwardly identified with Jesus, for "He" is the transcendent Lord of the world under whom Jesus also lived and died.

Much christological reflection has been occupied with trying to explain the sense in which Jesus is to be thought of as identical with God, and the sense in which he is distinct. I suggest that this essentially insoluble problem arose at least in part because from early on, instead of continuing to apply the name "Christ" to a range of events surrounding and including Jesus—the whole new order of relationships of humans to God and to one another within which the early Christian community understood itself to be living—

Christians increasingly used it to refer simply to the man Jesus; and thus, as the notion of God's incarnation in history was gradually worked into a fully articulated doctrine, it became identified exclusively with Jesus and Jesus' activities. But tying the incarnation in this way to a single individual renders it not only paradoxical almost to the point of unintelligibility; it also opens it to criticisms of another sort increasingly heard today: that the identification of this one particular man with the universal God has led inevitably to perpetuation of the historical parochialism and relativity of early Christianity, including its patriarchal sexism and its rather narrow religious chauvinism. These have had highly destructive and oppressive consequences in Christian history, and they are not suited to the problems of contemporary life. When interpreted in this way, then, it is not surprising that the notion of the incarnation appears to modern consciousness as archaic and even somewhat weird, and of very limited usefulness.

I want to suggest, however, that if incarnation is interpreted in the wider sense we have already identified in some New Testament passages, it becomes intelligible within the theological frame with which we have been working; indeed, it proves to be a significantly illuminating concept.[6] The traditional notion that God works through all of cosmic history—and is working in human history in particular toward the creation of a thoroughly humane order (that is, toward human salvation)—now becomes understood in terms of the modern notion of the evolutionary-historical process within which humanity has emerged and developed: the serendipitous creativity underlying and working through all reality is expressing itself here (over many aeons of time) in a trajectory toward human and humane orders of being. In a slow, long-term development of this sort the direction in which things are moving may, of course, remain unclear for a very long time. Not until a stage of considerable differentiation and specification has been reached is it possible to imagine, or make judgments about, what is really happening; and even then many quite diverse possibilities remain open. But each new stage of the ongoing biohistorical process specifies a bit more precisely what directions the movement is going and what outcomes may be expected, as some possibilities are cut off and eliminated, and others are opened up and increasingly realized; and there may come a moment of decisive "revelation" of what is going on in the process as a whole.

Thus, for example, at the moment of cosmic time in which the earth was gradually cooling and solidifying from the ball of fire it had earlier been, there would have been no way to anticipate or predict that in due course it would become a womb and home for living creatures. Later on, when living organisms began to appear in the sea, it would hardly have been possible to guess that they would eventually evolve into myriads of species of life—birds, insects, animals, plants with infinite varieties of flowers and fruits, and so on. Even with the appearance of mammals it could hardly have been suspected that anthropoids would appear further down the road. And with the emergence of fully formed *Homo* there was still no sufficient basis to foresee the development of ancient Egypt, Babylon, India, China, Greece, or Rome—and certainly not the various forms of modern civilization. However, if from the vantage point of modern humanity we look back over this long cumulation of events, we may begin to discern what appears to be a more or less continuous line of development up to the present. It is striking to realize that this line was not visible until the last half of the nineteenth century: before that (even one hundred years earlier) it could not be seen at all. It seems, thus, that with a trajectory of this sort what is going on is by no means evident at all points along the way; the events which give it its distinct character and significance become determinate only in the course of the process itself. Only as certain crucial thresholds were crossed did new possibilities appear and in due course become realized; and only after many such decisive thresholds were crossed did beings appear with a vantage point enabling them to see that it was possible to interpret this whole development as somehow implicit from the beginning. One speaks of a "process of development" when one can specify certain points or stages through which a particular trajectory has proceeded, the process as a whole being marked off and defined by some (at least implicit) beginning and end. "End" and "beginning" and "process of development" are thus all logically interconnected with one another; they illuminate and determine one another conceptually, and no one of them can be clearly understood—as the "end" or the "beginning" of "this particular process"—without the others. Because of these conceptual interconnections we are inclined to think of the end of a particular process of development as implicit from its beginning; and if it happens to be the process of our own development into humanness that we are considering, it will be of importance to us to attempt to see, on the basis of the direction it seems to have followed up to the point at which we humans now find ourselves, where it may be going.

Conceptual interconnections of this sort appear to lie behind the thinking which produced the Christian doctrine of the incarnation. In that doctrine the claim was made that what was already real and valid and true from the beginning of the world first became revealed—that is, became explicit and evident—with the appearance of Jesus Christ. As 1 Peter 1:20 put it: Christ "was destined before the foundation of the world but was made manifest at the end of the times for your sake." That is (to use the terms we have been developing in this volume), the humaneness of God—the tendency toward the human and the humane (toward "Christ") in the ultimate nature of things—has existed from the very beginning ("the foundation of the world"), but it has become evident and clear only now in the new order of relationships just coming into view. "Christ," thus, (this new order of relationships) provides a vantage point for ascertaining the direction in which the evolutionary-historical process—at least along this line—has been moving from its beginning. And it can be said that in a significant sense Christ is the "revelation of God"—that is, through Christ we see what is really expressing itself through this whole cosmic movement—what is truly *God,* and what God is really doing in human affairs. In this new order of relationships the nature of ultimate reality (as it bears on human life) becomes, as it were, visible to us; and in that sense God is *present* here (for us who are seeing this) as nowhere else. Some such pattern of ideas appears to lie behind the claim of the Fourth Gospel that the Word which was "with God" from "the beginning," and indeed "was God" (1:1)—that is, was the creative and ordering principie through which everything came to be—here (in Christ) "became flesh and dwelt among us" (1:14); or, as the writer to the Colossians so concisely put it, in Christ "the whole fulness of deity dwells bodily" (2:9). The contention here appears to be that at this point in human history (in the events surrounding and including and following upon the man Jesus) the direction in which the human trajectory is going—and thus what that trajectory really means, what human history is all about—has become visible to human eyes. This trajectory is moving, as Jesus himself put it in the parable of the Last Judgment, toward that "kingdom prepared for you from the foundation of the world" (Mt. 25:34), that community into which all shall enter who give food to the hungry and water to the thirsty, who clothe the naked and visit those who are sick and in prison (25:34–36). The claim here is that the trajectory bearing human history is moving in a particular direction: toward a community of mercy, peace, and justice. Those who do not order their lives accordingly will finally disappear into eternal darkness (25:41, 46).

Thus, though Jesus is just one particular creature among myriads of others, yet what has developed in connection with him—"Christ" (in the wider sense in which we are using this term)—can be characterized as "the image of the invisible God" (Col. 1:15). It is here that Christian faith finds its model or paradigm for understanding God: the ultimate mystery, as it bears on us humans, is to be construed in terms of what here becomes visible. Though it clearly would be an idolatrous error to worship the man Jesus or the community which grew up around him, yet to worship the God-revealed-in-Christ—the God defined and constructed with Jesus and the new order of human relationships surrounding him as the model—is to worship the true God. Thus, Christ (this new order of human relationships) and God (the ultimate mystery of things), though sharply distinct and not to be confused with each other, are nevertheless taken by Christians to be one in a significant respect. In and through Christ the serendipitous creativity, which underlies the evolutionary-historical trajectory that brought humanity into being, has revealed the direction it is moving with humanity, and what this means for human life; by making itself explicit and known within human culture and consciousness in this way, this directionality became in a new way a living and significant moment and force in human affairs and subsequent human history. And it now became possible for men and women deliberately and self-consciously to order their lives and activities in accord with God's human and humane purposes (as discernible in Christ). All those men and women caught up in this vision of what was really going on in human affairs, thus, now felt drawn to give themselves in work directed toward the transformation of our inhuman world—with its warring and self-destructive practices and institutions, selves and communities—into the "kingdom of God," that is, into those communities of love and peace and justice in which all could find their full integrity and self-respect. Christian talk about "God's incarnation in Christ," when interpreted along these lines, is clearly compatible with the developmental picture of the world and humanity with which we have been working; and the notion of incarnation turns out to be readily intelligible—provided we are prepared to make the central Christian affirmations: (a) that Jesus and the early Christian community present a paradigm for understanding true humanity and humaneness, and (b) that this christic paradigm reveals the meaning and direction of the evolutionary-historical trajectory which has brought us into being.

A christological emphasis of this sort, characteristic of Christian thinking from its earliest days, differs in important respects from the world-picture we have developed up to this point; attention should be called here to at least two issues. In the first place, this view focuses specifically on *Christ* (in the wider sense) as a definitive revelation or manifestation of God within the human sphere. Up to this point in our constructive work we have had to be satisfied with rather vague talk about humanness and humaneness, indicating by some general references to ideals of justice, peace, freedom, equality, and the like what was intended with these words: a world in which persons would be granted their full dignity and integrity, as they sought to take responsibility for themselves and their future. Both our conception of the human and our understanding of God (conceived as closely connected with the cosmic trajectory toward humanness and humaneness) were sketched in terms of these (essentially humanistic) values and ideals. Since, however, these ideals and values (as they developed in the West) were much influenced by Christian experience and reflection, it would not be a mistake to say that the understanding of human life which we have been sketching thus far has been similar to the Christian vision in some respects. Nevertheless, important differences have remained. For Christian faiths, Jesus and the new communal order of peace and love which grew up around him have provided the defining paradigm in terms of which both humanity and God have ultimately been understood. Even ideals of justice, love, peace, and the like were not appropriated by the Christian movement simply in their conventional meanings: they were reconceived in light of the vision of the human and the humane which had become visible in Christ. In the humanism with which we have been working up to this point, however, normative humanness has not been defined in this way with reference to a particular historical person and communal order. Rather, it has been given meaning by reference to a configuration of abstract ideals and values which are, in the nature of the case, never perfectly realized in any particular individual or community. Hence, though there is significant overlap between distinctively Christian perspectives and the vision of the human we have thus far been elaborating, the ultimate norms or standards in terms of which each understands and measures all things are sharply different: Christian perspectives nail their normative ideas and values down in a much more definite and inescapable way than is possible for most humanisms, through binding them to a particular historical figure and community.

This has the advantage of making the image of the truly human much sharper and more specific: it involves love and self-giving, reconciliation with all others (including even those enemies seeking to destroy us), a willingness to sacrifice our own interests to the well-being of others. Moreover, all this is focused and made concrete in the dramatic image of the actual life, suffering, and death of the man on the cross, and in the stories of his persecuted followers. In contrast with the rather loose commitments which abstract idealizations so often command, the New Testament stories of Jesus and the reconciling community make a powerfully evocative appeal in support of the heavy demands they lay on their adherents.

These very strengths, of course, carry with them the potential for serious perversions. For example, throughout most of Christian history the image of Christ was reified to the point of idolatry. In consequence, many took the teachings of Jesus (or other New Testament teachings) to be literally "words of God" or "commands of God"; these were to be unquestioningly believed, and human life was to be completely conformed to them—all of this even though such legalistic attitudes and practices directly contradicted the freedom and fulfillment, the openness and love, which Christian salvation was said to bring. Some Christians took the further step of persecuting in the name of Jesus those with whom they did not agree, thus adding to human suffering instead of helping to alleviate it. Any reification of Christ in this way into a kind of absolute standard to which all human ideas and values and conduct must conform is clearly a confusion and mistake which should be forthrightly rejected today. Our world is very different from that of Jesus and the earliest Christians; though much can be learned from the spirit manifested in their lives and activities, the views and ideas and attitudes which they held must not be regarded as normative in any literalistic or legalistic sense for us or our world.

The deleterious effects of the reification of Christ common in the tradition were significantly increased because the term "Christ" was not taken in the "wider sense" I am advocating here but rather as referring exclusively to the man Jesus, believed to be the "only begotten son of God." This made it necessary, in developing the Christian vision of the human, to attempt to see the nature and meaning of all human existence through the prism of one individual life and death. Although such a project might seem to be impossibly constricting, the figure of Jesus proved amazingly elastic for Christian interpreters: he could be seen as "gentle Jesus, meek and mild," as a bloodthirsty leader of crusades against the infidels, as a bourgeois family man and capitalist entrepreneur, as a sociopolitical revolutionary—whatever the needs of the time demanded. In recent years, however, a new and quite intractable difficulty for this understanding of normative humanness has arisen. Feminist theological analyses have shown that the traditional christological deification of Jesus, far from being salvific and fulfilling for all humans, has been significantly oppressive and destructive to women. The maleness of this Christian paradigm (taken to be the very "image of God") has reinforced and given theological legitimacy to patriarchal notions of the ontological superiority of males over females. Women, therefore, have often been seen in the Christian tradition as deficient or second-class humans who, for example, were not properly equipped to be priests or pastors, God's representatives here on earth; they were to take roles subordinate to men in church, in family, in the world at large. (Inferences of this sort were already drawn in a number of New Testament texts which continue to be cited all the way down to the present.) Under these circumstances women tended to understand themselves as significantly deficient or defective in their very being, no matter what compensatory honorifics were offered them.[7]

A second respect in which traditional christological ideas differ significantly from the theological construction in which we have thus far been engaged is not as adaptable to our contemporary needs as the first (with certain crucial modifications) appears to be; it derives from the largely dualistic language in which most Christian thinking has been expressed in the past. In the biblical imagery God is depicted as a "father" in heaven, and Jesus is his "son" come to earth; or God is one who sends forth his "word" and Jesus is that word here among us. Instead of employing the language of evolutionary and historical process (as we have been doing), we are presented with a divine reality come down from heaven to earth. It must be acknowledged, of course, that symbolic formulations of this sort bring out faith's meaning with an evocative power unavailable to the more abstract language we have been using. However, as we have seen, problems arise when we treat these pictorial symbols as literal representations of divine reality(s). The traditional christological language about Jesus as a divine being who came down from heaven, a man with a divine nature, should no more be treated in a literalizing and reifying way than God should be thought of as literally a "father" or "lord" who "lives in heaven."[8] Those who literalize the traditional christological symbolism all too easily begin to think of Jesus' words as the very words of God—eternally and forever true, absolutely binding upon humans in all respects. And they may be inclined to regard all those others who do not confess Jesus' deity in this way as somehow excluded from God's love and care, even condemned to eternal torment; as Cyprian put it in a classical phrase, "there is no salvation outside the Church."[9] It is important that Christians never forget that the crusades against those regarded as infidel Moslems were conducted in the name of the crucified one, and the tortures of the Inquisition were intended to compel submission to just this church that claimed to be the exclusive mediator of Christ's salvation. The literalizing moves of which Christians have often been guilty, far from promoting the more humane world for which Jesus died, have further undermined it by dividing humans from one another instead of reconciling them, by setting them at war with one another instead of bringing peace and love. The real enemy in all of this, that which made it possible, was the literalization and reification of the basic christological symbols. From early on Jews and Moslems realized that Christians were falling into idolatrous attitudes toward Christ (and the church), and they criticized these in the name of the One High God. But to this day Christians have seldom acknowledged this quite proper theological critique of their reified use of central religious symbols.

The reified mythic picture of Jesus as uniquely and exclusively God's son has helped to generate other theological problems: it has, for example, fostered a highly individualistic understanding of both humanity and God, an understanding in many ways incompatible with modern ecological and systemic ways of thinking. Since the normatively human is definitively represented in an *individual* man, in traditional Christian faith there are strong tendencies to understand human existence as essentially individualistic or atomic in character—instead of communal or social, as is implied by the wider conception of Christ that I am proposing here. Moreover, since this same individual man is regarded as the definitive revelation of divine reality, God also is taken to be an atomic individual being, a person—instead of, for example, an ecological-processive reality, as I am suggesting. From these two points it clearly follows that for traditional Christian faith the relationships between God and humanity will also be conceived in essentially individualistic terms, as one-to-one relationships between each individual soul and God.[10] In contrast, I have argued that humans are fundamentally social realities, constituted by the relationships—interpersonal and sociocultural, biological and physical—in which they stand; and their relationship with God, therefore, should not be understood as essentially a kind of direct personal encounter but rather as mediated in and through this social and ecological network.

As we can see, many features of the understanding of God and of the human (characteristic of much Christian piety) are largely products of the reification of the mythic language in which Christian faith was first formulated. When this is understood, it becomes clear that there is no good reason for contemporary Christians, with their modern understandings of human existence and the world, to feel bound to these traditional formulations; and in this volume I have proposed a quite different way of thinking about these matters. We need not, however, reject the traditional formulations completely. If we are careful not to literalize and reify the Christian myth of God's incarnation in Christ, and if we interpret it in the wider sense that I have proposed, it can remain significant and illuminating. For it expresses in powerfully evocative language the central Christian claim that the underlying cosmic movement toward humanness and humaneness has come to expression in human history in a paradigmatic, and even definitive, way: in the new order of relationships experienced (and aspired to) in the community which grew up around, and in consequence of, the ministry, death, and "resurrection" of Jesus, that which is truly human and truly humane became concrete reality in human consciousness and life; and thus the question of who or what God is—the question of the meaning for us humans of the ultimate mystery—received a significant answer. Something like this is what we can today mean if we say, in a sixth step of faith (along with two thousand years of Christian tradition), that God was incarnate in Christ.

I suggested (in Chapter 7) that bringing the symbol "Christ" into the threefold monotheistic categorial scheme does not really add a fourth category to the *structure* of theocentric faith, but instead qualifies in a fundamental way (for those committed to it) the three basic categories already in place. We can now see just what this means. The Christ-images—drawn from the ministry, teachings, and death of the man Jesus and the new orders of relationship experienced and aspired to in the early Christian community—are taken as principal criteria with reference to which the understandings of humanity, God, and the world are to be constructed. As the norm in terms of which authentic humanity and humaneness is now to be conceived, these images sharpen up and focus both the idea of the human in general and also the understandings of such particular qualities or virtues as peace and freedom, reconciliation and love (agape), justice and community. Thus, the character and the specific claims of what can properly be called *christic* life and faith come sharply into view, in contrast with perspectives which image and define human being in quite different ways—for example, as the power of will (as seen in a Napoleon or in Nietzsche's *Uebermensch*), or as intellectual or artistic genius (Faust), or as bourgeois middle-class conventionality and respectability, or as realized most fully in mystical experience or deeply religious piety, and so on.

Human being, however, does not exist simply in and of itself; it has its reality only within a context and a world which make it possible and which sustain it. This means that both the conception of God (the cosmic serendipitous creativity which has brought humanity into being) and the world which provides the context of human life (God's creation) must also be constructed in terms consistent with the Christ-images (for those who take these images paradigmatically to represent the truly human). For Christian faith, thus, what occurred in the historical events surrounding and including the man Jesus significantly shapes the understanding of all three monotheistic categories; and Christ becomes a principal criterion decisively influencing the construction of the entire world-picture. This does not mean, of course, that either Jesus or the early Christian community is taken to be God, or to be the only important reality in the world, or to be the only significant moment in human history. As we have seen, the ancient christological formulations were intended to protect against conclusions of just this sort; but the ambiguity of the terms in which they were expressed ultimately produced more confusion and disagreement than clarity of understanding. I suggest that the modern language of perspectives and world-pictures, of categorial structures, criteria of construction, and the like, enables us to express and interpret the christological concerns of contemporary Christian faith more precisely and clearly than is possible with the traditional reifying terminology of substances, natures, and persons.

Some aspects of the christological interpretation I am presenting here can be clarified, perhaps, with some simple diagrams. I have suggested that the basic structure of the Christian world-picture is provided by three categories: God, world, humanity, as in other monotheistic perspectives such as Judaism and Islam. For Christian faith, however, since the construction of all three of these is decisively influenced by the Christ-event, we do not have here a simply triangular or trilateral categorial structure:

Or a quadrilateral one:

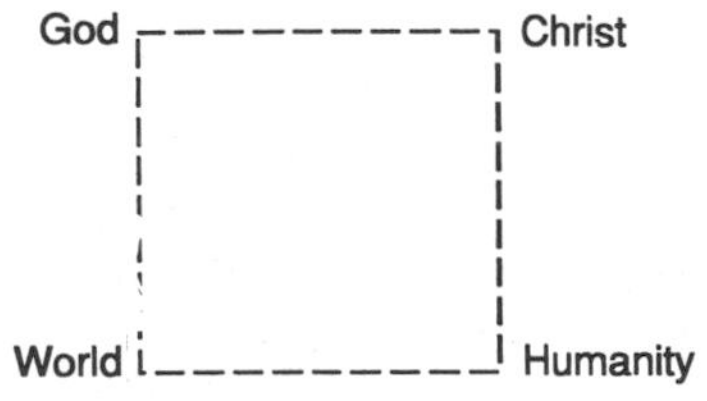

Rather, without detracting in any way from the fundamental theocentrism which Christian faith shares with the other monotheisms, we can, perhaps, represent the christocentrism I have been describing like this:

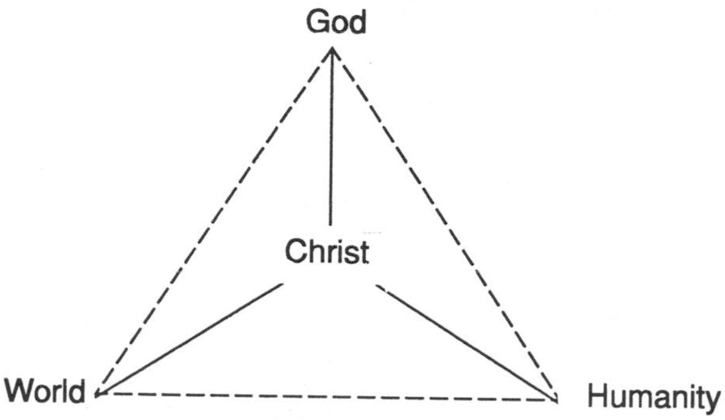

The somewhat vague humanistic theocentric faith (to which our five-step path of theological construction in Chapters 17–24 brought us) could be specified further in a number of quite different ways. What I am attempting to do here (without disparaging such other ways of moving in a sixth step of faith) is to sketch briefly what happens if we take seriously the Christian claim (and language) about the paradigmatic significance of the Christ-event for faith in God, and for our understanding of humanity in the world. In this chapter I have tried to show that a Christian faith-perspective, though sharply modifying the theocentric world-picture to which our constructive work had brought us, can nevertheless be developed quite straightforwardly in connection with it. It presents for our consideration, therefore, a potentially appropriate sixth step of faith. In the next chapter we will consider some further implications of such a step. Then in Chapter 27 we will discover that the introduction of *trinitarian* reflection into our consideration of christological issues leads to a much more radical transformation of the basic monotheistic categorial scheme than anything intimated up to this point.

26. Christ as Paradigm for God and for Humanity

New Testament uses of the word "Christ," we have observed, are somewhat ambiguous: in many cases this term refers simply and directly to the man Jesus of Nazareth; but in some important texts it has a wider meaning than this, and can be interpreted as designating the quality of the new transformative relationships which emerged in the community that grew up surrounding and including Jesus—a quality most dramatically epitomized, no doubt, in the memories and stories of Jesus' own relationships with his followers. The interpretations of Christ that developed in subsequent Christian history covered over this ambiguity by treating "Christ" and "Jesus" and "Jesus Christ" as all virtually interchangeable names for a single metaphysically unique, objective savior who, in a transaction with God in the crucifixion/resurrection, completely accomplished the salvation of humanity. As a result of this reification/deification of Jesus Christ and the culminating events of his ministry, the primary focus of Christian faith for the past two thousand years has been on that God-man of the past, with virtually everything of importance to human salvation traced back to that historical moment and interpreted in terms of it.

In contrast to this concentration of traditional Christian faith on a particular person and event, I am proposing here what I have called a "wider view" in which "Christ" is understood to refer to and name major features of the whole complex of events and relationships surrounding, including, and following upon the ministry and death of Jesus. On this view it is the appearance of a new communal ethos in history, rather than a metaphysically unique individual, that is the matter of central importance. Instead of narrowing the normatively human down to the image of a single supernatural individual—with all the limitations, one-sidedness, and distortions this inevitably brings to our conception of what is truly and properly humanizing and humane—this view presents the image of an inclusive egalitarian community that welcomes all sorts and conditions of women and men, no matter what their racial, religious, or ethnic background: "in Christ Jesus," as Paul put it, "There is neither Jew nor Greek, . . . slave nor free, . . . male nor female; for you are all one" (Gal. 3:28).[1] If this principle is made defining and then generalized, "Christ" will include (potentially) all the great diversity of ways of being human which we find in our world, so long as they are healing and reconciling and humanizing (in the christic sense) and do not seek to be oppressive of or otherwise destructive to others. Even though it gains great openness and breadth in this way, the symbol does not lose touch with the special significance of Jesus (so important to more traditional christologies): for Jesus remains, after all, the focal center around which, and in connection with which, this new (potentially all-inclusive) community was formed, and to which it continually has returned in memory, meditation, and ritual for renewed nourishment and further inspiration.

Retaining a certain focus on Jesus in this way has some advantages over a simply communal emphasis. It presents for the contemplation, devotion, and inspiration of all an image of a heroic figure, whose radical practices and teachings so threatened the social, political, and religious institutions and authorities of his day that they moved to execute him; this led to his passion and crucifixion, in which he did not waver in his expression of radical self-giving love even to bitter enemies ("Father, forgive them; for they know not what they do," Lk. 23:34)—ultimately the most powerfully evocative emblem of his life and work. Special emphasis on Jesus should not be given up entirely for the sake of the wider communal interpretation of Christ which I have proposed: in my opinion the ambiguity of the New Testament on this question of christological focus is itself of theological significance. Though centering on the man Jesus, the Christ-symbol is portrayed as extending beyond this solitary figure to include the community of reconciliation that grew up in response to his work—and in principle, thus, it can be extended to all communities of genuine healing, love, and justice. Thus, any community which becomes a vehicle in history of more profoundly humane patterns of life—as paradigmatically epitomized in the Christ-images of this seminal period—is to be understood theologically as helping to constitute (in its own distinctive way) the fullness of Christ.[2] Our christology provides us, thus, with a vision of human existence that extends from a focal point to wider and wider communities of reconciliation and love, justice and peace, freedom and creativity. Should we incorporate this vision (in a sixth step of faith) into the conception of God which we are here constructing? To answer that question we must consider more carefully just what this conception of Christ would mean if introduced into our understanding of God.

The image/concept of God (we have seen) provides communities and selves with a focus for devotion and service by means of which they can orient themselves in the world. I suggest that there are three desiderata in terms of which the adequacy of such a symbolic focus can be assessed: (1) it must provide sufficiently unified and clear images and concepts to concentrate the attention, interests, and affections of women and men in such a way that they can direct themselves toward God self-consciously and with some measure of confidence; (2) it must convey a sense of reality and truth, a sense that what these images and concepts present and represent is not just a product of human fancy; (3) it must give the men and women who respond to it the conviction that it is *God,* and not some idol—that which can provide adequate orientation in life, that which truly grounds human existence—with which they come into relation through these images and concepts. If our theological construction cannot satisfy these three desiderata, it is not adequate.

We were dealing with all of these, at least implicitly, in much of Chapters 21 to 23; what is required now, therefore, is to pull these matters together and bring them into relation with the conception of Christ that we have been developing. With respect to the first desideratum, I have tried to show that the image/concept of the creator/lord/father, although originally created as part of a now outmoded frame for orienting life, and reified in much traditional practice and belief into a particular being "up in heaven," contains within itself certain motifs that can help draw men and women forward toward fuller humanization, and which are, therefore, important for focusing human devotion and orientation—in particular, the motifs of *humaneness* (which tends to draw us out toward a more profound humanness) and *mystery* or absoluteness (which calls into question and relativizes our beliefs and values, our institutions and social practices, our anthropocentrism). This central symbol of our western religious traditions has, thus, valuable resources for orienting human life; and the important question is whether qualifying and modifying the traditional imagery of the creator/lord/father by (a) introducing a range of new metaphors to overcome the seriously misleading, indeed destructive and oppressive, effects which it has often produced in the past, and (b) reinterpreting it in light of the christological considerations we have been developing, transforms the symbol "God" adequately for today. I have argued that the word "God" remains a powerfully evocative name for identifying that evolutionary-historical trajectory which has brought us into being as human and continues to nourish us, drawing us on toward a more profound humanness and humaneness; and that so long as we do not reify the traditional imagery it continues useful as a way of symbolizing the ultimate reality with which we humans have to do. But our attention, interest, and devotion will be focused in one-sided and pernicious ways, if we do not significantly qualify and modify these metaphors (that have traditionally given content and meaning to "God") with others, such as Mother (as many feminists have suggested), Ground of Being (Tillich), the One who calls us into the future (Cobb, Pannenberg), Liberator (Cone), Creative Event (Wieman), World Spirit (Hegel), and so on; and I have especially urged that the notions of "serendipitous creativity" and "an evolutionary-historical trajectory toward the human and the humane" be given a central place in our conception of God. All these images and ideas (and more) can appropriately be used to help us conceive and image God, but none should be reified or given special status as *the* proper or definitive concept, that is, as literally true; a variety of symbols and images can (and should) be employed to make our God-talk concrete.

Not an unlimited variety, however (at least for Christian theology): this is where the normative significance of the symbol "Christ" comes into play. For example, symbols like Kali (the Hindu goddess of terror and destruction) or Satan (the personification of deceit and evil in the West) or simply Power or Energy (unqualified and unrestricted impersonal *force*) do not bring out—in fact they contradict—the sense of God as creative of and supportive of not only the impersonal world but also our humanity, our humanization, particularly as these are exemplified in the principal Christ-images; and hence these symbols are unacceptable to Christian faith. Image/concepts of these sorts do not symbolize well that dimension of reality, those tendencies and powers and movements in nature and history, on which God-talk (as normatively defined by christic imagery) is intended to focus our attention, our devotion, and our energies.

The central christic images and ideas—of the ministry, teachings, and death of Jesus, and of the primitive egalitarian community in which "all [are] one in Christ Jesus"—are sharp and clear. They present pictures of a dramatic and compelling figure, courageously facing death at the hands of those threatened by his radical ministry and teachings, and of a communal life among his earliest followers which seeks to overcome the barriers to meaningful and fulfilling forms of human existence created by status and class, race and gender, aggressiveness and hatred. However difficult it may be to emulate precisely or to instantiate in human life today what these images portray, they set before us a picture of life's possibilities which has powerfully attracted many women and men from the New Testament period onward; and for centuries (in those societies deeply affected by the Christian story) these images have shaped moral, religious, and more general cultural values and meanings, promoting the cultivation of loving, forgiving, and self-sacrificing attitudes and practices. Within the Christian cultus—in the worship of God—they continue to focus and form human affections and devotion at deep levels. For Christian faith it is in terms of these images and ideas that God and God's activity are to be understood; it is they that are to give life its unity and orientation, its center and meaning. Who and what God is becomes known in and through these patterns and norms, and in this way God continues to foster and move human existence toward the sort of realization and completion which they suggest.

An understanding of God defined in this manner contrasts rather vividly with the vaguer notions of a "cosmic ground" of our "humanity," to which we have heretofore been largely confined. To insure the universality and inclusiveness of these notions (and others we have been using up to this point), it has been necessary to present them in rather abstract and general terms. And for just this reason the guidance and orientation which they could provide for assessing and making the hard choices demanded of human beings remains somewhat amorphous. When God is defined in specifically christic terms, however, a clearer and sharper picture comes before us; and believers may well, therefore, understand themselves to be under rather specific and strenuous imperatives. Orientation on this God does not directly "solve," or even lessen, life's problems; indeed, they may become more difficult and demanding. More difficult, because it is by no means clear what a "Christ-like" mode of life requires of us in twentieth-century affluent America—"sell what [we] have, and give to the poor" (Mk. 10:21)? join a revolutionary cadre to overthrow the forces of oppression here and elsewhere? "bore from within" big government or IBM in order to bring about more humane policies and practices? become a Christian evangelist or pastor? Though the images of Jesus and the early Christian community are relatively sharp and clear and our devotion to God may be great, what does this really mean for our actual lives? for what we should do with ourselves, what policies we should pursue, and what concrete decisions we should make? However difficult it may be to answer questions like these, devotion to the Christian God is nevertheless more demanding than many other loyalties and styles of life which may attract us, because the standards implicit in the central christic images are so absolutistic, and they move so strongly counter to our "natural inclinations"—our desires for ease and comfort and wealth; for self-fulfillment and approbation; our laziness; our wishes for revenge; and so on. Jesus, whose gruesome crucifixion is at the center of the Christian picture, is one who appears to have sacrificed everything for the cause of God's kingdom. And the demands he lays on his followers are absolute, demands that would ordinarily be regarded as idolatrous and fanatical were it not believed that through the mouth of Jesus it is God who is speaking:

> I have come to set a man against his father, and a daughter against her mother . . . He who loves father or mother more than me is not worthy of me; and he who loves son or daughter more than me is not worthy of me . . . If any man would come after me, let him deny himself and take up his cross and follow me. (Mt. 10:35, 37; 16:24)

Absolute self-giving appears to be what is demanded of any serious follower of this figure.

The wider view of Christ with which we are working here, however, according to which "Christ" is understood to refer not simply to this Jesus who makes absolute demands upon his followers but also to the community of reconciliation that grew up around him and in consequence of his ministry, modulates this emphasis in certain respects. Instead of normativeness defined exclusively in terms of unqualified individual devotion and self-sacrifice to God's requirements (as dramatically epitomized in Jesus' life and death) the importance and the quality of *relationships among humans* now becomes central—relationships among the members of the Christian community, and relationships between that community (and its members) and those outside it. In both cases these are to be reconciling and healing, that is, community-building ("God . . . gave us the ministry of reconciliation . . . So we are ambassadors for Christ, God making his appeal through us," 2 Cor. 5:18, 20; cf. Gal. 5:22–26). Within the community itself, then, it is reciprocal love and self-giving that are truly responsive to God and are therefore to be normative, not complete self-sacrifice of each to the other (which would not even be intelligible as an absolutistic *communal* practice); beyond the community, however, where continuous efforts are to be devoted to overcoming barriers of class and caste, estrangement and indifference, hatred and warfare, fear and guilt, sacrificial initiatives toward others—by Christian communities as well as individuals—are appropriate and demanded. Here the image of the absolutely self-sacrificing Jesus presents a challenging picture of the sort of commitment and stance that Christian faith demands.

Thus, our first desideratum for an adequate conception of God can apparently be satisfied by theological construction guided by the symbol "Christ": the focus for orientation in life (the image/concept of God), created when the images of Jesus and the primitive community of reconciliation serve as paradigms, is relatively sharp and clear—however difficult may be its demands.

Let us turn then to our second desideratum, that the God of which we are speaking must impress us as *real*, not a mere figment of our imaginations. Throughout I have been suggesting that we identify God (or better: God's activity) with actual cosmic, vital, and historical powers or forces at work in the world (as we understand these matters today)—especially those which have brought us humans into being, which continue to sustain us in being, and which are drawing us onward toward a more profound humanization. These powers and forces and historical tensions are realities objective to us: together they constitute the evolutionary-historical trajectory which has produced us; it is not we who have made them. Although in the later stages of history human decisions and actions have become indispensable factors influencing the movement toward a free and responsible historicity, no persons or communities (until quite recently) have been able to try deliberately to move human historical development as a whole further in this direction; it has been the serendipitous creativity working in and through the evolutionary-historical process (and thus also working in and through human decisions and actions) that has brought this about. Contemporary women and men, with their desires to help forward the processes of humanization, are themselves products of this deeper movement of human history, not its creators. So there should be no question that we are speaking about something objectively real when we speak of God in terms of this serendipitous creativity. There are other ways to see and conceptualize the Real, of course, than as a serendipitous process expressing itself in directional movements; indeed, there are other frames of reference which have no place at all for talk of God. This plurality of ways of seeing and understanding the world is a plain fact of human history and culture, but it does not invalidate the frame of orientation which we have been putting together here. For our frame is specifically intended to give an important place to, and to interpret, precisely this pluralism of cultural orientations and lifestyles, this enormous variety of ways of being human which has emerged historically. The profound mystery pointed to by our historicity has been at the center of our theological concerns throughout; and it has affected in many ways the conception of God which we have developed.

The question now arises, however, whether this confidence about God's reality can still obtain if we understand God in terms of the further specifications which (as we have just seen) the Christ-symbol demands. For those who find the Christ-symbol compelling—that is, those for whom something genuinely valid for and true of human life comes into vivid focus in its images and demands—important features of what is truly *real* about human existence and the world doubtless seem to be shown forth here. To others, however—one thinks, for example, of Nietzsche and Freud—the overriding emphasis on self-giving love to others, for the sake of communal reconciliation and upbuilding, is a trap which is destructive of human possibilities and thus human reality; and to those who find christic imagery and stories beautiful and romantic but virtually useless for orientation in the cold "real world" where other quite different values and standards are in play, the "reality" presented here will be of little use in orienting actual human life; and so on. There can be no doubt, however, that many, when seriously confronting the christic images and meanings, have found them appealing and compelling, revealing something profoundly true about human existence. For such persons the notions of reconciliation, love, and peace, of self-giving, voluntary poverty, love for enemies, vicarious suffering, convey something of genuine importance about the human spirit—something about our deep interconnectedness with one another, something about authentic human fulfillment.

Moreover, they point us in the direction communities and individuals must move if our human world is ever to become more truly humane. Societies whose members respect one another and work together steadily for the common good, societies characterized by equality of opportunity and by freedom and justice and concern for all, will surely not be created as long as most of our activities are directed largely toward our own well-being and comfort, and we assert ourselves as aggressively as possible, whatever the cost to others; nor will our continuing celebration and exercise of violent power—whether political, economic, military, or religious—contribute much to their establishment. On the contrary, it is images (like those found in the New Testament) of communities of reconciliation—in which all recognize that they are "members one of another" (Rom. 12:5) in "one body" (1 Cor. 12:13), that they "are all one" (Gal. 3:28), with no discrimination among groups, classes, or sexes—that can focus our attention and our lives on the sorts of commitments we must make and loyalties we must maintain if we are to align ourselves with those cosmic and historical forces moving us toward a more humane world. In this sort of context of hopes and dreams the image of the self-sacrificial Jesus, who gives himself completely so that all may have "abundant life" (John 10:10), stands out in its full significance. Here is a vivid emblem of the radical transvaluation of values that is required if our world of violence and aggressive self-assertion is to become more truly humane and thus more human, an emblem that is simultaneously a powerful call for commitment to this expected and hoped for coming "kingdom of God."

Although we may not want to accord absoluteness to any of these images or ideas (as Christians have so often done in the past, especially with the image of Jesus), their continuing appeal suggests that they symbolize and focus something about human existence and the way human life ought to be comported which is genuine and true. The question which demands attention is not, then, whether that which is mediated through the Christ-symbol is to be regarded as reality in some sense or other: that point is obvious; but it leaves matters too vague and general for what is really at stake here. The important question is this: Is that which is presented in the christic imagery the *ultimate* reality with which we humans have to do, the reality of *God?* Is it that on which human life must in fact be oriented if it is to flourish? Or is this an idol, demanding our deepest commitment and loyalty, but certain to deceive and disappoint us if we give it? This brings us to our third—and crucial—desideratum.

Even if one were to maintain that Jesus and the early community of reconciliation symbolize a significant—even a magnificent—human possibility, why suppose that what is presented here is more than one among many possible modes of human existence? Why take the Christ-symbol as the normative or defining image of the human, and thus that point in human existence where the character and meaning of the evolutionary and historical movement toward the human and the humane most fully and definitively comes into view? Putting the question in the older, more traditional language: Why hold today that in these images and events *God* is revealing Godself, and that what is presented here, therefore, is more than just another example of the great diversity of human possibilities?

As we have seen in the course of our reflections in this book, when we introduce the name "God" into our discourse we are suggesting that the ultimate reality with which we have to do is not to be regarded simply as unqualified mystery: for now it is taken to be that which creates and sustains the vast panorama of life, including the enormously differentiated and complex process which has given rise to, and continues to nourish, our own human modes of being. To confess "faith in God" is to affirm that this mystery, with its tension or movement toward the human and the humane, is the adequate and proper ground for confidence in and hope for human life and its prospects—that it is our "creator and redeemer" (to use the more familiar words of tradition)—and we declare our loyalty and devotion to it and our intention to orient ourselves on it as we proceed through life. The primary issue, thus, with which the Christian claims present us is this: should we construct our understanding of this God along lines suggested by the central christic images and concepts? should we (to use more traditional language) regard these as the media of God's defining "revelation" to humankind? Or is the attempt to specify our conception of God in this way idolatrous?

This question poses two distinct issues which must be addressed if it is to be answered properly: (a) Do these images and concepts represent or exemplify what we can properly take to be the truly and authentically human, the model in terms of which humankind should be understood and measured, that which is rightly normative for women and men? (b) Even if they do, is there any reason why they should be regarded as the principal locus in human existence through which we come into contact with that which creates and sustains the truly human and humane (God our creator and redeemer), that which is bringing into being our full humanity? Or do the Christian concepts and images represent merely one of many such loci?—or perhaps even a delusory and misleading understanding of the human, which, if allowed to shape definitively our interests and affections, our reflection and activities, will lead us inevitably into idolatrous and destructive attachments? Clearly these questions must be addressed before we can seriously consider committing ourselves (in a sixth step of faith) to a specifically *Christian* understanding of God.

The Christian claims, as we can see from these questions, are momentous, and they raise wide-ranging issues that are difficult to grasp. The response we give to these claims will depend largely, I think, on three factors: (a) our understanding of the christic images and concepts themselves, (b) what we take to be "truly human and humane," and (c) our conception of what is (would be) required to bring about or create our true and full humanity. It is obvious that there is room for wide disagreements on each of these points, and the many extant varieties of christology are witness to the diversity of interpretations which have appeared in the past.[3] By now my view on each of these matters should be fairly clear: (a) the central christic images and concepts are those which emphasize activity that is healing and reconciling in situations of enmity and estrangement, poverty and despair, and that help build communities of reconciliation; (b) the "truly human" (to be understood, as we saw in Part II, in terms of our historicity) reaches its maximum in egalitarian communities characterized by love and respect for all and special care for the sick, the crippled, and those otherwise handicapped; and (c) such communities cannot be created through the violent exercise of power but only through gradual formation and transformation both of individual persons (so they are no longer self-aggrandizing) and of the social and institutional contexts of human life (so that basic human needs, both physical and psychological, are met).

Obviously, in suggesting that it is these particular concepts and images that are "central," I am making a selection from among many diverse New Testament motifs, deliberately omitting those which, for example, call for bloodthirsty revenge on enemies, those which promise an eternal beatitude in heaven for the faithful and torment in an everlasting hell for unbelievers, those which emphasize an exclusivistic church, and so on. It is a selection, however, which is clearly in keeping with the wider view of Christ with which I suggested we work here. The New Testament focus is on a story beginning with Jesus (whose ministry and teachings culminate in his own self-sacrifice in death) but whose work gives rise (after his death) to a new community of love and freedom, forgiveness and care for the needy, a community charged to become an agent of God's reconciling work in the world. This story is taken to present a paradigm both of God's way of addressing evil in the world—through love and forgiveness and healing even of enemies, vicarious suffering and self-sacrifice, the creation of communities of reconciliation and caring—and of what is expected and required of those women and men who seek to live in this world in faithful response to God's redemptive activity. That is, it is a paradigm that presents at once (as it was put at Chalcedon) true deity and true humanity: it shows us both who the true God is (in the Christian view) and what true humanity—humanity responding in faith and love to God—is. For those who accept this paradigm of the divine and the human, and who seek to order their lives in terms of what it prescribes, the way to break the vicious circle of bitterness and violence in human affairs is through building communities and institutions within which radical love/forgiveness/self-sacrifice is practiced in the hope of overcoming the hatreds and estrangements and debilitating conditions of life which are so productive of evil; the continuing use of violence in attacking evils in the human world seems always to beget more violence, instead of bringing the hoped-for new world of justice and freedom, peace and fulfillment. The earliest Christians believed both that they had been called by God to just this sort of ministry of healing and reconciliation in the world, and that it was the power of the divine spirit working among and within them (the power of what we have been calling the evolutionary and historical momentums moving in the direction of a more truly humane world) that led them to respond affirmatively to that call. This reconciling and healing power, imaged in and symbolized by the events surrounding and including Jesus, continues to call women and men today to respond to the need for, and to the forces working toward, such reconciling activity in the world.

In 2 Corinthians Paul expresses this central Christian self-understanding in this way:

> if any one is in Christ, he is a new creation; the old has passed away, behold, the new has come. All this is from God, who through Christ reconciled us to himself and gave us the ministry of reconciliation; that is, in Christ God was reconciling the world to himself, not counting their trespasses against them, and entrusting to us the message of reconciliation. So we are ambassadors for Christ, God making his appeal through us. (5:17–20a, including note)

Elsewhere he interprets the life of the Christian community in terms of a new "Spirit" which enlivens it: if Christians "walk by the Spirit" they will be led away from "immorality, . . . idolatry, . . . enmity, strife, jealousy, anger, selfishness, . . . and the like," and they will begin to bear "the fruit of the Spirit [which] is love, joy, peace, patience, kindness, goodness, faithfulness, gentleness, self-control" (Gal. 5:16, 20–23). Whether he uses the image of "Christ" or of "the Spirit" his central contention is the same: Christians are called to life in this new community in and through which their hatreds, enmities, and warfares with one another will be calmed, and where they will become bearers of a spirit that brings reconciliation and love, peace and freedom into human affairs. The Johannine writings go even further than Paul in their interpretation of the significance of the new quality of life aspired to and experienced within the Christian communities: this quality of life is identified here as itself the very presence of God.

> Beloved, let us love one another; for love is of God, and he who loves is born of God and knows God. He who does not love does not know God;

> for *God is love* . . . No man has ever seen God; if we love one another, God abides in us and his love is perfected in us. (1 John 4:7–8, 12; emphasis mine)

The salvation promised in these (and other) well-known texts is nothing else than that special quality human life is expected to take on within this new community, with its straining toward truly humane patterns of existence within itself and its larger task of fostering further humanization in the world through a ministry of healing and reconciliation.

I have noted a number of times that the various cultural streams of humanity seem today to be converging rapidly into a single interconnected human history. At this portentous moment, perhaps more than ever before, we need conceptions of the human and visions of history which will facilitate our movement toward an ordering of life and history that is at once humane and universal, an ordering in which the integrity and significance of each tradition and each community are acknowledged and the rights of every individual are respected; and it is important to identify, and to strengthen in every way possible, whatever historical momentums there are toward reconciliation of contending peoples, nations, cultures, religions. New cultural patterns of association and cooperation must be developed, new institutions must be invented, new ideologies that are at once universalistic and truly pluralistic must be created. For these sorts of things to come about a spirit of self-sacrifice for the well-being of the whole of humanity will be widely needed, a spirit which can subdue the instincts for self-preservation and self-defense (perhaps among the strongest that we possess) that so dominate our communal and national, as well as our personal, lives. It is just such a spirit of self-giving, love, reconciliation, the building of community, that is expressed in the symbol of Christ (as I am interpreting that symbol here). And to the extent that the Christian churches today actually express that spirit in their activities, they are historical bearers of the sort of reconciling and transformative activity so much needed in this historical moment.

We must not forget, however, that other images of the divine have also been strongly emphasized in the Christian tradition: for example, God as the *absolute Lord,* the tyrannical power who arbitrarily saves whomever "he" chooses, and damns to everlasting hell whomever "he" chooses (Rom. 9:10–24). Many today—I assume many of the readers of this book—are unwilling to fall down in worship before such a God as that. If this is so, why is it so? It is, I think, because we have made (whether knowingly or not), and we are prepared to keep, deep commitments to *humaneness* as a criterion to be used in identifying the True God. Precisely this criterion of humaneness and humanization has been given a prominent place in our construction here of a conception of God appropriate for today. The criterion may be formulated in this way: all attitudes and practices, institutions and ideologies, which help to create a more *humane* order, and an earth that can sustain it, are to be recognized as the present activity in human affairs of the True God (that is, as expressions of the evolutionary-historical trajectory which has created human life and continues to further it), and are thus to be supported; those attitudes and practices, institutions and ideologies, however, which create, support and promote *inhumanity*—that is, injustice and poverty and oppression, alienation and corruption, the destruction of the human environment—are to be regarded as anti-divine and to be opposed. Explicit recognition of the importance to us of this criterion puts us into a better position to distinguish the proper and legitimate center for our orientation, devotion and work—God—from the many idols demanding our attention and worship.

As we have seen, there is a second criterion for distinguishing God from the idols which must be employed along with this one, the criterion of relativization. Only to the extent that our theological world-picture, with God as its ultimate point of reference, continually calls us into question and enables us to recognize that true humanity—a truly humane and ecologically sustainable order in human life—is not yet here, and that we ourselves are not clear just what such an order would be like, can it help to protect us from the dangers of self-idolatry; only as we become open to radical criticism of our limited and biased perspectives and attitudes—our middle-class, western values and points of view, our parochial notions of where history is going, what movements beyond our present structures and ideas and ideals are required to bring about a "truly humane and ecologically sustainable order"—do we become free to move into the future with a concern wide enough to encompass all God's creatures and with a creativity that can promote the well-being of all. It is, thus, important that our devotion and activities be focused by images and concepts that locate the true humaneness and humanization for which we are striving outside of or beyond *us*, beyond our selves, our ideas, indeed our world—that is, in that Reality (or those realities) which can draw us beyond everything we now are or do or can imagine. The wealthy and the powerful in today's world particularly need to be relativized by such a transcendent center of orientation. The criterion of *relativization,* thus, is as essential for distinguishing God from the idols as the criterion of *humaneness*. The image/concept "God," understood and interpreted with the help of these two criteria, can focus our consciousness and devotion in such a way as to help draw us, or drive us, beyond our present ideals and values into a new and open future transcending anything we today can even imagine.

Unfortunately, the Christian churches early began to understand themselves in terms rather different from those I have just been sketching. They came to see their historical derivation from and thus connectedness with the man Jesus—whom they identified as "the Christ," the "Son of God," the "second Person of the Trinity"—as a kind of metaphysical guarantee that they were the true ongoing embodiment of his ministry and spirit and thus the special agents of God on earth. Roman Catholicism made this claim in largely institutional terms: since the bishops of Rome could trace their lineage and thus their authorization back through Peter directly to Jesus, the church was assured of its connection with the divine. Though the Eastern Orthodox churches remained more decentralized, they also held that only communities subordinate to and governed by duly ordained bishops could be assured of the ongoing presence of the spirit of Christ and God. The later Protestant churches, rebelling against such thoroughly institutionalized forms of authority and power, claimed instead that the visible presence of "word and sacraments" and/or verbal confessions of faith in the lordship of Christ were the proper marks of "the true church." In each of these cases the churches defined themselves *over against* the non-Christian world—"heathens," "pagans," "infidels," the "unsaved," those not "elect by God." Though Christians believed they were exercising a "ministry of reconciliation" in all of this, in actual fact their doctrines, practices, and institutions worked as one more divisive force among women and men. The proper forms of confession and ordination, and of the administration of the (other) sacraments, became more emphasized than loving one's neighbor as oneself, certainly more important than loving enemies and becoming reconciled with them. The churches all "confess" the revelation of God in Christ, but in many respects (from the perspective of the wider view of Christ with which we are working here) their actual institutional and communal lives belie it.

It has always been hard to take seriously the demands made by the Christ-symbol, especially as these were presented in the radical teachings of Jesus. Consider, for example, the parable of the last judgment (Mt. 25:31–46), which appears to address directly some of the issues with which we are here concerned. According to this parable, it is not those with nominal or institutional commitments to Jesus as Lord who will be acknowledged as his true followers at the last judgment, but rather those who perform simple acts of kindness or mercy "to one of the least of these my brethren" (25:40, 45)—giving a cup of cold water to the thirsty, clothing the naked, ministering to the sick. "Not every one who says to me, 'Lord, Lord,' shall enter the kingdom of heaven," Jesus says in another connection, "but he who does the will of my Father who is in heaven" (Mt. 7:21). That is, it is through participation in actual ministries of healing and caring for the suffering and the estranged wherever they are found, in loving our neighbors and our enemies, that the ongoing work of humanization—the work of God in the world to which Jesus' followers are called—is carried out, not through pronouncing certain verbal confessions or associating oneself with certain institutional structures and practices. It is precisely these sorts of reconciling and healing activities that are directed toward the overcoming of enmities and hatreds, poverty and oppression, and that are thus community-building, which are most urgently needed in today's world, as a historically, culturally, economically, and religiously divided humanity is being forced to grow together again, and as human life on planet Earth becomes a single interconnected network.[4]

This view of Christ presents us with a configuration of images and notions that can provide a powerful paradigm of both the human and the divine, that is, a paradigm which not only makes intelligible (in its own way) our understanding of human existence but also helps identify the evolutionary/historical trajectory that is moving it toward fuller humanization. It presents a coherent, meaningful—and, to some at least, a compelling—picture of human existence and human destiny, of our place in the world and our task(s) in life. Obviously this is not the only such picture available to us: there are many other (both religious and secular) ways of understanding the human situation, our deepest problems, the direction in which human history should be going. Some of these alternatives present quite convincing cases, and there is no excuse for not taking them seriously: one thinks of Freudian, Marxist, existentialist, deconstructionist, feminist, and other secular humanist perspectives; of contemporary forms of Buddhism, Hinduism, Confucianism, Judaism, Islam, and others of the great religious traditions; as well as of other quite different conceptions of Christian faith—each presenting its own (more or less fully defined) picture of the human condition today and its hopes for the future. My claim is not that Christian views of human existence and destiny are the only ones which need to be taken seriously, but rather the much more modest one that (at least some) Christian views are quite intelligible, and can be seen to make a certain kind of sense of the unfolding course of biological evolution and human history, and of the many urgent problems with which we humans must today come to terms. They present a coherent and comprehensible picture of human life within the world, one which contemporary persons can and should take seriously when deciding to what they should commit themselves, how they should orient themselves in life, to what complex of images, values, and meanings they should give their deepest loyalty, trust, devotion—that is, what God they should worship.

No coercive proof can be given that the Christ-symbol presents us with materials for constructing a conception of the True God (and not just one more idol)—our third desideratum; but it is possible, nevertheless, to see why one might be led to take such a position. For an understanding of God based on the christic paradigm (as presented here) does identify, bind together, and hold before us, in a configuration of powerful images and concepts, a conception of the (cosmic, biological, and historical) forces which both *humanize* and *relativize* us human beings; which draw us out and move us toward a more profound humaneness while simultaneously rendering questionable our proudest achievements as well as the overreaching claims we are inclined to make for ourselves—precisely the marks that we earlier decided (Chapters 21, 22, and 24) distinguish the True God from all idols. So we may be prepared, as a sixth step of faith, to commit ourselves to the humanizing and relativizing powers which are discernible with the aid of criteria derived from these images.

But of course the moment we are inclined to claim that this God-revealed-in-Christ is indeed the True God, not an idol, we must beware lest we convert this into a claim about ourselves: that it is *our* beliefs that are the true ones (in contrast with all those Hindus, Freudians, and positivists), that our community is specially elect of God, that our activities are guided by the Holy Spirit in a way not true of any others. For precisely at that point, with claims of that sort, instead of confessing the humanizing and reconciling Spirit(s) at work within history to be God, we are bowing down before the idol of our own beliefs and practices. Our lives are truly oriented on Christ (in the wider sense), and on the God who comes to expression in and through Christ, only to the extent that the spirit at work in us and our churches is the truly humanizing and reconciling Spirit that breaks down barriers among human beings, and builds communities of love, freedom, and justice in their stead (whatever may be the creed we utter with our lips).

It would be possible to spell out this understanding of the world much further, taking up the full range of traditional Christian doctrines; this is not necessary, however. That is the way in which the task of so-called systematic theology has often been conceived in the past, but it is probably no longer appropriate to think of theology in those terms.[5] What I have tried to present thus far is a meaningful and illuminating interpretation of the four central "categories" of the Christian perspective—humanity/world/God/Christ—enabling us to gain some sense of what a contemporary Christian world-picture might look like. We should note at this point, however, that the "Christian categorial scheme" has actually provided us with only a somewhat rough "table of contents" of the Christian world-picture. In the next chapter we shall see that trinitarian reflection requires—and enables—a rather drastic, and quite illuminating, reconception of the basic categorial pattern with which we have been working thus far.

I hope that by now it is clear that, however problematic the Christian picture of the world may be in many ways, it is neither unintelligible to modern consciousness nor irrelevant to modern life. There is still good reason to devote ourselves to God, not merely in some vague largely undefined sense, but to the God revealed in Christ. Our sixth and final step of faith is principally constituted by just such a movement beyond the largely humanistic understanding of God with which we have been concerned through much of this book. The doctrine of the trinity will fully integrate this step into a Christian understanding of God for today.

27. A Trinitarian God

The principal elements of a Christian understanding of God are now before us, and we are in a position to draw them all together in summary form; the concept of God as *trinity* is admirably suited to this purpose. It is widely acknowledged that the notion of the trinity is the most distinctive feature of the Christian conception of God; and such notable modern philosophers as Hegel and Whitehead have hailed Christian trinitarian reflection and speculation as introducing important original ideas into western philosophical thought. The trinitarian idea breaks decisively with the substantialistic assumptions of our philosophical traditions—that reality consists fundamentally of *substances* ("thing-like" somethings), and that it is with the concept of "substance," therefore, that we designate most precisely that which is truly real. With the development of the idea of the *perichoresis* of the three persons of the trinity (their interpenetration into one another), the notion of ultimate reality (God) as simple substance is displaced by a much more complex conception: on the one hand, the "persons" of the trinity are so involved with one another, so relationally interconnected in their very being, that it is simply not possible to conceive them as independent substances who have their being or can act in any way independently of the others *(una substantia, tres personnae);* on the other hand, the "one substance" that God is thought to be is precisely this exceedingly complex interpenetrative activity/being of the three "persons," a conception far removed from the simple oneness or unity which "substance" had previously designated. It would carry us far afield even to summarize briefly the reflection and elaborate argumentation which led to this extraordinary concept of God, but perhaps enough has been said to make it evident that some exceedingly complex notions were being generated in the course of Christian trinitarian reflection, and that along with them new dialectical ways of thinking were beginning to emerge. It is hardly surprising that both Hegel and Whitehead saw anticipations of their own thinking here; nor is it surprising that a good many others saw all of this Christian talk as unintelligible hocus-pocus, in which it is supposed that somehow in God 3 = 1 and 1 = 3.

In taking up the concept of the trinity now I do not intend to enter into these controversies. My interest in this idea does not derive from some desire to retain venerable Christian notions simply because they have been so important in the past: that would go against the most fundamental intentions of this constructivist approach to theology. It derives, rather, from my belief that the notion of trinity provides us with a pattern of ideas, and a dialectical understanding of the interconnectedness among ideas, which can pull together in a very illuminating way several major strands with which we have been working (perhaps not entirely consciously), as we have proceeded with our step-by-step construction of a Christian conception of God for today. With the concept of trinity I hope to draw together in compact summary form the understanding of God we have been developing, while also (incidentally) showing the continuing usefulness of the trinitarian concept for theological work today.[1] (For a schematic expression of the comprehensive drawing together and summing up which I shall undertake in my use of the concept of trinity, see Figure 4 in Chapter 20.)

The doctrine of the trinity purports to be above all about *God,* the Christian understanding of God. In our consideration of the desiderata which adequate conceptions of God must satisfy (Chapter 26), we noted that the most important question to be put to a proposed interpretation of God (the third desideratum) is: Is this really *God* we are dealing with here, or some idol? Precisely this issue is the first one addressed in the doctrine of the trinity: it is taken up in the doctrine of the so-called First Person, which confronts directly the question of the *godness* of God. We discovered in the course of this book (it is important to recall) that it is not possible to address this question in a theologically serious way until we have made reasonably clear to ourselves what we mean by "God," that is, until we have moved a considerable distance down the path of theological construction. In the order of theological construction, thus, the question about God and the idols is among the last to be directly addressed. However, when one wishes to state straightforwardly a doctrine of God, this is the first point to be made: it is *God* of which we intend to speak here, not something else; *God* is the subject to which we are seeking to attend. At the very beginning of this volume a similar announcement of intent was presented: the question about God and the idols was stated (in Chapter 1) to be central to our concerns. But at that point it was unclear just what kind of question this was and what sort of issues it involved; and it has taken several hundred pages to sort out and address those matters. Only toward the end (after a long process of construction/reconstruction), when we began to become clear about what we might justifiably mean by "God" today, did we move into a position from which we could ask, Who or what, then, is God? To have attempted to address that question earlier, before we had filled out our picture, would have led us to answer it in terms too abstract to be meaningful. We needed to work out the notions of humanness and humaneness, serendipitous cosmic creativity, evolutionary-historical trajectories, a wider christology, mystery, and so on, before we could see in some more concrete way just what the word "God" might today be taken to denote.

Though the question of the godness of God is, thus, one of the last to be taken up in the order of construction, the *reality* of the godness of God must be regarded as first in the order of being—and this is preeminently the order that is most important to faith. By "God" we mean to be referring to that which is "the Alpha and the Omega, the first and the last, the beginning and the end" (Rev. 22:13) of all that we are and all that we can imagine or know—the ultimate mystery with which we humans have to do. Only this can provide orientation for our lives appropriate to the world in which we actually live; this alone, therefore, is Reality suitable for our unqualified devotion. If we are not intending to call to mind this mystery when we utter the name "God," it is an idol with which we are concerned. The first intention of faith, then, when speaking of or to God is to address itself to the ultimate mystery of things, what is called (in traditional Christian language) the First Person of the trinity. And the early creeds usually opened with an affirmation such as, "I believe in [that is, I commit myself to] God the Father, almighty creator of heaven and earth."

For us humans today (as I have been arguing) it is the serendipitous creativity—which, working through the great evolutionary ecosystem that is our world, has brought us into being and is drawing (or driving) us on toward a fuller humanization—that best answers to this first intention of faith. The metaphors in which the early Christians articulated their faith are (as we have seen) overly anthropomorphic and sexist, and they suggest an anthropocentric picture of the universe; hence, in our theological reflection here, we have been replacing many of these with metaphors that express and evoke our modern understanding of ourselves and the world. Similarly, the traditional trinitarian technical (and subsequently liturgical) language—for example, the use of the term "person" in what is now an archaic sense—almost inevitably leads to many further sorts of misunderstanding today; therefore, in my analysis and interpretation of the trinity here I shall employ expressions such as the "first intention" or the "first motif" of this concept (instead of the "First Person").[2] Despite my reservations about the terminology in which traditional trinitarian doctrine was formulated and expressed, I believe that certain of the points which it makes are both clear and correct. Thus it is quite proper to say—as the doctrine of the "First Person" suggests—that when it is *God* we are attempting to address ourselves to or speak about, our "first intention" must be to concern ourselves with the ultimate Reality with which we have to do, the ultimate Mystery of things.

Much more than this is being intended, however, when the word "God" is employed in Christian discourse; in themselves, the notions of "ultimate reality" and "ultimate mystery" are so abstract as to be almost empty of meaning. To what do they refer? Certainly not to anything we directly experience: by what mark or criterion could we identify "ultimate reality" in our experience? Whatever else this term might signify, it does not seem to name anything experientially perceived. But concepts without percepts are utterly empty, as Kant pointed out long ago.[3] However significant for theology or religion such notions as "ultimate mystery" and "ultimate reality" may seem to be, then, unless they can be given content in some way, they will possess only the form of thought but have no genuine meaning. It is with respect to this issue that the other two "persons" or "motifs" of the trinity make their indispensable contributions: they provide experiential material, an experiential base, for the Christian understanding of God. The (Christian) notion of God, thus, is explicitly *synthetic:* it draws material from several different sources. The first motif of the trinity expresses the primary intention of our God-talk to be addressing itself to the transcendent, the mystery or reality beyond anything and everything we know or experience, *God;* other indispensable components of the idea of God are expressed by the second and third motifs of the trinitarian concept. Christian reflection on God has always recognized that unless we can say something specific and concrete about this transcendent "X"—can say something about who or what this "God" *is*—the intention to speak of God remains utterly empty.

What beyond the motif of transcendence is required to give the conception of God its full content and meaning, thus enabling it to function as intended? Two other quite distinct sorts of components are required: (a) God must be presented not merely as transcendent of, but also as significantly related to, the full range of reality(s) available to us in our experience and knowledge; (b) the image/concept of God must provide us with, and thus in some significant way include, norms and standards for the orientation of human life, that is, standards and norms which will significantly affect the way women and men comport themselves—the attitudes they hold, the aspirations they have, the decisions they make, the lives they lead. These two sets of issues are dealt with, respectively, by the doctrines of the Third and Second Persons of the trinity (the third motif and the second motif).

Let us take up the doctrine of the Third Person—the "Holy Spirit"—first. This doctrine expresses the understanding that God (the ultimate mystery) is everywhere present, is immanent in all that is: nothing could exist without God's (creative and preservative) activity, apart from God's presence "within" it. The world and God, thus, are not to be understood as radically *separated* realities or beings, divided from each other and existing over against each other, as the notion of God as creator, of God's radical transcendence (the first trinitarian motif), might seem, if taken by itself, to suggest; God is actually present to and "within" every created being. Ideas like these are difficult to think through clearly in the substantialist metaphysics of traditional theological reflection. According to that view, reality is made up of many individual objects or things, each more or less independent of the multitudes of other self-subsistent things in its environment, though related to them in many ways. How is it possible to understand distinct "substances" of this sort, each existing in its own separate space and standing over against all others in its distinctness, as "interpenetrated" by some super-substance? Though believers traditionally spoke of God's "omnipresence," it was virtually impossible to *think* clearly how this was to be understood; for God was also a substance—indeed, was substance *par excellence*—who occupied a distinct space ("heaven") sharply separated from the spaces which the creatures inhabited. How could God be in heaven and yet simultaneously everywhere on earth?

Although a substantialistic conceptual apparatus was the best available for early Christian reflection on theological issues, other quite different ways of thinking about reality and the world are at hand today. Modern sciences, for example, require conceptual schemes in which existent realities are thought of as interrelated "processes" of interconnected "events." Unlike the concept of "substance" (which suggests a something with relatively sharp boundaries distinguishing it from other "things"), the notions of "events" and "processes" suggest realities with much vaguer boundaries, realities which permeate one another in diverse ways. Today we think of the universe as a great ecosystem, with everything within it intrinsically interconnected and interdependent with all that is in its environment; in the modern understanding, moreover, this is not a static ecosystem with its various components balanced over against each other so as to maintain the same basic structure forever: this is an evolutionary ecosystem, a developmental whole, always in process of evolving into new patterns of events as time unfolds.

With a conceptual scheme of this sort, the notion of God's omnipresence can become intelligible in a new way. We have already noticed (in Chapter 19) the usefulness of the concept of "creativity" for interpreting the continuous in-breaking of novelty into the overall cosmic process. The traditional concept of the all-pervasive activity of the "divine spirit" can be connected with this notion, and we can speak of the "divine creativity" as that in the patterns of events and processes which is always and everywhere actively bringing into being whatever comes to exist; it is that, thus, which gives whatever exists its very reality, its being. (This move presupposes, of course, that we have made the several steps of faith that carry us beyond the bare notion of "serendipitous creativity" developed in Chapter 19 to an explicitly theological understanding of these matters.) The floor we stand on, the air we breathe, the words we speak, our bodies, our interactions with our friends—all these things so *real* to us are taken now to be (in a significant sense) the direct expression of God's continuous activity in the world, the presence of the "Holy Spirit," the Third Person of the trinity. One could go so far as to say that God (*qua* third motif of the trinitarian concept) *is* the very "reality" of all things—that is, by "God" we mean not only the ultimate mystery of things (first motif), but also that in the complex patterns of processes and events (whatever it may be) without which they would have no "reality," no "being" (third motif). That which we think of as ultimate mystery (first intention) is to be conceived in such a way that we simultaneously think of it as always present in all things (third intention), think of it as the "divine spirit" with us and in us and through us.[4]

Given this interpretation, the question whether God "exists" dissolves away. That is a question which can certainly arise for substantialist thinking, according to which the entire "three-personed" God is understood to exist as a particular something (an individual substance). Since to "exist" ordinarily means to be "somewhere," in some particular place, God must be thought of either as existing in a place to which we do not have access (heaven), or as existing somehow but not in any sort of place (an oxymoron). Not surprisingly, these issues have given rise to interminable disputes about God-the-trinity's reality. In the position I am setting out here, however, instead of holding that the trinity is some sort of mysterious substance, all three "persons" of which exist "out there" somewhere, "trinity" is regarded as essentially a conceptual device which holds together the three indispensable and inseparable strands in Christian thinking about God. Notions like "transcendence," "mystery," "absoluteness," and the like are understood to be important articulations of one dimension of the idea of God, the "first motif" (or intention) of the trinitarian concept; but this motif cannot be properly understood in abstraction from the equally indispensable second and third motifs. In contrast with the emphasis of the first motif on God's transcendence and radical otherness, the third motif (as we have just been noting)—the Holy Spirit—expresses the presence of God in and with the reality of everything that exists, and thus the presence of God to us and with us and in us in every moment of our lives (whether we are aware of this or not). As the creativity manifest throughout the cosmic process (first motif), giving everything that exists whatever reality it has (third motif), God is reality *par excellence,* the very principle of reality (first motif again).

According to the third intention of the concept of the trinity, thus, we are dealing with God in every moment of every day—whether we are concerned with getting food for our bodies, listening to a Mozart quartet, working desperately to save the planet from ecological destruction, enjoying sexual congress, synthesizing DNA in a laboratory, playing with children on the kitchen floor. In all these experiences and activities, *God's reality* is encountered in and through the finite realities directly experienced. This is, of course, a claim of faith, not an empirical observation: as we have seen throughout our program of theological construction (with its successive "steps of faith"), God is not to be understood as an empirical something, apprehended in experience in any ordinary way. This conceptual point (we can now observe) follows directly from the central emphasis of the first intention of the trinitarian concept: God's otherness, God's utter transcendence, God's mysteriousness. When this point is taken together with the concept of God's immanence, of God's presence to us in all the particulars of experience (third intention), it becomes clear that the divine reality cannot properly be thought of as one more particular being either in the world or "out there" in some transcendental heaven: God must be conceived in much more generalized (and vague) terms than that—for example, as the creativity at work within the unfolding evolutionary ecosystem, giving reality and directional movement and interconnectedness to the great multiplicity of particular events and beings in the world but not itself a particular being. By invoking the name "God," then, we mean to be focusing our consciousness on that process of or pattern in events (whatever it may be) which is at once creative and directional and unifying, which brings all that is into being and binds it into a *uni*verse—an ordered world that can sustain the web of life as a whole, and human historical existence within that web.

God's transcendence (first motif) and God's immanence (third motif) articulate different, but mutually reinforcing, aspects of the universality or all-comprehensiveness of God: they help to make clear what we mean when we say that it is *God* which is the primordial reality (mystery) at work behind and within and among *all* that is. Without such universal extension in its reference, the symbol "God" could not, of course, adequately perform its principal function—to orient human life properly in this world within which we lead our lives. But it also could not perform this function if it did not have another crucial component in its makeup: a criterial or normative dimension which can provide significant direction and guidance for ongoing human life. To say that God is involved in everything without exception gives us no help at all in making the many quite *particular* choices of which life is made up—to turn toward some things but away from others; to give ourselves to certain projects, causes, values, while working against others; to seek to shape our lives and our world in this way rather than that. To be oriented equally toward *everything*, all that is, would be to fly apart in all directions, to disintegrate as selves. No longer possessing centeredness and directionality, we would lose our agency, our power to act and choose and create, completely; and we would become beings simply acted upon, determined from without by the multitude of forces playing upon us from all sides. In short, we would lose precisely what is distinctive about our humanity: our freedom and creativity and self-consciousness, our historicity. As we saw in Part II, humans must have norms and standards which enable them to identify, from among the many forces playing upon them, those which will be creative of a better world and will assist them in their efforts to adapt to, and significantly contribute to, the coming of that world. Since a divine reality conceived entirely in terms of universalistic symbolism (however beautifully and thoughtfully articulated) would in no way bear upon these hard particulars of our many day-to-day choices, it could not significantly orient us in our actual living and dying as self-conscious historical beings. If it is to orient us effectively with respect to concerns of this sort, the divine reality mediated by the symbol "God" must (without negating its universality) manifest a *specific character* and a *specific directionality* in its activity, a character and directionality which suggest to us criteria and norms for ordering our lives in this world in which we find ourselves.

This is where the so-called Second Person of the trinity comes in. The second motif of the Christian understanding of God gives it a distinctive specificity and definiteness: God is thought to have "revealed" Godself in Christ; that is, Christ (understood in the "wider sense") provides a normative model with reference to which Christian image/concepts of God are constructed. According to this model, the universe is not taken to be simply what it presently appears to be; because of the activity of the God-revealed-in-Christ within it, the universe is going someplace, is being transformed in certain decisive ways, is moving on toward patterns not yet here—a "new heavens and a new earth," the "kingdom of God." For human beings to be oriented on this God means to labor within and promote those currents in history moving toward God's order of love and freedom (already foreshadowed in the early communities of Jesus' followers); that is, it means to form ourselves according to the paradigm of Christ. Of course, this entire configuration of theological images and ideas and claims is highly controversial; that it has this sort of normative significance must be understood (as we have seen) as essentially a faith-claim, not as something that can be established by evidence and proof. Precisely this faith-claim, however, is central to the Christian understanding of God, and thus an essential dimension of what is intended by Christians when they speak of God. This "second intention" or "second motif" of the trinitarian concept gives the conception of God concreteness and definiteness (without negating the divine universality expressed in the first and third motifs), the sort of concreteness and definiteness which can provide significant orientation in the evolutionary-historical development of the world, for those communities and selves that take it seriously. For Christian faith, thus, God is not simply "ultimate reality" or "ultimate mystery": "God" is the name used to integrally connect such notions as ultimate mystery and ultimate reality with that creative trajectory (to use the language we have been developing in this volume) of biohistorical forces and powers moving toward the transformation of all human existence into a truly humane order, a direction made paradigmatically visible by the ministry and death of Jesus and the new order of relationships in the early Christian communities. The inseparability of the several motifs of the trinity means that to devote oneself to God is to devote oneself to Christ, and to devote oneself to Christ (in our wider sense) is to devote oneself to God. The second intention of the trinitarian concept is as indispensable to its meaning (for Christian faith) as are the first and third.

It is important to recognize that when Christian faith affirms in this way a particular set of models or images as significantly revelatory of God, it is not thereby adding an extra something (not really essential) which other monotheistic positions can avoid. Characterizations of God as "ultimate reality" or "being itself" or "ultimate mystery"—though emphasizing important notes of universality and transcendence—are (as we have just seen) in themselves empty of any content that can provide effective orientation for human life. So far, then, as a notion of God (or any other metaphysical conception, for that matter) is claimed to provide some actual guidance for the way we live, it must present and accent (whether this is explicitly acknowledged or not) some specific configurations of value and meaning, or some particular images and models, as exemplary or paradigmatic of what is genuinely important for human beings—that is, as "revelatory" of the true character of the ultimate reality or ultimate mystery with which we humans supposedly have to do. The concepts of matter and power (or the will-to-power), of life or striving or struggle, of self-preservation, sexual fulfillment, beauty, pleasure, truth, creativity, and many others, have functioned in this way. In all such cases certain *particular* features of human experience or life are taken as keys or clues to the meaning of the whole of life, and on this basis criteria or norms for shaping and ordering life are proposed. (Even such notions as mystery or emptiness gain their meaning in part by contrast with everyday experiences of seeing clearly and understanding, or of solidity and fullness; they also, thus, express a certain particularity and definiteness, though so inchoately as to be virtually useless for orienting life.) No one, of course, is in a position to *know* that this or that particular meaning is the key or clue to all human life and all reality. In this respect, every recourse to such a paradigmatic notion is somewhat arbitrary: it expresses an act (or attitude) of faith in face of the mystery of things.

With these considerations in mind, one could argue that every religious or metaphysical position implicitly presupposes a threefold intention similar to that articulated in the Christian concept of the trinity: (a) it intends to address itself to or speak of Reality, what is ultimately true and real behind and beyond all appearances and illusions; (b) it is with the aid of certain particular (more or less ordinary) concepts and experiences, or configurations of experiences and concepts—evidently taken to represent and thus to *present* (incarnate?) this Reality—that it is characterized and interpreted, and thus is understood; (c) all the rest of experience and life—and the enormous diversity of realities and meanings that make it up—are now understood and interpreted in terms of their places within a Whole defined and characterized by the chosen paradigm.[5] Christian faith and theology, then, are distinctive not because they employ a finite model as key or clue to the proper understanding of humanity and the ultimate cosmic reality but because it is *Christ* to which they give this sort of paradigmatic significance.

Each of these three intentions or motifs is indispensable to the Christian understanding of God; each expresses something without which (from a Christian point of view) God would not be *God.* Apart from the first intention—that this is *God* with which we have to do here—the content of Christian faith would be limited largely to the tragic story of one human being, Jesus, and the first-century community of his followers. Without the second, the notion of God would be abstract and formal, essentially an "X" empty of any content which could provide orientation for life. Given these first two motifs, but absent the third—the all-pervasive Spirit of God—though God might be held to be present in and represented by the life of Jesus and the early churches two thousand years ago, the connection of this with our world and our lives today (and with all the rest of the biohistorical world of which we are part) would remain unspecified; God would remain, thus, largely irrelevant to us.

As traditional trinitarian reflection has emphasized, however, more can and must be said than simply that each of these motifs is indispensable: what we are really concerned with here is not three motifs or intentions but rather a single Reality, the *one God;* it is important, thus, that these three be conceived as dialectically interconnected in such a way as to be *one* with each other. This point can be explained most easily by noting difficulties that arise if it is denied. For example, assume that it is not truly the ultimate mystery of things (the first intention of Christian faith) that is present to and with and among us and all other realities (third intention): then *God* is not really present to us and with us, and the ordering principles and powers of our world and our experience are in fact something other than God. Or, assume that what we see and relate to in and through the symbol "Christ" (the second intention) is not the transcendent mystery (first intention): then devotion to and orientation on Christ is in fact idolatrous, such faith not being directed toward God at all. Or, assume that the hard facticity of our human existence (the third intention)—the material conditions with which we must come to terms, the social struggles in which we are engaged, the personal dilemmas we face, the intellectual quandaries we confront—is not caught up into, and shaped and ordered and given its proper significance by, the reality encountered in Christ (second intention): then this christic reality cannot provide adequate criteria and norms for ordering our actual lives and addressing our problems. What we have been treating as three distinct intentions, we can now see, will be seriously misleading if we do not recognize that they dialectically imply one another in such a way as to direct us toward a single, self-identical reality, the one God; our speaking in terms of three intentions was simply a way to articulate for ourselves the complexity of what is in fact a single intention—to direct ourselves to God. We mistakenly reify these three motifs employed in our speaking and thinking of God if we fail at any point to take note of this dialectical interconnectedness, and suppose that these three present truly distinguishable "parts" or "features" of the one God—instead of being simply our limping attempt to articulate the complexity of what we must finally regard as one and self-identical in God. We would have no way to represent this one God to ourselves without attending to each of these motifs; the three intentions can be distinguished from one another, therefore, in that each is directed toward a motif without which what Christian faith calls "God" would not in fact be *God*. But we must continually remind ourselves that it is the one self-identical God that (for Christian faith) is present to humankind in the dialectical interconnectedness of these three, and that it is this one God, therefore—ultimate mystery, paradigmatically represented in Christ, and manifest and active in all things—toward which Christian faith seeks single-mindedly to direct itself. As the tradition has put it: the three Persons interpenetrate one another so thoroughly that dividing or separating them in any way—either in their being or in their activity—is unthinkable.[6]

By "God," then, Christian faith and Christian theology (in the interpretation presented here) are far from meaning some mythic being "up in heaven" ruling the world from on high, a being who one day sent "his" son to earth to appease the wrath of the father and thus save humans from everlasting torment. (The early formulations of trinitarian doctrine already ruled out that sort of mythology as heretical.) In this articulation of the trinitarian idea, I have attempted to overcome the reifying effects of the traditional trinitarian metaphors ("substance," "persons," et cetera), thus freeing us to see "trinity" as a concept that specifies the central motifs of the Christian understanding of God while simultaneously holding them together in indissoluble unity—just the sort of concept that is needed to sum up and state clearly the unique logical structure of the central focus of Christian faith (as we have been construing it here). In this interpretation of Christian faith, the symbol "God" is intended to designate (a) the ultimate reality (mystery) with which we humans have to do, a reality regarded as the creativity which is at work in and through all things (first motif); that which (b) is thus present in and with all realities of our world—all that we can experience, know, or imagine—as that which enables them to be real, their very "reality" so to speak (third motif); and which (c) is at work, therefore, within the evolutionary-historical trajectory which has produced our humanness and is moving us toward a more profound humaneness, a trajectory manifest in and paradigmatically identifiable by the Christ-event (second motif).

It is important to note, now, how the concept of trinity is related to the fourfold categorial scheme employed up to this point to describe Christian perspectives, and to the threefold scheme said to be characteristic of monotheisms generally. The trinitarian conception, on the face of it, is not consistent with these basic patterns that have ordered much of the thinking in this book; and its introduction here, therefore, may seem to threaten the fundamental coherence of this whole project. Is the "God" of the threefold monotheistic categorial scheme now to be thought of as a trinity? If so, what could it mean to speak of Christ as a "fourth" category found in Christian monotheisms, when Christ is already included as a central "person" or "motif" of the trinity? But if the concept of trinity cannot be directly applied to what is called "God" in the monotheistic categorial pattern, to what does it refer—to "God" plus "Christ"? What place has the Holy Spirit, the "Third Person" of the trinity, in these categorial schemes? Perhaps these schemes must now be discarded?

If theological reflection and construction were understood to be essentially the activity of working out and filling in a basic pattern of ideas already present in principle when one begins one's work and not expected to change in any essential way as one proceeds, these sorts of problems and difficulties would certainly arise; for in our work here we have in fact ended with a conception that cannot be fitted directly into the categorial patterns with which we began. But from the beginning I have been arguing against the claim that in theological work we are engaged simply in making explicit what had been implicit all along: on the contrary, I have contended that theology is always an activity of *construction,* of bringing into being something that had not been there before. It is certainly true that we entered upon our theological work here by reflecting upon the fairly simple (and somewhat simplistic) notion that "God" is to be thought of as one term in a relatively straightforward easy-to-understand threefold (or fourfold) structure. However, the constructive work which has been necessitated in the course of our exploration of these several terms has carried us into complex notions of their interconnectedness and interdependence; and the concept of God-as-trinity, which can be seen as taking up and including within itself (so to speak) all else—the world, humanity, and Christ, though without canceling out or denying the distinctive reality and significance of any of these—turns out to be capable of drawing all the constructive work that went before into a new and illuminating systematic unity. The concept of trinity does indeed supply a different sort of conceptual pattern from the ones with which we had previously been working. This does not mean, however, that we are left, finally, with massive incoherency. From the beginning we have been employing concepts as heuristic devices intended to forward our thinking—not as windows opening on a vista of "the true nature of things"—and, as such, they are to be left behind as new more appropriate conceptions are constructed. The three- and fourfold categorial schemes served their purposes in the developing movement of our thinking, and there is no reason now to suppose it necessary, or even appropriate, to try to make them cohere systematically with the concept of trinity which has superseded them.

A path ordinarily is not expected to end where it began; it should not surprise us if an activity of step-by-step imaginative construction dealing with the profound mysteries of life ultimately concludes at a point scarcely intimated when it was initiated. The metaphor in terms of which theology should be understood is not that of a logically coherent timeless system of concepts in which our "end" is our "beginning" (T. S. Eliot)[7] but rather that of journeys to new lands, an ongoing pilgrimage into the unknown. The proper question to ask as we come to the end of this journey and look forward to others in the future is, Have we come to new and more profound insights into and understandings of Christian faith, human existence, and the realities with which they must come to terms? not, Does our conclusion reveal the same basic insights, ideas, and patterns with which we began? If the latter were the case, the hard "labor of the [theological] concept" (Hegel)[8] would hardly be worth the candle. We have come to an interpretation of Christian faith in which the symbol "God" designates and holds together in a unified conception the ultimate mystery of the cosmic ecosystem of which we are part (God's "transcendence") and the cosmic evolutionary-historical trajectory toward humanization (God's "humaneness"). For us historical beings, as we have seen, life is grounded on deep faith-commitments, patterns of trusting and hoping and loving that shape our attitudes and ways of thinking, our values and goals, our overall style of life and what it means to us. As our trinitarian construction emphasizes, Christian faith, in its concern with one God, makes two inseparable claims: it involves a basic commitment to *God*—that is, to a construal of the ultimate mystery of things as human-affirming, human-sustaining, and human-enhancing; and God is always understood in the light of *Christ*—the paradigmatic image of the human, and thus a principal clue to what is really going on in the world (what "God is doing") that is of ultimate importance to men and women.

An understanding of God—and of reality—of this sort may, of course, seem quite implausible to many, untrue to the world of today's experience. Certainly it is one that makes strenuous demands on believers, for there is so much in our world that is utterly inhuman, so much that needs radical transformation before any community of genuine love/equality/freedom could become well established. The ecosystem in which we live hardly seems to be moving toward bringing forth, and sustaining, a truly humane order of life in its midst; and a powerful act of faith is required, therefore, to believe that what is really going on in our world is anything like this—that, as Paul put it, although "the whole creation has been groaning in travail together until now" (Rom. 8:22), ultimately "the creation itself will be set free from its bondage to decay and obtain the glorious liberty of the children of God" (8:21). Nevertheless, as he went on to say, it is precisely "in this hope" that we are "saved" (8:24). However plausible or implausible this vision of the human situation in the world may be, it is still (for many) sufficiently coherent and meaningful to make a powerful appeal. The conception of the trinity, properly interpreted, sums up and ties together this whole Christian world-picture. It is not a world distinguished from others by virtue simply of a peculiar fourfold categorial structure; it is a world within which everything is ordered finally to that God "from [which] and through [which] and to [which] are all things" (Rom. 11:36), that God "in [which] we [humans] live and move and have our being" (Acts 17:28).

Part V

Faith and Life in Today's World

One lives and becomes conscious neither within a guarantee nor within a void . . . One can only live in faith. Life . . . is . . . the actualization of faith; pure self-consciousness of life is the awareness of faith, that is, the awareness of need and hope, of the lack of self-sufficiency and of possibility.

Mikhail Bakhtin

To discern the ways of God not in supernatural but in all natural and historic events, to respond to his intention present in and beyond and through all finite intentions, that is the way of responsibility to God.

H. R. Niebuhr

In our earthly experience the Divine Life is not One, but Many. But to apprehend the One in the Many constitutes the special character of love.

Ernst Troeltsch

If anyone says, "I love God," and hates his brother, he is a liar; for he who does not love his brother whom he has seen, cannot love God whom he has not seen.

1 John 4

Knowledge puffs up, but love builds up.

1 Corinthians 8

28. Theocentric Faith and the Churches

We now have before us a holistic construction of human existence within its proximate and ultimate contexts, a conception developed through a reconstruction of the Christian categorial scheme—God/world/humanity/Christ—in light of contemporary scientific and historical knowledge and philosophical reflection and understanding, and brought to completion in a version of the trinitarian idea. My own limitations in knowledge and insight, of course, have prevented many important points of view, many interesting and significant issues and problems and subject matters, from being taken up here; and this restricts the comprehensiveness and adequacy of the picture I have sketched. What I have attempted to do is reconstruct the Christian world-picture along lines that seem to me suggested—or demanded—by widely agreed macro-conclusions in several important contemporary fields of knowledge: evolutionary-historical understandings of human being generally, taken together with sociohistorical conceptions of human selfhood, mind, and spirit; modern astrophysical and ecological ideas of the universe and the situatedness of life; sociological and anthropological conceptions of the role, character, and significance of language and other types of symbolization (particularly religious) in human experience, activity, and mentality (including the implications of this for our understanding of the sciences and other forms of knowledge); philosophical and theological reflection on all of these and on their meaning for our understanding of human existence in the world. It is true, of course, that these (and other relevant bodies of contemporary knowledge) can all be understood in many different ways, and a wide range of interpretations of their theological implications could be offered. So the fact that I have taken certain positions on anthropological, cosmological, methodological, and other questions should not be regarded as implying that I think the issues which these various knowledges pose for theology have been settled. I hope that, as the theological conversation moves on, my proposals here will encourage others to take up these and other related issues, developing them further than I have been able to do and presenting other quite different interpretations.

The reconception of Christian faith and Christian ideas which I have worked out here is not intended as a mere academic excercise: the ultimate objective of theological reflection and construction (as I have emphasized from the outset) is practical, not speculative. It is my hope, therefore, that this re-construction of humanity's place in the world can serve as a kind of large-scale map helping men and women find their way in life today as they are carried forward inexorably into the unknown future, a map which will assist them in identifying and addressing—in faith—major problems with which life now confronts humankind. If it cannot (or does not) succeed in doing that, it must be reckoned a failure.

Although the basic symbolic pattern with which I have been working in this book is Christian, much of my language (as in the theological tradition generally) has been universalistic in intention, focusing on and attempting to address issues and problems that (I have claimed) today confront not simply the Christian churches, or some particular groups within the Christian churches, but humanity as a whole. Protest against such universalistic pretentions has been widespread in recent years. In religious circles, for example among so-called liberation theologians, it is often claimed that the concern of the theological tradition to address questions supposedly facing all women and men has in fact served to distract theologians from attending to the issues of injustice, prejudice, and poverty in the particular local situations in which they were living and working. And in academic and literary circles, among so-called deconstructionists and others (who have learned much from such practitioners of the "hermeneutics of suspicion" as Marx, Nietzsche, and Freud), it has become a commonplace that universalistic knowledge-claims are always deeply infected with the drive for power and domination of those who formulate them, and with the prejudices and biases of their distinctly limited and particular social positions and perspectives; they are in fact not "universal" at all, thus, but are instead essentially hypocritical masks for prejudice, power, and position. Undoubtedly each of these critiques is correct in its fundamental insights; but in neither case does this warrant dismissing or ignoring the important questions to which so-called universal statements and claims are presented as responses or answers.

The evils to which the liberation theologians' critique calls attention must certainly be acknowledged, repented for, and corrected (so far as possible). But in attempting to address these matters, we (and they) must not forget that the very God of whose liberating will and activity these theologians speak is in fact regarded (by them and their hearers) as the God of all creation, and thus of every nation and people; for them (or for us) to overlook or neglect this point, acting or theologizing as though it were simply some tribal god whom they (or we) were serving, or interested in serving, would be idolatry of a crude and obvious sort. Christian theologians dare not evade attempting to understand and to articulate what it means to believe in and serve the one God of all the world—even though this requires making judgments about "all the world," "all of humanity," and the like, and drawing pertinent conclusions from those judgments. And the deconstructionist insight into the particularity, prejudice, and pursuit of power concealed in all "universalistic" claims, making them masks for unsavory motives of all sorts, likewise calls for forthright acknowledgment and repentance from theologians today, accompanied by the request for continuing criticism of these aspects of our work wherever they appear. But (as with the liberation theologians' critique) this understanding and acknowledgment must never be allowed to justify overlooking, or refraining from attending to and carefully formulating, the (logically and linguistically) implied universalistic dimensions of the issues with which we are working: the very insistence that every insight and affirmation is located within and significantly shaped by some particular, and therefore limited and distorting, sociohistorical context and perspective is itself universalistic in intention and extension. Seeking to avoid or refraining to acknowledge these dimensions of our intellectual work does not in any way "purify" it. The urge to express ourselves in (the "universals" of) a common language—the drive to communicate—is itself a movement toward addressing a potentially unlimited audience, a push toward the universal. Although it is incumbent on theologians (as well as others) to acknowledge that our intentions on these matters are never adequately realized, shortcomings and failures can be better guarded against and corrected if this feature of language and thought is openly acknowledged and attended to.

The language, writings, and ideas found in the various "world religions" (if not in all human religiousness) often attempt to identify and address matters of such supposedly universal (human) interest and significance—sin, salvation, suffering, evil, Nirvana, Brahman, submission to Allah or God, human nature, the proper way to live, and so on. In all cases, of course, this speech and reflection have arisen and developed within the common language and perspectives of a particular society; in addition they (usually) have come to include notions, points of view, special interpretations and understandings which have emerged within a relatively small elite (priests, seers, teachers, writers, and others) within that society. The views expressed are, therefore, necessarily conditioned and limited (in many unrecognized ways) by the experience and practices of a fairly narrow base of language-users within a particular culture. In view of these circumstances surrounding the origins and evolution of the symbols and rituals, insights and perspectives, of the religions, one may quite properly ask what justification can be offered for the universalistic claims they make. Are these all not simply the product of the inclination to reify the imagination's creations, of the desire to bring improper closure to its pictures and conceptions of the context of human existence? Or do these universalizing tendencies manifested in religious imaginative creativity have more importance than this suggests, an importance that could hardly have come to the surface and been made explicit apart from the special attention and reflection which the emergence of just such specialized elites made possible?

These two questions, I think, are really complementary to each other, not in opposition: together they can help us see something of what is going on in religious symbolization, and in the communities that cherish and cultivate it, and what are its limitations. Religious rituals and symbol-systems (as we have seen in Chapters 3, 4, 6, 16, and elsewhere) orient, energize, and furnish guidance for human life by providing men and women with meaningful pictures or conceptions of the world, and of the place of human life within that world; and by offering ways to participate actively in that meaning. Human life and activity are experienced as "meaningful" when these conceptions and pictures are sufficiently convincing to provide a sense of purposefulness and value in times of cultural or personal crisis as well as in the routine activities of ordinary day-to-day existence. They can function effectively in this way, of course, only if they are believed "true," that is, only if they are taken to represent (more or less adequately)—and thus to present—"how things really are" with humanity, the world roundabout, and God (or the gods or other resources of life and meaning). It is hardly surprising, then, that most historical communities and societies have taken their religious symbolizations and rituals very seriously, protecting them (as much as possible) from attack from without and from the corrosion of doubt, disinterest, and unbelief within. The appearance in most cultures (on the one hand) of designated persons or groups with a mandate to preserve and protect the religious traditions and practices, handing them on unchanged to the next generation, and (on the other) of a universalistic or absolutistic quality in religious beliefs and claims, both came about quite naturally in response to the sociological and psychological necessities of ongoing sociocultural life. A society that failed to protect and transmit the symbolical and ritual resources which gave meaning and purpose to its existence could not survive for long.

Precisely this, of course, is a major problem in the modern era. Our religious traditions have become tattered and frayed, implausible or otherwise unacceptable to many; and our religious institutions are pluralized and often bickering with one another, and they are far from universally respected or appreciated. The fragmentation of modern religious life (particularly in societies emphasizing the "separation of church and state") into endless denominations, sects, and cults only adds to the sense that religion is more a matter of private interest and taste than of public concern and necessity. Moreover, powerful rival ideologies and institutions offered by modern science and technology have come to seem more persuasive in many respects than those offered by our religious traditions, and more effective in addressing many of the major problems of modern life. So the wariness in modernity of our religious institutions and ideologies is not surprising. The rise of a profoundly critical spirit during the Enlightenment, combined with the development of impressive methods for critical examination, analysis, and assessment of truth-claims in the sciences, history, and philosophy, has quite properly made the absolutistic claims of religious groups seem suspect; and the emergence of a democratic spirit in political and social life rightly calls into question the authoritarian exercise of power in many traditional religious institutions.

The so-called scientific worldview (to which modern technology and science have contributed and which they also presuppose)—promulgated now widely throughout the world—presents a picture of human existence as emerging within an utterly impersonal cosmic order that provides virtually no support for or sustenance to many of today's most central human concerns, for example, about freedom and justice and human flourishing in peaceful social orders (from local to global), about the meaning and value and purposefulness of life, about how humans ought to live and die. The ideologies and institutions of modern science and technology, therefore, though they have contributed much to the weakening of our religious institutions, practices, and beliefs, are themselves ill-equipped to provide significant spiritual sustenance and support, either for the ups and downs of everyday life or for times of profound cultural and personal crisis. It is not difficult to understand, then, why problems of emptiness and meaninglessness have been so widespread in modernity: at present our culture does not seem to have resources adequate to sustain and support, to orient and guide, to motivate and refresh ongoing human life.

The program of theological construction set out in this book is intended to address certain aspects of this problem. On the one hand, we have been examining one of the major religious resources profoundly formative of—and still (though much weakened) very much alive in—western culture: Christian faith. I have been concerned throughout to explore the pertinence of Christian faith to life in the modern world, its relevance to the special problems with which modernity today confronts women and men; and I have been sketching a reconception of Christian faith and its meaning that (I believe) enables it to bear more directly and effectively on these matters. On the other hand, I have recognized throughout this reconstructive work that a *modern secular faith*—involving a general acceptance of the basic outlines of (among other things) the scientific picture of the cosmos in which we live, the emergence and evolutionary development of life in this world up to and including the appearance of humanity, the sociocultural and historical shaping of the main features of human existence, important new ways of thinking about the roles and functions of symbolism and language (religious and other) in human life—in fact underlies and informs much of the experience and activity and thinking of many men and women today (at least in the West). I have been attempting to address myself, that is to say, to a deep bifurcation in the faith that actually orients the lives of many moderns, a division between certain Christian values, meanings, and commitments that continue to remain important and those many features of actual day-to-day living and believing that are largely defined and informed by modern (secular) ideas and practices. I have not argued here for the rejection, or even the downplaying, of either of these two important strands of commitment and faith in the name of the other. In my view our faith(s), our deepest-lying concerns and commitments, can neither be simply dropped by the wayside at will nor easily and deliberately transformed into something new and different. They define our very being—who we are, how we understand ourselves, what our existence is and what it means to us, what we value most highly and are devoted to—and they are not, therefore, easily subject to our direct manipulation. On the contrary, all our musings and thinking and reflecting, our intentions and our deliberate acts, are grounded in and emerge out of and are the expression of these deeper levels of our being. The most we can hope to do with respect to these matters, then, is try to articulate, and thus get clearer to ourselves, these deep-lying pictures and conceptions of life and the world which we take for granted; and then, perhaps—where we find tensions and contradictions and imbalances threatening to render us impotent or to pull us apart—attempt to adapt or fit these to one another in such a way that they can begin (in due course) to grow together, mutually fructifying and reinforcing one another, as they mature into a better integrated, more holistic faith.

In our constructive theological work here, therefore, I have attempted to bring into sharper consciousness the tensions between these two strands, thereby putting us into a better position to search out ways to adapt and fit them to each other. On the one hand, I have sought to move behind the many proliferations of Christian doctrine and praxis that have grown up over the centuries—and the disagreements within and among the churches about these matters—to the underlying historically developing categorial pattern that appears to have given the various versions of Christian faith and life their basic meaning and structure and import. And I have employed this Christian categorial scheme in developing the interpretation (construction) of human existence in the world which I present here. The Christian categorial scheme has been given this overarching organizing position because it has a means of holding all value and meaning and being together in systematic structural interconnection—the monotheistic idea of one God performs precisely this function (as we have seen)—something that modern scientific conceptions and pictures have (notoriously) been unable to do. On the other hand, since modern scientific and historical knowledges, and modern philosophical reflection, address much more directly and specifically many of the multifarious aspects and dimensions of our experience, life, and culture today, I have drawn heavily on these in filling out the specifics of the understanding of the world and all within it (including human being in particular) that I am proposing; and, indeed, in developing my basic conception of God. My central assumption in taking this approach has been, of course, that the overall Christian categorial scheme is broad enough and deep enough to accommodate the many perspectives and the enormous complexity and detail of our modern knowledges (without seriously distorting them).

As a first approximation, the position I have constructed shows reasonably well, I think, that the contributions of modernity to the patterns of faith that in fact order and orient much in our lives today can be integrated into an overall faith-perspective that is given its basic shape and meaning by the central Christian categories. It appears to be possible, thus (at least as an experiment in thought), to draw these two principal strands of contemporary living faith—modern secular, and Christian—together into one relatively coherent understanding of human life in the world. Each is thus enabled to contribute its strengths, and to have its weaknesses in some respects complemented, as they grow together into a wider and deeper and more unified new faith, appropriate for contemporary life—instead of continuing to struggle against and undermine each other within the minds and hearts of women and men today. The reader will have to decide the extent to which my proposals have succeeded in establishing such a faith-synthesis. I hope I have at least shown that the effort to reconstruct inherited religious categorial schemes, as we seek to articulate faith(s) appropriate for modern living, is worth pursuing; and I hope that others, with perspectives quite different from mine, will be encouraged to undertake such projects also.

To whom are the reconstructive suggestions in this book addressed? These are proposals about the overall orientation of life today, about the kind of symbolic frame that can provide guidance and motivation for women and men in today's world. Are these ideas simply cast forth on the wind in the hope they might attract the attention of various individuals and groups here and there who happen to have the leisure to pursue such vague and abstruse issues, or is there a more particular audience to whom these proposals are expected to be of especial interest? There is a simple and straightforward answer to this question. In our society (as in most others) there are well-established religious institutions—churches and synagogues and others—which have a special interest in and commitment to preserving and cultivating, disseminating and transmitting, the religious traditions of the culture; and supporting these institutions, as well as being supported by them, are the many "communities of faith" within which men and women seek and continue to find significant spiritual sustenance from these religious traditions and practices. There exists, thus, a large, quite distinct, institutional and communal public, which concerns itself explicitly and regularly with questions of orientation, meaning, and motivation for human living and dying in today's world, a public which seeks to address these issues with the help of the major religious symbols and rituals inherited (largely) from Christian and Jewish traditions. Although monotheistic—indeed, Christian—modes of symbolization belong by now to human existence generally (in the sense that they are openly accessible and frequently invoked in many different regions of modern culture, especially in the West), it is the religious institutions in our society that are especially attached to this symbolism in their liturgies, morality, and stated beliefs, and that continue to use and perpetuate it seriously. For them the symbols "God" and "Christ" have a significance not felt throughout the culture; and the power of these symbols—for the most part latent in the culture at large—continues here to bear more directly on ongoing human existence and its problems.

Thus, in certain significant respects the churches and synagogues and mosques in our culture function in sociologically different ways from other groups. They understand (to a greater extent than society at large) that their ultimate loyalty must be given to God alone, not to the nation within which they reside or the wider civilization of which they (and the nation) are part. And they may find themselves for this reason more sensitive than other groups to such major social and moral evils as poverty, injustice, nationalistic pursuit of power, and so on. Since the symbol "God" is important to them in ways not true of society at large, they take greater cultural responsibility for it than most other institutions or communities. Their concern to "remember" God's "mighty acts" in the past, to encourage orientations in life centered on God in the present, and to engender such orientations in each upcoming generation, has made them the principal historical bearers in our culture of monotheistic perspectives and symbolic patterns.

Today many are inclined, perhaps, to look upon these religious institutions as weak and largely irrelevant to main currents of cultural life. It is important to recognize, however, that without these sociocultural carriers our monotheistic patterns of symbolization would quite possibly not have survived into the present at all. Moreover, without continuing support from relatively strong communities and institutions explicitly devoted and committed to them, it seems unlikely that these frames of orientation will be able to play a vital role in western social and cultural life much longer—given the profound crises of cultural meaning and orientation today, crises to which the traditional imagery and conceptualization of God seems more and more irrelevant and remote. Support for theocentric patterns of life by the churches and other religious institutions will not be widely effective, however, if it is largely backward-looking and nostalgic, attempting to keep alive outmoded and irrelevant patterns of praxis and symbolization simply because they are believed to express "the faith . . . once for all delivered to the saints" (Jude 3). As I have argued here repeatedly, our inherited symbolism no longer fits the overall cast of life as it is lived, understood, and experienced in today's world. So it must change, and change in decisive ways, if it is to continue to function properly—that is, if it is not to die out.

Change in matters as deeply important to human life as religious symbolism is often difficult and painful; yet it happens all the time, as the history of every religion makes clear. The proper question to put with respect to Christian patterns of religious meaning, then, is not, Will (or should) change occur in the present modes of symbolization and praxis of the churches? but rather, Are the churches willing and able to support the kind of moves that will enable Christian rituals and symbolism to continue their life-giving functions? What we are speaking about here are quite momentous changes for the churches—changes in the conceptions and imagery with which they mediate (and interpret) God and Christ and which thus form and inform Christian devotion, experience, and worship at deep levels; changes in their understanding and practice of ministry, in their basic rituals such as the sacraments, in their attitudes toward the Bible, in many of their hymns; and so on. Can the churches really begin to self-consciously and directly embrace such all-encompassing change? Are they (and the other religious institutions in our society) prepared to undertake the sort of imaginative construction (as I have called it here) that can make available, on the basis of the symbolic, moral, and ritual resources inherited from our past, orienting and energizing meaning for the future? This can happen only, I think, if there is fairly wide recognition that this is really a life-or-death matter for the churches; and that they are, therefore, required by their own deepest commitments—their commitments to God and Christ—to adapt their practices and to reconstruct and reconceive the symbols which they cherish. The faith in God and Christ which the churches profess has built into it a powerful self-critical dialectic (though this has often not been emphasized), and it is this, and this alone, that gives the universalistic dimensions of their message some justification; it is also this, and this alone, that may be able to call them to changes as radical as those that seem demanded today.

The central focus of the churches' faith is God—God conceived in absolutistic and universalistic terms as the creator and judge of the world, "the Alpha and the Omega, the first and the last, the beginning and the end" (Rev.

22:13; cf. Isa. 44:6; 48:12), what I have called "the ultimate point of reference." It is not noted as often as it should be how difficult it is to conceptualize this universalizing and absolutizing dimension of God without falling into deep paradoxes: when we attempt to get clearly in mind just what it is we are trying to say here, God seems to dissolve into a kind of logical Archimedean point which, on the one hand, is that from which all else comes and to which it ultimately returns, that in terms of which, therefore, all else must be understood; but which, on the other hand, so utterly transcends everthing else (real or imaginable) that it cannot properly be conceived at all. This Archimedean point obviously is not to be identified with our ideas about it, or our act of conceiving it, or our language expressing it: these (and everything else we might imagine or say) belong to the "all else" which God "utterly transcends." But this implies, then, that when we speak of the divine "transcendence" or "wholly otherness" or "mystery," we really do not know what we are talking about; indeed, it is just our *not knowing* (as I have pointed out on several occasions in this volume) that these terms all emphasize. By "God" we mean that which calls us and all our claims and contentions—including especially our claims and contentions about God!—radically into question. Apart from this feature of the idea of God—which thoroughly undercuts any advantage with God that believers might imagine they have in comparison with their (unbelieving) neighbors—all our characterizations of God would in fact involve the (illegitimate) universalization of our own particular standpoint; and no claims about God's universality or absoluteness would be justifiable. To the extent that we forget these stringent rules of theological discourse, and suppose that our ideas and speech adequately represent, and thus present, the living God, we are idolaters—not devoting ourselves to *God* at all but rather to our own imaginings. To the extent, however, that we recognize that we also (and all our ideas, imaginings, and symbols) belong to the "all else" that is not to be confused with God, we are aware of ourselves as relativized and judged—and redeemed—from beyond ourselves. Just this sense of, and acceptance of, our creatureliness vis-à-vis God is faith.

This is obviously hard, and extraordinarily dialectical, doctrine; and it is not discussed as much or explained as well in the churches as it should be. In consequence the highly complex character of the notion of God which we have inherited is often not clearly recognized; and the symbol "God" is easily misused and may become quite dangerous. A nation or community or class or church, an entire people or a small elite group or sect, may come to believe God has authorized its particular practices, beliefs, and institutions; it is with *divine* authority, then, that certain activities and ideologies are enforced—both within the group and without—as right and true, others being opposed as false, even demonic. In consequence oppressive, repressive, and imperialistic behaviors of all sorts become justified in the name of God, and powerful religious fundamentalisms and fanaticisms develop. In view of the frequency with which this sort of perversion occurs, it may well seem that whatever positive significance the symbol "God" might have, it is simply too dangerous for human use: its dialectic is too complex for any but the most sophisticated to grasp, and its universalistic and absolutistic features, therefore—however valuable and important they might seem (in the abstract)—too easily and frequently tempt believers into highly destructive forms of self-idolatry and delusions of grandeur.

Whatever may be the dangers of the image/concept "God," it remains (at least in western cultures) our most profound and comprehensive symbol, particularly with respect to its powers to draw all that we humans know or experience or can imagine together into an all-inclusive yet open and thoroughly differentiated Whole. (It should not surprise us that a symbol with these capabilities would, when wrongly used, have great destructive potential.) Moreover, it does not seem likely that this symbol will completely die out very soon: indeed, the resurgence of modern fundamentalisms suggests that the greater probability, in the foreseeable future, is that it will grow in influence and power—perhaps with quite demonic and destructive consequences. It is important today, therefore, that the dialectical complexity, as well as the humanizing and healing potential, of the symbol "God"—each of them central themes of the theological position developed here—be brought out as clearly as possible. And it is of especial importance that these themes be stressed in those communities and institutions which are expressly committed to the meaning and importance of this symbol in human life—churches, synagogues, mosques, and others—and which are directly involved, therefore, in its cultural dissemination and transmission. When the humanizing side and the dialectical complexity of the image/concept "God" play their proper roles (as we saw in Chapters 21–24), precisely the universalistic and absolutistic qualities of this symbol (otherwise so dangerous) enable it to become the vehicle of significant self-criticism among believers. Theocentric symbolism, when rightly understood and interpreted, provides a point of reference in terms of which the ethnocentrism of its own bearer can be discerned and criticized; beyond this, it supplies a framework of orientation for human life which can overcome the anthropocentrism which we today see to be so destructive of the ecological web of life. It is the presence of this self-critical, and potentially self-correcting, principle at the very heart of this frame of orientation, and this alone, that can justify universalistic claims made in its behalf.

It seems clear, in light of these considerations, that those theologies which concern themselves with simply presenting straightforwardly what they take to be the faith, self-understanding, and convictions about life of one or another particular church, sect, or other religious group (or particular nation, race, or gender)—which understand themselves, thus, as essentially church-centered or tradition-centered or confession-bound—are especially dangerous. For they deal with religious symbolisms, even symbols like God and Christ, as though they were the possession of the particular group for which they speak; and the theologian seems to understand his or her responsibility to be primarily to this group instead of to God. Theologians of this persuasion, of course, never put the issue in this way: with parochialism built into the very foundation of their reflection and writing, the question whether loyalty to God might not demand something quite different from loyalty to the group seldom arises; and for just this reason theologies of this sort easily become self-idolatrous and demonic.

It is of the utmost importance that theologians understand themselves to be responsible first and foremost to God (and Christ), not to the churches that are the historical bearers of this symbolism, nor to the traditions in and through which this symbolism has been handed on to us today. The meaning of the symbol "God" (as we have seen) itself demands such a stance.[1] In addition, however, there is a broad sociocultural justification for it: the fact that the symbol "God" is widely accepted and employed not only in churches and synagogues but in western culture at large—and, indeed, throughout the world—shows that it is no longer (if it ever was) the private property of any church or tradition but now belongs to all of humankind.[2] And it is to all humankind, therefore, and not simply to some particular segment of humanity, that theologians who take this symbol seriously must today make themselves responsible. To the extent that the churches wish to contend that it is the God of all humanity, indeed all the world, to which they witness and which they serve, they must be willing to subject their own traditions, practices, and beliefs to criticism of the most fundamental sort in light of what this God may today be requiring of them. And they must be prepared to acknowledge that today God may well be calling many of the churches' long-standing traditions and practices into question, demanding that Christians and other believers move—in quite unprecedented ways—into reconciling conversations and relationships with the rest of humanity, indeed with all of life and the earth. It is no longer appropriate for Christian churches, Christian people, or Christian theologians to think of themselves as—in some significant way distinct from the rest of humankind—"a chosen race, a royal priesthood, a holy nation, God's own people" (1 Peter 2:9).

How, then, should the churches be thinking of themselves? What sort of self-understanding would give appropriate expression to the two great orienting symbols—God and Christ—to which they are committed? Historically, in my view, the churches have been much too concerned with defining precisely—and then showing that they exemplified properly—certain specific "marks" that established their truly Christian (and thus divinely warranted) character and mission.[3] This has led, not surprisingly, to self-justifying and self-magnifying claims, as various communions have each sought to prove they were the "true church" in contrast with the pretensions of their rivals; and it has also led to highly self-righteous stances, and brazenly imperialistic activities, with respect to other (non-Christian) religious communities and traditions. Though no attempts at self-definition and self-understanding are proof against human temptations to self-defensiveness and triumphalism (for direct concern with matters of this sort is always inherently self-centered), in my opinion it would be more in keeping with the churches' mission in the world if they saw themselves as essentially communities of reconciliation and humanization; that is, as communities whose central task was to respond to and cooperate with those movements in history and life (God's own humanizing activity) that are working to bring about a more humane and ecologically responsible existence for women and men today. The basic criteria of this humanizing and reconciling mission of the church are made quite clear (as we noted in Chapter 26) in the parable of the last judgment, where it is declared that those who truly do God's will in the world are those who feed the hungry, clothe the naked, visit the sick and imprisoned, welcome strangers—that is, those who give themselves over to activities that help to make human life more humane—not those who make formal obeisance to Christ or bear other identifying marks that distinguish them from their fellows (Mt. 25:31–46).

If the churches understood their mission in the world to be primarily reconciliation and humanization—if they understood themselves as basically agents of and witnesses to God's reconciling and humanizing activity in history and in nature—they would define themselves, not in terms of some "essence" or "identity" or "essential marks" which they (supposedly) possess, but rather in terms of their *relationships* with the larger human and natural world of which they are part. The life of the churches (worship services, administrative policies and practices, educational programs, working committees and task forces, and so on) would then be ordered in ways that made these specific kinds of relationship—humanizing and reconciling activities—the matters of central concern. Two principal foci would require ongoing attention:

1. The question of what it is to be a community of reconciliation and humanization, what it is to be an agent of and witness to God's reconciling and humanizing activity in the world, would become a matter of central importance. The community's humanizing and reconciling work should manifest itself through both (a) its own internal life of peace, love, equality, freedom, justice, ecological sensitivity, and the like; and (b) its reconciling and humanizing activities in the larger natural and historical world round-

about. The life of the churches should, then, be so organized as to maintain continuing attention to, and nurturance of, both these dimensions. How these matters would be worked out in any particular concrete situation would depend, of course, on how they were understood within (and especially by the leadership of) the particular communities involved, as well as on the actual character of the concrete sociocultural context within which each congregation lived—and the problems and possibilities that this opened up for its distinctive mission.

2. The continuing existence of a congregation as a community of reconciliation and humanization undoubtedly depends to a large extent on the objective sociological and political, psychological and historical, conditions obtaining in the sociocultural context within which it finds itself. The effectiveness with which its mission is pursued is, of course, partly within the control of the congregation itself, and depends heavily on the historical wisdom and understanding (as well as the shrewdness) of its leadership; but it is also in significant part beyond its direct control, depending on actions and attitudes, institutions and practices, in the concrete situation in which it is working—as well, of course, as on the serendipity of the wider historical and natural processes which pervade its context (what in an earlier period might have been called "the providence of God"). The churches can never carry out their mission effectively if they think that the main thing required of them is simply to draw on their own internal resources, attempting to see what their faith, ideology, world-picture, and related ideals seem to offer and demand. Only as they actually *succeed* in bringing about reconciliation among alienated parties, succeed in making the concrete historical processes which surround them (many of which may be moving in quite different directions) more humane and more ecologically responsive, do they in fact live and work as communities of humanization and reconciliation in their world. The specific character of the particular setting within which a church finds itself thus has a great deal to do with what can count as genuine reconciliation and humanization there.

It is not that a church's life must be one of continuous compromise between its ideals and the hard facts of historical existence. Sectarian movements have been inclined to express the issue in this way, with their insistence that the ideals of the church must be clung to, no matter how "unrealistic" they might seem. And in contrast, hardnosed "realists" have maintained that the Christian ethic does not, and should not, govern life in this world, and that the issue here, therefore, is not so much a matter of compromising and bearing the burden of a guilty conscience as of simply living "realistically" in the world. Though these two positions have usually been regarded as diametrically opposed, they in fact make the same dualistic mistake, though from opposite sides; and thus they both lose sight of their proper mission to be communities of reconciliation and witnesses to the God of humanization and humaneness in precisely *this* world. A mission of this sort requires churches, obviously, to live in the world in which they find themselves, performing their special task precisely here. On the face of it, this would not seem to be impossible; but it is a task which can easily be lost sight of when the churches think either that they must manifest some sort of "perfect" life (what Troeltsch called the "sect-type" alternative) or that they must allow the world roundabout them to define and determine their character (the "church-type" alternative).[4] Neither of these moves is satisfactory if the church's task in the world is to be both an agent of and (thereby) a witness to God's reconciling and humanizing activity in history and nature.

Are the churches prepared to take to heart these sorts of imperatives—which the symbols of God and Christ that they themselves confess, and to which they have committed themselves in loyalty, seem to lay upon them? Are they prepared to accept and support the open and universalistic theological stance that such a mission, defined in terms of reconciliation and humanization, demands? I do not know. There are many voices in the churches today calling for radical change: the voices of women, of blacks, of the poor and dispossessed, of those who find the message of the churches simply irrelevant or unintelligible. I would hope that the theological program which I have outlined in this book—a program which is intended to address theological dimensions of many of the problems to which these voices are seeking to call attention—will receive a hearing in the churches; and that it will become, thus, a living part of the ongoing theological conversation within and among these historical bearers of Christian religious symbolisms. During the two millennia of its history, Christian faith has shown a remarkable ability to take up into itself (and in this way adapt itself to) many different changes in the cultural faiths—the general patterns of belief and of orientation in life—of its adherents; and throughout this volume I have been arguing the importance of recognizing how thoroughgoing are the unprecedented changes which modernity and so-called postmodernity have brought about in the actual faiths by which people today live out their lives. Many aspects of modern and postmodern faiths are, of course, quite dubious from a Christian point of view, and Christians should subject these to drastic criticism, and work for their reform. But if criticism and reform of these matters is to be effective, it will have to be articulated in images and symbols and ideas that connect significantly with these faiths: that is the only way truly *reconciling* work can be carried out.

What I have called for here is reconstruction of Christianity's traditional symbolism in ways that will enable it to bear significantly on, and effectively transform as well as nourish, the faiths which actually orient the lives of women and men today. I do not regard this approach as involving a "watering down" of Christian commitment and belief to make it palatable to secular modernity—a charge often leveled against protestant modernism. On the contrary, my interest is in constructing an understanding of Christian faith that enables it more directly and effectively to address the major problems with which the world now confronts us. If such reconstructed Christian symbolism is to become effective in transforming today's powerful polytheistic and henotheistic faiths,[5] however, it will have to become a significant voice in the cultural debates of modernity and postmodernity, and that before the Christian strands that inform our "secular" culture die out completely. It is a large task indeed that confronts churches and theologians today.

29. Faith in God (II): Christian Theocentrism

In Chapter 27 I drew together and summarized, in terms of the Christian doctrine of the trinity, the conception of God being constructed in this book. This notion, I contended, holds together in dialectical interconnection the main claims about God which Christian faith seeks to make, articulating with precision both God's all-comprehensiveness and fullness of being—God's connectedness, and interconnectedness, with all that exists—and simultaneously God's utter distinctiveness, God's "wholly otherness" from all else, the ultimate mystery of the divine being. It is a doctrine, thus, the intention of which is to pull together and bring into focus the *object* of faith, that toward which Christian devotion and worship are directed, that in terms of which Christian faith seeks and gains its fundamental orientation in life and the world. Once one sees how complex the concept of trinity must be in order to articulate the Christian view of God, it is not difficult to understand why we men and women so often fall into idolatries of one sort or another even though we suppose we are worshipping the true God. It is hardly surprising, then (as we noted in Chapter 28), that it has been a difficult matter for the Christian churches—the historical bearers of this faith—to keep themselves directed toward this God which they profess. ". . . strait is the gate, and narrow is the way, which leadeth unto life, and few there be that find it" (Mt. 7:14 KJV): however much disagreement there might be about the specifics of my interpretation of the Christian conception of God, on this point many will agree, I suspect. The faith-situation of Christian believers and of the Christian churches is highly ambiguous and very difficult.

Instead of expounding further the object and situation of Christian faith, let us, in this concluding chapter, look more carefully at that faith itself, which seeks to focus on this object and which exists (thereby) in this ambiguous situation. In turning again now from the objective to the subjective side of Christian existence, we need to ask ourselves: In what ways and what respects is the human relationship to this trinitarian God a matter of *faith?* How is this faith to be characterized? What understanding and interpretation of it can be offered? In the course of this book I have devoted considerable space to setting out *reasons* which can be given for the positions taken on a great many different issues. This may give the impression—despite all that has been said about mystery and about the steps of faith involved in theological construction—that I regard the human relationship to God to be largely a rational matter, a matter of argument/debate/proof rather than a matter of faith/commitment/belief. Such a conclusion would be entirely mistaken. There is, of course, an important place in theological work for clear analysis and rational weighing of issues, for theology is essentially an intellectual activity. It is that analytic and constructive work by means of which we attempt to make as clear to ourselves as we can just what it is that faith trusts in, hopes for, believes. The rational analysis and construction in which we engage, however, are not to be confused with the actual believing and trusting and hoping in which we are continually involved in our ongoing day-to-day living; and the rational work of theology, in this respect, should be carefully distinguished from faith. But it is also true that we do not—and we cannot—trust or believe in a bare "X": belief and trust are evoked from us by reality(s) that we take to be worthy of them, reality(s) that we regard as trustworthy, belief-worthy. Christians (as well as others) have taken *God* to have this character. Hence love of God, trust in God, gratitude to God are regarded as proper attitudes for men and women to take up; they each express an important dimension of the appropriate stance of humans before God and toward God. For such a stance to be possible, certain things must be known, or at least believed—and thus must in some way have been learned—about this God whom we are to trust and love. This point was made long ago by Paul, when he emphasized that "faith comes from what is heard, and what is heard comes by . . . preaching" (Rom. 10:17). A major part of our theological work here has been devoted to getting this Reality, which can and does call forth faith for today, as clear in our minds as possible; we shall now try, in conclusion, to see a bit more directly how this faith-stance of the human subject toward God may be characterized and understood.

It was often suggested during the heyday of neo-orthodoxy that faith is (or involves) a kind of dramatic "leap," in and by means of which we commit ourselves and our lives to God despite an absence of evidence regarding either God's nature or God's reality—or, perhaps, even in spite of weighty evidence to the contrary on both counts. This kind of language has the value of underlining in a dramatic way our finitude: that we really do not know, indeed we cannot know, what human existence is all about; what is the true nature of the world in which we find ourselves; with what ultimate reality (or realities) we humans have to do. Hence, whatever may be our deepest commitments, our firmest beliefs, they always represent a kind of leap in the dark. This point about the ultimate mystery of life has been emphasized in this book in many ways, and we need not dwell on it further. The dramatic imagery of the existentialists expressed powerfully what is undoubtedly an important aspect of the truth about the human condition: that our biohistorical existence is ultimately grounded—at least with respect to its dimensions of conscious experiencing and thinking and acting—on faithing, on believing; for historical beings there are never any ultimate certainties.

But this existentialist language brings to our attention only one aspect of faith, an aspect which, if taken simply by itself, is seriously misleading. The image of religious belief as involving a blind "leap" tells us little or nothing about how persons ordinarily come to faith, or how faith arises in human communities. It is certainly not a matter of imaginatively confronting a huge abyss, then gathering all one's strength and leaping over it, so that afterward one is able to say, "Ah, at last I've done it; I've made the leap!" In the Christian tradition, we should remind ourselves, faith is often understood as a free gift of God, not something that we bring about by our own efforts.[1] As I have suggested from time to time, attitudes or postures of selves and communities such as faith and trust and love are *evoked* from us; they cannot be understood as simply and straightforwardly under our control, the direct expression of our own free decisions. It is important to acknowledge, of course, that we usually assent (in at least some minimal sense) to these attitudes that we take up. That is, we actively give ourselves over to them and in them; and sometimes we can (if we choose) withhold our assent (at least to some extent), turn in other directions, take up a somewhat different stance. The basic postures of selves and communities at their very deepest level, however—the basic trusting, believing, committing of themselves in various ways, as they engage in their interactions with other selves and communities—have been in place for a considerable time before they become matters of conscious awareness and can thus become (to some extent) matters of deliberate choice. These are the sorts of attitudes and commitments that constitute the very identities of communities and persons, that establish them as *this* particular community or person rather than that. Faithing, thus, whether in the ordinary affairs of everyday interpersonal interaction or in our relationship to God, is not simply a matter of our own doing—nor solely another's doing either, even God's: it is a *relational* stance that emerges only in the complex sorts of interaction within which human persons and communities are themselves created and which come to constitute them. Faith arises within, and itself becomes a feature of, wider ongoing processes; it is not a singular event or an unchanging state; faith is an essentially historical and social reality that comes into being through time. Neither Israel's faith, nor the (somewhat later) faith of the Christian communities, appeared simply in a moment—it always takes time for (a particular) faith to be(come) what it is.

I do not propose here to set out a phenomenology of the complex interaction-process(es) which we call faith, showing how faith in God arises in communities and in individuals,[2] and how it qualifies and transforms human lives and modes of existence. This would require careful psychological and sociological studies going far beyond anything we can undertake. What I do want to recall to our attention at this point—as a kind of example (however atypical in its systematic and deliberately constructive aspects) of faith's social and historical character—is the way and the respects in which faith has been involved in the developing process of theological construction in which we have been engaged in this book. I have emphasized throughout that we have not been engaged here simply in a process of analysis, construction, and persuasion, but that small increments of faithing—of believing, of committing ourselves—have also been involved at every point along the way. That is to say, we have not been engaged in purely intellectual activity, a process of producing a rationally plausible idea of God, at the end of which we could inquire whether we (were going to) "believe in" this God or not, whether we (could) trust and love and worship and commit ourselves to this God. Rather, I claimed, we have been making (or choosing not to make) decisions of belief and trust all along the way, decisions which—as we come now to the conclusion of this process of construction—incline us toward (or against) significant commitment to the trinitarian reality that has at last come into view.

It is true, of course, that we are now in a position to ask ourselves: Do we really believe in this God? Do we really want to commit ourselves to this God? to orient our lives in terms of this God? Or do we prefer to live out our lives in terms of some other frame of orientation, devote ourselves to some other center of value and meaning? Whatever we may say about these matters at this point, it will not be the expression of a completely free and unpredisposed decision ("leap"): there have been many smaller assents (or dissents), decisions, commitments along the course of our explorations in the preceding chapters; these have prepared the way for our concluding judgment now, and they incline us in one direction or another with respect to it. We have taken explicit note of a number of the more important of these junction points—these "small steps of faith"—on our path, and have built them into our intellectual journey; they have significantly shaped both our analyses and our constructions.

I want to summarize our constructive activity now in a way which will enable us to see more clearly how at every point a faith-dimension has been involved. It is convenient to identify here five major steps of faith which have carried us over the road we have traversed. For the most part, these are somewhat longer strides than the "six steps of faith" (displayed diagrammatically in Figure 4 in Chapter 20), which were outlined as we constructed conceptions of the world and God in Parts III and IV; the latter dealt with only a portion of the overall road to which we shall now give attention.

The first step of faith which I want to mention in this connection was not a part of the actual argument of this book itself, but rather set the stage for the processes of constructing—and of faithing—which have been sketched here, and which we have been following: the faith involved in the very decision to read this book. This was a decision which for most readers (I suspect) expressed a double commitment. First, it expressed a belief in and expectation that intellectual exploration of and analysis of our language and ideas about God—that is, the activity of reflecting on God—is, or can be, of significant value in coming to better understand who or what God is, and how we should live and act with respect to God. However amorphous and diverse such expectations and commitments may be, they surely are present to some extent in anyone who decides to undertake the lengthy and demanding task of reading a book of this sort; no one, I assume, would take on such a project fully expecting that the expenditure of time and energy would be of no use or value whatsoever. Second, the reading of this book presupposed not only a commitment (however tentative) to the general process of theological analysis and reflection, criticism and construction, but also some degree of faith in the author of this book: the author is one who, it was hoped and to some extent believed, may have something to say on these matters that is worth spending a bit of time reflecting upon, even though in the end one may not wish to accept it.

Commitments of this sort—acts of faith of this kind—are, of course, quite ordinary and common; in this case, however (unlike many others), they entailed some rather momentous issues—issues connected directly with faith in God. One might go so far as to say that these (quite ordinary sorts of) faith-commitments actually presupposed, in a sense, that (some) knowledge about and faith in God was already present in the prospective reader: for implicit in them there seems to be a belief or hope or faith that God may be susceptible of this kind of exploration, study, reflection; that is, that God (is the sort of reality that) can be to some extent learned about, reflected on, understood. For anyone who undertakes this kind of exploration, then (whatever the various readers of this book may have supposed as they began this project), God is not just a total blank, completely unknown, an absolute mystery; nor is God regarded as a matter of purely private experience, something not in any way communicable. On the contrary, in taking up a project of this sort readers presuppose that meaningful communication about God (in some sense) is possible for human beings, and that human language and reflection are capable—in some respects and to some degree—of dealing significantly with God. That is to say, for these readers, the symbol "God" (and thus *God!*) still carried meaning of some importance, meaning of sufficient significance that they were willing to give considerable amounts of time and energy to its exploration. (If the symbol "God" did not have at least this degree of significance for them, presumably they would not have made the effort to work through a study of this sort—just as they would not devote extensive time and energy to studies that took phlogiston seriously, or elves, or the idea that the earth is flat.) With these considerations in mind, we can see that some degree of *communal* faith in God (however minimal and tentative it might be) appears to be expressed in the continuing use of this symbol within the English-speaking community; and in our active participation in this ongoing use—through intensive theological reflection, for example—we also share (willy-nilly) in this underlying faith that funds the experience and activities of English language-users. This is, of course, a very minimal, and usually quite unselfconscious, faith; but it is an important opening which provides a basis upon which further steps of faith (of more explicit commitment) may be made—as we can see in the unfolding argument of this book as a whole.

So the reading of this book did not begin from Ground Zero, a complete absence of faith; on the contrary, it began with some important theological—important *faith*—presuppositions, presuppositions from which some significant consequences were to follow. For example, as readers sought to understand this book, they had to decide (at least tentatively) to consider seriously a constructivist approach to theology: that is, they put into temporary suspense (imaginatively) some of their own commitments (personal, ecclesiastical, or other) to other ways of thinking about theology—as grounded essentially in direct "divine revelation," perhaps, or in personal religious experience, or in tradition. In so doing they were led to entertain a significantly different way of thinking about theological responsibilities and about the tasks which confront theologians today. To the extent that the steps of theological construction—and thus of faith—suggested in this book seemed intelligible, and even convincing, to readers, they found themselves taking up personally (or perhaps in some respects modifying or refusing) the conception of God—and the sort of commitment to God—proposed here. Thus the reading of this book itself became a part of their own personal faith-pilgrimage.

Let us now (in summary) remind ourselves of the path of theological construction—and thus of faith decisions with respect to God—which the present work has taken up. The beginning point (presupposed in the very entry into a theological investigation of this sort)—and in this sense the "first step" of faith (for our purposes in these concluding remarks)—has just been briefly discussed: theological work begins in and with faith (implicit or explicit), a faith that includes the assumptions that it is worthwhile to expend time and energy reflecting on God, and that God is in some significant sense susceptible of inquiry, investigation, reflection. The entire project of theological construction proposed here follows from and builds upon this. It consists principally in the work of (a) excavating and articulating major themes and emphases (both implicit and those which earlier reflection over many centuries has made explicit) that give specific content to this faith—that is, developing a language and conceptual scheme within which the content of this faith can be made explicit; (b) critically assessing and appropriately reconceiving these ideas and this language in contemporary terms—that is, constructing (what today appear to be) more adequate formulations, concepts, and symbols than those inherited from tradition; and (c) extrapolating, filling in, and otherwise amplifying this understanding of humanity-in-the-world-under-God so as to take into account alternative contemporary views of the issues it poses—that is, constructing a holistic faith-perspective (world-picture) that can interpret intelligibly and meaningfully the wide reaches of human life as experienced and understood today.

We began to enter upon this activity of excavation, critical examination, and imaginative construction—our second step of faith—quite early in the book. We noted at the very outset that whatever that which we call "God" might turn out to be, this was not something known independently of—that is, entirely apart from significant relationship to—other realities. In the very first chapter I pointed out that our understanding of God is closely interconnected with and dependent upon the sharply contrasting notion of idols: without the notion of idolatry we could not make clear to ourselves what we mean by "God." Later I expanded much further on this interconnection of the concept of God with other concepts by arguing, on the one hand, that an important component of the concept of God is the (largely contentless) notion of mystery (Chapters 1, 4, and 5); and by contending, on the other hand, that the word "God" acquires significant dimensions of its positive meaning by virtue of the way it functions in a larger comprehensive categorial scheme that includes such other important concepts as "world" and "humanity" (Chapters 1, 6, and 7). It is in connection with the latter relationships—to our understanding of all else that exists, and to our understanding of ourselves as human beings—that "God" is given its (logically) dominating position in the semantic field in which it exists: in the monotheistic categorial scheme God is regarded as the "ultimate point of reference" in terms of which all else is understood. Moreover, for specifically Christian faith, as we saw, "Christ" must be added as a further major category determinative of the meaning of "God." To readers for whom this beginning analysis of the concept of God was persuasive, an important step of theological construction—and with it an expanded understanding of, and thus step of, faith—followed. We could now see that whatever might be the knowledge of God that we have (or come to have), our understanding is importantly shaped by conceptual issues, by the interconnections of our concept of God with other concepts such as world, humanity, mystery, Christ, idol. So what we today think or believe about the world and humanity (for example) significantly affects the way we think of, and what we believe about, God; and vice versa.

To anyone aware of these issues it is a serious theological mistake—and therefore, because of the conceptual structure of the idea of God, a serious mistake for faith as well—simply to take over traditional ideas of God uncritically: for this would mean that we were allowing our thinking about God to be given much of its content by antique ideas (of humanity and the world, as well as of God and idolatry)—ideas that do not connect well with either our experience or our world today, ideas that we, therefore, no longer actually accept or act upon. Obviously this point is not merely of intellectual or academic interest. It implies that religious faith cannot (logically cannot) be adequately nourished today simply by meditation on (ancient) scripture or by the attempt to live out of one's own (private) religious experience, however important each of these may be. For our very idea of God—that is, that in terms of which we seek to direct our religious devotion, that in terms of which we seek to relate ourselves to God—can perform these functions properly only when it is significantly interconnected with our (implicit and explicit) understandings of humanity and the world. Apart from such interconnection, it will not indeed be *God* with which we have to do in our faith and reflection, but instead a tradition—or experience—now become an idolatrous interloper between us and God. Our modern knowledges and understandings must, willy-nilly, bear significantly on our faith in and love of God—if God is indeed the ultimate point of reference for *our* life and world; just as, conversely, our faith in and love of God must bear on the way we understand ourselves and our world. The question about who or what God is, thus, is not merely of "theological" interest (in any narrow sense), nor is it simply a "faith issue"; it is a cosmological and anthropological and moral issue as well, that is, a question about all of life and the world. To take the mystery of God in this way—as having this kind of bearing on all of existence, and all of existence and reality as having this kind of import for what we worship and serve as God—is to make a significant second step of faith and commitment.

Awareness of this complex of largely conceptual considerations connected with faith in God prepared the way for a third step of theological construction and of faith: it now became necessary to give serious consideration to a number of material anthropological and cosmological issues, to see how these bear on our understanding of God and how our understanding of the divine mystery bears on them. Parts II and III of this work were devoted, therefore, to sketching a picture of the world, and of humanity within the world, based largely on widely accepted modern knowledges and on the modes of experience that ground these knowledges and are in turn significantly shaped by them—all understood as limited human attempts to come to terms with life in face of the ultimate mystery of things. There are, of course, in the late twentieth century, an enormous variety of understandings of humanity and the world. I argued (in Chapters 8–16) that the most plausible among these today are those which present humans as what I call "biohistorical beings"—beings which, though grounded in the evolutionary growth of the web of life on earth and continuing to exist in utter dependence upon it, have emerged into self-awareness, have gained some powers of freedom and deliberate creativity, and have become able, therefore, to take significant responsibility for themselves and their world. The plausibility of this conception of human existence derives especially from its ability (a) to assimilate, draw together, and interpret in an illuminating way current scientific and historical knowledges of many sorts, and (b) to give an intelligible explanation of the enormous diversity of anthropological, cosmological, and religious views, as well as of the multiplicity of social, cultural, and religious practices, followed by women and men over the long course of human history. According to this conception, the rich and wide pluralism of human life, and of human understandings of life, is to be seen as the product of human creativity attempting (with varying degrees of success) to come to terms with the enduring mystery within which life falls.

Such a biohistorical understanding of the human, including (as it does) this openness to mystery, can fit well into a monotheistic conceptual framework—provided the latter is developed in such a way as to be open to and genuinely appreciative of human diversity. (Historically, as we have noted, many monotheisms have been authoritarian and thus quite intolerant of differences.) As I tried to show in this book, such an open version of monotheism can be developed if prominence is given to the dimensions of humaneness and of mystery in the conception of God, thus undermining the tendency in this sort of conceptual scheme to emphasize dominative power and rigid order—a combination of motifs often used to provide religious legitimation for patterns of repression and domination in human affairs.

Of course, such a theocentric interpretation of the evolutionary and historical development of life on planet Earth is by no means necessary: the processes eventuating in the appearance of humanity, as we today think of them, can be understood in a number of quite different ways; and many moderns take our existence on earth to be a kind of cosmic accident with no intrinsic grounding in the ultimate scheme of things. It is also possible, however (I argued), to take precisely this emergence of human existence/history/historicity as a clue to the ultimate mystery of things—thus undertaking a third major step toward, and of, faith in God. When this idea is clarified and spelled out in further cosmological and theological reflection and construction, accompanied by several appropriate "small steps" of faith (Chapters 17–20), we begin to see that the universe of which we are part—and perhaps even the ultimate mystery of things—can be regarded as (in a way significant to us humans) "meaningful" and "good." To utterly deny this—thus attributing no cosmological or metaphysical grounding to the evolutionary and historical momentums toward the humane, toward freedom and justice and meaning, toward truth, beauty, and goodness—also, it must be noted, presupposes taking up some particular faith-stance or other, in the search for understanding of our historicity, our humanity; but it will obviously be one of a quite different sort.

These anthropological and cosmological explorations and interpretations prepared the way for another move forward in theological construction—and for the fourth major step of faith which both nurtures it and is nourished by it—that is, the construction of an image/concept of God which, as the ultimate point of reference in terms of which this developing picture of humanity-in-the-world is understood, provides us with a theocentric conception of our biohistorical existence (Chapters 21–24). In this step further critical analysis of the images and concepts which constituted the traditional symbolization of God was undertaken, combined with reconstruction of that symbol so that it could function more adequately as the ultimate point of reference for today's world. In my interpretation (in Part III) of the cosmic process as a whole, including especially those evolutionary trajectories within it which gradually acquired a measure of directionality, I suggested that we could appropriately speak of a kind of "serendipitous creativity" at work everywhere. The several notions, worked out in Parts II and III taken together, now provided us with images and metaphors for constructing an image/concept of God intelligible in today's world; they thus were seen to be mediating to us what we can today (in faith) regard as the divine grounding of all meaning, value, and being. This resymbolization, I argued, presents an appropriate center of orientation for contemporary human life, a center which transcends utterly the merely human and relates us significantly to all that is, a focus which thus overcomes the deep-lying anthropocentrism that ordinarily governs human existence, opening us to free and responsible participation in the complex and fragile ecological order which environs us. It is a center shrouded in mystery, but mystery now appropriated as significantly beneficent and trustworthy—to be believed in and loved "with all [one's] heart, . . . soul, . . . mind, and . . . strength" (Mk. 12:30).

It is possible, thus, to construct—on the basis of imaginative interpretation of human biohistorical existence and its cosmic context—a theocentric frame of orientation for life, an orientation which will facilitate the redirection of our energies, attitudes, and ideas in ways pertinent to many of the problems which today confront us. Many ecologically sensitive writers are already contributing (whether self-consciously or not) to the development of such a frame of orientation. Their attempts to creatively redirect our attitudes and our thinking, our policies and our institutions, are often grounded in profound moral concerns about the web of life on planet Earth as well as deeply religious attitudes of awe and respect for, and even love of, the magnificent cosmic order of which we are part; and their open expression of these things encourages similar attitudes and concerns in their readers. It may be that significant religious conversion away from the basic anthropocentrism of many of our traditions and patterns of life (both religious and secular) is beginning to get under way in our culture. Unfortunately, most of these (secular) writers do not attempt to articulate the broad conceptual frame—with its significant religious and moral dimensions—which seems implied by their work. Were this to be made explicit, it might well turn out to be a somewhat vague and general "soft monotheism" (not too far removed, perhaps, from the position just summarized)—a kind of extension of humanistic ideas and ideals, but with humanism's tendencies toward anthropocentrism strongly qualified by a quasi-theocentric emphasis.

All such moves which widen and deepen the moral and religious sensitivities in our culture are to be applauded: if we understand that all theologies are products of human imaginative construction, we cannot but welcome the attempts of others, from quite different perspectives, to address in their own distinctive ways the deep moral and religious problems of our society; the adversarial stance toward other points of view, so often expressed in theological writing in the past, no longer has any point. Faith in God, as I have tried to articulate it here, must express itself in appreciation for and cooperation with any and all moves toward a more truly humane and ecologically ordered world, for it is precisely such moves—and the communities and individuals contributing to them—that are understood to be the ongoing living expression of the divine activity in human affairs.

What does all this mean for Christian faith today? Christian faith has always been essentially a modification or transformation of the religious and cultural faiths already present in the society into which it came. This was obviously the case, of course, in its originary emergence within the Jewish world; but already in that earliest period it also drew heavily (in people like Paul and John) on Greek and Roman resources. And everywhere that it has subsequently moved, in its two-thousand-year history, it has imbibed deeply from the religious and moral resources in the cultures which became its new homes—however significantly it may have transformed and redirected what it drew from those resources.[3] I have tried to show in this book that the makings of a meaningful conception of God—capable of inspiring and focusing profound faith, loyalty, and affection—remain present (though largely latent) in contemporary western (secular and religious) culture and life. In many respects, of course, this (more or less humanistic) conception of God has pronounced Jewish and Christian features, since it draws heavily upon resources supplied to the culture at large by Jewish and Christian traditions. It cannot, however, be properly characterized as either Christian or Jewish, for it gives no significantly normative status either to specifically Jewish writings (including especially Torah and Talmud) or to Jesus Christ. Another step of theological construction (and of faith), therefore, further transforming this conception of God in important ways, is required to move from the generally theocentric cultural resources which it symbolizes to an understanding appropriate for contemporary Christian faith. (What would be required in this respect for Jewish believers today, I leave to Jewish writers and teachers to say.)

In Christian faith (as we have seen in Chapters 25 and 26) the conceptions of God and of humanity are not developed simply in terms of relatively vague notions of humaneness, freedom, justice, well-being, ecological responsibility, and the like, nor in terms of such widely admired human images as Socrates, the Buddha, Faust, the Nietzschean *Uebermensch,* the "common man"; it is, rather, Christ—the historical events "surrounding, including, and following upon" the ministry of Jesus of Nazareth (as I put it)—that is regarded as having paradigmatic, and thus normative, standing in the construction of these notions. What it is to be truly human and truly humane is depicted sharply and clearly and dramatically in the Christ-imagery and stories of the New Testament; these, thus, supply criteria for constructing both a Christian conception of what human life is and how it is to be lived, and a Christian understanding of God—the ultimate reality with which we humans have to do. Christians have developed their views of the normative conception of Christ in many different ways in the course of the past two thousand years, and they continue to do so today. (In our theological construction here "Christ" is understood in "the wider sense" that includes the life of the early Christian communities.) In this concluding chapter I want to emphasize again that it has always been the centrality which Christian faith has given to *Christ,* in its understanding of both humanity and God (Chalcedon), that has given Christian faith its distinctive marks; working out the meaning of that centrality for the theocentric framework developed in this book constituted the fifth (and final) major step of faith undertaken here.

This christocentrism introduces into the Christian frame of orientation a fourth category, thus substantially modifying—and complicating—the triadic structure generally characteristic of monotheistic faith-perspectives: without in any way giving up its theocentrism, Christian faith seeks to be christocentric as well. But is this really possible? Does not a move of this sort weaken the theocentric framework to the point where it may self-destruct? It was above all through their development of the concept of the trinity that Christian theologians attempted to address this problem, by drawing together the several strands that constituted their understanding of God in a way that insured both its christocentrism and its basic monotheistic intent (Chapter 27). What is affirmed in the trinitarian conception (as I have interpreted it here) is that (a) the ultimate mystery of things, the ultimate reality behind and working in and through all that exists, is to be construed (when it is the question of how we are to orient our biohistorical existence that is at stake) (b) in terms suggested by the images and stories of Christ (taken in the "wider sense"); these images and stories focus in the sharpest and most dramatic way what is required of us humans if our existence is to become truly humane, and they help women and men discern what it means to be living in a universe in which evolutionary and historical processes have produced and continue to sustain our biohistorical mode of existence, and which, it can be hoped (in the light of Christ), will continue to draw us toward a truly humane ordering of human life within our ecological niche on planet Earth; for (c) this is a universe in which serendipitously creative activity is everywhere at work. Stated in this way, the trinitarian doctrine sums up the central Christian claims about human life, the world, and God; and it does this in a manner that shows the trinity to be a *practical* notion having to do with the way in which life is to be lived (not a speculative concept pretending to set forth the inner structure of the divine being—something about which we can have no knowledge). The move into christocentrism, and into a trinitarian interpretation of this christocentrism, it should be clear, involves a fifth major step of faith—of life commitment—with implications significantly different from those of other monotheisms.

The form of life in which the trinitarian faith articulated here issues can be characterized conveniently in terms of the threefold pattern of the "Christian virtues": faith, hope, and love.* These three virtues taken together provide a nice summary framework for sketching the human situation in face of the ultimate mystery of things. As biohistorical beings we must, in the first place, live in *faith*—faith in some frame of orientation or other, faith in some

*Another formula that is often used to characterize Christian existence is derived from Jesus' double commandment to love God and love one's neighbor as oneself (Mk. 12:30–31). Here, however, attention is focused on only two primary objects for love—God and human beings. This formula, therefore, tends to reinforce a long-standing weakness of Christian faith, its tendency to see everything of importance in terms of human relations to God and to other humans, thus not giving proper attention to our embeddedness in, and responsibility for, the natural order within which human existence falls. When this emphasis is combined with the traditional tendencies to reify God into a position of utterly dominative importance, it becomes a poor guide in today's ecologically threatened world.

center of meaning and value. To the extent that our faith is placed in *God*—to the extent that we construe the ultimate mystery as God—it is possible to live with a deep confidence in the basic order and goodness and meaning of the world, and of human existence within the world. Faith in God, that is to say, can overcome the terror of historicity, enabling women and men to face both the problems of the present and the unknownness of the future with confidence and strength. Faith does this (in part) through giving rise to *hope* (Rom. 5:1–5), an attitude of positive expectation regarding the possibilities for human life that will emerge in the future: the relentless movement of time becomes the gift of openness and the prospect of creativity rather than the threat of dissolution and destruction. This hope, it must be noted, is not some mere abstract hope-in-general: it is the very specific expectation of a new human existence to be lived out in *love,* in relationships of interdependence and mutual support with our fellow humans and the rest of reality. Thus, the hope born of faith looks forward to a new order in which human life will be in full harmony with the entire ecological web of which it is part; in light of that hope it becomes possible, even now, to begin to take up a stance of love for all that is, what Jonathan Edwards called "benevolence to being in general."[4]

Nothing of the ultimate mystery of things is sacrificed in this version of Christian faith; on the contrary, the mystery is presupposed, and what is proposed here is a way of living in face of it. Nor is an openness to all of reality as it is—our own human reality and the reality of the world—in any respect restricted here; on the contrary, all of reality is to be affirmed, indeed loved. This faith, in its trinitarian emphasis on the interconnectedness of all that is, expresses, one could say, a kind of radical naturalism: not a reductive naturalism, of course, but one that affirms the deep value and meaning of our human historicity as well as of the wider world in which it emerges. In this vision of things meaning and value are no longer something extraneous to the natural order, something that must be super-added to it. Rather, they belong to it "naturally": in human beings this interconnectedness of value and being becomes visible as an empirical fact within the world; in God this interconnectedness takes on ultimate metaphysical meaning.[5] This is a faith, therefore, well suited to biohistorical beings like us. The word "biohistorical," which we have been using throughout to characterize the human, itself suggests precisely the inseparability of being and value in our own human existence; faith in God, as we have seen, is essentially a trust in and affirmation of the religious and metaphysical implications to be drawn from this biohistorical existence which we daily live out.

These considerations show in yet another way why it is important not to reify what we call "God" into a separate and distinct being thought of as "wholly other" from the world and humanity. When "God" is so reified, the world tends to lose its own intrinsic value, and humanity's significance as the locus of God's self-manifestation is diminished: with a move of this sort, thus, orientations supposedly theocentric move all too easily to the verge of self-destruction. Though the claim of our religious traditions that humanity was created in the "image of God" (Gen. 1:27) has lent itself to excessively anthropocentric (and thus problematic) interpretations, one implication that can be drawn from it—that humanity is that point in the finite order in which what we mean by "God" (the ultimate trinitarian interconnectedness of being and value) becomes, as it were, visible—articulates the indispensable epistemic grounding without which there could be no theocentric faith at all. Moreover, a God regarded as a separate self-sufficient individual being, utterly "outside" us and the world, really cannot even be *thought*. In theocentric faith properly conceived, we can see, though it is God who is placed at the very center of human life, indeed of all reality, a high place is also given to our distinctive human dignity within the created order. But not at the expense of the rest of creation: rather, the whole of nature—via the symbol "God" (which integrally connects material reality with value and meaning)—is seen to have its own proper dignity as well.

Faith in God, it is clear, is not the sort of thing that is either totally present or totally absent:[6] it admits of degrees; it is always living and changing, complexly intermixed with the many other faiths that help to constitute concrete human existence; it is always developing in various ways, adapting itself to changing circumstances of time and place. What I have done in this volume is attempt to link—by an activity of deliberate theological construction—the (implicit) faith manifest in certain assumptions about humanity and the world (which are widely accepted in contemporary western culture) with the (implicit) faith expressed in the continuing meaningfulness and use of the symbols "God" and "Christ" in our culture. Our succession of "steps of faith" has led to the construction of a theocentric world-picture appropriate, I believe, for orienting the lives of women and men today. Others, in their work of theological construction, would doubtless recommend rather different paths and ways of thinking about God and Christ, and thus about faith. And that is all to the good; for we are dealing here with issues beyond the imaginative and intellectual capacities of any of us—matters of ultimate mystery—and the participation of other voices, expressing quite different concerns and quite different ways of seeing things in this ongoing conversation of faith and about faith, is to be welcomed. This is a conversation, I want to emphasize, that is not to be confined to Christian voices; it must include the entire human family: Buddhists and Jews, Hindus and Marxists, Muslims and Freudians, humanists and feminists, racists and sexists and nationalists. The theological arrogance that claims the right to rule any voices out of the conversation, or attempts to silence any, can only be adjudged sin—that gross unfaith which refuses to acknowledge God's ultimate mystery, and in consequence feels free to appropriate the symbols of God and Christ for its own dominative and imperialistic purposes (Chapter 24).

I hope that I have succeeded in this book in showing that our basic faith—our orientation in life—and our religious and theological ideas (as well as many other ideas) are integrally interconnected, each shaping and otherwise affecting the other. Theological reflection and understanding are exceedingly important for faith, for they deal with the images and concepts in and through which the object of faith is brought to consciousness, thus becoming available for attention, interest, devotion, loyalty. Faith always lives out of the symbols created and continuously reshaped by the long line of earlier generations ("tradition"), but it also is always in process of adapting these symbols to new conditions of life and experience, and thus transforming them. Faith without theological images or concepts would be totally unfocused and would have no character or shape; it would, in short, have no meaning in or effect upon life. It is the particular task of theology, I have argued, to critically examine our inherited patterns of symbolization, and to develop criteria and methods by means of which this transformative activity can be carried on as effectively and responsibly as possible. The method of imaginative construction used in this book was developed with these concerns explicitly in mind.

It is obvious, of course, that the major Christian symbols were not originally created and shaped through deliberate imaginative construction in a series of clearly definable steps, such as those I have outlined here. They emerged within the mythic consciousness of the near eastern culture of four thousand years ago, and they developed in various ways, and were criticized and reshaped, during the two thousand years of Hebrew history which culminated in part (as Christians see it) in the ministry of Jesus of Nazareth and the establishment of the early Christian communities. It is not surprising that the earliest forms in which these images and symbols are still available to us (the Bible) have, after two more millennia of vast historical and cultural change, become in many ways strange to us. What I have tried to show in this book is that despite the fact that we no longer live in the mythic world within which the biblical writers experienced life and came to understand themselves, the central symbols for orienting human existence which they (together with their predecessors) created—"God" and "Christ"—can, if properly reconceived, still perform orienting functions in important ways today. To make this evident it was necessary to work out a version of those symbols which would be meaningful within our own horizons of experiencing and understanding, and above all of faithing. So our pathway here to faith in God and Christ—to what we today can properly regard as faith in God and Christ—could not begin simply and directly in and with the mythic perspectives reflected in the Bible, perspectives that, in their own rather diverse ways, were lived by Moses and Isaiah, Jesus and Paul, and even Aquinas and Luther: it had to begin within our own modern consciousness of human being and the world, moving within that consciousness to show (in several steps or stages) that God and Christ can still today serve as effective centers of devotion and life. Although these symbols themselves were significantly transformed in this process of theological reconstruction, I have attempted throughout to show that there remain important continuities with their earlier incarnations.

It is certainly not the case that all contemporary people must, or should attempt to, follow the particular pathway of faith and to faith which I have sketched here. Many will not recognize themselves or their world in the terms I have made central; others will regard this reconstruction as giving up matters indispensable to Christian existence. There is no need—in fact it would be quite inappropriate—to insist that such persons adopt this bio-historical framework for theological understanding. As I have frequently stated, a major intention in working out this perspective has been to make intelligible the enormous diversity of modes of existence, and patterns of self-understanding, within which women and men live (and can live), and to show how inappropriate—how inhuman!—it is to attempt to force everyone into the same mold. To the extent, however, that men and women of today live and work in a technical world, depend in many ways on modern medicine, watch the evening news on TV, expose themselves to contemporary university education, and so on, many of the features of experience and consciousness with which we have concerned ourselves here will inevitably be present in their minds and lives. However much, then, they may continue to suppose that the mythic world of the Bible provides them with a completely satisfactory faith, their actual lives are molded and shaped (in many ways) by these powerful currents in the modern world, together with the myths and faiths through which they are today interpreted—precisely the point of departure for the constructive theological work undertaken here. I do not believe, thus—I certainly hope it is not the case—that the version of Christian faith which I have sketched will be of value only to university and seminary students and professors.

The real test of the validity and significance of a configuration of theological proposals is to be found, as I said at the beginning of this book, in the success with which their methods and patterns of interpretation help mediate the meaning of Christian faith for the ongoing lives of a wide range of persons and communities, non-Christian as well as Christian. Without being in any way able to predict this, but with faith that God's continuing providential working in human affairs will properly sort these matters out, I gladly send these proposals forth into the world.

Notes

1. The Question of God

1. Various versions of these two aphorisms are often attributed to Ivan in F. Dostoyevsky's *The Brothers Karamazov.* However, though Ivan frequently expresses these ideas, he apparently never states them in this compact aphoristic form. For various expressions of the idea that "If there is no God, everything is permitted," see pp. 60, 72, 244, 561, 599, 616, and 662 of the Norton Critical Edition of *The Brothers Karamazov,* ed. Ralph E. Matlaw (New York: W. W. Norton, 1976). The entirety of chapter 4, "Rebellion," is devoted to discussion of the idea that "the suffering of just one innocent child makes belief in God intolerable."
2. Martin Buber, *Eclipse of God* (London: Gollancz, 1953), pp. 17–18.
3. See Francis Fiorenza, *Foundational Theology: Jesus and the Church* (New York: Crossroad, 1984), ch. 11.
4. Anselm, *Proslogion,* ch. 2.
5. Ibid., ch. 15.
6. For recent illuminating moves toward truly comparative theology, see W. C. Smith, *Towards a World Theology* (Philadelphia: Westminster Press, 1981); and Abe Nobuhiko, "Semiotics of Self in Theology: A Comparative Study of James and Nishida" (Th. D. diss., Harvard University, 1992).

2. Theology: One-Dimensional, Two-Dimensional, or Holistic?

1. Edward Farley's recent work *Ecclesial Reflection* (Philadelphia: Fortress Press, 1982) gives, in my opinion, the fullest and most illuminating discussion of the way in which traditional theology built up and relied upon what Farley calls "the house of authority." Farley also presents a devastating critique of all such authoritarian theology.
2. I preserve male gender language with reference to God when paraphrasing or summarizing biblical or other traditional texts which use such language.

When speaking in my own voice, however, I attempt to avoid all such sexist locutions; occasionally this necessitates the use of such neologisms as "Godself."

3. The outstanding exception to this has been, of course, Karl Barth, who attempted to develop a theology which was anchored at every point in the interpretation of scripture, and which did not in any way depend on resources outside of scripture—that is, a thoroughly "one-dimensional" hermeneutical theology. Any inspection of Barth's massive theological corpus, however, will reveal it to be permeated at every point by his vast knowledge of western theological and cultural history, and particularly by his awareness of the problems of modernity: it would have been impossible for him to formulate the major theological issues to which he addressed himself apart from this extra-biblical material. One cannot, after all, present a plausible interpretation of a text—even holy scripture!—without taking some account of readers' experiences and interests, their modes of speaking and understanding, their historical situations, et cetera; and Barth actually depended in many *positive* ways on extra-biblical materials for the central themes of his work (as he himself sometimes acknowledged). The significance of this, however, was not built into and made explicit in his methodological reflections; in fact he strove mightily to deny it: see, for example, his famous debate with Emil Brunner, English translation in *Natural Theology* (London, Geoffrey Bles, 1946). If he had found it possible to acknowledge that theology must inevitably be (at the very least) *two*-dimensional, his entire program would necessarily have been developed in a much different and—given Barth's exceedingly powerful theological imagination—much more subtle way.
4. Paul Tillich, *Systematic Theology* (Chicago: University of Chicago Press, 1951), vol. I, pp. 34–68.
5. This does not mean there is no longer any place for a concept or doctrine of "revelation" in more recent theological programs. It means, rather, that the primary use or significance of that notion is no longer understood to be the authorization or legitimation of particular theological doctrines or claims. "Revelation" often continues to have an important place as expressing one of the dimensions of God's relation to humankind (see e.g., pp. 352–355).
6. See especially David Tracy, *The Analogical Imagination* (New York: Crossroad, 1981) and Schubert Ogden, *On Theology* (San Francisco: Harper & Row, 1986).
7. See esp. F. D. E. Schleiermacher, *The Christian Faith* (Edinburgh: T & T Clark, 1928), esp. pp. 3–128; and *Brief Outline of the Study of Theology* (Edinburgh: T & T Clark, 1850), pp. 104–119.
8. First published in 1900 in German; translated into English and many other languages. For Harnack the essence of Christianity was its belief in the fatherhood of God and the brotherhood of all human beings (Lectures 1–3).
9. First published in 1903 as a series of articles in *Die Christliche Welt.* Now

available in English translation in *Ernst Troeltsch: Writings on Theology and Religion* (Atlanta: John Knox Press, 1977), pp. 124–181.

10. See especially Ernst Troeltsch, "The Place of Christianity among the Religions of the World," in Troeltsch, *Christian Thought: Its History and Application* (New York: Meridian Books, 1957).
11. In this country H. R. Niebuhr articulated a very attractive version of this sort of "confessional theology" more than a generation ago; see esp. *The Meaning of Revelation* (New York: Macmillan, 1946). And more recently Edward Farley, expressing and defending his version of confessionalism in terms of a "phenomenological method," has argued that this continues to be the most viable approach for Christian theology; see *Ecclesial Man: A Social Phenomenology of Faith and Reality* (Philadelphia: Fortress Press, 1975), esp. pp. xvi-xvii, and ch. 1. A much narrower kind of "confessionalism," which evinces little concern whether the Christian message is intelligible to those outside the circle of committed Christian believers, has recently appeared in some versions of the so-called narrative theology.
12. The most thorough discussion of these difficulties known to me is to be found in Francis Fiorenza's article on the method of correlation (to be published in *Beyond Hermeneutics* (New York: Crossroad, in press).
13. See note 6 above. So-called liberation theologies, with their interest in showing the bearing of the Christian message on contemporary concrete socio-political situations, also practice a method of correlation (in the sense discussed here). J. L. Segundo, for example—though he does not present himself as a "correlational theologian" in *The Liberation of Theology* (New York: Orbis, 1976)— explains the basic "hermeneutical circle" with which Latin American liberation theology operates (ch. 1) in essentially correlational terms (see esp. pp. 4–5, 8, 19, 31, and endnotes 22 and 55).
14. It should not be forgotten in this connection that Schleiermacher, the great founder of this approach, did not hesitate to speak of the superiority of Christianity to all other religions; see *The Christian Faith,* secs. 11–14.
15. A brief methodological discussion of why I regard the exploration of the symbol "God" to be "the proper business of theology" today can be found in the chapter by that title in my *Essay on Theological Method* (Atlanta: Scholars Press, 1975; rev. ed. 1979).

3. Theology as a Human Imaginative Task

1. For a more direct methodological argument that theology is fundamentally "imaginative construction," see my *Essay on Theological Method* (Atlanta: Scholars Press, 1975; rev. ed. 1979); chs. 1 and 10 of my *The Theological Imagination: Constructing the Concept of God* (Philadelphia: Westminster Press, 1981); and ch. 2 of my *Theology for a Nuclear Age* (Manchester: Manchester University Press; Philadelphia: Westminster Press, 1985).
2. Some of the paragraphs in the remainder of this chapter appeared in an earlier version in "Religious Diversity, Historical Consciousness, and Chris-

tian Theology," in *The Myth of Christian Uniqueness,* ed. J. Hick and R. F. Knitter (Maryknoll, N.Y.: Orbis Books, 1987).

3. Augustine makes this point in a number of places. Some of the more important texts are collected in Erich Przywara's *An Augustine Synthesis* (London: Sheed and Ward, 1945), pp. 53–63.
4. From Letter 73 and "The Unity of the Catholic Church," respectively. Trans. used here is from *Early Latin Theology* (Library of Christian Classics, vol. 5), ed. S. L. Greenslade (Philadelphia: Westminster Press, 1956), pp. 127–128, 169.
5. For brief further discussion of this point, see "The Idea of Relativity and the Idea of God," in my *The Theological Imagination;* and also "The Secular Utility of 'God-Talk,'" in *God the Problem* (Cambridge, Mass.: Harvard University Press, 1972). Paul Tillich, with his conception of "the protestant principle," and H. R. Niebuhr, with his conception of "radical monotheism," have also emphasized this point; see esp. Tillich, *The Protestant Era* (Chicago: University of Chicago Press, 1948), "Author's Introduction" and chs. 11, 13–15, and Niebuhr, *Radical Monotheism and Western Culture* (New York: Harper and Bros., 1960).

4. Theological Construction and Faith

1. An earlier version of much of what follows in this chapter, entitled "Mystery, Critical Consciousness, and Faith," was published in *The Rationality of Religious Belief: Essays in Honour of Basil Mitchell,* ed. W. J. Abraham and S. W. Holtzer (Oxford: Clarendon Press, 1987), pp. 53–69.
2. Paul Ricoeur, *The Symbolism of Evil* (New York: Harper and Row, 1967), pp. 350–357.
3. Anyone familiar with Karl Barth's commentary on *The Epistle to the Romans,* trans. by Edwyn C. Hoskyns (London: Oxford University Press, 1933) will recognize how heavily I am indebted to Barth for essential elements of my reflection here. I hope, however, that I have succeeded in avoiding the serious dialectical errors into which he fell (as it seems to me) in much of his all too definite and confident talk about the "wholly other" and about Jesus Christ, revelation, and salvation.

5. Mystery, Theology and Conversation

1. For some contemporary examples of this from quite different theological camps, see Karl Rahner, *Foundations of Christian Faith* (Seabury Press, 1978), ch. 2; Bernard Meland, *Fallible Forms and Symbols* (Philadelphia: Fortress Press, 1976), chs. 4–5; Karl Barth, *Church Dogmatics* (Edinburgh: T & T Clark, 1956–1969), I, 1, pp. 184–212; I, 2, pp. 122–202; II, 1, pp. 179–255.
2. Ludwig Wittgenstein, *Tractatus Logico-Philosophicus* (London: Routledge and Kegan Paul, 1961), p. 151.
3. Wayne Proudfoot has noted that the word "ineffable" functions in religious

discourse in ways similar to my characterization here of "mystery." See *Religious Experience* (Berkeley: University of California Press, 1985), pp. 124–136.

4. Compare Mikhail Bakhtin: "I occupy in singular existence a singular, unrepeatable, irreplaceable and impermeable place . . . No other is situated in the singular time and place . . . in which I am now situated . . . That which can be accomplished by me, can be accomplished by no one else, ever . . . For only I—the one-and-only I—can occupy in a given set of circumstances this particular place at this particular time; all other human beings are situated outside me." Quoted (and trans.) by Deborah Haynes in her "Creativity and Answerability: A Critical Theology of the Arts" (Ph.D. diss., Harvard University, 1990), pp. 98, 100–101.
5. M. M. Bakhtin, in *Speech Genres and Other Late Essays*, ed. C. Emerson and M. Holquist (Austin: University of Texas Press, 1986), p. 170. (Deborah Haynes called my attention to this quotation.)
6. In recent years there has been increasing interest among philosophers and theologians in conversation or dialogue as a proper goal for intellectual activity, instead of the more traditional pursuit of truth: see, for example, R. Rorty, *Philosophy and the Mirror of Nature* (Princeton: Princeton University Press, 1979) and *Consequences of Pragmatism* (Minneapolis: University of Minnesota Press, 1982); J. Habermas, *Theory of Communicative Action*, 2 vols. (Boston: Beacon Press, 1984, 1987); R. S. Bernstein, *Beyond Objectivism and Relativism* (Philadelphia: University of Pennsylvania Press, 1985); H. Peukert, *Science, Action and Fundamental Theology: Toward a Theology of Communicative Action* (Cambridge, Mass.: M.I.T. Press, 1984); F. Fiorenza, *Foundational Theology* (New York: Crossroad, 1984); D. Tracy, *Plurality and Ambiguity* (San Francisco: Harper and Row, 1987); P. Hodgson, *God in History: Shapes of Freedom* (Nashville: Abingdon, 1989). My suggestion that (religious) truth should be understood to be specifically dialogical (and thus pluralistic) in character is in harmony, I think, with this growing interest in conversation and "communicative action."
7. I do not mean by these remarks about the distinctive task of academic theology to suggest that all theologians in the academy should address themselves to metatheological issues—that is, should work on an abstract plane which locates and interprets all other theologies, theological methodologies, and theological claims in its own terms. On the contrary (as can be seen, I hope, from the conception of pluralism worked out in this book), in my opinion (a) every theological position (including so-called metapositions) is grounded in and thus relative to the particular sociopolitical and religio-cultural context from which it emerges, and (b) it is precisely the concrete struggle and mutual criticism of these different theological perspectives—of which "academic theology" is only one!—that is indispensable to the health of the theological work of all these participants. So a variety of advocates of significantly distinct theological perspectives must be present in the ongoing conversation which the academy fosters, if that conversation is to be fruitful, each representing her or his position as forcefully and effectively as

possible. It is the conversation and debate among these concrete "advocacy" positions—with so-called academic theology itself being but one among the many voices—that is desired; only this can assure that the dialogical theology of the academy will make significant contributions to the wider theological conversation. The pluralistic view of academic theology that I am suggesting here should be sharply distinguished from the more traditional one which looked toward a single all-inclusive abstract theological "system" that supposedly had a "place" within itself for all the other concrete but "parochial" theologies. For further discussion of this notion of the special task of academic theology, see my article "Critical Theology as a University Discipline," published in the *Festschrift* for John Cobb, *Theology and the University,* ed. D. R. Griffin and J. C. Hough, Jr. (Albany: State University of New York Press, 1991), ch. 2.

6. The Christian World-Picture (I): The Monotheistic Categorial Scheme

1. According to the *Oxford English Dictionary* (Compact ed.), the word "orient" comes from a Latin word meaning "to rise," and it indicates in particular the direction of the rising sun, the east; the verb "to orient" means to place or arrange something so that it faces the east. By extension, it means "to place or adjust in any particular way with respect to the cardinal points [of the compass] or other defined data; . . . also, to ascertain the position of (anything) relatively to the points of the compass"; figuratively, it means "to adjust, correct, or bring into defined relations, to known facts or principles; . . . to put oneself in the right position or relation; also, to ascertain one's 'bearings', find out 'where one is'." According to the *Encyclopedia of Religion,* ed. M. Eliade (New York: Macmillan, 1987), "orientation" is a centrally important religious activity. "Orientation is the conscious act of defining and assuming proper position in space. Fixing the human place in existence in a significant way is a religious act when it orients a human being toward the sacred . . . In relation to the sacred, inhabited space and history become apprehensible . . . Since orientation involves relating an entity to a reality other than itself, it always entails a conjunction of beings and, in this sense, creates a center where all realities meet. . . . orientation situates human living space in meaningful relation to the beings around it. It requires a grasp of the total human situation, a sense of the whole of existence at all its levels . . . Orientation effects what it symbolizes: the proper relation of the human situation to the very ground of being within which human life finds itself. For this reason orientation—taking one's place in the world—is conceived of in many religious traditions as the first act of fully human beings living in habitable space. By symbolically assuming one's proper position in the world, one communicates with significant powers at work in the cosmos and gains a sense of one's unique significance in relation to all else" (vol. 11, pp. 105, 107). It should be noted that these remarks in the *Encyclopedia of Religion* are largely about orientation toward "sacred" reality; they thus

presuppose a dualism of sacred/profane. In this book (as we shall see) I am interested in overcoming this dualism; hence, the "orientation" which I take to be at stake in religious symbolisms is with respect simply to *reality.* Theology is concerned with finding the best possible symbolism (whether "secular" or "religious") for accomplishing this.

2. See H. R. Niebuhr, *Radical Monotheism and Western Culture* (New York: Harper and Bros., 1960).
3. Portions of what follows in this chapter and the next are excerpted from, or paraphrases of, material in ch. 4 of my *The Theological Imagination: Constructing the Concept of God* (Philadelphia: Westminster Press, 1981).
4. For some elaboration of this point see my *God the Problem* (Cambridge, Mass.: Harvard University Press, 1972), esp. pts. II and III.
5. Karl Barth does not hesitate to make this a matter of central dogmatic significance in his interpretation of the doctrine of creation; see *Church Dogmatics,* III, 1 (Edinburgh: T & T Clark, 1958), pp. 94–228.
6. An early and widely known article making this point is that of Lynn White, Jr., "The Historical Roots of Our Ecologic Crisis," *Science* (1967), 155:1203–1207.
7. For the classical discussion, see T. W. Adorno (and others), *The Authoritarian Personality* (New York: Norton, 1950).
8. Cf. Bruno Snell, *The Discovery of the Mind* (New York: Dover, 1982), pp. 123–132.
9. S. Kierkegaard, *Fear and Trembling* (Princeton: Princeton University Press, 1945).

7. The Christian World-Picture (II): The Category of Christ

1. The text used here is taken from *Christology of the Later Fathers,* ed. Edward Rochie Hardy, Library of Christian Classics, vol. 3 (Philadelphia: Westminster Press, 1954), p. 338.
2. Text (slightly altered) cited from ibid., p. 373.

8. Historicity and Biology

1. Soren Kierkegaard, *The Sickness unto Death* (Princeton: Princeton University Press, 1941), p. 17.
2. Immanuel Kant, *Critique of Judgment,* trans. J. H. Bernard (New York: Hafner, 1951), p. 55.

9. Humanity in the World

1. This point has now been recognized in modern astrophysics with the emergence of the so-called anthropic principle. For discussion see John D. Barrow and Frank J. Tipler, *The Anthropic Cosmological Principle* (Oxford: Oxford University Press, 1986).

2. Clifford Geertz, *The Interpretation of Cultures* (New York: Basic Books, 1973).
3. Ibid., p. 64.
4. Ibid., p. 67.
5. Ibid. The sociobiologists C. J. Lumsden and E. O. Wilson, with their concept of "gene-culture coevolution," appear to concur with this judgment; see *Promethean Fire: Reflections on the Origin of Mind* (Cambridge, Mass.: Harvard University Press, 1983).
6. Ibid., p. 49. In the paragraph immediately preceding Geertz supplies more detail: "there is no such thing as a human nature independent of culture. Men without culture would not be the clever savages of Golding's *Lord of the Flies* thrown back upon the cruel wisdom of their animal instincts; nor would they be the nature's noblemen of Enlightenment primitivism or even . . . intrinsically talented apes who had somehow failed to find themselves. They would be unworkable monstrosities with very few useful instincts, fewer recognizable sentiments, and no intellect: mental basket cases. As our central nervous system—and most particularly its crowning curse and glory, the neocortex—grew up in great part in interaction with culture, it is incapable of directing our behavior or organizing our experience without the guidance provided by systems of significant symbols. What happened to us in the Ice Age is that we were obliged to abandon the regularity and precision of detailed genetic control over our conduct for the flexibility and adaptability of a more generalized, though of course no less real, genetic control over it. To supply the additional information necessary to be able to act, we were forced, in turn, to rely more and more heavily on cultural sources—the accumulated fund of significant symbols. Such symbols are thus not mere expressions, instrumentalities, or correlates of our biological, psychological, and social existence; they are prerequisites of it. Without men, no culture, certainly; but equally, and more significantly, without culture, no men."
7. See esp. Ernst Troeltsch, "The Place of Christianity among the World Religions," in *Christian Thought: Its History and Application* (New York: Meridian Books, 1957).

10. Toward a Normative Concept of the Human

1. See, for example, A. M. Abraham Ayrookuzhiel, *The Sacred in Popular Hinduism* (Madras: Christian Literature Society, 1983).
2. My attempt to sketch a pluralistic/dialogical notion of truth itself, along lines implied, perhaps, in these last remarks, can be found in the references cited in the footnote to Chapter 5, p. 68.

11. Agency and Self-Reflexiveness as Sociohistorically Constituted

1. For an excellent brief analysis of the concept of imagination and its uses, see Alan R. White, *The Language of Imagination* (Oxford: Blackwell, 1990).
2. There are some peculiar exceptions to this rule. For example, in English

"we" can be and is sometimes used in a second-person sense. For examples and discussion, see Peter Mühlhäusler and Rom Harré, *Pronouns and People: The Linguistic Construction of Social and Personal Identity* (Oxford: Blackwell, 1990), ch. 7.

3. The book cited in the previous note makes this argument in detail, drawing on a wealth of comparative linguistic material to support it.
4. For very thoughtful discussion of this history, see Charles Taylor, *Sources of the Self* (Cambridge, Mass.: Harvard University Press, 1989), pt. II, "Inwardness."
5. On women's consciousness, see (among others) Carol Gilligan, *In a Different Voice* (Cambridge, Mass.: Harvard University Press, 1982), and Jean Baker Miller, *Toward a New Psychology of Women* (Boston: Beacon Press, 1976); in regard to Japanese group consciousness, I have found the writings of Thomas Kasulis, for example, *Zen Action, Zen Person* (Honolulu: University Press of Hawaii, 1981), and Takeo Doi, *The Anatomy of Dependence* (Tokyo: Kodanshu International, Ltd., 1973), quite illuminating.
6. See esp. ch. 5 of *Pronouns and People,* "I: the Indexicalities of Responsibility and Place."
7. Our very sense of temporality, with its three modalities of past, present, and future, is closely connected with—if not derivative from—this threefold self-reflexiveness belonging to the "I." The distinctive ways in which past and future are each connected with the "I" (which lives always in the present) gives these two modalities the peculiar shadowy semi-reality which is their mark, in contrast with the full-bodied actuality of the present. Memory makes available to us what we have suffered in the past and what we have done, what projects we have attempted and how they have fared, and thus it shapes our sense of the sorts of actions that are possible and desirable, as well as those that are undesirable. On the basis of this past experience we make our decisions and perform our actions in the present with reference to the future. Thus, without memory (the presence of the past) deliberate action (projection into the future) would not be possible. Conversely, however, if we had not already been agents (to some degree) in the past—if we had never tried to *do* anything, to move into the future—and if we were not aware of our past interactions with other agents, we would have nothing to remember that could assist our acting in the present (though we would be, like other animals, conditioned to respond to particular stimuli in certain definite ways). Our capacity to remember a significant past is thus interconnected with our awareness that we always face an impending future. Future and past, (potential) action and memory, are mutually interdependent; neither could exist for us without the other. And both, of course, require body, our having available to ourselves—and our being aware that we have available—the physical resources to move, to do, to effect some changes in the world. What I *remember* is what this embodied "I" has done and what has happened to it; and what I *intend* I intend for this embodied "I," and for those others with whom I stand in interrelation.
8. Conversation is no merely mechanical or biological process entirely deter-

mined by physical forces or physiological impulses or prior conditioning. It is conscious and deliberate: we speak when we so choose, and we are silent when we choose; and what we say (except for inadvertent "slips of the tongue") we intend to say. For this reason we quite properly *hold ourselves responsible* for what we have said: it was *our own doing*, and we are well aware that we could have spoken otherwise had we chosen so to do. It is for us—no one else—to determine what the next sentence will be.

12. Subjectivity, Experience, and Freedom

1. Cf. Talcott Parsons, *The Social System* (New York: Free Press, 1951), and Talcott Parsons and Edward Shils, eds., *Towards a General Theory of Action* (Cambridge, Mass.: Harvard University Press, 1951), for a much fuller discussion of these matters.
2. See esp. Ludwig Wittgenstein, *Philosophical Investigations* (Oxford: Blackwell, 1958); also *The Blue and Brown Books* (Oxford: Blackwell, 1960); *On Certainty* (Oxford: Blackwell, 1969); and *Zettel* (Berkeley: University of California Press, 1967).
3. The fullest and most convincing discussion of this matter of which I am aware is to be found in Peter Mühlhäusler and Rom Harré, *Pronouns and People: The Linguistic Construction of Social and Personal Identity* (Oxford: Blackwell, 1990), esp. ch. 5. According to these writers, subjectivity is apprehended in quite different ways in different linguistic contexts. Particularly striking is the very diminished sense of subjectivity and agency among speakers of Inuit (Eskimo). Certain "features of [this] language suggest strongly that while the uses of English favour a theory of the person conceived not only as a location, but as a substance qualified by attributes, in Eskimo persons are rendered as qualifications (for instance, as locations) of substantialized qualities and relations. . . . the content of 'I hear him' would be expressed in Eskimo by . . . [words meaning] literally 'his making a sound with reference to me' . . . Perceiving and cooking are things we [English speakers] do; Inuit favours expressions that display such things as happening to us . . . In so far as vocabulary and grammatical form can be cited as evidence, Eskimos seem to distinguish their own emotions and those of others by referring them to locations in the array of persons, the grammatical forms emphasizing the public display rather than the private feeling . . . Important aspects of the passive Eskimo conception of action are revealed in the theory of art. . . . there are no Eskimo equivalents for our concepts of 'making' and 'creating'; carving, for instance, is described in terms of releasing or revealing what is already there. The concept of active individual agency plays scarcely any role . . . Eskimo morality is centred on a sharp distinction between communal matters and personal and private matters. Only the former are appraised as good or bad . . . Fair dealing in an individualistic person-to-person sense or truth-telling are at best secondary virtues. Theft from persons . . . is not conceived as a serious misdemeanor

. . . Eskimo culture seems . . . to have been built on a moral order in which individuals are defined as conduits through which forces from sources extrinsic, and often external, to themselves issue in action, and in which moral responsibility both is to the group and devolves on the group" (pp. 110-112).

4. An excellent analysis of the concept of "free action" will be found in A. I. Melden, *Free Action* (New York: Humanities Press, 1961).

13. The Interpenetration of Action with Reflection

1. My reflections on the different degrees in which reflection comes to interpenetrate action were initially stimulated by the notion of "levels" of action set out by H. D. Aiken, *Reason and Conduct* (New York: Knopf, 1962), ch. 4, and Maurice Mandelbaum, *Phenomenology of Moral Experience* (Baltimore: Johns Hopkins Press, 1969); I shall, however, develop this idea in a rather different way than they did.
2. There may well be some circumstances in which we hold ourselves or others responsible in certain respects even for what we regard as "unconscious" behavior, since this behavior may sometimes be subject to some human control and may be transformable—even if only in very complicated and indirect ways (and certainly not without someone becoming in some way conscious and deliberate about bringing about such transformation). I cannot take up this matter here, however.
3. It is important to Christian ethics that we hold this "spontaneous" level of human behavior to be morally significant, for Christian faith regards *loving* action as normative for humans. Kant pointed out that love cannot be commanded and cannot be deliberately chosen: for this reason, he argued, love is morally ambiguous in comparison with *duty,* which he took to be the paradigm of the moral; see "Foundations of the Metaphysics of Morals," in L. W. Beck's translation of Kant's *Critique of Practical Reason and Other Writings in Moral Philosophy* (Chicago: University of Chicago Press, 1949), pp. 60–61. But, though Christian faith certainly regards doing one's duty to one's neighbor as important, it values much more highly *loving the neighbor,* responding spontaneously to the neighbor's need (cf. the parable of the Good Samaritan). If we are ultimately to develop a Christian interpretation of human action and morality, therefore, "spontaneous acts" of this sort must be given a significant place in our overall scheme.
4. H. R. Niebuhr, in *The Responsible Self* (New York: Harper and Row, 1963), has attempted to work out an entire ethic in terms of the concept of the fitting. I am indebted to him for developing this notion, but, as will become evident, I do not think it illuminates all the aspects of moral action and reflection to which we need to pay attention here.
5. In recent years Alan Gewirth has presented a position similar in a number of important respects to the one I am setting forth here; see *Reason and Morality* (Chicago: University of Chicago Press, 1978). His position, how-

ever, appears to be much more rigidly rationalistic on its normative side than mine.

6. A similar but much fuller and more detailed analysis of moral concepts than I am able to provide here will be found in J. M. Brennan, *The Open-Texture of Moral Concepts* (New York: Barnes and Noble, 1977).
7. This is the way in which I interpret Kant's point about morality being reason's autonomous "self-legislation," in which reason "gives a law to itself" and is thus not to be regarded as a matter of heteronomous obedience to alien commands. See "Foundations of the Metaphysics of Morals," pp. 84–97, 103–107.
8. The issues arising in connection with Circle 4 will not be discussed at this point. They are the subject matter of Chapter 16 and of Parts III and IV.

14. An Ecological Ethic

1. Aristotle also, though he failed to distinguish clearly the end-seeking characteristic of acts (what I call their "expedience") from their moral quality, nevertheless included as a part of his analysis a discussion of this central feature of acts without which moral considerations could not arise at all, that is, their distinctly *voluntary* character; see Book III of the *Nicomachean Ethics.*
2. Kant, "Foundations of the Metaphysics of Morals," in L. W. Beck's translation of *Critique of Practical Reason and Other Writings in Moral Philosophy* (Chicago: University of Chicago Press, 1949), pp 72–84, 89–92.
3. Ibid., p. 80; cf. p. 94.
4. Peter Mühlhäusler and Rom Harré have especially emphasized, with reference to contemporary linguistic theory, that human conversation would be impossible (in any language or culture) in the absence of such basic moral attitudes and practices; *Pronouns and People: The Linguistic Construction of Social and Personal Identity* (Oxford: Blackwell, 1990), pp. 29–33.
5. Kant, "Foundations of the Metaphysics of Morals," p. 87; cf. pp. 94–96.
6. Ibid, pp. 92–93.
7. Ibid., p. 89.
8. Ibid, pp. 90–91, 96–109.
9. On pp. 91–96 of the "Foundations of the Metaphysics of Morals" Kant discusses his notion of the "realm of ends," but he does not formulate precisely this imperative (though he comes quite close on pp. 95–96).
10. ". . . if we abstract from the personal difference of rational beings and thus from all content of their private ends, we can think of a whole of all ends in systematic connection, a whole of rational beings as ends in themselves . . . This is a realm of ends . . . Morality . . . consists in the relation of every action to that legislation through which alone a realm of ends is possible" (p. 91). Kant's doctrine of community has often been ignored in presentations of his ethics, and this has led to a widely held atomistic misunderstanding of his position. For a good discussion of these matters, see Jennifer

Moore, "The Role and Meaning of Community in Kant's Ethics" (Ph.D. diss., Harvard University, 1986).

11. See Kant's several writings on the philosophy of history, conveniently gathered together in *On History* (Indianapolis: Bobbs-Merrill, 1963); see also *Religion within the Limits of Reason Alone* (New York: Harper and Bros., 1960), esp. Book III. For discussion of Kant's philosophy of history, see Michel Despland, *Kant on History and Religion* (Montreal: McGill–Queen's University Press, 1973).
12. See Kant, "What Is Enlightenment?" in *Critique of Practical Reason and Other Writings in Moral Philosophy,* pp. 286–292.
13. Kant, "Foundations of the Metaphysics of Morals," pp. 93–97.
14. For discussion of these issues see Nancy Chodorow, *The Reproduction of Mothering* (Berkeley: University of California Press, 1978).
15. See Evelyn Fox Keller, *Reflections on Gender and Science* (New Haven: Yale University Press, 1985), esp. ch. 5.
16. Carol Gilligan *(In a Different Voice)* and others have presented evidence that women's moral consciousness in our society is more sensitive to our social interconnectedness—and that women value relationships with other persons, indeed often define themselves in terms of such relationships to a much greater extent—than is true of males, who often value autonomy and independence more highly than social connections. (See also Keller, *Reflections on Gender and Science.*) Sharon Welch has argued that our moral traditions generally take for granted that an "ethic of control" is what is required to order human life properly; but this presupposes a social position of prestige and power. New insights into human moral existence can be gained if we examine the "ethic of risk" with which many humans have actually had to live out their lives; Welch, *A Feminist Ethic of Risk* (Minneapolis: Fortress Press, 1989).
17. Tillich, *Systematic Theology* II (Chicago: University of Chicago Press, 1957), pp. 33–36.
18. This may be particularly true of persons with a highly developed sense of individual ego, persons whose original social sensitivities have been weakened as they have acquired a powerful sense of their own autonomy and power, their own agency. For such persons (as we have noted) the intuitive and immediate moral sensitivities often originally present in Circles 0 and 1 may have somewhat diminished, and therefore when moral considerations arise (in Circle 2), with their various rules and principles seemingly external to the immediate situation and imposed upon it, they may have a largely heteronomous feel about them. It may be true, as some have held, that most women in our society are not socialized toward autonomy and independence in this way but rather toward a special sensitivity for the social connections that bond them to others. However, even if this is so, its principal effects are often limited largely to face-to-face "primary group" relationships where immediate interpersonal connections are central, while the more complex moral issues connected with the wide ramifications of action throughout

society as a whole remain unaddressed. In our complexly interconnected world of today, these "wide ramifications" must be understood to include human relations and ecological concerns both around the globe and extended indefinitely into the future. Matters of this scope can hardly be directly intuited or sensed by anyone, for our very awareness of them depends on considerable knowledge drawn from a wide range of fields—economics, politics, history, sociology, international relations, the physical and life sciences, et cetera. Since moral and ethical consciousness today, thus, must extend far beyond what is given intuitively in the immediacy of concrete interpersonal relations, it will probably always seem more remote than, and can never have the motivational immediacy of, the expedient and aesthetic dimensions of action.

19. Hobbes, *Leviathan,* ch. 13.
20. It should be remembered that notions of humanity's radical difference, or alienation, from nature are not mere modern inventions: their roots go far back into our religious traditions which focused so much attention on the distinctiveness of the human *soul.*

15. The Corruption of Historicity: Freedom and Evil

1. In certain main lines of the position I develop here, I am following Paul Tillich's illuminating discussion of anxiety; see esp. *The Courage to Be* (London: Nisbet and Co., 1952), esp. chs. 2–3; and *Systematic Theology* I, (Chicago: University of Chicago Press, 1951), pp. 191–192; II (Chicago: University of Chicago Press, 1957), pp. 34–36, 67–68. For a similar analysis by a psychologist, see Rollo May, *The Meaning of Anxiety* (New York: Ronald Press, 1950).
2. For Niebuhr's discussion, see *Nature and Destiny of Man* (New York: Scribners, 1949), pp. 181–186, 250–254; for Kierkegaard, *The Concept of Anxiety* (Princeton: Princeton University Press, 1980). Freud's discussions of anxiety have also influenced contemporary theological interpretations. An excellent discussion of Freud's two quite different theories of anxiety, and their significance for understanding human religiousness, has been developed in an unpublished paper by Christopher Chapman, "The Freudian Critique of Religion in Relation to Theories of Anxiety in Psychoanalysis and the Theology of Paul Tillich."
3. Tillich, *Courage to Be,* p. 33.
4. Herbert Fingarette, *The Self in Transformation* (New York: Basic Books, 1963), pp. 78–79.
5. For discussion of the relation of "responsiveness" to "responsibility" or "accountability," see H. R. Niebuhr, *The Responsible Self* (New York: Harper and Row, 1963), pp. 61–65.
6. G. W. F. Hegel, *Phenomenology of Spirit,* trans. A. V. Miller (Oxford: Oxford University Press, 1977), pp. 111–119.

16. Historicity and Religion

1. See note 1 to Chapter 6 for a brief discussion of the concept of *orientation* as a key to understanding the significance of religion.
2. See esp. Niebuhr, *Radical Monotheism and Western Culture* (New York: Harper and Bros., 1960), pp. 100–113.
3. A similar understanding of religious meaning as that which funds in basic ways the life of a culture is found in the work of Paul Tillich (as well as many others) and is well expressed in Tillich's aphorism: "Religion is the substance of culture, culture is the expression of religion"; see *The Protestant Era* (Chicago: University of Chicago Press, 1948), p. xvii; see also pt. II, as well as *Theology of Culture* (New York: Oxford University Press, 1959), and many other texts in his work. Cf. also Bernard Meland, *Faith and Culture* (London: George Allen and Unwin, 1955). In this connection Wittgenstein's remarks on the underlying "picture of the world" which humans presuppose in all their living, acting, and reflecting are also very interesting; *On Certainty,* for example, sec. 85–299. And see Clifford Geertz, "Religion as a Cultural System," in *The Interpretation of Cultures* (New York: Basic Books, 1973), ch. 4; Peter Berger, *The Sacred Canopy* (New York: Doubleday, 1967); Hans Mol, *Identity and the Sacred* (New York: Free Press, 1976); and many others.
4. See W. C. Smith's Ingersoll Lecture on "Eternal Life," presented at Harvard Divinity School on June 15, 1966.
5. Buddhist thinkers, particularly in the Mahayana traditions stemming from Nagarjuna (second century C.E.), have been aware of these problems for many centuries. For discussion of Nagarjuna's work, see F. J. Streng, *Emptiness: A Study in Religious Meaning* (Nashville: Abingdon Press, 1967), and D. J. Kalupahana, *Nagarjuna: The Philosophy of the Middle Way* (Albany: State University of New York Press, 1986).
6. The sort of comparative analysis of religious symbol systems which I have in mind here is suggested in my (very brief) sketch of the basic symbolic patterns of Buddhism and Christianity in "Religious Diversity and Religious Truth," in *John Hick: A Festschrift,* ed. A. Sharma (London: Macmillan, forthcoming).
7. A much fuller (early) statement of this elusive and paradoxical problem will be found in my paper "A Problem for Theology: the Concept of Nature," *Harvard Theological Review* (1972) 65:337–366; at that writing the paradoxes seemed to me virtually insoluble. By the time that paper was reprinted, however (with some small changes), as ch. 8 of *The Theological Imagination* (Philadelphia: Westminster Press, 1981), I was beginning to see some glimmers of light. But only quite recently have I begun to feel that I am finding a way to address the issues posed in that paper of twenty years ago.
8. This conception of metaphysics is sketched more fully in "Metaphysics and Theology," ch. 9 of *The Theological Imagination.*

17. Small Steps of Faith

1. It should be noted here that the program of theological construction which we will be following in these chapters is not precisely the same as that projected in my *Essay on Theological Method* (Atlanta: Scholars Press, 1975, 1979). There I described an "order of construction" (p. 46) consisting of three moments: first, a moment of phenomenological and scientific description of experience and the world, in which a concept of the world was developed without regard to the question of whether that concept stood, or could stand, in any intelligible relation to the symbol "God"; second, the actual construction of a concept of God, which could serve as a relativizing and humanizing focus for the devotion and work of human beings; and third, the necessary adjustment of the first and second moments to each other through the imaginative construction of a picture of the world and humanity "under God." Here, however, we will not be following precisely this pattern, at least not in this sequential order. Rather, in these chapters I will bring moments I and III into much closer relation with each other than I had anticipated would be possible or appropriate in that earlier sketch. On the one hand, I shall continue to emphasize accurate phenomenological and scientific description of humanity and the world, as these appear to modern experience and knowledge. On the other hand, however, I shall be regularly noting, as we proceed, the considerable variety of plausible metaphysical and religious interpretations to which these phenomenological and scientific conceptions are open; and we shall undertake to make a number of small steps (or leaps) of faith, as we carefully build up an interpretation of the world to which the concept of God can be significantly related, an interpretation within which faith in God (in a sense still to be determined) is plausible. So, when we take up the construction of the concept of God itself, we will not really be moving into the *second* moment of a sequence of three; rather, we will be moving to the climactic moment of a single gradual process within which we have been constructing a picture of the situation of humanity in the world. Logically, the same features are present in this pattern of theological construction as in the program I originally proposed: (1) the world and the human as these are given in and to our modern experience and knowledge; (2) the symbol or concept of God; (3) an interpretation of humanity in the world which has a significant place for both of these. But in our order of construction we will not have taken up these three points in sequence; rather, we will have worked at (1) and (3) in tandem with each other, in order to develop a position from which we could address the central problem of theology (which in the earlier proposal was first to be sketched in moment II and then to be completed in moment III), namely, constructing the image/concept of God itself.
2. See Sallie McFague, "Cosmology and Christianity: Implications of the Common Creation Story for Theology," in *Theology at the End of Modernity:*

Essays in Honor of Gordon D. Kaufman, ed. Sheila Davaney (Philadelphia: Trinity Press International, 1991).

3. Not only positivistically inclined writers, but also many influenced by the later Wittgenstein, have emphasized this point. See, for example, O. K. Bouwsma, *Without Proof or Evidence* (Lincoln: University of Nebraska Press, 1984), pp. 1–25; James C. Edwards, *Ethics without Philosophy* (Tampa: University Presses of Florida, 1982); Richard Rorty, *Philosophy and the Mirror of Nature* (Princeton: Princeton University Press, 1979) and *Consequences of Pragmatism* (Minneapolis: University of Minnesota Press, 1982).
4. See Walpola Rahula, *What the Buddha Taught* (London: Gordon Fraser, 1967), pp. 12–15.
5. For a fuller analysis and justification of this point with respect to Buddhism, see my paper "Some Buddhist Metaphysical Presuppositions: A Response to Ryusei Takeda's Paper, 'Pure Land Buddhist View of Duhkha,'" *Buddhist-Christian Studies* (1985) 5:25–48.
6. I have benefited in my reflection on these matters from Helmut Peukert's discussion in *Science, Action and Fundamental Theology* (Cambridge, Mass.: M.I.T. Press, 1984), pp. 217–221.

18. Cosmic Visions and Human Meaning

1. Buddhism represents an exception to this dichotomy. For it, radical flux or change has apparently been primary, but this was not conceived in terms of historical process or development (though the idea of karma implies certain kinds of historical connectedness).
2. For illuminating discussion of the difference between "cosmic" and "historical" interpretations of the ultimate context of human existence, see M. Eliade, *Cosmos and History* (New York: Bollingen Foundation, 1954); see also P. Tillich, *The Protestant Era* (Chicago: University of Chicago Press, 1948), pt. I; and E. Voegelin, *Israel and Revelation* (Baton Rouge: Louisiana State University Press, 1956).
3. For detailed philosophical investigation of modern cosmological theory which shows clearly the extent to which this is all a product of the constructive powers of the human imagination in face of ultimate mystery, see Milton Munitz, *Cosmic Understanding: Philosophy and Science of the Universe* (Princeton: Princeton University Press, 1986). See also Michael Arbib and Mary Hesse, *The Construction of Reality* (Cambridge: Cambridge University Press, 1986).
4. Cf. L. Wittgenstein, *On Certainty,* sec. 126–475.
5. Rudolf Bultmann, "The New Testament and Mythology," in *Kerygma and Myth,* ed. H. W. Bartsch (London: S.P.C.K., 1953).
6. James Gustafson, in his *Ethics in a Theocentric Perspective,* 2 vols. (Chicago: University of Chicago Press, 1981, 1984) has performed a notable theolog-

ical service in his strong attack on the undue anthropocentrism of much of the Christian tradition. But he has not sufficiently nuanced his discussion of these matters. He seemingly supposes (a) that modern science and cosmology are not anthropocentric at all, and (b) that anthropocentrism is never legitimate, for any reason or in any respect, in theology or ethics (or in science). There is, thus, in Gustafson's work, both an undue naiveté with respect to science and also an inadequate perception of the purposes and functions of conceptions of God in human life; the "theocentrism" which he wishes (quite rightly) to promote is therefore less persuasive than it might be. For a full analysis of these matters, see my article "How Is *God* to Be Understood in a Theocentric Ethics?" in *James M. Gustafson's Theocentric Ethics,* ed. H. R. Beckley and C. M. Swezey (Macon, Ga.: Mercer University Press, 1988), pp. 13–37.

7. The term "spirit" is generally used in our language in contrast with "body" or "matter"; it designates experiential dimensions that seem difficult to interpret as simply bodily or material—for example, meaning, mind, purpose, values such as truth and justice, mathematical and logical concepts, etc. Cf. Wittgenstein: "Where our language suggests a body and there is none: there, we should like to say, is a *spirit.*" *Philosophical Investigations* (Oxford: Blackwell, 1958), pt. I, sec. 36.
8. For elaboration of the idea that metaphysical thinking is built up on the basis of different "root metaphors," see Stephen Pepper, *World Hypotheses* (Berkeley: University of California Press, 1942), and Dorothy Emmet, *The Nature of Metaphysical Thinking* (London: Macmillan, 1946). See also Ian Barbour, *Myths, Models, and Paradigms* (New York: Harper and Row, 1974), and Sallie McFague, *Metaphorical Theology* (Philadelphia: Fortress Press, 1982); these two cite much of the extensive literature which has recently appeared on the significance of "models" and "metaphors" in human thinking.
9. Cf. J. Bronowski: "In a history of three thousand million years, evolution has not run backward. . . . the building up of stable configurations . . . [has] a direction . . . which cannot be reversed . . . It is evolution, physical and biological, that gives time its direction . . . And it is not a forward direction in the sense of a thrust toward the future, a headed arrow. What evolution does is to give the arrow of time a barb which stops it from running backward; and once it has this barb, the chance play of errors will take it forward of itself." "New Concepts in the Evolution of Complexity: Stratified Stability and Unbounded Plans," *Zygon* (1970) 5:28, 31–32, 34. In Chapter 20 below, we shall take up some problems (important for theological reflection) posed by simplistic interpretations of the "chance" aspects of the forward movement of evolutionary processes.
10. A brilliant expression of the faith-stance which denies that the cosmos has any real human or humane meaning is to be found in Bertrand Russell's "A Free Man's Worship": "The life of Man is a long march through the night, surrounded by invisible foes, tortured by weariness and pain, towards a goal

that few can hope to reach, and where none may tarry long . . . Brief and powerless is Man's life; on him and all his race the slow, sure doom falls pitiless and dark. Blind to good and evil, reckless of destruction, omnipotent matter rolls on its relentless way; for Man, condemned to-day to lose his dearest, to-morrow himself to pass through the gate of darkness, it remains only to cherish, ere yet the blow falls, the lofty thoughts that ennoble his little day; disdaining the coward terrors of the slave of Fate, to worship at the shrine that his own hands have built; undismayed by the empire of chance, to preserve a mind free from the wanton tyranny that rules his outward life; proudly defiant of the irresistible forces that tolerate, for a moment, his knowledge and his condemnation, to sustain alone, a weary but unyielding Atlas, the world that his own ideals have fashioned despite the trampling march of unconscious power." *Mysticism and Logic* (Garden City, N.Y.: Doubleday Anchor Books, 1917), pp. 53–54. A life can certainly be built on this sort of ultimate despair about the meaning and place of the human and the humane, but it will be of a quite different sort from one lived out of a confidence that our human existence and projects have a significant place in the ultimate scheme of things.

19. Serendipitous Creativity

1. In the recent discussions of "the anthropic principle" by physicists, astronomers, and other scientific cosmologists, the importance of this issue for physical science theory is now being debated. For some of the discussion, see John D. Barrow and Frank J. Tipler, *The Anthropic Cosmological Principle* (New York: Oxford University Press, 1986).
2. Paul Ricoeur, *Freud and Philosophy* (New Haven: Yale University Press, 1970), pp. 459–493.
3. For a sustained argument on this point from a biological point of view, see Ernst Mayr, *Toward a New Philosophy of Biology* (Cambridge, Mass.: Harvard University Press, 1988), esp. chs. 2–3, 6–9.
4. I have worked out this argument in more detail in *Theology for a Nuclear Age* (Philadelphia: Westminster Press; Manchester, England: Manchester University Press, 1985).
5. In what follows in the next few paragraphs, I have benefited from insights found in W. Pannenberg, *Anthropology in Theological Perspective* (Philadelphia: Westminster Press, 1985), pp. 371–376, and H. N. Wieman, *The Source of Human Good* (Chicago: University of Chicago Press, 1946), pp. 56–69.
6. Cf. R. Scharlemann, *The Being of God* (New York: Seabury Press, 1981), pp. 72–74, 121.
7. Mayr, *Toward a New Philosophy of Biology,* p. 150. For full discussion see chs. 6–9.
8. Ibid., p. 145.
9. Cf. Stephen Toulmin's discussion of the evolution of patterns of thought in

Human Understanding: The Collective Use and Evolution of Concepts (Princeton: Princeton University Press, 1972).

10. This breakdown of teleological thinking is widely acknowledged; for a recent theological example see Peter Hodgson *God in History: Shapes of Freedom* (Nashville: Abingdon Press, 1989). Hodgson has proposed a rather different resolution of this problem than I am suggesting, namely the idea of occasionally and variously emergent "shapes of freedom," as the basic expression of God's activity in history.
11. This appears also to have been true for the emergence of the very universe (as we think of it) itself: "If the rate of expansion one second after the big bang had been smaller by even one part in a hundred thousand million million, the universe would have recollapsed before it ever reached its present size." Stephen W. Hawking, *A Brief History of Time* (Toronto: Bantam Books, 1988), pp. 121–122.

20. Directional Movements in a Serendipitous Universe

1. Ernst Mayr, *Toward a New Philosophy of Biology* (Cambridge, Mass.: Harvard University Press, 1988), p. 435.
2. J. Bronowski states flatly that "It is evolution, physical and biological, that gives time its direction." "New Concepts in the Evolution of Complexity: Stratified Stability and Unbounded Plans," *Zygon* (1970) 5:34. See also the quotation cited in Chapter 18, note 9.
3. Even so resolutely antiteleological a writer as Ernst Mayr cannot avoid acknowledging that looking backward from where we stand, an almost teleological movement comes into view: ". . . who can deny that overall there is an advance from the prokaryotes that dominated the living world more than three billion years ago to the eukaryotes with their well organized nucleus and chromosomes as well as cytoplasmic organelles; from the single-celled eukaryotes to metaphytes and metazoans with a strict division of labor among their highly specialized organ systems; within the metazoans from ectotherms that are at the mercy of climate to the warm-blooded endotherms, and within the endotherms from types with a small brain and low social organization to those with a very large central nervous system, highly developed parental care, and the capacity to transmit information from generation to generation?" (*Toward a New Philosophy of Biology*, pp. 251–252.)
4. It is possible, thus, as Kant suggested, to *think* (though not to know in any scientific way) of a deep underlying harmony or connectedness between nature and freedom: for Kant, as Adina Davidovich has put it, "there is a *perspective* from which we can *think* of nature as teleological." See Davidovich's important new study of the bearing of the Third Critique on the Kantian philosophy as a whole, *Religion as a Province of Meaning: The Kantian Foundations of Modern Theology* (Ph.D. diss., Harvard University, 1990), p. 64; emphasis mine.

5. It has recently begun to appear possible, even likely, that the continuous increase in entropy over time in the universe may itself, in the natural course of events, give rise—through the development of so-called dissipative systems—to increasingly complex forms of organization, eventually including living systems. "... the picture that is emerging in ... recent thermodynamic analyses ... [suggests that] the movement of the [entropic] stream *itself* inevitably generates, as it were, very large eddies *within* itself in which, far from there being a decrease of order, there is an increase first in complexity and then in something more subtle—functional organization ... There could be no self-consciousness and human creativity without living organization, and there could be no such living dissipative systems unless the entropic stream followed its general, irreversible course in time. Thus does the apparently decaying, randomizing tendency of the universe provide the necessary and essential matrix (*mot juste!*) for the birth of new forms—new life through death and decay of the old." Arthur Peacocke, "Thermodynamics and Life," *Zygon* (1984) 19:430.
6. See Karl Löwith, *Meaning in History* (Chicago: University of Chicago Press, 1949), intro. and chs. 2–4.

21. Functions of the Symbol "God"

1. Rudolf Bultmann, "New Testament and Mythology," in *Kerygma and Myth*, ed. H. W. Bartsch (London: S.P.C.K., 1953), p. 10, note 2.
2. For fuller discussion of each of these metaphors, see my *Systematic Theology: A Historicist Perspective* (New York: Scribners, 1968), esp. ch. 9; see also chs. 18–22.
3. Despite the great importance of Whitehead's cosmological thinking for theologians, helping to reorient our conceptual habits from structural-substance modalities to those of process and creativity, this direct attention to the *functions* which traditional God-talk performed (and performs) seems to be lacking; nor has it been carefully addressed by Whitehead's theological followers.

   An exception to this claim is suggested by the approach of Bernard Loomer in the recently published paper on "The Size of God," in *The Size of God: The Theology of Bernard Loomer in Context*, ed. William Dean and Larry Axel (Macon, Ga.: Mercer University Press, 1987), esp. pp. 41–42. Loomer, however, does not carry through this functional approach consistently in his paper; see my analysis in "Empirical Realism in Theology: An Examination of Some Themes in Meland and Loomer," in *New Essays in Religious Naturalism*, ed. C. Peden and L. Axel (Macon, Ga: Mercer University Press, 1992).

   Whitehead did indeed find an "X" in his cosmological scheme which he labeled "God"; and it is not surprising that some theologians have, for this reason, seized upon his thought as providing a basis for doing contemporary theological reflection. This may be all to the good—if Whitehead's God in fact can and does perform the central functions of the traditional image/concept "God"—or it may be seriously misleading. Obviously, the question as to which of these judgments is correct will be determined not primarily by the plausibility of Whitehead's cosmology but rather by our understanding of the functions of God-talk. In my view a central responsibility of the theologian is to think through carefully the meaning and proper use of the symbol "God" and make proposals for its reconstruction today. Failure to do this can all too easily result in the subordination of theology's proper and indispensable autonomy to the disposal of philosophy, or psychology, or comparative religion, or some other (nontheological) framework which supplies the basic perspective and criteria governing one's work. For discussion of the theological inappropriateness of such subordination, see my "Theology as a Public Vocation," in *The Vocation of the Theologian,* ed. T. W. Jennings (Philadelphia: Fortress Press, 1985); "Metaphysics and Theology," in *The Theological Imagination: Constructing the Concept of God* (Philadelphia: Westminster Press, 1981), ch. 9; and "The Proper Business of Theology," in *An Essay on Theological Method* (Atlanta: Scholars Press, 1975; rev. ed. 1979), ch. 1.

4. For an earlier version of portions of what follows in the next pages, see *The Theological Imagination,* pp. 32–46.

22. Reconstructing the Concept of God

1. The Bible is not entirely consistent in this emphasis; some "theophanies," for example, are reported in the Bible, but these seem to be more manifestations of God's *power* than of God in Godself. However, Enoch "walked with God" (Gen. 5:22, 24), we are told; God "appeared" to Abraham (Gen. 17:1; 18:1) and spoke to him; Jacob wrestled with "a man" all night long (Gen. 32:24), and then later said he had "seen God face to face" (32:30); after hearing the voice from the whirlwind, Job does not hesitate to say, "now my eye sees thee" (42:5). But it is not evident that much should be made of these stories theologically, especially in view of the explicit statements that humans cannot "see" God.
2. See Rudolf Bultmann, "The New Testament and Mythology," in *Kerygma and Myth,* ed. H. W. Bartsch (London: S.P.C.K., 1953); also *Jesus Christ and Mythology* (London: SCM Press, 1958).
3. Immanuel Kant, *Critique of Pure Reason,* trans. Norman Kemp Smith (New York: Humanities Press, 1950), A395 (cf. A384).
4. In thinking about the distinction between metaphors and concepts, I have found Sallie McFague's work especially helpful. See *Models of God* (Philadelphia: Fortress Press, 1987), ch. 2; and *Metaphorical Theology* (Philadelphia: Fortress Press, 1982).
5. Some recent feminist writers have argued that the source of the notion of the solitary autonomous agent is the distinctively male experience of defining one's self and establishing one's identity through *dis*sociating and *dis*tinguish-

ing one's self from the mother, the female; but that it presents what is actually a highly abstract and misleading picture of selfhood, since actual agency cannot exist apart from this very social matrix. See, for example, Nancy Chodorow, *The Reproduction of Mothering* (Berkeley: University of California Press, 1978).

6. See Richard Rubenstein, *After Auschwitz* (Indianapolis: Bobbs-Merrill, 1966).
7. In *Models of God,* Sallie McFague shows how thoroughly these three metaphors, if taken seriously, can reorient our thinking about God.

23. Faith in God (I)

1. For detailed examination of the peculiar "ungrounded" character of propositions expressing or describing features of our underlying "picture of the world" (Wittgenstein's phrase), see L. Wittgenstein, *On Certainty,* esp. secs. 94–178, 204–209, 555–560.
2. Karl Popper, *Logic of Scientific Discovery* (New York: Basic Books, 1957).
3. Cf. Philo's remark in David Hume, *Dialogues on Natural Religion* (New York: Hafner Publishing Co., 1953), p. 56: "All religious systems, it is confessed, are subject to great and insuperable difficulties. Each disputant triumphs in his turn, while he carries on an offensive war, and exposes the absurdities, barbarities, and pernicious tenets of his antagonist. But all of them, on the whole, prepare a complete triumph for the *sceptic,* who tells them that no system ought ever to be embraced with regard to such subjects: for this plain reason that no absurdity ought ever to be assented to with regard to any subject. A total suspense of judgment is here our only reasonable resource. And if every attack, as is commonly observed, and no defence among theologians is successful, how complete must be *his* victory who remains always, with all mankind, on the offensive, and has himself no fixed station or abiding city which he is ever, on any occasion, obliged to defend?"
4. The most careful analysis (with which I am acquainted) of these issues, showing that a thoroughgoing skepticism rests on deep confusions and is in fact impossible, is to be found in Wittgenstein's *On Certainty.*
5. W. C. Smith, *Belief and History* (Charlottesville: University Press of Virginia, 1977), and *Faith and Belief* (Princeton: Princeton University Press, 1979).
6. For a thorough philosophical analysis of this use of the word "belief," see H. H. Price, *Belief* (London: George Allen and Unwin, 1969), esp. pp. 426–454.
7. In taking this position I am aligning myself in certain respects with the position outlined by R. B. Braithwaite in *An Empiricist's View of the Nature of Religious Belief* (Cambridge: Cambridge University Press, 1955), though I hope my interpretation is somewhat more nuanced than his early statement was.
8. The argument of these chapters, that faith in God today both gives rise to, and simultaneously is grounded upon, a retrospective assessment and inter-

pretation of the meaning of a particular trajectory of evolutionary and historical events, may at first sight seem weak and dubious. It should be noted, however, that something like this reflective movement of thought must have been involved in the origins (as well as the ongoing strengthening and reinforcing) of Israel's faith in Yahweh's action in and through the natural order and the processes of history. Though the early stories of the rise of Israel's faith—for example, the "call of Abraham" to leave his home and go wherever God led him (Gen. 12) and the commissioning of Moses to bring the children of Israel out of Egypt and into a "promised land" (Ex. 3)—have the form of promises about what God will do in the *future,* we must remember that these texts themselves were all produced hundreds of years *after* the events described. From that subsequent vantage point storytellers and writers, who themselves believed Yahweh had made possible this succession of events, put together these histories which spoke of God's intention to lead Abraham to a new land and to bring Moses' people out of Egypt into Canaan. The notions of God's "promises" and of the "fulfillment" of those promises were originally generated, thus—and have continued to be sustained over many centuries—in *retrospective* reflection; we have no reason to suppose (on the basis of such historical evidence as is available to us) that the actual *historical* Abraham and Moses had ever heard of such promises of Yahweh, and that it was because of these that they engaged in the activities attributed to them. The "promise and fulfillment" pattern, which eventually provided a way of seeing the entirety of the future activity of Yahweh—and became thus the basis for hopes and faith about the future of Israel and, in due course, of all humankind—was itself actually generated in retrospection. (This same pattern underlies later Christian eschatological expectations and hopes, these being grounded particularly in memories and retrospective interpretations of Jesus' ministry and death.) My suggestion, then, that contemporary faith in God simultaneously is grounded upon, and gives rise to, a retrospective interpretation of a particular trajectory of the evolutionary-historical movement is not all that different from the way in which Israel's faith in Yahweh both was grounded upon, and also made possible the generation of, a conception of the meaning of Israel's history. In both cases patterns (believed to be) discerned in the past provide the basis for hopes and convictions about the future, and thus generate a framework within which life in the present can be lived meaningfully.

9. It is sometimes supposed that a constructivist approach to theology implies that our religious symbols consist in *nothing more* than our own fanciful and arbitrary imaginings. That is, however, a seriously misleading oversimplification. Theological reflection and construction are human responses to what is (believed to be) *really there* in the world, what has brought us into being as human and sustains us in being; responses, thus (using specifically theological language now), to God's own activity. It is true, of course, that this whole framework of orientation centered on God could be false. The world may in fact have a meaning for humans of a quite different sort

than our theocentric conceptual frame suggests. Our talk about divine revelation should not, therefore, be taken as in some way validating a theistic position over against other alternatives, as establishing its greater truth. The concept of revelation expresses, rather, the point that if the symbol "God" actually stands in some significant relation to the realities of the world in which we live—and there are in fact genuine cosmic tendencies toward humanization, some real groundings in the cosmic scheme of things for such distinctively human concerns as love and care, justice and truth, purposive activity and meaning—then our groping efforts to formulate and express these notions are not just the product of our own ungrounded imaginings: they represent instead our quite proper human responses to the activity of these cosmic humanizing powers upon us (the "self-revealing of God"). And what we are doing in our theology is not just speculating wildly about how things are: we are seeking better to hear God's revelatory word (to "know God"), that we might better respond with faith and love and the service of our lives.

10. Shailer Mathews, *The Growth of the Idea of God* (New York: Macmillan, 1931), ch. 8.
11. My teacher H. R. Niebuhr, more sharply and clearly than anyone before him, framed this question as the central one for theological ethics; see, for example, *The Responsible Self* (New York: Harper and Row, 1963), chs. 4–5 and pp. 161–173. I want to acknowledge fully my heavy debt to him for this notion as well as many others elaborated in this book.

24. Sin and Evil

1. B. Spinoza, *Ethics,* pt. IV.
2. The basic root experience underlying the concept of evil may well be the feeling of *pain,* a feeling which seems to be grounded directly on the responsiveness of individual organisms to what is happening to them. Pain appears to be the mode in which various sorts of malfunctioning or injury or threat of danger or destruction most primitively impress themselves on an organism; it is, thus, originally connected directly with the organism's survival. In (self-conscious) human beings, of course, the awareness of pain becomes symbolically overlaid and colored in various degrees and ways by patterns acquired during socialization and enculturation—and these widen and deepen its originary meaning. I suggest that it is this primitive organismic sensing of potential destruction, combined with (later) awareness of power(s) capable of and bent on such destruction, that is the germ of the concept of evil, a concept which (as we shall see) is susceptible of much broader and more profound religious and moral interpretation than is pain itself. For further discussion of some of these issues, see "Evil and Salvation: An Anthropological Approach," ch. 6 in *The Theological Imagination: Constructing the Concept of God* (Philadelphia: Westminster Press, 1981).

3. S. Kierkegaard, *Fear and Trembling* (Princeton: Princeton University Press, 1941), Problem I.
4. Believers in such a God all too often take it for granted that God is *their* special protector, a supreme defender against their enemies, one who has authorized their particular projects and who empowers them to bring these projects to realization (a clearly ideological use of the symbol). Whether such believers are political conservatives, seeking to preserve and strengthen the present order, or revolutionaries attempting to overthrow it, they easily come to suppose that their enemies are God's enemies as well—"devilish" beings, the very "focus of evil" (Ronald Reagan), whom God wills that they destroy by any means possible. Thus, on the one hand, in the name of God arise holy wars and revolutions, inquisitions, the free use of torture, napalm, nuclear weapons—even against innocent bystanders caught in this great struggle between the supposed forces of light and forces of darkness. On the other hand, those who are powerless and oppressed may come to believe that this very same God wills precisely their condition of misery and servitude. So piety may seem to them to require acquiescence in utterly dehumanizing social, political, and economic arrangements; and the cultivation of such virtues as humility, patience, acceptance of whatever befalls oneself or one's group, may be seen as the proper expression of faith. In both these cases—whether God is believed to authorize and sanctify our humanly desired goals and our humanly contrived means of achieving these goals, or God is believed to be the ultimate author of what are in fact humanly created evils of injustice and other forms of dehumanization—the symbol "God" serves to provide a powerful, and thoroughly demonic, ideological reenforcement of evil. In these sorts of situations, instead of relativizing these evils, and opening up paths toward humanizing transformation, the invocation of God only intensifies and deepens those forces already working toward the destruction of human being and well-being. Moreover, faith in this God further exacerbates the anxiety, guilt, and shame, the social tensions and disorders, the oppressiveness of unjust social institutions, which (as we noted in Chapter 15) develop directly out of violations of the moral requirements of human historicity. The symbol "God," thus, and faith in God, are far from unambiguously good; they may in fact work as further powerful evils in human affairs.
5. Jonathan Edwards, *The Nature of True Virtue* (Ann Arbor: University of Michigan Press, 1960).
6. If our sin has progressed to the point at which we directly identify our judgments with God's truth, and our actions with God's will, then, of course, the will and truth, righteousness and justice, of God no longer stand over us, calling us into question and opening us to possibilities we had not previously seen, relativizing our firmest convictions and what we take to be our profoundest insights. When religious believers no longer can distinguish, sharply and clearly, God's will from their own, there is nothing to prevent them from plunging deeper and deeper into perdition, as in their false

consciousness they increasingly seek to play God on earth. Forgiveness of sin—that is, genuine dissolution of the human drive to be God—continues to be possible only so long as the *distinction* between ourselves and God remains effective in consciousness, relativizing our judgments and actions, calling us into question.

25. A Wider Christology

1. For the translation followed here (with slight alterations) see *Christology of the Later Fathers,* ed. Edward Rochie Hardy, Library of Christian Classics, vol. 3, (Philadelphia: Westminster Press, 1954), p. 373.
2. Paul Tillich, *Systematic Theology* (Chicago: University of Chicago Press, 1951), I, p. 27.
3. Much of what follows in the next few pages is drawn from my *Theology for a Nuclear Age* (Manchester: Manchester University Press; Philadelphia: Westminster Press, 1985), ch. 4.
4. In what follows I will be drawing heavily on the analysis of John Knox in *On the Meaning of Christ* (New York: Charles Scribner's Sons, 1947), ch. 2.
5. For the translation used here, see *Christology of the Later Fathers,* p. 373.
6. I might just note in passing that in a recent book Peter Hodgson also appears to be proposing what I am here calling a "wider Christology": "God was 'incarnate,' not in the physical nature of Jesus as such, but in the gestalt that coalesced both in and around his person—with which his person did in some sense become identical, and by which, after his death, he took on a new, communal identity . . . For Christians the person of Jesus of Nazareth played and continues to play a normative role in mediating the shape of God in history, which is the shape of love in freedom. Jesus' personal identity merged into this shape insofar as he simply *was* what he proclaimed and practiced. But Jesus' personal identity did not exhaust this shape, which is intrinsically a communal, not an individual shape. . . . the *communal* shape of spirit is the true and final gestalt of God in history." *God in History: Shapes of Freedom* (Nashville: Abingdon Press, 1989), pp. 209–210.
7. The classical feminist analysis of these matters is to be found in Mary Daly's *Beyond God the Father* (Boston: Beacon Press, 1973).
8. I earlier argued (Chapter 22) that the ancient symbolic language of the churches can continue to be used in connection with the theological picture we are developing, provided we do not literalize and reify it, as has happened so often in the past. I should add now that this caution about reification applies not only to what has happened in much traditional piety, but also to sophisticated theological formulas widely influential in Christian history—for example, Chalcedon's talk of two distinct "natures" being present in the one person Jesus Christ, or the trinitarian formulation which referred to three distinct "persons" in one divine substance.

9. Cyprian in Letter 73, *Early Latin Theology,* Library of Christian Classics, vol. 5, ed. S. L. Greenslade (Philadelphia: Westminster Press, 1956), p. 169.
10. Cf. Augustine: "I desire to know God and the soul . . . Nothing more." "The Soliloquies," in *Augustine: Earlier Writings,* Library of Christian Classics, vol. 6, trans. J. H. S. Burleigh (Philadelphia: Westminster Press, 1953), pp. 26–27.

26. Christ as Paradigm for God and for Humanity

1. For a historical analysis of the evidence which reaches the conclusion that at least some of the earliest Christian communities were radically egalitarian, see Elisabeth Schüssler Fiorenza, *In Memory of Her* (New York: Crossroad, 1985), pt. II.
2. It is imperative that this "fullness" of Christ be understood to include that unrestricted *openness* to the many diverse forms of the human which truly reconciling love (even of "enemies") requires, and that it in no wise be permitted to become yet one more form of destructive, all-consuming Christian imperialism and triumphalism.
3. Significant variations in our understandings of these several factors lead to quite different responses to the question whether we should give the symbol of Christ categorial status in our theocentric world-picture. Three examples will make the point: (1) If we take the principal christic image to be that of *Jesus humble, meek, and mild*—the man who sacrifices himself completely and without reservation to the hands of his enemies—but we think that what is required to bring about a more humane order in human life is violent overthrow of the powers of evil; then, of course, we will not believe devotion to what we see portrayed in this paradigmatic image to be of much help in joining us with those historical processes that can actually bring into being a more human and humane order. That is, in this case devotion informed by what we take to be the central christic image(s) will do little to connect us with the kind of power that we believe to be required to further our humanization, and which is to be regarded, thus, as the truly divine creative power at work in our human world. (2) If we believe that a properly ordered human society would be essentially hierarchical in structure, with governing positions held by persons of special talent and intelligence and with most ordinary folk serving and obeying the great and powerful; then devotion and reflection guided by images of one who blesses the poor and calls down woes on the rich, whose birth is celebrated with a song about "put[ting] down the mighty from their thrones, and exalt[ing] those of low degree" (Lk. 1:52), who calls publicans and sinners to be his followers and rebukes the righteous solid citizens of his day, will hardly seem conducive to bringing about a better-ordered human society. (3) If we consider human salvation—that is, true human fulfillment—to consist in a supernatural life with God after death, and we take Christ to be an omnipotent and omniscient supernatural being come down from heaven to attract our loyalty and devotion so that

we will not become overly concerned with "things of this world"; then it should be clear that although "Christ" will be the mediator of salvation, commitment to Christ will have little to do with overcoming the structures of evil and oppression here on earth, thus establishing a more humane order. Other examples could easily be supplied of the ways in which various combinations of differing convictions about our three factors lead to quite diverse conclusions—both about what the central christic concepts and images are and what they mean, and about what significance they might have for further humanization here on earth.

4. Many liberation theologians appear to doubt that a strong theological emphasis on reconciliation and "nonviolence" is appropriate in situations of severe oppression. I do not want to enter that debate here, but I would like to call attention in this connection to the sharp distinction made by the "Minjung" theologian Kim Yong-Bock—working under very difficult conditions in South Korea—between various kinds of "political messianism" and the "messianic politics" of Jesus. The latter, based on the image of Jesus' "powerlessness," he argues, is the proper course for Christian communities—even under conditions of extreme oppression—to follow. See "Messiah and Minjung: Discerning Messianic Politics over against Political Messianism," in *Minjung Theology: People as the Subjects of History,* ed. Commission on Theological Concerns of the Christian Conference of Asia (Maryknoll, N.Y.: Orbis Books, 1983), pp. 183–193.
5. Many sorts of criticism can be leveled against the general conception of systematic theology; from the vantage point we have reached in this book, two in particular may be mentioned here. (1) Projects in systematic theology (including my own venture some years ago) seem to presuppose that theological "truth" is dispersed among, and resides in, the many Christian "doctrines" (or "dogmas") that have been handed on from generation to generation in the churches; the task of the theologian, then, is to gather the most important of these doctrines together, arrange them so as to show their systematic interconnectedness, and thus present a compact synoptic view of the Christian faith as a whole. This approach presupposes a semi-atomistic conception of theological truth; and, because of its general presumption that "all" of the "major" Christian doctrines are worthy of inclusion in the systematizing exercise, it is quite conservative in its consequences. As we have seen, however, much that has been taken for granted in traditional Christian faith is highly questionable—even quite dangerous. In my view, only a holistic constructivist approach to theology (the present work is intended to be an example of such) can make possible the critical scrutiny of Christian perspectives that is today so much needed. (2) Since projects in systematic theology are concerned primarily with the retrieval and contemporary restatement of traditional Christian doctrines, their purview is basically *internalistic,* that is, it is defined largely by previous formulations of Christian doctrine and the criticisms which have been made of these. Today, however, with our heightened awareness of the significance of other religious

(and secular) perspectives for the orientation of human life, it has become more important (as we have seen) to examine carefully and assess the *overall perspective* of Christian faith than to concern ourselves so scrupulously with the fine points of detailed traditional arguments. The very conception of systematic theology tends to conceal or obscure these sorts of issues rather than to open them up. The holism required by constructivist approaches to theology, however, encourages continual comparison of Christian perspectives with other points of view—not simply on matters of detail, but in terms of their overall impacts on and meaning for human existence; such approaches, therefore, are much better fitted to address the major issues confronting theologians today.

27. A Trinitarian God

1. The connection of the interpretation of the trinity which I elaborate in this chapter to more traditional formulations can easily be discerned, I think, through examination of my earlier discussions of the trinity in chs. 6 and 17 of *Systematic Theology* (New York: Scribners, 1968). Though I now regard the understanding of theology presented in that volume as "pre-critical," in that I did not yet fully realize what it meant to take theology as essentially "imaginative construction," as argued in my *Essay on Theological Method* (Atlanta: Scholars Press, 1975; rev. ed. 1979), the interpretation of the idea of trinity presented there is similar in important respects to that outlined here.
2. Some might object that it is not legitimate to substitute such terms as "intention" and "motif" for "person" in interpreting trinitarian ideas, since they obviously carry quite different meanings. However, as we discovered in our earlier analysis of the symbol "God," it is frequently necessary today (in our attempt to enable this symbol to continue to function properly) to make rather drastic changes in the metaphors that traditionally provided much of its distinctive content; and these changes result in significant transformations in the way God is understood. The concept of the trinity is no different from other traditional theological notions in this respect. The proper question to ask about my proposed substitutions is whether they enable us to employ trinitarian ideas in an intelligible and illuminating way that is continuous (at least in some important respects) with earlier ways in which these notions were employed, and whether this significantly clarifies and otherwise enhances the conception of God which we are constructing; not whether the terms I use are essentially synonyms of the more traditional ones.
3. Kant, *Critique of Pure Reason,* A51/B75.
4. The appropriateness of speaking of the divine immanence in all things in terms of the metaphor spirit is well expressed by Sallie McFague: "the spirit of God [is] the divine wind that 'swept over the face of the waters' prior to creation, the life-giving breath given to all creatures, and the dynamic move-

ment that creates, recreates, and transcreates throughout the universe. Spirit, as wind, breath, life is the most basic and most inclusive way to express centered embodiment. All living creatures . . . depend upon breath. Breath also knits together the life of animals and plants, for they are linked by the exchange of oxygen and carbon dioxide in each breath inhaled and exhaled. . . we literally live from breath to breath and can survive only a few minutes without breathing . . . Spirit is a wide-ranging, many-dimensional term with many meanings built upon its physical base as the breath of life. We speak of a person's spirit, their vigor, courage, or strength; of team spirit, the collective energy of a people at play; of the spirit of '76 or the spirit of Tiananmen Square, the vitality, grit, and resolution of a people banding together in a common cause to oppose oppression; of a spirited horse or the spirit of a sacred grove . . . All these connotations are possible because of the primary meaning of spirit as the . . . 'breath of life' (Genesis 2:7) . . . We 'live and move and have our being' in God (Acts 17:28) . . . That is, perhaps, the most basic confession that can be made: I owe my existence at its most fundamental level—the gift of my next breath—to God . . . And so does everything else in creation . . . [The concept of Spirit] underscores the connection between God and the world as not primarily the Mind that orders, controls, and directs the universe, but as the Breath that is the source of life and vitality. The connection is one of *relationship* at . . . the level of life, rather than *control* at the level of ordering and directing nature." *The Body of God: An Ecological Theology* (Minneapolis: Augsburg Fortress, forthcoming), ch. 4.

5. For an earlier discussion of this (implicit) "trinitarian structure" of metaphysical thinking, see my *Systematic Theology*, pp. 97f. A more general discussion of the formal similarity of metaphysical reflection to Christian theology (though not worked out in trinitarian terms) can be found in "Metaphysics and Theology," ch. 9 of *The Theological Imagination: Constructing the Concept of God* (Philadelphia: Westminster Press, 1981). A similar understanding of metaphysics as based on generalization of specific paradigms is developed in Stephen Pepper, *World Hypotheses* (Berkeley: University of California Press, 1942).
6. To some readers these remarks may suggest that I am setting out an "economic" conception of the trinity here since I work out God's threefoldness in terms of God's relations to the world (and to us humans) instead of as belonging to God's inner "essence," supposedly independent of the world (the so-called immanent trinity). This judgment, however, is based on oversimplification. The point I am making is that all three motifs are essential to the Christian concept of God, that is, that God (for Christian faith) cannot be conceived apart from these three. To insist, now, that it is theologically requisite that it be God-in-Godself that we are conceiving here (with our three motifs)—as opposed to God as we humans conceive God—would be to imply that we are able to conceive God-in-Godself somehow independently of our human conceiving of God. This is, of course, nonsensical and

impossible, a claim based on (fallaciously) abstracting what we call "God-in-Godself" from our conception of God, and then reifying this abstraction and supposing (mistakenly) that when we attend to our reified abstraction it is really God-in-Godself that we are (at last!) contemplating. It is of course true that we can distinguish (mentally) between "God-in-Godself" and our concept of God(-in-Godself). But in the case of God (unlike the epistemic situation with respect to finite objects) this distinction is in fact empty, since we have no independent access to or experience of God with which to compare our concept. The contrast often made between the economic and the immanent trinity, then (at least as it applies to the position I am articulating here), depends upon confusions introduced by reification of our concepts (a problem that repeatedly arises, as we have seen, in much traditional Christian thinking). Once one sees that the real issue here is misplaced reification, it becomes clear (a) that (the Christian) God can be claimed to be truly *God* only in and through something like a trinitarian conceptual pattern; and (b) that since there is no way to move beyond such a trinitarian concept to a supposedly "deeper" understanding of God(-in-Godself), the significance of the contrast between the economic and immanent trinities falls away.

7. T. S. Eliot, "East Coker," in *Four Quartets* (New York: Harcourt, Brace, 1943).
8. Hegel, "Preface," *Phenomenology of Spirit,* paragraph 70.

28. Theocentric Faith and the Churches

1. I have developed these ideas more fully in my essay on "Theology as a Public Vocation," in *The Vocation of the Theologian,* ed. T. W. Jennings (Philadelphia: Fortress Press, 1985).
2. This point has been developed (in a slightly different way) in ch. 1 of my *Essay on Theological Method* (Atlanta: Scholars Press, 1975; rev. ed. 1979).
3. The traditional four historic marks of the church were unity, holiness, catholicity, and apostolicity (Niceno-Constantinopolitan Creed, 381 C.E.); in mainline Reformation teaching the church was said to be wherever the word is truly preached and the sacraments rightly administered. See, for example, *Augsburg Confession,* art. 7; Martin Luther, *On the Councils and the Church,* pt. III; John Calvin, *Institutes,* book IV, i, 8–12.
4. See Ernst Troeltsch, *The Social Teachings of the Christian Churches* (London: George Allen and Unwin, 1931), 2 vols., for full discussion of these notions. Despite the many problems which critics have brought up with Troeltsch's position, his wide-ranging and insightful historical treatment of the ways in which the churches have related themselves to their social contexts remains the classical treatment of these issues.
5. H. R. Niebuhr has shown the usefulness of the notions of "henotheism" and "polytheism" as instruments for the interpretation and critique of modern

culture; see *Radical Monotheism and Western Culture* (New York: Harper and Bros., 1960).

29. Faith in God (II): Christian Theocentrism

1. "For by grace you have been saved through faith; and this is not your own doing, it is the gift of God" (Eph. 2:8; cf. Rom. 5; Gal. 3–5, and passim.) That salvation—including faith—was to be understood as entirely God's free gift to humans was, of course, a central emphasis of the main-line Reformers.
2. I attempted to sketch briefly something of that sort a good many years ago in the chapter "The Foundations of Belief" in *God the Problem* (Cambridge, Mass.: Harvard University Press, 1972).
3. For a very suggestive interpretation, along these lines, of the historical spread of Christianity around the globe, see Lamin Sanneh, *Translating the Message: The Missionary Impact on Culture* (Maryknoll, N.Y.: Orbis Books, 1989).
4. Jonathan Edwards, *The Nature of True Virtue,* ch. 1.
5. Cf. H. R. Niebuhr on God as the unity of value and being; see esp. *Radical Monotheism and Western Culture* (New York: Harper and Bros., 1960), chs. 1–2, supplementary essays 2–3.
6. Cf. the prayer of the father of the child possessed of an evil spirit: "Lord, I believe; help thou mine unbelief" (Mk. 9:24 KJV).

Name Index

Subject Index

Index of Scriptural References